The Design of
Organizations

The Design of Organizations

Pradip N. Khandwalla

McGill University

HARCOURT BRACE JOVANOVICH, INC.
New York / Chicago / San Francisco / Atlanta

To all my teachers, those who
taught me questions, and
those who vexed me with theirs.

ISBN: 0-15-517366-9
Library of Congress Catalog Card Number: 76-53988

Printed in the United States of America

Preface

This book is about organizations—profit-making as well as non-profit corporations, giant organizations like the U.S. government or General Motors as well as tiny ones like the corner grocery store. In the book we take the position that a single body of knowledge—*organization theory*—can explain the structure and functioning of the great variety of formally set-up collectivities we call organizations and that we do not need one theory for hospitals, another for political parties, a third for corporations, a fourth for governmental organizations, and so on.

Our unit of analysis then is the organization. It is *not* individuals or groups, except to the extent that their behavior affects the organization they are operating in or are themselves affected by the way the organization is operating.

The Design of Organizations aims to systematize an amorphous and rapidly growing body of knowledge about organizations and to show how this knowledge can be applied to the practical work of designing effectively performing organizations. The exercise is rather like one of applying economic theory to design more effective decision-making systems, or applying the physical and the social sciences to engineer and market better products. Organization *theory* does not tell us what to do. It provides explanations for what is going on, predicts the consequencs of alternative courses of action, and leaves it to us to use this knowledge as best we can. Organization *design* is the attempt to apply this knowledge constructively to improve organizational performance, or at least to avoid making the mistakes that lead to disaster. The power of this knowledge becomes evident when we realize how much of the good of society is tied up with the performance of its organizations, as, of course, is the well-being of those who work in them.

This book is intended for use in undergraduate or graduate courses on organization theory. (The latter are known also as courses on complex organizations, formal organizations, the management of organizations, etc.) Because of its strong emphasis on strategic variables, the book can be used as a supplement in courses on policy or strategy. Its coverage of management theory and its emphasis on the design of organizations enable it to be used as a supplement in courses on management. And its review of the behavioral science literature as well as its equally strong emphasis on situational and structural variables make it useful also in courses on organizational behavior.

The Design of Organizations is divided into two parts. The first part explores the foundations of organizational analysis. Chapter 1 introduces organizations. Chapters 2 and 3 subject the organization to economic, political, sociological, and social psychological analyses, with an emphasis on identifying interesting questions in organizational analysis. Chapters 4 through 6 describe the history and the major orientations of organization theory. Many of the latter have been palpably influenced by the disciplines of economics, political science, sociology, and social psychology. The orientations discussed are the bureaucracy school founded by Weber, the principles of management school founded by Taylor and Fayol, the human relations school founded by Mayo, the human potential or human resources school founded by Argyris and McGregor, the bounded rationality school founded by Simon, systems orientation, and contingency theory.

Part I ends in Chapter 7 with a model of how organizations function. It stresses relationships among situational or contextual, strategic, structural, behavioral, and performance variables. The model is a fusion of the many strands in organization theory, especially from the contingency theory and systems orientation perspectives, and it forms the basis for the second part of the book.

Part II draws on a more recent body of research and systematically explores the design implications of the model outlined in Chapter 7. It attempts to summarize organization theory in the form of testable propositions and to use these as the bases for suggestions about the design of organizations.

Chapters 8 and 9 discuss what may be called situational or contextual variables, the demographic properties of organizations—their size, age, and type—and the external environment of organizations. Chapters 10 and 11 treat what in Chapter 7 were termed strategic variables, variables that have major and long-term consequences for the organization. Chapter 10 goes into the goals of organizations, and Chapter 11 the ideology and style of the top management. In both chapters, the influence of situational variables is described. Chapters 12 and 13 take up structural variables. Chapter 12 discusses the organization's operations and information technology and workflow, and Chapter 13 outlines organizational structure—that is, the durable and formal relationships in the organization, which include departmentalization, bureaucratization, hierarchy, decentralization, and control and information systems. In these two chapters, the effects of situational and strategic variables are described. Chapter 14 discusses the design of human behavior in organizations, in particular the strategies available to the designer to influence motivation and morale, conflict and cooperation, creative behavior, and innovative behavior. Chapter 15 describes the determinants of organizational performance and the strategies available to the designer to raise performance on key goals.

Many colleagues have given generously of their time in reading drafts of the chapters. I am especially grateful to Walter Morley Balke, Manfred F. R. Vets de Vries, Richard Marshall, and Henry Mintzberg of McGill University, Lawrence A. Gordon of the University of Kansas, and Alfred Kieser of the Free University of Berlin. Andrew Van De Ven, the Wharton School, University of Pennsylvania, and W. Richard Scott, Stanford University, did a thorough job of reviewing the manuscript and made very valuable suggestions for improvement. Any remaining lapses in the book are, of course, my responsibility. My students—undergraduate, graduate, and doctoral—have provided invaluable help in making this book more readable. I am particularly grateful to Roger Gosselin, student and colleague. Debbie Currie, Margaret Dunnette, and A. S. Nair have provided fine secretarial support. I am grateful to my wife Anjali for remaining relatively calm even when the book began to absorb a frighteningly large percentage of my waking (and sleeping) hours. I am also beholden to my father for his support and assistance, especially during the final revision of the book. Finally, Gary Burke at Harcourt Brace Jovanovich was helpful with patience, suggestions, and support.

Pradip N. Khandwalla

Contents

ORGANIZATIONAL ANALYSIS FROM THE PERSPECTIVES OF ECONOMICS AND POLITICAL SCIENCE   41

SOCIOLOGICAL AND SOCIAL PSYCHOLOGICAL ANALYSIS OF ORGANIZATIONS   71

THE STRUCTURAL ORIENTATIONS IN ORGANIZATION THEORY 130

THE BEHAVIORAL ORIENTATIONS IN ORGANIZATION THEORY 176

THE SYSTEMS AND CONTINGENCY APPROACHES TO ORGANIZATION THEORY   223

7

A MODEL OF ORGANIZATIONAL FUNCTIONING   260

THE DEMOGRAPHIC CHARACTERISTICS OF ORGANIZATIONS: SIZE, AGE, AND TYPE   291

THE EXTERNAL ENVIRONMENT OF ORGANIZATIONS   326

THE GOALS OF ORGANIZATIONS   355

THE STYLE OF TOP MANAGEMENT   392

WORKFLOW AND TECHNOLOGY   446

13

THE STRUCTURE OF ORGANIZATIONS   482

14

THE DESIGN OF HUMAN BEHAVIOR IN ORGANIZATIONS   530

15

THE DESIGN OF ORGANIZATIONAL PERFORMANCE   572

APPENDIX A
A BRIEF DESCRIPTION OF KHANDWALLA'S STUDY OF CANADIAN FIRMS   637

The Design of
Organizations

1

"Can the strength of a hundred people be greater than that of one thousand people? It can and is, when the one hundred are organized."
V. I. Lenin

Introduction to Organizations *All Text*

THE NATURE OF ORGANIZATIONS

Introduction

Imagine a world without organizations! There would be no schools in which to get a formal education (or to while away time), no hospitals and medical clinics, no clubs or associations, no political parties, no government, no firms. Individuals—at best families—would have to fend pretty much for themselves to satisfy their myriad needs, much as in paleolithic times. Indeed, one way of measuring civilization is to look at the diversity of organizations in a given society. At one extreme today are communities with tribes as the sole organization. At the other extreme are societies, such as those of North America, in which not only are there many categories of organization, but there are innumerable subcategories within each organizational class. For example, the manufacturing firm is one of several different types of firm (some of the others are banking firms, insurance firms, advertising agencies, food retailing firms) the firm itself being one of several different types of organization. But the manufacturing firm is further classified, in the U.S. Census of Manufactures, into several *hundred* industrial

1

categories (e.g., steel-producing firms, chemical and drug firms, electronics firms, machinery-manufacturing firms). Or, take medical institutions, another major type of organization. Here one finds general hospitals, dental clinics, orthopedic units, pathology laboratories, psychiatric clinics, eye clinics, cancer research institutes, and so on and on. A similar range of organizations can be found in governmental institutions. One has but to look at the index of the Yellow Pages of a large city to get some idea of the variety of organizations in a modern society, while the several hundred pages of the directory itself give some indication of the number of organizations in a modern city. Indeed, there typically is nearly one organization for every ten people living in such a city.

Why this great variety and density of organizations? One reason is that the organization is a highly efficient way of satisfying a great many human needs. And it is highly efficient (as compared, for example, to the individual, the family, or a friendship group) because it can assemble and coordinate relatively large magnitudes of specialized resources under one roof, so to speak, for achieving specific objectives. It is able to do so, not only because it is legally allowed to do so, but, more importantly, because it has a number of essential properties. Let us take a look at these.

Properties of the Organization

The essential properties of organizations that make them so highly productive are:

Hierarchy of authority. In every organization some individuals carry out the orders of other individuals, and the latter in turn carry out the orders of their superiors. This is the hierarchy of authority. In some organizations, this vertical differentiation of authority is very elaborate. For example, in one cement company, there are eleven levels of authority. On the other hand, in a company manufacturing locomotives to the specifications of customers, there are only seven, despite the fact that both companies are of approximately equal size. Organizations are hierarchically organized because this helps in supervising employees and in coordinating and making decisions. Even a cooperative society, democratic as it is, has a hierarchy of authority. At the very top is the membership body to make policy decisions. Below this is the managing committee to carry out the decisions of the membership body and to supervise the actions of the administrative staff. Below the managing committee may be other committees and/or the administrative staff to deal with daily problems. The modern corporation parallels this structure, with the board of directors at the top overseeing the actions of the chief executive, who in turn supervises other corporate officers, and so on down the line. Individuals as well as groups (such as committees) can be part of the hierarchy.

Rules, procedures, controls and techniques. All organizations, even the most loosely organized, have rules, procedures, controls, and techniques. Many rules are formalized and officially enforced. In schools, for example, there is often a rule of not smoking in class, and that rule is rather conspicuously made known to the students. Sometimes there are informal rules that are enforced through informal means. For example, in one plant, the informal rule was for each worker not to produce more than x units per day despite a piece-rate system, because of the workers' fear that if they produced more management would raise standards. Whenever a worker exceeded x units during a day and tried to produce more, he would be "binged"—that is, given a painful blow on the shoulders by one or more of his mates. This "rule" was enforced quite effectively.

Organizations also have standard operating procedures, controls, and techniques. A *standard operating procedure* is a standardized way of responding to recurring problem situations. In firms, every time the inventory falls below a certain level, a standard operating procedure for replenishing it is put into effect. The individual in charge of the inventory does not have to run to his boss for directions because he knows what needs to be done. Standard operating procedures, by routinizing responses to problem situations, vastly increase the efficiency of an organization and cut down the amount of needed personal supervision.

Controls are summary measures of behavior, whether of machines or humans. For example, one very common control is the statement of final accounts. At a glance it tells the organization's financial position. Other common controls are audit reports and reports disclosing how the actual costs of operations compare with standard costs. Controls are a primary means by which an organization remains close to its charted path. They are a powerful homeostatic mechanism, for they tell management what, if anything, went wrong (or right) and to what extent. On the basis of this information, appropriate remedial action can be taken.

Techniques are the relatively standardized means by which given ends can be achieved. If the production system of an organization is inefficient, for example, management may turn to operations research techniques to make it more efficient. If morale is low, or workers seem alienated, management may turn to human relations techniques to improve morale. The production technology itself is a technique, and so are modern marketing, financial management, and personnel management. Techniques can be quite complex and often require quite skilled personnel to operate them. Often, a technique incorporates many rules, procedures, and controls.

Formality of communication. The language employed in organizations is quite a bit different from language employed at home or in purely social settings. In organizations, the work of each member is usually very closely linked to what some others are doing. In such a context, use of a standardized, work-related, technical vocabulary avoids ambiguity and misunderstanding and thus becomes a necessity for speedy communications. When the blast furnace supervisor gives the order to fire the furnace, that order must be understood unambiguously and simultaneously by everyone whose job it is to fire the furnace. When a doctor instructs a nurse as to what treatment to give to a patient, the nurse must understand exactly what the doctor wants done. Often, for the sake of accountability as well as for clarity, communication is reduced to written form. The content of most interpersonal verbal communication, too, tends to be formal, work related, and precise, and, at work, individuals conversing with one another are rather conscious of the organizational roles they are playing.

Specialization of functions and division of labor. Long ago, Adam Smith (1723–90) demonstrated the huge advantages of specialization and division of labor. In *division of labor,* work is divided up so that no one is saddled with too great a burden. In *specialization,* individuals are asked to perform only a narrow range of functions so that they can develop a great deal of competence in the performance of these functions. For a given magnitude of work, the greater the division of labor, the larger is the *number* of individuals required to perform it. The greater the specialization of functions, on the other hand, the larger is the *diversity* of personnel and the greater is the *range* of roles that are played in the organization.

Employment of skilled personnel. Unlike families, in which wives often employ rank amateurs as husbands (and vice versa), organizations generally make it a point to employ persons that are skilled in performing the many functions of the organization. Although nepotism surely exists in organizations, the guiding principle is to hire competent persons. Much of the work in modern organizations is fairly technical and cannot be discharged by the untrained. It therefore would be a waste of scarce resources to hire individuals totally untrained for their jobs. On the other hand, competent individuals, when motivated, can be highly productive. Skill levels, of course, vary from one part of an organization to another and from organization to organization. In one aerospace firm, no supervisors are hired unless they have at least a bachelor's degree. In a printing plant, on the other hand, there are many supervisors that are not high school graduates. In professional organizations such as hospitals, there are marked differences in the amount and type of training among doctors, nurses, administrators, lab technicians, and other staff. This spread of skills is equally observable in most sizable, modern organizations.

Specificity of purposes. Generally speaking, families and communities do not have specific purposes; they are all-purpose collectivities. Not so organizations. Most have highly specific purposes. A school is set up for the purpose of educating students; if it is an elementary school, then it teaches only elementary classes. A political party has as its purpose persuading the electorate in a specific area to put it in power. A firm's purpose is to produce and market goods or services. A government bureau is set up, often by an act of the legislature, to provide certain quite specific services to the citizenry. This specificity of purposes can vary, of course, between organizations. Some conglomerates put no limitation on the kinds of goods or services they may do business in. Government as a whole has quite wide-ranging and somewhat nebulous purposes. Smaller organizations, such as a school, or the corner drugstore, or a cooperative, have much narrower and usually more precise purposes.

Not only do organizations have specific purposes, they *organize* themselves to achieve these. Most activities in an organization are undertaken in the belief (sometimes mistaken) that they help the organization achieve its purposes. In a firm, for example, raw materials are purchased, processed, and marketed to earn the firm a profit. Individuals are hired, trained, or fired for the same purpose. Machinery is acquired, repaired, overhauled periodically, for the same purpose. Similar litanies can be repeated for other types of organization. This specificity of purposes and of the means by which these purposes are attained is a highly visible and important characteristic of organizations.

Thus, organizations are those collectivities that have *all* of the following in at least *some* degree: a hierarchy of authority; rules, procedures, controls, and techniques; formal communications; specialization of functions and division of labor; employment of skilled personnel; and specific purposes that are the focuses of the organization's activities.

Notice the functions that these properties perform for the organization. Division of labor, specialization, standard operating procedures, and techniques permit the organization to carry on very diverse activities efficiently. But the specificity of purposes provides an integrating focus to these diverse activities. So do formal communication, hierarchy of authority, rules, and controls. It is precisely because the organization is able to carry on a variety of activities in a coordinated manner that it is so wonderfully more productive than a mere collection of people, and justifies Lenin's assertion that a hundred organized individuals are stronger than a thousand unorganized individuals.

But just because every organization must have these properties in some measure to be called an organization does not mean that all organizations are alike. Indeed, they differ widely, even dramatically. Part of the difference stems from the fact that organizations emphasize the above properties to varying degrees. Some, like well-established government bureaus, emphasize them strongly; others, like research laboratories and artistic organizations, emphasize many of these properties much less. In other words, we have a variety of organizational forms. Besides different emphases on these properties, organizational differences arise also from other features that are not as universal as the ones listed above. Not every organization has committees, but organizations such as universities and legislatures are chock-full of committees. The activities of some organizations may be geared to the mass production of standardized products or services, those of others to production to individual customers' specifications. Some organizations greatly emphasize technocracy and planning; others may have no use for it.

Thus, while organizations share some properties, their different emphasis on these as well as on other not-so-common properties cause *organizational differences*. A major task of organization *theory* is to explain why these differences arise. A major task of organization *design* is to put together effective combinations of these common and not-so-common properties.

The difference between other collectivities and organizations is often a matter more of degree than of substance. The family, a friendship group, community, caste, and society are some of the other collectivities that traditionally are not called organizations. But they share a great many of the attributes of organizations. A family often has goals, a hierarchy of authority and influence, division of labor, specialization of functions, and so on. If it differs from an organization, it is in its smaller size and the great intensity of the *emotional* bonds among its members. The collectivities larger than the organization—community, society, etc.—often exhibit hierarchies of power and status, specialization of functions, a certain amount of formality in communications, and some formal as well as nonformal norms or rules. If they differ from the organization, they do so in the degree to which their goals are more diffuse, and in the degree to which activities within the collectivity are not subject to central coordination of some kind. As March and Simon put it, organizations are the largest assemblages in society that

TABLE 1–1

The Organization Versus the Family, the Friendship Group, and the Community

	Organization	Family	Friendship group	Community
Properties distinguishing organizations				
Specificity of purposes	✓			
Employment of skilled personnel	✓			
Formality of communication	✓			
Formal rules, procedures, controls, techniques	✓			
Hierarchy of authority	✓	✓		
Specialization and division of labor	✓	✓		✓
Other common properties of collectivities				
Strong emotional bonds between members		✓	✓	
Values and ideology	✓	✓	✓	✓
Status differences	✓	✓	✓	✓
Nonformal relationships (cliques, friendship ties, etc.)	✓	✓	✓	✓

NOTE: The absence of a check mark means that the property is not found *universally* in the type of collectivity in question; it may be found in some collectivities of the type but not in all.

have anything resembling a central coordinative system.[1] Perhaps it is best to think of the *typical* organization as being fairly distinct from the *typical* family or the *typical* community but also to concede readily that, occasionally, a family or a community may rather strikingly resemble an organization, and vice versa. Table 1–1 highlights some similarities and differences between the typical organization on the one hand and the typical family, the typical friendship group, and the typical community on the other.

Activities and Resources of Organizations

To be able to survive and achieve the goals for which it is set up, an organization—any organization—carries on a number of activities. Bakke has classified these activities into five different types:[2]

1 Activities designed to ensure the *availability of resources* to the or-

ganization. These include, among others, attempts to identify sources of raw materials or inputs; to recruit, select, and train personnel; and to acquire the necessary plant and fixtures.

2 *Workflow* activities, comprising all that is done, once the organization has acquired the necessary human and material resources, to create and distribute the output of an organization. In a manufacturing organization, the production and sales operations would comprise workflow activities. In a school, the actual teaching and the placement of graduates would comprise workflow activities.

3 *Control* activities, aimed at the coordination of operations. These comprise activities such as directing employees what to do and how, motivating them by rewards and punishments, evaluating employees and projects or courses of action, and communicating information to members of an organization to enable them to do their jobs.

4 *Identification* activities, which define the organization (and differentiate it from other institutions) for its members and outsiders, such as when the chairman of a company, addressing the annual general meeting, says, "We in this company believe that we are in the transportation business, and our motto is service to the customer!" Public relations activities, image-building activities, starting an organizational newsletter, and the like are all instances of identification activities.

5 *Homeostatic* activities, a residual category. It includes activities through which the preceding four activities are integrated so that the organization remains in a state of dynamic equilibrium (that is, it adapts to changing circumstances and does not fall apart in the process). Many of the activities of the organization's top management are of this type. Homeostatic activities include activities designed to integrate the needs and interests of the organization, its members, and other institutions with which it has relations. They include problem-solving activities. And they encompass the leadership processes that provide imagination and initiative to the organization, as well as the legitimization processes, such as registering the organization's charter with the appropriate governmental authority, by which an organization tries to convince society that its activities are legal and legitimate.

Bakke argues that various kinds of resource are needed to carry on these activities. He identifies six different resources: human resources, material resources (such as plant and machinery, inputs for processing), financial resources (short- and long-term finance), natural resources (such as land), ideational resources (the ideas used by the organization and the language in which these are expressed and communicated), and the resources constituting the operating field—the "market"—of the organization (e.g., the electorate for a political party, a market segment for a firm).

Organization as a Unit of Analysis

An organization need not be an autonomous legal unit, although this is the most visible organizational form. Departments and divisions of an organization can also be regarded as organizations. The essential points are that they be set up to achieve some goal or goals and that they exhibit the properties of organizations, such as a certain amount of formality in transacting business, some minimum hierarchy of authority, and so forth. Naturally, in studying such embedded organizations, we must keep track of their relationship with their parents, for these relationships are likely to affect the former's behavior quite powerfully, much as the environment of independent organizations affects their behavior. In one subsidiary of a corporation, the vice president of operations insisted to the author that the subsidiary was quite autonomous. Nonetheless, it turned out that the president of the subsidiary was a headquarters man and that once every six months a book of detailed rules and regulations arrived from the headquarters to serve as a "guide" (somewhat like Mao's little red book) to executive action. The policies of the subsidiary reflected more the policies of the corporate headquarters than was warranted by the subsidiary's business situation.

It is a bit futile to try to fix the boundaries of an organization. Some people are obviously members of an organization because they are employed by it or hold office in it. Others are on the borderline. For example, one normally thinks of university students as members of the university organization. Are the clients of a bank members of the particular banking organization? Are citizens members of the governmental organization? The answer is not at all clear cut. Like an onion, an organization consists of multiple layers of affiliates, not all of whom may have equally strong bonds with the organization. One person may choose to consider only the inner layers; another may be interested also in the outer layers. Like beauty, the outlines of an organization are in the eyes of the beholder!

The purpose of inquiry dictates what are considered the boundaries of an organization. For example, a researcher may be interested in comparing the different pathological and research laboratories of a hospital in order to find evidence for the hunch that the research laboratories should be more loosely organized than the pathological laboratories, in view of the more creative, novel, and nonroutine nature of the work of the former. Here the unit of analysis is not the hospital but rather small suborganizations embedded in the hospital. On the other hand, another researcher may be interested in comparing hospitals of different sizes to determine whether the size of the hospital affects staff-patient relationships adversely and thus results in the delivery of poorer health care to patients. Here one is justified in treating individual hospitals as units of analysis. A third researcher may be interested in studying the effectiveness of the entire health delivery system in an area, comprising public and private hospitals, clinics, consulting and general physicians, and so on. For this purpose, an entire network of individuals and organizations may justifiably be treated as an organization, even though normally it would not be regarded as such.

So long, therefore, as one clearly *defines* the unit of analysis, and it is reasonably obvious that the unit one is studying has *all* the *properties of an organization*, the unit of analysis in question is a fit subject for organizational research and analysis. Organization theory is designed to explain the behavior of all such units of analysis, and prescriptions about organizational design are meant to apply to all such units, be they small or large, embedded or independent entities.

Why Study Organizations?

We study organizations because they have such a great influence on our lives, for both good and bad, and also because they are highly interesting arenas for studying human behavior. We get our education largely—but not exclusively—in organizations such as schools, colleges, and universities. We are treated, when our health breaks down, in organizations such as clinics and hospitals. We get a good part of our entertainment from organizations that run television and radio stations and theaters and publish newspapers and periodicals. Cataclysmic decisions such as those of declaring or terminating wars are made by organizations—the governments of nations—as well as the more mundane but important decisions relating to social security, environmental protection, taxes, highway construction. The belief in the importance of the individual—as a voter and as a consumer—is still the central myth of both democracy and capitalism. There is far greater evidence, however, that organizations are the primary units of decision-making, resource allocation, and innovation in a complex modern society. Indeed, modern society is inconceivable without the extremely complex network of organizations that mushrooms to service the varied and insatiable needs of its members. The organization as a social invention is fully comparable in importance to the family and will probably play as major a role in the further cultural evolution of mankind.

The study of organizations is likely to lead to more effective ways of satisfying the needs of society. The huge multinational enterprises as well as the vastly larger governmental institutions of today could hardly be possible—certainly would not function effectively—without an understanding by their managers of the way organizations function. There was a time when one capable individual could run an organization reasonably well, trusting largely to common sense and intuition. That is still possible for many small organizations, although what the study of organizations has to offer probably would improve significantly the chances of their survival. As the human race grows more literate, more affluent, and more "picky," it must learn to operate organizations with more and more complex technologies, structures, ideologies, and human relationships. These organizations cannot be built or operated without a sound grasp of the principles of organizational functioning. Research into and study of the latter is vital for the continued well-being of society.

Not only do organizations serve a variety of needs, but they affect quite vitally the people associated with them—and half or more of the population works in organizations at least eight hours a day. Organizations satisfy—and sometimes frustrate—a great many needs of the people associated with them. Some of these needs are: the need for security and stability of occupation; the need for companionship and social support; the need for power over others as well as for dependence on others; and the need for personal growth and the actualization of one's potential. Organizations have, through largely increased productivity, become much better paymasters. There is little question that working conditions have improved vastly over the years— from fourteen-hour days on semi-starvation wages to eight-hour days on wages that in North America, Western Europe, and Japan enable the employee to have a car, home, television, washer, dryer, and many other amenities. There is also evidence, however, that the modern organization is a psychologically stressful place of work. Because organizations are hierarchical, they often give rise to severe competition among the supervisory personnel wanting to climb the management ladder. Because efficiency often requires extreme specialization and division of labor, work becomes boring. Because a host of controls and standard operating procedures is often necessary for efficiency and coordination, they overly circumscribe the autonomy of employees and cause them frustration. There is evidence that a whole host of psychosomatic disorders including ulcers and heart disease may be linked to the stresses of organizational life.[3]

If we understand organizational dynamics more fully, we may be able to design better organizations, just as a better understanding of our physical environment has led to a more secure and productive world. Of course, there is no unanimity about what is a "better" organization, and, as in other branches of knowledge, greater knowledge may be used for nefarious purposes as well. But the two widely accepted organizational objectives are efficiency in the pursuit of socially acceptable organizational purposes and the happiness of the organization's members; a third, concern for the community, is growing in acceptance. Based on research to date, it seems possible to design organizations that can achieve their objectives more efficiently and also perhaps increase the satisfaction of their members' needs.

Research on organizations has been highly productive. In a period of about seven decades, the growing volume of research has not only provided a much better understanding of the common organizational form of bureaucracy (especially why it fails) but also unearthed novel organizational forms. The haul has been rich. Participatory management, mechanistic and organic management, "professional" management, management by objectives, Theory X and Theory Y, "tall" and "flat" structures, divisionalization, centralization and decentralization, integration and differentiation, matrix structure, and other organizational forms have been discovered or developed. The end is not in sight. Journals such as the *Administrative Science Quarterly, Human Organization, Journal of Management Studies, Academy of Management Journal,* and many others in English and other languages continue to publish huge quantities of research on various facets of the structure and functioning of organizations. The subject of organization is easily one of the most prolific and dynamic components of the social and the management sciences. It has attracted and continues to attract sociologists, psychologists, anthropologists, economists, political scientists, administrators, and even mathematicians and philosophers. Many spend their research lifetimes exploring one aspect or another of the organization's fabulous mosaic.

Not only has organizational research furnished many alternative organizational designs, but attempts to solve the problems that organizations run into have given birth to an equally fascinating range of techniques. Operations research, planning, job enrichment, organization development, market research, financial analysis, and other techniques were developed and are being refined to help the organization function more effectively.

Another reason for studying organizations is that knowledge of how organizations function can help an individual—particularly a manager—navigate organizational eddies and currents with greater wisdom and probability of success. Organizations are incredibly complex. They must solve a great many problems to stay afloat.[4] For example, every organization has to confront the problem of how to acquire the right members, retain them, and motivate them to be productive. Almost every organization experiences interpersonal and intergroup conflicts and must face the problem of managing such conflicts. Practically every organization is a system of power and authority and must address itself to the question of what kind of power distribution is most useful. Every organization must learn to adapt to its environment to remain viable. Clearly, a greater understanding of how

FIGURE 1–1
Benefits of Organizational Research

people can be motivated, how and why conflicts arise and what can be done to prevent them from becoming destructive, what effects different power structures have, or how organizations can adapt to the characteristics of their environment can be useful to a manager in playing the many roles he has to play: those of an effective monitor, resource allocator, spokesman, disturbance handler, leader, negotiator, and so on.[5]

To the behavioral sciences, the organization offers a great natural laboratory for studying human behavior. The organization is not only just one more behavioral setting. It has distinctive features, like formality of relations; a careful and constant evaluation of performance; competition for power, influence, and money; the necessity for people to work in close interdependence with one another; and organizational policies and procedures that intensively shape behavior. The human responses to these offer rich insights into human behavior; and, indeed, the fields of industrial and managerial psychology, concerned as they are with behavior in industrial settings, have made significant contributions to social psychology.

In sum, the study of organizations is enormously productive (see Figure 1–1). Civilization is stuck with organizations, for a great deal of good and for some evil as well. Without organizations we may still, of course, have a society, possibly a happy society—of cave-dwelling humans that have survived child mortality, famines, predations of wild animals (including other humans), and disease. With organizations we still have problems, some of them stemming from our working in them, but we also live longer, develop a great many skills, open ourselves to a wide range of experiences, and pursue pleasure and avoid pain more expeditiously.

But alas! Bountiful as the study of organizations is, it is not without its costs. The field is extremely complex. It requires the student to be aware of behavioral, structural, technological, environmental, and performance variables affecting organizations. Each of these groups of variables consists in turn of a myriad of lesser variables. The interrelations of these variables, too, have to be borne in mind. On top of that, because the field is relatively young, there are no standardized definitions of variables. Reliable measurement of these variables can be a horrendous problem. A confusing variety of research methods is employed in organizational research. The quality of research is highly variable. Often research findings conflict with one another. Quite commonly there is simply no research evidence available to support or refute a point in contention. With these difficulties, endemic to most young and rapidly growing fields in the social sciences, the task of the student is not enviable. To be a successful organizational analyst requires a lot of hard work, a high tolerance for ambiguity, a sound judgment that comes with the practice of systematic organizational analysis, and a strong motivation to penetrate the complexities of organizational functioning. Organization theory has much to offer—except pat answers and neat formulas!

In the remainder of the chapter we discuss first the nature of organization theory and next the different methods for studying organizations.

THE NATURE OF ORGANIZATION THEORY

The Nature of Theory

Organization theory, like theory in every other field, tries to *explain* as parsimoniously as possible a mass of observations and hunches. In order to explain facts, organization theorists *devise concepts* and *define* them. For example, the concept of decentralization has been developed to label that class of organizational phenomena in which somebody with a formal authority to decide on a set of tasks voluntarily allows subordinates to make some or all such decisions.

But it is not enough simply to have concepts. Organization theorists are interested in relating concepts, in explaining how a phenomenon such as decentralization is affected by another phenomenon such as the size of the organization. To do so, they formulate *hypotheses* that can be tested by systematically gathered data. For example, one such hypothesis might be: Large organizations are more decentralized than small ones. How did the theorist come to believe this? He may have *come across* a few large organizations that were highly decentralized and a few small ones that were highly centralized. And so he might have felt that perhaps this was a universal condition. Or, he might have *conjectured* that as an organization grows larger it employs more people and undertakes a larger range of activities. Since the boss cannot supervise all these extra individuals or have the expertise to take the many technical decisions that need to be taken in an organization with many activities, the boss is bound to decentralize some authority.

Notice that the theorist needs to make *assumptions* in making a hypothesis: (a) that as organizations grow larger they employ more people and undertake a larger range of activities, and (b) that one person cannot supervise too many people or have the expertise to take a great variety of decisions, especially those of a technical nature. These assumptions may be the intuitions of the researcher, or the beliefs of authorities on organization theory, or facts confirmed by previous empirical research.

Organization theory, like any other theory, is a *network* of interconnected concepts, definitions, assumptions, and hypotheses. The hypotheses in organization theory take several forms. The more common forms are:

1 A theorist may hypothesize that large organizations are decentralized. This hypothesis simply states an attribute of large organizations without indicating whether large organizations are more or less decentralized than small organizations. Another example is: "Organizations have a hierarchy of authority." A third example is: "Organizations try to protect their core technologies from environmental turbulence." These hypotheses are of the form: organizations (or X types of organization) have Y characteristic(s); or, organizations (or X types of organization) do Y types of thing.

2 A more complex form of hypothesis is one where a relationship is postulated between two or more variables. For example, a theorist may hypothesize that decentralization of authority and the organization's use of sophisticated control systems are positively related—that is, they

co-vary. Notice, however, that the theorist is not saying which causes which. These hypothesis are of the form: The organizational phenomenon Y is positively (or negatively) related to X.

3 In a still more complex form, the theorist hypothesizes a causal relationship. For example: "The more the organization's environment is dynamic, the more loosely structured and organic is the organization caused to be." Here, a property of the environment causes the organization to possess specific characteristics. By and large these are the kinds of proposition developed in this book. They are of the form: The organizational phenomenon Y is a positive (or negative) *function* of X. A variant of these are hypotheses of reciprocal causality. For example, "The more decentralized the organization, the more the organization uses sophisticated controls, *and* the more the organization uses sophisticated controls, the more decentralized it gets." Here the form is: Y is a function of X at time t, and X is a function of Y at $t + 1$.

4 In the most complex form, the theorist not only hypothesizes a causal relationship and gives the sign of the relationship but goes on to give the *form* of the relationship. For example: "A given change in the degree of automation of the organization's technology causes a 150 percent greater change in the number of operatives connected with the technology in the opposite direction." This would be represented as $\Delta Y = -1.5 \Delta X$ where ΔY = change in the number of operatives, and ΔX = change in the degree of automation of technology. Research in the organizational field has not yet advanced to the point where these kinds of precise hypothesis can be commonly made. The form of such hypotheses, quite common in the natural sciences and in economics, is: $Y = f(X);\ \partial X / \partial Y = 0$. Here, $f(X)$ is a precise specification of the relationship between X and Y, and the null partial of X with respect to Y indicates that while Y is affected by X, the vice versa is not true.

The Nature of Organizational Laws

The laws of organization theory, as indeed of all the *social* sciences, are laws of tendency or probability. They are not deterministic like the laws of the natural sciences. For example, other things being equal, the pressure in a gas *invariably* will rise as the temperature of the gas goes up. On the other hand, organizations *tend* to get decentralized as they grow larger; they *tend* to get vertically integrated as they use a mass production technology; they *tend* to have a flexible structure as they function in a dynamic environment. In other words, organizations commonly but not invariably respond in a manner Y given a stimulus X.

What good are organizational laws if they are so tentative? First of all, they help us predict what is likely to happen to organizations as we change their circumstances. This is certainly better than not knowing at all what is going to happen as we increase the size of the organization or automate its technology or divisionalize it. Meteorological information is also couched in terms of tendencies or probabilities. "There is a good chance of showers tomorrow," the meteorologist may say. Though it is not certain that it will rain, the probability of rain helps us arm ourselves with an umbrella or a raincoat and helps us decide whether we want to go on a picnic or not. Thus, knowledge of organizational tendencies, tentative though it may be, is useful for planning precautionary or other action.

Actually, the laws of organizations are useful not only for their predictions of organizational consequences but also for their implicit ruling out of opposite consequences. If it is probable that an organization gets decentralized as it grows larger, it is *very* improbable, other things being equal, that it will survive or function effectively should it instead get centralized as it grows larger. If functioning in a technologically sophisticated environment makes it probable that the organization get technocratic—that is, employs specialists and operates with sophisticated techniques—it is very unlikely that an organization functioning in a technologically sophisticated environment would survive by relying exclusively on personnel with common sense but no technical expertise. Organizational laws not only point to what is probable but help to rule out the opposite of what is probable. To the designer of an organization this is very useful knowledge, for it drastically narrows the search for design alternatives in a given situation.

The Ambit of Organization Theory

Pugh has defined "organization theory" as "the study of the structure and functioning of organizations and behavior of groups and individuals within them."[6] The structure of organizations—their anatomy—covers those aspects and relationships in organizations that are relatively stable, such as the hierarchy of authority, the purposes for which an organization is set up, its rules and standard operating procedures, its technology, its principal activities, its operating policies, its organizational chart. The physiology of organizations—the way they function—covers organizational aspects that are more fluid and unpredictable, such as the chains of events that culminate in decisions; the interpersonal relations tied to the input-process-output cycle; organizational conflicts and politics; nonformal communications (e.g., the grapevine); the processes by which organizations change, innovate, and resuscitate themselves or die. Organization theory is interested, not only in the structure and functioning of organizations, but also in how these are influenced by technological, economic, political, and social forces.

The interest of organization theory in groups and individuals associated with or working in organizations is of a special kind. Organization theorists are less interested in the psychology of group or individual behavior than in how these behaviors are affected by organizational properties such as the organization's pyramidal authority structure, the extensive role specialization and division of labor, or the use of controls and standard operating procedures. In other words, organization theorists take their cues about the dynamics of human behavior from psychologists and then like to theorize about, as well as do empirical work on, how behavior is influenced by the way organizations are set up to function. Equally, they are interested in studying how the needs, motivations, and perceptions of individuals shape organizational structure and process. Put another way, organization theorists like to look at the responses of humans to organizational stimuli and at the responses of organizations to human stimuli.

Organization Theory and Organizational Practice

There is a rich interrelationship between organization theory and organizational practices. In the past, administrators and businessmen like Henri Fayol (1841–1925), Colonel L. Urwick (1891–   ), Chester Barnard (1886–1961), and Alfred Sloan (1875–1966) felt the need to give coherent expression to their administrative experiences. Each came up with significant theories of how organizations function. Professional researchers, too, were spurred to try explaining their experiences with organizations. Elton Mayo (1880–1949), for example, accidentally found that the productivity of a group he was studying went up no matter what happened to the lighting arrangements in the work place. This led him to an insight into the nonformal relationships at work and the power of group phenomena in affecting productivity. More recently, a number of consultants with a behavioral science orientation, like Douglas McGregor (1906–64), have utilized their management experiences to articulate theories of healthy organizations and sick organizations. These days, of course, much of organizational research is highly professionalized and systematic. Nonetheless, it continues to be influenced heavily by emerging organizational practices. For example, the so-called matrix organization, with its highly flexible structure, began to be practiced widely in the sophisticated aerospace industry before theories appeared attempting to explain its use.

But just as theorists have drawn on their observations of organizational practices, so have practitioners drawn on theories. In the early part of this century, "principles of management" theories were in vogue. Many businesspeople and also administrators of nonprofit organizations read these theories and tried to pattern their organizations after the principles enumerated in them. Later, the human relations movement took root, and a great many businesspeople turned to the writings of such men as Mayo and F. J. Roethlisberger (1898–   ) to design their organizations more effectively. Currently the contingency theories of organization are being studied by many a corporate planner and developer as guides to organizational design. The publication of business journals such as the *Harvard Business Review, California Management Review, Canadian Business,* and *Business Horizons* to which the practitioners as well as the professional organizational researchers contribute articles, attests to the highly stimulating traffic from theory to practice and vice versa. The general steps of this traffic are outlined in Figure 1–2.

Organization Theory and Organizational Design

Developing a theory is a scientific enterprise. It is designed to *explain phenomena.* If the phenomena that are the object of study can be explained by a theory, then the theory can facilitate *predictions* about the future behavior of these phenomena. If these predictions are borne out, the theory gets confirmed, and this gives the scientist greater *control* over the domain of the phenomena. The time, then, is ripe for making applications of the theory. In the world of physics, for example, Einstein's theory of relativity sought to explain the relationship between matter and energy. That theory predicted that time slows down as an object moves faster. This prediction was tested by round-the-world flights with extremely precise atomic clocks. Time did slow down as predicted, and so the theory was confirmed. That confirmation in turn means that if photon rockets capable of traveling at close to the speed of light can be developed, people could make interplanetary and interstellar flights during a lifetime.

Most social and management sciences are, of course, very far from this ideal of the natural sciences. Organization theory is no exception. And yet a sufficient body of research in this field has been accumulated to make possible at least some prescriptions about the overall forms of organizations. In other words, the present corpus of organization theory and research can support prescriptions about the design of organizations.

The word "design" means putting different parts together so that the whole is more valuable than the sum of the parts. This is the great challenge

FIGURE 1–2
The Traffic Between Theory and Practice

STEPS IN THE TRAFFIC	MAIN RESPONSIBILITY
Observation of organizational practices and problems	Administrators, consultants, organizational researchers
↓	
Development of organization theory to explain observations	Researchers
↓	
Testing of theory	Researchers
↓	
Refinement of theory	Researchers
↓	
Practical applications based on theory (including suggestions for organizational design)	Consultants, staff specialists within organizations, researchers
↓	
Assessment of the practical applications	Consultants, staff specialists, researchers
↓	
Observation of discrepancies between reality and hoped for results	Administrators, consultants, staff specialists, researchers

before organization theorists—to construct coherent alternative designs for organizations out of the seeming chaos of thousands of disparate hunches and empirical findings. This book takes up the challenge in a modest way. It does so first by trying to build up a body of law-like propositions about organizations from past and present research, or from informed guesswork, and next by trying to sketch out the implications of these propositions for an imaginary designer of organizations.

Organization theory, like economics or psychology, is a reactive field. Unlike physics, whose laws cannot be affected by humanity's knowledge of them, the "laws" of organizations, if so dignified a term may be applied to them, can be. For example, suppose that on the basis of research, a theorist proposes: "The greater the use of psychological tests in selecting employees, the better is the organization's performance." Now, let us suppose thousands of managers read about this proposition in the *Harvard Business Review*. They all busily set about installing psychological testing services for their employees. Since every organization does it, nobody has a comparative advantage, and indeed, there may be a slight decline in performance because of the costs of psychological testing. A researcher making the scene at this point might find a null or even a negative relationship between psychological testing of employees and organizational performance. Thus, organization theory and organizational design must be continually updated. There can be no definitive work on this subject.

Next we turn to the different methods by which we add to our knowledge of how organizations function.

METHODS FOR STUDYING ORGANIZATIONS

Introduction

Research is really nothing but *systematic* search for the truth. Organizations have been studied through many different methods. A *method* is a systematic and consistent manner of studying something. Casual observation is not a method, but participant observation is. Social chats with an organization's executives or personnel are not a method, but interviewing is. There is an element of rigor in a method. A method is a well-established sequence of premeditated actions. It is a program for gaining valid knowledge.

Methods

Some of the more common methods by which organizations have been studied are case studies, field studies, participant observation, interview or questionnaire surveys, field experiments, natural experiments, laboratory experiments, computer simulations, management games, and mathematical models of organizational behavior. Organization theory has been influenced by a number of social sciences, particularly by sociology, social psychology, political science, and economics. It has adopted not only many of the ideas and approaches of the social sciences (Chapters 2 and 3) but many of their research methodologies. For example, it has borrowed the field study and the questionnaire and interview survey from sociology, mathematical model building and simulation from economics and the applied economics field of operations research, and field and laboratory experimentation from social psychology. The research methods employed by organizational researchers are described briefly below.

Case studies. The researcher interviews a few individuals in the organization to determine the background and facts about an organizational occurrence like a strike, or severe conflict between organizational groups, or breakdown in communications, or poor organizational performance. This is not a very systematic method; it is likely to yield incomplete information because of the few individuals interviewed. Its advantage is that it is a quick way of getting the story and is a good pedagogic device for giving the student insights into organizational phenomena. There are many books of cases. To give a few examples: The book of cases by Wegner and Sayles, *Cases in Organizational and Administrative Behavior*, examines incidents in a large variety of organizations from the human relations viewpoint.[7] Newman's *Cases for Administrative Action* examines incidents from an administrative viewpoint. Dalton, Lawrence, and Lorsch's *Organizational Structure and Design* gives fairly detailed case studies of organizational structure and processes. A list of topics, as an aid to a fairly comprehensive case study, is reproduced as an appendix to this chapter.

Field studies. Field studies are usually much more thorough and much more time consuming than case studies. Researchers try to interview a representative sample of organizational members—sometimes all of them. They may structure the interviews; they may pass out questionnaires; they may examine relevant documents and records. They are likely to attend to the reliability and validity of their measures. They are likely to focus on a great many variables in explaining how an organization functions. Many organizational researchers with a sociological or anthropological background have given us field studies. The journal *Human Organization* frequently publishes field studies of organizations. Some classic field studies are: Selznick's *TVA and the Grassroots*, Crozier's *Bureaucratic Phenomenon*, and Whyte's *Human Relations in the Restaurant Industry*. Though a field study yields very valuable information, its limitation is that it involves the study of only one or a very few organizations. For a thorough treatment of the subject, see W. Richard Scott, "Field Methods in the Study of Organizations."

Participant observation. The researcher is a member of the organization studied and, being one of them, is likely to earn the confidence of the people in the organization. But emotional involvement with them may also give the researcher certain biases. Also, as a member, he may have limited access to other parts of the organization since his duties may constrain him to spend most of his time in the department to which he is assigned. Still, the participant observer is in an excellent position to observe how those around him really feel and what really goes on in his department. Dalton's *Men Who Manage* and Roy's "Banana Time—Job Satisfaction and Informal Interaction" are classics.

Interview or questionnaire surveys. A good deal of organizational research that is being done today is of the interview or questionnaire survey type.

Its great advantage is that information on a large and representative sample of organizations can be gathered quickly. This makes possible sophisticated statistical analysis of the data if they are in a quantifiable form. Whether the data so analyzed are informative or not depends, of course, on how good the instruments are by which the data are gathered. If the interview schedules and the questionaires are thoroughly pretested, then the information they yield is likely to be valid and reliable. Woodward's study of 100 British firms (*Management and Technology*), the study by Pugh and his associates of about fifty organizations in the English Midlands ("An Empirical Taxonomy of Structures of Work Organizations"), and Lawrence and Lorsch's study of ten U.S. firms (*Organization and Its Environment*) are examples. A comprehensive questionnaire utilized by the author for the study of corporate designs has been reproduced in Appendix A to this book. The *Administrative Science Quarterly* and the *Academy of Management Journal* are two of the more prolific publishers of survey-type research.[8]

Field experiments. Unlike a field study, in a field experiment the researcher tries to control and manipulate some aspects of the organization's functioning in order to study the effects of the manipulation on other aspects of the organization's functioning. Field experiments are rare because managements generally do not like to make guinea pigs of their organizations. A well-known example of a field experiment is Coch and French's experiment on participative decision-making in the Harwood Manufacturing Company; another example is Morse and Reimer's experiment on decentralization of decision-making in an insurance company. The extension of the findings of a field experiment to organizations in general is restricted because the field experiment is usually confined to one organization.

Natural experiments. In these, it is management, not the researcher, that decides what variables are going to be manipulated. For example, the management decides to install a computer-based information system. This is a major change. Researchers come in and request permission to study the effects of such a change. If management agrees, they may take measurements on the organizational variables that interest them, such as the level of job satisfaction before the installation of the system and again after its installation. This way, they can identify the effects of the change in the data-processing system. The many studies of the effectiveness of management training programs carried out in organizations are examples of natural experiments. An example is the 1966 study by Blake and Mouton.

Laboratory experiments. A laboratory situation affords the researcher maximum control over the manipulation of variables. But it is difficult to create a facsimile of an organization in the laboratory setting. An ongoing organization is very complex. A laboratory organization should reflect the properties of an ongoing organization like hierarchy of authority, rules and procedures, specialization and division of labor, specificity of goals, formal communications, and so on. Without these properties, one cannot generalize the findings from laboratory experiments to real life organizational settings. The communications-networks experiments of Leavitt, Bavelas, and others are fairly good examples of laboratory experiments with possible generalization to organizations. The laboratory study of the effects of tall and flat hierarchies on organizational performance by Carzo and Yanouzas is another example. For a review of laboratory experiments designed to study organizational phenomena, see Weick's "Laboratory Experimentation with Organizations."

Computer simulation. Since organizational laws are tendency laws, analytical solutions to organizational problems are not very useful. They have, of course, been tried by economists with respect to price and output behavior of firms, but under very restrictive and artificial assumptions that grossly simplify reality. Computer simulation offers a way of retaining the enormous complexity of real organizations and permitting the use of probabilistic hypotheses to see at a glance how the system as a whole responds to the manipulation of organizational variables. Naturally, the results are as good as the model of organizational relationships that is plugged into the computer. Computer simulation is not a hypotheses-testing strategy but a hypotheses-generating strategy. It is relatively cheap and flexible. A study such as the computer simulation of a firm by Bonini is a good example of the analytical power of this method. Clarkson's *Portfolio Selection: A Simulation of Trust Investment* is another example.

The management game. The management game usually consists of teams representing companies competing with one another. The game is usually played over a period of time and can be made as realistic and complex as need be.[9] At best, however, the behavior of teams presents the behavior only of the top management of firms, not of the entire organization. Management game is more useful as a pedagogical device than as a research method for studying organizations. Bass's use of the management game to study the effects of sensitivity training on team performance is an example.

Action research. Kurt Lewin, the social psychologist, once commented that an effective way of studying a group or an organization is to study it as it grapples with a problem. Many consulting behavioral scientists have refined this insight into what is known as action research. Typically, it occurs when researchers are called into an ailing organization to serve as consultants. As a first step, they interview or survey a representative number working in the organization to get an assessment of what is going on. Next, the findings are shared with all or most of the members of the organization and jointly evaluated. Out of such a meeting come proposals for future action. The accent in action research is on action, not on research. Still, action research does help in providing crude tests for models of organizational change. The *Journal of Applied Behavioral Science* has published some fairly good action research studies. A sophisticated version of action research is to be found in Mann's "Studying and Creating Change: A Means to Understanding Social Organizations."

Literature search. Literature search is the common adjunct of almost any research effort. However, it is an important source of information about organizations in its own right. The researcher reviews the published material on those aspects of organizations in which he is interested, such as the way organizations solve problems and make decisions, or the exercise of power and authority in organizations, or organizational growth and development. Out of this review of many disparate studies, usually a model or a theory may be developed that better explains the known facts. March's *Handbook of Organizations* is an outstanding example of literature searches being undertaken to study various organizational phenomena, various methods for studying organizations, and various types of organization.

Mathematical model-building. Except in the hands of economists, this is as yet an infrequent method in organizational research. Williamson's model of discretionary managerial behavior is a good example of mathematical models pressed into the service of research on organizations.[10] Other examples are in Simon's *Models of Man.*[11]

Criteria for Choosing a Research Method

The important point to bear in mind is that each of these methods has its advantages and disadvantages. (See Table 1–2.) Some of the criteria that guide research are: How much control does the researcher have on the manipulation of variables? How generalizable to all organizations are the results got through the use of the method? How valid and reliable are the measurements of organizational variables? How economically can we get the information we want? How speedily can we get it? How easy is it to use the method? The table summarizes the advantages and disadvan-

TABLE 1–2
The Advantages and Disadvantages of Research Methods

Research method	Control over manipulation of variables	Generalizability to all organizations	Validity of measures*	Expense	Speed	Ease
Case study	Low	Low	Low	Low	High	High
Field study	Low	Low	High	Fair	Low	Low
Participant observation	Low	Low	Fair	Low	Low	Low
Survey	Fair	High	Fair	Fair	Fair	Fair
Field experiment	Fair	Low	High	High	Low	Low
Natural experiment	Fair	Low	High	Fair	Low	Fair
Laboratory experiment	High	Low	Fair	Fair	Fair	Low
Computer simulation	High	Low	N.A.	Fair	Fair	Low
Management game	Fair	Low	Fair	Fair	Fair	Low
Action research	Low	Low	Fair	Fair	Fair	Low
Literature search	Low	Fair	Low	Low	Fair	Fair
Mathematical models	High	Low	N.A.	Low	Fair	Fair

* "Validity of measures" means, "Do the measures employed measure what they are intended to measure?"

tages of these research methods in terms of these criteria. It should be obvious that there is no one best research method. If speed is essential, the case study is the ideal method. If coverage of a large number of organizations is essential, a survey is desirable. If control over the manipulation of variables is important, the laboratory experiment is best, and so on. The researcher's goals and the constraints within which the work must be done ultimately determine which method or which combination of methods must be used.

Generally speaking, however, when an area of organizational research is more or less a *terra incognita,* "tight" research methods such as laboratory experimentation, mathematical model-building, or computer simulation may not be appropriate. The need is for "quick and dirty" methods to get an overview of the terrain. Case studies and field studies fit the bill well, as do loosely structured surveys. Once the terrain becomes reasonably familiar, it makes sense to develop closely reasoned hypotheses and to test them with more rigorous research methods such as field or laboratory experiments and carefully structured surveys.[12]

SUMMARY AND PLAN OF THE BOOK

Summary

The organization is one of the vital social inventions of mankind, and modern societies are characterized by an enormous number and variety of organizations. The minimal characteristics of organizations, which explain why they are so productive, are a hierarchy of authority; rules, procedures, techniques, and controls; formal interpersonal communications; specialization of functions and division of labor; organizational membership based more on expertise and achieved status than on ascribed status, family connections, and the like; and fairly specific purposes, which become the focus of the organization's activities. While all organizations must have these properties in at least some degree to be called organizations, they vary considerably in the extent to which they possess these as well as other characteristics.

The typical organization differs from the typical family in the much lower intensity of the emotional bonds between members in the organization and in its larger size. It differs from the typical community or society in the much greater specificity of the organization's objectives and in the much greater central coordination of its activities.

The organization carries on a number of activities, principally activities designed to acquire resources; workflow activities; control and coordination activities; identity-building activities; and homeostatic activities designed to keep the organization healthy and well adjusted to its environment. To carry on these activities, the organization uses different kinds of resource, chiefly human resources, material resources, financial resources, physical resources, ideational resources, and the "market" or operating field.

The organization has no fixed boundaries, nor need it be a completely independent body to be called an organization. Any body of individuals that shows the characteristics of the organization, whether it is an independent body or a group of individuals functioning within a larger organization, can be studied as an organization. It is the purpose of inquiry that sets the boundaries of what constitutes an organization.

There are a number of reasons for studying organizations. First of all, they are the primary means by which society gets its work done and its needs satisfied. And they vitally affect the lives of the millions of people who work in them. The study of organizations can lead to more effectively functioning organizations and to improvements in their design such that people may have more of their needs satisfied and experience less stress. Research on organizations has been an enormously productive enterprise. Because of research we understand much better the different forms or designs that organizations can take. Research on the problems organizations have to deal with has led to the development of a great many techniques such as operations research, management training, and organizational development. The knowledge of how organizations function, what problems they run into, and the ways in which these problems can be approached is indispensable to those who manage organizations. Finally, the organization offers to the social psychologist a remarkably fertile research setting. How human beings respond to the various stresses, strains, and opportunities in the organization is a rich source of insight into the dynamics of human behavior and has led to a better understanding of why we function the way we do. The organization is a giant psychological laboratory. However, the complexity of the organization makes its study difficult.

Organization theory's purposes is to explain, as economically as possible, the multitudes of facts about organizations. For this purpose, theorists devise concepts to describe with brevity organizational phenomena and form hypotheses that link concepts. They form hypotheses on the basis of their observations and/or on the basis of a set of assumptions. Thus, organization theory is a network of interconnected concepts, assumptions, and hypotheses. The hypothoses take on several forms. The simplest are of the form: "organizations (or X types of organization) have Y characteristics." More complex ones have the forms: "the organizational phenomenon Y is positively (or negatively) related to X"; "the organizational phenomenon Y is a positive (or negative) function of X"; and "$\Delta Y = k\Delta X$." Most hypotheses developed in this book are of the form: "Y is a function of X."

The laws that govern organizations are not deterministic or universal like those of the natural sciences but probabilistic, and some of them may possibly also be culture bound. However, they still help in explaining and predicting organizational phenomena. For the organizational designer, they helpfully narrow the area of search for design alternatives.

The subject matter of organization theory is the study of the structure of the organization, the processes by which it functions, the determinants of its structure and functioning, the way groups and individuals working in the organization affect the organization, and how they in turn are affected by the properties of the organization.

There has been a rich interaction between organization theory and organizational practices. Many executives and administrators have tried to theorize about organizations on the basis of their experiences, and, of course, many managers try to employ the tenets of organization theory in designing their organizations. There are many business journals to which both practitioners and researchers contribute.

Once a theory gets support from systematically gathered data, its propositions become helpful in designing organizations. However, human behavior is reactive, and so, periodically, organization theory and design must be updated.

There are many methods for studying organizations. Chief among these are case studies, field studies, participant observation, surveys, field experiments, natural experiments, laboratory experiments, computer simulation, management games, action research, literature search, and mathematical models. The criteria by which each of these can be evaluated are: control over the manipulation of variables, generalizability of the findings resulting from the use of the method to organizations in general, validity of the measures of organizational variables, expense, speed in gathering the needed information, and ease of using the method. In terms of these criteria, the different research methods have different advantages and disadvantages. The researcher must select that method, or that combination of methods, that is most appropriate given the research goals, the researcher's situation, and the state of knowledge in the area of the research.

The Plan of the Book

This book is about organization theory and the implications of this theory for the design of organizations. The first part of the book introduces the reader to organizations and organizational design and is intended to lay the groundwork for a more detailed treatment of organization theory and design issues in the second part of the book. The second part of the book deals with the design of organizational components such as management philosophy, organizational goals, organizational structure, organizational technology, organizational behavior, and organizational performance. The attempt is to identify the environmental and organizational forces that shape these and to identify combinations of these components that seem particularly effective. A number of propositions are developed in the course of this odyssey.

In the first part of the book, the next two chapters attempt to view the organization through the perspective of each of four major social sciences—namely, economics, sociology, political science, and psychology. The emphasis is on the kinds of question they raise for the study of organizations and the kinds of perspective they provide that could be helpful in dealing with something as complex as organizations.

The fourth chapter provides an outline of the structure-oriented schools in organization theory, particularly the early schools founded by Weber and Fayol, their key concerns, and their evolutions to the present. The kinds of question they raise for organizational analysis are particularly stressed. The fifth chapter similarly treats the human-behavior-oriented schools in organization theory, particularly the human relations, participative management, human resource development, and "bounded rationality" versions. The sixth chapter outlines the "open systems" and contingency approaches. Drawing on the material in the preceding chapters, Chapter 7 describes a model of the way organizations function and get shaped. The balance of the book is then a more detailed exposition of the broad relationships outlined in the model.

SUGGESTED READINGS

"The Nature of Organization Theory," pp. 1–24, in A. H. Rubenstein and C. Haberstroh. *Some Theories of Organization* (Homewood, Ill.: Irwin-Dorsey, 1966).

"Introduction," pp. 1–26, in P. Blau and W. Scott, *Formal Organizations* (San Francisco: Chandler Publishing, 1962).

James March and Herbert Simon, *Organizations* (New York: Wiley, 1958), pp. 1–6.

"Strategies of Research," Ch. 2, in W. F. Whyte, *Organizational Behavior: Theory and Application* (Homewood, Ill.: Irwin-Dorsey, 1969). An excellent discussion of the different strategies of research.

QUESTIONS FOR ANALYSIS

1 "Business is simply a form of human competition, greatly resembling war," said Clausewitz, the famous Prussian general (1780–1831) who wrote extensively on war and the management of large armies at war. If business

competition is like a war, then should the organization of a firm be similar to that of an army?

2 Is a typical class at school or college an organization? Is a street corner gang an organization?

3 Sociologists have fun analyzing one organizational type as if it is a different organizational type. For example, they may look for the features of a gang in a cooperative. How about the firm as a gang, and vice versa? How would each look if organized along the lines of the other?

4 If your uncle came to you for help in understanding why there is such a large turnover in his garment-manufacturing factory (employing 50 individuals), what would be your research strategy? Would it be any different if the plant employed 5,000 workers?

5 Suppose you and your friends decide to market a new concept in housing that greatly cuts down construction costs. Aside from incorporation, patenting of the invention, and the raising of capital, what *must* be done to turn a group of friends into a full-fledged organization? (*Hint:* essential properties of organizations.) Be as specific as you can.

6 Form yourselves into study groups of five members each. Utilize the Appendix to this chapter as best you can to study various aspects of an organization of your choice.

Footnotes to Chapter One

[1] See James March and Herbert Simon, *Organizations*, p. 4.

[2] See E. Wight Bakke, "Concept of the Social Organization."

[3] Stephen Sales and James House, "Job Dissatisfaction as a Possible Risk Factor in Coronary Heart Disease."

[4] See Warren Bennis, *Changing Organizations*, pp. 190–91.

[5] See Henry Mintzberg, *The Nature of Managerial Work*, Ch. 4.

[6] See D. S. Pugh, "Modern Organization Theory: A Psychological and Sociological Study."

[7] Additional information on this and the other research examples cited in the following discussion can be found in the Bibliography at the end of this book.

[8] For a useful description of the "do's" and "don't's" of questionnaire construction and interview procedure, see Arthur Kornhauser and Paul B. Sheatsly, "Questionaire Construction and Interview Procedure."

[9] See K. J. Cohen, et al., "The Carnegie Tech Management Game."

[10] Oliver Williamson, "A Model of Rational Managerial Behavior."

[11] For a review of mathematical application to organizational studies, see W. H. Starbuck, "Mathematics and Organization Theory."

[12] See Joseph E. McGrath, "Toward a 'Theory of Method' for Research on Organizations," for an interesting discussion of what research methods are appropriate in different circumstances.

[13] H. Levinson, with Janice Molinan and Andrew C. Spohn, *Organizational Diagnosis*, pp. 55–65.

A List of Topics for the Case Study of an Organization[13]

I. **Genetic Data**
   A. *Identifying Information*
      Organization name
      Location
      Type of organization
      Organizational affiliation
      Size
         a. Financial condition
         b. Stockholders
         c. Employees
      Situation of the initial contract
         a. Consultation
         b. Research orientation
      Circumstances of the study
      Special conditions affecting validity of the study
      First overall impressions

   B. *Historical Data*
      Chief complaint or events leading to the initiation
         of the study
      Problems of the organization as stated by key
         figures
         a. Long-range
         b. Short-range
      Background of the organization
         a. Key development phases
            (1) As reported by organizational
                participants
            (2) As reported by outsiders
            (3) As reported by the consultant
         b. Major crises experienced by the organization
            (1) Natural catastrophies
            (2) Loss of key personnel
            (3) Labor problems
            (4) Financial emergencies
            (5) Technological changes
         c. Product-service history
            (1) Change and development of organiza-
                tional goals
            (2) Sequence of development in product or
                service
            (3) Relative success or failure in various
                stages of service or (product) history
            (4) Geographical patterns
            (5) Special skills of the organization
            (6) Performance reputation and record
         d. Organizational folklore

Circumstances surrounding study

II. **Description and Analysis of Current Organization as a Whole**
A. *Structural Data*
Formal organization
a. Chart
b. Systems concept
c. Formal job description
Plant and equipment
a. Location: territory covered
b. Value
c. Kinds of equipment: size, function
d. Relative efficiency: age, obsolescence
e. Special demands plant and equipment make on people
f. Varieties of work environment
Ecology of the organization
a. Spatial distribution of individuals
b. Spatial distribution of activities
c. Implications of the data on spatial distribution
Financial structure
Personnel
a. How many people are employed
b. Where do they come from and what is their ethnic composition
c. What are the various educational levels
d. What is the average tenure
e. What is the range of skills
f. What is the absentee rate
g. What is the turnover rate
h. What is the accident rate
Structure for handling personnel
a. Recruitment
b. Orientation
c. Training
d. Growth on the job
e. Promotion
f. Compensation
g. Performance analysis
h. Kind and intensity of supervision
i. Rules and regulations for employees
j. Medical program
k. Safety program
l. Retirement program
m. Recreation program
n. Other fringe benefits
o. Labor contract
Policies and procedures
a. Scope

        d. How they are communicated
        c. Who knows about them
        b. What discretion is left to lower supervisory
           levels
    Time span and rhythm
        a. Seasonal cycles
        b. Diurnal cycles
        c. Planning spans
        d. Degree activities are regulated by time
        e. Attitudes about punctuality
        f. Urgency
        g. Concern about deliveries

B. *Process Data*
    Communication systems
        a. Incoming: reception and routing
           (1) Amount and types of materials
           (2) Modes of transmission
               (A) Oral or written
               (B) Formal or informal channels
           (3) Timing, rhythm, urgency
               (A) According to plan
               (B) Erratically or spontaneously
           (4) Source and audience
        b. Processing: integration, decision
           (1) Amount and types of material
           (2) Modes of processing
               (A) Oral or written
               (B) Formal or informal channels
           (3) Timing, rhythm, urgency
               (A) According to plan
               (B) Erratically or spontaneously
           (4) Source and audience
        c. Outgoing: routing and response
           (1) Amount and types of materials
           (2) Modes of distribution
               (A) Oral or written statements
               (B) Formal or informal channels
           (3) Timing, rhythm, urgency
               (A) According to plan
               (B) Erratically or spontaneously
           (4) Source and audience
    Current and previous studies in, and reports to, the
    organization
        a. Consultant reports
        b. Special staff studies
        c. Marketing studies
        d. Engineering studies
        e. Accountants; audits and reports.

III. **Interpretative Data**
    A. *Current Organizational Functioning*

Organizational perceptions

  a. Degree of alertness, accuracy, and vividness
    (1) To stimuli from within the organization
      (A) From personnel
          i. Employees to management and vice versa
         ii. Supervisor to subordinate and vice versa
        iii. Departments to each other's needs
      (B) From physical plant
    (2) To stimuli from without
      (A) Primary external stimuli
          i. Marketing conditions
         ii. Purchasing conditions
        iii. Labor conditions
      (B) Secondary external stimuli
          i. Legislative (tariff and tax laws)
         ii. Transportation
        iii. Competitors
        iv. Research developments
         v. Economic, social, and political trends

  b. Direction and span of attention (selectivity)
    (1) Dominant foci of interest
      (A) Long-term framework
      (B) Short-term framework
    (2) Significant neglected foci

  c. Assessment of the discrepancy between reality and perceived reality
    (1) Of reality within the organization
    (2) Of reality outside the organization

Organizational knowledge

  a. Acquisition of knowledge
    (1) Methods of obtaining new knowledge
      (A) Related to personnel and plant
      (B) Related to products, services, or competitors
      (C) Related to financial resources
      (D) Related to forces and trends affecting the organization
      (E) By whom (sources within and outside the organization)
      (F) Reservoir of intellectual sources
          i. Talents and skills within the organization
         ii. Consultants
        iii. Affiliations with specialized institutions or universities

iv. Library facilities and
services
(2) Degree of receptivity to new knowledge
(A) By whom
(B) To what
(3) Level and range of knowledge
(A) Concerning themselves, their
products, their services and
related factors
(B) Outside their immediate area of
interest
b. Use of knowledge
(1) How is it brought together
(A) Who thinks about it
(B) Level of abstraction
(2) How is knowledge organized and sys-
tematized
(A) Committee system
(B) Records and storage system
(C) Other modes of organization and
systematization
(3) Amount and kind of use (retrieval)
(4) Organizational conditions affecting the
use of intellectual sources
(A) Ability to deal with abstract problems
(B) Flexibility
(C) Characteristic style and variations
c. Dissemination of knowledge
Organizational language
a. Themes and content of employee publications
b. Organizational ideology
c. Advertising themes
d. Organizational symbols and slogans
e. Language of policies as distinct from the
policies themselves
f. Language of customs, taboos, prohibitions,
and constrictions; direct and implied.
Emotional atmosphere of the organization
a. Prevailing mood and range
b. Overall stability of variability of mood
(1) Intensity of reactions
(2) Duration of reactions
(3) Appropriateness to stimulating factors
c. Intraorganizational variability
(1) By hierarchical level
(2) By department
(3) Other (geographical location,
profession)
Organizational action
a. Energy level

        (1) Consistency or variability of application
              (rate of discharge of energy)
        (2) Points and periods of peak expenditure
              energy
   b. Qualities of action
        (1) Degree of directness
        (2) Degree of flexibility
        (3) Planning and timing
        (4) Degree of persistence
        (5) Effectiveness
        (6) Constructiveness or destructiveness

B. *Attitudes and Relationships*

   Contemporary attitudes toward, and relationships
     with, others
     a. Range, diversification, depth, and constancy
         (1) Customers
         (2) Competition
         (3) Employees
         (4) Occupational associations and
              representatives
         (5) Stockholders
         (6) Legislative bodies
         (7) Executive and regulatory bodies
              (governmental)
         (8) Control bodies (internal)
         (9) Suppliers
       (10) Financial community
       (11) Host community
       (12) Dealer organizations
       (13) Plant builders
       (14) Consultants
       (15) Others
     b. Major attachments
         (1) Positive
         (2) Negative
     c. Masculine-feminine orientation
         (1) Of organization
             (A) Masculine
             (B) Feminine
             (C) Degree of achievement
             (D) How pervasive
         (2) In relation to the industry
     d. Transference phenomena
         (1) Related to the consultant
         (2) Related to the organization
         (3) Related to each other
   Relations to things and ideas
     a. Quality and intensity of relations to plant,
        equipment, raw material or supplies, prod-
        uct, and services

      (1) Symbolization
      (2) Unconscious personification
  b. Time: how is it regarded
      (1) Past, present, future orientation
      (2) How is future planned for
      (3) Is time valued as an investable
         commodity
      (4) View of work cycles
  c. Space: how is it conceptualized
      (1) As a local concern
      (2) As a cosmopolitan concern
  d. Meaning of work for the organization
      (1) As a device for coping with the environ-
         ment
         (A) In economic terms
         (B) In terms of skill
         (C) In terms of thinking
         (D) In terms of psychological defense
      (2) As a device for fulfilling psychological
         contract
      (3) As a device for channeling energy
         (A) Constructively
         (B) Destructively
         (C) As a process of regression
            i. Within the work setting
           ii. In nonwork activities
  e. Authority, power, and responsibility
      (1) How does the organization regard power
         (A) The power of others
         (B) Their own power vis-à-vis the
            world outside
         (C) Power internally
            i. Generally
           ii. By ranks
      (2) How does the organization handle
         authority
      (3) How does the organization handle
         responsibility
         (A) Outside the organization
         (B) Inside the organization
  f. Positions on social, ethical, and political
    issues
Attitudes about self
  a. Who do they think they are and how do they
    feel about it
  b. Where do they think they are headed and
    how do they feel about it
  c. What are their common aspirations
  d. How do they look to themselves
Intraorganizational relationships
  a. Key people in the organization

    b. Significant groups within the organization

    c. Implications of a and b

IV. **Analyses and Conclusions**

    A. *Organizational Integrative Patterns*

    Appraisal of the effect of the environment on the organization

        a. Historical

            (1) Beneficial

            (2) Harmful

        b. Contemporary

            (1) Beneficial

            (2) Harmful

        c. Anticipated

            (1) Beneficial

            (2) Harmful

    Appraisal of the effect of the organization on the environment

        a. Historical

            (1) Beneficial

            (2) Harmful

        b. Contemporary

            (1) Beneficial

            (2) Harmful

        c. Anticipated

            (1) Beneficial

            (2) Harmful

    Reactions

        a. Of the environment

            (1) To the injury

            (2) Toward source of the injury

        b. Secondary reaction from the organization

    Appraisal of the organization

        a. Special assets

            (1) Material or tangible (financial, patents, physical plant, equipment, geographical distribution, transportation, communication, personnel)

            (2) Functional (including leadership and mental set, or attitude)

                (A) Reality orientation

                    i. To external environment

                    ii. To internal environment

                (B) Values and ideals

                    i. Degree of institutionalization

                    ii. Congruence with reality

                (C) Task mastery

                    i. Psychological contract unfulfillment

                    ii. Growth and survival

                    iii. Task-directed behavior

b. Impairments
    (1) Material or tangible (financial, patents, physical plant, equipment, geographical distribution, transportation, communication, personnel.)
    (2) Functional (including leadership and mental set, or attitude)
        (A) Reality orientation
            i. To external environment
            ii. To internal environment
        (B) Values and ideals
            i. Degree of institutionalization
            ii. Disparity from reality
        (C) Task mastery
            i. Psychological contract unfulfillment
            ii. Growth and survival
            iii. Task-directed behavior
c. Level of integration
    (1) Normal adaptive activities
    (2) First-order adaptive activities
    (3) Second-order adaptive activities
    (4) Third- and fourth-order adaptive activities
d. Overall effectiveness and facade

B. *Summary and Recommendations*
    Present status
    Explanatory formulation
      a. Genetic
      b. Dynamic
    Prognostic conclusions
    Recommendations

Organizational Analysis from the Perspectives of Economics and Political Science

INTRODUCTION

Organization theory has been an interdisciplinary field. A number of social scientists have contributed to its development. *Economists* have studied price, output, and resource allocation behavior of firms. Although their ideas are relevant principally to firms (one type of organization), with some imagination they can be extended to many other organizations, because other organizations, too, are economic entities. They, too, have limited resources to achieve their goals, and they, too, for the most part, are subject to market forces. *Political scientists* have studied the phenomenon of power and its institutionalization, particularly in the government. But in most organizations the exercise of power and its legitimation are of central importance, so the ideas of political scientists have implications for all organizations. Every organization is a miniature society. Every organization, as it evolves, develops traditions, exhibits a stratified power and status structure, develops the structures and processes that help it survive, and contains within it some incompatibilities or inadequacies that impel it to change. Hence, *sociology*, or the science of society, is of great relevance to organizations. Finally, organizations are assemblages of interacting human beings.

41

TABLE 2–1
The Core Concerns of Social Sciences and Core Questions for Organizational Analysis

Social science	Core concerns	Questions for organizational analysis
Economics	Allocation of society's scarce resources to alternative ends	How do organizations make decisions regarding the allocation of their resources?
Political science	The legitimate and nonlegitimate use of power	How is power handled in organizations? With what consequences?
Sociology	The structure and functioning of society	What are the anatomical and physiological properties of the organization as a social system?
Social psychology	The behavior of human beings in a social setting	What are the organizational implications of different models of the human being?

The perspective from the study of human behavior and human mentality in a social context—*social psychology*—is of obvious and immense relevance if we want to understand why people in organizations behave the way they do.

Each of these four social sciences is a discipline, a state that organization theory is yet struggling to attain. A discipline, as distinguished from a field of knowledge, is characterized by a *disciplined* way of conducting inquiry. This requires fairly broad agreement among the scientists practicing the discipline on a number of issues: key concepts and variables, their definitions, and modes of analysis. These make for rigor and depth in analysis, but also for narrowness and biased explanation of events. Economists, for example, can bring to an analysis of inflation powerful tools of macroeconomic theory, such as the Keynesian multiplier and accelerator, the velocity of circulation of money, and so on. But they will tend to ignore political factors, such as the form of government, the motivations and perceptions of key groups in society, and long-term sociological trends in population composition and life styles. Like a laser beam, the perspective of each discipline is powerful but narrow; when applied to organizations, it illumines only partly the extremely complex goings on. Ultimately, organization theory must learn to absorb this melange of perspectives and develop a disciplined way of its own of extending its explanatory power. Building on the analytical perspectives offered by social sciences, as well as by the various schools of organization theory influenced by these social sciences, we present a synthesized mode of analysis for organizations starting in Chapter 7.

First, however, we must cull what we can from each of the four social sciences mentioned above. Each of the four is enormous. We cannot possibly make an inventory of their concepts and findings for use in this book. We shall, therefore, content ourselves with outlining some of their key concepts or approaches that are of particular relevance to the analysis of organizations. The value of this lies in outlining *questions* that can be raised in studying organizations. These questions can lead to important theoretical insights and, hopefully, to attractive practical applications too. Table 2–1 gives a quick overview of the core concerns of each social science and the kinds of question they raise in organizational analysis.

In this chapter we identify the questions central to an economic and a political analysis of organizations. In the next chaper we describe the sociological and social psychological approaches to the study of organizations.

ECONOMIC ANALYSIS OF ORGANIZATIONS

What Is Economics?

Economics is "the study of how men and society *choose*, with or without the use of money, to employ *scarce* productive resources, which could have alternative uses, to produce various commodities over time and distribute them for consumption, now and in the future, among various people and groups in society."[1] This definition by a famous economist underlines the *social* nature of economics and its attempts to shed light on three troublesome social problems: what goods and services to produce, how to produce them, and for whom.[2] Economics covers many areas, notably studies of resource allocation, pricing, and output decisions by firms in different market structures (microeconomic theory and industrial organization); welfare economics; the economics of national growth and development; and the economics of income, employment, money, and fiscal policies (macroeconomics). Our primary concern will be with microeconomic theory, since it is most directly related to the analysis of organizations, certainly of business firms. Microeconomic theory is the theory of how firms make pricing and output decisions. It tries to explain how much of each factor of production is optimally employed. The theory also seeks to relate the structure of the market in an industry (for example, whether it is competitive or monopolistic) with the conduct of firms in the industry. This conduct may be competitive or collusive, aggressively advertising and promotion oriented or not, oriented toward the innovation of new products or toward the continued marketing of true and tried products. This aspect of economics, seeking to relate the structure of an industry to the market conduct and performance of firms in the industry is called "industrial organization."[3]

The Logic of Optimal Production

Economics has to do with economizing—that is, with the "optimal" allocation of finite resources to alternative, and seemingly insatiable, human needs. Economists generally regard resources (factors of production)—land, labor, capital, management, and technical know-how—as each having multiple uses, as each being, within limits, a substitute for the others. What this implies is that if one of these—say labor—gets scarce, its market price relative to those of the other factors will go up, and therefore other resources—say capital—will be used by organizations as partial substitutes for labor. Thus, while the use of each one of these resources is essential to the functioning of any organization, managerial rationality consists in making *marginal adjustments* in the use of these resources, deemphasizing the use of the relatively expensive resources and emphasizing the use of the relatively cheap factors, so that for a given level of organizational output, the total cost is minimized. To achieve a condition of minimum cost per unit at a given level of output, the organization must so deploy its various resources that the ratio of the marginal productivity of the last unit of each resource to its marginal cost is equal for every productive resource employed in the organization. The relations between some factors of production may be complementary—that is, a greater use of one factor requires a greater use of the complementary factor. For example, if more managers are hired, more secretaries and other staff may also have to be hired; if there is an expansion of facilities then more labor and raw materials will have to be secured. In this case, the marginal productivity of the last composite unit of the jointly varying factors of production and its cost will have to be assessed.[4]

The logic of optimal production has powerful implications for organizational design. If we think of organizational design as putting together various combinations of *organizational* components like technology, structure, management ideology, and human behavior, to achieve effectively the goals of the organization, then by analogy from economic analysis it follows that (a) none of these components may be useful in isolation; (b) for effective functioning the combination of these components is of greater importance than the use of individual components; (c) the identification of the optimal combination for the organization, given its specific situation, is a key managerial function; and (d) the process by which this optimal combination is identified is essentially an adaptive trial-and-error process, guided, however, by the insights afforded by organization theory into the organizational consequences of variations in these components. Economic theory therefore points to a useful set of questions for organizational analysis:

1 What *organizational* variables that are crucial for the effective functioning of an organization are capable of being altered by management?

2 How do alterations in their magnitudes affect the performance of the organization?

3 If some of them are changed, which other organizational variables might have to be changed?

4 What would be effective combinations of these variables?

5 What would be an effective *process* for changing organizational variables?

Take for example a school whose students are generally several years behind those of the average school in reading skills, a problem quite common in ghettos. An economist organizational analyst is likely to ask: What variables are under the control of the school's administrators? Can they change the physical location of the school? Can they change teachers? Can they change the attitudes of teachers toward the students? Can they alter the technology of instruction? Can they change the composition of the student body? Can they change their attitudes towards reading and learning? Once the economist gets some idea of what the administrators *can* do (and what they *cannot* do because of legal or economic or social constraints), he can ask: Change(s) in which of the variables that can be altered by the school's administration will provide the greatest payoff, dollar for dollar, in terms of improved reading skills? Suppose that a change in the teaching technology from rote learning to a greater use of audio-visual aids is found to be the best means. What other variables (such as the capacity of the teachers to handle audio-visual equipment) will have to be altered? How *much* of a change in the use of audio-visual equipment and in the teachers' ability and willingness to handle this equipment is needed for best results? What would be an effective strategy for securing the needed changes?

Typology of Market Structures

The economists' classification of the firm's business environment into monopolistic, oligopolistic, monopolistically competitive, perfectly competitive, and so on affords a way of viewing the environment, not only of firms, but of other types of organization, such as political parties, hospitals, or governmental agencies, that experience competition for power, personnel, funds, and the like.

The principal types of market structure studied by economists are:[5]

1 The competitive market, characterized by numerous relatively small sellers of homogeneous products, none of whom can control the price of its product. Price is set wholly by market demand and supply. Examples of perfectly competitive markets are few, but the dairy industry, the livestock industry, and the timber industry are examples of many relatively small producers of homogeneous products.

2 The imperfectly competitive market, characterized by perfect competition in one part and monopoly in another. The typical example is of a domestic monopoly such as The Bell Telephone Company, or a nationalized airline monopoly, that also operates in highly competitive foreign markets. In an imperfectly competitive market, the firm can control the price of its product in the part that is monopolized by it but has no control over price in the competitive portion of its market.

3 The monopolistically competitive market, in which the *somewhat* similar products of different sellers compete with one another. Competition in this case is muted by the attempts of each firm to differentiate its product from those of rival firms by such devices as minor product changes, advertising and promotion campaigns, and the like. Monopolistic competition is common in industries in which economies of scale are not very large, there are many firms, and the product of different firms can be differentiated at least in the minds of relatively naive customers. Many consumer goods industries, especially the nondurable-goods ones such as garments, brand food products, and retailing are of this type. Some control over price is made possible by market differentiation.

4 Price leadership, a market structure in which a dominant firm sets the market price that several much smaller firms take as given. The U.S. Steel Corporation, for many decades, was the price leader in the U.S. steel industry. Price leadership tends to be common in industries with large scale economies and a homogeneous product.

5 Oligopoly, in which a few large firms dominate the market. The automobile industry in the United States or Japan is a good example. So are the U.S. aluminum industry and the Canadian tobacco products industry. A variant is duopoly, in which just two firms constitute the market. Duopolies are more prevalent in local markets than in national or international markets. Oligopoly is the most frequent market structure in industries with large economies of scale. In some oligopolies the industry's products are highly differentiated (e.g., the automobile industry); in others they are quite homogeneous (e.g., aluminum). Oligopolies may be highly competitive, as in the case of the automobile industry, or they may operate as cozy cartels.

6 Monopoly, which is a single-firm industry. The so-called natural monopoly arises because the economies of scale are so vast that the market can be most efficiently serviced by just one firm. Having more than one firm in the industry would raise the unit cost of production. The natural monopolies tend to be either nationalized or stringently controlled by government legislation. The railways are a prime example of a natural monopoly. In India they are nationalized.

Just as one can classify the market structure in the product market—that is—the market in which the firm operates as a seller, one can similarly make a classification of the market in which the firm operates as a buyer. For example, monopsony is a situation in which the firm is the only buyer of a product; oligopsony is where it is one of a few large buyers; and so on.

A number of economists in the area of industrial organization have tried to establish links between the structure of a market and the price, promotion, and innovation policies of firms in that market. For example, it has been found that the closer a market resembles an oligopoly, the less the firms in it compete on the basis of price. Instead they tend to compete furiously through advertising and promotion.[6] It has also been found that research and development activity tends to be stronger in moderately competitive markets than in competitive or monopolistic markets.[7] Now, heavy advertising and promotion imply a strongly market-oriented management—that is, a management that is especially sensitive to the needs of the customers and to creative ways of selling its products. And heavy emphasis on the development of new products or services implies that the organization must hire many different kinds of specialist, encourage innovation and experimentation, engage in careful market analysis to see which products it should place its bets on, set up divisions or other units to market these products (a form of decentralization), and so on. Thus, what kind of market structure a firm (or some other kind of organization) may face has far-reaching implications, not only for the pricing, marketing, and new product introduction *policies* of that organization vis-à-vis its rivals, but also for the *design* of its organization. Table 2–2 indicates some relationships between market structure, the market behavior of firms, and the administrative consequences of the latter.

The study of the relationship between market structure and market conduct and of the possible links between market conduct and organizational design raises a number of questions for organizational analysis:

1 What is the organization's "market" (or "markets")? It is relatively simple to identify the market of a firm. But what is the market of a political party? Of a school? Of a union? Of a hospital? Is a department of engineering of a university in the education industry or in the engineering industry? As students are its clients, it may be thought to be in the higher education industry. But since it exports its "products" (skilled students) to the engineering profession, is it not also in the engineering industry? In economics, the concept of the market refers to the set of individuals or organizations that are producing goods or services that are at least partial substitutes for one another in the minds of their clients or customers. If we apply this definition to the department of engineering, we are likely to say that its market is the set of

TABLE 2–2
Market Structure, Market Behavior of Firms, and the Administrative Consequences of Market Behavior

Market structure	Market behavior of firms	Likely administrative consequences of market behavior
Regulated monopoly (e.g., A.T.&T.)	Pricing designed to yield the legally permitted rate of return on investment	A good deal of market analysis, long-range forecasting, and planning, to secure no more or less than the permitted rate of return
Unregulated monopoly (e.g., a firm that patents a revolutionary process or product)	Profit maximization pricing, or pricing below it to prevent the entry of rival firms into the market	A somewhat slack and wasteful administration; overstaffing
Oligopoly in which the products are differentiated (e.g., the automobile industry)	Frequent introduction of new models; heavy advertising and promotion	The departments of product design, marketing, and distribution enjoy a great deal of power and status; the hiring of researchers, engineers, and other technocrats
Oligopoly in which the products are homogeneous (e.g., the aluminum industry)	Attempts to suppress price competition	Since production efficiency is crucial, the manufacturing department has great power and status; the hiring of researchers to improve the manufacturing process

organizations competing with it to "sell" qualified engineering students to industry—that is, the departments of engineering of other universities in the region.

2 What is the structure of the organization's market (or markets)? Is it oligopolistic, monopolistic, or competitive? Are the products or services in the industry homogeneous or differentiated? Are there barriers to the entry of new organizations into the market? Are the customers many or few, large or small, naive or sophisticated? Answers to these questions will shed light on the pricing, advertising, and innovation policies that the organization is likely to have to follow and on the probable administrative consequences of these.

The Cost Function and the Behavior of Organizations

Economists (and accountants) pay a great deal of attention to what they call the firm's cost function (the changes in the unit cost of production that

Market structure	Market behavior of firms	Likely administrative consequences of market behavior
Monopolistic competition (e.g., the garment industry)	Similar to oligopoly with differentiated products	The departments of marketing and distribution enjoy a great deal of power and status; the hiring of technocrats hampered by the small size of the organization
Perfect competition (e.g., the flour-milling industry)	Severe price competition	Since production efficiency is crucial, the manufacturing department has great power and status; tight control of operations; the hiring of technocrats to reduce costs inhibited by the small size of the organization
Imperfect competition (e.g., an airline that has a monopoly of domestic routes but competes in the international market)	Competitive pricing "abroad," regulated monopoly pricing or unregulated monopoly pricing "at home"	One division set up for "home" market, another for "foreign" market

take place as a result of increases or decreases in the quantity produced by the firm). The nature of organizational costs are of great importance in understanding the behavior of organizations. Consider, for example, two firms of equal size, one of which has very large fixed costs (that is, those costs—e.g., rent, that do not vary with the level of output), while the other has rather low fixed costs. Two steel makers, one with a brand new plant (high fixed costs) and the other with a similar but highly depreciated plant (low fixed costs) are ready examples. If the other costs are identical, and both get the same price for their products, the firm with high fixed costs is clearly under much greater pressure to keep on producing and selling at or near its full technical capacity, because only then can it make enough surplus over its variable costs (those that vary directly with production) to pay for its fixed costs. In the accountant's language, the high-fixed-costs firm has a much higher break-even point than the other one.

One can imagine the plight of such a firm if there is a recession in its industry. It can, in a recession, sell only a fraction of its output at acceptable prices and thus may not be able to cover its fixed costs. If this persists for a while, it may even have to go out of business—unless it *diversifies* its operations in such a way that when the demand for some of its products falls, that for others remains stable or perhaps even rises. Or perhaps it can save itself by more forceful marketing of its products.

Diversification has been observed to result in divisionalization.[8] Greater marketing effort means that people with a different orientation from that of production people enter the organization—the packagers of products, the ad representatives, the distributors, the sales representatives. Obviously, this is going to affect the prevailing norms and values and may even introduce serious conflicts between the production and the marketing personnel. Thus, high-fixed-cost firms may well get differently designed (more divisionalized, more marketing oriented) than low-fixed-cost organizations. There is no reason why these pressures may not be felt by organizations other than firms, such as hospitals and universities. Obviously, therefore, in organizational analysis, it is important to ask: What is the cost structure of the organization's operations? Are costs mostly fixed or mostly variable? If the former, what strategies is the organization pursuing to keep its facilities fully utilized? What are the administrative consequences of these strategies?

Conclusion

Economics is a discipline, and because it is a discipline it is biased in favor of economic explanations of organizational phenomena. Without necessarily sharing such a bias, we can acknowledge the value of economic concepts, theories, and modes of analysis for organizational studies. Of particular value are the questions economists habitually ask when analyzing a firm: How does the firm allocate its scarce resources to achieve its goals? How are factors of production related? What does the production function or the cost function look like? Are there substantial economies of scale? What is the nature of the demand for the firm's products or services? What is the structure of the market in which the firm is functioning? How does the firm respond to the market structure? If these questions are pursued systematically, much insight is likely to be gained into the operations of any type of organization that may be under study. Indeed, if organization theorists were to think about the *administrative* consequences of different types of cost functions, market structures, and so on, a line of inquiry economists have been reluctant to pursue, organization theory would mature rapidly.

Economic thinking is a vital part of organizational decision-making, and indeed the techniques of operations research have been developed precisely by subjecting many organizational operations to these questions. Unfortunately, too many organization theorists have been put off by the artificiality of the economist's assumptions and use of sophisticated mathematics. There is surely more to organizational behavior than economic forces. But the pervasive, long-term effects of these forces on the organization need badly to be acknowledged and explored.

POLITICAL ANALYSIS OF ORGANIZATIONS

The bailiwick of the political scientist is power, politics, and polity. *Power* is the ability, through the actual or implied use of force, to secure one's goals. *Politics* is the study of the tactics and strategies employed by individuals, groups, or organizations in their quest for power. *Polity* is the political organization of a body of people under a system of government that reflects an ideology, a set of values and beliefs about what the system of government ought to be. It has been pointed out that the "political desires shared by the members of a society impel them to create a government and a political system. The desires that they do not share will lead to struggle within the society and within the political system which is a part of it."[9] Thus, the basis of a polity, at least in democratic societies, is consensus about what a government ought to be like. The basis of changes in polity is disagreements about this. The basis of political behavior or politics is conflicts of interest among actors in the social drama.

Political science has emerged from political philosophy, which in turn goes back to the pre-Christian era. The Chinese Mencius (5th century B.C.), the Indian Kautilya (4th century B.C.), and Plato (4th century B.C.) speculated about alternative forms of government or the way the state should be run. In more recent centuries, Locke, Hobbes, and Rousseau looked into the origin of the state, Machiavelli probed statecraft, and Jefferson and Hamilton the structure of polity. Marx provided an explanation for changes in polity based on conflicts between classes. The study of political philosophy or ideology is still an important aspect of political science. So is the study of government and its institutions.

What is distinctive about contemporary political science is that besides the study of political ideology and the institutional aspects of the government, in both a national and a comparative context, there is an increasing emphasis on a *systems* study of political *behavior*.[10] The ambitious attempt of contemporary political science is to establish links between social structure and process; personality formation; and political structure, process, and behavior. The increasing emphasis in political science is on interest groups (lobbies, political parties, associations, unions), how they emerge, how they articulate their interests, and how they affect the polity.[11] This has led political scientists to integrate sociological and anthropological concepts such as culture and socialization (the transmission of cultural values from one generation to the next) into their conceptual armory.

Now one can think of organizations in general (and not merely the government) as polities. Every organization can be thought to have a policy- and rule-making system even if it does not possess a legislature. It can be thought to have an executive system to carry out the policies, even if the executive is not an elected one or has no formal constitutional sanction to exercise authority. And it can be thought to have a judicial or rule-interpreting system, even if it does not have formal appeal boards. These legislative, executive, and judicial *functions* may or may not be formalized, may or may not be separated as in most contemporary governments, and may or may not be highly developed. But if all organizations can be thought to engage in them, in however rudimentary a form, the questions political scientists raise in their analysis of polities can be applied to the analysis of organizations. Table 2–3 lists some key questions pursued by political scientists.[12] Many of these, with suitable adaptation, can, as the table shows, be pressed into the service of organizational analysis.

Questions About Power

The nature of power. There are many definitions of power,[13] but, generally speaking, *power* is the ability to secure one's goals through the explicit or

TABLE 2–3
Questions for the Political Analysis of Organizations

	Political science questions	Questions for the political analysis of organizations
About power	What is power? What are the sources of power? How does power get allocated? How is power acquired? What are the uses of power? What are the restraints on the use of power? What are the consequences of the use of power?	What is power in an organizational context? What are the sources of power in organizations? How does power get distributed in them? What are the uses of power in organizations? What are the restraints on the use of power? What are the social and economic consequences of political action?
About politics	What are the forms of politics? What are the causes and consequences of politics?	What forms does politics take in organizations? What are the causes and consequences of organizational politics?
About polity	What makes people create institutions that limit their freedom? What alternative forms do polities possess? Why do polities differ from society to society?	What impels organizational participants to accept the constraints of organizational life? What alternative forms do authority systems take? Why do authority systems differ so much?

implicit use of force. In the *organizational* context, power is the degree to which an individual or a group or an administrative unit is able to influence decision-making in its favor.

The exercise of power may be regarded by those subject to it as legitimate or nonlegitimate. Authority, as Max Weber pointed out, is the exercise of power accepted as legitimate by subordinates. When the exercise of power is accepted as legitimate, it is not seen as coercive. Weber distinguished between three forms of authority: traditional, rational-legal, and charismatic.[14] Traditional authority, such as the authority of a baron over his serfs during the Middle Ages, is rooted, not in law or contract, but in custom and tradition. Rational-legal authority is rooted in law and in contracts. The authority of a freely elected president or prime minister has its source in a constitution. The authority of a factory supervisor to order workers to do or not to do certain kinds of work is rooted in a contract that the supervisor and the workers have entered into with the organization. Charismatic authority, such as that of a Gandhi or a Mao Tse-tung, resides in the intense loyalty and devotion followers feel towards charismatic figures or their ideas.

Sources of power. French and Raven suggest that there are five bases or sources of an *individual's* power.[15] An individual may have power because of the ability to reward the compliant behavior of others. He may have power because of his ability to punish the noncompliant behavior of others. He may have power arising out of his formal position in the organizational hierarchy, because his superiors have let it be known that he has certain formally delegated powers. He may have power because of his technical or other expertise, because he is the one to ask in certain types of problem situations. And he has power because of some charisma he has, because others identify with him on account of his magnetic personality or ideas.

As to *groups'* power within an organization, it has been suggested that groups or administrative units whose work cannot be substituted by other groups or units are likely to be more powerful than those whose work can be substituted.[16] The more interconnected the work of a group or a unit is with that of other groups or units within the organization, the more power it has. The more immediately a unit affects the final outputs of the organization, the more power it has. And, last, the more a group or a unit helps the organization cope with uncertainty, the greater power it has. These factors help us see why the top management group is generally so much more powerful than other groups in an organization. The kinds of decision it makes are not allowed to be made by any other group; its work is highly pervasive; its decisions immediately affect the outputs of the organization; and its analysis and interpretation of the complex goings-on in the environment enable the organization to cope with uncertainty. By the same token the union often has great power. It has a monopoly over negotiating with management the wages and working conditions of the workers. Through its control over workers it has a pervasive influence on the activities in the organization. And, of course, it can grind the organization to a halt and affect its outputs drastically by a decision to strike.

Allocation of power. In a competitive system, be it a society or an organization, power flows to those who have something to offer to the system or the constituents of the system. In such a system, the allocation of power is somewhat like the allocation of resources, which, as we noted in the section on the economic analysis of organizations, tends to be done on the basis of their relative marginal productivities. Indeed, in such a system, the power a person possesses approximates that person's marginal productivity compared to that of other members of the system, so one can visualize an economics of power. In this conception of power, power of a person or perhaps even a group is roughly equal to his or its ability to reward the system by offering his or its services (or punish it by withholding them).

All systems are not competitive, however, or at least not equally competitive. In traditional societies or organizational systems, traditional norms and values govern how much power individuals and groups have. The power hierarchy is rigid, and the power one possesses comes by birth or other social ties. It is not, except in extraordinary circumstances, the result of deeds.

We noted earlier the various sources of power in an organization: formal position, expertise, charisma, ability to reward and punish, uniqueness of tasks, pervasiveness, immediacy of effect on the organization's outputs, ability to remove uncertainty faced by the organization. It is easy to see how and why the high-ranking organizational elites, the managers, the owners, and the senior staff people, get their power. What is fascinating to study is the way people much lower down in the organization, the rank and file, get *their* power.

One source of power of the organizational rank and file clearly is a *united front* against the higher ranking members of the organization—the power of the formal or the informal union. But besides this, the very necessity of division of labor and *specialization* in sizable, complex organizations means that even relatively junior members can wield considerable power over the elites. If the ground maintenance crew walk off their jobs, especially during a winter, the whole airport can grind to a halt. Specialization makes the organization a system of interdependent work units, any one of which can, by withholding its services, veto the functioning of the rest.

Besides the power that unionization and specialization confers, lower level members of an organization can (and often do) acquire considerable power through intimate *knowledge* of the organization.[17] In government bureaucracies, for example, the politically appointed head, initially at least, is at the mercy of the career officer old-timers who know all the rules and all the ropes. Thus, familiarity with the complex workings of the organization is an important source of power. Another is the *dependence* of the higher ranking person on his subordinate. In hospitals, the ward physicians are responsible for the care and treatment of each ward patient, and often there are dozens of them. Medicine, seclusion, sedation, and transfer orders all require the doctor's signature. A physician would never be able to attend to these unless he or she could unofficially delegate responsibilities to the supervisory attendant. Now if the doctor gets tough with this attendant on any issue, all the latter has to do is to stop doing the unofficial chores for the doctor to bring him or her to heel.[18]

Technical expertise is another source of power. The generals often get their way in the funding of new and esoteric weapons systems because their nontechnical civilian bosses and the equally lay legislature simply have no way of assessing reliably these weapons systems. Doctors in hospitals, invoking the sacred norm of saving human life, sometimes get esoteric equipment for far-out experiments, especially if the administrators of the hospitals are not medically trained.

Finally, being in a central position or a *mediating* position can confer considerable power. The secretary or the assistant to the president of a corporation sometimes has power rivaling that of the president, for, like Haldeman who controlled access to President Nixon, he or she often determines what papers the president will see, whom he or she will talk to, what meetings he or she will attend, and so forth.

Considering all these factors that confer power on lower level members of organizations, one writer has claimed that organizations are continuously at the mercy of their lower participants[19] and another that authority is really delegated upward, not downward.[20]

Uses of power. Power is nearly indispensable for the coordination of activities in a society. Without some concentration of power in a government, the vast work of protecting society and ministering to its many economic and cultural needs would be all but impossible. In organizations, too, power and authority serve these functions. Here is a story about a French cooperative that tried unsuccessfully to do without power differences:

> After the chaos of World War II, some French companies were reconstituted on the basis of cooperative ownership. In one of these firms, the workers, as owners, were to receive equal pay and shares of profit. In addition, all would participate in important decisions. Finally, all were to work at all jobs. In Marx's relatively rare speculation about future communist society, he suggested that eventually each man will be able to decide for himself what he will work at each day. A social commitment by the individual should insure that all necessary duties are performed. This French cooperative attempted to give such choice; each worker could choose his job for each day. So, the free, equal, worker-owners began to labor in their business without hierarchy. But utopia was not to be.
>
> Jobs were not the same. Some were dirty or boring or hard; others were clean or interesting or easy. After a period of voluntary selection of the former, men began to choose the latter. Free choice did not work; the necessary jobs were not filled. In order to correct the imbalance in job selection, an assignment system was needed. Therefore, a worker of integrity and popularity was chosen by his fellows to set up and run such a system. It was to be a fair method for rotating people equally through all positions.

Our honored worker was to labor at the regular jobs as well as make the necessary assignments. He was to continue to receive the same equal share of profits.

Pierre was honest and trustworthy, but there were problems. First, what was fair? Should he assign weak, sickly André to arduous duties just as often as he assigned the strong, healthy Jacques? Should he make this decision himself, or should he raise the question with the entire work force? Even more difficult, although he was scrupulously honest in seeing that everyone worked at desirable and undesirable jobs equally, André and Jacques did not perceive themselves as putting in equal time. Exaggerating their assignments to difficult positions, some workers accused Pierre of bias. He began to feel lonely—alienated from his friends and distrusted by his associates. In short, his election turned out to be no privilege.

After some time and much unhappiness, unlucky Pierre went to his fellow workers with an ultimatum: either he gave up his unpleasant duties, or he received a greater reward. In the cooperative described, he eventually received a reduction of duties and an increase in pay. Voila!: managerial hierarchy—complete with differentiated power, prestige, and pay.[21]

Though power commonly gets used to further organizational objectives, it also, of course, is commonly used to advance the personal goals of those with power. Whether power will be used to further personal goals or organizational goals depends, of course, on the goals of the individual or the group wielding power. If they feel a commitment to the manifest goals for which the organization is set up, such as achieving a social revolution (in the case of a revolutionary party), or spreading information about birth control and family planning (in the case of a family planning unit), then their power is likely to be utilized to further the ends of the organization. Commitment comes from organizational processes such as careful selection of personnel, training, and indoctrination programs and simply working together to meet grave threats to the organization.[22] A sound control system also helps to ensure that power is not used entirely for personal purposes. This is because a control system monitors performance, provides feedback, and provides to the hierarchy performance information that can become the basis of regulatory action. However, controls and commitment can work at cross-purposes sometimes. A too harsh or arbitrary control system can drastically reduce commitment.[23]

Restraints on the exercise of power. In organizations, as in society, there are important constraints on the exercise of power. Governments in democratic countries are subject to many checks and balances. In the United States the doctrine of separation of powers means that the judiciary, the legislature, and the executive are separate but equal, each supreme only in areas specified to be its domain by the Constitution. In Britain, the executive is subordinate to the legislature, but the judiciary is not. This separation of power acts to limit the power of any one organ of government.

Even if this were not the case, the sheer size of modern government would imply considerable limitations on the exercise of power by even the chief executive. Power is diffused throughout the governmental apparatus by an intricate network of specialist departments, bureaucratic rules and procedures, traditions, and what not. Any executive wishing to move quickly is likely to throw up his hands in despair, as President Kennedy is reported to have done with the Department of State.[24]

In organizations in general, there are two sets of forces that limit the exercise of power. One set is environmental in character—for example, the law or public opinion. The other set of forces is internal to the organization and resides in rules and regulations, the sheer size and diversity of operations, countervailing political coalitions within the organization, and the ability of the relatively powerless to find alternative employment. Large organizations are more visible and therefore more subject to environmental pressures. And because they are large the internal forces blocking the exercise of power are also formidable. As a consequence, the arbitrary exercise of power is often more feasible in small than in large organizations.

Consequences of political acts. In an organization, as in a society, the relationship between political, social, and economic activities is quite strong. Every *decision* is a political act, for it involves the exercise of power and authority. But in an organization every decision has some economic consequences, for managerial decisions are primarily resource-allocating decisions. And since most decisions affect what work people do and how they work together, they also tend to affect the social activities going on in an organization. An example is a dean's decision to hire a new faculty member. Being a decision, it is a political act. Its economic consequences are an increased budget allocation for staff salaries. The social consequences are the arrival of a new person with specialized training, some unique personality characteristics, a distinctive philosophy of life, and some personal idiosyncrasies—a person whose presence is going to affect or modify existing friendship relations and patterns of communication or create new ones.

So long as resources are scarce in relation to human aspirations, and so long as there are conflicting claims on these limited resources, the criteria that govern economic decisions will not be purely rational in an economic sense. They will be subjected at least partly to political considerations. Equally, of course, whatever the distribution of power in an organization, political decisions will not be totally divorced from economic realities.

Questions About Politics

Political philosophers and scientists have been concerned, not only about how power gets used legitimately, but also about how it gets used in non-legitimate ways. We may call the latter politics, to distinguish it from the socially acceptable, legitimate use of power. For example, majority rule is a legitimate use of power in a democratic institution. But the use of majority power to crush all opposition, or to promulgate rules that amount to harassment of the minority, is nonlegitimate political behavior.

Forms of politics. The use of tactics such as blackmail, doublecross, and coercion is as old as statecraft. The Indian Kautilya wrote a great treatise, called *Arthashastra,* in the fourth century B.C. that details many such tactics.[25] He wrote that to get his way, the king could use four different types of strategem. He could use flattery, bribery, coercion, or treachery. Kautilya then indicated the circumstances under which each should be used. Machiavelli, the Florentine writer of the sixteenth century, had similar advice for the ruler when the survival of the state is at stake.[26] Antony Jay's *Management and Machiavelli* is an attempt to apply Machiavelli's precepts to the management of firms. As an example, Machiavelli's advice to the management of a firm that has just absorbed another might be to plant a few of its managers in the key departments of the absorbed firm. Otherwise, it would have to use up a great deal of its energy in giving orders to the absorbed firm, asking for information, and checking up to see whether the orders had been executed. It might be better, Machiavelli might add, either to get rid of the absorbed firm's senior managers *or* to make them part of the team. If they are down-graded, they could become disgruntled, a source of sabotage or at least of noncooperation.

Political behavior is gaming behavior. It is trickery and manipulation. It is building coalitions. It is self-serving intrigue. It is the behavior of the organizational politician. It is a far cry from the almost puritanically rational behavior assigned to the manager by economists or the good Samaritan behavior hoped for by the behavioral scientist. Indeed, Cyert and March, in their behavioral view of resource allocation and decision-making in firms, have pointed to coalition-building and coalition-maintaining activities as crucial in understanding organizational behavior.[27]

A number of political tactics can be identified. Newman, in a fascinating description of power tactics, gives the example of a shoe company in which all purchasing was centralized at the headquarters.[28] A branch first asked to buy some minor supplies locally. The request was granted. A little later, repair parts of the machinery were requested to be bought locally; and this was allowed, too. The next year, the manager successfully requested that the branch purchase even machinery locally, since engineers at his plant knew best what was wanted and how to get it, and anyway he had a full-fledged purchasing department going. By these tactics, the branch ultimately was able to do most of its purchasing locally. Newman calls this tactic "camel's head in the tent." In another instance, a salesman, when questioned about his expense account, started talking about the danger of competitors stealing a large account—Newman calls this "throwing a red herring across the trail." In a company having difficulty making its shipments promptly and correctly, the manufacturing department suggested to management that the shipping department be transferred to it from the sales department for better coordination. The sales department countered by requesting that warehousing be transferred to it from manufacturing for the same reason! In yet another situation, the chief engineer tried to strengthen his position among senior executives by playing off the manufacturing and sales departments against each other. Quite commonly, the chief executive deliberately stays out of a union-management conflict until a critical point is reached. Then he enters the negotiations playing the statesman, expecting that his presence, untarnished by the preceding battle, will carry greater prestige and weight.

Cause of politics. The kinds of politics discussed above are common to all organizations. However, organizations vary a great deal in the *intensity* of politics. There may be some intrigue in all organizations, but clearly some organizations are hothouses of political back-biting and back-scratching, and some are far less conducive to it. An interesting question is: What explains the variation in organizational politics?

Political behavior is behavior of individuals or groups in conflict with one another. If A's desserts in no way depend on B's efforts, nor are they in any way affected by what B gets, then there is little reason for A either to make a political friendship with B or try to do B in. Thus, some form of interdependence is a necessary condition for political behavior. But the extent and intensity of political or conflict behavior depends on disagreement as to goals (personal and organizational) and the means by which these ought to be attained. It may also depend on a breakdown in the means by which conflicts can legitimately be resolved.[29]

Where interdependent parties or groups are substantially in agreement about goals as well as means, there is little conflict and little political behavior. This happens occasionally in governments and other organizations during severe crises. The Labour and the Conservative parties formed a successful coalition government in Britain to prosecute the war against

Hitler. This can also occur in what Etzioni calls "normative" organizations, such as religious institutions and political parties with strong ideologies.[30] It happens partly through brainwashing and thought control and partly through self-selection of members. When organizational members are agreed as to goals and means, all that remains is the design of a program or plan to attain the goals. But this state of perfect agreement is rare, even in normative organizations.

Most frequently there is at least reasonable agreement as to goals, particularly organizational goals, but disagreement as to *how* to attain the goals. In corporations, an important goal is to make profits, but the different department heads may be at loggerheads about how to increase profits. The marketing vice president is likely to see aggressive sales and promotion as the key, while the production vice president is likely to emphasize modern mass production equipment. The controller is likely to emphasize a sophisticated control system, while the personnel manager is likely to emphasize good human relations and motivating the employees through better pay and working conditions. Assessments of costs and benefits of various alternatives as well as some horse trading are likely to occur when there is disagreement on the means by which agreed upon goals are to be achieved.

The most virulent forms of political behavior arise when there is agreement neither as to goals or means nor as to general procedures for resolving disputes. These situations are emotionally charged and are characterized by mutual suspicions and grave distrust. Governments antagonistic to one another often exhibit this behavior, as do antagonistic political parties. Union-management relations, too, sometimes deteriorate to this level. When this happens, character assassination, lists of enemies, public lip service to agreements but private sabotage, spying, strikes, and acts of violence characterize organizational behavior. What the cynical consider normal organizational behavior is actually an extremum in organizational pathology and relatively rare in its virulent forms.

Questions About Polity

Acceptance of constraints. Two centuries ago, the British philosopher Locke raised the question as to why man, born free, creates a state to regulate his behavior. Locke felt that by setting up a state with jurisdiction over all, people expect to get a better protection of their lives and property than in a stateless state of nature. In a stateless society, the inherent selfishness of people and their tunnel vision lead to grave hardships. Rousseau, too, advanced the notion of the social contract under which individuals handed over to the state certain rights in return for the protection and benefits afforded by the state.

One may argue quite validly that all organizations, not just governments, arise because organizations as organizations achieve far more than their founders can, acting alone. And so, in return for the conveniences afforded by the organization, people give up some of their free-wheeling ways.

Organizational life is undoubtedly constraining. Routines have to be followed, as do the directives of one's superiors. The place of work is fixed. Interpersonal relationships on the job are often quite formal. These discomforts are borne because organizational members secure the benefits of steady earnings, often a fair degree of job satisfaction, fair treatment, the warmth of relationships with friends on the job, possibilities of promotion and personal growth, and more. Barnard and later Simon advanced their inducements-contributions theory, which in effect suggested that the contributions that members of an organization make to it by way of compliance with the job requirements must be at least matched by the inducements offered by the organization to do so.[31]

Forms of polities. Polities of nations differ widely. Some of them are democratic; others are totalitarian. Within these two classes are many subclasses. Dahl, for example, has suggested that one can think of polities as varying along two somewhat related dimensions.[32] One dimension is public contestation in the conduct of government—whether, for example, public offices are elective or not. The other dimension is participation—that is, the proportion of the population that can participate in public contestation. For example, in South Africa public contestation is limited largely to white adults, while in democratic countries all adults have the right to participate in the conduct of the government. Dahl calls polities low on public contestation *and* participation *closed hegemonies.* At the other extreme are polities high on both, called *polyarchies.* The ones that are high on public contestation but low on participation (e.g., South Africa) he calls *competitive oligarchies,* while the ones that are low on public contestation but high on participation (e.g., the Soviet Union) he calls *inclusive hegemonies.*

Dahl has tried to explain the circumstances sustaining each of these forms. For example, some of the conditions most favorable to polyarchies are historical sequences like competition between oligarchies preceding wide participation in the conduct of the government, a high level of socioeconomic development, reasonably low inequality of income, freedom from foreign domination, a widespread belief that polyarchy is effective in solving major problems, a reasonably high degree of trust among political activists, partly competitive and partly cooperative political relationships, and the acceptance of the necessity and desirability of compromise. Opposite conditions are likely to lead to a more hegemonic, totalitarian form of government.

Organizational polities can be classified in many ways. Following Dahl, one can think of organizational polities as being closed, highly centralized hegemonies. Or they can be classified as competing oligarchies—that is, organizations in which powerful elite groups are vying for power, as is often the case with large organizations such as the federal government, with its various departments locked in a fierce struggle for funds and power. Another class is the inclusive hegemonies, such as the Yugoslav factories or the Chinese communes, in which everybody participates in the making of decisions that must, however, be consistent with the party line. Or, they may be classified as polyarchies, such as democratic organizations like cooperative societies and professional associations.

Organizational polities can be classified also in terms of the form of the mechanism used to control the behavior of lower level members. Etzioni has classified *control modes* (or means of control) into utilitarian, normative, and coercive.[33] Organizations (or parts of organizations) that greatly emphasize the rewarding of conforming or "desirable" behavior (such as exceeding the production quota) and punishment of deviant or "undesirable" behavior (such as failure to reach the production quota) are said to have a utilitarian mode of control. Business firms are common examples. Organizations that seek to control behavior through getting the members to accept certain beliefs and certain norms of behavior, or to give unquestioned loyalty to the leaders of these organizations, are said to have a normative mode of control. Evangelical organizations and revolutionary political parties are examples. Organizations, such as jails and custodial institutions, that control the behavior of members through the threat of physical punishment are said to employ a coercive mode of control. Etzioni has argued that each mode of control elicits a distinctive form of involvement with the organization on the part of those subjected to it. Alienation is associated with the use of coercion, a calculative involvement with the use of a utilitarian mode of control, and commitment with the use of a normative mode of control.

Thus, the extent to which there is contestation in the conduct of the organization's major functions, the degree to which the rank and file is permitted to participate in making decisions related to these functions, and the means of control utilized to control the behavior of the rank and file offer ready criteria by which to classify an organization's polity. In terms of these criteria, organizational polities can fall into one of twelve different classes and can range from polities that are polyarchic and normative to those that are closed hegemonies and coercive, including in between such exotic concoctions as polyarchic and coercive, and hegemonistic and normative.

Factors accounting for polity differences. The members of an organization are drawn from a wider culture and bring into the organization the values of this wider culture. Within the organization, too, through continuous interaction, they may develop a distinctive organizational culture. Thus, if the wider culture puts a premium on authoritarian values, the organizational culture will tend to be authoritarian, and an authoritarian, centralized, regimented polity or authority system will find support in such a culture. Crozier's study of French bureaucracies indicates that aversion to interpersonal confrontations between individuals in superior-subordinate relationships in France often translates into a highly depersonalized authority system bureaucracies.[34] Professionals (doctors, lawyers, accountants, professors, etc.) as a class have distinctive values, such as a commitment to the profession or the discipline, self-regulation, and autonomy at work. In organizations dominated by professionals, such as universities and hospitals, these values reinforce a highly decentralized authority system characterized by a great deal of autonomy to the professional in his or her area of expertise.[35]

Ideologies of the organizational elites (managers, owners, senior staff) have a considerable influence on the form of the organizations's authority system. The ideologies that have been discussed widely in the organizational literature concern the assumptions organizational elites make about human nature and the nature of work and consequently about the most effective means of achieving the organization's goals. Generally, these ideologies tend to fall into two groups, the authoritarian and the participative.[36] In the first it is assumed that people resist work because work is painful; the best way to achieve the organization's goals therefore is to direct and supervise work very closely. This leads to a centralized authority system in which all discretionary authority is centered at higher levels in the organization. In the participative ideologies, the assumption is that, when motivated by interesting and challenging work, people can regulate their own conduct quite effectively without the assistance of outside controllers; therefore, letting the worker have the authority to carry out the work is the best way the organization can achieve its goals. This ideology leads to a highly decentralized authority system with lower levels exercising a great deal of discretionary authority.

Besides cultural and ideological factors, the size of the organization, its technology, and the fluidity of its business situation also are known to affect its authority system. Large organizations tend to have a highly bureaucratized authority system, with a strong emphasis on hierarchical relationships, rules and regulations, specialization in decision-making, and so forth. Small organizations have much looser polities.[37] Mass production technologies tend to be associated with more structured authority systems than non-mass production technologies, because of the former's greater need to plan ahead for efficient workflows.[38] Organizations in stable environments tend to develop bureaucratic authority systems, while those in turbulent environments tend to have looser, organic authority systems.[39] Indeed, *within* an organization, polities may differ markedly. They tend to be more decentralized, organic, and participative in parts of the organization where tasks are creative or involve the continuous solving of complex, novel problems. They tend to be centralized, bureaucratic, and nonparticipative in parts of the organization where tasks are reduced to a routine.[40]

Conclusion

Like economics, political science is a discipline. It is predisposed to a *political* explanation of social and organizational phenomena. An exclusive reliance on such explanations is hazardous, for there is more to human behavior than a striving after power and dominion. But a political analysis does afford valuable insights, especially when integrated with insights secured through an economic analysis.

SUMMARY

Organization theory has been an interdisciplinary field. This chapter has been concerned with economic and political analyses of the organization. The principal concern of economics is with the optimal use of relatively scarce resources. The logic of optimal production in a firm argues for marginal adjustments of factor (resource) inputs. As applied to all organizations it implies an approach to design characterized by a managerial search for optimal combinations of organizational variables (goals, ideology, technology, structure, human behavior, etc.). Organizational design has to be a trial-and-error process, guided, however, by the predictions of organization theory.

The typology of the firm's market structures—perfect competition, oligopoly, monopoly, and so on—provided by economic theory is a useful way of regarding the business environment of other organizations as well. The links economists have sought to establish between market structure and market conduct of firms are useful in assessing the external policies of organizations and their internal administrative consequences.

The organization's cost or production function may have major organizational consequences. The behavior of organizations with high fixed costs and a high break-even point is likely to be rather different from those with low fixed costs and a low break-even point. The pressure to operate at full capacity is likely to be much greater in the former organizations. That, in turn, is likely to pressure them into attempts at diversification of activities and forceful marketing. These, in turn, may have consequences like divisionalization or conflicts between marketing personnel and those engaged in operations.

For organizational analysis, the questions economists habitually ask are particularly useful—such as: How does the firm allocate its scarce resources? How are the factors of production related? What are the characteristics of the firm's costs? What are the characteristics of the demand for its products or services?

The subject matter of political science is power, politics, and polity or political organization. The ideas of political philosophers like Mencius, Kautilya, and Machiavelli, Locke, Hobbes, Rousseau, and Marx have shaped modern political science. Modern political science seems to be moving in the direction of a systems study of political behavior. All organizations have polities—that is, authority systems—and therefore can be subjected to political analysis. Table 2–3 takes major political science questions and converts them into questions for the political analysis of organizations.

Power is A's ability to get B to do something the latter may be reluctant to do. Authority is the legitimate exercise of power and is rooted in tradition, law, contract, or charisma. There are several sources of the power an individual may possess. These are: A's ability to reward B; A's ability to punish B; B's identifying with A's values or personality; A's formal positional power; and A's expertise. Groups and administrative units derive their power from the uniqueness of their tasks, the pervasiveness of their activities, the immediacy with which they affect the organization's outputs, and their ability to reduce uncertainty faced by the organization.

In a competitive system, be it a society or an organization, power flows to those who can make the greatest contribution to the achievement of the goals of the system. In a traditional system, however, power is ascribed, not achieved.

In organizations, power is often wielded by lower level members. This occurs if they band together (say, in a union), if work in the organization is highly specialized and interdependent, if the lower level members have an intimate knowledge of how the organization operates that is not shared by their superiors, if the latter are dependent on them for nonformal favors, if the lower level members have technical expertise not fully understood by their superiors, or if the lower level members mediate access to powerful members of the organization.

Power is indispensable in coordinating the myriad activities of an organization. Whether power will be used to further personal goals or organizational goals depends on the degree of commitment that the powerful have to securing the organization's goals and on the existence of a control system that monitors performance.

There are many restraints on the arbitrary exercise of power. Some stem from outside the organization, in the form of the law and public opinion. Others are internal to the organization and stem from established rules and regulations, precedents, the size of the organization and the diversity of its operations, countervailing political coalitions against those with power, possibilities of alternative employment, and so forth.

Political acts in organizations have economic and social consequences. The relationship between political acts such as decisions and economic acts such as allocation of resources is particularly close.

Politics takes many forms. The intensity of organizational politics depends on whether the different groups in an organization disagree on the goals of the organization, the means for achieving them, and the procedures for resolving conflicts.

Organizational life is constraining, but people form or join organizations because (a) the organization can achieve what they cannot achieve acting alone and (b) because the economic and psychological inducements they get from their association with organizations equals or exceeds the contributions they make to the organization.

Organizational polities vary greatly. A classification adopted from Dahl based on public contestation in organizational functions and the degree of participation of the rank and file in decision-making enables one to classify organizational authority systems as closed hegemonies, competing oligarchies, inclusive hegemonies, and polyarchies. Etzioni's classification, based on the kind of control mode utilized to regulate the behavior of the rank and file, permits an organization to be classified as normative, utilitarian, or coercive.

Several factors account for differences in the polities or authority systems of organizations. The norms and values members of an organization import from the wider culture affect the organization's authority system. The ideology of the organization's elites shapes it, too. Other factors that influence the authority system are the size of the organization, its technology, and its business environment. Indeed, not only do authority systems differ in different organizations; they also differ from one part of the organization to another, this variation being accounted for by the kinds of task performed by each part.

SUGGESTED READINGS

Robert Averitt, *The Dual Economy* (New York: Norton, 1968), particularly Chs. 4, 5, and 6.

Chs. 6, 7, and 8 in Amitai Etzioni, *Modern Organizations* (Englewood Cliffs, N. J.: Prentice-Hall, 1964). For a more advanced treatment by this author, see "Organizational control structure" in J. March, ed., *The Handbook of Organizations* (Chicago: Rand McNally, 1965).

Ch. 6 in Michel Crozier, *The Bureaucratic Phenomenon* (Chicago: University of Chicago Press, 1964).

Dorwin Cartwright, "Influence, Leadership, Control," in J. March, ed., *The Handbook of Organizations* (see Reading 2, above). The article represents a review of various concepts of power from a social psychological viewpoint.

QUESTIONS FOR ANALYSIS

1 "Human beings desire both *power* and *money*. Therefore, all political decisions in organizations have an economic basis, and all economic decisions have a political basis." Do you agree? How about the takeover of one firm by another? Or the decision to abolish separate departments of production and marketing and instead to set up product divisions, each with its own marketing and production personnel?

2 Was I.T.T.'s involvement in Chilean politics for economic or political reasons?

3 Why did Protestantism break up into various independent sects and the Roman Catholic Church, despite some recent losses, remain a relatively monolithic organization? What mechanisms of control are holding the Church intact?

4 Could the control mechanisms that Stalin used to run the Soviet government be used in today's Soviet government?

5 How do you think economic crises affect organizations? Suppose that the demand for large automobiles falls off because of an oil crisis. How would it affect those departments of the General Motors Corporation that produce mostly large cars? How would it affect the organization of its Vega plants? Consider the effects on centralization or decentralization of decision-making, the use of control mechanisms, political behavior, and the morale of managers and workers.

6 Why are there only two major political parties in the United States? Why are there only three major firms in the American automobile industry? Do you see any common reasons for the two oligopolies? Do you see any similarities in the organizations of these firms and the two political parties? Would these organizations change if half a dozen other political parties entered the U.S. political scene and similarly a large number of new firms entered the automobile industry?

7 Here are the basic facts of a case reported by Wegner and Sayles.[41] Subject the case to a political and economic analysis.

1. Hamilton Engines is a hundred-year-old company with a very good record of labor peace. It has been unionized for the last 25 years by an industrial union hitherto dominated by the Italian employees of Hamilton. The Italians control most of the top union jobs.

2. In recent years the company has been hiring more and more Mexican-Americans. Supervisors have been encouraged to learn Spanish, and an expensive training program has been instituted to turn workers into machinists. Few supervisors, however, have learned Spanish.

3. Thirty-five percent of the work force is of Italian descent; 40% is Spanish-speaking.

4. The union elections are due next month and both the Mexican-Americans and the Italians have nominated a slate of candidates.

5. Hamilton Engines is in a highly competitive industry. It pays relatively low wages compared to other firms in the area in which it is located.

6. Two weeks ago, Manuel, the Spanish-speaking candidate for vice president and chief steward, was suspended for two weeks without pay for having someone else punch his time card. Manuel was reportedly seen in the parking lot 10 minutes before his shift ended by an Italian oldtimer.

7. Manuel argued that he left early only because he suddenly remembered that he might have left his parking lights on that morning because of the heavy fog. In the meantime, some other worker punched Manuel's card by mistake and kept quiet about it for fear of being criticized. When Manuel got back, he found his card punched, and so he simply left for the day.

8. The union has charged top management with favoritism. It alleges that the supervisor rescinded the disciplinary action to avoid displeasing the Mexican-Americans. The supervisor has been heard to say that top management did get involved in the case.

9. Manuel and his friends deny this. They say the union is out to get him. What kind of a union is it, they argue, that wants workers to be penalized?

10. The union has threatened to call its first walkout to protest favoritism. The Mexican-Americans in turn have threatened that if such an action is taken, they will start their own union.

Footnotes to Chapter Two

1 Paul A. Samuelson, *Economics*, 7th ed., p. 5.

2 *Ibid.*, Ch. 2.

3 See Richard Caves, *American Industry: Structure, Conduct, Performance*, 3rd ed., for a brief and lucid treatment of industrial organization.

4 See Samuelson, *op. cit.*, Ch. 27, for a more elaborate description of the economics of production.

5 For details, see R. M. Cyert and Kalmen Cohen, *Theory of the Firm: Resource Allocation in a Market Economy*, Chs. 4, 9, 10, 11, 12, and 13.

6 See F. M. Scherer, *Industrial Market Structure and Economic Performance*, Ch. 6, for the evidence on the suspension of price competition in oligopolistic industries, and pp. 99–100, 341–43, for the evidence linking advertising and promotion to market structure.

[7] See *ibid.*, pp. 347, 363–77, 410, and 436, for the evidence linking research and development activity to market structure.

[8] See Alfred Chandler, *Strategy and Structure*, p. 44.

[9] Philippa Strum and Michael Schmidman, *On Studying Political Science*, p. 10.

[10] Gabriel A. Almond and Bingham G. Powell, Jr., *Comparative Politics*, Ch. 1.

[11] Strum and Schmidman, *op. cit.*

[12] *Ibid.*, p. 19.

[13] See Robert A. Dahl, "The Concept of Power," and James March, "The Power of Power," for discussions of the many meanings of power.

[14] Max Weber, *The Theory of Social and Economic Organizations*, tr. 1947, pp. 324–28.

[15] J. R. P. French, Jr., and B. Raven, "The Bases of Social Power."

[16] C. R. Hinings, D. J. Hickson, J. M. Pennings, and R. E. Schneck, "Structural Conditions of Intraorganizational Power."

[17] David Mechanic, "Sources of Power of Lower Participants in Complex Organizations."

[18] Thomas J. Scheff, "Control Over Policy by Attendants in a Mental Hospital."

[19] Mechanic, *op. cit.*

[20] Chester Barnard, *Functions of the Executive.*

[21] D. Hampton, C. Summer, and R. Webber, *Organizational Behavior and the Practice of Management*, pp. 188–89.

[22] Muzafer Sherif, "Experiments in Group Conflict."

[23] Chris Argyris, *Integrating the Individual and the Organization.*

[24] Arthur Schlesinger, Jr., "The United States Department of State."

[25] R. Shamasastry, *Kautilya's Arthashastra.*

[26] Niccolo Machiavelli, *The Prince*, tr. 1950.

[27] R. M. Cyert and James March, *A Behavioral Theory of the Firm*, Ch. 3.

[28] William H. Newman, *Cases for Administrative Action*, pp. 86–98.

[29] James March and Herbert Simon, *Organizations*, Ch. 5.

[30] Amitai Etzioni, *Modern Organizations*, Ch. 6.

[31] Barnard, *op. cit.*, and Herbert Simon, *Administrative Behavior.*

[32] What follows is based on Robert A. Dahl, *Polyarchy.*

[33] Etzioni, *op. cit.*, Ch. 6.

[34] Michael Crozier, *The Bureaucratic Phenomenon.*

[35] See Etzioni, *op. cit.*, Ch. 8, for a discussion of the authority of professionals versus that of administrators. Also see Richard H. Hall, "Professionalization and Bureaucratization."

[36] See H. Rush, *Behavioral Science: Concepts and Management Application*, for a summary of the views of McGregor, Argyris, Likert, and others pertaining to this.

[37] See, for example, D. S. Pugh, D. J. Hickson, C. R. Hinings, and C. Turner, "The Context of Organization Structures."

[38] P. N. Khandwalla, "Mass Output Orientation of Operations Technology and Organizational Structure."

[39] T. Burns and A. M. Stalker, *The Management of Innovation.*

[40] Richard H. Hall, "Intraorganizational Structural Variation: Application of the Bureaucratic Model."

[41] R. Wegner and L. Sayles, *Cases in Organizational and Administrative Behavior*, pp. 62–64.

3

Sociological and Social Psychological Analysis of Organizations

INTRODUCTION

In the previous chapter, we analyzed the organization from the perspective of economics and political science. The structure of the organization's "market" and the characteristics of the costs of operating the organization were some of the key tools of economic analysis we pressed into our service. The political science perspective was invoked to examine the organization as a polity and to identify the determinants of political behavior in organizations.

In this chapter we continue to examine organizations from the perspective of social science disciplines—this time, sociology and social psychology. They both attempt to view human behavior in a social context rather than in a physiological or neurological context. But, while sociologists like to study the *institutions* people set up because they are social animals, social psychologists tend to be more interested in the way the *individual responds* to social settings.

Sociologists are interested primarily in the modal behavior of social institutions—for example, what are the reading habits of the "typical" North

71

American family. They may, of course, find that there are several "typical" North American families, such as the affluent "typical" family, the middle class "typical" family, the poor "typical" family, and so on. Sociologists may then go on to try to explain the reading habits of each of these "typical" families in terms of its income, level of education, occupational structure, and the like.

Sociology seeks its explanations for "typical" behavior in *structural* rather than psychological terms. What are the structural conditions in organizations, it asks, that cause strikes regardless of the personality dispositions of labor and management leaders? In response to this query, the researcher is liable to examine structural conditions like the level of wages of the workers relative to the wages of other kinds of workers, the kinds of controls that are being used by management, the rate of automation. Obviously, these structural conditions affect behavior by affecting the motivations, perceptions, cognitions of individual workers and their leaders. But the sociologist prefers to ignore these or make some quite simple-minded assumptions about human motivation. This is so partly because sociologists are generally not trained in psychology. It is also partly because they prefer to stick to the overt and the easily measurable and observable explanatory variables. In part it is also because they are interested in the behavior of the "typical" individual or institution and feel that introducing psychological concepts or taking cognizance of personalities would simply muddy up this analysis.

Social psychologists are not uninterested in structural conditions like the rapidity of automation, the management control system, or the workers' relative wages. They are interested primarily in how workers in organizations *react* to these and why they react the way they do. Their point is that people react—not to objectively real structures or events—but to their subjective perception of them. That is why some workers perceive automation as a threat while others do not. Social psychologists are liable to invoke sophisticated psychological theories of motivation, perception, and attitude formation to explain these reactions. Their concern is not with the "typical" worker's "typical" reaction to the "typical" structure of the work situation. It is likely to be rather with the co-variation or correlation between personality dispositions of workers and worker reactions, mediated perhaps by the nature of the organization's structure. After the sociologist and the social psychologist are through studying strikes in organizations, they are liable to come up with the following types of generalizations.

Sociologist. Workers "socialized" in urban areas are more likely to participate in strikes than workers "socialized" in rural areas. The typical strike is precipitated by the fear of imminent automation, low wages relative to those earned by workers of comparable skill, and the arbitrary use of authority by management.

Social psychologist. Workers with strongly active social and power needs are more likely to participate in strikes than workers with weak social and power needs. Workers with strong achievement needs and with strong needs to accept and submit to authority are less likely to participate in strikes than those with weak achievement and submission needs. The greater the frustration of the need for job security, and the greater the deprivation of self-esteem through such factors as perceived low wages relative to those earned by workers of comparable skill and the perceived arbitrary exercise of authority by management, the more prone the worker is to participate in a strike.

It is clear that these explanations usefully supplement each other and point to usefully different avenues for remedial action. The sociological explanation may point to structural solutions like the slowdown of automation and/or councils for joint management-worker decision-making. The psychological explanation may point to human relations training for supervisors, confrontation meetings between management and workers to air the differences and explore possible avenues of future collaborations, and better procedures for selecting and training workers.

SOCIOLOGY

The Domain of Sociology

Sociology is the "study of systems of social action and of their interrelations."[1] Social action is noninstinctual human behavior to satisfy basic human needs. Sociology is the study, not just of what people do socially or how institutions function, but of how social or institutional acts are *interrelated* to form a pattern or system. Sociology has the widest coverage of any social science. It covers the study of single social acts, social relationships, organizations and institutions, communities, and societies.[2] Organizations are regarded as one of the primary units of social life. Among the various topics in sociology, the "sociological perspective" and "fundamental social processes" are of particular importance in the sociological analysis of organizations, the first for obvious reasons and the second for cuing us to the processes that may go on in organizations, since organizations resemble miniature societies.

The Sociological Perspective

In the course of studying systems of social action, sociologists seek to explain the nature not only of social order but of social disorder.[3] Social order is not the equivalent of social good, and social disorder does not imply social evil. Rather, social order means observed *regularities* or recurrences in social behavior that allow us to draw hypotheses about the nature of the relationship between events. For example, one may observe that old societies such as those of India and China are heavily stratified, while younger societies such as those of North America are much less so. This may lead to a hypothesis that as a society grows older it gets more stratified. If this hypothesis is confirmed, then increasing stratification with age becomes an accepted regularity of societies. Through such hypotheses sociologists try to understand how the seemingly random social behavior of individual members of a society amounts to a social system—irrespective of whether this is a "good" or a "bad" system—that is, how the coordination and integration of social acts occur in an orderly and regular rather than a chaotic way.

Sociologists also study sporadic social behavior—mainly social disorders such as violence, crime, revolutions, and strikes. They seek to understand why and how they occur. As society is a moving equilibrium of forces working toward social order and forces working toward disorder, sociologists are also interested in understanding how social changes take place—how, for example, attitudes towards sex have changed in North America over the past few decades. But, while social changes are interesting to sociologists, so is social continuity—why, for example, capitalism has persisted in the Western world for so many centuries; why the caste system has persisted in India for so many millennia.

Whether sociologists are studying social order or disorder, they seek the causes not in terms of chance personality factors but, as we noted earlier, in terms of more durable structural factors.

The sociological perspective then, seeks the structural causes of order, disorder, continuity, and change in societies and institutions. It prompts the following questions for organizational analysis: (a) What structural forces ensure stability and *order* in the operations of organizations? (b) What structural forces cause *disorders* in organizations? (c) What structural forces lead to *continuity* in the life of the organization? (d) What structural forces lead to *changes* in the operations of the organization?

Stability and order. Insight into social stability or regularity is afforded by the equilibrium model of society.[4] The basic notion in this model is that when the equilibrium of a society is disturbed, forces are set in motion that restore equilibrium. The process is one of homeostasis. Homeostasis is analogous to the thermostat that maintains room temperature at a preset level, or to the process by which the body produces antibodies to fight a bacterial infection and restores itself to its normal healthy condition. In societies, the homeostatic forces are organized around widely shared norms about what needs to be done in case of a social disturbance. In a democratic society, for example, an attempt by someone to seize absolute power will trigger countervailing attempts by the public and by various institutions to preserve democracy. The attempts are likely to take the form of articulating the social consensus through the press, through demonstrations, through pressuring the legislators, through court challenges, and so forth.

What are the mechanisms by which the *organization* maintains internal order and regularity in its operations? First of all, organizations are generally set up to pursue some specific goals. A firm is set up to earn profits. A club is set up for the entertainment of its members. If an organization's goals are not being achieved, the organization, especially its management, will set out to improve matters. Quite commonly, organizations design a sensitive control and information system in order to forewarn management of a change or a possible change from the charted course so that remedial action can be taken. Standard operating procedures and organizational traditions and precedents are other mechanisms that work for operating stability. The sheer size of an organization can be a force for stability because change may require the agreement of a large number of individuals, each of whom may try to make sure that the change does not rock the boat too much—certainly not his portion of it. Last, loyalty felt by members toward the organization and the punitive power of management are factors that lend stability to organizational operations.

But just because there are many mechanisms keeping the organization's operations stable hardly means that the organization is operating optimally. Indeed, the organization may continue to operate inefficiently for many years because of inertia or traditions or cumbersome procedures that no one is willing to change, as sometimes happens with bureaucracies. All we have tried to do is to indicate the forces that keep the organization operating in a stable manner at whatever average level of efficiency it is operating.

Disorder. Insight into social disorders comes from the conflict model of society. The conflict model of society says that usually there is little harmony among different segments of society. In fact, many segments of society have sharp conflicts of interest. One example is the conflict of interest between workers and capitalists over their respective claims to profits. In totalitarian societies there often are powerful if hidden conflicts between technocrats and party cadres in the running of factories. Marx specifically forecast recurrent disorders in capitalist societies until, as he saw it, the contradiction between private ownership of the means of production and a deprived but solidified proletariat was resolved.[5]

In organizations, too, there are disruptive forces. Just as the magma swirls beneath the relatively placid crust of the earth, so do human passions and the hidden contradictions of organizational life create turbulence beneath apparent organizational stability. Brown has been a machinist with the company for twenty-one years but is in danger of a layoff because other, younger men are available at lower rates and with more up-to-date skills. So he seethes with anger and anxiety, railing against the "irresponsibility" and "immaturity" of the younger men and at the venality of management. And Ken, the young machinist, is, of course, disgusted at the slow-motion ways of bumbling old Brown, who, as best he can tell, still lives in the 1950's. The vice president who was passed over for the presidency is planning to leave to form a rival corporation and is trying to hire away the best talent in the company to the new corporation. In the large general hospital, the doctors and the administrators are constantly squabbling—the doctors want the best equipment to "save life," regardless of cost, and the administrators are squirming over the apparent duplication and under-utilization of medical equipment as well as the high-handed ways of the doctors. In a health care bureaucracy, the management is committed to the values of communication only up or down the line of command and the exercise of authority strictly according to explicit job specifications. But the demand by a senior government official that the bureaucracy undertake a number of innovative projects, such as seeking the participation of the community the bureaucracy serves, has caused great consternation because the ideas, the imagination, and the expertise needed to plan the projects are simply not available except among some of the junior staff. But to give them responsibility would violate the norm of seniority and the hierarchy of authority.

In the above examples, note the *structural* causes of the various conflicts: management's having to choose between experienced but expensive and somewhat obsolete older workers and inexperienced but cheaper and technically better trained younger workers; the pyramidal shape of the organizational hierarchy, which is guaranteed to produce a few winners and many losers; the disagreement between professionals, with their norm of service at any cost, and bureaucrats, with their norm of efficiency and parsimony; and, finally, the conflict between a seniority system that rewards loyalty and a meritocracy that requires the crossing of hierarchical and departmental barriers. In all these examples, a sociologist may argue plausibly that conflict is inevitable because of structural factors, regardless of who the actors are.

A number of organizational researchers of sociological persuasion have pointed to the structural contradictions of organizational life, particularly within bureaucracies, that lead to changes—often unanticipated, unlovely changes. For example, the impossibility of managing everything forces top management to delegate authority. But the new wielders of authority have their own selective perceptions, motivations, beliefs, and technical skills. As a result, differentiation of interests and approaches takes place within the ranks of management. This adversely affects coordination of organizational activities.[6]

Another classic syndrome has been identified by Gouldner.[7] The need for control of operations impels management at higher levels to formulate rules and standard operating procedures. But since these are set impersonally in bureaucracies, usually with minimum involvement of those subject to them, employees tend to do only what is minimally required of them. For example, a clerk pays attention only to his own work and does not attend a client who wants some information; a professor regularly teaches the required hours per week but makes no time available to students after the class is over; a machinist does not lend a hand when someone's equipment breaks down. This, of course, adversely affects the overall performance of the organization. Feeling distressed, upper management tightens the screws further, and the cycle of noninvolvement, minimum acceptable performance, and deterioration in performance is repeated.

And so, whatever the personal idiosyncracies of organizational actors, powerful structural factors can create a field of forces in which conflict becomes inevitable or at least highly probable. This conflict may erupt as any of the common disorders of organizational life—back-biting, strikes, sabotage, or worse.

Continuity. One of the questions sociologists pursue is: What makes for the continuity of social patterns of behavior despite the turnover in the membership of a society? To paraphrase Tennyson—men may come and men may go, but society goes on forever. Why? One way sociologists have tried to answer this question is by imagining society to be some kind of an organism with specific needs. Just as an organism develops the anatomical structures necessary to satisfy its needs, society is supposed to develop the structures necessary to satisfy its recurring needs. This is the famous structural-functional view of society propounded by anthropologists like Malinowski and Radcliffe-Brown and developed further by Talcott Parsons and his associates.[8] Succinctly put, social life "persists because societies find means (structures) whereby they fulfill the needs (functions) which are either pre-conditions or consequences of organized life."[9] As examples, society sets up the institution of the family (a structure) because of its need for socialized members to replace the ones that die out or become nonproductive; it meets its need for security by setting up the state with military and police powers at its disposal.

The structural-functional view prompts the following questions for organizational analysis: (a) What kinds of need do organizations have? (b) What kinds of structure do organizations develop in response to these needs? These are very broad questions, and here they can be only superficially tackled. Obviously, the needs of every organization, like those of every human being, are to some extent unique. But, just as it has been argued by psychologists that most human beings have certain common needs, such as the need for security, the need for social communication, and the need for autonomy and self-actualization,[10] it has been argued by some organization theorists that most organizations have certain common needs. Bennis, for example, has indicated that to survive, all organizations need to confront the following problems:[11]

1 How to integrate or synthesize the needs of the organization for efficiency and growth with the needs of organizational members for self-actualization, autonomy, pleasant social relations, security, and the like. If this problem is not confronted, then the organization may have either happy, satisfied members but inefficient operations or superficially efficient operations but unhappy, alienated, uncooperative organizational members.

2 How to secure adequate interpersonal and intergroup cooperation and prevent destructive conflicts. An organization consists of individuals and groups with specialized functions. Such specialization is likely to lead to a self- or group-oriented perception of problems rather than one that emphasizes the goals of the organization as a whole. Since specialization implies interdependence, unless individuals or groups are willing to cooperate, the organization as a whole is likely to suffer.

3 How to distribute power and authority in the organization. Authority is indispensable for coordination of operations and for taking remedial action should plans go awry. But concentration of authority and power in the hands of a few can lead to alienation and stifling of initiative in the many. Hence, questions such as use of controls or centralization/decentralization are important questions of organizational design.

4 How to adapt to changes in the business environment of the organization. Just as adaptation to nature has been necessary for human

TABLE 3–1
Organizational Needs and Common Organizational Structures

Need or function	*Organizational structural responses*
Integration of the needs or goals of the organization with the needs or goals of its members	A system of incentives; participative decision-making; careful selection and training of organizational members
Intergroup collaboration	Profit-sharing; planning; management training in intergroup collaboration
Distribution of authority to secure coordination of activities without stifling initiative	Hierarchy of authority but with substantial decentralization of authority; establishment of management controls combined with participative decision-making
Adaptation to the environment	A good information and control system; divisionalization; marketing
Organizational renewal	Organizational development programs; systematic gathering and feedback of reliable information concerning organizational health

survival, organizations too must adapt to the changes in the social, economic, technological, and legal environment in which they operate. The accurate perception of the nature of environmental change and the kinds of response an organization should make to environmental changes are key concerns of organizational designers.

5 How to revitalize the organization when it gets sick. Organizations may get sick from failing to respond to any of the four organizational needs mentioned above. Just as human beings need to know how to treat themselves or how to get proper treatment in the event of sickness, organizations, too, need to know how to get a cure should disease creep in. Alienation, apathy, high absenteeism or turnover, excessive organizational politics, persistently low performance, and the like are symptoms of organizational disease.

If the organization can develop appropriate structures to deal with these problems or needs, it is likely to continue to survive, even if its managers, staff, technicians, and workers die or leave and are replaced by others. We will elaborate in later chapters on the kinds of structure needed to deal with these problems; in Table 3–1, however, we indicate briefly a few of the structures or mechanisms organizations develop to deal with these problems.

One should not get the impression from the table that to survive all organizations need to develop identical structures. Organizations differ in the intensity of the five needs listed in the table. These needs differ because of differences in goals, environment, technology, size, age of the organization, and so on. Hence, since the intensity of needs differs from one organization to the next, the deployment of the structures listed in the table will also differ from organization to organization.

Consider for example the research and development laboratory of an electronics firm and its production department. Let us treat both as individual organizations. In the lab the need to integrate the needs of the scientists with the goals of the laboratory is very important. Creativity would suffer gravely unless the scientists are highly motivated. At the same time, unless research results in useful products, the research effort would be wasteful from the company's viewpoint. Thus, it is imperative to have a highly sophisticated incentive system that takes into account not only the pecuniary needs of the scientists but also their needs for autonomy and self-actualization. Careful selection and training and participative decision-making are also very important. In the production department there is extensive use of machinery and a great deal of specialization in the work performed by work groups. Because of this, there is considerable potential for intergroup conflict. In this organization the structures necessary for securing intergroup collaboration assume strategic importance. If we were to consider the needs of the marketing department of this company, perhaps the need to adapt to environmental changes would be the strongest need, and therefore the structures that facilitate this, such as a good information and control system, would be of strategic importance.

In summary, all organizations have the needs listed in Table 3–1, but to varying degrees, and so, to survive, each organization needs to emphasize the structural responses listed in the table to a different extent.

Change. Models of social evolution provide insights into questions of organizational evolution. The question that sociologists explore is: "Are societies subject to evolutionary changes?" Some sociologists believe that all societies go through fixed stages of development. Karl Marx believed, for example, that all societies go through the stages of feudalism, capitalism, socialism, and communism, each stage preceded by a fundamental change in technology. Auguste Comte believed that all societies go through the three stages of conquest, defense, and industry. Emile Durkheim believed that there is an evolutionary trend in societies from a low division of labor and specialization to a high division of labor and specialization. In the low division of labor society there is "mechanical solidarity." In this society people are held together by tight religious and familial bonds. In the high division of labor society, which emerges as a consequence of industrial development, there is "organic solidarity." In such a society, relations are less intimate and personal and are governed mainly by common interests, by contract, and the like. Other sociologists believe that while every society need not go through a fixed sequence of stages, humanity as a whole demonstrates an evolutionary sequence. Leslie White, for example, believes that the evolution of culture proceeds in spurts as new sources of energy are harnessed. Cultures are moving, he feels, toward a world culture marked by a world government.[12] William Ogburn sees inventions as the principal engine of evolutionary change, and has argued that there is a "culture lag." In other words, our ideas and social arrangements invariably lag behind changes in technology and inventions.[13]

From the point of view of organizational analysis, the question that sociological models of evolution prompt is: "Do organizations exhibit some kind of propensity to change over time?" The question is a difficult one to answer. We do not have reliable information on organizations of centuries other than the present one. What information we do have suggests that large organizations even in ancient times exhibited some of the same properties as large contemporary organizations exhibit—namely, a hierarchy of authority, delegation of authority, division of labor and specialization, and standard operating procedures.[14] But there may be some important qualitative differences between older and contemporary organizations. For one thing, today's organizations employ a far more automated, capital intensive, sophisticated technology than earlier organizations of the same type. As a consequence, their personnel needs to be better educated than the personnel needed in bygone centuries. The authoritarian or paternalistic mode of management, which has been the prevalent mode of management during much of history, is far less acceptable in today's organizations. Human-relations oriented, participative management is becoming the order of the day. For another thing, today's organizations function in a far more turbulent technological and cultural environment than older organizations. Professional management (planning, forecasting, marketing, the use of operations research) and the management of change and innovation are far more important today than in earlier centuries. As Alvin Toffler has suggested, the need to confront frequent change means "adhocracy"—that is to say, the perpetual setting up and dismantling of temporary organizational structures.[15]

Figure 3–1 suggests lines of evolution of organizations. The comparison is between organizations in earlier times and organizations of the *same type* today and in the near future (one cannot compare, say, governments of today with inns of the Middle Ages). Also, it is worth stressing that what is contemporary or prospective is not necessarily better than what was in the past. Indeed, in some ways, present or future organizational arrangements may be a good deal worse, especially for the managers of organizations. The organizational life of the Roman administrator or of the

FIGURE 3–1
Organizational Evolution over the Centuries

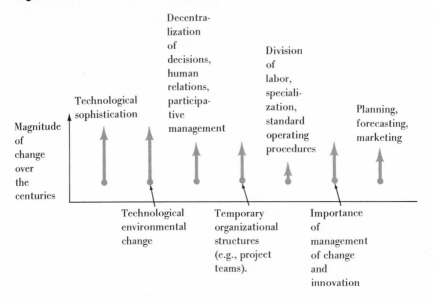

NOTE: The dots represent the past, the arrows the direction of change, and the length of the arrows the estimated magnitude of change.

proprietor-manager of an eighteenth-century English factory was probably a good deal easier than that of the contemporary governmental administrator or factory manager. Contemporary managers have to keep up with technical changes. They are expected to be good at human relations. When making decisions, they are expected to listen to the advice of a battery of experts. Their decisions must be made quickly under great pressure. They must learn to live with the rapid pace of organizational changes. All these requirements mean a degree of flexibility, drive, and tolerance probably uncommon in ancient times.

Social Processes in Organizations

Social processes are a major subject of sociological study. A large number of processes go on in society. Most of these processes occur in organizations too, and Table 3–2 lists some of the more important ones, along with the organizational forces that aid or impede them. For example, one of the most important and widely studied social processes is differentiation and stratification of people into status or wealth categories. The process is an important one for assessing the inevitability of class conflict suggested by Marx.

TABLE 3–2
Social Processes Occurring in Organizations

Processes occurring in organizations	*Forces reinforcing processes in organizations*
Differentiation and stratification of organizational members on the basis of status	Division of labor and specialization; differences in abilities; differences in formal authority; differences in control over the organization's resources
Mobility (upward and lateral mobility of organizational members)	Meritocracy aids upward and lateral mobility; seniority system aids upward mobility; educational qualification requirements impede upward mobility of blue-collar operatives; nepotism impedes upward mobility
Cooperation, accommodation, and assimilation of organizational members; integration of members into organizational community; their socialization and indoctrination	Work interdependence; common fate; social interaction at work; participation in decision-making; personnel selection procedure and training
Conflict within the organization (interpersonal and intergroup conflict)	Differentiation and stratification; incompatible interests of organizational members; many rivals for powerful positions due to the organization's being a pyramid of authority
Opinion formation, articulation, and interpersonal communication	Shared work interests; common work-related vocabulary; work-related interdependence; proximity; common interests
Nonformal control of organizational members	Informal control systems centered in work groups; common fate and interdependence in work group resulting in work group norms, which guide the behavior of group members
Deviant behavior in organizations (behavior antithetical to the dominant values of the organizational culture)	Weak hold of the organizational community on its members; disorganization; inability of organizational members to satisfy their urgent needs by legitimate means; managerial attitude of indifference or contempt toward subordinates
Changes in attitudes and norms of organizational members	Technological or market change resulting in infusion of new members, regroupings of personnel, modification of jobs, and so on

If indeed there are clearly distinguishable social classes, differentiated on the basis of possessions, status, common attitudes, and the like, and if, in addition, their interests are incompatible, then class conflict is inevitable.

Within organizations, too, one finds status hierarchies. In corporations, the owning and managing elites form a high status class, while the clerical personnel and blue-collar workers form a low status class. If the interests of these classes are not reconciled, then class conflict, marked by many overt and covert struggles, may take place in organizations. Strikes are only the most dramatic form of these class struggles.

Another example of a social process that has been studied widely by sociologists is deviant behavior such as crime, juvenile delinquency, prostitution, drug addiction. Deviant behavior is behavior antithetical to the dominant norms of a culture. In *organizations* deviant behavior is likely to take the forms of thieving, disobedience, rebellion, absenteeism, malingering. A number of sociological studies have tried to identify the causes of deviant social behavior. One important cause has been found to be normlessness due to rapid social change and weak hold of the community on its members.[16] Another cause is a broken family or a childhood deprived of parental care and affection.[17] A third cause is the nonavailability to the deviant of legitimate paths for attaining socially approved goals—for example, the difficulty or impossibility of getting a "fair deal" in jobs or housing.[18]

One may expect somewhat analogous forces to create deviant behavior in organizations. For example, organizational norms may not have crystalized if the organization is young or has had a very rapid rate of change in its operations technology or nature of business. This may give rise to a feeling of normlessness or to a weak affiliation with the organization's culture. Another cause for deviant behavior in organizations may be the feeling of some members that they are unjustly blocked. Many blue-collar workers and junior level supervisors feel that because they lack paper qualifications they can never rise in the organizational hierarchy. This may lead some of them to become disgruntled "rotten eggs."

Conclusion

As we have seen, a good deal of sociological theory is usable in the analysis of organizations. Over and above this, a great many sociologists have contributed directly to organization theory, since the study of organizations has been an important subject in sociology. As we noted in Chapter 1, organizations play a vital function in the well-being of society. No wonder then that sociologists have a strong interest in the workings of organizations. Sociologists such as Max Weber, Robert Merton, Philip Selznick, Alvin Gouldner, Tom Burns, Richard Hall, Peter Blau, Michel Crozier, and many others have contributed significantly to our understanding of how organizations function.

What is distinctive about the sociological approach is its emphasis on uncovering the durable or structural factors shaping the functioning of organizations.[19] For example, in trying to explain conflict among individuals within an organization, the sociologist will try to seek structural reasons rather than personal ones. Instead of saying that Manager A and Manager B are quarreling because they are both cantankerous individuals, the sociolologist will seek underlying structural reasons for their quarrel. It may be that they are fighting because both are competing in the race to succeed their common boss. Here, the structural reasons are: (a) that upward mobility is highly valued by the managerial class (of which the two are members) and (b) that in organizations generally an ever-shrinking number can be promoted as one climbs the organizational hierarchy. Given these structural factors, the observed rivalry is seen as inevitable, regardless of the two managers' actual dispositions.

But while sociologists tend to ignore personalistic factors, they do not necessarily ignore the human personality. If two managers are fighting, they *assume* that the fight arises because the two managers have a high need for power, since managers "typically" have a high need for power. In other words, rather than confronting the complexity of the actual personalities in a situation, they like to simplify their analysis by *attributing* some behavioral tendencies to the individuals on the basis of presumptions of what these individuals should be like given their training, class affiliations, and so on. To take another example: to explain observed conflict in an organization between the line managers and the advisory staff who provide most of the technical analysis for the decisions the line managers make, the sociologist will assume that managers are "locals" (that is, their primary loyalty is to the organization) and the staff are "cosmopolitans" (that is, their loyalty is to their respective professions or areas of expertise).[20] Since the norms of the two groups differ, conflict between them in this organization is "inevitable."

Perrow gives a fine example of structural analysis in a situation in which personal factors appear at first sight to be dominant.[21] One large assembly plant of an automobile company had a poor performance record. Its manager, one Mr. Stewart, seemed to be an autocrat who did not solicit suggestions from his subordinates, often bypassed his immediate subordinates, and ruled by fear. He was replaced by a Mr. Cooley, who mingled with lower level managers, sought their cooperation and suggestions, encouraged group meetings, engaged in long-range planning, and modernized the plant. The performance of the plant quickly improved. Superficially, one may be inclined to attribute the poor performance of the plant to Stewart's being a poor leader and the improvement in performance to Cooley's being a good leader. Perrow, however, draws attention to structural factors behind these two managers' performance. It appears that Stewart earlier had demonstrated competent management of a plant. When, however, he was given charge of the assembly plant, the latter had obsolete, run-down equipment and was performing poorly. The headquarters failed to recognize this and blamed Stewart for poor performance. Consequently they exerted tremendous pressure on Stewart and kept on issuing detailed directions not only to him but to his subordinates. Since Stewart had little discretionary authority, he could grant little to his subordinates; since he was under tremendous pressure, he transmitted some of this pressure to his subordinates.

Fortunately for Cooley, he was seen by the headquarters as a competent man and therefore was given a great deal of discretionary authority. Since he had this authority, he could grant a great deal to his subordinates, and since he was not under great pressure, his subordinates too were relieved of some of this pressure. There was relaxation of tensions, less alienation, greater motivation, and the performance of the plant improved. What Perrow is suggesting is that had Cooley been in Stewart's position his behavior would have been very like Stewart's, and vice versa. As Perrow says, "If organizations are to be studied, rather than individuals or group processes, then the structural view, characteristic of sociology, is superior" to the social-psychological perspective.[22]

It is because of the sociological preoccupation with structural explanations and with the study of the whole organization, rather than of just groups and individuals within it, that organization theorists of sociological training have sought to explain the structure and functioning of organizations in terms of variables like the nature of the organization's environment, its goals, size, technology, and types of business. (These theorists have been some of the principal votaries of the so-called contingency approach in organization theory discussed in Chapter 6.)

Let us now see what the social psychological perspective has to offer.

SOCIAL PSYCHOLOGY

The Domain of Social Psychology

The roots of the word "psychology" are *psyche*, meaning "mind," and *logos*, meaning "measure, order, structure." Thus, psychology is the science of the mind or mental processes—the science of human nature—and since mental processes are intimately connected with behavior, it is also a science of human behavior. The contributions of psychology, particularly of social psychology, to understanding human behavior in organizations have been enormous.

Social psychology is a major branch of psychology. It treats many of the same subjects as the other branches, such as perception, cognition, motivation. But it is distinctive in focusing on the *social* factors that influence how individuals perceive, believe, get motivated, form attitudes, and so on. Social psychology is the study of the individual in a social context.

The study of the formation and change of attitudes is a major focus of social psychology because of the obvious social content of attitudes. We pick up most of our attitudes from others—our family members, friends, neighbors, colleagues at work, the reference group with which we identify. Another major focus of social psychology is the study of groups and how groups affect the thinking and behavior of individuals.

Both of these focuses are, of course, of considerable interest to students of organizations. Attitudes of organizational members substantially determine their behavior at work and thus affect the success or failure of the organization. The organization can be viewed as a system of interlinked groups. Whether these groups are functioning in a collaborative manner or in a destructively competitive manner determines whether the organization can achieve its goals or not. Whether each group is itself a cohesive team or a collection of warring members vitally affects the achievement of each group's goals. Much of what is known as behavioral science consists of techniques for changing negative attitudes and for making work groups function more effectively. More than sociology and political science, social psychology has been the knowledge resource for many management *applications*. In this regard it rivals economics, which is the knowledge resource for operations research and financial management.

There are five major orientations in social psychology.[23] These are: the gestalt orientation, the field theory orientation, the reinforcement or behavioristic psychology orientation, the psychoanalytic or depth psychology orientation, and the role theory orientation. Each of these orientations represents a model of human beings and their social behavior. Individually, each provides only a partial explanation of the immense complexity of human behavior. Put together, they can provide a fascinating multifaceted perspective of human behavior in organizations.

We briefly review each orientation, remembering that each is a major field of research, rivaling in magnitude the study of organizations, and that we cannot, therefore, expect to "cover" it in any depth. Our objective is to outline the model of the human being and his social behavior that each orientation provides and to sketch out a few insights into human behavior in organizations. Table 3–3 provides a summary of the principal concerns of each of these orientations and the organizational issues illumined by the orientation.

TABLE 3–3

Orientations in Social Psychology, Their Major Concerns, and Organizational Issues Illuminated by Them

Social psychological orientation	Major focuses	Organizational phenomena illuminated
Gestalt orientation	Perception, cognition, and problem-solving	Beliefs held by organization members; the way they define reality; the way problems are solved in organizations; administrative rationality
Field theory orientation	Motivation and conflict	Intrapersonal and interpersonal conflict in organizations; styles of leadership; levels of aspiration of organizational members; strategies for changing attitudes
Reinforcement orientation (behavioristic psychology)	Learning, or behavior modification	The design of rewards and sanctions in the organization; behavioral change in organizations and its permanence
Psychoanalytic orientation	Personality and pathological behavior	Neurotic behavior of leaders and subordinates; the role of personality in decision-making
Role theory orientation	Role, or socially expected behavior	Conformity and deviant behavior in organizations; role conflicts and role ambiguity; the effects of role on personality

Gestalt Orientation: Model of Human Being

The word *gestalt,* a German word, means "form, structure, organized whole." Implicit in gestalt psychology is the assumption that an important influence on human behavior is our need for an organized, coherent (as opposed to chaotic) view of the world and our relations to it. Because of this need we strive to organize what we perceive—that is, to arrange into meaningful patterns the millions of bits of information that we take in through our senses.

A key notion of this psychology, advanced by Kohler[24] and Koffka,[25] two of its founders, is that psychological phenomena occur in a "field." A "field" is a system of interdependent parts or factors in which the properties of the system are not inferrable from the properties of the isolated individual elements—the whole is greater than the sum of its parts. The whole affects the parts—a group powerfully influences the behavior of its members. The parts, in turn, affect the behavior of the whole—a single false note can ruin an aria, as can a slight excess of salt a meal.

The other key notion is that psychological processes act to make our perception as orderly or "good" as conditions will allow. For example, as Koffka has suggested, either we accentuate the similarity or relationship of elements in the perceptual field or we exaggerate the differences.[26] The former is called "assimilation," and the latter is called "contrast." In general, stereotypes are examples of assimilation, while the ethnocentrist's tendency to view foreigners and ethnic minorities as very different from his own group is an example of contrast.

There have been many interesting experimental demonstrations of the gestalt principles at work. In an experiment by Asch, two sets of subjects were given a list of adjectives describing a person. The lists were identical except that the adjective "cold" in one list was replaced in the other by the adjective "warm." The subjects were asked to give their impressions of the person. The subjects given the "warm" list had far more positive impressions of the person than the subjects who were given the "cold" list. The former set of subjects thought the person to be happier, better natured, more generous, more humorous, more popular, more humane, and so on, than the latter set of subjects did. The whole impression of the person, a gestalt, was radically changed by the change of one part, a single adjective.[27]

Gestalt theories such as that of Heider suggest that lack of balance or the presence of incongruity in the perceptual field can lead to attitude change because of the need to restore balance or remove the incongruity.[28] Festinger's famous experiments on "cognitive dissonance" are a demonstration of this. In these, individuals who were given $1 to tell the experimenter's accomplice what was patently not true (that they had enjoyed a very boring laboratory task) told the experimenter that they in fact enjoyed the task more than those subjects that were given $20 to say the same.[29] Here the incongruity or dissonance lay in receiving very little for violating the norm of truthfulness. The incongruity was removed by the subject's coming to believe that he had in fact enjoyed the task.

The foregoing and other experimental work suggests:

1 Our perceptions are highly selective. In the welter of information that besets us, we pick out those bits that have the most meaning to us on account of our preconceptions and current operating needs. That is to say, consciously or unconsciously we exercise choice in what we perceive. This choice is not exercised capriciously; it is exercised rationally in terms of the mental frame in which we may be operating.

2 We seek meaning in what we perceive. Sometimes we impose a meaning on even random phenomena such as seeing the hunter in the constellation of stars known as Orion or the old man on the moon.

3 We are uncomfortable with mutually inconsistent perceptions or beliefs. To get rid of this discomfort we try either to synthesize the opposing beliefs or perceptions or to suppress, devalue, or deny one of the opposing beliefs or perceptions.

Obviously, social factors play an important role in shaping our perceptions and beliefs. Social interaction helps us crystallize our norms and shapes our goals and needs. These, in turn, play a part in the selectivity of our perception. The very process of imputing a meaning to ambiguous phenomena is affected by social factors. In a primitive culture, boils on the body may be interpreted as a manifestation that malignant spirits have taken possession of the body. In science-dominated cultures, they may be interpreted as an attack of smallpox.

The gestalt contribution to the understanding of insight and problem solving has also been notable. A problem can be thought of as a perceptual field. Insight, or the "aha" experience we get when we see a possible solution to a vexing problem, represents a change in the perceptual field. Some fascinating experiments with monkeys in the early part of this century suggested that even monkeys are capable of intelligent, problem-solving behavior.[30]

The gestalt-initiated research on problem solving suggests the following picture:[31]

1 Problem solving is fundamentally different from habitual behavior. In habitual behavior a given stimulus elicits a more or less invariant response. In problem solving, stimulus has to be seen as a problem situation. The response to it may vary greatly on the way the perceiver structures the problem.

2 A situation is seen as a problem if some goal cannot be achieved with the means at one's disposal. This may be because the goal is too vague, or the required means are not available, or the process by which the available means can be utilized to secure the goal is not well understood.

3 Problem solving proceeds in a number of distinctive, if overlapping phases. The first phase consists of the perception of the problem situation through some stimulus. In the next phase, the concepts involved in the problem situation are sought out or clarified. This phase marks the definition of the problem in some detail. In this phase the problem solver makes some key decisions as to which parts of the situation to react to and what strategies to adopt in responding to the problem situation. In the third phase, the problem solver assesses the courses of action available to him. In this phase the problem solver may exhibit some preferences such as for risky versus conservative alternatives or for complex and comprehensive versus simple alternatives. The fourth phase is the decision-making phase, in which the actual choice of alternative is made. In the final, fifth phase, the chosen alternative's effectiveness is verified.

4. There are various obstacles as well as various aids to creative problem solving. Stereotyped perception is a key obstacle. Functional fixedness—the inability to see functions for a thing other than its conventional uses—is an important form of stereotyped perception. A stick may be seen merely as a weapon. It may not readily be seen as a lever, as a pole, as a measuring rod, as a material to carve or engrave, as a wall hanging, as firewood, and so on. Defensive beliefs, fear of failure, and mental rigidity are other examples of obstacles. Brainstorming is an important aid to creative problem solving. It is a process in which the production of potential solutions is separated from their evaluation. It is a technique for preventing premature killing of ideas. Other examples of techniques that draw on gestalt principles for creative thinking are the synectics method based on imaginative use of analogies and the method of attribute listing, in which the attributes of an object are listed exhaustively with a view to stumbling on some novel improvements or uses.[32]

It is obvious that a person's social experiences affect the problem-solving process. Whether a situation is seen as a problem situation or not often depends on the person's socialization. In a study by Dearborn and Simon, executives from different departments of a large company were asked to identify the key problem in a business case.[33] The sales executives tended to see marketing and sales as the most important problem area, and the production managers identified the need to "clarify" the organization as of most importance. The choice of goals is largely a matter of one's social experiences and training. Since the problem-solving process is initiated by the frustration of some personal goal, it is clear that social factors affect the triggering of the problem-solving process. The problem solver's training will also affect the way he structures the problem and the way he goes about solving it. In an organization, a person with training in planning is likely to insist on first getting all the facts, on clarifying and possibly quantifying the goals or objectives, on searching systematically for alternatives, and so on. On the other hand, a person without much formal training in planning may prefer to go on readily available facts and to pick the first alternative that promises to meet the major goals.

What the foregoing implies is that even the most rational person is only *subjectively* rational. In organizations a "rational" decision maker may choose the best of the alternatives *known* to him. But this is only the tip of the iceberg. First all possible alternatives have to be perceived. But selective perception may prevent that. It may also prevent the perception of all the consequences of those alternatives that are perceived. Add to that the possibility that the decision maker may have perceived the initial problem situation itself selectively. What this boils down to is that administrative rationality is quite limited, and though there are programs like that of Kepner and Tregoe[34] to extend it, perfect rationality such as is assumed by economists is probably unattainable.

The Gestalt Orientation:
Model of Organization

Gestalt psychology is the psychology of the individual's perceptions, cognitions, and problem-solving processes. It has been extended to take into account the influence of social factors. The gestalt view prompts the following picture of the organization.

The subjectively rational perceptions, beliefs, and problem-solving processes of the individual members of the organization are influenced by those of others with whom they come into contact, and they, of course, in turn influence the perceptions of the others. Thus, the organization is a system of interlinked perceptions, beliefs, and problem-solving processes. The organization is almost like a giant brain that receives sensations from a great many sources, each sensation being sorted, filed, and assessed for its implications. If the receptors in the brain are defective, or the paths connecting the receptors are defective, or the brain mechanisms that interpret the sense signals to derive some meaning are defective or paralyzed, then the brain is likely to malfunction. Similarly, if in the organization the perceivers of the key information, the decision makers whose beliefs shape the organization's policy, and the key problem solvers are either incompetent or not properly interconnected, then the organization is likely to operate poorly. From the standpoint of organization design, the gestalt orientation makes us pay attention to the *removal of blocks* to clear perception and fresh, creative problem solving, if not among all members of the organization, at least among those whose decisions matter a great deal. These are blocks such as defensively closed minds, fear of failure, mental rigidity, reluctance to explore novel ideas, and an excessive tendency to categorize things as "good" or "bad." Similarly, the gestalt orientation suggests that attempts be made to inculcate in key decision makers *habits that favor creative problem-solving*, such as brainstorming. The foregoing implies that the organization set up personnel selection, training, and promotion procedures that maximize the probability that key personnel do not have blocks to productive thinking and have the ability and motivation to engage in creative thinking. A premium on intel-lectual brightness, an organizational tolerance for creative if somewhat nonconformist individuals, an organizational climate that encourages wide-ranging discussion, exploration of novel suggestions, and free and open communication channels are all likely to be helpful.[35]

The Field Theory Approach: Model of Human Being

Field theory, derived from gestalt conceptions, is associated primarily with the name of Kurt Lewin, a German gestalt psychologist who emigrated to the United States during the Hitler years, and his colleagues and students, particularly Leon Festinger. Unlike the gestalt theorists, who focused pri-marily on perception, Lewin concentrated on the dynamics of *motivation.* He examined the factors that underlie behavior and determine goals toward which (or away from which) behavior is directed. Lewinian terminology liberally incorporated terms from the physical sciences like valence, force, tension, locomotion, space. He tried to invent a physics of psychology. He believed that human behavior takes place in psychological *force fields.* These may have properties similar to those of the gravitational and other force fields that determine the behavior of material objects. The psychological force field consists of all the forces acting on the individual that can change his behavior. Principally, these forces stem from the individual's motives, intentions, perceptions of reality, and the demands made on him by other entities.

The central tenets of field theory may be summarized as follows:[36]

1 Needs and goals create tension in people. People attempt to reduce this tension by trying to satisfy their needs and reach their goals. Thus, human behavior is goal directed. Some goals are approach goals, such as wanting to make money. Others are avoidance goals, such as wanting to stay out of jail.

2 Needs are in one of three states: deprivation, satiation, or over-satiation. Oversatiation is a state of undertension. An oversatiated need prompts a person to seek the gratification of other needs.

3 Needs and goals are often interrelated and interdependent. One structural relationship among human needs is indicated by Abraham Maslow, who suggested that needs form a hierarchy.[37] Physiological and security needs, social needs, ego needs, and self-actualization needs form a hierarchy of successively less urgent needs. As the currently most urgent need is satisfied, the next most urgent need becomes dominant. There are other structural relations among needs, such as those of mutual incompatibility, interdependence, and substitutability in the fulfillment of one need by another.

4 People can experience various forms of conflict in their attempts to satisfy needs. They may have to choose betwen equally attractive alternatives—or between unattractive alternatives. Or, they may have to exercise choice with respect to alternatives that have some attractive features and some unattractive features. These conflicts may be termed "predecisional conflicts." In every case, the conflict is a source of tension. It sets into motion tension-reducing behavior. In the case of conflict from having to choose between two desirable alternatives, there is a post-choice tendency to devalue the forsaken alternative and raise in value the chosen alternative. In conflicts arising from having to choose between unpleasant alternatives, the person will either try to escape from the situation, or if this is not possible, transfer his dislike to the forces blocking his escape. In the case of conflict caused by an alternative having pleasant as well as unpleasant characteristics, whether the alternative is picked will depend on the potency of the goal to be reached through the alternative. If the alternative is picked, the good points will be revalued and the bad points devalued.

5 Human goals arise not only from physiological forces but from social forces acting on the individual. Social interaction can create "own" forces for change or "induced" forces for change (or both). "Own" forces arise from the activation of one's own needs for change through social interaction. "Induced" forces are requirements imposed on the individual. When individuals participate in a group decision, they get the feeling of having had a say in the decision—that is to say, they have an ownership interest in the decision. When a decision is imposed by the group leader, the individuals are induced to cooperate because of the fear of being punished. In some famous experiments on styles of leadership, Lewin and his associates were able to demonstrate that democratically led groups were as productive as autocratically led groups. In addition, in crisis situations and in situations in which the leader was absent, the democratic groups showed greater resourcefulness and continuity of effort than autocratically led groups.[38] These experiments have been one of the foundations of the participative management movement in industry.

6 Changes in attitudes and behavior come about either through the person's changing, or through a change in the person's perception of the situation. Brainwashing is one way of eliciting compliance; making compliance lucrative is another. Dissonant or contradictory information also is a powerful motivator of attitude change. As we noted earlier, in some interesting experiments by Festinger, it was found that subjects who were asked to lie for a paltry sum reported themselves more strongly in agreement with what they were told to say than individuals who were rewarded munificently to dissemble.[39] The former presumably found it unacceptable to lie for a small sum, and therefore got rid of their tension by actually coming to believe the falsehood.

7 Not only do individuals have goals, but these goals are subject to systematic changes of magnitude. The individual's level of aspiration with respect to a goal is equal to the expected utility of success in achieving the goal less the expected disutility should failure occur. The expected utility of success is equal to the utility or satisfaction from succeeding times the subjective probability of success. The expected disutility from failure is equal to the dissatisfaction from failing to reach the goal times the subjective probability of failure. The level of aspiration depends on the past experience of the individual in trying to reach the goal; the trend—that is, whether one is improving, stagnating, or deteriorating; the most recent success or failure; the standards of the group to which one belongs; personality factors such as self-confidence. The phenomenon of the level of aspiration explains many social phenomena like the apathy of the lowest social classes and their revolutionary fervor *after* things have improved somewhat. When failure has been the predominant experience, the level of aspiration is likely to be very low, for the subjective probability of success is low and that of failure is high. But after things improve for a while, the subjective probability of success rises and that of failure falls, and so the level of aspiration rises rapidly.

8 There is a structure to human attitudes as well as to stable social relations. Both are characterized by sets of opposing forces that keep them in a sort of equilibrium. If force is increased on one side, the chances are that force on the other side will also be increased. The new situation will not be very different from the old, except that the level of tension will have gone up. Similarly, a reduction of force on one side will tend to be matched by a reduction on the other. The level of tension will fall as a consequence. For example, the nature of prejudice is such that if a male chauvinist is provided with evidence that women are the equals of men, he will simply find loopholes in the evidence or discover some additional evidence refuting women's equality with men. The Cold War offers a striking example of increased force on one side being matched by increased force on the other side, with greater tension resulting from each increment in force. Détente hopefully offers an example of matched reductions in force with a lowering of tension.

9 Individuals like to be members of a group for a number of reasons, one of which is the need to evaluate one's abilities and opinions, and even emotions, especially if one experiences some doubts concerning them.[40] This need for self-evaluation gets individuals to search for somewhat similar individuals who can act as sounding boards. Group solidarity is fostered by perception of interdependence in achieving a common goal. Group solidarity or cohesiveness has a number of interesting consequences.[41] One consequence is greater willingness on the part of group members to divide up work, accept one another's influence, and evaluate one another's actions more positively. In other words, a cohesive group begins to resemble a close-knit small organization. There are three sources of pressure to communicate within groups. One stems from pressures toward uniformity in a group. Another stems from attempts to get the group to its goal. And the third arises from the existence of emotional states within the group. Through these group processes or group dynamics, membership in the group comes to be highly valued. This has the effect of increasing the efforts by group members to influence group decisions and also of increasing the magnitude of opinion change that occurs when there is a discrepancy of opinion within the group. Strong pressures for uniformity within a group lead to concerted efforts to break down deviant opinion, including, as a last resort, the psychological expulsion of the deviant.[42] In short, membership in a cohesive group profoundly affects the beliefs, motivations, perceptions, and behavior of its members. The individual as a group member develops attributes that are absent outside the field of forces represented by the group.

Field theory has become the intellectual foundation of a good part of attitude-change technology—what today is known as organizational development, management development, conflict-resolution technology, or sensitivity training.[43] This technology is examined at greater length in Chapters 5 and 14. Changing attitudes and getting rid of stereotypes and intergroup conflicts is a major and continuing undertaking in most organizations because of the dynamic character of modern operations. In Lewinian terms, attitudes are, like status quos in social relations, quasi-stationary equilibria. By analyzing the forces acting on the individual to maintain an attitude at a given level—say, a very negative attitude of workers toward management—management often can change it by weakening the forces supporting the current attitude and strengthening the forces opposing the current attitude. If gestalt psychology helps our understanding of how people perceive the world, how they form impressions, and how they solve problems, field theory helps us understand the dynamics of motivation so that we can more effectively motivate a change in people's perceptions, impressions, and modes of problem-solving.

Field Theory: Model of Organization

Field theory suggests the following model of the organization.

The organization consists of interlinked individuals—that is, of interlinked motivational fields. Each individual has a unique motivational field, consisting of active approach and avoidance goals. What goals are active depends on the "own" and "induced" forces acting on the individual. Since the motivational fields are interlinked through interpersonal communication, forces that affect the motivation of one individual may have surprising effects on the motivations of other individuals in the organization. Thus, if one individual is punished (or rewarded), some predictable as well as unpredictable consequences may follow for the motivation and behavior of others in the organization. In other words, the motivational fields of organizational members are not static but dynamic and are only partially within the control of the organization.

A major problem before the organization is to design the organization so that the bulk of the individuals are motivated to work for—or at least not against—the goals of the organization. In other words, the problem is of so shaping the motivational forces within individual members that the resulting behavior supports the organization. The organizational strategy becomes one of strengthening supportive forces and weakening hostile forces in its members. Supportive forces can be strengthened if members are convinced that their important needs can be met by working for the organization. Hostile forces can be weakened if the members feel that the psychological cost of working for the organization is not excessive. But just as the organization tries to get the best deal it can from its members, the members in turn try to strengthen forces supporting them and weaken forces hostile to them. The members can strengthen supportive forces by convincing the organizational hierarchy of their readiness to cooperate in helping the organization achieve its goals. Hostile forces can be weakened if the organizational hierarchy feels that the cost to the organization of retaining its members is not excessive.

A number of strategies are available to the organization to strengthen supportive forces and weaken hostile forces in its members. Some, such as job enrichment and participative decision-making, not only strengthen supportive forces by satisfying important needs for autonomy and self-actualization, but weaken hostile forces by decreasing boredom on the job. Other common strategies are good pay scales and fringe benefits, rewards tied to performance on the job, and humane supervision. Competition among organizational members, such as among sales personnel to secure the largest increase in sales, or among divisional heads for profitability, is a strategy for trading hostility to the organization for interpersonal hostility.

In organizations, as in society, groups are a major source of need gratification, including security from arbitrary organizational action. Thus, members of an organization seek memberships of groups. Groups may crystallize around people who work close to one another, or people who for some reason must interact frequently, or people who share a common fate, or people whose work is similar. If the interests of such groups are in conflict with one another, inimical relations may develop among them. If cooperation between these groups or their members is necessary, such enmity could harm the organization. The organizational imperative, therefore, is to strengthen forces supporting cooperation among such groups and to weaken hostile forces. Commitment of such groups to an overarching, superordinate goal can do the trick. So can a periodic examination of the stereotypes the groups hold of one another, and an airing of hostile feelings, with a view to restoring more objective perceptions. A third strategy is to create strong incentives for collaboration. An instance of this is worker and management participation in the profits of the company.

Reinforcement or Learning Theory Orientation: Model of Human Being

Reinforcement theory—"rat learning" to its detractors—has been an old and very productive tradition in psychology. Its origins may be traced to the writings of the eighteenth-century utilitarian philosopher Jeremy Bentham, who noted the curious habit of the human to seek pleasure and avoid pain! In recent times, two names have been preeminently associated with this orientation. One is that of Ivan Pavlov, the Russian psychologist who made classical associative learning famous by the paradigm of the salivating dog. The other is B. F. Skinner, the progenitor of instrumental or operant conditioning and of learning machines. In Pavlovian learning, the reinforcement or reward is simultaneous with or immediately precedes desired behavior; in Skinnerian conditioning, the reward is conditional upon the desired behavior being emitted.

In sharp contrast to the mentalistic, multicausal-behavior models of the gestalt and the field theorists, the learning theorists concentrate on one observable stimulus at a time. Machine-like control of human and animal behavior is their goal. Their key assumption is that all complex human behavior that we observe, even the learning of language and thinking itself, can be explained in terms of reinforcement learning. They are undoubtedly right up to a point. Where they go wrong is in asserting without proof that all behavior can be explained in terms of reinforcement and only in terms of reinforcement. Reinforcement theory readily explains the usual and the conventional. It does not sound very plausible in explaining novel and creative behavior.

The basic findings of Skinnerian learning (also called behavioristic psychology) are the following:[44]

1 Any organism (including the human being) tends to engage in a desired behavior more frequently after it is begun to be positively reinforced or rewarded on emitting it. The organism tends to engage in a behavior less and less frequently should the rewards not be offered, or if the organism is punished or negatively reinforced for emitting the behavior. Thus, behavior is strengthened by positive reinforcement and extinguished by null and negative reinforcement. The closer in time the reinforcement is to the behavior in question the more effective is the reinforcement.

2 Reinforcers may be extrinsic to the behavior, or intrinsic to the behavior, or both. When money is paid to elicit routine responses in a factory, the reinforcer (money) is extrinsic. When a person works because work is interesting and challenging, the reinforcer (interesting work) is primarily intrinsic.

3 There are two dimensions of learning or behavioral change. One is the *frequency* with which the desired behavior is emitted or undesired behavior is not emitted. The other is the *duration* over which learned behavior persists after the reinforcement is cut off. When desired behavior is reinforced every time it is emitted (continuous reinforcement), the frequency with which the desired behavior is emitted is *lower* than when desired behavior is intermittently or partially reinforced. As an implication, if a bonus for exceeding quota is given to sales representatives every now and then, then sales representatives are likely to try to exceed quota more frequently than if they are given a bonus every time they exceed their quota. Alternatively, if work is so arranged that a bonus can be earned only once in a while because the quota can be exceeded only once in a while, the sales representatives are likely to try harder than if a bonus is assured because the quota can be exceeded every time.

4 Partial reinforcement comes in several forms. If desired behavior is reinforced every n^{th} time it occurs, it is an instance of a fixed ratio reinforcement. If on an average $1/n$ of the desired responses is reinforced in a random pattern, it is an instance of a variable ratio reinforcement. If reinforcement is provided only a certain time interval after the desired behavior is begun to be emitted, it is an instance of an interval schedule, which can also be fixed or variable.

5 The variable ratio schedules tend to produce more durable behavioral change than both the fixed ratio and continuous patterns of reinforcement. Ratio schedules lead to a faster rate of desired behavior than interval schedules. However, interval schedules produce quite long-lasting behavioral changes.

6 In a given situation, an organism may have available to it a hierarchy of responses. For example, when frustrated at work, a manager half the time may try to get more information and resources to solve the problem, a third of the time may relieve the frustration by bawling out a secretary, and a sixth of the time may do nothing. In this example, the prepotent response is the desired one of attempting to solve the problem. The reinforcement or behavior change strategy would be to strengthen the problem-solving response through positive reinforcement and weaken the undesirable weaker responses of aggression and withdrawal by neutral stimuli or negative reinforcement.

7 There are important side effects of the use of rewards (positive reinforcement) and punishments (negative reinforcement). The most important side effect of positive reinforcement is that the individual begins to like the *source* of reinforcement and therefore is more willing to collaborate with it. The side effect of negative reinforcement is dramatically opposite. The individual builds up an antipathy towards the source of reinforcement and actively tries to avoid this source or overwhelm it as well as the reinforcement situation. If escape or aggression is possible, either physically or mentally, punishment simply becomes a positive reinforcer of escape or aggressive behavior. These facts are of considerable importance in understanding social behavior, whether in or outside organizations.

Several social psychologists have been influenced by learning theory. The work of Homans and of Thibaut and Kelley is particularly significant for understanding behavior in organizations. George Homans, a social psychologist and sociologist, has employed the behaviorist psychology of Skinner (as well as economic theory) in his study of human interaction, particularly within groups. He views human behavior, as Skinnerians do, "as a function of its payoff: in amount and kind it depends on the amount and kind of reward and punishment it fetches."[45] His key concepts are activity or behavior, sentiment (activity that signifies feelings), interaction, and norm. Interactions and activities within a group result in sentiments and give rise to norms of behavior within the group. The intensity of interaction between any two individuals depends on how rewarding their activities have been to each other, and these mutual rewards selectively reinforce behavior by each that the other finds satisfying. However, the value of A's behavior to B may diminish (through satiety) with increasing emission of A's behavior. Also, a person in an exchange relation (that is, exchanging rewards) with another expects that the rewards of each are proportional to that person's costs or investments. Homans calls this the law of distributive justice, the violation of which to a person's disadvantage is likely to cause anger. Homans has tried to apply these ideas to many forms of social interaction.

Based on his assumptions about human interaction, he has advanced several propositions about small groups.[46] Some of his more interesting propositions throw light on friendships within a group, leadership in the group, and the patterns of interactions within the group:

> The more frequently persons interact with one another, the stronger are their sentiments of friendship.[47]

> The higher the rank of a person within a group, the more nearly his activities conform to the norms of the group,[48] and the wider his range of interactions.[49]

> In a group, a person of a higher social rank than another originates interaction for the latter more often than vice versa.[50]

> The closer an individual or a subgroup comes to realizing in all activities the norms of the group as a whole the higher will be the social rank of the individual or subgroup.[51]

> The higher a man's social rank in a group, the larger is the number of persons for whom he originates interaction, either directly or through intermediaries, and the larger is the number of persons that originate interaction for him, either directly or through intermediaries.[52]

Thibaut and Kelley share the assumption of Homans that the persistence and intensity of a social interaction is a function of the rewards received and the costs incurred by each participant in an interaction.[53] However, Thibaut and Kelley state that the value a participant places on a given outcome in an interaction is determined, not by the outcome's absolute magnitude, but rather by its comparison with two standards. One standard is the person's estimate of the average or usual value of such outcomes; Thibaut and Kelley call it the "comparison level." The other standard is called the "comparison level of alternatives" and is the lowest acceptable outcome needed for the person to remain in the social interaction situation, in the light of the available alternatives. Thus, in social interaction, indeed in any situation in which a decision has to be made, the individual tends to ask: "Is the outcome likely to be as good or better than in the past? How does the outcome compare with those of other possibilities before me?" By using these decision rules, the individual is likely to get the most out of the decisions he makes. Obviously, these decision rules are similar to the ones that follow from the theory of the consumer in economics.

Thibaut and Kelley have proposed that the various contingent payoffs in a social interaction can be represented in a matrix form. These matrices are, of course, identical to the ones that game theorists are fond of constructing. Different types of interdependence between social interactors— competitive, cooperative, partly competitive and partly cooperative—can be illustrated by constructing different payoff matrices, as shown in Figure 3–2. Hypotheses can be derived from these matrices as to how individuals go about maximizing their payoffs under different conditions of interdependence, and these can be tested under laboratory conditions.

On the basis of their experiments, Thibaut and Kelley have identified several forms of control that one participant can exercise over the other. In "fate control," B is totally at the mercy of A, as shown in Figure 3–2(a). Regardless of what B chooses, A can get 5 units. But if A chooses red, B can only get a unit whether he picks black or red. There can also be mutual fate control, as shown in Figure 3–2(b). A has "behavior control" over B when, by varying his behavior, A can make it worth B's while to change his. In other words, B's outcomes depend on A's choice as well as his own. Mutual behavior control is illustrated in Figure 3–2(c) and (d).

Figure 3–2(d) illustrates the famous "prisoner's dilemma." If both A and B try to maximize their payoffs, both will be losers. Only by learning to trust each other, restrain their greed, and cooperate can both expect to win some payoffs. That is evidenced by both consistently choosing black and eschewing the temptation to choose red. That presumably is the meaning of détente between old enemies like Russia and America, India and Pakistan, Israel and Egypt. Horrible as the thought may be, war games depicting alternative payoffs and strategic actions are devised and played (acted out?) at the military headquarters of many a nation to provide insights into the psychology of the enemy and the options he possesses.

Those social psychologists who have adopted the propositions of learning theory tend to conceptualize humanity the same way that economists do.[54] People are maximizers of utility; they engage in a social interaction until the costs of further interaction outweigh its benefits. This does not mean that people are selfish; but it does mean that they are self-centered. It

FIGURE 3–2
Several Different Types of Social Interdependence

(a) FATE CONTROL

		B	
		Black	Red
A	Black	A = +5, B = +5	A = +5, B = +5
	Red	A = +5, B = +1	A = +5, B = +1

(b) MUTUAL FATE CONTROL

		B	
		Black	Red
A	Black	A = +5, B = +5	A = +1, B = +5
	Red	A = +5, B = +1	A = +1, B = +1

(c) BARGAINING

		B	
		Black	Red
A	Black	A = +4, B = +2	A = −1, B = −1
	Red	A = −1, B = −1	A = +2, B = +4

(d) TRUST AND SUSPICION

		B	
		Black	Red
A	Black	A = +1, B = +1	A = −2, B = +2
	Red	A = +2, B = −2	A = −1, B = −1

NOTE: Numbers represent payoffs. For example, in (a), if A and B both choose red, A gets 5 units and B gets only 1 unit. If, on the other hand, A chooses black and B chooses red, both get 5 units.

implies that the human being is a hedonist, that the governing principle of human behavior is the pleasure principle rather than the need to comprehend the world, or the need to actualize one's potential, or the need to sacrifice one's life for an ideal. There is much evidence for this view. But there is also evidence that the human animal is a thinker, an idealist, a striver after the elusive and the mysterious.

Learning theory, with its focus on rewards and punishments, the way these are administered, the degree to which they alter human behavior, and the degree of permanence of alterations in behavior, provides fruitful insights into understanding many organizational phenomena. Learning theory is useful in diagnosing the effectiveness of an organization's reward and punishment system and in indicating what it *should* be like for greater organizational effectiveness.

Learning theory has been applied fruitfully in many organizations. Allyon and Azrin observed patients in a mental hospital to determine what activities they engaged in when they had the opportunity. After that, they dispensed tokens to these mental patients based on their accomplishment of certain desired tasks. These tokens could be used by the patients to "buy" the activities they preferred to engage in. The results were quite astonishing. Five schizophrenics and three mental defectives served as subjects. They performed regularly and adequately, in sharp contrast to the erratic and inconsistent behavior characteristic of such persons. When tokens were no longer tied to desired performance, the performance consistency dropped to zero.[55]

In a remedial school in a lower class black area of Kansas City, tickets were given as rewards for superior academic performance. These tickets could be exchanged for things the children liked, such as movies, food, toys, shopping trips. After this reinforcement system was introduced, the average grade of the children rose from a D to a C. Scores on standard achievement tests progressed over twice as fast as in the previous year and twice as fast as those of a control group.[56]

The applications of learning theory to industrial organizations are legion. Piece-rate incentive systems are common examples, for in these, productive behavior is immediately rewarded and in proportion to the amount of the effort. More ingenious is the example of a St. Louis hardware company that uses a lottery system approximating a variable ratio schedule to cut down late arrivals for work and absenteeism.[57] Under the system, a person who is daily on time for work at the start of the day and after breaks is eligible for a drawing at the end of the month. Prizes worth $20 to $25 are awarded to the winners, on a 1 winner to 25 eligibles ratio. At the end of six months, people who have had a perfect attendance record for the entire period are eligible for a drawing for a color television set. Management reports that sick leave costs have been reduced by 62 percent, and nearly 40 percent of the employees have become eligible for the monthly drawings.

Learning Theory: Model of Organization

Learning theory suggests that the organization is, or can function as, a machine. This is because human behavior is precisely controllable through rewards and punishments. It suggests that we can forget about unobservable phenomena like feelings and thoughts and concentrate instead on the control of human behavior. Indeed, all behavior in organizations, whether conformist or innovative, can be traced to the conditioning undergone by the emitters of such behavior.

Such a view of organizations has several implications for organizational design:

1 The designer should know what constitutes desirable behavior in an organization. This is likely to vary greatly. The desirable behavior of the production operative is not the same as the desirable behavior of the salesperson or the research scientist. Thus, the designer needs to have an inventory of desirable behaviors for different roles in the organization.

2 The designer needs to be aware of the positive and negative reinforcers of desirable role behaviors by the members of the organization. Higher salary may reinforce salespeople but not necessarily research scientists; and even among salespeople or scientists there may be individual differences in what are successful reinforcers and what are not. These reinforcers may change over time, for individuals' comparison standards may undergo change over time. For example, a salesperson who put out more work with a 5 percent bonus last year may now need a 10 percent bonus because rival firms now offer an 8 percent bonus for exceeding quota.

3 The designer needs to have careful measurements of the performance of all individuals and to note the variation in performance attendant upon variations in the magnitude and type of reinforcers. Without such careful measurements, the designer would be unable to identify an "optimal" reinforcement system for each individual and therefore for the organization.

It is clear that in such an organization, accountants, time and motion study experts, operations researchers, industrial engineers, statisticians, and the like would be the elite. Such an organization would be the delight, perhaps, of economists and behaviorists.

The Psychoanalytic Perspective: Model of Human Being

Psychoanalysis is identified with the most famous of all psychologists, Sigmund Freud. The core of Freudian psychology is that our mentality has three interacting parts. The first is the id, our animal heritage, the hothouse of our impulses and instincts, the source of our sexual and aggressive energy. The second is the superego, which is the repository of our ideals and of society's commandments of do's and don't's, which we have internalized and which, if we break them, cause us feelings of guilt. The third is the ego, our faculty of perception, memory, reason, and contact with reality, which mediates between the powerful, often antagonistic forces in our id and the conscience. Our psychic life—our dreams and our hang-ups, our wit and our imagination, even our "mistakes"—are the results of the interactions of these triple forces of instinct, ethics, and practicality. The blocking of our instincts for practical reasons or to prevent us from feeling guilty is the major energizer of these phenomena. Psychoanalysis, culminating in catharsis or the discharge of intense emotions attended by insight, is a powerful technique for getting neurotic individuals well.

The Freudian conception of the human being is an awesome, tragic one. Rational faculties are forever caught in the cross-fire between impulses and the directives of conscience and self-image. What we call civilization is largely an acting out of this incessant conflict. In this sense this internal conflict is highly creative, for it forces the individual to seek symbolic means of disguising anxiety and guilt. Who knows? Perhaps the organization was itself invented to provide relief from anxiety and guilt through routinizing and ritualizing the waking hours!

Psychoanalytic theory has helped social psychologists to understand better the human *personality*. Particularly interesting is the insight it has provided in the authoritarian aspect of personality.[58] The basic idea is that when a child's impulses are suppressed by arbitrary and harsh parental authority, the hostility he feels cannot be expressed towards the punitive parents. Having submitted to their authority, he also develops a view of himself as dependent on his parents and thus unable to defy or even question them. The child's solution is to displace hostility onto those that cannot easily retaliate, such as younger siblings, subordinates, and members of low status minority communities; and to idealize as perfect those with legitimate authority, such as parents, government leaders, and so on. Such a child comes to regard socially unacceptable impulses as sinful. Rather than recognizing these impulses in himself and reconciling himself to his humanity, he projects onto others, especially persons weaker than himself, those of his impulses that he cannot accept. He may also invent an ideology of righteousness that permits him to be destructive without feeling guilty. Such children grow up to be conventional, moralistic, mentally rigid, and power oriented.

The authoritarian personality is a syndrome: rigidity, conventionality, deification of authority, and an exploitative, contemptuous relationship with the weak and the helpless. Research suggests that within a given culture, people who are highly authoritarian "are more likely to be lower class, less educated, less intellectually sophisticated, less liberal politically, more prejudiced, less successful as patients in psychotherapy, more religious and stricter in their child-rearing practices" than people who are less authoritarian.[59] Rokeach has shown that dogmatism (a defensively rigid and closed belief system), an authoritarian trait, is found at the extremes of both sides of the political spectrum.[60] It is not necessarily tied only to a belief in God or to a conservative ideology as much as it is a commitment to a dogma, whether it is right wing or left wing, atheist or theist.

The study of the authoritarian personality is sometimes helpful in understanding the attitudes one finds among organizational members. Conventionality and respect for authority are fairly common. But when someone has them to excess, we may be able to explain them in terms of a predisposition to authoritarianism rooted in repressed hostility. Excessively domineering behavior and excessive scapegoating may be similarly attributed. It may be that the leaders and possibly many of the followers in fanatical organizations such as the Ku Klux Klan may be highly authoritarian individuals. Quite possibly, one of the reasons dictatorship persists in some societies may be that the child-rearing practices in these societies result in relatively high levels of authoritarianism in the population. Organizations in such societies, including their governments, are likely to be more centralized than in other, nonauthoritarian societies.

Indeed, the fascinating work of Kardiner and other psychoanalytically inclined anthropologists suggests that a relatively homogeneous and closed society develops distinctive child-rearing practices.[61] These in turn lead to a distinctive personality structure among the members of this society. This "basic personality" in turn gives to the organizations and institutions of this society a distinctive pattern of structures, processes, and ideologies. Several organizational researchers, such as Whyte and Crozier, have sought to explain organizational differences between, say, Peruvian firms and American firms or French bureaucracies and American bureaucracies in terms of the differences in the basic make-up of the personality of the respective peoples.[62]

The study of personality has revealed a number of ways that individuals typically respond to others. These are called interpersonal response traits. Table 3–4 lists some of the interpersonal traits that researchers have identified.[63] In the table, role dispositions are ways in which the individual performs roles in social situations. For example, at a party, one individual may usually play a dominant, assertive role. Another may commonly play a more submissive role. Sociometric dispositions are the individual's tendency to like or dislike, accept or reject others in social settings. Expressive dispositions are the modes of self-expression in responding to others; for example, is the individual constantly showing off or usually self-effacing.

The development of these traits may be traced to the relationship between the individual as a child and the adults (usually parents) who had power over him or her. These traits can be viewed as the child's strategies to

TABLE 3–4
Interpersonal Response Traits

Disposition		*Spectrum of response traits*
Role dispositions	Socially timid (reticent, withdraws quickly into a shell)	⟵⟶ Ascendant (defends own rights, forceful)
	Submissive	⟵⟶ Dominant (assertive, power oriented)
	Socially passive	⟵⟶ Socially active (an organizer and energizer of groups)
	Dependent	⟵⟶ Independent (prefers to chart own course)
Sociometric dispositions	Rejecting others (critical, suspicious of others)	⟵⟶ Accepting others (nonevaluative, trustful)
	Unsociable	⟵⟶ Sociable (likes to be with people)
	Unfriendly	⟵⟶ Friendly (genial, warm, open, approachable)
	Unsympathetic	⟵⟶ Sympathetic (concerned with the feelings and wants of others)
Expressive dispositions	Noncompetitive	⟵⟶ Competitive (sees every relationship as a contest)
	Nonaggressive	⟵⟶ Aggressive (attacks others, quarrelsome)
	Self-conscious (easily embarrassed)	⟵⟶ Socially poised (not easily embarrassed)
	Self-effacing	⟵⟶ Exhibitionistic (ostentatious, shows off)

gratify needs at the least psychic or physical cost. If home life is explosive, then withdrawal, timidity, passivity may be learned as the best means of keeping out of harm's way. With doting parents, ascendence, dominance, and the like may be seen as effective. Of course, social and cultural factors also play a part, not to mention purely genetic or physiological factors. Whatever the causes, these traits define the personality of the individual as revealed in social interactions.

In organizations we are often interested in designing work groups, task forces, and project teams. Aside from technical qualifications and mental abilities, one must bear in mind the personality of the members of these groups and teams. If all the members of a policy-making group are ascendant or dominant types, little agreement on policies is likely. If the sales manager, whose job is to motivate the salesforce and deal with irate customers, is an unsocial type, the sales department is likely soon to distintegrate. If the principal assistants to the president of a country are domineering, rejecting, unsociable, unfriendly, and unsympathetic types, as President Nixon's assistants were perceived to be, then powerful antagonisms will be generated toward not only the assistants but the president himself.

Psychoanalytic Orientation: Model of Organization

Psychoanalysts are likely to perceive the organization as a system of interacting personalities, each carrying its big or little burden of internal conflict between impulses and norms of good behavior. They may see the organization itself as adding to the conflict by imposing additional norms of "good" behavior, such as punctuality, respect for rules and procedures, obedience to the boss, friendliness and sociability. So psychoanalysts may see in the organization a good many obsessive and compulsive patterns of behavior indicative of varying levels of mental disturbance, and they would be particularly alert to such neurotic behaviors as scapegoating, denial, withdrawal, ritual, explosive rage, fantasying.

Psychoanalysts are likely to be intrigued by patterns of leadership and subordination, particularly because superior-subordinate relationships are in a way a resurrection of parent-child relationships. They would then look for the strategies superiors follow for controlling subordinates and the strategies subordinates adopt for escaping from the control of the superiors.[64]

They are likely to identify the institutionalized means of control in the organization, such as hierarchy, formal controls and directives, indoctrination, sanctions for misbehavior, rewards for good behavior, and so on. They are likely to wonder about the supervisory personality structures needed to set up these modes of control and the personality structures of subordinates who find these control modes acceptable. For example, it is unlikely that organizations that heavily accent hierarchy and rules, such as military establishments, can retain this particular control structure without fairly high levels of authoritarianism in their personnel. Nor is it likely that democratic institutions can retain their character with too liberal a sprinkling of authoritarian individuals.

Psychoanalysts would tend to pay close attention to parts of the organization in which discretionary behavior is most feasible. Professors in faculties, doctors in hospitals, and top managers in corporations are some of the charmed individuals with a good deal of discretionary authority. Psychoanalysts would probably watch their behavior closely, for they have the latitude needed to display their personal idiosyncrasies. If these individuals are powerful, their neurotic behavior can have major repercussions in the organization. It is said that one American entrepreneur, imbued with Spartan ideals, used to compel his managers to go riding with him every morning, come hail, fire, or brimstone. Delinquents and weaklings were summarily fired. One of the victims was notified of his dismissal by having his desk burned outside his office as he was arriving for work! The vast human suffering caused by the whims of insane tyrants as also the vast amelioration wrought by sane leaders, throughout history, bear testimony to the power of the personality of the powerful in shaping human affairs. Indeed, a famous political scientist and statesman, Henry Kissinger, once noted that although as a Harvard political science professor he believed that structural factors were very important in determining political outcomes, his dealings with the world's statesmen convinced him that personality factors were sometimes more important.

Psychoanalysts would encourage an organizational design that minimizes stress on the organization's members. That is to say, they are likely to advocate a design that lowers levels of anxiety, frustration, conflict, and tension. They would want to get rid of guilt-inducing organizational norms and repression- and suppression-inducing organizational controls, and to provide ready availability of individual and group therapy in the organization to increase people's contact with reality. Such therapy can help strip away the unrecognized and unconscious forces that impede rational functioning of people in organizations. In a climate of greater realism, the pursuit of phantom individual and organizational goals would be replaced by the pursuit of more realistic goals. In the Glacier Metal Company, where such therapy was used, it did not democratize the organization or lead to sweeter superior-subordinate relations.[65] Far from it, the romantic democratic notions the management was harboring were recognized as illusory in the tight, competitive market the firm was operating in. The political nature of labor-management relations came to be acknowledged frankly. These relations got institutionalized in the Works Council, which consisted of the representatives of management and workers. The primacy of managerial decisions was made explicit. If workers did not like any decisions, they were encouraged to put pressure on the management in the Works Council to change or modify their decisions.

Role Theory Orientation:
Model of Human Being

If "personality" is the similarity in the responses an individual makes to different situations, "role" is the similarity in the responses of different individuals to the same situation. Role theory, enriched by psychologists as well as sociologists, offers insights into the roles people play—e.g., the roles of parent, spouse, child, worker, citizen. It is also helpful in understanding the conflicts they experience in playing these roles—e.g., the conflict a manager often experiences in the role of being a morale booster and an evaluator of subordinates. Role theory sheds light on the relationship between role performance and personality, the development of the self concept, the reference groups that affect one's self concept, and deviant roles.

What is a role? In a given culture, a role consists of a range of socially expected behaviors associated with a given status or position. For example, the role of the father may be that of the provider of necessities of life, disciplinarian, provider of psychological security, and so on. But within this set of expectations, there is a permissible range. For example, one father may be strict, but not to the point of abusing his child. Another may be permissive, but not to the point of allowing his child to wreck the house or hurt others and damage their property. Roles are learned in social intercourse through imitation, or brainwashing, and through prodding by the family, the social group one belongs to or aspires to (called the "reference group"), and those who speak for the community.

From the point of view of organizational studies, three elements of role theory are significant. One is role conflict, the conflicting demands made on people by the multiple roles they perceive they have to play. Another is the relationship between personality and role. And the third is deviant behavior—that is, why people sometimes do not play the social game.

Role conflict. In an organization, individuals play multiple roles. Mintzberg has identified a large number of roles that managers have to play.[66] For example, they have to play the roles of monitor and disseminator of information, of leader and figurehead, of allocator of resources, of negotiator, of external representative. Sometimes, at least, these roles must conflict, as when a manager acts as an adviser to a subordinate and then at year's end evaluates the subordinate for a pay raise or a promotion. Conflicts may arise also because of impossible demands on a limited resource, such as time. Should a manager go to a ceremonial meeting honoring a retiring colleague? Or read a massive report on the new information system? Or catch up on correspondence? Or review a subordinate's work? All between 4 P.M. and 5 P.M. of some work day! Also, a manager's perception of the managerial role may be at variance with the role his or her boss, peers, or subordinates expect him or her to play. For example, an authoritarian boss may expect the manager to be autocratic in dealing with subordinates, and the young manager, imbued with McGregor's democratic Theory Y notions, may find this intolerable. Sometimes a person may simply not know how to act in a given situation. Thus, playing organizational roles can sometimes be a source of frustration, conflict, and anxiety.

For the most part, organizations and their members get by without rough consequences from role conflict. One of the reasons is that individuals play different roles at different times or in different contexts or with different people and thus avoid serious tensions. But there are situations in which role conflict is chronic and others in which it is infrequent. In organizations that have to adapt to a great deal of change, roles cannot be designed too well because behaviors required in changing, often unforeseeable circumstances, cannot be specified properly in advance. And so, as the work of Burns and Stalker indicates, role conflict and role stress are quite high in changing organizations.[67] As a product manager in such an organization observed, "One of the troubles here is that nobody is very clear about his title or status or even his function."[68] Role conflict is rarer, on the other hand, in organizations that evolve stable operating procedures and job descriptions because they function in a relatively changeless environment.

Jaques and Brown, noticing peoples' need to have their role and status clearly defined in a way that is acceptable to themselves as well as to others in the organization interacting with them, have worked out a program for role clarification that has apparently been quite successful.[69] Essentially, consultants interview all individuals in the organization who volunteer to be interviewed and ask them to specify in detail their job or roles. After clearing with them the distribution of their role perceptions to other relevant members of the organization, a meeting is called at which role conflicts, role ambiguity, and conflicting perceptions of roles are discussed. For example, the purchase manager may say, "I have the responsibility for purchasing, but not the authority to determine the specifications." This role conflict may be discussed at length, and the engineering and the production managers may agree to let the purchase manager have limited authority in determining specifications of goods or equipment to be purchased—say, with regards to routine items. At the end of a meeting or several meetings, there is (it is hoped) far less role conflict than before.

Role and personality. There is a fascinating relationship between role and personality. In almost any role there is a range of acceptable behaviors. For example, the staff manager can be quite passive, letting line managers come to him with their problems. As the personnel officer of a cement company said, "I don't believe in imposing my services on the departments. I let them come to me when they have problems. That way I get more respect." However, as the personnel manager of a drug company said, "How do I operate? Well, I introduce myself to different line managers. I inform them of the kinds of services I can offer. I have my staff surveying the organization for opportunities where our skills can be used." Such differences in approach depend on a manager's personality.

Conversely, as Merton has argued, the nature of the role may well alter the personality of the individual playing it.[70] In popular folklore, presidents, prime ministers, and others in high authority are supposed to grow in their office—that is, to develop a bipartisan viewpoint. Nixon, the arch anti-Communist, became a great friend of the Russians and the Chinese during his presidency.

In the face of the pressure in organizations for method, prudence, and discipline, Merton says, individuals internalize these as ends in themselves and acquire a bureaucratic personality. Lieberman's research on a medium-sized home appliance manufacturer suggests that some aspects of the personality, such as attitudes toward the company and perception of various aspects of the job situation do undergo a change with a change in role.[71] He found that workers who were promoted to the position of foreman developed more positive attitudes toward management and more negative attitudes toward unions. Workers who became union stewards developed attitudes in the opposite direction. Due to a recession, the company had to demote some of the promoted workers back to the position of operator. The attitudes of these individuals again became relatively more antimanagement and pro-union. Thus, people who are placed in a role will tend to take on or develop attitudes that are congruent with the expectations associated with that role. At the same time, it is not clear how permanent these changes are.

It is very likely that the organizational roles individuals play induce *some* changes in their personality, just as their personality causes *some* variation in the roles they are expected to play. Changes in personality are likely to be substantial among those individuals who have to adapt to major changes in their tasks. Changes in roles are likely to be substantial where these roles cannot be defined too well, as in upper levels of management or in creative organizations—that is, in roles that require a considerable amount of discretionary behavior.

Deviant behavior. In societies, as in organizations, we commonly observe behavior that is considered deviant—i.e., behavior that departs from normal or prescribed role behavior, as when a student starts lecturing to a professor or a worker gives orders to his supervisor. Organized crime, insurrection, dropping out, and living in communes are examples of socially deviant behavior. Strikes, sabotage, apathy, absenteeism, and soldiering are examples of deviant behavior in organizations. What are the different types of deviant behavior and why do they arise? Merton has provided a neat scheme for analyzing socially deviant behavior that can also be applied to deviant behavior in organizations.[72]

Merton has identified five different types of social adaptation. (a) First is *conformity*, which is when the individual accepts a culture's goals as well as the institutionalized means of achieving these goals (for example, an MBA starts a business to get rich). (b) The second is *innovation*, in which the individual accepts the culture's goals but rejects the institutionalized means of achieving the goals in favor of new or even nonlegitimate means (the MBA turns a professional muckraker of business). (c) The third is *ritualism*, in which the goals of the culture are rejected but the individual adheres to the institutionalized means for achieving the goals (say, the bureaucrat who has given up on getting ahead in the department but slavishly works his eight hours daily shuffling papers). (d) The fourth is *retreatism*, in which the individual rejects the culture's goals and the culture's institutions. (e) The fifth is *rebellion*, in which the individual substitutes the culture's goals and seeks substitutes for the institutionalized means as well (e.g., the terrorist group that wants to overthrow white middle-class values and democratic decision-making by assassinations and sabotage, or the hippie group that substitutes spiritual growth for material acquisitions and living in rural communes for living in suburbia). Obviously, what may be called rebellion in one culture may be conformity in another culture because goals differ from culture to culture and so does the nature of the institutions established to achieve these goals. Of these five, all but conformity may be regarded as deviant behaviors.

In organizations, we do see conformity; employees generally do turn up on time and often enthusiastically do what they are told by their bosses. We also see ritualism, retreatism, rebellion, and innovation. In universities, for example, a great many students accept academic goals and the system of classes, textbooks, examinations, and specialization. There are also students who see little value in academic learning but go through the motions of being students because of parental pressure or because a degree is necessary for getting a job. These are the ritualists. Then there are the students who reject academic learning as well as the means by which it is imparted—the students on the roll but not in the class. These are the retreatists. In recent years the rebellious students with their fiery speeches and acts of violence have made many a campus come alive. And then there are the innovators, too few of them, who have come up with revolutionary but feasible proposals for making university education a more meaningful experience, such as the proponents of the open university. Merton's typology of social adaptation is a useful first step in labeling various forms of deviant behavior in organizations and in formulating tentative first explanations of their causes.

But the question that remains, of course, is: Why do some people reject cultural or organizational goals and/or the institutionalized means by which these are achieved? The answer, according to sociologists, lies in the reference group theory. One's behavior is determined, according to sociologists, not only by the group one belongs to, but also by the norms and values of the group one *aspires* to belong to—in other words, the reference group. For example, many children of workers wish to become professionals and may therefore acquire the values of the latter and reject many values of the working class. If the group an individual is in coincides with his reference group, his behavior is likely to be conformist. If his reference group is radically different from the group he is forced to be in, he is likely to engage in deviant behavior.

Even if this is true, we still do not know why a deviant individual may be a rebel, innovator, ritualist, or retreatist. The answer may lie in personality dispositions. It makes sense to try to correlate deviant behavior with personality structures. The social or organizational rebel may be one who not only happens to be in the wrong group but has personality traits of dominance and activism. The social or organizational ritualist or retreatist, similarly, may be not only in the wrong place but also be a rather passive character. The innovator may be in the right group but may be a bright, creative individual with high aspirations.

Conclusion. Role theory views the person as an actor on the social stage.[73] It sees behavior as shaped by the logic of one's tasks and the social expectations as to what is the permissible range of proper behavior. It therefore gives primacy to technical and social factors in the shaping of behavior and to internalized norms and values. It points to the conflicts people experience because of incompatibilities in the many, many roles everyone has to perform. In some ways these conflicts are similar to the conflicts experienced because of the collision of instincts and conscience. In a sense, the roles any one of us must play *are* his superego. Role conflict is, therefore, conflict between the different elements of the superego. To that extent, role theory provides a useful supplement to the psychoanalytic perspective of the human being.

Role Theory: Model of Organization

Role theorists are likely to view the organization as an elaborate stage, with many actors enacting a prolonged and complex, if repetitive drama, their well-coordinated roles leading to a somewhat prosaic denouement, that of the achievement of the organization's goals. The social and technical factors that shape roles are likely to receive particular attention, as is the tension between the human needs and predispositions of role incumbents and their prescribed role behavior. Role theorists would be as interested in why individuals conform to the roles they are supposed to play as in why they choose to deviate from their roles. They would try to categorize roles, to distinguish between main roles and subsidiary roles, roles that involve a great deal of conflict and those that involve little conflict, roles that are prescribed in detail and those with considerable discretionary element, roles that are clearly spelled out and roles that are ambiguous, roles that are technical in nature and roles of a social nature, prestigious roles and low status roles, and so on. They may question why so many different kinds of role need to be played in the organization and try, in this regard, to chart the roles in order to identify interconnected roles or role clusters and isolated roles. From such a chart reasonable guesses may then be made about the social relationships in the organization, on the assumption that incumbents filling highly interconnected roles are likely to be more socially integrated in the organization than those filling relatively isolated roles.

Role theory raises several interesting questions for organizational design:

1 Should roles be clearly and explicitly defined or left largely to the interpretation of role incumbents? When work is relatively routinized and the work that an individual performs is closely related to the work performed by others, it makes sense to define roles clearly and explicitly. When the work is not routine and is not closely related to the work performed by others in the organization, roles need not be defined too precisely because discretionary behavior is feasible and indeed necessary.

2 Should role conflict be permitted in the organization? A role incumbent experiences role conflict when exposed to contradictory expectations. For example, workers may expect a supervisor to be warm and supportive, while management may want a strict disciplinarian. Role

conflict is a source of anxiety and stress, but limited role conflict is unavoidable in organizations and not without merit. It can be a source of innovations. The resourceful foreman can secure discipline and improve morale by instituting group discussions of management proposals and group decisions for implementing them.

3 How much and what kind of deviant behavior should the organization tolerate? Certain types of deviant behavior, particularly rebellion, ritualism, and retreatism, represent a failure of the existing control system of the organization. The control system can be strengthened to weed out these three forms of deviant behavior. After all, selection procedures can be devised to eliminate those who do not agree with the goals of the organization or the means employed to achieve them; supervision can be tightened; attempts can be made to indoctrinate members; and so on. The price, however, may be loss of innovative behavior. The best and the brightest tend to leave the organization that tries to overdetermine the behavior of its members. President Nixon lost many able men like Hickel, Finch, Schultz, Connally, and others because he expected them to toe his line. As with role clarification so with the control of deviant behavior, what may be appropriate in one part of the organization may not be appropriate in another. In parts of the organization in which highly efficient routines have been developed, much less deviant behavior need be tolerated. In parts of the organization in which creative problem-solving is important, a good deal of deviant behavior needs to be tolerated, perhaps encouraged. This implies that in such parts of the organization (research labs, strategy formulating groups, etc.), both the established organizational goals and the established means for securing these goals should be open to frequent questioning.

Conclusion

We have examined five orientations in social psychology. Each has a distinctive model of the human being. Each adds to our understanding of the immense complexity and variety of human behavior. The central tenets of each orientation give rise to a distinctive model of organizations and some distinctive suggestions for their design. The latter are summarized in Table 3–5.

Social psychology has been an important knowledge resource for at least two schools in organization theory—namely, the human relations movement and the human potential or human resources movement. These two are discussed in Chapter 5. Social psychology has also been an important knowl-

TABLE 3-5
Psychological Orientations and Organizational Design

Psychological orientation	View of organization	Suggestions for organizational design
Gestalt view	Organization as a system of interlinked perceptions, beliefs, and problem-solving processes	Emphasis on securing correct and full information; an accurate assessment of this information; use of techniques of creative problem-solving
Field theory view	Organization as a system of interlinked motivational fields, each field characterized by approach and avoidance goals	Emphasis on integrating the needs and goals of organization members with the goals of the organization; the widespread use of attitude change technology (organizational development) by the organization
Learning theory view	Organization as a system of behaviors conditioned by rewards for desirable behavior and sanctions for undesirable behavior	Need for information on desirable role behaviors, the reinforcers of different individuals engaged in role behaviors, performance in response to variations in reinforcement, and so on
Psychoanalytic view	Organization as a system of interlinked personalities	Reduction of anxiety, tension, guilt, conflict, and frustration in organization members; elimination of excessive organizational morality; availability of individual and group therapy
Role theory view	Organization as a system of interlinked roles or prescribed behaviors; organization as a stage	Minimize deviant behavior, role ambiguity, and role conflict in individuals whose work is relatively routine but permit some deviant behavior, role ambiguity, and role conflict in individuals whose tasks are changeable and require the exercise of a good deal of discretion

edge resource for mounting an attack on the structural orientations in organization theory, discussed in Chapter 4. There is little doubt that as social psychology develops and provides us with a more integrated model of people and their social behavior, it will continue to be one of the greatest knowledge resources for the development of organization theory and theory of organization design.

If sociology alerts us to the underlying structural conditions that shape events within organizations, social psychology brings to our attention the richness of the human personality that reacts to, interprets, modifies the underlying structural conditions and leaves its indelible impress on organizational events. Take Churchill's role in the British government during the Second World War or Mao Tse-tung's role in Communist China. A sociologist may accurately argue that in societies faced with grave exigencies, conditions are ripe for the emergence of a charismatic leader. Good as this insight is, it does not begin to explain the behavior of the British or Chinese governments under the impact of gargantuan personalities such as Churchill and Mao. For understanding this, we need to probe the norms, values, ambitions, and goals of these leaders and their close subordinates and the way they interacted to make and implement decisions. This is where social psychology comes in. But these are big persons in big organizations. Even in the smallest organizations psychological variables have a great impact. How else is one to explain the enormous variation in performance of organizations in the same industry in the same society? There are many industries in which the profitability of firms consistently varies by a factor of 2, or even 5, between firms of approximately the same size.[74] It is difficult to avoid the conclusion that behavioral variables play at least as potent a role as underlying situational or structural factors in shaping the functioning of organizations. The conjoint use of the sociological and social psychological approaches, as well as those of economics and political science, is likely to yield best results in organizational analysis.

SUMMARY

In this chapter, the organization has been viewed from the perspective of sociology and social psychology. Sociology is primarily interested in the typical behavior of social institutions and tries to explain this behavior in terms of structural rather than psychological conditions. Social psychology stresses the fact that people react not to actual stimuli but to their perception of stimuli. It stresses needs, motivations, beliefs, perceptions, personality dispositions, conditioning, and positive or negative feelings toward objects in explaining how people behave. It also stresses the social forces that shape human needs, motives, beliefs, perceptions, attitudes, and behavior.

Sociologists attempt to identify the structural factors underlying social order, disorder, continuity, and change. The sociological analysis of organizations therefore raises four questions: What structural factors ensure the stability and orderliness of organizational operations? What structural factors cause disorders in organizations? What structural factors lead to continuity in the operations of organizations despite change in their personnel?

What structural factors lead to changes in the design of organizations over time?

Insights into organizational stability are afforded by the equilibrium or homeostatic model of society. Specificity of organizational goals and assessment of the organization's performance regarding these goals through a control and information system constitute powerful homeostatic mechanisms. Others are standard operating procedures, the size of the organization, the loyalty of the organization's members to the organization, and the punitive power of management.

Insights into organizational disorders are provided by the conflict models of society, which view antagonistic class interests as the wellspring of social disorder. Some of the structural factors underlying organizational disorders are: the pyramidal shape of the organizational hierarchy, which limits the upward mobility of power-oriented executives; the nature of modern technology, which limits the upward mobility of those without adequate educational qualifications; the rapid rate of technological change, which creates organizational tensions between the experienced but obsolete senior staff and the qualified but inexperienced junior or younger staff; the conflict between line and staff, line having strong loyalty to the organization and staff having strong cosmopolitan, professional orientation; the conflict between the norm of seniority and the norm of meritocracy; the conflict between the necessary delegation of authority and top management's need to control operations; the endless cycle of impersonal rules, minimum acceptable performance, deterioration in organizational performance, and more stringent rules.

The structural-functional model of society provides insights into organizational continuity. The structural-functional view is that society continues because its needs are met by social structures. Applied to organizations, it raises two questions: What kinds of need do organizations have? What kinds of structure do organizations develop to meet these needs? Major organizational needs are: (a) to meet the needs of its members and at the same time make sure that the organization's needs for growth and survival are also met; (b) to secure adequate interpersonal and intergroup collaboration; (c) to distribute power, authority, and influence in the organization in such a way that operations are coordinated but initiative and creativity are not stifled; (d) to adapt effectively to changes in the business environment; (e) to keep the organization healthy and quickly remedy organizational maladies. Table 3–1 indicates the more common structural responses of organizations to the foregoing organizational needs. Since different organizations are likely to have these needs to different degrees, they are likely to emphasize these structural responses to differing degrees.

Models of social change and evolution provide insights into questions of organizational evolution. While organizations of the same type probably have exhibited considerable similarity over the millennia, some notable changes have occurred. These seem to be in the direction of far more sophisticated and automated technology; far more rapid technological change; far greater decentralized and participative decision-making; far greater use of temporary, ad hoc structures; far greater importance of the management of innovation and attitude change; and far more attention to planning, forecasting, and marketing.

The study of social processes offers important insights into organizational processes. Some of the more common social processes are stratification, mobility, cooperation and assimilation, opinion formation, nonformal control, deviance, and attitude change. Table 3–2 lists these in organizational terms and summarizes the organizational factors that reinforce or impede these processes.

Since sociologists are very interested in uncovering the structural factors underlying organizational phenomena, it is natural that organization theorists of a sociological persuasion should seek explanations for organizational phenomena in terms of such structural factors as the nature of the organization's technology, type of business, environment, and size. The contingency orientation in organization theory, reviewed in Chapter 6, owes much to these theorists.

Social psychology is the study of the individual in a social context. There are five major orientations in social psychology—namely, the gestalt orientation, the field theory orientation, the learning theory or behavioristic orientation, the psychoanalytic or personality theory orientation, and the role theory orientation. An overview of their major concerns and the organizational phenomena they illumine is provided in Table 3–3.

The gestalt orientation assumes that human beings have a great need to have an organized, coherent view of the world. This implies that our perception is selective and organized, and that in our beliefs we strive to eliminate inconsistencies. In the gestalt view, problem-solving occurs when there is a dramatic reordering of the perceptual field. The gestalt orientation stresses the importance of patterns, of the whole being greater than the sum of the parts. The gestalt view indicates the subjective elements in human rationality. It prompts the view of the organization as a giant brain. From the point of view of organization design, it suggests that attention be paid to the removal of mental blocks to clear perception and creative problem-solving, to formal training in creativity, and to organizational arrangements whereby the key positions are staffed by bright, creative individuals.

Field theory, founded by Lewin and influenced by gestalt conceptions, has been much concerned with the dynamics of human motivation. Each person is seen as having many goals and needs that are related in complex ways. Some of these are approach goals, and others are avoidance goals. The pursuit of goals can cause many different types of conflict in the individual. The forces activating these goals may be "own" (internal) or "induced" (externally imposed). Human goals are not static. The level of aspiration of these goals varies systematically with such factors as experience. The need to assess one's opinions, abilities, and emotions is a force causing individuals to join groups. Communication within groups has several functions, particularly to achieve the group's goals, to deal with dissenting opinions, to confirm opinions and beliefs, and to release tension. Cohesive groups take on the characteristics of well-knit small organizations. Human attitudes as well as social relations generally appear to be in a sort of equilibrium because of the parity of opposing forces. Changes in attitudes or social relations can be accomplished if forces resisting change are weakened and those supporting change are strengthened. Field theory has been utilized extensively in the development of attitude change technology, management development, and organizational development. Field theory suggests that a major problem for organizations is to motivate members to work for the organization. Available strategies are to design cohesive work groups and to assure good intergroup collaboration, job enrichment, participative management, humane supervision, good fringe benefits, the accenting of superordinate goals, the airing of stereotypes, profit-sharing, and the like.

The reinforcement orientation identified with Skinner, also called learning theory orientation and behavioristic orientation, avoids imputing motives or goals to human beings and views them as passive instruments of their environment. It argues that all of human behavior, other than purely instinctive behavior, is a product of conditioning. The basic findings of this orientation are that rewards increase the frequency of desired behavior and punishment decreases the frequency of undesired behavior. Intermittent reinforcement generally is more effective than continuous reinforcement. Social psychologists have utilized these basic findings in explaining social interaction, leadership in groups, and behavioral strategies in game-type interpersonal situations. Learning theory suggests that the organization should be viewed as a system of rewards and punishments within which the behavior of members can be so precisely conditioned as to yield a trouble-free, smoothly operating organizational machine. From the point of view of organizational design, this would require a great investment in measurement, experimentation, and assessment.

The psychoanalytic orientation, identified with Freud, presents a conflict model of man, with ego, impulses, and conscience perpetually in conflict with one another. Creative as well as destructive activities are designed to afford relief from this conflict. This conflict shapes personality. One well-researched personality syndrome is the authoritarian personality. Whether organizations have authoritarian control structures or not may depend on how authoritarian their key decision makers are. Psychologists have identified a large number of interpersonal response traits that define the social personality of the individual. In the design of teams or groups set up to accomplish organizational tasks, it is important to know which personalities would be needed to accomplish the tasks and which ones would hinder them. The psychoanalytic orientation usefully draws attention to the organizational conditions that add to conflicts experienced by the organization's members and calls into question the organizational norms and practices that cause mental illness. It suggests that individual and group therapy should be a strategic element in the design of organizations.

Role theory views the person as an actor called upon to play several more or less appointed parts on the social stage. Role conflict arises because of incompatible demands on the same individual. Although most individuals adapt well to role conflict by playing different roles in different situations or at different times, such conflict can be a source of stress. In organizations some degree of role conflict is unavoidable, especially for those individuals whose tasks are too variable to be predesigned because of the variable character of the organization's business. Role conflict can also give rise to innovations. The roles that people play influence their personalities and vice versa. In organizations, the personality changes are likely to be substantial among those members whose tasks change dramatically over time. Role changes are likely to be substantial when roles have a considerable discretionary content and therefore can be shaped by the personality dispositions of the incumbents. Deviant behavior arises when individuals do not play their appointed roles because they reject or substitute either the cultural goals or the institutionalized means for reaching them. In organizations, deviant behavior can be drastically cut down by stringent selection procedures, careful training and indoctrination, show of authority, and other similar steps. But the price is the stifling of creativity and innovation. In parts of the organization in which creativity and innovation are desirable, there should be tolerance for deviant behavior. The role theory view of organization indicates that the analyst should identify the social and technical forces that shape roles, the tension between personality needs and expected role behaviors, the different categories of roles played in the organization, the interconnectedness of roles, and so on.

A summary of the different orientations in social psychology and their respective implications for organizational design are listed in Table 3–5. If the sociological approach increases our awareness of the structural, situational conditions that shape the functioning of organizations, social psychology alerts us to the equally important behavioral variables that also shape organizational processes. They complement each other.

SUGGESTED READINGS

Chs. 1, 2, and 3 in Alex Inkeles, *What Is Sociology?* (Englewood Cliffs, N. J.: Prentice-Hall, 1964).

Ch. 1 in Charles Perrow, *Organizational Analysis: A Sociological View* (Belmont, Calif.: Wadsworth, 1970).

Morton Deutsch and Robert M. Krauss, *Theories in Social Psychology* (New York: Basic Books, 1965). For the student of organizations, a comprehensive but also somewhat technical introduction to the different orientations in social psychology.

Walter R. Nord, "Beyond the Teaching Machine: The Neglected Area of Operant Conditioning in the Theory and Practice of Management," *Organizational Behavior and Human Performance*, Vol. 4, No. 4 (Nov. 1969), pp. 375–401. A stimulating exposition of the application of learning theory to organizational design.

QUESTIONS FOR ANALYSIS

1 The White House staff has grown over the decades from a few dozen men and women to a few thousand. What sociological factors can account for this enormous increase in the men and women needed to advise the President and do his chores? What type of organization would you predict that the White House staff will become in the future? Would you say that the office staffs of the chief executives of all large organizations tend to grow as the White House staff has grown?

2 What kind of organization will the prisons of the future be? Will they resemble cooperative societies or military organizations?

3 Marx claimed that under communism the state will wither away. What were his reasons for saying so? Is this likely to happen?

4 Michels, a German sociologist, thought that democratic organizations sooner or later turn into oligarchies—that is, organizations managed by a few. Can you find any sociological and psychological factors that support or contradict this view? Would you say that unions today are getting more or less democratic? Why?

5 The *Chicago Daily Herald* was on the brink of going out of circulation a couple of years ago. It was a local paper and devoted more space to local events and social gossip than to national or international issues. To stanch the loss of advertisers, the publisher brought in a dynamic young editor, Bill Bentley, who gave a face lift to the daily and ran controversial but highly informative series on the plight of the blacks, political corruption, the decay of American cities, and shady business practices of large corporations. The circulation and advertising revenue increased dramatically, and the paper captured national attention. But now the publisher and the board of directors feel that the paper has gone too far. They feel that people do not want to hear constant bad news, that influential politicians and corporate chiefs are muttering angrily about the "excesses" of the paper. They are afraid of bad publicity and loss of major advertisers. They are pressing the editor to soften the tone of the paper and give up "muckraking." The editor, of course, will have none of this.

In the post-Watergate era, what factors could be behind this confrontation between the editor on the one hand and the publisher and the board on the other?

6 Take a look at the organization of your school. Then try to analyze it from sociological and social psychological viewpoints.

7 Here is an incident published in *Encounters in Organizational Behavior*.[75]

What's Wrong with Wong?

It was brown bag time for the night shift maintenance mechanics. Pike and Monico were ahead eating at a small work bench next to the parts storage bins when Hazard arrived.

"Where have you been?" asked Pike.

"Servicing the conveyor belts in department B-9," replied Hazard, as he snapped open his lunch bucket and took out a sandwich.

"You did that last week," said Pike. "Isn't that a monthly preventative maintenance job?"

"I guess so," said Hazard, "but Jimmy Joe wanted me to re-check the bearings and look for belt wear."

"Please," said Monico, "let us speak more respectfully of our great leader. You know we should refer to him as Mr. James Joseph Wong."

"Oh, no," countered Pike, "I believe the master of night shift plant maintenance would prefer to be called General Wong."

"Most certainly, General Wong . . . the Oriental autocrat," said Monico, playing along.

Monico and Pike bowed their heads ceremoniously.

"I think you guys are being too hard on Jimmy Joe," said Hazard, between bites.

"Come on, Hazard," said Monico. "Face it. Ever since they promoted Wong to supervisor three months ago he's been different . . . a regular dictator."

"That's right," added Pike. "Wong was completely different when he was just one of us guys in maintenance. But he really began to give the orders the moment he took over."

Pike continued, "None of the old procedures were good enough for him. He had to re-schedule everything. Then he promised management even more output on our shift. He really changed when he was given more power."

"I've seen this before," said Monico. "Promote a good guy from the ranks and he turns on you. When a man gets a blue stripe* on his badge he's not the guy you used to know."

"Hey, that's clever. That's exactly how to describe Wong," said Pike smiling broadly. "Try this fellas . . . where's the Joe I used to know?"

Monico and Pike roared with laughter and even Hazard smiled.

"I've got another," said Monico. "How about . . . what's wrong with Wong?"

"Crazy!" said Pike applauding.

"Well, I don't know," said Hazard, pouring coffee from his thermos. "I don't see Jimmy Joe that way. He's certainly nice to me and I don't feel I've been working any harder since he took over. In fact, I think Jimmy Joe has improved our operation. You have to admit it was a little sloppy when Haney ran it."

"You rate busting kinds never seem to learn," said Pike shaking his head. "We have pre-set standards for charging our time which allow for emergencies you can't predict. So, even though battery replacement in a lift truck takes only twenty minutes, we charge thirty minutes. The extra time is for emergency repairs as they come up . . . that's what you and General Wong don't seem to understand about the maintenance business."

"Right," said Monico. "Wong is squeezing out all our emergency time to make himself look good at our expense. Boy, will it hit the fan around here the first time we have a major breakdown."

"I don't happen to feel that way," said Hazard finishing his coffee. "I think new standards are fair . . . they correct some excesses created by equipment changes over the years."

Hazard stood up and closed his lunchbox.

"Look you guys," he said, "I've got to get back to check that conveyor again. But if you're that upset about the rates why don't you talk to Jimmy Joe?"

"That won't do any good," said Pike. "He's locked in like granite."

"Can't talk to him about anything anymore now that he's such a big, important man," added Monico as Hazard left.

"Got time for a cigarette?" asked Pike.

Monico glanced at his watch. "Yea, I guess we have five minutes yet."

The two mechanics lit up and exchanged predictions about the coming Sunday's pro football schedule.

"Mind if I join you guys?" It was Wong holding a vending machine sandwich and a cup of coffee.

---

* Blue stripe. In this instance a color pattern on a standard employee identification badge to draw visual distinction between supervisors and nonsupervisors. Color coding of employee badges is quite common.

"No, not at all, Jimmy Joe," said Pike as he put out his cigarette. "But, I've got to get back and finish that assembly department repair job."

"Me too," said Monico. "I'm behind schedule now."

James Joseph Wong ate alone.

What psychological concepts and orientations can you use to explain the attitudes of the men towards Wong? Can you think of any structural factors that may also usefully explain the facts of the case?

8 In a century-old New England mental hospital founded by the state, two forms of psychotherapy are being used. One is oriented to the concepts of restoring psychological health in the patients—that is to say, to recreating a healthy, conflict-free personality that is able to face life without the use of psychological mechanisms of repression. The other is a behavioristic group oriented to control of behavior through positive and/or negative reinforcement. A researcher found the mental health group of therapists somewhat demoralized, pessimistic about effecting cures of their patients, and a little bit unwilling to interact with their patients. The behavioristic therapy group, on the other hand, seemed to be in relatively high spirits, optimistic about effecting cures, and looking forward to interacting with their patients. What might be the structural and psychological factors underlying these findings?

Footnotes to Chapter Three

[1] Alex Inkeles, *What Is Sociology?* p. 16.

[2] *Ibid.*

[3] *Ibid.*, pp. 25–27.

[4] See, for example, Talcott Parsons, *The Social System*.

[5] For later work on conflict models of society, see Ralf Dahrendorf, *Class and Class Conflict in Industrial Society*.

[6] Phillip Selznick, "An Approach to a Theory of Bureaucracy."

[7] Alvin Gouldner, *Patterns of Industrial Bureaucracy*.

[8] See Talcott Parsons, *The Structure of Social Action*, for an exposition of the structural-functional view.

[9] Inkeles, *op. cit.*, p. 35.

[10] See Abraham Maslow, *Motivation and Personality*.

[11] Warren Bennis, *Changing Organizations*, Epilogue.

[12] Leslie White, *The Science of Culture*.

[13] William Ogburn, *Social Change with Respect to Culture and Original Nature*.

[14] See Claude S. George, Jr., *The History of Management Thought*.

[15] Alvin Toffler, *Future Shock*.

[16] Clifford Shaw, et al., *Delinquency Areas*.

[17] S. Glueck and E. Glueck, *Unraveling Juvenile Delinquency*.

[18] R. Cloward and L. Ohlin, *Delinquency and Opportunity*.

[19] See Charles Perrow, *Organizational Analysis: A Sociological View*, Ch. 1.

[20] See R. K. Merton, "Patterns of Influence: Local and Cosmopolitan Influences"; see also Inkeles, *op. cit.*, Ch. 4, for the conceptions of man in sociological analysis.

[21] Perrow, *op. cit.*, pp. 11–14.

[22] *Ibid.*, p. 175.

[23] See Morton Deutsch and Robert M. Krauss, *Theories in Social Psychology*, for an excellent review of these five orientations.

[24] Wolfgang Kohler, *Gestalt Psychology*.

[25] Kurt Koffka, *Principles of Gestalt Psychology*.

[26] *Ibid.*

[27] Solomon Asch, "Forming Impressions of Personality."

[28] Fritz Heider, "On Perception, Event Structure, and Psychological Environment."

[29] Leon Festinger, "The Motivating Effect of Cognitive Dissonance."

[30] See Kohler, *op. cit.*

[31] See R. M. Gagné, "Problem Solving and Thinking," for a summary of this research.

[32] For a review of blocks to creativity as well as methods of creative problem solving, see A. F. Osborn, *Applied Imagination*, 1957.

[33] D. C. Dearborn and Herbert Simon, "Selective Perception: A Note on the Departmental Identifications of Executives."

[34] See C. Kepner and B. Tregoe, *The Rational Manager: A Systematic Approach to Problem Solving and Decision Making.*

[35] See Gary Steiner, ed., *The Creative Organization*, for a fuller view.

[36] See Kurt Lewin, *Field Theory in Social Science.*

[37] Maslow, *op. cit.*

[38] Kurt Lewin, Ronald Lippitt, and R. K. White, "Patterns of Aggressive Behavior in Experimentally Created 'Social Climates.'"

[39] Leon Festinger and J. Carlsmith, "Cognitive Consequences of Forced Compliance."

[40] See Leon Festinger, "A Theory of Social Comparison Processes," and Stanley Schachter, *The Psychology of Affiliation.*

[41] See Morton Deutsch, "A Theory of Co-operation and Competition," and "An Experimental Study of the Effects of Cooperation and Competition upon Group Process."

[42] Stanley Schachter, "Deviation, Rejection, and Communication."

[43] See Edgar Schein, "Management Development as a Process of Influence"; R. R. Blake, H. A. Shepard, and J. S. Mouton, *Managing Intergroup Conflict in Industry*; and Richard Beckhard, *Organization Development: Strategies and Models.*

[44] B. F. Skinner, *Science and Human Behavior.*

[45] George C. Homans, *Social Behavior: Its Elementary Forms*, 1961, p. 13.

[46] George C. Homans, *The Human Group.*

[47] *Ibid.*, p. 133.

[48] *Ibid.*, p. 141.

[49] *Ibid.*, p. 145.

[50] *Ibid.*

[51] *Ibid.*, pp. 180–81.

[52] *Ibid.*, p. 182.

[53] J. W. Thibaut and H. H. Kelley, *The Social Psychology of Groups.*

[54] See Ch. 2.

[55] T. Allyon and N. H. Azrin, "The Measurement and Reinforcement of Behavior of Psychotics."

[56] Walter R. Nord, "Beyond the Teaching Machine: The Neglected Area of Operant Conditioning in the Theory and Practice of Management."

[57] *Ibid.*

[58] T. W. Adorno, et al., *The Authoritarian Personality.*

[59] Deutsch and Krauss, *op. cit.,* p. 163.

[60] Milton Rokeach, *The Open and Closed Mind.*

[61] Abram Kardiner, et al., *The Psychological Frontiers of Society.*

[62] W. F. Whyte, *Organizational Behavior: Theory and Application,* Ch. 32, and Michel Crozier, *The Bureaucratic Phenomenon,* Ch. 8.

[63] See D. Krech, R. Crutchfield, and E. Ballachey, *Individual in Society,* p. 106.

[64] See Abraham Zaleznick, "The Dynamics of Subordinacy," for an interesting account of the various types of subordinate behavior.

[65] Elliot Jaques, *The Changing Culture of a Factory.*

[66] Henry Mintzberg, *The Nature of Managerial Work,* Ch. 4.

[67] T. Burns and G. M. Stalker, *The Management of Innovation.*

[68] *Ibid.,* p. 94.

[69] Rowbottam, *Hospital Organization,* 1973.

[70] R. K. Merton, *Social Theory and Social Structure,* p. 198.

[71] S. Lieberman, "The Effects of Changes in Roles on the Attitudes of Role Occupants."

[72] Merton, *Social Theory.*

[73] See E. Goffman, *The Presentation of Self in Everyday Life,* for an interesting exposition of the role player as actor.

[74] See the *U.S. Newsfront Directory* for the annual variations in profit rates of public companies in each of a very large number of industries.

[75] Robert D. Joyce, *Encounters in Organizational Behavior,* pp. 40–41.

*"People are trapped in history
and history is trapped in them"*
James Baldwin

The Structural Orientations in Organization Theory

TIME AND ORGANIZATION THEORY

A Historical Review

In the two preceding chapters we looked at the organization from the perspective of four social sciences: economics, political science, sociology, and psychology. The exercise was a bit like examining a rock or a fossil from the point of view of chemistry, biology, and geology. In this and the next two chapters, we sketch out organizational concepts as they developed over time.

Men have had ideas about organizations and their management since time immemorial. Here is some advice, culled from a 5,000-year-old manuscript, from an Egyptian father to a son who is about to start a business:

> Proclaim thy business without concealment. . . . One ought to say plainly what one knoweth and what one knoweth not. (A call for honesty in managerial dealings.)
> The leader ought to have in mind the days that are yet to come. (The need for planning.)

Great is a great one whose counselors are great. (The value of staff advice to a manager.)

Write with thine hand, read with thy mouth, and ask counsel of them that have more knowledge than thou. . . . Persevere in asking counsel, neglect it not. . . . (The use of staff by managers.)[1]

And here are the eight methods by which a king governs his country, as set out in the nearly 3,000-year-old Chinese Constitution of Chow:

Eight methods he holds to govern the country. The first is ritual and worship, so as to control its spirit. The second is statutes and regulations, so as to control its great officers. The third is removal and appointment, so as to control its petty officers. The fourth is emolument and rank, so as to control its scholars. The fifth is taxes and tributes, so as to control its resources. The sixth is ceremonies and customs, so as to control its people. The seventh is punishment and reward, so as to control its strength. The eighth is farming and other employments, so as to control its multitude.[2]

Note the great variety of control modes that the constitution suggests should be used by the emperor for controlling his subjects.

Another Chinese, Mencius, writing about 2,500 years ago, pointed out the great advantages of using systematic procedures. As he put it, "Whosoever pursues a business in this world must have a system. . . . The skilled may at times accomplish a circle and a square by their own dexterity. But with a system, even the unskilled may achieve the same result."[3]

Plato, in his *Republic*, anticipated Adam Smith by 2,000 years when he wrote this about the benefits of specialization and the greater possibilities for specialization when the market is large:

Which would be better—that each should ply several trades, or that he should confine himself to his own? He should confine himself to his own. More is done, and done better and more easily when one man does one thing according to his capacity and at the right moment. We must not be surprised to find that articles are made better in big cities than in small. In small cities the same workmen makes a bed, a door, a plough, a table, and often he builds a house too. . . . Now it is impossible that a workman who does so many things should be equally successful in all. In the big cities, on the other hand . . . a man can live by one single trade. Sometimes he practices only a special branch of a trade. One makes men's shoes, another women's, one lives entirely by the stitching of the shoe, another by cutting the leather. . . . A man whose work is confined to such a limited task must necessarily excel at it.[4]

Here is Alfarabi's 1,000-year old suggestion for the manager's traits and for collective leadership should a single superman manager not be found:

In the model state there must be a hierarchy of rulers coming under the control of a supreme head or prince. The prince, head of the model state or of the whole earth, must possess certain traits: great intelligence, excellent memory, eloquence, firmness without weakness, firmness in the achievement of good, love for justice, love for study, love for truth, aversion to falsehood, temperance in food, drink and enjoyments, and contempt for wealth.

All these traits must be found in one man alone placed in charge of directing the complicated machinery of the state. In case all these traits cannot be found in one man alone, then inquiry should be made to determine whether there are two or more who possess the required traits jointly. If there are two, they should both rule the model state. If there are three, then these three should rule. If more are needed, more should rule.[5]

And here is Sir James Steuart, an eighteenth-century contemporary of Adam Smith, advocating the virtues of the division of work between managers and workers and the advantages of a piece-rate system:

In the first supposition, it is the head of the Master which conducts the labor of the slave, and turns it toward ingenuity; in the second, every head is at work, and every hand is improving in dexterity. Where hands therefore are principally necessary, the slaves have the advantage; where heads are principally necessary, the advantage lies in favor of the free. Set a man to labour at so much a day, he will go on at a regular rate, and never seek to improve his method; let him be hired by the piece, he will find a thousand expedients to extend his industry. . . . From this I account for the difference between the progress of industry in ancient and modern times.[6]

The Appendix to this chapter charts the stream of thinking about how organizations are or should be managed from immemorial times down to about 1970. The stream has become a flood in recent years and must await the efflux of time before the significant contributions are sifted from the trivial. But in it lie the sources of modern ideas about the management of organizations.

The Evolution of Modern Organization Theory

Over the centuries, more thought appears to have been devoted to individual institutions (the government, democracy, the church, capitalism, socialism, etc.) than to organizations as a *class* of collectivities. With the advent of the nineteenth century, however, capitalism, with its luxuriant growth of firms as well as other organizations, became the dominant institution in Western Europe and America. Toward the end of the nineteenth century, the business firm became the object of lively scrutiny by economists. Alfred Marshall was the first major economist to systematize the economic theory of the firm. That theory has evolved into one of the most sophisticated of all theories in the social sciences. It is also, however, open to the charge of resting on unrealistic, perhaps impossible, assumptions and of describing the behavior of a more or less fictitious entity.

The development of organization theory proper began in the first decade of this century with the work of the German social scientist Max Weber. Since then, organization theory has shown remarkable vitality and many-sided growth. It began about 1910, when Weber described bureaucracy as the "ideal" form of organization.* As an organizational form it was particularly suitable, he felt, in a society that was getting increasingly dependent on nonprofit institutions to meet its varied needs for education, health, sanitation, security, and so on. Soon thereafter, about 1916, Henri Fayol, a French executive, propounded his principles of effective administration. Both Weber and Fayol seemed to regard the organization as a kind of machine, which, if properly designed, would efficiently achieve its objectives. About 1930, the human relations movement, founded by Elton Mayo, appeared. It emphasized the importance of social relations at work. It mounted a major critique of the unhuman aspects of Weber's and Fayol's conceptions. In the mid-forties, Herbert Simon expounded his view of the administrative decision maker with limited reasoning, perceiving, and information-processing abilities. His was an attack on the omniscience that the economists had been according to decision makers and on the universalistic prescriptive character of classical organization theory. In 1950, Eric Trist brought the socio-technical systems viewpoint to bear on organization behavior. It stressed that a work group is subject to social, psychological, technical, and economic forces. In 1958, Joan Woodward founded contingency organization theory by showing that differences in the structures of organizations depend on differences in the technology employed by these organizations. She showed the inappropriateness of universal principles of organizations and brought out their situational character. In the mid-fifties, Chris Argyris and Douglas McGregor developed their models of desirable organizations in which human needs could be more fully satisfied and a fuller use could be made of the human potential. (See Figure 4–1.)

These major orientations of organization theory—the study of bureauc-

* The word "ideal" does not, in Weber's conception of bureaucracy, mean "perfect." It simply means the *abstract form* of bureaucracy as distinguished from the real-life manifestations. At the same time, there is little question that he did think highly of the form because of its many advantages that he perceived.

FIGURE 4–1
Major Schools in Contemporary Organization Theory

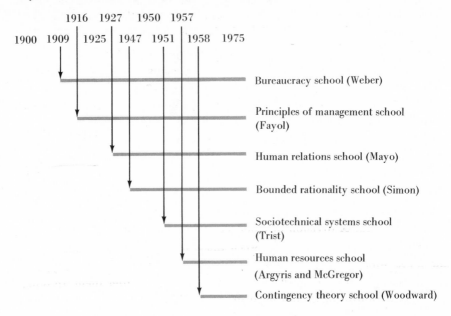

racy, the principles of management, human relations, administrative decision-making, contingency theory, the systems approach, and the human resources movement—are examined at some length in this and the following two chapters. In this chapter, we take a look at the bureaucracy school founded by Weber and the principles of managment, or management theory, school founded by Fayol. In examining each of these schools, we will concentrate on their basic orientation, especially the assumptions they make about the organization man, and what they regard as strategic variables in the study of organizations. In addition, we shall indicate their lines of development or evolution and the key questions they raise in organization theory as well as in the study of a particular organization.

THE BUREAUCRACY SCHOOL

In this section, we shall review Max Weber's conception of the properties a bureaucracy should possess, the critique of bureaucracy, the search for different forms of bureaucracy, and the comparative analysis of organizations.

Weber

Unlike the political philosophers, who studied mainly the government, and the economists, who studied mainly the business firm, Weber examined the nature of all organizations.[7] The question he posed at the beginning of this century was: "What is the organizational form than can service the increasingly more complex needs of an urbanizing, industrializing society?" Since society's form was that of competitive capitalism, organizational performance was highly important for attracting society's scarce resources, and hence organizational roles would have to be staffed on the basis of *technical competence* rather than on the basis of social status or kinship or heredity. Earlier, Adam Smith had demonstrated that division of labor and specialization are enormously productive. Therefore, *division of labor* and *specialization* would also have to be necessary features. Since, in an organization with a great deal of division of labor, coordination of activities would be a problem, some differentiation between those who gave orders (managers) and those who carried them out (operatives) would be necessary, and indeed managers would have to have others in turn to order them. In other words, the organization would need to have a *hierarchy of authority.* Since organizations engage in repetitive tasks, it would be economical to develop *rules* and *standard operating procedures* so that work would become habitual. Also, rules and procedures preclude arbitrary supervisory behavior and erratic responses of subordinates to work situations. For the same reasons, it would be necessary to have explicit rules regarding the rewarding of superior performance and the punishing of poor performance and the *specification of the exact work duties and authority* of every employee.

Weber also felt that in this organizational form, the *property of the organization* would have to be kept completely *distinct* from the *property of the staff* (a principle well recognized in corporate law). He insisted, on not very convincing grounds, that the administrative *staff* of an organization should *not own* the organization in part or full. Such a dictum, however, would rule out cooperatives, partnerships, proprietorships, and firms in which the owner also works as the manager. He also insisted upon the *recording* of administrative acts, decisions, and rules in writing, a requirement that, if faithfully carried out, would soon bury an organization under a mountain of paper. Despite the formidable *impersonality* of this form, Weber allowed it to have a nonbureaucratic, even charismatic head. Such a chief would hold the organization together because of the loyalty he would evoke, and he would also get social acceptance or legitimacy for the organization.

These, then, were the properties of bureaucracy as an "ideal type" of organization. Bureaucracy as an "ideal type" was meant by Weber to imply not a perfect organization, but only a type of an organization with certain desirable properties that might be particularly suited for operating institutions like government agencies, departments, and public institutions. The force of competition might keep business firms efficient. But public institutions do not ordinarily engage in competition for patronage, and, therefore, unless they are carefully and rationally designed, they might not be able to provide services efficiently to the public.

Response to Weber

Weber's work has led to three distinct reactions, mostly from sociologist students of organizations. One is a critique of his work designed to show that his abstract form of bureaucracy is in practice not so rational after all, that there are a great many unanticipated consequences of his dicta, quite a few of which are "dysfunctional" (a polite term for "harmful"). Another reaction is to show that there really are not one but several different types of bureaucracy, each appropriate in different circumstances. A third response is what has been called the comparative analysis of organizations. The attempt here is to compare and contrast the specific dimensions of the structures of different types of organization such as firms, hospitals, prisons, and government agencies and thereby to identify the similarities between superficially dissimilar institutions and the dissimilarities between superficially similar organizations. Let us review briefly each of the three responses to Weber's work.

Unanticipated Consequences of Bureaucracy

THE BUREAUCRAT'S PRAYER

Oh, Thou, who seest all things below
Grant that Thy servants may go slow;
That we may study to comply
With regulations till we die.

Teach us, O Lord, to reverence
Committees more than common-sense;
Impress our minds to make no plan
And pass the baby when we can.

And when the Tempter seems to give
Us feelings of initiative,
Or when, alone, we go too far
Recall us with a circular.

'Mid fire and tumult, war and storms,
Sustain us, Blessed Lord, with forms,
Thus may thy servants ever be
A flock of perfect sheep for Thee.

— Anon.[8]

This "prayer" may be more a caricature than the reality of bureaucracies. But the dysfunctionalists have argued that while a bureaucracy is intended

FIGURE 4–2
The Anticipated and Unanticipated Consequences of the Bureaucratic Form

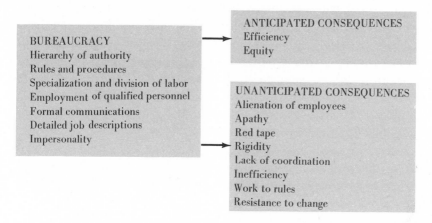

BUREAUCRACY
Hierarchy of authority
Rules and procedures
Specialization and division of labor
Employment of qualified personnel
Formal communications
Detailed job descriptions
Impersonality

ANTICIPATED CONSEQUENCES
Efficiency
Equity

UNANTICIPATED CONSEQUENCES
Alienation of employees
Apathy
Red tape
Rigidity
Lack of coordination
Inefficiency
Work to rules
Resistance to change

to be highly efficient, in practice its properties give rise to many unanticipated harmful consequences (see Figure 4–2). For example, division of labor and specialization force top administrators to delegate authority to subordinates. But subordinates introduce sectional interests and values into decision-making, and this hampers the coordination of organizational activities.[9] Nixon was not the first top administrator to claim that he ought not to be punished for the misdeeds of subordinates to whom he had delegated authority.

The formulation of rules and procedures impels employees to do what is minimally required of them and to pay attention to the letter rather than the spirit of the regulations. This, in turn, generates bureaucratic rigidity and red tape. The performance of the organization deteriorates, and tighter rules are enacted, leading to further rigidity and red tape.[10] For example, in a school, the teachers were spending several extra hours a week helping students with sports and with extracurricular activities. The new principal sent a circular to the teachers to the effect that some teachers were leaving early and that henceforth no teacher was to leave before 4:30 P.M., the official school closing time. Many teachers felt that it would force them to wait in the school even when they had nothing particular to do during a day when their classes finished early. They retaliated by refusing to stay beyond 4:30 P.M. Sports and extracurricular activities suffered, and many students left the school.

Industrial psychologists such as Argyris and Herzberg also have attacked bureaucracy for its effect on human motivation. Argyris has argued that division of work, formal rules and regulations, and hierarchy of authority lead to so much alienation of employees from management that eventually the organization's performance suffers.[11] Herzberg has argued that job enrichment—the design of challenging jobs—is preferable to narrowly specialized jobs in motivating superior performance.[12] However, it is an open question whether everyone, or even a majority of those who work in bureaucracies, look for stimulation and self-actualization in work. As Strauss has pointed out, many individuals do not like to be bothered with responsibility or are afraid of taking on challenging assignments.[13] Many prefer just to put in their scheduled hours of work and do their "own thing" outside the organization, at home or in the community. The roots of these differences in dispositions towards jobs may, as noted in Chapter 3, lie in early childhood experiences, rather than in organizational practices.

Many of bureaucracy's critics are undoubtedly right, but in respect of parts of some bureaucracies some of the time. There *are* many efficient bureaucracies, in business, in government, in other social institutions, as there are some that are malfunctioning. Besides, as researchers have shown, there are different forms of bureaucracy, so it is not very helpful to blast "the" bureaucracy with a shotgun. Each form of bureaucracy has its own advantages and disadvantages. It is possible to so design a bureaucracy as to make it an efficient mechanism in the particular situation in which it finds itself.

Different Forms of Bureaucracy

A number of sociologists studying formal organizations have sought to determine the extent to which real-life bureaucracies exhibit the characteristics Weber thought bureaucracies should possess. Their evidence suggests that there are a number of different types of bureaucracy operating in different situations of organizational size and with different types of task.

Tasks. A number of studies indicate that organizations or parts of organizations engaging in technically complex tasks tend to have a strongly professional orientation, while organizations or parts of organizations engaged in routine tasks tend to have a strongly clerical orientation. In terms of Weber's criteria, a professional orientation implies a strong emphasis on technical competence as a basis for hiring, firing, and promotion of personnel. A clerical orientation, on the other hand, implies a strong emphasis on hierarchical relationships and rules and procedures. For example, in a study by Hall, the positive intercorrelation between hierarchy, division of labor, rules, procedures, and impersonality was fairly strong, suggesting that organizations vary in the degree to which they are clerical bureaucracies.[14] He also found that emphasis on technical qualifications, a characteristic of the professional bureaucracy, was *negatively* correlated with all of the above except rules. This suggests that organizations vary in the extent to which they employ professional norms and that professionalization tends to be found where the clerical features of a bureaucracy are not so strong, and vice versa.

In another study, Hall found that *within* an organization, departments handling nonuniform and difficult-to-routinize tasks, such as the research department, were significantly more professionalized and had fewer of the features of a clerical bureaucracy than departments handling routine tasks with traditional skills, such as the accounting department.[15]

Other studies have not contradicted these findings. For example, one measure of professionalization may be the ratio of the professional and skilled personnel to managerial personnel. In a study by Rushing, it was found that this ratio was highest for capital goods industries (such as machinery manufacturing), next for consumer durable goods industries and producer goods industries (such as the automobile industry and the steel industry), and lowest for consumer nondurable goods industries (such as the food and clothing industries).[16] Since, generally speaking, the technology employed in capital goods industries tends to be most sophisticated and the technology employed in consumer nondurable goods industries tends to be least sophisticated, again the inference is that the degree of professionalization varies systematically with the complexity of the technology. In the same vein, Stinchcombe reported that the ratio of professional and skilled personnel to managerial personnel was much higher in mass production manufacturing industries than in the relatively simple craft technology construction industry, indicating again that professionalization is associated with technological complexity.[17] Figure 4–3 shows the three forms of bureaucracy indicated by these studies.

Size. Like the complexity of the tasks or technology, size also seems to affect bureaucratic form.

Pugh and his associates have identified seven different kinds of bureaucracy on the basis of their study of a diverse sample of British organizations.[18] Differing size appears to be the strongest factor accounting for the differences among these seven forms. They are as follows:

1 **Full bureaucracy.** This kind is characterized by a considerable programming of activities, sophisticated control procedures, extensive documentation, considerable control over decision-making by staff experts, and substantial centralization of decision-making in policy matters at the top. A government department or agency is a typical example.

FIGURE 4–3
The Nature of Organizational Tasks and the Forms of Bureaucracy

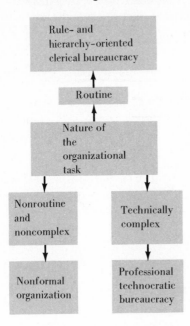

2 Nascent full bureaucracy. This kind is similar to the full bureaucracy, but the characteristics are less pronounced. It is the full bureaucracy in the making.

3 Workflow bureaucracy. The workflow bureaucracy, primarily the large manufacturing organization with standardized workflows for mass production, has even more programming of activities and sophisticated control procedures than the full bureaucracy but is more decentralized.

4 Nascent workflow bureaucracy. This form shows the characteristics of workflow bureaucracies but not to a pronounced degree, and it also is smaller in size than the workflow bureaucracy.

5 Pre-workflow bureaucracy. This type is less structured, less subject to sophisticated controls, less formalized, and smaller than the two preceding workflow bureaucracies. But like these two kinds, it too, shows the combination of decentralization of decision-making authority and impersonal control mechanisms.

6 Implicitly structured organization. Such organizations have low structuring or programming of activities, few sophisticated controls, dispersed rather than centralized authority for making decisions, and considerable control of activities by line managers as opposed to a system of impersonal controls. These are typically small organizations, family owned and controlled and not in the business of mass production.

7 Personnel bureaucracy. This is similar to the implicitly structured organization except that it tends to be owned and controlled by an outside body such as the government or city council. Decision-making is highly centralized, and procedures for selection, advancement, and the like are highly standardized.

Pugh, Hickson, and Hinings consider three dimensions of organizational structure as particularly relevant in determining what kind of bureaucracy an organization is. One is the *degree of decentralization of authority*, another is *the extent to which work is structured*, and a third is the *extent of control wielded by technically trained staff*. The personnel bureaucracy is low on all three; the workflow bureaucracy is high on all three. These authors suggest that there is a definite developmental sequence among workflow bureaucracies. That is to say, small, custom manufacturing organizations with few standard operating procedures, little formalization of roles, few sophisticated controls, and control of operations by supervisors (rather than technically trained staff), if and when they graduate to the status of large, mass production organizations, develop standardized procedures, formally defined roles, many sophisticated controls, and considerable influence of technically trained staff in decision-making. Among nonworkflow bureaucracies, too, such as government departments and service units in manufacturing organizations, there may be a similar developmental sequence from little structuring, standardization, formalization, and professionalization to much of these as the organizational unit grows larger.

Comparative Study of Organizations

One of the growing points of organizational research influenced by Weber has been the comparative study of organizations.* In this, superficially different organizations such as firms, hospitals, and schools are compared on a number of dimensions that the organization theorist considers important in organizational analysis. It has been undertaken primarily by organizational researchers of a sociological persuasion. A comparative study enables one to make stronger generalizations than a study based on only one

---

* At its broadest, the comparative study of organizations has been described as any "attempt to establish general principles about organizations from the study of more than one organization at once"—see S. H. Udy, Jr., "The Comparative Analysis of Organization," p. 679. We have restricted the meaning of comparative study to the study of superficially different *types* of institutions on certain important dimensions to determine whether they are in reality similar or dissimilar.

class of organizations. Also, it often makes possible the development of new theory.

For example, Etzioni has argued that organizations in which coercive means of control are utilized (such as prisons and custodial institutions) are characterized by alienated members; those in which remunerative means of control are used, such as firms and government departments, generally evoke a calculative involvement in the members; while organizations that use normative power (one that rests on identification with some norms, values, or dogma, such as in the church) evoke in the members primarily a moral, conscience-based involvement with the organization.[19] Another example is the work of the so-called Aston group we reviewed in the previous section, who studied a sample of assorted British organizations, some being firms and some being government departments, local municipal agencies, and the like.

The interesting point about comparative studies is that they uncover surprising similarities between organizations that on the face of things look dissimilar. One may think that firms and hospitals are grossly dissimilar organizations. Their goals are clearly different. And yet the study of their organizational structures and the technologies they use may reveal striking similarities. For example, just as large firms try to standardize their workflow, so do large hospitals. Just as large firms use various controls and techniques to monitor performance, so do large hospitals.

In a study by Hall, Haas, and Johnson, the authors classified a sample of assorted organizations two ways.[20] First, they used the Etzioni typology based on the means utilized to control the behavior of the organizational rank and file. Next, they classified them utilizing a typology developed by Blau and Scott, based on the criterion of whom the organization is set up to benefit (whether it is the owners, as in the case of firms; clients, as in the case of service organizations; members of the organization, as in the case of mutual benefit organizations; or the public-at-large, as in the case of commonweal organizations).[21] Table 4–1 shows the results of their classification of these organizations utilizing the two typologies. Notice that a private school and a private university, as well as a religious service organization, were classified as service organizations. A bank and a government regulative agency, as well as a labor union, were classified as utilitarian organizations. A private television station, a church, and a city recreation department were classified as normative organizations.

On the other hand, there may be surprising differences between organizations of the same institutional form. In Table 4–1, a state hospital is classified as coercive, while a private hospital is classified as normative; a private television station is classified as a business organization, while an educational television station is classified as a commonweal organization.

As Burns and Stalker's study shows, there were striking differences in the organizations of firms in the electronic industry depending on whether the firms were operating in its dynamic segment or in its stagnant segment.[22] Similar striking differences can surely be found among other institutional forms.

The great advantage of the comparative study of organizations is that it forces us to give up looking at organizations merely on the basis of their institutional forms and compels us to start looking for distinctive *organizational* types. It moves us away from common stereotypes to organizational reality. It opens up the possibility that large firms may have more in common with large hospitals, large bureaus, or large parties than with small firms. It points to the universality of organizational forms in given contexts of size, nature of the environment, and so on. By implication, it enables us to learn much about a particular organization by examining the evidence about other organizations of basically the same organizational form even if they have other institutional labels. Thus, if we know a lot about large corporations, by extrapolating that knowledge with due care we may be able to make reasonably good guesses about large political parties or large private hospitals.

THE PRINCIPLES OF MANAGEMENT AND MANAGEMENT PROCESS ORIENTATION

Start

Introduction

Another powerful tradition in organization theory, derided somewhat but quite persistent, is that of the principles of management. It has also been described as the management process school. Like Weber, the attempt of management theorists has been to identify the principles or norms that should govern the management of enterprises, particularly firms. They have also explored such issues as: What is the essence of management? What is the domain or process of management? Is management culture bound or culture free? Is management a science or an art?

Management is perhaps the most influential element in the design of organizations. It is the element that coordinates current organizational activities and plans future ones. It allocates resources. It arbitrates disputes. It provides leadership. If it is dynamic and progressive, the organization is likely to fare well. If it is reactionary and stupid, the organization is likely to disappear like the dodo, especially if confronted with changes in its environment. Management is the organizational element that adapts the organization to its environment and often shapes the very environment to make it more suitable to the organization. No organization can function without a management. However, the form and functions of management are likely to vary from culture to culture and possibly from organization to organization.

Just as the bureaucracy school takes its bearings from sociology, the management process school takes its bearings from economics and, increasingly, from social psychology. This is because this school is oriented to the study of corporate management, and, since corporations compete for patronage more than most other types of organization, it is strongly concerned, as economists are, with questions of efficiency in resource allocation and with profit-maximizing market behavior. In addition, management is very much a social psychological process since it involves intense interaction among decision makers and between managers, staff, and operatives. Also,

TABLE 4–1

Classification of Assorted Organizations Utilizing the Etzioni and Blau and Scott Typologies

Blau-Scott Typology	*Etzioni Typology*
Mutual Benefit	Coercive
County medical association	Juvenile detention center
County political party	Law-enforcement agency
Farm cooperative	State hospital
Farmers' federation	State penal institution
Labor union organization	State school
Private country club	
Religious-fraternal organization	Utilitarian
State church organization	Bank
Trade association	Farm cooperative
	Government regulative agency
Service	Hotel-motel
Civil rights organization	Insurance company
Delinquent reformatory	Labor union organization
Insurance company	Manufacturing plant
Juvenile detention center	Marketing organization
Parochial school system	Medical association
Private hospital	Municipal airport
Private school	Post office
Private welfare agency	Public transit firm
Public school system	Public utility
Religious service organization	Quarry
State psychiatric hospital	Railroad
State school	Restaurant
University	Retail store
	Trade association
	Trucking firm

organizing and leadership are important elements of management process, so this school draws heavily on social psychology for insights into *how* managers should build teams, raise morale, motivate personnel, communicate effectively, and exercise leadership.

The Founders

The founders of the modern principles of management school may be said to be Frederick Winslow Taylor and Henri Fayol. Taylor was the American who, about the beginning of this century, advocated the scientific management of factory production involving time and motion study, the standardization of parts and processes, and so forth.[23] His approach was to study operations and, after careful observation and experimentation, determine

Table 4–1 (continued)

Blau-Scott Typology	*Etzioni Typology*
Business	Normative
Bank	Church
Hotel-motel	City recreation department
Manufacturing plant	Civil rights organization
Marketing organization	County political party
Newspaper	Delinquent reformatory
Private television station	Educational television station
Public transit firm	Farmers' federation
Public utility	Fund-raising agency
Quarry	Local religious organization
Railroad	Military supply command
Restaurant	Newspaper
Retail store	Parochial school system
Trucking firm	Private country club
Commonweal	Private hospital
City recreation department	Private school
Educational television station	Private television station
Fund-raising agency	Private welfare agency
Government regulative agency	Public school system
Law-enforcement agency	Religious-fraternal organization
Military supply command	Religious service organization
Municipal airport	State church organization
Post office	State psychiatric hospital
State hospital	University
State penal institution	

SOURCE: Richard H. Hall, J. Eugene Haas, and Norman J. Johnson, "An Examination of the Blau-Scott and Etzioni Typologies," *Administrative Science Quarterly*, Vol. 12, No. 1 (June, 1967).

the principles by which operations could be performed optimally. Taylor believed that the essence of management was getting individuals and groups to perform organizational activities. He separated mental work from manual work and particularly emphasized that planning was management's function just as "doing" was the function of workers. He enumerated four principles of scientific management:

1 Workers should be scientifically selected, trained, and given jobs for which they are best suited physically as well as intellectually.

2 Work should be analyzed scientifically instead of by rules of thumb. Here Taylor pointed to the need for technocracy and professionalism.

3 Close cooperation should exist between the planners and the doers, the managers and the workers, so that work is done in accordance with scientific principles. Here, Taylor pointed to the interdependent nature of the organization's activities, to the fact that the whole can be greater than the sum of the parts only if the parts are properly integrated.

4 Managers and workers should share equal responsibility, with each group doing the work for which it is best equipped. Here Taylor pointed to organizational ethics.

Taylor also advocated continued research to increase productivity. He believed in a system of rewards and punishments geared to performance and output. He also advocated setting up a system of controls so that supervisors would be burdened only with the exceptional problem situation and not with moment to moment personal supervision of their subordinates.

Taylor was criticized unfairly for ignoring the needs of the workers and for viewing workers as "slobs." While he was by no means a socialist, or a great votary of human relations, as the four principles enumerated above indicate, neither was he a tyrant. He emphasized the application of science. But he also emphasized the fact that without the cooperation of workers, mere scientific management cannot work. His view of workers was no worse than the prevailing business view of workers and a good deal more humane than that of many of his contemporaries in management.

While Taylor and his followers were oriented to the management of production, Fayol, a French executive and engineer, sought to systematize the whole of management. He argued, in a book published in 1916, that management is an indispensable element in the running of all business and nonbusiness enterprises.[24] The domain of management, he felt, is *planning and forecasting,* the setting up of appropriate structures for carrying out various organizational activities—that is, *organizing leadership, coordination* of activities and *control.* The domain of management that Fayol staked out has not changed appreciably over the years. Most management theorists

believe that however management may differ from culture to culture and organization to organization, there is no management that does not do or provide at least some planning and forecasting, organizing, coordination, control, and leadership.

Fayol also enunciated several principles of good management. A manager, he wrote, must have enough authority to discharge his responsibilities. Each man should have only one boss to avoid conflicting demands on him (the principle of unity of command). He advocated the principle of unity of direction—that is, that people engaged in the same activities be assigned identical objectives in the organizational plan. Hierarchy of authority was another principle—every employee must report to some boss. He enunciated the principle of equity—a combination of kindliness and justice in treating employees. He also thought that all personnel must be allowed to show initiative, and that management must foster the morale of its employees.

There are two principal strands in the work of the founders. One is that there are universal principles of management that should be observed for any organization to run properly. The other is that the process of management is characterized by certain activities like planning, organizing, leading, controlling, and coordination. Let us examine how each of these strands developed.

Principles of Management

In the mid-twenties, James D. Mooney pursued Fayol's notion that principles of administration could be applied to the management of all organizations. Mooney was an interesting fellow. For years he doubled as a corporate executive and a spy for the American Office of Naval Intelligence! He teamed up with a Fordham University history professor, Alan Reiley, to write *Onward Industry!* The message of this book was that the world could be saved from the Great Depression through increased organizational efficiency. Mooney and Reiley wrote,

> Management is the vital spark which activates, directs, and controls the plans and procedure of organization. . . . The relation of management to organization is analogous to the relation of the psychic complex to the physical body. Our bodies are simply the means and the instrument through which the psychic force moves toward the attainment of its aims and desires.[25]

This was perhaps the first attempt to attribute spiritual qualities to management!

Mooney and Reiley enumerated principles that are similar to the ideas of Weber. Two of their principles are worth noting:

1 In every organization there is a functional differentiation of duties or specialization of functions. Mooney and Reiley talk of determinative, applicative, and interpretive functions, corresponding to the lawmaking functions of the legislature, the law-enforcement functions of the executive branch, and the interpretation of law functions of the judiciary in democratic governments.[26]

2 Staff activities should be clearly distinguished from line activities. Line represents, they wrote, "the authority of man . . . staff, the authority of ideas."[27] Line commands; the staff advises.

Mary Parker Follett, a political scientist, social worker, and writer on management, anticipated the orientations of several contemporary schools in her four fundamental organizational principles.[28] These principles are: (a) The responsible people must be in direct contact regardless of their position in the organization. "Horizontal" communication is as important as hierarchy in achieving coordination. In this principle she anticipated the organic management style described by Burns and Stalker.[29] (b) Concerned or affected individuals should be involved in policy or decisions while these are being formed and not simply brought in afterwards. In this principle she anticipated the participative management movement. (c) In a decision situation, all factors need to be related, and these interrelationships themselves must be taken into account. In this principle she anticipated the systems theorists. (d) Since so many people contribute to the making of a decision, the concept of ultimate responsibility is an illusion. Authority and responsibility should derive from the actual function to be performed, not from the place in the hierarchy. Here, too, she anticipated organic management.

The real explosion in the number of principles of management came with Colonel L. Urwick. He assembled a large number of principles under each of Fayol's managerial functions of planning, forecasting, organizing, leading, coordinating, and controlling.[30] His assumption was that a logical structure based on (his) principles of management was better for efficiency in operations as well as morale than one governed by personalities and personal idiosyncrasies. Some of the several dozen principles he advocated are: (a) There should be a clear line of authority, as in the military, from the top management down to the lowliest employee. (b) The duties, responsibilities, and authority of each role should be communicated to its incumbent in writing. (c) Each individual should perform a single function only. (d) The span of control of any manager (the number directly reporting to him) should never exceed six. (e) Authority can be delegated, but not responsibility—a superior must take absolute responsibility for what his subordinates do.

Chester Barnard, for many years a president of the New Jersey Bell Telephone Company, advanced the then revolutionary notion that organizations are cooperative systems and that authority is really delegated upward rather than downward.[31] Unless employees are willing to accept the authority of management to issue orders, the prerogative of management to issue orders is meaningless. He argued that organizations cannot function unless individuals within it can communicate with one another and are willing to contribute action towards the achieving of some shared goals. That contribution, he said, depends on their subjectively valued contributions being equaled or outweighed by the subjectively valued inducements they receive from the organization. He felt that the managerial or executive task is the specialized work of maintaining the organization in operation and consists of three subtasks or principles:

1 The executive must maintain organizational *communication*—that is, link those who are willing to work for the organization with the common purposes. He should do this, first, by defining organizational positions or roles; next, by getting the personnel to fill these roles; and, last, by helping to develop an informal communication system good enough to spread the word of what needs to be done, so that formal orders need only relatively rarely be issued. In other words, he stressed the importance of a *cohesive organization with well-informed members.*

2 The executive must *secure essential services* from individuals by maintaining *morale* through incentives, restraints, controls, supervision, training, and education.

3 He must *formulate the purposes and objectives* of the organization and disseminate these right down to the organization's lowest levels, to enable the organization to work as an organic whole.

Another executive who was also quite influential was Alfred Sloan of General Motors. In his book, *My Years with General Motors*, Sloan enunciated the principle of *coordinated decentralization*[32]—that is, that decentralization of operating authority is necessary for fostering initiative. This is best done by creating autonomous divisions. However, policy should be made centrally and, to facilitate coordination, preferably by committees of executives; and certain functions, such as the control of cash, should be centralized for purely economic reasons. Corporate decision-making should be aided by groups of experts (staff) in matters of forecasting, research, and the like. The organization of General Motors, which Sloan shaped, has been adopted by a great many large American corporations.

Another major management writer is Wilfred Brown, the chief executive of a British firm. He has argued that good management implies the recognition and development of three systems in a company: (a) an executive system of formal positions as shown on an organization chart; (b) a representative system that may or may not be formalized but consists of mechanisms by which subordinates convey their views and feelings to their superiors (e.g., deputations of subordinates, suggestion boxes, evaluation of superiors' performance by means of questionnaires filled out by subordinates); and (c) a legislative system that formally or informally sets limits to what a company may do, exemplified by the meetings of shareholders, the board of directors, works councils that consist of representatives of the corporation's various publics, and so on.[33] At his Glacier Metal Company, he has tried to put his ideas into practice and has worked particularly to develop good representational and legislative systems as exemplified by councils composed of representatives of workers and management.

Critique of Principles of Management

The standard of the principles of management votaries has been carried forward ably by men like Koontz and O'Donnell and Newman and Summer.[34] Their work tries to incorporate the human relations viewpoint and is generally less dogmatic than the work of the founding fathers. But they, too, are subject to the principal criticisms leveled against this entire school. One major criticism is the readiness to generalize principles from a few case histories rather than insisting on rigorous empirical research. Also, these principles are often stated as unconditional statements of what ought to be done in all circumstances when what is needed are conditional principles of management. For example, it makes little sense to say that a manager's span of control should be no greater than six. But it could make sense to say that *if* the work the subordinates of a boss do is fairly uniform, *then* for greater efficiency or coordination, the span of control should be larger than six, and *if* the work they perform is varied, *then* the span should be smaller than six.

Indeed, whenever these principles have been tested empirically, they have fallen like autumn leaves. For example, Dale found considerable variation in the span of control of the chief executive even among highly successful firms,[35] and Woodward found that the span of control varied with the technology used by the firm.[36] The Urwick principle that each individual should perform only a single function flies in the face of the work of Argyris[37] and Herzberg,[38] which suggests that enlarged and enriched jobs, presumably involving a number of operations, lead to greater worker motivation than highly specialized jobs. Also, as Burns and Stalker have shown, in organizations in a technologically turbulent environment, the concepts of a strict hierarchy and an explicit specification of the duties, responsibilities, and authority of each employee, two of the principles of Urwick, make no sense at all. They cite the example of the head of one concern in the electronics industry who attacked the very idea of the organization chart (an embodiment of the hierarchy concept). He thought having an organization chart was a "dangerous method of thinking about the working of industrial management. The first requirement of a management, according to him, was that it should make the fullest use of the capacities of its members; any individual's job should be as little defined as possible so that it will 'shape itself' to his special abilities and initiative."[39] There simply is no scientific evidence yet that any of the myriad "principles" contributes anything to organizational performance or is universally used.

These principles of management are like proverbs—they are wise in a vague sort of way. They may well be applicable in a number of organizational situations, but we need better data than have been presented by their progenitors to believe that. The contribution of the principles of management theorists is an important one in a historical sense. They were among the first to have developed some interesting concepts that became useful later on in organization theory—such concepts as the span of control, different types of departmentalization, the essential functions of management, separation of line and staff functions. Their orientation, that of organizing for efficiently achieving the goals of the organization, is a powerful one from the point of view of the design of organizations, but it has also been attacked as by and large neglecting the human factor in organizations.

The Domain of Management

Earlier, we noted that according to Fayol, the domain of management is planning and forecasting, organizing, leading, controlling, and coordinating (see Figure 4–4). Indeed, many management theorists believe these to constitute the process of management. Since so much has been written about these functions, it may be useful to note briefly what they mean today. Their design is substantially the design of the organization.

Planning and forecasting. Organizations operate in a world of at least some uncertainty and one in which the ability to anticipate problems is of considerable value. Planning and forecasting are processes by which the organization keeps adapted to its environment. Forecasting requires the gathering of pertinent information about the future in order to be able to form some idea of that future. If the organization is a firm, that may mean gathering information on the size of next year's market. If it is a university, it may mean estimating next year's enrollment. Planning, on the other hand, is the fixing of targets, for the organization as a whole as well as for its various departments and divisions. Naturally, targets are set on the basis of the forecast of operations.

The process of planning does not stop with target setting. It extends to setting up policies and standard operating procedures and the development of work schedules. At each of the many phases of planning, decisions must be made. Problems must be diagnosed, alternatives must be sought and evaluated, and the alternative that appears the most suitable must be selected.

There are various levels of planning. Strategic planning is long-term planning, and it involves questions such as: What business should the organization be in a decade from now? What should the organization look like in five years? Tactical planning is short-term planning, and the typical questions pursued are: What should be the level of our operations a year from now? How should we adjust our marketing strategy? What are our short-term financial and personnel needs? Contingency planning takes into account possible occurrences; it is planning for what to do if there is a recession or if there is a change in government policy. The Soviet government, for example, has a minimum plan and a maximum plan. The minimum plan (relatively low targets) goes into effect if the harvests turn out to be bad, there are exceptional Cold War pressures, and so forth. The maximum plan (relatively high targets) goes into effect under conditions of good harvests, international relaxation, and the like.

Planning may be comprehensive or limited in scope. There are organizations that plan to the last detail; others rest content simply with setting broad targets for the next financial period. Planning may be done by an army of experts using sophisticated forecasting techniques and simulation models; or it may be done in a seat-of-the-pants manner, by a number of executives sharing their judgments over a cup of coffee. Planning may be done from the top down, with the top executives deciding on targets that are then passed down; or it may be done from the bottom up, with the lowest sections formulating plans and targets and sending them up for evaluation and coordination. Planning may be done participatively, with a great many members of the organization chipping in with their ideas and judgments, or it may be done in an elitist manner by a few executives or technocrats. Thus, there are many dimensions and types of planning, and planning practices are likely to vary from organization to organization.

Organizing. Organizing involves assigning various tasks to different members of the organization, grouping them into sections, divisions, and departments, formalizing the hierarchy of authority into an organization chart, and so on. Organizing has two aspects. One is the technical aspect of finding the individuals with the right technical abilities to fill the organizational

FIGURE 4–4

The Domain and Functions of Management

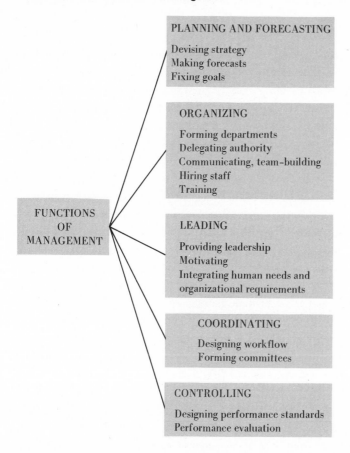

slots and of putting them together for easier coordination and greater efficiency. The other is the social aspect of dealing with members not as machines but as individuals with unique motives, abilities, and limitations and as members of nonformal groups. Recruitment, training, departmentalization, delegation of authority, line-and-staff and human relations are some of the principal elements of the process called organizing.

Recruitment and training have been extensively researched.[40] The point to note is that recruitment and training of personnel offer two powerful alternative (but not mutually exclusive) strategies for controlling human behavior in organizations. By instituting proper recruitment and selection procedures, organizations can cut down the cost of training employees—the employees come into the organization at least partially trained. The use of various test scores, such as the A.T.G.S.B. score in admitting MBA students, is a way of trying to ensure that individuals with the right mental attitudes and sufficient intelligence are recruited. The process of educating them is thereby made a less impossible task! On the other hand, by instituting proper training procedures, the organization secures an access to a wider, more heterogeneous personnel market.

There are several ways of grouping organizational members. Functional departments are formed when individuals are grouped together on the basis of the organizational function, such as marketing or manufacturing, to which they contribute their efforts. Thus, all personnel having expertise (or intending to have expertise) in marketing may be grouped together in the marketing department; all those having expertise in production operations may be grouped together in the production department. On the other hand, complementarity rather than similarity in skills may be the basis for grouping people. The maintenance personnel may be allocated to the production department to assure better coordination between maintenance operations and production operations. The allocation of nurses, doctors, and secretaries to wards serves the same purpose. Divisionalization is another example of grouping complementary personnel. A third way of grouping people, called the matrix structure, involves allocating individuals to their functional specialization group as well as to project groups. In situations in which technical skills of a high order are needed, but the work is relatively routine, as in pathological laboratories, functional departmentalization tends to be commonest. In situations in which quick coordination between personnel with diverse training is essential, the divisional form tends to be commonest. In situations in which technical expertise and quick coordination between diverse personnel are essential, and the organizational tasks are in the form of highly variable projects, the matrix structure may be most common.[41]

There are limits to the ability of managers to make decisions. They also have only a limited amount of time. Hence delegation of authority for making decisions is inevitable as an organization grows larger and/or engages in more varied and complex activities. Management by exception has become a common feature of decentralized organizations. In this, the manager delegates to his subordinates most of the routine decisions charged to him and reserves to himself the power to make decisions in exceptional, novel, or crisis situations. Management by objectives is another form of decentralization. Under this, the superior encourages his subordinates to develop objectives for themselves that are consistent with the organization's objectives and helps them draw up plans for achieving these objectives. Profit decentralization is yet another form of decentralization. Under this, the subordinate manager is held accountable for a certain return on investment (or some other performance measure in the case of nonprofit organizations) and given a free hand to develop the procedures that can help him achieve the target. A number of researchers have found that decentralization and the use of a system of sophisticated controls and procedures go hand in hand.[42] In other words, an impersonal system of control is a substitute for personal supervision and control.

Many management writers have made a distinction between line and staff. As we noted earlier, Mooney and Reiley advised that line managers make decisions and the staff provides information and advice. In large organizations, such as the General Motors Corporation, the staff groups are located at the headquarters for economy. For less sophisticated and more routine tasks, the departments and divisions may have their own staff as well. In theory staff is advisory. In practice, staff personnel often make decisions or have a very great say in the making of decisions. In the Nixon administration, Nixon's staff often superseded the decisions of his line managers. Where decisions require extensive technical analysis or where the staff have the "ear" of the powerful, they, rather than the line managers, are in the driver's seat. Line and staff relationships are, as a consequence, often strained. They represent the collision of two antagonistic cultures, that of the technocrat and that of the perhaps unsophisticated but experienced administrator.

Organizing encompasses not only designing the organization's structure but also dealing with individuals, communicating information to them, treating them fairly and humanely—in short, human relations. Individuals are not automatons. They have feelings, needs, motives. They often react to information in unanticipated ways. They often form groups and cliques that may work at cross-purposes to the organization. A vast amount of research has been done in the area of human relations in industry.[43] We will deal with it at a greater length in the next chapter.

Leading. As Newman and Summer have noted, "Leadership . . . involves the way a manager behaves in his man-to-man relationships with his subordinates. In leading, a manager strives to integrate the needs of people with the welfare of his company or department. . . . In short, a leader tries to act to maintain a good balance between individual motivation *and* cooperative efficiency."[44] As a leader, the manager draws on a number of power sources—that of his formal authority, his power to punish and reward his subordinates, his personal qualities, his administrative and technical acumen, and his being the symbol of the organization's ideology.

There has been a great deal of social psychological research on leadership.[45] An important finding is that leadership is partly situational and partly intrinsic to the person. In other words, there are very few individuals who are accepted as leaders in all situations, but there are many whose leadership may be acceptable in a number of similar situations because of abilities that are relevant to these situations. Another finding is that in most task-oriented groups there are two leadership roles. One is that of the task leader, who organizes the group for action; the other is that of the maintenance leader, who, through his empathy and good humor, keeps the group in a state of emotional equilibrium. A third finding is that in task-oriented groups the leader who is concerned with both the achievement of the group tasks *and* the well-being of the group members tends to be more effective than one who is only task oriented or oriented only to the needs of the group members. A fourth finding is that there is greater commitment to the group task, greater cohesion, and greater self-reliance in the members of democratically led groups than in groups with either autocratic or laissez-faire leaders.

Fiedler's early research suggested that the leader who is detached enough to have preferences among workers is more effective than one who prefers not to feel differentially toward subordinates. His further work on the contingency model of leadership, however, suggests that the interpersonally oriented leader—that is, the leader who does not like to discriminate between workers—tends to be quite successful in raising group performance in task situations that are moderately favorable to him (see below). On the other hand, in task situations that are either very favorable to him or very unfavorable to him, the discriminating, task-oriented leader is likely to be needed to raise group performance.[46] Fiedler considers a task situation as favorable to the leader if the leader is well liked by subordinates, if the group task is structured and the group performance is quantifiable, and if the leader has considerable positional and expertise-based authority. A task situation is considered to be unfavorable if the leader is disliked, if the group task is ambiguous, and if the leader does not have much authority over subordinates.

Controlling. Controlling is the process by which an organization periodically takes its bearings. It is the "process of measuring progress, comparing it with plans, and taking corrective action."[47]

There are many controls that organizations use. Preparation and analysis of periodic financial statements, budgeting, the internal audit, establishment of standard costs and the comparison of the actual costs with the standard costs, quality control, and performance appraisal of employees are all examples of management controls. Like planning, control has many dimensions. It can be simpleminded or sophisticated, extensive in coverage or directed at only a few organizational activities, remedial in intention or punitive, arbitrarily imposed or developed through members' consent and participation.

Research on controls indicates that they tend to proliferate as the organization's size increases and as it operates in an increasingly turbulent environment.[48] Their use makes possible management by exception—that is to say, it allows managers to attend to the exceptional, novel, or emergency situations, since the routine problems are taken care of by the system of controls and established procedures.

Several authors have noted the dysfunctional consequences of controls.[49] If performance is measured in terms of only a single criterion, it may lead to the neglect of other unmeasured aspects of performance. For example, in a public employment agency, the employment interviewers were appraised on the basis of the number of interviews they conducted but not on the basis of the number of jobs they found. As a consequence, many interviews were conducted, but few jobs were found!

Where multiple criteria for assessing performance are used, such as profits, production, quality, and morale, organizational participants may be torn among conflicting goals. Should the production manager accept a large order that may help meet the production quota but may lower the profit rate and overextend the department and its workers? Frequently, the response is to attend to one criterion (the one in terms of which current performance is lowest) at one time and to the other criteria at other times. The net result may be "fire-fighting" behavior that results in merely mediocre performance on all the criteria. Control mechanisms involving measurement of performance on one or multiple criteria are likely to breed a calculative involvement in organizational members. In other words, they are likely to be motivated to get away with as little as they can for as long as they can. As Drucker has pointed out, since organizations have in fact many objectives, it is necessary to identify what the priorities are, spell them out, and get managers to make decisions based on these priorities—something he calls "management by objectives."[50] Perhaps that way, the dysfunctions of controls may be minimized, for then individuals would be assessed on the basis of *their* objectives and not in terms of criteria imposed from above.

Coordinating. Coordinating is the management of interdependence in work situations. For example, in a hospital, the activities of doctors, nurses, ward attendants, lab technicians, and clerks must be coordinated if the patient is to receive good care. How is coordination achieved? Hierarchy is the simplest and most common device. By putting interdependent units under one boss, some coordination among their activities is ensured. The specification of rules, procedures, and policies is another common coordination device. Rules and policies are particularly useful in coordinating the activities of groups or individuals of equal status and authority. If the sales and the credit departments bicker a great deal, the establishment of a credit and sales policy by top management may improve coordination between the two. Planning is a way of anticipating interdependencies and thus forestalling or mitigating coordination difficulties. Through proper planning, for example, enough raw materials can be purchased in advance so that production does not suffer. Participative, committee, or group decision-making is another common coordinating device. Fostering a climate of mutual trust and collaboration is also a coordinating mechanism. Providing interdependent units with an incentive to collaborate, such as a profit-sharing plan, is another mechanism. Indoctrinating organizational members with the goals and mission of the organization, a device used commonly in religious and military organizations, is still another coordinative device. Thus, a large variety of coordinative devices are available to management.

Critique of Management Process

Recently, it has been questioned whether planning, organizing, leading, controlling, and coordinating provide an adequate description of the management process. After an intensive observation of what six top executives *actually* did during the course of a few days at work, Henry Mintzberg concluded that these labels do not adequately capture the reality of what managers do.[51] He suggested that instead the manager should be regarded as playing some ten different roles, played in no particular order.

A distinction should, however, be drawn between the roles that an individual manager plays and the functions discharged by the managerial *system* in an organization. Put another way, the output of the various roles performed by managers may be the major organizational functions of planning, organizing, and the rest. By way of an analogy, members of a family engage in a variety of behaviors that then can be summarized in terms of roles of father, mother, child, symbolic head, external representative, and so on. But these roles in turn make possible certain social functions, such as child rearing, the acquisition of property, the maintenance of the family unit, the transmission of culture from generation to generation. Thus, planning, organizing, leading, coordinating, and controlling provide an inadequate description of managerial behavior. They may, however, provide a reasonable description of what *functions* management serves in an organization.

Comparative Management

The comparative management school is an offshoot of the management process tradition. This school identifies itself with the basic management issues of the management process tradition (planning, organizing, leading, etc.), but it breaks away in seeking to identify the *conditions* under which these issues

TABLE 4–2

Dale's Classification of Organizational Problems at Seven Stages of Growth

Stage of growth	Number of employees*	Organizational problem and its possible consequences
I	3–7 (any size)	Formulation of objectives (division of work)
II	25 (10)	Delegation of responsibility (accommodation of personalities)
III	125 (50–100)	Delegation of more management functions (span of control)
IV	500 (50–300)	Reducing the executive's burden (the staff assistant)
V	1,500 (100–400)	Establishing a new function, or functional-ization (the staff specialist)
VI	5,000 (100–500)	Coordination of management functions (group decision-making)
VII	465,000 (over 500)	Determining the degree of delegation (decentralization)

* The first figure indicates the actual size of the company studied. The parenthetical figure indicates very broadly the size of the company when the particular organizational problem may arise for the first time. The likely consequence of each organizational problem is shown in parentheses.

SOURCE: E. Dale, *Planning and Developing the Company Organization Structure*, AMA Research Report No. 20 (New York: American Management Association, 1952), p. 22.

might assume particular importance. It does so by comparing what different firms *do* in response to the need for planning, organizing, and the rest. It tries to draw its conclusions from systematic empirical work. Dale, who surveyed American firms to discover how they used classical concepts,[52] is the principal luminary of the comparative school. Table 4–2, which shows the different management issues that become critical as a company grows in size, indicates the kind of work done in the comparative management school.

A corollary to comparative management is international management, the attempt to compare and contrast management practices in different countries and cultures. The basic idea is to identify the relationships between each of the elements of management and different aspects of the cultural environment, in order to get some idea of the extent to which principles of management are universal and the extent to which they are only locally applicable. Farmer, Richman, Negandhi, Massie, and Estafan are some of the leading members of this school. The following table, Table 4–3, gives an idea of the focus of enquiry of the comparative international management school.[53]

start

TABLE 4–3
Environmental Factors Affecting Managerial Functions

Managerial functions	ENVIRONMENTAL FACTORS			
	Educational	Sociological-cultural	Legal-political	Economic
Setting objectives	Technical and higher educational systems	Role of religion; view of management goals and values important in culture	Government influence/regulations	Fiscal and monetary policies
Policy formulation and implementation	Educational match with requirements	Attitude toward management and managers	Political stability	Economic stability
Research and development	Scientific orientation	Acceptance of change	Government support: financial investment	View of risk taking and progress
Production and procurement	Supply of engineers and technicians	Attitude toward efficiency	Government support: defense and other government contracts, industrial zoning	Availability of resources; adequate infrastructure
Finance	Specialized training in accounting and economics	View of savings and investment	Tax reliefs, subsidies, financial restrictions	Central banking system; foreign aid and private investment
Marketing	Literacy level	Attitude toward material possessions	Import-export and foreign exchange regulations	Market size; degree of competition; per capita annual income; price stability

ENVIRONMENTAL FACTORS

Managerial functions	Educational	Sociological-cultural	Legal-political	Economic
Planning and innovation	Technical capability for budgets, schedules, and basic policies	View of time and change; use of new knowledge and statistical data; population growth	National planning by central government	Inflationary-deflationary tendencies
Organization	Functional specialists and type of education	View of authority; group decision-making; inter-organizational cooperation	Predictability of legal actions; political influence	Division of labor; factor endowment
Staffing	Education level	Interpersonal cohesion; class structure; individual mobility	Status of management vis á vis government; labor laws	Labor union influence; attitude toward unemployment
Direction, supervision, motivation	Management development	View of achievement; dedication to work; language barriers to communication	Tolerance of bribes, fraud, and tax evasion	Worker participation in management; use of monetary and fringe benefits; incentives
Control	Ability to use feedback for corrective action	Attitude toward scientific method	Accounting data; reports for government regulation	Private property rights; quotas

SOURCE: From J. L. Massie, *Essentials of Management* (Englewood Cliffs, N. J.: Prentice-Hall, 1971), pp. 39–40.

For example, Massie suggests that the managerial function of setting organizational objectives is likely to be affected by a society's system of higher education; the important values and goals of the society, particularly religious values and the social view of management; the legal framework governing the society; and the role that the government plays, especially its fiscal and monetary policies. In a society such as that of the United States, where higher education is widespread, the acquisitive instinct is strong, and the legal and political framework supports decentralized, competitive economic activity, management is generally likely to engage heavily in the goal-setting process. In more traditional, less developed societies such as that of India, with extensive regulation of economic activity by the government, setting of long-term objectives may not be a very important management function.

The work of the international management researchers, though still in its infancy, raises an interesting issue: Can U.S. style modern, professional management be exported to very different cultures? There is tentative evidence supporting both a "yes" and a "no." U.S. style management seems to be flourishing in Europe, but not yet in Japan and not during the Allende period in Chile. It is very doubtful whether it would function effectively in China or the U.S.S.R.

The empirical work of Negandhi and Prasad sheds some light on this issue. They did a comparative study of the business management of firms in Argentina, Brazil, India, the Philippines, and Uruguay by interviewing a number of executives from each of the selected firms. The depth of inquiry was greatest in the case of India. In each country, they studied selected pairs of U.S. subsidiaries and local firms matched for type of industry. They postulated that, in general, management philosophy or policy toward consumers, employees, suppliers, distributors, government and community, and stockholders would, in conjunction with environmental variables, affect the process of management, which in turn would affect enterprise and managerial effectiveness as judged by the firm's profitability, growth in profits, growth in market share, consumer good will, employee satisfaction, and so on.[54] Their model is shown in Figure 4–5.

On an average, as we would expect, U.S. subsidiaries turned out to have a more "progressive" management philosophy than local firms. In other words, the management of U.S. subsidiaries displayed greater concern about consumer, employee, supplier, distributor, government, and stockholder good will toward the company than their local counterparts. They also had more formalized planning, forecasting, organizing, control, and coordinating practices. The important point, however, is that the index of the progressiveness of management philosophy was strongly *correlated* with the formalization of management planning, organizing, and related practices as well as with an

FIGURE 4–5
The Negandhi-Prasad Model for Cross-cultural Management Research

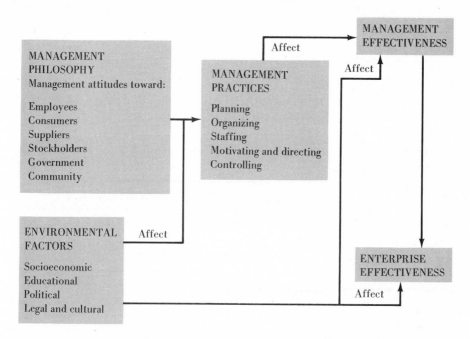

index of management effectiveness. The latter was based on such factors as management ability to attract and retain high-level manpower, employee morale and job satisfaction, low employee turnover and absenteeism, cooperative interpersonal relationships at work, cooperative interdepartmental relationships, the primacy of overall objectives rather than departmental objectives, utilization of high-level manpower for strategic planning rather than routine operations, and the adaptability of the organization to its environment.[55] It would appear, therefore, that U.S. style "progressive" management philosophy and practices, regardless of whether they are practiced by U.S. subsidiaries or local firms, increase managerial effectiveness. It is less clear from the study whether they also increase enterprise effectiveness in terms of profitability, growth rate, and the like.[56]

COMPARISON OF BUREAUCRACY AND MANAGEMENT PROCESS ORIENTATIONS

In this chapter, after sketching briefly the evolution of organization theory, we examined two great founding orientations, one of the bureaucracy school, the other of the principles of management (or management process) school.

There are similarities between them but also some notable dissimilarities. These are explored briefly below.

The Model of the Individual

In both orientations there is a rationalistic flavor. Human beings are thought of as reasonable creatures who accept efficient organizational arrangements if only these are properly explained to them. They are willing to tolerate routinization of work, accept orders from their bosses, be shifted around from one section to another if necessary for the organization efficiently to achieve its objectives. No real account is taken of personality—the richness of a person's impulse life, perception of reality, need structure—things we explored in Chapter 3. While several management process theorists, notably Taylor, Follett, and Barnard showed some understanding of the human element in organizational life, the bureaucracy school, wedded as it has been to the structural-functional perspective in sociology, has operated on quite naive assumptions about human nature. Only a few, such as Selznick,[57] took the trouble to explore how the human members of an essentially impersonal organization might respond to it. While neither orientation regards people as automatons, as some writers have alleged, they both seem to be content with the common stereotype of the average person as reasonable, self-interested, and quickly adaptable to rewards and sanctions.

Strategic Design Variables

Both orientations heavily accent the structural aspects of organizations such as hierarchy of authority, rules and procedures, formal role relationships, departments, delegation of authority, and the like. Neither particularly probes organizational *processes* such as the workflow, the way decisions actually get made, the way conflicts arise and scores get settled, the way organizational goals get formed. Underlying much of the writing in the two orientations, with the exception of a few theorists like Selznick, Follett, and Barnard, is a machine conception of organization and possibly a belief that if only a sound structure could be constructed, trouble-free organizational processes would follow.

There is a subtle but important difference between the two orientations with respect to organizational goals. Weber outlined the design of bureaucracy he considered best for efficient achievement of whatever goals a bureaucracy set for itself. Indeed, he was thinking primarily of public service organizations such as government departments and agencies. Although a good many of the ideas of the principles of management writers came from their study of traditional military or religious institutions, their focus was clearly the business firm, and the preeminent goal was the *managerial* one of profit, not the social goal of public service.

This focus has had important consequences. The management process theorists have quickly caught on to insights and research findings that promised to work—human relations in management, ideas about profit decentralization, management by objectives, and others. The bureaucracy researchers have been, by contrast, less interested in what works (partly because it is always difficult to assess what works in public service type organizations) and more interested in developing theoretical models of organizations and doing systematic organizational research. One cannot help but notice the rigor with which sociological research on organizations has been pressed and the sloppiness—but operating relevance—of much of the research of the management process theorists.

Evolution of Theory

Bureaucracy researchers as well as management process researchers have been moving towards a comparative, contingency view of organizations. Though both started with universalistic conceptions of organization, both now recognize the obvious fact of vast organizational differences. Both recognize that the explanation for these differences may lie in environmental or task differences. This stream of thought, called contingency organization theory, will be examined in a later chapter.

Questions for Organizational Analysis

The two orientations provide somewhat different sets of questions for organizational analysis and for further development of organization theory. These may most conveniently be shown in a tabular form (see Table 4–4).

SUMMARY

People had ideas about organizations and their management in ancient times. The Appendix shows the evolution of thinking about how organizations are or should be managed from those times to the present day.

Modern organization theory began with the work of Max Weber, who wrote about bureaucracy as an ideal-type organizational form. Frederick

TABLE 4–4
Questions for Theory and for Analyzing an Organization

	Questions for organization theory	*Questions for analyzing an organization*
Bureaucracy school	What are the properties of an efficient organization?	What are the structural strengths and weaknesses of the organization?
	What different forms of bureaucracy are there? What are the environmental and technological determinants of these forms?	What kind of a bureaucracy is the organization? What factors made it assume this form?
	What are the anticipated and unanticipated consequences of each form of bureaucracy?	What anticipated and unanticipated consequences have this form had?
Management process school	What are the principles of efficient management?	What are the principles that the management of the organization tries to use? Do they make sense?
	What are the functions of management?	How does the organization's management fulfill its functions? How well?
	Are the principles and functions of management universal or culture bound?	Are there other principles or other ways of discharging functions that could make better sense?
	What managerial functions become strategically important at different stages of an organization's growth?	What managerial functions are currently strategic? Which ones are likely to become strategic in the future?

Taylor and Henri Fayol about the same time founded the principles of management or management process school. The human relations movement was founded about 1930. The administrative decision-making school was founded in the forties, systems theory in the early fifties, the human resources orientation in the mid-fifties, and the contingency theory in the late fifties.

Weber described the properties of bureaucracy as the use of technical competence, division of labor and specialization, hierarchy of authority, rules and standard procedures, specification of work duties and authority, recording of all administrative acts, impersonality.

The response to Weber was threefold. One response was that bureaucracy is not really a workable organizational form because of the harmful unanticipated consequences of its properties. Another reaction was to show that there are, in reality, many different kinds of bureaucracy. A third response was to compare superficially different organizational forms and find real similarities and differences among them.

The principles of management (or management process) school is oriented to the study of principles of effective management and to the study of the domain of management—namely, planning, organizing, leading, controlling, and coordinating. A series of executives such as Fayol, Mooney, Urwick, Barnard, Sloan, and Brown have made valuable contributions to this school. This school has been criticized for inadequate empirical work, the propounding of universal principles of management on flimsy evidence, and an oversimplified description of the management process. Comparative management and international management are important extensions of this school. These tend to take a more conditional view of management functions.

Both the bureaucracy and the management process schools stress heavily the importance of structural variables and underemphasize the importance of personality variables. They view human beings as essentially reasonable and pliable. Both schools have been moving gradually toward a comparative, contingency view of structures and processes. The questions that these schools prompt for further development of theory and for the analysis of an organization are indicated in Table 4–4.

Stop

SUGGESTED READINGS

Claude S. George, Jr., *The History of Management Thought* (Englewood Cliffs, N. J.: Prentice-Hall, 1972). More emphasis on the developments in management than on organization theory. Traces sources of modern ideas to ancient times.

Tom Lupton, *Management and the Social Sciences*, 2nd ed. (Harmondsworth, Middlesex, England: Penguin Books, 1971).

Joseph L. Massie, *Essentials of Management*, 2nd ed. (Englewood Cliffs, N. J.: Prentice-Hall, 1971).

D. S. Pugh, "Modern Organization Theory: A Psychological and Sociological Study," *Psychological Bulletin*, Vol. 66 (1966), pp. 235–51. A fairly sophisticated account of its evolution.

QUESTIONS FOR ANALYSIS

1 Are there any differences in planning, organizing, leading, controlling, and coordinating between a restaurant and a food-processing firm? Between a general hospital and General Motors? How does the general hospital as a bureaucracy differ from General Motors as a bureaucracy?

2 During a stroll through the plant, the foreman told the visitor, "We were proud of our safety record in this plant. A year ago, on the recommendation of a management consultant we set up a separate safety department in the personnel office. Since, accidents have gone up a quarter." Why?

3   The study of the Egyptian government through the periods of the Old Kingdom, the Middle Kingdom, and the New Empire provides us with illustrations of their recognition of the principle of control of an extended operation through a centralized organization.

They first established in their empire a loosely decentralized form of government. From 2160 to 1788 B.C. the government was so highly decentralized that the tax commission was the only real tie between the central government and the sub-states. The head of each of these states, of course, owed his loyalty to the Pharaoh. However, control was so remote that these states could easily be compared to the feudal estates of middle European history.

The rulers of the New Empire period, beginning around 1600 B.C. began recentralizing by means of a military take-over. Since it was a military take-over, the officers of the army stepped into administrative positions and reorganized the central government. This centralization placed all the land into the hands of the royal officials with the Pharaoh at the head. Authority was centralized in the Pharaoh who delegated local authority to the territories through governors or mayors appointed by the central government. The new governors did not operate independently, as did the governors of the Old Kingdom, but merely carried out the directives of the Pharaoh. The army was maintained by the central government and taxes were collected by it. To aid him, the Pharaoh had a prime minister who actually took part in administering the state, making frequent inspections of the territories. . . .

Later during the New Empire (1530–1050 B.C.) the provincial governments of the Old Empire completely disappeared, and the royal power became real as well as titular. The centralization of the government was accomplished during the rule of the Hyksos, who drove out the foreign invaders in the provinces and assumed complete control. The king thereby came to own all the property in Egypt and to exact an annual rental payment from the country, usually 20 percent, and in the form of grain.[58]

What forms of control did the Egyptian central government exercise during the different phases of history? Why?

4   The Dashman Company was a large concern making many types of equipment for the armed forces of the United States. It had over 20 plants, located in the central part of the country, whose purchasing procedures had never been completely coordinated. In fact, the head office of the company had encouraged each of the plant managers to operate with their staffs as separate independent units in most matters. Late in 1940, when it began to

appear that the company would face increasing difficulty in securing certain essential raw materials, Mr. Manson, the company's president, appointed an experienced purchasing executive, Mr. Post, as vice president in charge of purchasing, a position especially created for him. Mr. Manson gave Mr. Post wide latitude in organizing his job, and he assigned Mr. Larson as Mr. Post's assistant. Mr. Larson had served the company in a variety of capacities for many years, and knew most of the plant executives personally. Mr. Post's appointment was announced through the formal channels usual in the company, including a notice in the house organ published by the company.

One of Mr. Post's first decisions was to begin immediately to centralize the company's purchasing procedure. As a first step he decided that he would require each of the executives who handled purchasing in the individual plants to clear with the head office all purchase contracts which they made in excess of $10,000. He felt that if the head office was to do any coordinating in a way that would be helpful to each plant and to the company as a whole, he must be notified that the contracts were being prepared at least a week before they were to be signed. He talked his proposal over with Mr. Manson, who presented it to his board of directors. They approved the plan.

Although the company made purchases throughout the year, the beginning of its peak buying season was only three weeks away at the time this new plan was adopted. Mr. Post prepared a letter to be sent to the 20 purchasing executives of the company. The letter follows:

Dear ———

The board of directors of our company has recently authorized a change in our purchasing procedures. Hereafter, each of the purchasing executives in the several plants of the company will notify the vice president in charge of purchasing of all contracts in excess of $10,000 which they are negotiating at least a week in advance of the date on which they are to be signed.

I am sure that you will understand that this step is necessary to coordinate the purchasing requirements of the company in these times when we are facing increasing difficulty in securing essential supplies. This procedure should give us in the central office the information we need to see that each plant secures the optimum supply of materials. In this way the interests of each plant and of the company as a whole will best be served.

Yours very truly,

Mr. Post showed the letter to Mr. Larson and invited his comments. Mr. Larson thought the letter an excellent one, but suggested that, since Mr. Post had not met more than a few of the purchasing executives, he might like to visit all of them and take the matter up with each one of them per-

sonally. Mr. Post dismissed the idea at once, because, as he said, he had
so many things to do at the head office that he could not get away for a
trip. Consequently he had the letters sent out over his signature.

During the two following weeks replies came in from all except a few
plants. Although a few executives wrote at greater length, the following reply
was typical:

> Dear Mr. Post,
>
> Your recent communication in regard to notifying the head office a
> week in advance of our intention to sign contracts has been received.
> This suggestion seems a most practical one. We want to assure you
> that you can count on our cooperation.
>
> Yours very truly,

During the next six weeks the head office received no notices from any
plant that contracts were being negotiated. Executives in other departments
who made frequent trips to the plants reported that the plants were busy,
and the usual routines for that time of year were being followed.[59]

Why isn't Mr. Post getting any advance notices of contracts over $10,000?
Are any of the management functions discharged by Mr. Post in conflict
here?

Appendix

The Managerial and Organizational Continuum[60]

Approximate year B.C.	Individual or ethnic group	Major managerial or organizational contributions
4000	Egyptians	Recognized need for planning, organizing, and controlling.
2700	Egyptians	Recognized need for honesty or fair play in management; therapy interview—"get it off your chest."
2600	Egyptians	Decentralization in organization.
2000	Egyptians	Recognized need for written word in requests. Use of staff advice.
1800	Hammurabi (Babylon)	Use of witnesses and writing for control; establishment of minimum wage; recognition that responsibility cannot be shifted.
1491	Hebrews	Concepts of organization; scalar principle; exception principle.
600	Nebuchadnezzar (Babylon)	Production control and wage incentives.
500	Mencius (China)	Recognized need for systems and standards.

Approximate year B.C.	Individual or ethnic group	Major managerial or organizational contributions
400	Socrates (Greece)	Enunciation of universality of management.
	Cyrus (Persia)	Recognized need for human relations; use of motion study, layout, and materials handling.
	Plato (Greece)	Principle of specialization enunciated.
321	Kautilya (India)	Science and art of statecraft.
175	Cato (Rome)	Use of job descriptions.
A.D.		
20	Jesus (Judea)	Unity of command; Golden Rule; human relations.
284	Diocletian (Rome)	Delegation of authority.
900	Alfarabi (Arab)	Listed traits of a leader.
1436	Arsenal of Venice (Venetians)	Cost accounting; checks and balances for control; numbering of inventories, parts; interchangeability of parts; use of assembly line technique; use of personnel management; standardization of parts; inventory control; cost control.
1525	Niccolo Machiavelli (Italy)	Reliance on mass consent principle; recognized need for cohesiveness in organization; enunciated leadership qualities; described political tactics.
1767	Sir James Steuart (Britain)	Source of authority theory; impact of automation; differentiation between managers and workers based on specialization and comparative advantages.
1776	Adam Smith (Britain)	Application of principle of specialization to manufacturing workers; control concepts.
1799	Eli Whitney (U.S.)	Scientific method; use of cost accounting and quality control; applied interchangeable parts concept; recognized span of management.
1800	James Watt Matthew Boulton (Britain)	Standard operating procedures; specifications; work methods; planning; incentive wages; standard times; standard data; employee Christmas parties; bonuses announced at Christmas; mutual employee insurance society; use of audits.
1810	Robert Owen (Britain)	Recognized and applied need for personnel practices; assumed responsibility for training workers; introduced clean row homes for workers.
1832	Charles Babbage (Britain)	Scientific approach emphasized; specialization emphasized; division of labor; motion and time study; cost accounting; effect of various colors on employee efficiency.

Approximate year A.D.	Individual or ethnic group	Major managerial or organizational contributions
1856	Daniel C. McCallum (U.S.)	Use of organization chart to show management structure; application of systematic management to railways.
1886	Henry Metcalfe (U.S.)	Art of management; science of administration.
1900	Frederick W. Taylor (U.S.)	Scientific management; systems applications; personnel management; need for cooperation between labor and management; high wages; equal division between labor and management; functional organization; the exception principle applied to the shop; cost system; methods study; time study; definition of scientific management; emphasis on management's job; emphasis on research, standards, planning, control, and cooperation.
1909	Max Weber (Germany)	Listed the characteristics of bureaucracies.
1916	Henri Fayol (France)	First complete theory of management; functions of management; principles of management; recognized need for management to be taught in schools.
1923	Oliver Sheldon (U.S.)	Developed a philosophy of management; principles of management.
1927	Elton Mayo (U.S.)	Recognized the importance of group affiliation and group dynamics in the functioning of organizations.
1930	Mary P. Follett (U.S.)	Managerial philosophy based on individual motivation; management as a group process; usefulness of conflict.
1931	James D. Mooney (U.S.)	Principles of organization recognized as universal.
1937	Talcott Parsons (U.S.)	Viewed structures of organization in terms of the social functions they facilitated.
1938	Chester I. Barnard (U.S.)	Theory of organization; functions of the executive; management as a cooperative process; need for communication; the notion that authority is delegated upwards rather than downwards.
1940	Robert Merton (U.S.)	The molding of the human personality by work in bureaucracies.
1943	Lyndall Urwick (Britain)	Collection, consolidation, and correlation of principles of management.
1943	Philip Selznick (U.S.)	Theory of organization; nonformal aspects of the organization.

Approximate year A.D.	Individual or ethnic group	Major managerial or organizational contributions
1947	Rensis Likert and Chris Argyris (U.S.)	Placed emphasis on psychology, social psychology, and research in human relations in organization theory; emphasized the incompatibility of human needs with rigid organizational requirements.
1947	Herbert Simon (U.S.)	Viewed management as decision-making; emphasized the limited rationality of decision makers.
1951	Eric Trist and K. W. Bamforth (Britain)	Viewed the organization as a social, psychological, and techno-economic system.
1952	Ernest Dale (U.S.)	Comparative management.
1954	Peter Ducker (U.S.)	Enunciated management by objectives.
1954	Alvin Gouldner (U.S.)	Described the dysfunctional consequences of bureaucratic rules and impersonality.
1958	Herbert Simon and James March (U.S.)	Studied cognitive aspects of human behavior in organizations; viewed decision-making as an identifiable, observable, and measurable process; viewed organization structure as resulting from the cognitive properties of human beings.
1958	Joan Woodward (Britain)	Studied the relationship between organizational structure and the production technology.
1960	Douglas McGregor (U.S.)	Enunciated Theory X and Theory Y.
1960	Wilfred Brown (Britain)	Viewed the organization as an executive, representative, and legislative system.
1961	Amitai Etzioni (U.S.)	Comparative analysis of organizations; classification of organizations on the basis of the mechanisms used to control the organizational rank and file.
1961	Rensis Likert (U.S.)	Described an effective organizational design based on participative management and "linking pins."
1961	Tom Burns and G. M. Stalker (Britain)	Identified two contrasting management styles, the organic and the mechanistic.
1962	Richard Hall (U.S.)	Described structural variations within bureaucracies.
1963	Richard Cyert and James March (U.S.)	Wrote a behavioral analysis of decision-making in firms.
1963	D. Braybrooke and C. Lindblom (U.S.)	Behavioral analysis of decision-making in political institutions.
1964	Michel Crozier (France)	Examined the cultural and political roots of bureaucratic practices.

Approxi-mate year A.D.	Individual or ethnic group	Major managerial or organizational contributions
1965	Richard Farmer and Barry Richman (U.S.)	Comprehensive model for a comparative, cross-cultural study of management.
1966	Daniel Katz and Robert Kahn (U.S.)	Synthesized the systems and psychological frameworks in the study of organizations.
1967	Charles Perrow (U.S.)	Framework for the comparative analysis of organizations based on technology.
1967	Paul Lawrence and Jay Lorsch (U.S.)	Refined the contingency theory of organizations through their research.
1967	James Thompson (U.S.)	Organizational structure as a function of its environment and its technology.
1969	The Aston Group (Britain)	Large-scale studies of organizational structure; related properties of organizational structure to size, technology, and so on.

Footnotes to Chapter Four

[1] As quoted in Claude S. George, Jr., *The History of Management Thought*, p. 6.

[2] *Ibid.*, p. 12.

[6] *Ibid.*, p. 13.

[4] *Ibid.*, pp. 15–16.

[5] *Ibid.*, p. 31.

[6] *Ibid.*, p. 55.

[7] Max Weber, *The Theory of Social and Economic Organization*, tr. 1947.

[8] Quoted in Ernest Dale, *Readings in Management*, p. 177.

[9] Phillip Selznick, "An Approach to a Theory of Bureaucracy."

[10] Alvin Gouldner, *Patterns of Industrial Bureaucracy*.

[11] Chris Argyris, *Personality and Organization*, 1957.

[12] F. Herzberg, *Work and the Nature of Man*.

[13] George Strauss, "The Personality Vs. Organization Theory."

[14] Richard Hall, "The Concept of Bureaucracy: An Empirical Assessment."

[15] Richard Hall, "Intraorganizational Structural Variation: Application of the Bureaucratic Model."

[16] William A. Rushing, "The Effects of Industry Size and Division of Labor on Administration."

[17] Arthur Stinchcombe, "Bureaucratic and Craft Administration of Production: A Comparative Study."

[18] D. S. Pugh, D. J. Hickson, and C. R. Hinings, "An Empirical Taxonomy of Work Organizations." Another taxonomy of bureaucracies based on empirical work in Israel is provided by Y. Samuel and B. Mannheim, "A Multidimensional Approach Toward a Typology of Bureaucracies."

[19] Amitai Etzioni, *Modern Organizations*, Ch. 6; see also Amitai Etzioni, ed., *A Sociological Reader on Complex Organizations*, 2nd ed., Part 3, for empirical studies.

[20] Richard H. Hall, J. Eugene Haas, and Norman J. Johnson, "An Examination of the Blau-Scott and Etzioni Typologies."

[21] Peter Blau and Richard Scott, *Formal Organizations*.

[22] T. Burns and G. M. Stalker, *The Management of Innovation*.

[23] Frederick W. Taylor, *The Principles of Scientific Management*.

[24] Henri Fayol, *General and Industrial Management*, tr. by Storrs.

[25] James D. Mooney and Alan Reiley, *Onward Industry!*, p. 13.

[26] *Ibid.*, p. 26.

[27] *Ibid.*, p. 34.

[28] See H. C. Metcalf and L. Urwick, eds., *Dynamic Administration*.

[29] See Burns and Stalker, *op. cit.*

[30] L. Urwick, *The Elements of Administration*. See pp. 119–29 for a list of his principles.

[31] Chester I. Barnard, *Functions of the Executive*.

[32] Alfred P. Sloan, Jr., *My Years with General Motors*.

[33] Wilfred Brown, *Explorations in Management*.

[34] See H. Koontz and C. O'Donnell, *Principles of Management*, and William H. Newman and Charles F. Summer, *The Process of Management*.

[35] Ernest Dale, *Planning and Developing the Company Organization Structure*.

[36] Joan Woodward, *Technology and Organization*.

[37] Chris Argyris, *Integrating the Individual and the Organization*.

[38] Herzberg, *op. cit.*

[39] Burns and Stalker, *op. cit.*, p. 92.

[40] See Marvin Dunnette, *Personnel Selection and Placement*, for a summary of the research on the subject.

[41] See Jay Galbraith, "Environmental and Technological Determinants of Organizational Design."

[42] See John Child, "Organization Structure and Strategies of Control."

[43] See, for example, Arnold Tannenbaum, *Social Psychology of the Work Organization*, and Keith Davis, *Human Relations at Work*.

[44] Newman and Summer, *op. cit.*, p. 11.

[45] For a good review of findings on leadership, see D. Krech, R. Crutchfield, and E. Ballachey, *Individual in Society*, Ch. 12. See also Elmer Burack, *Organizational Analysis*, Ch. 9, for a review of the evidence from an applied management viewpoint.

[46] Frank Fiedler, "A Contingency Model of Leadership Effectiveness."

[47] Newman and Summer, *op. cit.*, p. 12.

[48] See P. N. Khandwalla, "Control Systems: What's Best for Your Profitability?"

[49] See, for example, V. F. Ridgway, "Dysfunctional Consequences of Performance Measurements."

[50] Peter Drucker, *Managing for Results*.

[51] Henry Mintzberg, *The Nature of Managerial Work*.

[52] Dale, *op. cit.*

[53] Joseph L. Massie, *Essentials of Management*, pp. 39–40.

[54] Anant Negandhi and Benjamin S. Prasad, *Comparative Management*, pp. 20–21, and 23.

[55] See *ibid.*, Appendix A.

[56] *Ibid.*, pp. 144–47.

[57] See Phillip Selznick, "Foundations of the Theory of Organization."

[58] George, Jr., *op. cit.*, pp. 7–8.

[59] G. W. Dalton, Paul Lawrence, and Larry Greiner, *Organizational Change and Development*, pp. 13–14.

[60] Based partly on George, Jr., *op. cit.*, pp. vii–viii.

5

"In great matters, men behave as they are expected to; in little ones, as they would naturally."
Chamfort

The Behavioral Orientations in Organization Theory

INTRODUCTION

In the previous chapter we examined two orientations in organization theory that heavily emphasize organizational structure—namely, the bureaucracy orientation and the principles of management orientation. We noted that they underemphasize the human element influencing the behavior of organizations. In this chapter we examine three orientations that are strongly behavioral in their analysis of how organizations operate and should operate. One is the human relations orientation, which gathered momentum in the 1930's. The second is the closely allied human resources orientation, which took root in the mid-1950's. The third is the "bounded rationality" orientation of the Carnegie theorists, which originated in the late 1940's.

These three orientations are behavioral in the sense that they start with a fuller view of human nature and behavior than the structural orientations that were examined in the previous chapter. Yet they do not ignore organizational structure. Indeed, each of these behavioral orientations has important things to say about the structure of organizations. But they tend to view the structure of organizations as being shaped by human needs, abilities, and

176

limitations, and they see the structure, in turn, as shaping the behavior of those that work in organizations. Besides, they have a strong interest in the *processes* that go on in organizations, such as the formation of cliques and coalitions and the development of new performance programs.

There are some important differences among these three orientations, which will be amplified later. For the moment we may note that the human relations orientation gives primacy to the social and ego needs of people. It makes its greatest contributions to the understanding of what effective leadership is and to the delineation of the network of nonformal communication patterns and friendship relations known as the nonformal organizational structure. The human resources orientation leans heavily on full utilization of the human potential in organizations. It has made its greatest contribution to conflict management, the management of change, and the development of human resources. The Carnegie theorists have emphasized particularly the cognitive limitations of human beings and have drawn the implications of these limitations for decision-making and program development in organizations.

THE HUMAN RELATIONS ORIENTATION

Introduction

The attempt to measure human productive behavior scientifically, with a view to establishing standards of performance—an attempt that is linked inseparably with the name of Frederick Winslow Taylor—had several consequences. One was scientific management, followed by industrial engineering, human engineering, and operations research. The other was the human relations movement. The latter emerged from a serendipitous discovery by Mayo and Dickson of group processes affecting motivation and productivity in what was a straightforward industrial engineering project (a study of the effect of varying illumination on output) at the Western Electric Company.[1]

The human relations movement has several related strands (Figure 5–1). One is group dynamics, or the study of how groups function and how they affect human behavior in organizations. Another is the study of the nonformal organization—that is, of the activities, norms, relationships, and patterns of communication (over and above those sanctioned by the organizational hierarchy) that arise spontaneously in organizations. A third is the style of supervision and management, with particular emphasis on being employee oriented and participative.

FIGURE 5–1
The Main Strands of the Human Relations Orientation

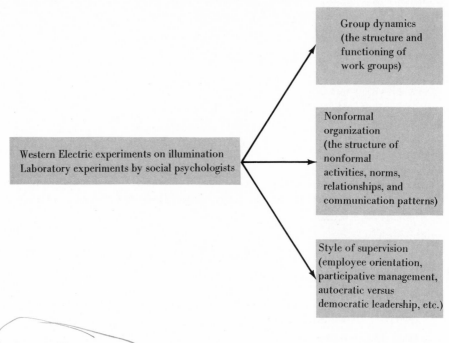

Group Dynamics

The experience at the Hawthorne plant of Western Electric Company had a profound impact on the thinking of organizational researchers. Productivity went up despite reduction in illumination. The researchers who conducted the experiment felt that group processes had something to do with this curious phenomenon. They felt that the subjects valued their membership in the work group, and since the work group had high performance norms, its members worked hard even in physically uncongenial surroundings. In other parts of the company, the researchers uncovered group pressures that depressed the productivity of group members.[2]

From the simpleminded notion that all one has to do for greater efficiency is to design jobs and equipment very carefully and then train employees to do the jobs, there was an advance to the notion that the work group has many unanticipated effects on the employee who works in it. The work group is a source of satisfaction for its members. It satisfies their social needs, such as the need to be wanted by others, the need for friendship, the need to communicate with fellow beings. It also satisfies their security needs (the group can protect an individual against a hostile supervisor) and knowledge needs (the group can help one another solve their on-the-job problems). Since the individual needs the group, the group can strongly affect the behavior of the individual. Thus, whatever the incentive system, if there is work group pressure to go slow, the chances are that each person will. By the same token, whatever be the individual's inclinations, if the norm of the work group is high productivity, the chances are that the individual will strive to produce at a high level.

The workings of the work group, or "group dynamics" as it came to be known among social and industrial psychologists, became a focus of intensive inquiry. Much research was done in field sites as well as in the laboratory. Cartwright and Lippitt, summarizing the wisdom about groups, made the following points:[3]

1 *Groups have a psychological reality.* Group decisions may produce changes in individual behavior much larger than those that normally result from attempts to change the behavior of individuals as isolated individuals.

2 *Groups are inevitable and ubiquitous* and are found in all reaches of society.

3 *Groups mobilize powerful forces* that produce effects of the utmost importance to individuals. Such variables as the extent of interaction within a group, the degree of group cohesiveness, identification of members with the group, and competition with other groups affect the strength of the group's pressure on the individual members and ultimately influence the choices each considers and the decisions each makes.[4]

4 *Groups can produce both good and bad consequences.* If cohesive groups in work situations can be induced to accept the goals of management, such as high productivity, low wastage, and high quality, then, as Seashore has shown, productivity of individuals in the group will tend to be high because of group pressure.[5] But, if the cohesive group is set against management objectives, this group cohesiveness will work against management. A group can be a more productive problem solver than individuals acting alone, because of the interaction within the group, the examination of many alternatives, and the convergence of many skills on the problem situation. However, a group can turn into a cabal, intolerant of any deviant opinion or dissonant information, and this can lead to disaster.[6]

5 *A correct understanding of group dynamics can help us enhance desirable consequences and inhibit undesirable ones,* for knowledge is power, power to modify—and to manipulate—behavior.

FIGURE 5–2
The Linking Pin Function

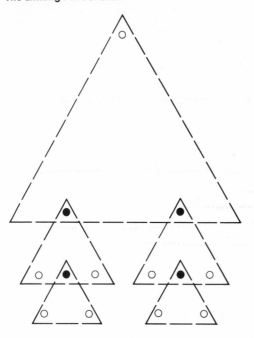

NOTE: Each circle in the figure represents a group member. The triangles made by the dashed lines represent groups. The linking pin is designated by the dark circle. The linking pin need not be the formal leader of the group.

Efforts to understand groups better, spurred by Kurt Lewin, the eminent social psychologist, led to a great many studies of such aspects of their functioning as leadership, communication within the group, intergroup relations, morale within the group, the group's productivity and its determinants, and group problem-solving.[7]

From the point of view of organizational design, the implications of group dynamics have led Likert to develop the idea of the *linking pin*. For the proper functioning of the organization, it is necessary to have, not only cohesive work groups, but work groups whose goals are mutually consistent and consistent with the goals of the management of the organization. This, Likert feels, can be achieved by having groups linked together by competent, trained group coordinators, or linking pins, with membership in more than one group (see Figure 5–2).[8] These linking pins communicate the consensually determined preferences of one group to the members of any other groups that have work interface with the first group. In turn, the preferences of the other groups are communicated by the linking pin to the first group. The linking pin function is quite important because in large organizations interfacing groups often experience conflicts due to mutually incompatible goals as well as to stereotypes and selective perception. The linking pin performs three functions. (a) He helps the group achieve consensus on an issue. (b) He communicates this consensus to the other interfacing group or groups of which he is a member. (c) Finally, in case of intergroup conflict, he attempts to facilitate the resolution of the conflict. His task is unenviable. In the event of conflict, he is pulled in opposite directions. If he sides with one group, his other group may accuse him of betrayal. A study by Lawrence and Lorsch indicates that linking pins who share the norms of interfacing groups, or whose norms are intermediate between the norms of interfacing groups, and who can speak the lingo of the interfacing groups are likely to be more effective than those whose norms are much closer to those of one of the interfacing groups or who are not familiar with the special terminology employed by one of the interfacing groups.[9]

The Nonformal Organization

The organization as shown on the organization chart or described in official manuals is a very pale version of the living organization. Consider the following brief descriptions of the business faculty of a university. The first describes its formal structure, the second the nonformal relationships and norms of its members.

The formal organization. The business faculty consists of the dean, forty-five professors, twelve secretaries, and an associate dean. The professors are allocated to five departments, those covering organization behavior, managerial economics, marketing, finance and quantitative methods. Each group elects a chairman who holds office for two years. The chairmen are responsible for drawing up the departmental budgets and for recommending hirings, firings, and promotions within their departments. In addition, there are several faculty committees, one for research, another for promotion and tenure, a third for student affairs and admissions, and a fourth for program evaluation and development. Although in practice decision-making is considerably decentralized, the final authority for all administrative decisions resides in the dean, while the final authority for all academic decisions resides in the faculty as a whole.

The nonformal organization. Although the dean is the head of the faculty, two other individuals wield greater power. One of them is an old-timer who has been with the faculty for over twenty years and has had a hand in hiring practically everybody else in the faculty. He is a good friend of the dean and his principal counselor. Another is a younger professor who is academically very competent. He has earned many laurels and has a fine reputation in his field. He is the leader of the younger block in the faculty. This group is somewhat unhappy with the old-timers in the faculty, whom they perceive as obsolete and conservative. In decisions involving faculty promotions, the dean is seen by this group to favor the old-timers. The departmental heads vary a great deal in their style. The head of the managerial economics group is quite autocratic. He conducts his meetings in a "businesslike" fashion and, after listening to his colleagues, announces his decisions by saying, "The consensus appears to be such and such." The head of the organizational behavior group is warm and friendly but a bit ineffective in dealing with an obstreperous flock. The head of the quantitative department is very concerned about "sound" structures and "proper" procedures. The head of the finance department prefers a policy of laissez faire. Departmental loyalties are fairly to extremely strong. These loyalties seem to be exacerbated by a reduction in the operating budget due to financial stringency. Indeed, there is a fair degree of hostility between the organizational behavior group and the quantitative departments, the former viewing the members of the latter as engaging in irrelevant mathematical exercises. The members of the quantitative department refer scornfully to the members of the organizational behavior group as "those charlatans." At faculty meetings the votes are more and more along departmental lines. Indeed there is increasing pressure to reconstitute faculty committees so they consist of representatives of departments rather than of the dean's appointees. Officially, excellence in teaching, research, or administration is rewarded. Unofficially, research and contributions to the administration of the faculty seem to be weighted more than teaching ability in promoting faculty members.

Just as the organization has a structure of official roles, procedures, rules, departments, it also has a *structure* of unofficial, nonformal communication patterns, relationships, and norms.[10] In studying an organization, one can (and should) ask the following questions:

1 Which members of an organization get along well together, and which do not? Which prefer to work with one another, and which do not? The science of sociometry has been developed to study patterns in these types of choice.

2 Who converses most commonly with whom? How far do the formal lines of communication coincide with the nonformal lines of communi-

cation? What is the content of nonformal communication? How far do rumors supplement formal announcements?

3 Who are the informal leaders? What accounts for their popularity? What kinds of pressure do these leaders exert on the administration?

4 Are there strong nonformal norms and traditions that govern who is hired, under what circumstances people are fired, and what constitutes proper supervision, what is a fair day's work, and other such matters?

From the point of view of organizational design, one may ask: Is it desirable to permit the growth of the nonformal organization? The short answer is that it is impracticable to prevent the growth of the nonformal organizations, just as it is impracticable to have an organization without at least some formal structure. The formal organization arises because the organizations are set up to achieve some goals. The nonformal organization arises because the formally designed organization is insufficient in meeting the very human needs of its members for support, friendship, social interaction, and so on. Clearly, what is harmful is a punitive or harsh formal structure that gives rise to an opposing nonformal structure—a nonformal structure that works at cross-purposes to the goals for which the organization is set up. If the formal design is sensible and humane, the probability of a contrary nonformal structure is likely to be minimized. In any case, it may be desirable for key decision makers periodically to *find out* what the nonformal structure is so that the formal as well as the nonformal structure may be intelligently modified. The Michigan Survey Research Center has developed a program for gathering and feeding back to the organization information about such important aspects of the nonformal organization as the state of morale, intergroup or interdepartmental conflict and cooperation, and so on.[11]

The Style of Supervision

Following the experiments at the Western Electric Company, the luminaries of the human relations movement came to believe in the efficacy of employee-oriented supervision. If the employees could be made to feel that their opinions mattered and that they could communicate them freely to their superiors, and if they realized that management cared for their needs, then, the argument went, they could reciprocate by giving loyalty to the company and by working more productively. Many courses for training supervisors in human relations came to be marketed. The following is a very short "Course."

A Short Course in Human Relations

The Six Most Important Words:
"I admit I made a mistake"
The Five Most Important Words:
"you did a good job"
The Four Most Important Words:
"what is your opinion?"
The Three Most Important Words:
"if you please"
The Two Most Important Words:
"thank you"
The One Most Important Word:
"we"
The Least Important Word:
"I"[12]

A large amount of research has been done on topics related to the style of supervision. In brief, the findings are:

1 One of the findings of the famed Ohio State Leadership Studies was that leadership seems to consist of two main dimensions. One is called "initiating structure." The other is called "consideration."[13] Initiating structure means directing and organizing activities, such as by the leader making his attitudes clear to the subordinates, by his making sure that his role is understood by the members, by his maintaining definite standards of performance. Consideration means the leader expresses concern and sympathy for subordinates by, for example, finding time to listen to their complaints, being friendly and approachable, and looking out for their welfare. A leader high on the dimensions of initiating structure "organizes and defines the relationship between himself and the members of his crew. He tends to define the role which he expects each member of the crew to assume, and endeavors to establish well-defined patterns of organization, channels of communication, and ways of getting jobs done."[14] On the other hand, a leader high on consideration is "indicative of friendship, mutual trust, respect, and warmth in the relations" with subordinates.[15]

2 Neither of these dimensions seems to be related unequivocally to a supervisor's performance on the job. When management is asked to rate the performance of supervisors, initiating structure tends to be correlated positively with the performance of supervisors as judged by management. In other words, the higher the supervisor's score on initiating structure, the higher the performance rating that supervisor is

likely to receive from management. The relationship between consideration and supervisor's performance on the job as rated by management tends to be either negative or inconsequential.[16] However, when the supervisor's proficiency on the job is rated by subordinates, the tendency is for such ratings of performance to be correlated with the supervisor's score not only on initiating structure but on consideration.[17] Thus, the ability to provide structure in a work situation is more certainly necessary for *perceived* high performance than the ability to be considerate to subordinates.

3 The leadership dimension of consideration tends to be correlated with the morale of subordinates.[18] While there is no strong evidence that morale of employees is correlated with their productivity, high employee morale tends to be associated with low turnover and absenteeism.[19] It therefore stands to reason that a supervisor who is able and willing to provide a fair amount of direction to subordinates *and* show them a good deal of consideration (go to bat for them, listen empathetically to their problems and suggestions, etc.) *generally* speaking may be a more effective leader than one who emphasizes either only consideration or only structuring the work group's task.

4 Studies conducted by the University of Michigan's Institute for Social Research indicate that supervisors of high productivity sections practice a highly supportive employee-oriented style that has many of the same features as consideration. Furthermore, supervisors of low productivity sections practice an authoritarian, nonsupportive style. The supervisors of high productivity sections tend to practice general supervision, while those of low productivity sections tend to practice close supervision—that is to say, watch over every detail of the subordinates' work.[20] The problem with these findings is that it is not clear whether supportive and general supervision cause productivity of work groups to be high or vice versa. Both explanations are plausible. Supportive and general supervision may motivate grateful subordinates to put forward their best efforts. On the other hand, high productivity may cause the supervisor to relax and be congenial to the workers. Quite possibly, the causal arrow may go both ways. In other words, supportive and general supervision may be necessary for high productivity, but without high productivity supportive and general supervision may quickly evaporate.

5 Efforts to change supervisory behavior through human relations training have not been very successful.[21] In one study, though foremen showed an increase in the consideration dimension immediately after a training program, the amount of their consideration, as judged by their own subordinates, several months after the completion of training was lower than that of a control group of foremen who had undergone no human relations training![22] Further analysis indicated that for trained foremen to maintain high levels of consideration it was necessary for their supervisors to be high in the consideration dimension. The study suggests that unless behavioral or attitudinal change is reinforced at work, it is likely to be transient. Cognitive change needs to be accompanied by an appropriate change in the system of rewards and sanctions to ensure the permanence of such change.

6 Participative management is a mode of democratic *decision-making*. It requires a substantial erosion of the power and status difference between superiors and subordinates. It implies decision-making by consensus or majority vote after a full discussion of all sides of an issue. A good deal of experimental and field research has been done on participative management.[23] The main findings are:

(a) Participatively managed or democratically led groups are more self-reliant than autocratically led groups, especially during the leader's temporary absence. Members of autocratically led groups exhibit greater apathy, dependence, frustration, and aggression toward the leader.[24]

(b) It is easier to change the beliefs and behavior of individuals when they are handled together and when they are allowed to participate in a group discussion than when they are merely told to change their beliefs and behavior.[25] A group discussion leads to a wider awareness of the issues and a feeling on the part of members of having participated in the making of decisions. A group position emerges from such a discussion and thus acts as a force for keeping individual members in line.

(c) Productivity may increase under a more participative style of management, but there is no clear evidence that the gains are greater than those under a more nonparticipative or authoritarian style of management. The evidence is stronger, however, that the organizational climate and morale change for the better should management become more participative and change for the worse should it become more authoritarian or nonparticipative.[26]

(d) Not all organizational members react favorably to participative management. Those with strongly authoritarian personalities react indifferently or negatively to participative management.[27]

(e) There is some evidence that the power-sharing characteristic of participative management increases not only the feeling of control of lower level employees but also the feeling of control of the management.[28] In nonparticipatively managed organizations the management has the authority to make decisions but not necessarily control over the *outcome* of its decisions. The latter depends to a great extent upon the cooperation extended by employees. In participatively managed organizations, the management forgoes some of its formal authority to make decisions but gains in exchange a greater assurance that the decisions made participatively will be implemented expeditiously because of employee cooperation.

Human Relations Orientation and Organization Theory

The human relations viewpoint by no means represents a comprehensive theory of what organizations are and how they function. But it does make some useful contributions to organization theory. These may be summarized as follows: The human factor in organizations is of the highest importance. The needs, feelings, beliefs, and attitudes of organizational members should be taken into account if we wish to understand how organizations operate, for they quite dramatically modify formally approved operations. They give rise to what is known as the nonformal organization. Of particular importance are ego needs and social needs. If these needs are satisfied, organizational members may reward the organization by higher productivity, lower absenteeism and turnover, and greater cooperation with management. Ego and social needs are likely to be satisfied by employee-oriented, group-centered, participative supervision and management. In securing improvements in organizational operations, the importance of group pressures on individual members should be recognized. A strategy of change should concentrate on achieving consensus within a relevant group as to the desirability and mechanics of change. This, too, calls for an employee-oriented, participative management. Since an organization consists of interfacing groups, it is necessary to have competent linking pins for integrating and coordinating the operations of the organization.

This theoretical perspective has given rise to some important notions about organizational design. These notions have come to their most complete flowering at the hands of Rensis Likert. Likert has described four models of organization design: the authoritative, the benevolent authoritative, the consultative, and the participative.[29] These models cover a number of important organizational functions, such as leadership, motivation, communication, interaction and influence, decision-making, goal setting, and control. The authoritative and the participative models offer the sharpest contrasts, with the benevolent authoritative being more similar to the authoritative than the participative, and the consultative being more similar to the participative and the authoritative. The key elements of the authoritative and the participative designs are reproduced in Table 5–1. Needless to say, Likert is totally in favor of the participative design and opposed to the authoritative design.

TABLE 5–1
Likert's Models of Organizational Design

	Authoritative	*Participative*
Leadership	Superiors have little or modest trust and confidence in subordinates; subordinates feel constrained in discussing job-related matters with their bosses; superiors seldom seek ideas and opinions of their subordinates in solving on-job problems	Superiors have trust and confidence in subordinates; subordinates feel free to discuss any job-related matters with their bosses; superiors always seek ideas and opinions of their subordinates in solving job-related problems
Motivation of organizational members	Threats, punishments, and rewards; responsibility for achieving organizational goals concentrated at upper management levels	Participatively designed reward system; participatively set goals and improvement programs; participative evaluation of progress; responsibility for achieving organizational goals shared by personnel at all levels
Communication	Little two-way communication; communications from superiors received with suspicion by subordinates; upward communication distorted by the desire to keep the boss happy; bosses have little knowledge of the problems faced by subordinates	Great deal of upward, downward, and horizontal communication; subordinates accept communications from above but feel free to question them; accurate upward communication; bosses aware of their subordinates' problems
Interaction and influence	Little and cautious interaction with superiors; little cooperative teamwork	Extensive, friendly interaction between superior and subordinates; great deal of cooperative teamwork

A Critique of Human Relations

The human relations orientation has been criticized on a number of counts. These may be briefly noted:

1 The assumption of the human relations orientation is that it is always possible to find a solution that satisfies everybody. But often there are sharp conflicts of interest between, say, workers and management, that are structural in character and not merely psychological. In a recession, a company may have to lay off 30 percent of its work force. No amount of participative management or employee-oriented supervision can sugarcoat this unpleasant reality. By creating false expectations in both management and employees, human relations may mask such conflicts

	Authoritative	Participative
Decision-making	Policy and many operating decisions made at the top; some formal delegation of authority to lower levels; lower level organizational members largely unaware of organizational problems; technical and professional knowledge used if available at higher levels or in formally designated staff groups; subordinates seldom involved in decisions related to their work; decision-making not designed to motivate the implementation of decisions	Decision-making done throughout the organization, integrated through interlinked groups; awareness of organizational problems throughout the organization; most of the technical and professional knowledge available in the organization used irrespective of where it is located; subordinates fully involved in decisions related to their work; decision-making designed to motivate the implementation of decisions
Goal setting	Goals set through the issuance of orders; goals generally are accepted overtly but resisted covertly	Goals generally established by group discussion and consensus; goals fully accepted overtly and covertly
Control	Control function concentrated at upper levels; informal organization (cliques, friendship groups, etc.) opposed to organizational goals; control reports used to police the organization, punish the stragglers, and reward the high producers	Widespread participation in the control function; formal and informal organization committed to organizational goals; control reports used not punitively but for self-guidance and coordinated problem-solving

for a while and cause a realistic solution to be temporarily evaded until the situation gets so bad that naked force is invoked to impose a solution.

2 Human relations in practice sometimes degenerate into mere manipulation. Consider the following example of an employee-oriented, participative manager quoted by Rensis Likert, the great votary of humane management:

One way in which we accomplish a high level of production is by letting people do the job the way they want to so long as they accomplish the objectives. I believe in letting them take time out from the monotony. Make them feel that they are something special, not just the run of the mill. As a matter of fact, I tell them if you feel that job is getting you down get away from it for a few minutes. . . . If you keep employees from feeling hounded, they are apt to put out the necessary effort to get the work done in the required time.

I never make any decisions myself. Oh, I guess I've made about two since I've been here. If people know their jobs I believe in letting them make decisions. I believe in delegating decision-making. Of course, if there's anything that affects the whole division, then the two assistant managers, the three section heads and sometimes the assistant section heads come in here and we discuss it. I don't believe in saying that this is the way it's going to be. After all, once supervision and management are in agreement there won't be any trouble selling the staff the idea.

My job is dealing with human beings rather than the work. It doesn't matter if I have anything to do with the work or not. The chances are that people will do a better job if you are really taking an interest in them. Knowing the names is important and helps a lot, but it's not enough. You really have to know each individual well, know what his problems are. Most of the time I discuss matters with employees at their desks rather than in the office. Sometimes I sit on a waste paper basket or lean on the files. It's all very informal. People don't seem to like to come into the office to talk.[30]

The above example illustrates the strengths and the weaknesses of the participative, human relations approach. "Make them feel that they are something special. . . ." That is good. But is it not also manipulative in intent, getting others to do what you want by flattering them? "I believe in letting them take time out from the monotony." Fine. But why have monotonous jobs? "Once supervision and management are in agreement there won't be any trouble selling the staff the idea." But what if the staff does not buy the idea? What does the manager do? "My job is dealing with human beings rather than with the work." Sounds great. But what happens when a job has to be done in a hurry and much depends on the accomplishment of the job? Would the manager take his chances with "letting people do the job the way they want to" or with letting anyone "get away from it for a few minutes"? Etzioni and others have hurled precisely these kinds of question at the practitioners of human relations in management.[31]

3 There is a tendency for the supporters of human relations to overemphasize the benefits of human relations and to underemphasize its costs. Moreover, there is no systematic theory as to the circumstances under which the benefits from the practice of human relations outweigh the costs or vice versa. How far, for example, can a platoon commander, under orders to capture a hill, practice human relations in the thick of battle? When decisions have to be made very quickly, when secrecy is important, when work is reduced to an unfailing routine, or when subordinates do not particularly care to be consulted, human relations with its expensive supervisory training and its somewhat leisurely process of decision-making, may be infeasible. Under opposite circumstances, the cost of human relations may be justifiably borne by the organization.

4 The human relations approach undervalues, often ignores, necessary managerial qualities other than initiating structure and consideration. Surely, initiative, drive, imagination, the ability to make tough decisions, resourcefulness, the ability to play politics are equally important attributes of a good leader.

5 The conception of the individual utilized by the human relations theorists overemphasizes the importance of social needs and need for recognition and support and underemphasizes the need for security and self-actualization. It practically ignores other aspects such as the human mind's limited information-processing and problem-solving abilities.

6 The human relations orientation demands from superiors a degree of goodness and a willingness to give up the exercise of power that is perhaps unrealistic. A desire for power is one of the main reasons people seek to become managers. Can these individuals realistically be expected to give up this desire permanently? Can the injunction to be good and kind survive in a competitive organizational world? As Machiavelli has pointed out, a person who wishes to make a profession of goodness will necessarily come to grief among so many who are not good!

THE HUMAN RESOURCES ORIENTATION

The Founders

If Likert and his associates seized on the bolstering of the individual's self-worth (an ego need) and social nature as a seemingly inexhaustible mine of motivated behavior, Douglas McGregor and his associates struck the gold mine of another human need, the need for self-actualization, and have been busily working it for its organizational and managerial implications. In a landmark book, McGregor outlined his famous Theory Y, counterposing it against an unsavory Theory X of an authoritarian, manipulative management and lazy, submissive workers.[32] McGregor argued that what we know about human behavior is inconsistent with the assumptions of Theory X but congruent with those of Theory Y. Under Theory Y, there is no differentiation between good, responsible managers and lazy, passive workers. All humans have the potential for seeking and accepting responsibility. People are not inherently lazy—the expenditure of energy in work is (or can be) as natural as play. We are all potentially capable of self-direction and self-control. Creativity is not as rare as is imagined. And there is great scope for utilizing the average person's intellectual potentialities in contemporary industrial life. As a practical consequence of Theory Y, McGregor proposed management by objectives, a system under which the subordinate takes the responsibility for setting his or her own objectives, with the help and collaboration—not supervision—of the superior. Supervisors, however, do not abdicate responsibility. In matters that they judge are within their province, they exercise authority, but after a full discussion with subordinates.

Chris Argyris, arguing in a similar vein as McGregor, has deplored the wastage of human resources in modern formal organizations. He has argued that organization people find themselves in an existential dilemma. Arriving in the organization unfettered and innocent, they find themselves in regulatory chains. The organization, through its principles of specialization, hierarchy, and impersonal controls, frustrates their individual needs for maturity, autonomy, responsibility, and the exercise of their gifts as human beings, and ultimately leaves them either impotent and passive, or actively, sometimes explosively, fighting the organization.[33] Argyris has suggested participative management, and an enlargement of the individual's job (to make it more interesting) as two ways out of the impasse. In recent years, he has turned to sensitivity training to educate management into greater interpersonal competence.[34]

Argyris has described six organizational properties, which, he says, determine whether organizational members get psychologically sicker or

TABLE 5–2

Argyris' Organizational Properties, Psychological Health, and Psychological Sickness

Organizational properties contributing to psychological sickness of organizational members	Organizational properties contributing to psychological health of organizational members
One part controls the whole (organization)—for example, in a hierarchical organization, the top management controls the rest of the organization	The whole is created and controlled through the *interrelationships* of all parts; the situational logic, not the whims of one part, guides the behavior of the whole
Awareness of plurality of parts but not of their relationship — specialization may cause this	Awareness of *patterns* of parts, of how various departments are linked together
Achieving objectives related to the parts (suboptimization)	Achieving objectives related to the whole organization
Inability to influence internally oriented core activities; internal core is the organizational structure, goals, processes, and so on (a rigid structure is what Argyris has in mind)	Ability of the organization as an organism to influence internally oriented core activities "it" desires; flexible organizational structure
Inability to influence externally oriented core activities—that is, activities aimed at the environment; an organization that feels fenced in by its environment	Ability of the organization as an organism to influence externally oriented core activities "it" desires; pro-active (as against a "reactive") organization
Nature of core activities influenced by the present only (shortsightedness)	Nature of core activities influenced by past, present, and future

healthier. For example, does one part of the organization (such as the management) control the whole? If so, psychological sickness (immaturity, aggression, alienation) is likely. If the functional interrelationship between the parts of the organization controls the whole, psychological health (maturity, responsibility, autonomy, self-actualization) becomes probable. Table 5–2 shows the organizational properties that make for psychological sickness and those that contribute to psychological health.

Herzberg has been another industrial psychologist who has anchored some notions he calls a motivation—hygiene theory in self-actualization.[35] He has suggested that there is a fundamental difference between the effects that factors intrinsic to the job have on human motivation and the effects that factors peripheral to the job have. Such factors as how challenging the job is; what recognition one gets in it; the possibilities of advancement, growth, and achievement he regards as factors intrinsic to the job. Factors

TABLE 5–3
Herzberg's Principle of Vertical Job Loading

Principle	Motivators involved
Removing some controls while retaining accountability	Responsibility and personal achievement
Increasing the accountability of individuals for own work	Responsibility and recognition
Giving a person a complete natural unit of work (module, division, area, and so on)	Responsibility, achievement, and recognition
Granting additional authority to an employee in his own activity; job freedom	Responsibility, achievement, and recognition
Making periodic reports directly available to the worker rather than to the supervisor	Internal recognition
Introducing new and more difficult tasks not previously handled	Growth and learning
Assigning individuals specific or specialized tasks, enabling them to become experts	Responsibility, growth, and advancement

such as company policy, supervision, working conditions, interpersonal relations, salary, job security are regarded by him as extrinsic to the job. He calls intrinsic factors "motivators" and the extrinsic factors "hygiene factors." He has claimed that the presence of motivators leads to a *durable state of motivation*, but their absence does not depress motivation, while the presence of hygiene factors does not lead to a durable state of motivation, but their absence can lead to alienation. Herzberg has recommended enriching the jobs—that is, making them more stimulating and challenging —as a way of *motivating* employees and the use of the hygiene factors to *maintain* the motivation. Table 5–3 shows how jobs may be enriched through what he calls "vertical job loading."[36]

Herzberg's theory has been tested in a number of cultures and organizational settings and has received mixed support. His methodology has been attacked, and his theory has also been termed too simplistic.[37] There may well be a difference between what people say motivates them and what in fact motivates them. Herzberg claims that money is a hygiene factor, not a motivator. Undoubtedly for some it is. Yet, the evidence of common observation is overwhelming that a great many people work very hard to earn more money.

Organization Development

The themes of self-actualization and interpersonal competence and the need for the effective management of complex organizations have been synthesized into several programs for organizational redemption. These programs collectively go under the rubric of organization development (O.D.). The question the O.D. theorists pursue is: "How can we optimally mobilize human resources and energy to achieve the organization's mission and, at the same time, maintain a viable, growing organization of people whose personal needs for self-worth, growth, and satisfaction are significantly met at work?"[38]

Beckhard defines O.D. as "an effort (1) *planned*, (2) *organization-wide*, and (3) *managed* from the *top*, to (4) increase *organization effectiveness* and *health* through (5) *planned interventions* in the organization's 'processes,' using *behavioral-science* knowledge."[39] He lists the following characteristics of successful O.D. efforts:

1. There is a *planned* program involving the whole system.

2. The top of the organization is *aware of* and committed to the program and to the management of it. (This does not necessarily mean that they participate exactly the same way as other levels of the organization do, but that they *accept* the responsibility for the management.)

3. It is related to the *organization's mission*. (The organization development effort is not a program to improve effectiveness in the abstract. Rather it is an effort to improve effectiveness aimed specifically at creating organization conditions that will improve the organization's ability to achieve its mission goals.)

4. It is a long-term effort.
    . . . usually at least two or three years are required for any large organization change to take effect and be maintained. This is one of the major problems in organization-development efforts, because most reward systems are based on rewarding the achievement of short-term "profit" objectives. Most organization leaders are impatient with improvement efforts which take extended time. Yet, if real change is to occur and be maintained, there must be a commitment to an extended time, and a willingness to *reward* for the *process* of movement toward goals, as well as toward the specific achievement of short-term goals.

5. Activities are action-oriented.
    (The types of interventions and activities in which organization members participate are aimed at changing something *after* the activity.)
    In this respect, O.D. activities are different from many other training efforts where the activity itself, such as a training course or a management workshop, is designed to produce increased knowledge, skill, or understand-

ing, which the individual is then supposed to transfer to the operating situation. In O.D. efforts, the group builds in connections and follow-up activities that are aimed toward *action programs*.

6. It focuses on *changing attitudes and/or behavior*. (Although processes, procedures, ways of work, etc., do undergo change in organization-development programs, the major target of change is the attitude, behavior, and performance of people in the organization.)

7. It usually relies on some form of *experienced-based* learning activities.

The reason for this is that, if a goal is to change attitudes and/or behavior, a particular type of learning situation is required for such change to occur. One does not learn to play golf or drive a car by getting increased knowledge about how to play golf or drive a car. Nor can one change one's managerial style or strategy through receiving input of new knowledge alone. It is necessary to examine present behavior, experiment with alternatives, and begin to practice modified ways, if change is to occur.

8. O.D. efforts work primarily with groups.

An underlying assumption is that groups and teams are the basic units of organization to be changed or modified as one moves toward organization health and effectiveness. Individual learning and personal change do occur in O.D. programs but as a fallout—these are not the *primary* goals or intentions.[40]

Beckhard indicates a number of situations in which an O.D. effort is called for. He says that O.D. is likely to be utilized when a need for change is felt by somebody in a strategic position in the organization. He lists the following kinds of condition or felt need that evoke a demand for an O.D. intervention in the organization:

1. The perceived need to change managerial strategy. For example, O.D. consultants were called in by the president of a small but successful materials handling company. He felt that his father's strategy of total direction and control and centralized decision-making was inappropriate in the changing times and was not suited to his own temperament and desire for a more participative style.

2. The felt need to make the organization climate more consistent with both individual needs and the changing needs of the environment. Historically, a bank had been managed in a benevolently autocratic manner. In the face of increased competition management decided to go in for a program of branch expansion, methods improvement, and computerization of operations. But the program was not functioning too well because of the resistance of old-line middle managers. The personnel department induced the top management to call in O.D. consultants to start a pilot project to demonstrate the effectiveness of O.D.

3. The perceived need to change the cultural norms of the organization.

Some of the members of a family owned large and successful food company became concerned about the familial rather than the professional way the organization was managed. They started a large O.D. program to change the organization's culture to a more professional one.

4. The need to change structure and roles, such as the felt need to change from a functionally organized organization to a divisionalized organization.

5. The need to improve intergroup collaboration. In a manufacturing division of a large consumer products company, the division manager found a poor relationship between the personnel of the production plants and the headquarters staffs. Outside O.D. consultants were brought in to assist with the diagnosis and with a program to change mutual attitudes.

6. The felt need to improve the communications system.

7. The felt need for better planning.

8. The need for coping with problems of merger.

9. The felt need for change in the motivation of the work force through job enrichment programs, the Scanlon plan, etc.

10. The felt need for adaptation to a new environment.[41]

The Strategy of Organizational Change

Organization development, we noted earlier, is a response to the need for change felt by important members of an organization. Two alternative strategies of change and development are discernible. One is a global strategy aiming at massive and long-term revamping of the entire organization, exemplified by the managerial grid of Blake and Mouton.[42] The other is less ambitious and capitalizes on small, successful changes.[43]

The Blake and Mouton program of organizational change, called the "managerial grid," aims at extensive and long-term changes in management philosophy and organizational practice. It assumes that the best style of management is one that exhibits high concern for employees as well as for the tasks at hand. This is not very different from the style considered ideal by human relaters. The style that emphasizes concern for employees but not for the tasks confronting the management or the one that emphasizes concern for the tasks but not for employees is regarded as a deficient style. What is new is Blake and Mouton's actual program of organizational development, spread over several years. It consists of successive phases. These phases aim at the following:

1 Managers are made aware of their own behavioral patterns and how they interact with others, through sensitivity training sessions. Out of this awareness, they may see a need to change their attitudes and be-

havior. The managers learn these new attitudes and behaviors with the help of skilled trainers.

2 Managers learn effective modes of team-building.

3 Managers learn effective ways of securing intergroup cooperation.

4 Managers learn effective modes of planning the growth and development of the entire organization.

The completion of these training phases takes several years. The program is an expensive one. Apart from the cost of hiring trainers, the principal cost is managerial time. In contrast to this rather comprehensive program of organizational development, there are programs that are oriented more to the solution of specific problems. The steps are roughly as follows:

1 A client calls in consultants to deal with a problem. For example, in a railway cargo assignment department, the problem was one of gross inefficiency.[44] Compared to other departments doing the same kind of work in the region, this one had the worst efficiency. An industrial engineering study had revealed several weaknesses, but the management was too paralyzed by a sense of powerlessness to even try to implement the recommendations.

2 The consultants talk not only to the senior managers but to samples of junior and middle level managers and workers. The objective is to identify a problem that most interviewees agree is an urgent problem *and* one that can be tackled immediately. In the railway cargo assignment department, the supervisors agreed to deal with the problem of the conveyer belt. Luggage moving on a round conveyer had to be lifted off the conveyer by a gang of workers. As the luggage came on the conveyer, one by one the workers pulled out the pieces of luggage and assigned them to separate destination channels. The system resulted in frequent misplacement of luggage. Also, if workers failed to lift off a piece of luggage, it had to go the full conveyer round. This took a full hour, during which time the workers had to remain in the conveyor area to pick up the luggage on its next pass.

3 The consultants call a meeting of workers and managers to elicit suggestions for dealing with the problem. One suggestion at a meeting called by the consultants for dealing with the conveyer problem was that workers should specialize in picking up the luggage. One worker should pick up the luggage destined for all northern towns, another for all southern towns, and so on. Small gangs of workers should be stationed alongside the conveyer, so that if a piece of luggage "escaped" from one gang it would be picked up by a member of the next gang. This suggestion was enthusiastically adopted.

4 Consultants plan in great *detail* the implementation of the accepted suggestion. In the conveyer case the planning was done with the team of workers and managers selected for implementing the suggestion. The plan was committed to paper in great detail. Individuals were requested to indicate the precise steps they proposed to follow. These steps were carefully evaluated and synchronized. Performance was continually evaluated, and the team met periodically for this purpose. The objective of this elaborate planning and control procedure was to help the team members learn the mechanics of successful implementation of innovations.

5 Once the innovation is successfully implemented, the result is generally considerable enthusiasm for tackling larger, more complex problems. The gestalt of futility and failure is broken. The possibility of further successful innovations releases the creative energies of the organizational members. One successful innovation triggers many others. In the process, important problem-identifying, problem-solving, interpersonal planning, and control skills are learned by different groups in the organization.

Which of these two O.D. strategies is more successful? This is hard to say. No systematic, large sample evidence is available on the point. It is probable, however, that the comprehensive, Blake and Mouton style O.D. is feasible in organizations in which there already is a lot of commitment to organizational change. The necessary reservoir of faith in O.D. already exists. On the other hand, the piecemeal O.D. strategy is likely to be more feasible in innovation- and change-*resisting* organizations with deep-seated interpersonal and intergroup conflicts. In these organizations what works is likely to carry more weight than the distant pie-in-the-sky possibilities offered by the comprehensive approach.

O.D. and Organizational Design

The assumptions that O.D. theorists make about the nature and functioning of organizations provide clues for the organizational design that they prefer. These assumptions are:

1. The basic building blocks of an organization are groups (teams). Therefore, the basic units of change are groups, not individuals.

2. An always relevant change goal is the reduction of inappropriate competition between parts of the organization and the development of a more collaborative condition.

3. Decision-making in a healthy organization is located where the information sources are, rather than in a particular role or level of hierarchy.

4. Organizations, subunits of organizations, and individuals continuously manage their affairs against goals. Controls are interim measurements, not the basis of managerial strategy.

5. One goal of a healthy organization is to develop generally open communications, mutual trust, and confidence between and across levels.

6. "People support what they help create." People affected by a change must be allowed active participation and a sense of ownership in the planning and conduct of the change.[45]

These assumptions suggest that O.D. theorists prefer an organization to emphasize healthily functioning groups and cooperative rather than competitive intergroup relationships. They prefer dispersed rather than centralized decision-making and decision-making by situational experts rather than by formal title holders. Management should be oriented to the achievement of organizational objectives rather than to ensuring that procedures are followed. The interpersonal and intergroup relationships should be characterized by open communications, mutual trust, and confidence. Changes must be instituted participatively. Emphasis should be put on training to upgrade the knowledge, skills, and ability of lay personnel at all levels. This organizational design is virtually identical to that preferred by Likert (see previous section) and subject to the same basic question: Is it appropriate in all circumstances of culture, economic conditions, technology, and so forth?

A Critique of the Human Resources Orientation

The charge of manipulating subordinates that has been leveled against the human relations orientation cannot be sustained against the human resources orientation because the latter emphasizes openness, frankness, and confrontation of issues, rather than the sugar-coating of hostile feelings. However, some O.D. proponents could be accused of promoting a program of O.D. on ideological grounds rather than on grounds of its demonstrated capability for improving organizational performance. The objective of designing organizational processes in a way that enables members to actualize their potential is a laudable one. It should not, however, be furthered by attempts to convince management that O.D. is profitable in the absence of any clear proof that it is.

The human resources orientation shares some of the deficiencies of the human relations orientation: an overemphasis on the motivational properties of people and an underemphasis on cognitive properties; a tendency to aspire to one cure-all organizational design regardless of differences in technological, cultural, or economic circumstances; a somewhat naive faith that good intentions can overcome structural conflicts; an unwillingness to confront some of the beneficent aspects of conflict.

Conclusion

From an applied management standpoint, the work of Likert, McGregor, Argyris, Herzberg, and their respective associates and disciples has been very influential. They have corrected the unhuman bias of the bureaucracy and management process orientation and made human motivation an important strategic variable in the design of organizations. But they have neglected a very important dimension of the human being, that of the imperfect problem solver. That dimension has been exploited brilliantly by Simon, March, and Cyert, all at one time or another professors at the Carnegie Institute of Technology in Pittsburgh. The Carnegie school, consisting of these three and their students and associates, has had a profound impact on organization theory. The Simon-March-Cyert perspective is that organizations consist of individuals with limited rationality and information-processing skills interacting with one another to make organizational decisions. Two of their principal foci are: How does an organization get a structure—that is, how does it go about developing operating programs that stabilize human relationships in it? And, how do decisions get made in organizations?

THE CARNEGIE ORIENTATION

The Founder

Herbert Simon, initially a political scientist, and one of the truly seminal contributors to organization theory (besides being a renowned psychologist and management scientist), set out his view of the organization member in his early work.[46] He viewed the individual as intendedly and adaptively rational, having goals and seeking to achieve these goals, but with imperfect information and information-processing capacities. Because we process information serially rather than simultaneously, it is difficult for us to pursue several goals simultaneously. Hence, we tend to pursue goals sequentially. Because we have a limited capacity to process information, we try to build simplified models of causality based on the little information we have digested. Often we are very selective in what we choose to perceive. Because we have a limited capacity to endure cognitive strain, we try to program our lives and reduce search behavior. Because the future for most of us is uncertain, we tend to follow the maxim that a bird in hand is worth two in the bush—we "satisfice." If the environment is benign and we strike it rich, naturally we raise our aspirations and look some more in the bush; but if it is not, we rest content with the bird in hand, and sometimes with only a few feathers! Such are the human decision makers of organizations.

In their acclaimed book, Herbert Simon and James March further explore the implications of administrative man with his selective perception, bounded or limited rationality, and "satisficing" proclivities.[47] They explore the determinants of what motivates an organization member to participate in the activities of the organization, what motivates the member to "produce," why intra- and inter-individual conflicts arise, how they get resolved, and how the organization responds to routine and novel situations. In the course of their odyssey, they generate approximately 150 hypotheses about behavior in organizations and behavior of organizations. Table 5–4 gives a quick overview of the human model utilized by Simon and the other Carnegie theorists and some of the organizational implications of this model.

Organizational Programs

Of particular importance to the design of organizations is the March and Simon typology of the programs that organizations use.[48] These programs are basic to understanding how organizations function under ordinary as well as novel or extraordinary circumstances. A program is a sequence of activities and is evoked by some stimulus, such as a customer's order or the failure of the delivery truck to arrive in time or a worker's quitting a job. If the stimulus is one of those that keeps on recurring, a routine will be developed to handle the situation promptly and efficiently whenever it occurs. Once such a routine is developed, there is little problem-solving activity with regard to stimuli of the kind for which the routine is developed. This way, a program minimizes cognitive strain, because solutions to recurring problems need not be discovered over and over again. A program serves as a control device since it specifies what must be done in specific circumstances and is an important part of the mechanics by which

TABLE 5–4

The Carnegie Model of the Human Being and Its Organizational Implications

Human nature	Organizational implications
Intendedly rational behavior	Goal-means hierarchies (work organized to achieve the organization's goals)
Limited information-processing capacity	Development of programs to attend selectively to information; use of staff "filters" to simplify information
Selective perception (subjective rather than objective perception; perception affected by needs and preconceptions)	Interdepartmental and interpersonal conflicts; overspecialization; excessive attachment to departmental rather than organization-wide goals; coalitions based on identity of interests
Satisficing (search for the good enough rather than for the best)	Suboptimal decision-making and limited planning; limited and sequential pursuit of multiple goals; compromise-based coalitions
Bounded or limited rationality (search for simple and proximate causes of events rather than for complex and distant causes of events)	The use of rules of thumb in decision-making; incremental changes rather than sweeping, global changes; development of routines and programs; problem-initiated rather than anticipatory decision-making

activities in an organization are coordinated. A program has the property of making human behavior in organizations more predictable.

March and Simon distinguish between routines or programs with little or no discretionary content (such as the inspection of the military barracks every morning, the ordering of a specified amount of fresh inventory when stocks fall below a certain level, the punching of the time card when arriving at or leaving the factory premises) and those that do have substantial discretionary content. Examples of the latter are the formulation of the budget for the next year, the development of a number of new products to replace obsolete products, the learning of better methods of teaching so that student ratings improve next year. These involve problem-solving and choice —they are the occasions for genuine decision-making. They are discretionary performance programs.

Discretionary programs are of several types. When the sequence of activities is specified, but not the end product or output of the activities, as in budgeting for next year, the discretionary element resides in the choice of the nature of the output—e.g., the size of the budget and the priorities it incorporates. This usually happens when activities constituting the program are relatively easy to observe and supervise but the output is difficult to observe, supervise, or measure or is contingent on many events or conditions. Under opposite conditions, programs will have discretionary content in the choice of activities but not in the choice of the output—e.g., a program to secure a rate of return on employed capital of 15 percent, a program to achieve a cost reduction of 10 percent, a program to capture the capital city of the enemy, a program to defeat the opposing candidate.

Another force tending to determine whether a program will or will not be discretionary in its activities or output is the need for coordination. If a program is in a strongly interdependent relationship with other programs— e.g., the program of maintenance of equipment and production programs, or sales and the extending of credit to customers—then the program will tend to be routinized to make life easier for those who manage the other programs, since predictable behavior is the very essence of interdependent functioning. If interdependence resides only in activities, then the discretionary element may characterize the output of the program; if it resides only in the output of the program, then there may be some discretion left in the activities constituting the program. Thus, the degree of recurrence, observability, controllability, and interdependence with other programs will determine whether a program is discretionary or not and, if it is discretionary, whether it is so in activities or output or both.

The importance of programs lies in the fact that they are the physiological counterparts of what we call organizational structure. If one looks at the organizational chart of an organization, the positions one finds on it can be described as a number of roles. Each of these roles, such as that of the controller, is a program or a set of programs, and each of these programs is an element in the skein of programs that describes the functioning of the organization. The workflow of the organization is nothing more than a congregation of individual programs subject to a master sequencing program. Also, one finds that roles and programs at the higher reaches of the organization have greater discretionary elements than those at lower levels. In other words there is greater frequency of problem-solving and decision-making at higher levels than at lower levels. This, of course, means that the design of the organization at upper levels must differ substantially from that at lower levels—for example, greater use of staff expertise, greater consultative decision-making, more open and flexible communications channels, will characterize the upper organization. (See Figure 5–3.)

March and Simon describe the general process by which programs get developed or changed in organizations (see Figure 5–4).[49] Variables that are largely within the control of those formulating or changing a program will be considered first, and a serious attempt will be made to elaborate a program of activity based on the control of these variables. Failing this, the decision makers will try to influence variables not directly under their con-

FIGURE 5–3
Consequences of Discretionary Element in Organizational Roles

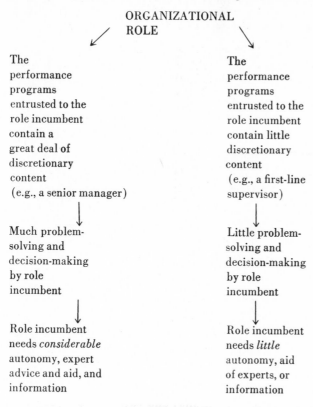

ORGANIZATIONAL
ROLE

The performance programs entrusted to the role incumbent contain a great deal of discretionary content (e.g., a senior manager)	The performance programs entrusted to the role incumbent contain little discretionary content (e.g., a first-line supervisor)
↓	↓
Much problem-solving and decision-making by role incumbent	Little problem-solving and decision-making by role incumbent
↓	↓
Role incumbent needs *considerable* autonomy, expert advice and aid, and information	Role incumbent needs *little* autonomy, aid of experts, or information

trol, beginning with the most easily or predictably influenced, and then going on to the more difficult or more chancy variables.

For example, in a food products company, the personnel department was asked to take over the recruitment of supervisory personnel and was given a certain budget for the purpose. It was told by top management that the recruited supervisors must have some technical qualifications. The personnel department then developed a program of recruitment based on advertising in local newspapers and magazines and visits to local campuses. These could be financed within the budget constraints, but the results were disappointing. So the department attended to other variables not under its direct control. It sought to involve area divisions in recruitment work. They were requested to interview candidates in their areas and advertise in their local papers for candidates. This, too, was not fully effective. Next the personnel department sought a larger budget for intensive recruitment nationally rather than just locally and asked top management for permission to upgrade salary offers. The results were still somewhat disappointing, so the

FIGURE 5–4
Program Development in Organizations

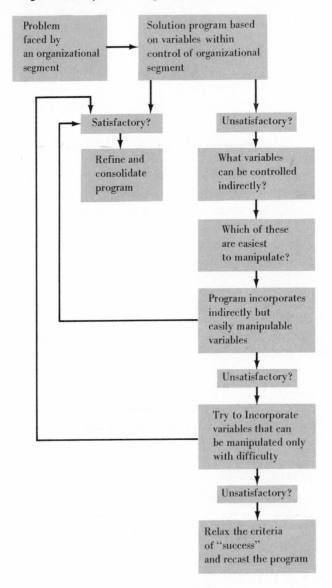

department tried to get the top management to relax the criteria for re-cruitment by lowering minimal qualifications. Notice that the personnel department did not begin by trying to get top management to lower the minimal qualifications, for that would have been both very difficult and very chancy. They exhausted their simpler alternatives before venturing into the more difficult ones.

Organizational Decision-Making

Cyert and March, building on the ideas of Simon and March, further explored organizational decision-making, particularly in sizable firms functioning in moderately competitive, oligopolistic markets.[50] Of the two, Cyert is an economist and March a political scientist. Both have administrative experience in educational institutions.

They viewed an organization such as a large firm as being managed, not by a single, omniscient chief executive (as microeconomic theory implies), but by a shifting *coalition* of staff specialists, managers, union representatives, powerful customers, bankers, suppliers, and others who must somehow agree on what objectives the organization should pursue. Since their interests may partially conflict, members of the coalition must bribe one another by money, backscratching, or otherwise so that agreement on some coherent objectives emerges. But the inherent conflicts of interest of pressure groups in this fragile coalition imply that the organization attends to the goals of the key decision makers at best sequentially, not simultaneously. Some years back, the liberals in the U.S. government successfully pressed for detente with the Communist countries. That upset the die-hards. To keep the right-wingers happy, the government liberalized trade restrictions against the white regime of Rhodesia and granted the colonial regime of Portugal a large subsidy. This is what Cyert and March call the *quasi-resolution of conflict*, the perpetual covering up of internal conflicts through "side payments."

The cognitive properties of decision makers—their bounded rationality and limited information-processing capacity—give rise to a number of additional characteristics of organizational decision-making. Some of these are:

1 *Uncertainty absorption*. The organization must somehow reduce the highly varied, complex, and unreliable information coming to it from the environment into something that is recognizable, simple, and believable. The use of market forecasts is an example.

2 *Uncertainty avoidance*. Since uncertainty makes planning difficult, organizations try to reduce uncertainty. For example, firms often integrate vertically to secure surer supplies and channels of distribution or enter into long-term contracts with suppliers of key inputs and with their major customers for the same purpose.

3 *Problemistic search*. Organizations evolve standard operating procedures to meet most recurrent situations, such as a routine for replenishing stocks when they get depleted. When, however, a problem situation arises—that is, a situation in which routines cannot readily be applied—the organization undertakes search for a solution. But the solution is local, superficial, and incremental more often than global and planned, and usually it is in the neighborhood of a solution that has worked in the past. For example, in a factory when a worker was crushed by a crane, the organization set up a committee to look into the acquisition of newer, safer cranes, since it was known that these were readily available. The committee was not asked to look at all the possible alternatives such as the redesign of the workflow, additional training for crane operators, a better warning system, and so on.

4 *Organizational learning.* Organizations learn from their experience. They learn to modify their goals in the light of their past aspirations and achievement. They also modify their goals in the light of the achievements and expectations of their reference group (e.g., their competitors, in the case of firms). They learn to pay attention more selectively to their environment, viewing some classes of event as being of more importance than others. For example, in the United States, universities have learned to pay more attention to the prospects for governmental grants than to the discomfort of parents over rising tuition fees! Organizations learn to emphasize some measures of their performance more than others. For many decades auto firms paid more attention to styling than to safety, and now, under pressure from consumers and the government, some welcome reversal of priorities seems to have taken place. Finally, organizations also learn to change their problem-solving process or search rules, emphasizing those rules that yield satisfactory solutions and dropping those that do not. The U.S. Defense Department under Secretary McNamara made the use of rigorous cost-benefit analysis mandatory in the making of major decisions regarding weapons systems. Pentagon generals initially found this unpalatable, used as they were to relying on their personal judgments of how good weapons systems were. When President Nixon got rid of the mandatory use of cost-benefit analysis, contrary to expectations, cost-benefit analysis did not wither away, because by then the Pentagon had learned to live with it and had found it quite a useful technique.

Despite the seeming indeterminacy of organizational decision-making, in practice it is remarkably predictable, particularly with respect to recurring situations. This is because organizations evolve "heuristics," or rules of thumb, which they can use in recurring decision situations. For example, one pricing heuristic in many industries is, "Follow the leader." A common advertising heuristic is, "Cut down on institutional advertising in a recession." Indeed, armed with the knowledge of organizational programs and the heuristics used by the organization's decision makers, one can make reasonably accurate predictions of the organization's decision-making behavior. Cyert and March were able to simulate the pricing and ordering decisions of a department store reasonably accurately,[51] and they also report Clarkson's simulation of the decisions of an officer of an investment trust.[52] To the extent that prediction is an aim of science, the contribution of the Carnegie theorists, particularly of Cyert and March, is quite significant. Their model of organizational decision-making is summarized in Figure 5–5. It shows how the various elements of organizational decision-making —uncertainty avoidance and absorption, quasi-resolution of conflict, problemistic search, sequential attention to goals, and organizational learning— are tied together.

A Critique of the Carnegie School

An interesting question that the work of the Carnegie theorists does not satisfactorily answer is: Does the character of decision-making vary from organization to organization, and if there is such a variation, what factors account for it? For example, quasi-resolution of conflict and uncertainty absorption are two of the principal features of organizational decision-making. Is there an equal amount of quasi-resolution of conflict and uncertainty absorption in every organization? That seems unlikely. Small organizations probably have less superficially resolved internal conflicts and have fewer mechanisms for predicting the future than large ones. Organizations functioning in dynamic, turbulent environments are also likely to have more of both than organizations functioning in static environments. We need a theory that predicts the properties of an organization's decision-making process given the properties of its size, nature of business, environment, and so on.

The work of the Carnegie theorists is not normative; it is descriptive. It tells us what organizations are really like, not what they should be like. In this respect, their orientation differs sharply from the orientation of the human relations and the human resources theorists. And yet, by providing a fairly accurate picture of what really goes on in organizations, they help the organizational designer avoid those aspects that debilitate the organization and strengthen those that invigorate it.

Finally, while the Carnegie model of the individual is far more sophisticated than the model utilized by the human relations or the human resources orientations with respect to *cognitive* matters (problem-solving, perception, etc.), it is not so sophisticated when it comes to *affective* factors, particularly the structure and dynamics of human needs. They do not adequately

FIGURE 5–5
Carnegie Model of Organizational Decision-making

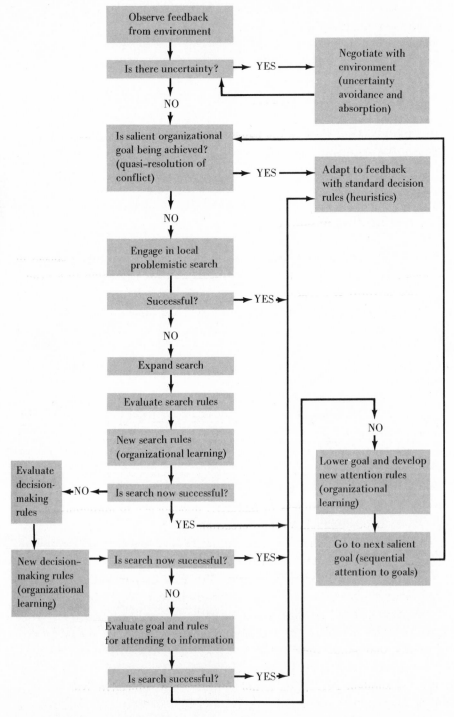

SOURCE: Adapted from R. M. Cyert and J. G. March, *A Behavioral Theory of the Firm* (Englewood Cliffs, N. J.: Prentice-Hall, 1963), p. 126.

explore the implications of a hierarchy of needs. For example, how is organizational decision-making affected when the dominant need in key decisions makers is for self-actualization? Ego gratification? Such questions are left not only unanswered but unasked.

COMPARISON OF THE THREE BEHAVIORAL ORIENTATIONS

Now that we have reviewed the human relations orientation, the human resources orientation, and the "bounded rationality," or Carnegie, orientation, let us briefly compare them.

Model of the Human Being

The human relations orientation focuses on the motivational aspects of people, particularly the need for self-esteem and for belonging to a group. The ego is frail; it needs constantly to be boosted by the supportive behavior of those with whom the person interacts. Human beings are gregarious and dependent on others, especially the group in which they work, for satisfying a variety of their needs. They internalize many of the norms and values of the work group. They are not at all the self-reliant, aggressive, individualists of the old American West.

The human resources orientation also focuses primarily on the motivational aspects of the human personality, but on the need for self-actualization rather than on the need for self-esteem and group belonging. The need is not, therefore, so much for a supportive climate that makes one feel good as for a climate in which doing one's own thing is an accepted way of life. The model is that of efflorescence—growth from a frail bud to a full-blooming flower, from childishness to maturity, dependence to autonomy, superficiality to depth, random play to creation.

The Carnegie "bounded," or limited, rationality school views the human being as rational in intention if not always in actions. Given their goals, people try to reach them economically. But they may make mistakes. Or, they may not know of ways to reach the goals very efficiently. In a world of uncertainty they "satisfice"—that is, settle for the "good enough." They strive for understanding but, lacking omniscience, settle for simple models of reality that guide their behavior. They live by proverbs and rules of thumb because in a world of uncertainty these come out right, not always, but often enough. Perception is not objective but subjective. And yet it is not totally emotional or erroneous. It is right enough to serve its purposes and distorted enough to meet important needs for balance and harmony. In a world buzzing with information, much of which is just noise given our needs and goals, we perceive selectively and subjectively and most of the time succeed in seeing the world as coherent.

Strategic Organizational Variables

In both the human relations and the human resources orientations, the strategic variable is the organizational climate. Is it oppressive, unsupportive, and hostile? Or is it supportive and friendly? If it is the latter it motivates productive, cooperative, creative behavior. If it is the former it motivates alienation, apathy, and hostility. In the organizational climate, the superior-subordinate relations and the peer relations within the work group loom the largest, for the group, not the individual, is viewed as the basic organizational decision unit.

In the Carnegie orientation, one strategic organizational variable is the way human behavior is programmed through standard operating procedures and the use of heuristics. Another strategic variable is organizational decision-making, and in this, the political aspects of decision-making involving coalition-building, bargaining, side payments, and quasi-resolution of conflict are especially emphasized. Also emphasized are the mechanisms that reduce cognitive strain, such as uncertainty avoidance and absorption and problemistic and sequential search.

Evolution of Theory

As we noted in the preceding chapter, Fiedler has proposed a contingency view of leadership effectiveness that suggests that task-oriented leadership is effective in situations that are either very favorable or very unfavorable for the leader, while interpersonally oriented leadership is effective in situations that are moderately favorable to the leader.[53] Since leadership behavior is one of the linchpins of the human relations movement, we may expect a gradual shift to a more situational view of the effectiveness of traditional human relations.

The writings of O.D. theorists suggest a growing awareness that O.D. effectiveness—and by implication the effectiveness of the underlying organizational ideal—may be contingent on a number of factors, such as environmental change that makes established organizational structure and processes obsolete, realization on the part of top management of a need to change, support of top management for organization-wide change efforts, a willingness to take the risk of making radical changes in the design of the organization, and so forth.

Contingency approaches are being developed with respect to the process of organizational decision-making that the Carnegie theorists heavily emphasized. Mintzberg, Raisinghani, and Théoret have trichotomized strategic organizational decisions into opportunity decisions, problem decisions, and crisis decisions.[54] Opportunity decisions (such as perceiving a market potential and seizing it) are a function of managerial will. At the other extreme, crisis decisions, such as the effort of Rolls Royce to stay afloat when the developmental and production costs of its engine for the Lockheed Tristar airbus vastly exceeded the value of its bid, are evoked primarily by external environmental pressures. These authors go on to develop a basic model of strategic decision-making that incorporates phases such as the identification of threats, problems, or opportunities; the development of strategic alternatives; and the selection of the alternative eventually adopted. After that, they list seven types of strategic decision processes that are variants of their basic model. Administrative decision theory may evolve rapidly toward a typology of the process of decision-making. With that may come attempts at linking each type with situational variables like the nature of the organization's environment, the size and business of the organization, its goals, and so on.

Questions for Organizational Analysis

The three behavioral orientations discussed in this chapter prompt several questions for organization theory and organizational analysis that are listed in Table 5–5.

SUMMARY

One response to the mechanization of factory work was an emphasis on human relations. Following experiments at the Western Electric Company, the work group was recognized to have a great influence on its members, and the style of supervision came to be acknowledged as a crucial factor in the working of the group. The human relations orientation has branched out into intensive studies of the workings of groups, of the nonformal organization, the style of supervision, the relationship of supervisory style and productivity, of job satisfaction and productivity, and the like. The human relations orientation usefully has drawn attention to the social and ego needs of organizational members and to the implications of these needs for sound management practice. But it has also been criticized on a number of grounds—chiefly, that it tries to mask structurally irreconcilable con-

TABLE 5–5
Questions for Theory and for Analyzing Organizations

	Questions for organization theory	Questions for analyzing an organization
Human relations orientation	What constitutes the psychological climate of organizations?	What is the organization's psychological climate? Does it vary from one part to another?
	How does psychological climate affect motivation and productivity?	How does the organization's psychological climate affect the motivation and productivity of groups and individuals functioning in it?
	What factors determine the level of psychological climate an organization has?	What factors in the environment, technology, nature of business, and so on make the climate what it is?
Human resources orientation	How do organizational structures and processes affect the development of the human personality?	How do the organization's stucture and operating process affect the growth needs of the people working in it?
	How are human developmental needs and organizational requirements integrated? How should they be integrated?	How are growth needs and the organization's requirements for efficiency, survival, and growth integrated? How should they be integrated?
Carnegie orientation	How do the cognitive properties of humans affect the structure and functioning of organizations?	What are the information-processing and problem-solving capabilities of the key administrators of the organization? How do these capabilities affect the development of routines and discretionary programs in the organization?
	How do organizations make decisions? What factors underlie different processes of decision-making?	How do decisions get made in the organization? What coalition has the greatest influence? What rules of thumb, or heuristics, are being used in making decisions? How "optimal" are the decisions?

flicts, that it is manipulative in intent, that it is deficient in taking note of the cognitive properties of human beings, and that it is universalistic and fails to take into account the cultural, technological, and economic differences in the circumstances in which organizations operate.

Argyris, McGregor, Herzberg, and others founded and nurtured the human resources movement. Its central tenet has been that formal organizations involve a vast waste of human resources through excessive job specialization, hierarchical relationships, and other similar rigidities. Very few human abilities are tapped by the formal organization, and, indeed, many are stunted or even destroyed by organizational arrangements.

The technology of organization development has been developed to better integrate human needs and organizational requirements. Its features are that it is a planned, organization-wide effort, managed from the top, to increase organizational effectiveness and health through interventions in the organization's processes using behavioral science knowledge. Organizational development has been found useful in a number of situations. Its assumptions point to an organizational design substantially similar to the one proposed by Likert.

The Carnegie theorists, Simon, March, and Cyert, have explored the organizational implications of the individual's limited information-processing and problem-solving capacity. Their contributions, particularly regarding how human cognitive properties affect the development of organizational programs and the way decisions get made in organizations, are notable. They have distinguished between routine and discretionary programs, identifying the determinants of the latter, and they have described elements of organizational decision-making like quasi-resolution of conflict, uncertainty avoidance, problemistic search, and organizational learning.

SUGGESTED READINGS

Ch. 6 in Richard M. Cyert and James G. March, *A Behavioral Theory of the Firm* (Englewood Cliffs, N. J.: Prentice-Hall, 1963), which describes the major decision-making concepts of Cyert and March.

Ch. 26 in Harold Leavitt, *Managerial Psychology*, 3rd Ed. (Chicago: University of Chicago Press, 1972). A lucid explanation of organizational decision-making as viewed by the Carnegie theorists.

Pp. 80–86 and 108–11 in D. S. Pugh, D. J. Hickson, and C. R. Hinings, *Writers on Organizations* (Hammondsworth, England: Penguin Books, 1971). Brief essays on Simon and on Cyert and March.

Pp. 1–55 in Benjamin Rush, *Behavioral Science* (New York: National Industrial Conference Board, 1969). A very good review of the works of Likert, Argyris, McGregor, Blake and Mouton, Herzberg, and others.

QUESTIONS FOR ANALYSIS

1 Take a look at the following case from the human relations and human resources perspectives. What would you have done in Mr. Springer's place?

What would you do if you took over Bainbridge House at the end of the fourth quarter? What does the case reveal about decision-making at Bainbridge House?

The Fall of Bainbridge House

A year ago last July, Arthur Bainbridge carefully placed the ball on the seventeenth tee of the Carolina Valley Golf Course in suburban Raleigh, North Carolina, and took several practice swings. He wiped his brow and lowered his cap, shielding his eyes from the hot afternoon sun. Then, he dug in his spikes firmly, swung with unusual accuracy, and drove the ball into a very long high arc. It dropped just at the edge of the green and rolled within a scant yard and a half of the hole. While his golf partners applauded, Bainbridge threw both arms upward in sheer joy; then, without warning, he faltered and fell to the ground.

Bainbridge House began to die that very day although to outsiders it still appears to be well and flourishing. But to anyone familiar with the customs, traditions, and attitudes of the firm it is clear that it is unlikely to survive much longer.

Curiously, this is not the story of the indispensable man but rather of an unusual but not uncommon sequence of events which has brought the firm to near ruin.

Raised in a family of furniture builders, Arthur Bainbridge was a master furniture craftsman by his mid-twenties. He started his own firm a few years later and Bainbridge House soon earned the distinction of being one of the finest small furniture manufacturers along the Atlantic Seaboard. Bainbridge House had generally avoided fabrics and coverings and concentrated instead on a limited line of custom crafted wood tables, chairs, and decorative pieces.

Arthur Bainbridge was always aware that it took a number of skills to run his High Point factory and that he did not have them all. Over the years he hired a small, but efficient, front office staff and an excellent finance man, Jess Forster. Two master designers were brought in from larger firms nearby and the finest furniture builders in the business soon began to gravitate to Bainbridge House. A solid network of representatives placed the line in custom furniture houses across the country.

No, Arthur Bainbridge was not indispensable and did not intend to be. Drawing upon scholars from Duke University and North Carolina State, Bainbridge House developed a modest, but workable internal organizational development plan which became a model for graduate student analysis for several years. The small team was at least as strong and capable as any in the industry.

Charlotte Bainbridge, now the sole owner, ran the firm in absentia for six months. The existing management team functioned reasonably well after the sudden loss of the president but profits were cut sharply by a sudden drop in demand for custom specialty furniture.

An attorney, and long time family friend, advised Charlotte to sell Bainbridge House, which she finally consented to do. Jess Forster headed a small group of management personnel who attempted to obtain adequate financing for its purchase. They were successful in obtaining the necessary financial backing but unsuccessful in the purchase itself. With great reluctance, Charlotte Bainbridge accepted a significantly larger offer from a Boston financial conglomerate.

only interested in money

formal vs informal

The new owners were noted for using a return-on-investment ratio for all of their holdings. Elston G. Springer, a vice-president, was assigned operating responsibility for Bainbridge House and began a series of moves to return it to an acceptable level of profitability.

In capsule form, the following happened:

First Quarter
1. Springer orders two speciality "losers" cut from the line.
2. The marketing manager objected vigorously.
3. Austere budgets were imposed on all departments.
4. The office staff was reduced.
5. A loss in the prior quarter was partly offset by a small profit in the first quarter.

specialization loss of motivation

Second Quarter
1. Early retirements among the older, higher paid furniture builders and finishers were encouraged.
2. Capital equipment expenditures were deferred.
3. Jess Forster objected vigorously. — *no consideration for employees*
4. Several local suppliers were dropped in favor of a new low-bid procurement policy.
5. Second quarter profits were up sharply.

No Loyalty Non productive

Third Quarter
1. Inspection standards were lightened to reduce the reject and rework rate.
2. The production manager submitted his resignation.
3. The new production manager instituted the design of a low cost furniture line using some molded plastic parts to replace traditional hand sculpturing.
4. Jess Forster left Bainbridge House to accept a management position with another firm.
5. Toughened inspection procedures were introduced after numerous field complaints.
6. Profits rose to record levels.
7. Elston Springer, lauded at Corporate for his achievement in "turning

around" Bainbridge House, was dispatched to revive another "sick" acquisition.

Fourth Quarter
1. Turnover among craftsmen increased.
2. The new General Manager scrapped plans for the line of low-cost furniture.
3. Quality problems forced a new look at using local suppliers and materials.
4. An abortive attempt at unionization was made.
5. A personnel survey revealed that only 37 percent of those now with the company had been employed before Arthur Bainbridge died.
6. Eight major accounts dropped the Bainbridge House lines near the end of the quarter.
7. Profits were off from the second and third quarter levels but the General Manager was optimistic about the future.[55]

2 Identify quasi-resolution of conflict, problemistic search, uncertainty avoidance and absorption, sequential attention to goals, and organizational learning in the following study of an organizational decision. After you identify and label appropriately the events in the case, flow chart them, and compare the flow chart with Figure 5–3.[56]

The decision is part of a larger decision regarding the installation of an electronic data-processing system. The company, a medium-large manufacturing concern, had made some preliminary investigation of the problem and decided that a consultant was necessary. At the beginning of the process of deciding which firm should be chosen, there was no clear program as to how many firms would be evaluated. A list of possible consultants was prepared, but a series of chance circumstances led to a meeting with Alpha, a relatively new consulting firm specializing in the design of electronic data-processing systems.

On February 21 consultants from Alpha and people from the company discussed the problem of improving business methods. By March 23 Alpha had submitted a step-by-step program that would survey and analyze the company's operations and data-processing procedures. Alpha stated that the objective of this program would be (1) the estimation of savings that could be realized through the use of electronic equipment and (2) the specification of the price class and characteristics of equipment required. The fee expected for this work was stated as $180 per man-day (i.e., $3600 per month assuming one man works a 20-day month). The initial consulting task was to be limited to 100 man-days, and consequently the fee was limited to $18,000. Traveling expenses of some $4000 would also be charged.

The report was well received by company officials, who generally agreed that Alpha would be retained until the question of investigating other alternatives was raised. As will be obvious, this was a crucial point in the process, but it is not clear what prompted the suggestion for additional search effort. The suggestion was rather quickly accepted, and a list of about a dozen potential consultants, which had been prepared earlier by a staff member, was presented. The controller decided that only one more firm, Beta, should be asked to submit a proposal. Beta was more widely known, older, and larger than Alpha, although it did not specialize in electronic data-processing feasibility studies.

Following analysis of the problem, Beta submitted a contract-proposal covering an investigation of the company's problems. The stated objectives were two: (1) to reduce the costs of the accounting and clerical operation and (2) to improve the quality of information available for accounting and control. Beta stated in the contract proposal that employing electronic data-handling equipment was to be considered as a possible means of attaining these objectives. This contract outlined service charges that would not exceed $5000 a month. The initial study was to be completed and a report submitted three to four months after active work began.

After Beta had submitted a report, it became necessary to choose between the two firms. At the request of the controller a staff member wrote a memorandum that listed the criteria on which the decision should be based and also evaluated the two firms on each of the criteria. The results of this memorandum are summarized in the Table below.

Comparison of Consulting Firms

Criteria	Alpha	Beta
Quality of personnel	Depth in quality of computer personnel	More experienced in business problems
Cost of services	$180 per man-day ($3600 per month); $18,000 maximum charge plus traveling expenses	$5000 per month maximum plus traveling expenses
Commitment made	Committed themselves primarily to study of feasibility of application of E.D.P. equipment	Will give consideration to both methods and possibility of using E.D.P. equipment, in order noted
Estimated time	100 man-days maximum; possibility of doing work in 15 weeks	Longer time allowed because of greater commitment (actual time stated in contract was 3-4 months)
Availability and scope	No quantitative evaluation mentioned.	
Geographic situation	Main office approx. 2500 miles from company's office	Main office approx. 500 miles from company's office

The staff member who wrote the memorandum believed that as far as the quality of personnel, cost of services, and estimated time were concerned the two firms were equal or could be made equal by negotiation. Regarding the other criteria—commitment made, availability and scope, and geographic situation—he felt Beta had an advantage. He was supported in this opinion by an academician who had previously served as a consultant to the company. Analysis of the memorandum seems to show, however, that the only advantage that can objectively be given to Beta is its geographic situation. Even here, aside from availability, it is difficult to see any advantage; the only possibility would be higher traveling expenses for Alpha, but presumably this would mean a reduction in some part of the fee. Again it should have been possible to negotiate on availability and scope, assuming that geographic proximity is divorced from availability. It is quite obvious that the commitment could have been negotiated because Alpha, as a new organization in the field, was open to suggestion with respect to the kind of commitments it should make.

On the cost side (ignoring possible negotiation) there was some ambiguity. The approximate monthly charges were $1400 less for Alpha than for Beta. The total charge for Beta to the company varied according to the length of time it would take. The estimated length of time for Beta was three to four months, which would mean a price between $15,000 and $20,000. Alpha, on the other hand, had a maximum price of $18,000. Exact price comparisons under the circumstances were difficult to make. Since Alpha gave a maximum total price whereas Beta used only a maximum monthly charge and no upper limit on the time, what advantage there was in the cost situation was probably in Alpha's favor. However, the costs were close enough and the circumstances blurred enough so that relative cost was difficult to evaluate.

This fact was recognized by the staff members involved, who proposed that the decision be made on collateral grounds (e.g., geographic proximity, possible future uses). As noted above, the grounds specified seemed to favor Beta, and this preference of the staff was apparent almost from the moment that the decision to expand the search to Beta was made. That is, the staff members most closely involved seemed to view Alpha as a reasonable solution until the suggestion for further search was made. There is some suggestion that they interpreted the instruction to expand their search to include Beta and only Beta as a preference for Beta by their supervisors. The controller and assistant controller, on the other hand, felt that the final decision was based on the independent recommendations of their staff members and did not acknowledge the possibility that such an outcome was implicit in the decision not to accept Alpha until further investigation. The firm decided to hire Beta.

3 What differences, if any, in the nature of decision-making would you expect between the way a restaurant goes about hiring a waiter and the way a faculty goes about hiring a new professor? What differences would you expect between the way a company makes a decision to invest $30 million in a new plant and the way it decides to buy $3,000 worth of new furniture? Would you expect the same decision-making process if the industry was facing a possible recession?

Footnotes to Chapter Five

-¹ F. J. Roethlisberger and W. J. Dickson, *Manager and the Worker*, pp. 14–18.

² *Ibid.*

³ D. Cartwright and R. Lippitt, "Group Dynamics and the Individual."

⁴ J. G. March and Herbert Simon, *Organizations*, pp. 59–82.

⁵ Stanley Seashore, *Group Cohesiveness in the Industrial Group*, 1954.

⁶ See B. Collins and H. Guetzkow, *A Social Psychology of Group Processes for Decision Making*, Ch. 2, for propositions about individual versus group productivity. See Irving Janis, *Victims of Groupthink*, for adverse aspects of group functioning.

⁷ See A. P. Hare, E. F. Borgatta, and R. F. Bales, *Small Groups*, for a very wide range of studies on groups; and Collins and Guetzkow, *op. cit.*, for an inventory of propositions about group behavior.

⁸ Rensis Likert, *New Patterns of Management*.

⁹ P. Lawrence and J. Lorsch, *Organization and Its Environment*.

¹⁰ For some classic studies of the nonformal organization, see Donald Roy "Banana Time: Job Satisfaction and Informal Interaction"; C. R. Walker and R. H. Guest, *The Man on the Assembly Line*; and M. Dalton, *Men Who Manage*.

¹¹ See F. C. Mann, "Studying and Creating Change: A Means to Understanding Social Organization."

¹² Source unknown. The author is indebted to Mr. Stephen Lebner for bringing this "course" to his attention.

¹³ See A. Halpin and B. Winer, "A Factorial Study of the Leader Behavior Descriptions."

¹⁴ *Ibid.*, pp. 42–43.

¹⁵ *Ibid.*, p. 42.

¹⁶ *Ibid.*

¹⁷ *Ibid.*

¹⁸ See *ibid.*; see also D. Katz and R. L. Kahn, "Leadership Practices in Relation to Productivity and Morale."

¹⁹ See R. L. Kahn, "Productivity and Job Satisfaction"; and Victor Vroom, *Work and Motivation*.

²⁰ See Likert, *op. cit.*

²¹ See Arnold Tannenbaum, *Social Psychology of the Work Organization*, p. 80.

²² E. Fleishman, "Leadership Climate, Human Relations Training, and Supervisory Behavior."

²³ See Tannenbaum, *op. cit.*, Ch. 7, for details.

²⁴ R. White and R. Lippitt, *Autocracy and Democracy: An Experimental Inquiry*.

²⁵ Kurt Lewin, "Group Decision and Social Change."

²⁶ See Nancy Morse and E. Reimer, "The Experimental Change of a Major Organizational Variable"; and L. Coch and J. R. P. French, Jr., "Overcoming Resistance to Change."

²⁷ Victor Vroom, *Some Personality Determinants of the Effects of Participation*.

28 Arnold Tannenbaum and R. L. Kahn, "Organizational Control Structure: A General Descriptive Technique as Applied to Four Local Unions."

29 Likert, *op. cit.*

30 *Ibid.*, pp. 7–8.

31 Amitai Etzioni, *Modern Organizations*, pp. 41–49.

32 Douglas McGregor, *The Human Side of Enterprise.*

33 Chris Argyris, *Personality and Organization.*

34 Chris Argyris, *Integrating the Individual and the Organization.*

35 F. Herzberg, *Work and the Nature of Man.*

36 F. Herzberg, "One More Time: How Do You Motivate Employees?"

37 For a review of Herzberg's theory and research, see N. King, "Clarification and Evaluation of the Two-factor Theory of Satisfaction."

38 Richard Beckhard, *Organization Development: Strategies and Models*, Ch. 3.

39 *Ibid.*, p. 9.

40 *Ibid.*, pp. 15–16.

41 *Ibid.*, pp. 16–19.

42 R. Blake and J. Mouton, *The Managerial Grid.*

43 As an example, see J. Baker and R. Schaffer, "Making Staff Consulting More Effective."

44 The author is indebted to Dr. Harvey Thomson for this example.

45 Beckhard, *op. cit.*

46 Herbert Simon, *Administrative Behavior.*

47 March and Simon, *op. cit.*

48 *Ibid.*, pp. 142–50.

49 *Ibid.*, pp. 179–80.

50 R. M. Cyert and J. G. March, *A Behavioral Theory of the Firm.*

51 *Ibid.*, Ch. 7.

52 *Ibid.*, Ch. 10.

53 F. Fiedler, "Validation and Extension of the Contingency Model of Leadership Effectiveness: A Review of Empirical Findings."

54 Henry Mintzberg, Duru Raisinghani, and André Théoret, "The Structure of 'Unstructured Decisions.'"

55 Robert D. Jayce, *Encounters in Organizational Behavior*, pp. 46–49.

56 The following case is from Cyert and March, *op. cit.*, pp. 60–63.

"The only argument available with an east wind is to put on your overcoat."
James Russell Lowell

The Systems and Contingency Approaches to Organization Theory

to 235

INTRODUCTION

In Chapter 4 we reviewed two founding orientations of contemporary organization theory—namely, the bureaucracy school and the management process school. In Chapter 5 we reviewed three behaviorally oriented schools of organization theory, the human relations school, the human resources school, and the Carnegie "bounded rationality" school. In this chapter we review the systems approach and the contingency approach to organization theory. These two differ from the others in emphasizing the "openness" of the organization to its task environment. The organization is seen as influenced heavily by its markets, its technology, the culture within which it subsists. Since these vary widely, so must organizational structures and processes.

THE SYSTEMS APPROACH

The Meaning of "System"

The word "system" has several connotations: a set of interdependent, interacting elements; a group of units so combined as to form an organized

223

whole whose output is greater than the output of the constituent units would be were they to function independently. The human being, for example, is a system. It consists of a number of organs and limbs, and only when these are functioning in a coordinated way is the human effective. Similarly, one can think of the organization as a system consisting of a number of interacting parts. For example, a manufacturing firm has a section devoted to manufacturing, another devoted to marketing, a third devoted to financing, and various others. None of these is of much use all by itself. But when a firm has all these sections, and when they are properly coordinated, it can hope to function effectively and make a profit.

To a large extent a system is what one chooses to perceive as a system: it is a gestalt, a perceived configuration that somehow seems to make sense as a whole, as a unit. In this universe, everything can be shown to be related to everything else. The smallest thing has an infinite gravitational field; the smallest atom reaches out to grasp the entire universe and is affected in turn by the other atoms in the universe. And yet, the relationship between an atom on earth and one out in the Crab Nebula is so infinitely weak that we ignore it. It is because of our ability to fail to see many weak relationships that we are at all able to perceive "systems." The organization is perceived as a system simply because we fail to see or choose to minimize the relationships between the people constituting an organization and their friends and relations and, in turn, the relationships between the latter and their friends and relations, ad infinitum. Otherwise, the whole world—three billion of us—would constitute the organization!

The Development of Organizational Systems Theory

The application of systems theory to the analysis of organizations shows a number of distinct elements, which we will enumerate first and then discuss in more detail.

1 The *attributes* of the living system, exposed to and dependent on its environment, have been sought in functioning organizations. Katz and Kahn, for example, have tried to identify the input-throughput-output cycle in organizations, as well as the processes of entropy, dynamic homeostasis, differentiation, and equifinality.[1]

2 Identification of the major *parts* of the organizational system has been sought. Parsons has identified the institutional, managerial, and technical subsystems of the organization.[2] Katz and Kahn have identi-

fied three additional subsystems: the adaptive, maintenance, and production supportive subsystems.[3]

3 The _forces_ shaping organizational systems have been identified. For example, Emery and Trist have made the important point that a change in any one of social, technical, or economic forces acting on a system may trigger a change in the other two.[4]

4 The process of _interaction_ between subsystems has been examined. Leavitt has suggested that a change in any one of the tasks of the organization, its structure, the techniques and technology utilized in it, or the human or "people" part of the organization can trigger changes in the other three.[5]

5 Attempts have been made to apply systems theory to aid managerial decision-making and _administrative action_. Seiler's effort in this regard is noteworthy.[6]

Properties of the Organization As an "Open," "Living" System

One can distinguish a closed system that does not import energy from outside or "export" outputs to the rest of the universe, such as a nucleus or a solar system, from an open system that does interact with its environment and indeed survives because it does so. Societies, organizations, the family, human beings, the cell, and many mechanical systems such as a car are open systems. The open system is a system that ingests energy from the environment, transforms it, and then exports energy back to the environment, usually in a form different from the form in which it was ingested.[7] According to Katz and Kahn, the following characteristics seem to define all open systems including, particularly, organizations:[8]

Input. Every open system imports energy in some form or other from its external environment. Cars import gas and human labor; cells import blood and oxygen; organizations import fuel, manpower, machinery, information, and so on.

Throughput. Every open system processes the energy available to it. The body converts starch and sugar into heat and action. The organization processes raw materials and other inputs to create a product or service.

Output. Every open system has an output that it exports to the environment. The body exports carbon dioxide, water, and feces. The organization exports products or services.

Cycles of events. The energy exchange is cyclical, repetitive. The export of an output makes possible an input or import, which makes possible processing and output, which makes possible a fresh input, ad infinitum. In organizations it may be helpful to view the cycle as one of events (purchase-production-sale, etc.). This cyclical character of events gives organizations their structure. Each event in turn may be thought to have a cyclical activity pattern; so organizational structure is a series of linked cycles of activities.

Negative entropy. Entropy is the natural process of decay, disorganization, and death. A system must counteract this process to keep on being healthy and alive. Negative entropy is the process by which decay is arrested through importing more energy than is exported by the system—that is, by storing energy. Organizations try to do so by building up assets, especially cash, resources, and morale. These come in handy in bad times when the process of disorganization picks up strength.

Information input, negative feedback, and the coding process. Living open systems, such as organizations, import not only energy but information. Negative information about their performance (negative feedback) helps them correct their deviations from course like a thermostat. Since a vast amount of information is directed at every living system, each must devise a code by which it knows which information is useful to it and which is not.

The steady state and dynamic homeostasis. Open systems that survive by importing energy to offset entropy are characterized by a steady state. However, this does not mean that the system does not change over time. Since its environment may change, the system must change, too, but it changes just enough to counteract the disruptive force in environmental change. This it usually does by preserving its character but allowing its form to change. Over time, this process of adjustment may be characterized as dynamic homeostasis. The adjustment of government policies to the wishes of the people is an example of dynamic homeostasis. On the other hand, a spreading war is an example of the breakdown of dynamic homeostasis and the ascendance of entropy. Over time, living systems learn to anticipate disturbances and, indeed, often grow by excessively storing energy to meet future difficulties.

Differentiation. Open systems move in the direction of differentiation, elaboration, and greater specialization in the functions performed by their parts. The bodily sense organs and nervous system over millennia have become more differentiated, elaborated, and specialized. Open systems move from a dynamic, somewhat uncoordinated interaction of their parts to central coordination of the interaction of highly specialized parts. Family-owned organizations often evolve from a state in which everybody makes decisions and thereby gets into the others' way to a state of hierarchy, standard operating procedures, and formal delegation of authority and responsibilities. The force motivating differentiation is greater efficiency through specialization of functions.

Equifinality. It is usually possible for open systems to reach the same final state from differing initial conditions and to reach different final states from the same initial conditions. One organization may choose to grow by acquisitions, another by building plants, a third by subcontracting part of production. One hospital can use its staff and facilities to promote research, another to promote teaching, a third to promote cure of common diseases, a fourth to promote the cure of rare diseases. Equifinality is an important principle. It points to the possibility of choice in organizational design.

The Major Subsystems of the Organization

Drawing on the work of Parsons previously mentioned, Katz and Kahn have identified a number of organizational components or subsystems that enable the organization to function efficiently. These are: a production or technical component; a production supportive component (purchasing, sales); a maintenance component (for preserving the productive capacity of personnel and machinery—the personnel department, rewards and sanctions, the maintenance crews); an adaptive component seeking to adapt the organization to new processes and products (research and development department, organization and methods, market research, operations research, etc.); an institutional component whose function it is to obtain social support and legitimacy for the organization; and a managerial component that coordinates internal and external activities and resolves conflicts.[9]

Since each component has a fairly specialized function, each develops a distinctive nucleus of operating procedures and values. For example, the production component is keyed to efficiency, rationalization, and careful programming of activities. The adaptive component is change oriented and oriented toward the environment and the future. The managerial component is oriented toward growth, coordination, efficiency, and quickness in decision-making. But because these components are highly interdependent (there would be no production without purchasing and sales, no adaptation without managerial support, no management without maintenance, etc.), conflict from differences in values and operating procedures is inevitable. Thus, the system must pay attention to devices for reducing conflict—that is, to leadership and communication processes aimed at conflict reduction and to a strategy of organizational change and development that can foster a climate of collaboration. These, presumably, would create a synergistic interaction among organizational components. Table 6–1 shows the various subsystems, the functions they perform, their orientation or thrust, and the mechanisms they employ.[10]

The Forces Shaping Organizational Systems and Subsystems

While each subsystem may develop distinctive properties through specialization in the functions it performs, each subsystem operating in an organization, as well as the organization as a whole, is a social, technical, and economic unit. Each system or subsystem consists of humans working together, and hence it is a *social* unit. It employs a variety of techniques and technologies, and therefore it is a *technical* unit. Its resources are limited in relation to the goals it might wish to secure, and therefore it is an *economic* unit. Thus, each organizational system or subsystem is subject to social, technical, and economic forces, and these forces are interrelated. A modification of any of these forces may have powerful repercussions on the other forces, giving the system its distinctive properties. This is the perspective of Emery and Trist.[11] (See Figure 6–1.)

The social-technical-economic systems perspective of Emery and Trist grew out of a fascinating study by Trist and Bamforth of the mechanization of British coal mining.[12] The long-wall method of coal mining was installed because it was believed to be more economical than other methods. It required a degree of mechanization and the breakup of the old work groups. Under the new system, work was individualized rather than being a team

FIGURE 6–1
The Forces Shaping Organizational Systems and Subsystems

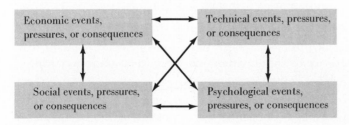

NOTE: Each set of events and pressures may originate in the unit or outside it. Each set of consequences may be limited to the unit or may have ramifications outside it.

228 *The Systems and Contingency Approaches to Organization Theory*

TABLE 6–1
Formal Subsystems of Organizations: Their Functions, Dynamics, and Mechanisms

Subsystem structure	Function	Thrust	Mechanisms
Production: primary processes	Task accomplishment: energy transformation within organization	Efficiency—get the most at the least cost	Division of labor: setting up of job specification and standards
Maintenance of working structure	Mediating between task demands and human needs to keep structure in operation	Maintenance of steady state; conservation of productive resources	Formalization of activities into standard procedures; setting up of system rewards; socialization of new members
Boundary systems			
Production-supportive: procurement of materials and manpower and product disposal	Transactional exchanges at system boundaries	Specific manipulation of organizational environment	Acquiring control of sources of supply; creation of image
Institutional	Obtaining social support and legitimation	Societal manipulation and integration	Contributing to community; influencing other social structures; public relations
Adaptive	Intelligence, research and development, planning	Pressure for change	Making recommendations for change to management; technical analyses of problem areas and opportunities
Managerial	Resolving conflicts between hierarchical levels	Control	Use of authority and persuasion

TABLE 6–1 (Continued)

Subsystem structure	Function	Thrust	Mechanisms
	Coordinating and directing functional substructures	Compromise or integration	Alternative concessions; setting up machinery for adjudication; planning and budgeting
	Coordinating external requirements and organizational resources and needs	Long-term survival: optimization, better use of resources, development of increased capabilities	Increasing volume of business; adding functions; controlling environment by absorbing it or changing it; restructuring organization

SOURCE: Based on D. Katz and R. Kahn, *The Social Psychology of Organizations* (New York: Wiley, 1966), p. 86.

effort. Under conditions of seclusion and danger, thousands of feet below surface, the miners were deprived of the company of other miners. The new technique of production caused great disaffection, and productivity suffered. Thus, economic factors had technical, social, and psychological consequences. The technique of production was subsequently modified to permit greater interaction on job. Morale improved, and productivity rose.

Interaction Between Subsystems

Leavitt has drawn on the sociotechnical perspective to propose that organizational change, whether it originates in a change in the structure of the organization, or the tasks performed by it, or the techniques by which tasks are performed, or the organization's human component, is likely to have repercussions for the other three.[13] For example, suppose a large trade union supports a new political party to further its interests. This represents a change in the tasks performed by the organization, for now not only is the trade union trying to protect the interests of its members, it is trying to mold the government of the country to its own ideology and interests. One possible structural implication may be the setting up of a new administrative unit whose mission would be to secure resources for fighting elections and mobilizing public opinion in favor of the new party. A technological implication may be a much greater use of market research techniques to find out what the electorate wants, what programs may "sell," and how they should be "packaged." The human consequences of the decision to work with a new political party may be the influx of politicians into the trade union, with possibly differing personal habits, feelings, norms about right and wrong, and preferences about political strategy.

The installation of a computerized information system represents a change in the techniques employed in the organization to achieve its goals. This has been shown to have substantial structural and human consequences, such as the regrouping of certain work units, the elimination of certain clerical personnel, and a better quality of decision-making by managers.[14] Walker's study of automation in a steel mill affords another illustration of technical changes triggering a wide variety of other changes in the organization.[15]

The Leavitt framework can be utilized both to analyze what happens in any of the subsystems identified by Katz and Kahn and also to trace the implications of a change in a subsystem for other subsystems in the organization. A structural change in the managerial subsystem, such as decentralization of decision-making authority, may trigger technical, human, and goal-related changes within the managerial subsystem, such as a greater reliance on impersonal control systems, higher managerial motivation, and greater diversification in the goals pursued by the organization. Thus, the managerial subsystem, through a process of dynamic homeostasis, will reach a new equilibrium forged by the new set of social, technical, and economic forces. It will now have a different set of tasks, structure, techniques, and characteristics of people working in it. But these in turn may have spill-over effects on the technical, maintenance, adaptive, institutional, and production-supportive subsystems interfacing with the managerial subsystem. For example, the greater decentralization in the managerial subsystem may imply a greater autonomy for the production manager, who now feels free to institute changes in the production processes that require the retraining of personnel. The Leavitt framework enables us to foresee the structural, task-related, human, and technological *organization-wide* consequences of a change in any part of it. The interactions between subsystems are illustrated in Figure 6–2.

Administrative Uses of Systems Theory

Consider the adage "For want of a nail the shoe was lost; for want of a shoe the horse was lost; for want of a horse the general was lost; for want of the

FIGURE 6–2
Interaction Within and Between Organizational Subsystems

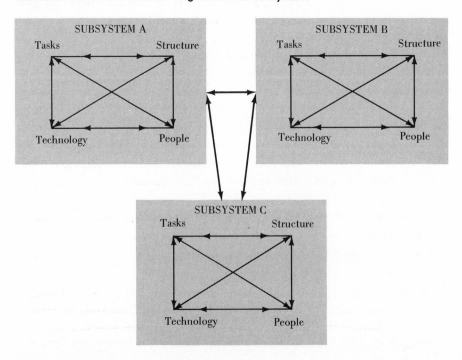

general the battle was lost; for want of the battle the war was lost; ... This systemic property of events, that their ultimate causes may be extremely remote, makes the task of the *applied* systems theorist a difficult one; it would simply be too time consuming to trace through in detail all the multiple chains of causes impinging on an event. Seiler, therefore, proposes that in systems analysis of behavior in organizations, the manager be *selective* in the phenomena chosen for study.[16]

We have seen that systems consist of subsystems. For example, the universe is a system consisting of successively smaller subsystems, like clusters of galaxies, star clusters, stars, planets, satellites. The organization as a system consists of departments, which are subsystems, and in each department there are sections, each section in turn being a subsystem whose subsystems are work groups and individuals. Since the intensity of interrelationships within a subsystem is greater than the intensity of the relationship between the subsystem and the system to which it belongs, it would be desirable to locate first of all the major system relevant to an event but then to focus on the subsystem most closely affecting the event to see how it affected the event. For example, if there is a volcanic eruption on the moon, we identify the solar system as the relevant supersystem but then focus on the properties of the moon as the most appropriate subsystem. If a few workers vandalize a plant, we locate the organization, or perhaps the factory, as the relevant system but concentrate our attention on the work groups to which these workers belong. Naturally, once we understand better how the properties of the focal subsystem affected the event, we can ask whether the nature of the relationship between a subsystem and the next higher system may play a part in explaining why the event took place. If sabotage by a worker took place in a work group that was disaffected with management, the relationship between the work group and management—for example, the nature of supervision, the nature of the remuneration given to the workers—would be considered. If the remuneration appears to be exploitative, the nature of the relationship between management and society (the next higher system) might be considered—whether society, through its laws and norms sanctions, perhaps encourages, exploitation, as in early forms of capitalism and communism (see Figure 6–3).

Second, Seiler proposes that we need not know everything we can know about a relevant system before we act. We must exercise judgment if we are not to be swamped by information. To be able to do this, we need to

establish who we are, what our role is, what our competence is, and what our goals are. Then we choose to analyze the internal workings of those systems whose internal condition is something we can and want to do something about. Other systems whose internal condition is beyond our compe-

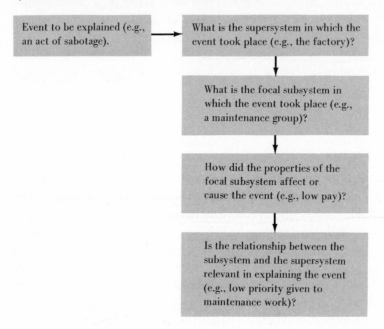

tence or role or desire to influence are taken into account only insofar as their effects impinge on the internal workings of systems we *are* trying to influence.[17]

When a disturbed worker is brought before a psychiatrist, the latter concentrates on the internal motivational state of the worker and the stresses being experienced, only tangentially taking into account the characteristics of the work group, the nature of the management system affecting the work group, and so on, since these are not areas in which the psychiatrist has much influence.

What systemic forces or inputs are most relevant in organizational analysis? Seiler identifies four that should be considered in analyzing any organizational *situation*.[18] The first are *human* inputs, such as the personalities, attitudes, skills, knowledge, expectations, and values of organizational participants. Next are *technological* inputs, such as the nature of operations technology—for example, whether it is mass production or custom type, automated or labor intensive, undergoing rapid or only minimal technological change. The third set of inputs are *organizational* inputs, such as operating procedures, policies, the structure of authority—for example, whether it is decentralized or centralized and what are its control mechanisms such as incentives, sanctions, controls. Finally, there are _social_ inputs, such as the attitudes and norms of work groups, nonformal leadership, and the like. These four sets of forces, often interrelated in complex ways in a given situation, affect activities (walk, talk, work with hands, sit and think, etc.); interactions between individuals; and sentiments or attitudes. (See Figure 6–4.) Seiler gives many examples of systems analysis applied to practical situations.

Conclusion

The systems approach is undoubtedly mind broadening. It calls attention to social, psychological, economic, and technical forces; to goals, roles, norms, structure, technology, people, and environment; to the various subsystems of the organization, their functions and orientations. It indicates that these are interrelated and that the relationships are dynamic. What it fails to do is to spell out the precise relationships among these. It is one thing to say that economic forces trigger social, technical, and psychological changes in the organization. But this is not enough. What we need is a statement of _what_ economic forces initiate _what_ social, technical, and psychological changes. It is the difference between saying X is related to Y and saying a change in X leads to an increase (or decrease, as the case may be) in Y. To a limited extent, the contingency orientation in organization theory fills this lacuna.

FIGURE 6–4
Inputs and Outputs in Organizational Systems Analysis as Indicated by Seiler

FIGURE 6–5

A Comparison of Carnegie, Systems, and Contingency Paradigms

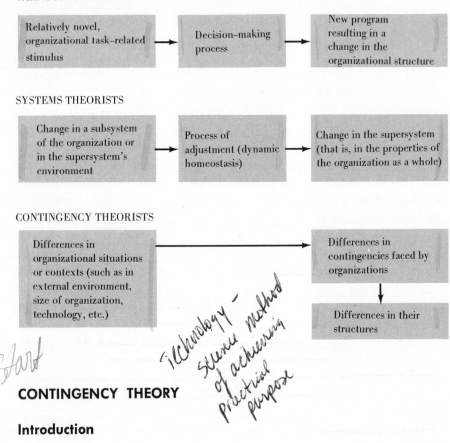

CARNEGIE THEORISTS

| Relatively novel, organizational task–related stimulus | → | Decision–making process | → | New program resulting in a change in the organizational structure |

SYSTEMS THEORISTS

| Change in a subsystem of the organization or in the supersystem's environment | → | Process of adjustment (dynamic homeostasis) | → | Change in the supersystem (that is, in the properties of the organization as a whole) |

CONTINGENCY THEORISTS

| Differences in organizational situations or contexts (such as in external environment, size of organization, technology, etc.) | → | Differences in contingencies faced by organizations |
then ↓
| Differences in their structures |

(handwritten annotations: "Start", "Technology – science method of achieving practical purpose", "Chance or possible event / liable to happen")

CONTINGENCY THEORY

Introduction

The so-called contingency theorists—Woodward, Burns and Stalker, Thompson, Lawrence and Lorsch, and Perrow, to mention a few—like the systems theorists, give a great deal of weight to the interface between the organization and its task environment. But unlike the systems theorists and the Carnegie theorists, their emphasis is not so much on the dynamics of the process by which an organization adapts as on the end result itself (see Figure 6–5). The paradigm is similar to the stimulus-response model of the Skinnerians, who also more or less ignore the *process* by which a stimulus results in the emission of a response.

The basic idea of the contingency theorists is that the nature of the organization's technology, its size, its legal incorporation, the character of its markets, and other factors confront the organization with some opportunities as well as constraints and problems and therefore set the tone of the organization's adaptation as revealed by its structure. The idea is an elaboration of the biologist's functionalist view of the adaptation of living forms to their environment. For example, elephants have trunks to enable them to feed from their great height, and apes have prehensile fingers and toes to enable them to swing from trees. Contingency theory indicates the kinds of structure that may be appropriate responses to each of several different organizational contexts or situations.

Contingency theory has had a profound impact on contemporary organization theory and on the applied field of organizational design. Its most notable contributions are in identifying the variables that have a major impact on the overall design of the organization, such as size, technology, and the nature of the environment, and then in *predicting* the differences in the structure and functioning of organizations that arise because of differences in these variables. The rest of this book is largely an elaboration of this perspective. It will not, therefore, be amiss to review some of the landmark studies that have shaped contemporary organization theory.

A Brief Chronicle of Major Studies

Woodward. In 1958, Joan Woodward published her study of one hundred English manufacturing firms.[19] Her original intention was to see whether the principles of management enunciated by Mooney, Gulick, Urwick, and others (Chapter 4) were observed in business or not. She found that the so-called principles of social organization were widely ignored. What is more important, she found that differences in technology accounted for differences she found in organizational structures. She developed a scale for measuring technology. In her scale, technologies ranged from those designed for custom manufacture to those designed for continuous process production of liquids, solids, and gases, with large batch and mass production technologies being intermediate on her scale. She called her scale a scale of technological complexity, with custom technology being regarded as the most noncomplex and continuous process technology being regarded as the most complex. She classified the firms by the technology they predominantly used.

In the expanded version of her original work, she has graphically shown her major findings and discussed these at length.[20] Table 6–2 summarizes some of the findings in Chapter 4 of this work. Her work has been criticized as being methodologically sloppy, and later attempts to replicate her findings often failed to find the same or similar relationships,[21] but hers was a pioneering study, and it firmly established the importance of technology as a determinant of organization structure.

TABLE 6–2
Some of Woodward's Findings

	Custom production	Mass production	Continuous process production
Median number of management levels	3	4	6
Average number of employees controlled by first-line supervisors	25	50	11
Median number of industrial workers per single member of staff	8	5.5	2
Percentage of costs allocated to wages	30	26	15

Burns and Stalker. Tom Burns, a sociologist, and G. M. Stalker, a psychologist, examined twenty British firms in the electronics industry.[22] For their conclusions they relied primarily on unstructured interviews with the executives and staff of the firms they studied. Though they did not quantify their information, they were able to form insightful impressions of how technological and market changes affected the firms they studied.

They identified two radically opposite management styles, which they called the organic style and the mechanistic style. The organic style is characterized by a highly flexible and informal organization, with individuals communicating not only with their immediate superiors, subordinates, and colleagues, but with anyone else in the organization with whom they have a task-related need to communicate. Formal authority is not nearly as important as situational authority. In other words, the degree of influence a person has in a given situation depends on what contribution that person can make to the solution of the problem rather than to formal rank in the organization. Duties and responsibilities, too, are constantly reshaped by situational demands. The awareness of organizational goals permeates not only the upper echelons but also the rank and file. Burns and Stalker observed a tendency for firms facing rapid technological and market change to practice this style. They felt that this style is appropriate to unstable conditions in which novel problems continually arise. In such conditions, specialists must continually interact and readjust their plans. This becomes possible if management philosophy encourages vertical and horizontal interactions that ignore departmental boundaries and channels of communication laid out in the organization chart.

The mechanistic style has many of the elements of bureaucracy: strictly defined duties, responsibilities, and authority; highly structured channels of communication; a highly formalized hierarchy of authority; and so forth. In addition, it has some of the elements of traditional management, such as highly visible status differences between the upper and the lower echelons of management and a great deal of insistence on personal and departmental loyalty. Burns and Stalker observed a tendency for firms in technologically static parts of the electronics industry to use this management style.

Burns and Stalker noted the difficulty mechanistic firms had in adapting to technological innovation. Internalized bureaucratic values impelled their managements to try essentially bureaucratic means for solving organizational and technical problems created by innovation. Burns and Stalker call these "pathological systems." In one pathological system, the decisions related to innovation are continually referred up to the chief executive because subordinates do not feel competent or confident to make decisions in novel situations. As a consequence, the chief executive not only is overburdened, but since the information relevant to the decision is available with the subordinate who pushed up the decision in the first place, the chief develops a number of dyadic relationships with lower level subordinates. This is, of course, quite upsetting to those in the organization who feel that all communication from the top should pass through proper channels.

Another pathological system, called "the mechanistic jungle" by Burns and Stalker, involves the creation of liaison officers, contract or project managers, and committees to deal with problems of change. The problem is that the power and authority of liaison officers, project managers, and committee heads is tied to the perpetuation of their groups—that is to say, to the perpetuation of the difficulty that forced management to set up these groups. As a consequence, the organization swarms with small bureaucracies that keep busy creating justifications for their continued existence.

The organic and mechanistic styles are ideal types. In actuality organizations are likely to show different combinations of elements of the two styles. There are few organizations, if any, that are purely mechanistic or purely organic.

Lawrence and Lorsch. One basic idea of these two professors at the Harvard Business School has been that different parts of the organization face different task environments. For example, in a typical manufacturing firm, the environment of the marketing department is competition, market fluctuations, customer preferences. The environment of the research and development department, on the other hand, is technical innovations that are taking place in the industry, innovations in product design, the development or discovery of new products.

P. Lawrence and J. Lorsch have argued that these differences in the task environment inevitably imply that the organization gets differentiated.[3] In other words, its different parts develop distinctive structures, values, attitudes, and orientations. For example, if the task environment of the production department is more "certain" than that of the research and development department, the former may be more structured than the latter. Production people may have more formal interpersonal relations than people in research and development. The planning horizon of production managers may be shorter than that of R and D managers. The production managers are likely to have strongly held efficiency goals. The R and D managers may instead have goals of fostering creativity and innovation. This idea of differentiation is rather similar to the idea of Katz and Kahn, discussed earlier in the chapter, that different subsystems of the organizational system, because of differences in their orientations and functions, employ structures and processes that differ from subsystem to subsystem (see Table 6–1).

Lawrence and Lorsch argue that in highly differentiated organizations, integration of activities becomes very important. By integration they mean "the quality of the state of collaboration that exists among departments that are required to achieve unity of effort by the demands of the environment."[24] In other words, the more the organization is characterized by differential structures and by differences in departmental goals, interpersonal orientations, attitudes, beliefs about what is good management practice, and the like, the more the organization must try to create a unity of purpose and the more it should encourage a willingness on the part of different personnel and departments to collaborate in achieving the goals of the organization as a whole. Organizations try to achieve this unity of purpose by using a number of mechanisms: by designing a chain of command; by having integrating committees or liaison individuals and groups; by setting up standard operating procedures; or by training managers in human relations, to name just some. Figure 6–6 shows the Lawrence and Lorsch model.

The novel aspect of the Lawrence and Lorsch model is, not that organizations are differentiated or that they need to have their activities properly coordinated, but that the organization, in order to be effective, needs to be *both* differentiated and integrated and that the *degree* of differentiation and integration depends on the degree of diversity in the task environments of the organization's different departments.

Lawrence and Lorsch studied ten organizations in three industries—six in the plastics industry, two in the container industry, and two in the consumer food industry. They gave questionnaires to between thirty and fifty upper-level and middle-level managers in each organization and interviewed several as well. They gathered data (a) on the perceived uncertainty in the task environments of the production department, the marketing department, and the research and development department of each of these organizations and (b) on the extent to which the departments in each organization were dif-

FIGURE 6–6
The Lawrence and Lorsch Model of Organizational Differentiation and Integration

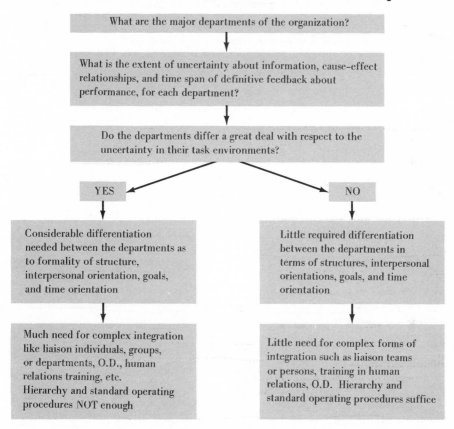

ferentiated and the extent to which the organization as a whole was integrated. They found what their model predicted—namely, that organizations, such as the plastics organizations, whose departments had varying degrees of uncertainty in their task environments, were more differentiated and employed more complex forms of integration or coordination than organizations, such as those manufacturing containers, whose departments had little variation in task environment uncertainty. What is more, they found that the higher performance organizations in each *industry* had higher levels of integration of activities than the lower performance organizations, although not necessarily higher levels of differentiation.[25] Several students of Lawrence and Lorsch have extended this type of work.[26]

Thompson. The death of James D. Thompson, a sociologist by training, deprived organization theory of a major contributor. As he put it, "uncertainty appears as the fundamental problem for complex organizations,

Contingency Theory **241**

and coping with uncertainty is the essence of the administrative process . . . . the tighter the norms of rationality, the more energy the organization will devote to moving toward certainty."[27] This is because the planning of operations clearly is easier under conditions of certainty—that is, when the future is perceived to be predictable rather than unpredictable and capricious. The oil embargo by the Middle East oil producers made the future full of uncertainty for many governments: the oil embargo might or might not be lifted; oil might or might not be available in sufficient quantity or at acceptable prices; further war might or might not break out; protectionist policies might or might not be initiated by other governments; domestic industry might or might not cut back on capital spending; and so on and on. It is clear that decisive, rational, efficiently planned action becomes very difficult in situations such as this.

Since uncertainty is disruptive, Thompson proposed: "Organizations under norms of rationality seek to place their boundaries around those activities which if left to the task of environment would be crucial contingencies."[28] Thus, an organization employing mass production technology (called "long-linked technology" by Thompson) will be inclined to acquire control over sources of crucial raw materials and channels of distribution if there is persistent uncertainty about the availability of these raw materials or channels of distribution. Many oil and steel firms integrated vertically for this reason. Without vertical integration, there might be no assurance of operating the plant at full capacity and reaping thereby the benefits of economies of scale. On the other hand, an organization employing an "intensive" technology, such as the intensive care unit of a hospital, is likely to seek as much control over the object worked upon, whether it is a patient or a respirator. An organization using a "mediating technology"—that is, a technology that connects different users of the product or the service—such as an employment agency or a telephone network, is likely to try to diversify the market it serves so that it does not get too dependent on any one market.

Thus, organizations grow to anticipate contingencies and in the process acquire components whose capacities are often not balanced or matched. This creates excess capacity in some components, which generates a tendency for the organization to grow further to make fuller use of these partially idle components. As Thompson put it: "The multicomponent organizations subject to rationality norms will seek to grow until the least reducible component is approximately fully occupied. . . . Should the organization as a whole have excess production capacity, it will seek to enlarge its domains, that is, try to reach out into new markets or new areas."[29]

Thompson proposed a fourfold classification of the organization's environment: stable and homogeneous, stable and heterogeneous, unstable and homogeneous, and unstable and heterogeneous. The corner grocery store is likely to have a stable and homogeneous environment. The department store on the other hand, catering as it does to a great variety of customers and customer needs, is likely to have a stable and heterogeneous environment. The electronic data-processing systems firm catering to specialized clients is likely to have an unstable and homogeneous environment (unstable because of the rapid rate of innovation in computer hardware and software). The multinational corporation, such as Litton Industries, I.B.M., or General Motors, is likely to have an unstable and heterogeneous environment.

Thompson argued that environmental heterogeneity and instability have significant implications for organizational structure—for example, that "organizations facing heterogeneous task environments seek to identify homogeneous segments and establish structural units to deal with each."[30] Thus, there may be a tendency for divisionalization in a diversified organization. Moreover, "boundary-spanning components facing homogeneous segments of the task environment are further subdivided to match surveillance capacity with environmental action." For example, the marketing department may set up sections to deal with different regions or types of customers. The U.S. State Department has various country "desks."

In another context, "the organization component facing a stable task environment will rely on rules to achieve its adaptation to that environment." When the environment is stable, the organization has ample time to learn a few simple rules that have proved effective in the past. The book-lending rules of libraries are an example. And, "when the range of variation presented by the task environment segment is known, the organization component will treat this as a constraint and adapt by standardizing sets of rules." This is the typical situation of bureaucratic government departments. They develop a system for categorizing persons or events and then develop rules for responding to each category of persons or events. For example, a welfare department may first categorize its clientele into senior citizens, unemployed but able-bodied persons, and unemployables. Then it devises rules for responding to the needs of each class of clients.

On the other hand, "when the range of task-environment variations is large or unpredictable, the responsible organization must achieve the necessary adaptation by monitoring that environment and planning responses, and this calls for localized units." This seems to suggest decentralized decision-making and planning in organizations facing unpredictable, highly variable, contingency-rich environments.

Figure 6–7 summarizes the organization's response to properties of its environment.

Besides the characteristics of the organization's task environment, another major force shaping the organization is the various types of dependency relationship in its workflow. Thompson distinguished between

FIGURE 6–7
Thompson's View of Organizational Adaptation to Environment

	Homogeneous environment	*Heterogeneous environment*
Stable Environment	Rules and categories for applying rules	Divisions; sections; rules and categories for applying rules
Unstable Environment	Uncertainty absorption (monitoring); contingency planning; decentralized decision-making	Divisions; sections; uncertainty absorption (monitoring); contingency planning; decentralized decision-making

reciprocal dependencies, sequential or serial dependencies, and pooled dependencies. When two individuals, A and B, depend on each other for their work, as a buyer and a seller often do, then the dependency is reciprocal. When B depends on A but not vice versa, and C depends on B but not vice versa, the relationship is a serial or sequential dependency. Assembly line relationships are of this type. When A, B, and C draw on a common pool of resources, such as when three professors share the same secretary, the relationship is called a pooled dependency. Figure 6–8 illustrates these various dependencies in a divisionalized organization.

Thompson argued that activities must be coordinated wherever there is a situation of dependency. He suggested that organizations minimize the costs of coordination, first, by grouping the reciprocally dependent parts together and, next, by grouping together or linking the serially dependent parts. Thereafter, coordination costs are minimized by assigning personnel to functionally homogeneous units. For example, in a university, professors teaching complementary courses that lead to a specialization are located together in faculties or departments to minimize coordination costs. Thus does a business school end up having statisticians, mathematicians, economists, behavioral scientists. Within a faculty, professors who teach sequentially dependent courses tend to be grouped together. For example, professors teaching organization behavior and organization theory tend to be grouped with behavioral scientists because the course succession usually is a course in behavioral science followed by courses in organizational behavior and organization theory. This way, coordination costs are decreased.

FIGURE 6–8

Dependencies in a Divisionalized Organization

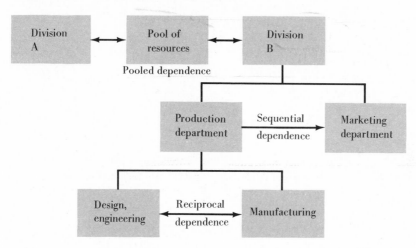

NOTE: The arrows point to the source of the dependency.
SOURCE: The author is indebted to Professor Andrew Van de Ven for suggesting this diagram.

Finally, professors teaching different sections of the same course are linked together to facilitate standardization in course offerings. When it is not practicable to group together personnel that have some dependency on one another because they have been assigned to groups on some other basis, the organization tries to minimize coordinative costs by applying standardized rules of conduct to the interdependent personnel. For example, secretaries may be assigned to different professors. But rules regarding leave, working hours, pay scales, and so on are devised to minimize coordination and supervision costs. Other coordination devices employed by the organization are liaison positions, committees, and task forces to link interdependent units that cannot be grouped together for any reason.[31]

Thompson also discussed the forces that shape the form of the organization's structure. In the *absence* of a strong, continuing dependency between the technical core of an organization (such as the manufacturing department of a firm) and its boundary-spanning units (e.g., the marketing department), the organization is likely to have centralized decision-making for scheduling technical and boundary-spanning operations, and the organization will be functionally departmentalized. This is the common organizational structure for mass production organizations operating in a stable environment. But when there is a strong, continuing dependency between the technical core and the boundary-spanning units, they will be clustered together into divisions.[32] Organizations designed to handle unique or custom

custom

tasks try to minimize coordination costs by basing specialists in functionally specialized departments for administrative purposes but deploying them into task forces for operational purposes." This often results in what is nowadays called the "matrix structure."

Thompson tried to fuse together the view of the systems theorists that the task environment is a powerful shaper of the organization and the "bounded rationality" perspective of the Carnegie theorists, especially of March and Simon, which stressed that organizations develop structures precisely because their human members have limited information-processing and problem-solving capability (see Chapter 5). He also took cognizance of organizational economics, especially the notion that organizations try to minimize the costs of coordinating their multitudinous activities.

Perrow. Like James Thompson, Charles Perrow is an organization theorist with training in sociology. He has identified two dimensions of work situations that he proposes have major consequences for organizational structure. One dimension of work situation is variability, the other is search.[34] A work situation may be stable (or uniform), or it may be variable because of variability in the materials worked upon. A doctor cannot treat all patients identically because patients differ a great deal. The work situation may be readily analyzable, or a fair degree of search may be required before the problem can be solved. Sniffles and sneezes may readily tell the doctor that the patient has a cold and that aspirin may be the appropriate remedy. Little search is needed. But symptoms of fever and painful spasms in the region of the liver may require blood and urine analysis before a diagnosis can be made and medicine prescribed. A lot of search is needed here—and a fair degree of thinking on the part of the doctor about how to proceed.

Perrow labels work procedures or the technology employed in a work situation as *craft* when the work involved is fairly uniform ("few exceptions") and search is fairly difficult ("unanalyzable search"). *Routine technology* is employed when the work involved is fairly uniform ("few exceptions") and not much search is needed to solve any work-related problems ("analyzable search"). *Nonroutine technology* is employed when the task stimulus is variable ("many exceptions") and search is fairly difficult ("unanalyzable search"). *Engineering technology* is used when the task stimulus is variable ("many exceptions") and readily analyzable ("analyzable search").

Perrow says that "in the interests of efficiency, organizations wittingly or unwittingly attempt to maximize the congruence between their technology and their structure."[35] Thus, if different organizations use different technologies, they will end up with differing structures. He identifies three di-

Variable = many exceptions

FIGURE 6-9
Perrow's Analysis of Technology and Organizational Structure

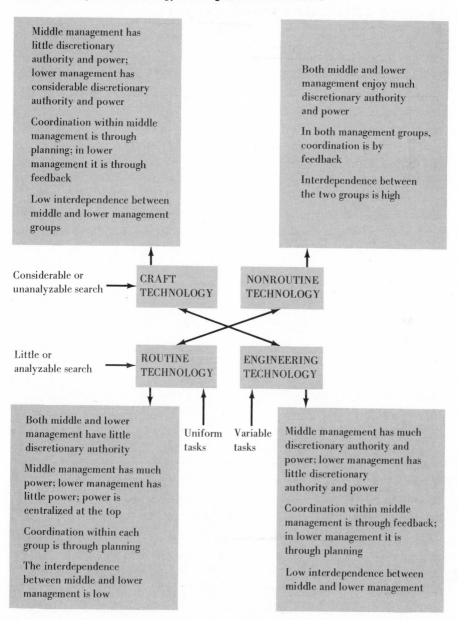

Middle management has little discretionary authority and power; lower management has considerable discretionary authority and power

Coordination within middle management is through planning; in lower management it is through feedback

Low interdependence between middle and lower management groups

Both middle and lower management enjoy much discretionary authority and power

In both management groups, coordination is by feedback

Interdependence between the two groups is high

Considerable or unanalyzable search → **CRAFT TECHNOLOGY**   **NONROUTINE TECHNOLOGY**

Little or analyzable search → **ROUTINE TECHNOLOGY**   **ENGINEERING TECHNOLOGY**

Uniform tasks   Variable tasks

Both middle and lower management have little discretionary authority

Middle management has much power; lower management has little power; power is centralized at the top

Coordination within each group is through planning

The interdependence between middle and lower management is low

Middle management has much discretionary authority and power; lower management has little discretionary authority and power

Coordination within middle management is through feedback; in lower management it is through planning

Low interdependence between middle and lower management

mensions of organizational structure: the discretionary authority of middle and lower management groups and their power;[36] the basis of coordination within each group; and the interdependence of the two groups. Figure 6-9 indicates the organizational structure associated with each of the "craft," "nonroutine," "routine," and "engineering" technologies. The organizational structure associated with nonroutine technology is very similar to the organic management of Burns and Stalker. The organizational structure associated with routine technology is very similar to their mechanistic management. The organizational structure associated with craft technology is decentralized. The structure associated with engineering technology is flexible but centralized.

Perrow's hypotheses are appropriate to work groups. He has unfortunately extrapolated them to whole organizations on the assumption that the technology of the entire organization can be categorized as craft, engineering, routine, or nonroutine. Sizable complex organizations utilize many different technologies. The most one can say is that in each part of the organization, the technology employed is likely to produce the comparable structure. Thus conceived, the Perrow perspective usefully supplements the Lawrence and Lorsch view that parts of the organization differ from one another because of differences in their task environments.

Conclusion

A good deal of organizational research can be called "contingency theory research." Some of the pioneering work has been reviewed in this chapter. Some other work, notably that of the Aston group, which we reviewed in Chapter 4, is also in this tradition. In succeeding chapters we will be drawing upon a good deal more research of this type, including the author's own.

At the moment, contingency theory is perhaps the most powerful current sweeping over the organizational field. The history of many fields shows a movement from universalistic principles to *situational* relationships and principles. The current prominence of contingency theory suggests that organization theory is entering a period of scientific maturity. Because of the intellectual efforts of men and women like Woodward, Burns and Stalker, Lawrence and Lorsch, Thompson, and Perrow, a decade from now organization theory will be fleshed out much more fully by the findings of systematic empirical work.

And yet there is something unsatisfactory about contingency theory, a tendency to see unique organizational responses to environmental and technological stimuli. Contingency theorists have tended to underemphasize, often ignore, the possibility of more than one feasible organizational response to the same task environmental stimulus. Child has drawn attention to this mechanistic flavor of contingency theorists.[37] The chances are that the task environment constrains the choice of organizational design; but it does not constrain it to just one possibility. The further development of organization theory may well depend on the identification of *alternative* feasible organizational responses to the same task environmental stimuli.

A COMPARISON OF SYSTEMS AND CONTINGENCY ORIENTATIONS

Model of the Human Being

The systems theorists usually employ a much richer model of the human animal than contingency theorists. The former take into account, as Emery and Trist, Katz and Kahn, and Seiler do, the full range of human needs and motivations. The contingency theorists on the other hand are, by and large, much more interested in structural adaptations of organizations to their task environments and generally content themselves with a naive, "average person" model. One of the reasons for this is that social psychologists have been some of the principal contributors to systems theories, while sociologists have been the main contributors to contingency theory.

Strategic Organizational Variables

Systems theories are all encompassing: they try to cover personal, social, technical, structural, and environmental variables. Contingency theorists so far have concentrated on structural adaptations of organizations to their task environments. Systems theorists like to describe the process by which an organization moves from one situation to another. Contingency theorists like to slur over this process and predict instead the ultimate outcome of a disturbance of the organizational equilibrium by a change in the task environment.

Evolution

It is possible that the two orientations may merge—or at least profoundly influence each other. Systems theorists may learn to try to make precise predictions of how an organizational system will behave under different contingencies. Contingency theorists may become more interested in (a) the process by which organizations adapt to their task environments and (b) the systems notion of equifinality—that is, the notion that several different adaptation strategies may be available to an organization facing a particular contingency.

Questions for Organization Analysis

The two approaches prompt the following questions for organization theory and for analyzing any particular organization (Table 6–3).

SUMMARY

In this chapter, we have examined two related orientations in organization theory. The systems orientation and contingency orientation both emphasize the importance of the task environment and the need for the organization to adapt to its task environment.

A number of aspects of the systems analysis of organizations were explored. These were: (a) the properties of the organization as a living, open system—principally, input-process-output cycle, entropy, differentiation, and equifinality; (b) the principal subsystems of the organizational system—namely, the institutional, managerial, technical, production-supportive,

TABLE 6–3
Questions for Organization Theory and for the Analysis of Organizations

	Questions for organization theory	Questions for organizational analysis
Systems orientation	1. What are the major subsystems of organizations? What are their properties? How do they interact?	1. What are the major subsystems of the organization? What are their properties? How do they interact?
	2. What are the properties of organizational systems? What kinds of relationship do they have with the environment? What are the processes by which organizations adjust to changes in their environments? Are there alternative paths to the same ultimate state?	2. What are the properties of the organization as a whole? What kind of relationship does the organization have with its environment? How does the organization adjust to changes in its environment? Does it use multiple modes of adjustment?
	3. How do organizational changes affect subsystems and how do changes in any subsystem affect the properties of the whole system?	3. How do changes in the organization affect its various subsystems, and how do changes in any of its subsystems affect the organization as a whole?

adaptive, and maintenance subsystems; (c) the social, technical, and economic forces shaping organizational systems or subsystems; (d) the interaction between task-related, structural, technological, and human variables; and (e) the administrative uses of systems analysis in identifying the *key* organizational systems or subsystems affecting an event and in formulating an input-output analysis of organizational situations.

Contingency theory is the most powerful orientation in organization theory today. Contingency theorists have concentrated on relating differences in organizational structure to differences in the task environments of organizations. Since this book relies heavily on this orientation, an attempt was made to sketch the contribution of the founders. Woodward observed that in the sample of firms she studied, the form of technology used by the organization appeared to determine the organization's structure. Burns and Stalker identified the organic and the mechanistic styles and associated them with dynamic and stable environmental conditions respectively. Lawrence and Lorsch observed that different parts of the organization tend to

	Questions for organization theory	Questions for organizational analysis
Contingency orientation	1. What are the different dimensions of the task environments of organizations? What contingencies, constraints, etc. does each dimension pose to organizations?	1. What are the major dimensions of the organization's task environment? What contingencies, constraints, threats, and opportunities do they pose to the organization?
	2. What are the principal dimensions of organizational structure that are sensitive to the influence of the task environment? How does each structural dimension get affected by the properties of the task environment?	2. What are the chief elements of the organization's structure, and how have they been shaped by the properties of the organization's task environment?
	3. Are there systematic differences in the task environments of the different parts of organizations? How do they introduce structural differentiation within organizations? How do organizations counteract this differentiation?	3. Are there notable differences in the task environments of the major departments of the organization? Have these caused significant structural differences between the departments? What integrative mechanisms is the organization using?

have distinctively different task environments. Where these environmental differences are pronounced, the parts of the organization get highly differentiated from one another, and the organization must utilize complex, integrative mechanisms to keep the activities of the different parts coordinated. In other words, high levels of environmental differentiation beget high levels of organizational differentiation as well as integration. Thompson identified uncertainty as a crucial problem for organizations since it makes rational, efficient planning of operations difficult. He found that organizations using different kinds of technology employ different devices to circumvent uncertainty. He also argued that organizations respond differently to heterogeneous or dynamic environments than to homogeneous or stable environments. He felt that dependency relationships in the organization's workflow are the basis for grouping individuals together in organizations. Perrow basing his analysis on the extent of needed search and the variability of tasks facing an individual or a group, identified four different technologies—namely, craft, engineering, routine, and nonroutine. His analysis suggests that parts of the organization employing craft technology (much or unanalyzable search, little variability) tend to be decentralized; those employing engineering technology (little or analyzable search, much variability) tend to be centralized but flexible; those employing routine technology (little or analyzable search, little variability) tend to be mechanistically organized; and those employing nonroutine technology (much or unanalyzable search, much variability) tend to have an organic structure.

Many systems theorists in the organizational area have been social psychologists, while many contingency theorists have been sociologists. This probably accounts for the much greater attention paid to personality and process variables by systems theorists and to structural variables by contingency theorists. In future, the systems theorists may take to formulating hypotheses the way contingency theorists do; the latter may pay more attention to the principle of equifinality and to the processes by which the organization adapts to its task environment. The questions the two orientations prompt for organization theorists and for organizational analysts are shown in Table 6–3.

SUGGESTED READINGS

Chadwick J. Haberstroh, "Organizational Design and Systems Analysis," pp. 1171–1212 in James March, ed., *Handbook of Organizations* (Chicago: Rand-McNally, 1965). A survey piece. For a compendium of readings, see Frank Baker, *Organizational Systems* (Homewood, Ill.: Irwin, 1973).

Chs. 2, 3, and 4 in D. Katz and R. Kahn, *The Social Psychology of Organizations* (New York: Wiley, 1966).

Chs. 1, 8, and 9 in Paul Lawrence and Jay Lorsch, *Organization and Environmen* (Homewood, Ill.: Irwin, 1967).

Chs. 2, 3, and 4 in Charles Perrow, *Organizational Analysis: A Sociological View* (Belmont, Calif.: Wadsworth, 1970).

Chs. 1, 2, and 8 in John A. Seiler, *Systems Analysis in Organizational Behavior* (Homewood, Ill.: Irwin, 1967).

QUESTIONS FOR ANALYSIS

1 Suppose that two large American equipment-manufacturing companies bid for a job to set up a huge steel plant in Iran. One of them gets the bid; the other one loses. How would the different subsystems in the winner be affected? How would the different subsystems in the loser be affected? How would the organization as a whole be affected?

2 Consider the following case. Refer to the questions in Column 3 of Table 6–3, and try to answer as many of them as you can.

Utility Power Company

Members of engineering management at the Utility Power Company were, in 1959, searching for a method to increase the work capacity of the distribution section. Pressures for expansion of the company's electrical distribution system were increasing rapidly, calling for a marked improvement in the speed with which construction and renovation designs were made available to field construction crews.

The Utility Power Company held a franchise covering a large area of the midwestern part of the United States. Its distribution territory was divided into four regions, each responsible for the construction, maintenance, and operation of power substations, transmission lines, and auxiliary equipment, as well as for commercial activities related to customer service. The regional offices relied upon a central engineering group, the distribution section, for the design and cost information required in expanding their service facilities.

The distribution section was housed at company headquarters, located approximately 150 miles from any one of the regional offices. Two teams, in each an engineer and a draftsman, reported to the assistant section manager. Their exclusive assignment was to design and estimate costs for power substations throughout the company's franchise area. The section manager directly supervised four teams, each composed of an engineering supervisor, three engineers, and two draftsmen. Each of these four teams was responsible for designs and cost estimates for all other equipment requested by a particular distribution region. Regional work loads and priorities varied from time to time. There was a certain amount of transfer of personnel between teams as a result, although, because all regions were exerting pressure to have their work completed, team supervisors usually found reasons to hold onto their team members.

The distribution engineering teams had each developed close, friendly working relationships over the years. Engineers and draftsmen were salaried and nonunion. The men of each team had considerable opportunity to work closely together. It was the custom for all members of a team working on a particular engineering problem to travel together for several days at a time surveying some portion of a region's extensive territory. On their survey trips, and at the home office, each draftsman felt himself to be as closely integrated into his team as were the engineers. Although there were obvious distinctions of technical status (for example, each supervisor had his own office, the engineers of each team were located together, and the draftsmen of all teams worked in one large room), there appeared to be little formal barrier between team members as they worked together. Even across team lines, there appeared to be a great deal of informal, friendly interchange of information.

The draftsmen of each team, in addition to routine drafting duties, were frequently assigned those elementary design and estimating problems of which their engineering colleagues found them capable. The availability of such work made technical and salary advancement for the draftsmen a readily attainable goal. Furthermore, some of the engineers showed considerable interest in helping draftsmen, particularly those who were enrolled in correspondence schools or courses, to improve their technical skills.

The distribution section had operated in the foregoing manner for many years. Since World War II, a number of engineers and a few draftsmen had been hired as replacements and as increases to the overall engineering capacity of the section. In spite of these additions, however, a backlog of essential projects from the field had steadily mounted. Repeated efforts to obtain qualified new men, particularly draftsmen, had met with little success.

In 1959, Philip Hawkins, the distribution section manager, proposed to his superior, James Preston, that the distribution section be reorganized along more efficient and more highly productive lines.

Hawkins' plan entailed the establishment of a draftsmen's "pool." Under this proposal, all draftsmen would be removed from team affiliation, to be placed under the supervision of a chief draftsman. . . . The new supervisor would assign to draftsmen the work received from engineers according to his estimate of the individual capacities of his men and by reference to a predetermined priority schedule. Hawkins predicted that the new system would increase available drafting time and, through greater specialization, would enhance the productivity of engineers and draftsmen alike.

The proposed system was to have several additional benefits. It would remove the causes for the "sloppy setup" in controlling supplies and in operating printing and duplicating machinery. Stocks of drafting supplies had traditionally been haphazardly maintained, with occasional depletions of materials occurring unnoticed. Similarly, reproducing machinery had not been giving good service because, it was believed, each draftsman was operating the equipment to secure his own print requirements. The pool arrangement would make it possible to assign to the chief draftsman a girl who would be in charge of the stock room and the duplicating and printing equipment.

Preston agreed to study Hawkins' ideas in preparation for further discussions a few days hence.

After several discussions of the plan to reorganize the distribution section, the engineering vice president agreed with the section manager that the institution of a drafting pool would improve the section's capacity to meet its work schedule. The following implementary plan was considered by both men to be essential.

Key to the success of the pool would be the choice of a chief draftsman. It was agreed that the job would require a man with obviously superior technical ability. Since the new supervisor would have to be chosen from the ranks of the present drafting group (no outsider being available for consideration), he would have to have won the respect of all the men who were to report to him. One of the draftsmen, Roger Manson, was believed to be "head and shoulders" above the rest. Hawkins reported that Manson was working hard to increase his drafting skill, that he was more objective and aggressive in his work than the others, and that he had been given more advanced engineering work than any other draftsman. Manson had been with the distribution section for six years, somewhat less than had the majority of the draftsmen. Previously, he had spent five years as a Utility Power Company substation maintenance man. He was 33 years old, about average for the drafting group. While supervisory experience would have been desirable, none of the draftsmen possessed that qualification.

It was decided, first, to advise Manson in confidence of the new plan in order to ascertain his willingness to accept the supervisory position. Manson would be warned that he would have to rely upon the leadership which the respect for his ability would generate, rather than upon his formal position. In no case would heavy-handedness be advisable.

Assuming that Manson would accept the new job, Hawkins was to call a meeting of the entire section, including clerks and stenographers as well as engineers and draftsmen. At this meeting, he would carefully explain the nature of the change and the reasons for it. The new chief draftsman would be introduced and his duties outlined. Questions would be solicited and discussed until it appeared that the change was well understood. On the presumption that this meeting would proceed successfully, the new organization would be put into effect the next day.

Early in October, 1959, Hawkins, in a confidential meeting, proposed to Manson that the latter assume the duties of the new section post, that of chief draftsman. After listening to Hawkins' description of the job and the authority limits within which he would be expected to function, Manson eagerly accepted the position. Over the next week, the two men met several times to plan for the organization of a drafting pool. Both men were enthusiastic about the potentialities of the new plan.

On October 12, a meeting of the full section was called, the plan was explained in detail, and the chief draftsman's appointment was announced. A number of questions arose and were discussed. By the end of the meeting, everyone involved appeared to understand the change and its implications for each individual. On October 13, the plan was put into effect.

During the remainder of October and through November, the pool system seemed to be shaking down well. There were minor grumblings now and again from engineers who believed a job of theirs had not been given sufficient priority by the chief draftsman. But in the drafting room, co-operation seemed high, and the production of drawings was much improved. The chief draftsman had introduced several new techniques for correcting and reproducing drawings which had significantly reduced the need for tedious corrections and redrawing. The supply situation was brought under control, files were straightened out, and the appearance of the drafting room, in general, was radically improved.

The persistence of one custom, a holdover from the team system, seemed to be reducing the potential for further increases in the production of drawings, however. Engineers continued to take former teammate drafts-men on field survey trips. On these trips, which lasted several days, draftsmen took notes, and even carried some of the less complex jobs through the cost-estimating stage of design upon their return to the section office. In consequence, these men were out of Manson's control for a week or more at a time. Despite the problems which this custom posed for the chief drafts-man's effective scheduling of work, production of the pool was more than satisfactory.

Then, through December and the early months of 1960, Hawkins began to observe signs of increasing discontent. He heard from some of the engineers that their draftsmen friends had confided in them their growing impatience with the chief draftsman. They reported such comments as: "I used to like that guy; but now that he's got his new job, he thinks he can push any kind of petty job on me and expect me to thank him for it." Others remarked: "The work just isn't interesting like it used to be. You never know what's going on with a job. You draw a piece of it, and it gets whipped away from you before the ink is dry."

Hawkins also observed a mounting friction between the engineers and the chief draftsman. Manson and Hawkins had agreed that the chief drafts-man would have to know a good deal about each job in order to schedule drafting work properly. Particularly, Manson felt that this knowledge was critical for his ability to check drawings, as he always did, before returning them to the engineer for final authorization. However, several of the engineers referred to Manson's efforts as "interference." They remarked, in Hawkins' presence, that they could not help being impatient with having to "go through the whole story again" for Manson's benefit. They talked as though Manson stood between them and the draftsman, with whom they were "anxious to get down to cases."

In February, 1960, Hawkins began to notice the production of designs for field construction crews was falling off. The engineering supervisors reported to Hawkins that their engineers and a number of draftsmen were highly discontented. The supervisors warned that something had to be done before a full-fledged explosion occurred. One of them even suggested that the pool idea be abandoned and that the section revert to the team system of operation.

By the middle of March, 1960, Hawkins was convinced that some immediate action would have to be taken to reverse the productivity trend to his section. The situation had been alleviated for a time by a change in the policy for capital plant additions. Formerly, every addition in excess of $1,500 net estimated cost was the responsibility of his section. That amount had been raised to $2,500 thus eliminating about three fourths of that minor estimating work which draftsmen were capable of handling on their own. However, Hawkins felt sure that with increasing labor and materials costs, many of these small jobs would soon be back under his jurisdiction.

Hawkins discussed the worsening situation with the chief draftsman. Manson, however, was convinced that the new capital-additions policy would provide the relief needed to make the pool system operable. Nevertheless, Hawkins felt that the pool idea had proved unsuccessful, and he determined to abandon it in favor of a modified team system.

After consultation with the engineering supervisors, Hawkins decided to retain the centralized supply and reproduction facilities in charge of a girl who would report to one of the substation design engineers. Otherwise, the pool idea was to disappear altogether. The teams were to be reconstituted, with the express provision that each supervisor was to arrange for the loan of draftsmen between teams whenever the need arose. Whenever these mutual arrangements failed, the matter was to be brought to the attention of the assistant manager.

Manson was to be reincorporated, at his present salary level, into one of the teams. Hawkins, in discussion with Manson, stressed that this action was not to be construed as a reprimand of the chief draftsman. In fact, it was simply a response to an unworkable organization which had been initiated by the section manager. Hawkins told Manson that he realized the ex-chief draftsman would probably feel awkward at first about his new status but that he should do his best to adjust to it. Simultaneously, Hawkins met alone with the engineering supervisor in whose group Manson would work. He received assurances from the supervisor that the pool system and Manson's position in it were closed issues.

Shortly thereafter, a general meeting of the section was called. Hawkins explained that the pool idea had not succeeded, as everyone knew; that its failure was no one's fault, except possibly his own; and that a modified team arrangement, as previously described, would go into effect immediately. The assignment of draftsmen to the teams was also announced at this time.

In December, 1960, Hawkins reported that the revised team system of operation in his section had proved successful. By means of several follow-up efforts on Hawkins's part, excellent cooperation between teams had been achieved, and draftsmen were often sent on temporary loan to other teams whenever drafting commitments warranted. There had been some anxiety at first about the adjustment of Manson; but after several months, he appeared to be reasonably well integrated into his team. The productivity of the section seemed to Hawkins to be at an all-time high.[38]

3 Suppose you are given the following information about two organizations. How would your recommendations differ with respect to their designs?

	Firm A	Firm B
Size	Large	Medium-sized
Type of industry	Manufacturing	Service
Business	Cars	EDP Systems
Environment	Stable, heterogeneous	Dynamic, heterogeneous
Technology	Mass production	Custom
Differences in uncertainty faced by major departments	High	Low

Footnotes to Chapter Six

[1] D. Katz and R. L. Kahn, *The Social Psychology of Organizations*, pp. 19–26.
[2] Talcott Parsons, *The Structure and Process in Modern Societies*, pp. 63–64.
[3] Katz and Kahn, *op. cit.*, pp. 84–99.
[4] F. E. Emery and E. L. Trist, "Socio-technical Systems."
[5] Harold Leavitt, "Applied Organizational Change in Industry."
[6] John A. Seiler, *Systems Analysis in Organizational Behavior*.
[7] L. Von Bertalanffy, "General Systems Theory."
[8] Katz and Kahn, *op. cit.*, pp. 19–26.
[9] *Ibid.*, pp. 84–99.
[10] *Ibid.*, p. 86.
[11] Emery and Trist, *op. cit.*
[12] E. L. Trist and K. W. Bamforth, "Some Social and Psychological Consequences of Long-wall Method of Coal Mining."
[13] Leavitt, *op. cit.*
[14] Charles Hoffer, "Emerging EDP Pattern."
[15] C. W. Walker, "Life in the Automatic Factory."
[16] Seiler, *op. cit.*
[17] *Ibid.*, pp. 7–8.
[18] These are rather similar to the factors that Leavitt, *op. cit.*, considers in his model of organizational change.
[19] Joan Woodward, *Technology and Organizations*.
[20] Joan Woodward, *Industrial Organization*.

21 See D. J. Hickson, D. S. Pugh and D. C. Pheysey, "Operations Technology and Organizational Structure: An Empirical Reappraisal," for a critical review of Woodward's work and an attempt at replicating her results.

22 T. Burns and G. M. Stalker, *The Management of Innovation.*

23 Paul Lawrence and Jay Lorsch, *Organization and Environment.*

24 *Ibid.,* p. 11.

25 *Ibid.,* Ch. 6.

26 Jay Lorsch and Paul Lawrence, eds., *Studies in Organization Design.*

27 James D. Thompson, *Organizations in Action,* p. 159.

28 *Ibid.,* p. 39.

29 *Ibid.,* p. 46.

30 This and the several quotations immediately following are from *ibid.,* pp. 70–72.

31 See *ibid.,* pp. 59–64, for a discussion of the various strategies organizations employ to minimize coordination costs.

32 *Ibid.,* p. 75.

33 *Ibid.,* p. 80.

34 Charles Perrow, *Organizational Analysis: A Sociological View,* p. 75.

35 *Ibid.,* p. 80.

36 Perrow distinguishes between discretionary authority and power, but the distinction is without much of a difference.

37 John Child, "Organizational Structure, Environment, and Performance: The Role of Strategic Choice."

38 Seiler, *op. cit.,* pp. 32–49.

7

"The formed world is the only habitable one."
Thomas Carlyle

A Model of Organizational Functioning

start

THE NOTION OF DESIGN

Introduction

The word "design" connotes skillful or elegant form, pattern, structure, to achieve one or more objectives. Inherent in the idea of design are several notions:

1 There is someone who has the power or the authority to design. The designer has some control over the material being fashioned—that is, the material is pliable.

2 The designer has a choice of shape to give to the material—in other words, there are alternative forms. However, this choice may be circumscribed by the potentialities, constraints, and contingencies of the material; the preferences and properties of the designer; and the constraints and contingencies of the processes employed to transform the material.

3 The designer has some idea of how to go about giving the desired form to the material. In other words the designer has some idea of what

causes what and how different aspects of the material are interlinked.

Organizational design has to do with how the elements of organizational structure and processes can be interrelated, given the organization's business situation, to achieve efficiently the objectives of the designer. Let us apply the ideas about design to organizations.

Designer

Organizations being complex entities, a great many forces participate in their designing. Some of these forces arise from the nature of human needs; some from the economics of the organization's functioning and from its environment; some from the values and goals of the key members of the organization; some from organizational necessities such as motivating the organization's members, coordinating their actions, and the like. The principal *agency* through which organizations are shaped, regardless of how many or how diffuse the forces shaping them, is management. For it is management, like the ego in Freudian psychology, that reconciles and manipulates the various pressures on the organization and, through its decisions and directives, gives the organization's structures and processes distinctive form.

Management designs the organization, though not always to its own liking. For example, management, under pressure from the union, may set up an arbitration board to review worker grievances—but not like it one bit. On the other hand, many aspects of organizational design do reflect the wishes of top management. In a large, diversified tar and chemical company that was about to go broke, the chairman installed a strong accounting-oriented executive. The latter ordered the rationalization of the accounting procedures used by the different divisions. He also set up profit decentralization. Despite some initial opposition, he managed to get them installed. The company's organization changed fairly drastically as a result of this and more closely reflected the philosophy of top management.

Thus, in organizations the principal designer is management. The papacy in the Roman Catholic Church, the presidency in the executive branch of the U.S. government, the officers in the case of firms, the medical and administrative boards in the case of hospitals are all examples of designers of their respective organizations because of their top management roles.

But it is worth noting at this point that "management" is not necessarily the same as the formally designated officers of the organization. Some of the latter may be playing purely ceremonial functions, such as the British monarch or the chancellor of McGill University. Some others may not be designated as officers and yet may be playing crucial decision-making roles in the organization. The faceless heads of mafia-controlled firms are examples. The union boss whose approval for major policy changes is sought as a matter of course is a member of management though seldom designated as such. In professional organizations such as hospitals, the professionals may not be in administrative positions. And yet, in many a hospital, powerful doctors have a greater say in design decisions than many administrators. Thus, though generally speaking the formally designated top officers constitute management, sometimes others not designated as such may also be considered to be members of top management and, therefore, as members of the designing group by virtue of their nonformal power and influence.

Material of Design

In organizations, the "material" that management shapes is very diverse and varies greatly in pliability. This "material" consists of people; roles, positions, structure, and action programs; technology; goals and values; and the environment. For example, management can hire or fire individuals. It can train them. It can develop new programs or modify existing ones. It can change the structure of the organization—say, from one that is centralized to one that is decentralized. It can alter the production process—for example, by buying highly automated equipment. It can change the goals of the organization, from a purely growth and efficiency orientation to one that includes job satisfaction and environmental protection as well. And it can try to modify the environment, too, by, for example, changing its markets, changing the constituency to which it appeals if it is a political party, lobbying to government for more munificent grants if it is a university, and so on.

Management cannot, of course, change all the elements of design (people, structure, technology, goals, environment, etc.) with equal facility or speed. Management can hire and fire individuals without great delay, but it would take it much longer to alter their attitudes and abilities, and then with only a modest probability of success. If this were not true few organizations would suffer from "people problems." Structure is more amenable to managerial direction, and indeed there are many examples of dramatic changes in the structure of many a corporation in a fairly short period of time. Chandler has described how some very large U.S. corporations, such as General Motors, Du Pont, Sears Roebuck, and Standard Oil, got divisionalized almost overnight under the pressure of market forces.[1] New programs are continually being developed and old programs modified in many organizations. And yet, the force of tradition and pressures from vested interests can delay—sometimes indefinitely—changes in structure. Minor changes in technology can be executed fairly quickly—if unions will allow them—but major changes are expensive and take much longer to effectuate. For example, the big auto makers in Detroit declare the impossibility of meeting legal antipollution standards by the mid-seventies. So expensive and complex is the plant in many industries that putting in a new technology must take years rather than months.

Goals are related intimately to the function for which the organization is set up and, therefore, not very amenable to management control. Management scarcely can change the hospital's goal of providing health care facilities for patients, or the firm's goal of doing business to make a profit, or the political party's goal of fighting elections. What management can do, however, is to decide what *targets* to pursue—what rate of return to shoot for, what quality and quantity of hospital services to provide, the number of senate seats to contest. Finally, for most organizations except the very large or monopolistic ones, the environment is, by and large, a constraint. Marketing, lobbying, public relations may soften environmental constraints somewhat, but in the short run at least, management just has to accept them. In the long run, however, it has more freedom. A firm can develop one market and get out of another; a hospital can gradually establish itself as a specialized hospital catering to a specific class of patient and move away from being a general hospital; and so on. Thus, while all the elements of organizational design are alterable by management, some are more so than others, and some take longer to change than others.

Choice

To the untrained eye, all organizations appear alike. Actually there are great differences in the designs of organizations, and this is so even in organizations of the same class. Take firms, for example. Some are highly centralized, some are highly decentralized, and a great many fall in the middle range of decentralization. Some go first and foremost after profits, others after growth, and still others after liquidity and stability. Some firms use mass production techniques; others use custom technology. In some firms, managers are mostly professionals, as in aerospace and pharmaceutical firms; in others they are mostly nonprofessionals, as in print shops. Many other differences can be identified. The point is that not only corporations but hospitals, schools, governments, and other organizations as well, all exhibit a great deal of variation, so management has a considerable choice of design.

Constraints on Choice

Naturally, not every design is equally good. Some designs are more appropriate to the organization's situation than others. For example, Burns and Stalker found that what they called an organic style of management (open communications, relatively loosely defined roles, power vested in situational expertise rather than in position in formal hierarchy) fitted better firms confronting changing markets and technology, while the mechanistic style typical of bureaucracies was more appropriate to firms functioning in stable markets with little or no technological change.[2]

Size is another factor that constrains the choice of design. Large organizations tend to be decentralized because otherwise the top management would be overloaded. Thus, centralization (except of certain aspects of decision-making such as raising capital, declaring dividends, charting out a strategy of growth) is not a feasible alternative for large organizations. The type of organization—for example, whether it is a firm or a cooperative or a government agency—also constrains some choices. A cooperative is founded on democratic principles and therefore, unlike a firm, cannot be organized and run like a dictatorship at the discretion of its management. A government agency in a democratic country is generally vulnerable to attacks in the legislature and often must adopt many rules and regulations to be able to defend the propriety of its actions, a necessity that forces it to be bureaucratic.

The social function of the organization, whether it is a producer of goods or services and what kinds of good or service it produces, is also sometimes a source of constraints. An advertising agency and a restaurant are both service-oriented firms, but their functions are different. An advertising agency must come up with creative copy for its many clients and must therefore hire a number of artistic, creative individuals. Since creativity cannot flourish in a rigid, bureaucratic climate, the organization has to be flexible, informal, and decentralized. The restaurant may have a creative chef, but the economies are in attracting customers (good service, decent decor) and in watching food costs carefully. The organization needs usually to be run as a tight ship, which means close personal supervision by the manager of most aspects of the business. A juvenile rehabilitation center and a juvenile custodial institution both have inmates. But the purpose or function of the former is to restore wholeness to truncated psychic lives, while that of the latter is to protect society from the capers of delinquents. As a consequence, the climate, the system of rewards, the nature of supervision, and so forth tend to be vastly different.

The goals of an organization's designers—growth, profits or efficiency, stability, high morale, a good public image, etc.—will also affect the choice of design. A Montreal auto dealer has a tremendous yen for growth. He has no great use for sophisticated controls and a formal organization chart, but he does use a powerful incentive system for salesmen that has rapidly increased his sales. On the other hand, stability is so important to a Montreal savings institution that in a hundred years of operations it has not ventured beyond the city limits and in fact opens new branches only if it can find people from inside to work in them—outside recruitment being taboo because, as its president said, "It would unsettle the employees."

The technology employed by the organization is another powerful force acting to limit the choice of design. In a firm using a custom technology—that is, a technology geared to producing to the specifications of individual customer's orders such as that of a printing plant—the marketing of the product (that is, registering an order) precedes its design and manufacture, and coordination between the activities needs to be intense. In a mass production firm, greater separation of the three functions is possible, and departmentalization often follows functional lines. In the custom technology firm, on the other hand, whatever be the type of departmentalization, the necessity of coordinating marketing, design, and manufacture for major orders often implies a matrix structure or a structure in which a team is assigned to each such order.

The properties of the designer—the management of the organization—will also be a source of limitations on the choice of design. The management is, of course, a group of individuals. Their individual preferences, values, limitations, and styles inevitably will color the choices they make. If the chief executive is a democratic type, the top management group may resemble Likert's Type 4 management style—democratic, group decision-making, open communications, and so on. If the chief executive is the autocratic type, the top management of the organization is likely to take on the Type 1 style—autocratic, manipulative decision-making, restricted communication channels, and the rest.[3]

Besides the personal idiosyncrasies of management, their human limitations also affect choice. Organizations with traditional managements often find it difficult to cope with newfangled management tools like computers, information systems, and organizational development. The use of these would require so much re-education for them that they shy away from them. Technocratic managements, often staffed by MBA's, feel more at home with these techniques and so use them quite frequently. The cognitive limitations of management are, therefore, another major constraint on the choice of design.

Another source of limitations on the choice of organizational design is culture. Culture sets the bounds on what may or may not be done, on what is desirable and what is not. The members of an organization, bringing into

FIGURE 7-1
Freedom and Constraints in the Choice of Organizational Design

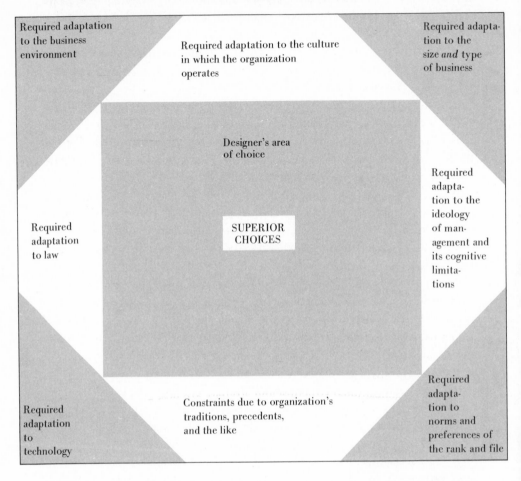

Required adaptation to the business environment

Required adaptation to the culture in which the organization operates

Required adaptation to the size *and* type of business

Designer's area of choice

Required adaptation to the ideology of management and its cognitive limitations

Required adaptation to law

SUPERIOR CHOICES

Required adaptation to technology

Constraints due to organization's traditions, precedents, and the like

Required adaptation to norms and preferences of the rank and file

it values of the wider culture, will simply not put up with actions that seriously undermine the dominant values of the wider culture. The resistance to Nixon's autocratic ways from within the U.S. government is a case in point. Firms in North America tend to be more decentralized than firms in, say, Germany; American culture sanctions, in fact supports, decentralization of authority, whereas German culture does not, at least not to the same degree.[4] Within the North American culture, the cotton textile industry is more tradition bound and conservative in its management than the organic, technocratic aerospace industry. A new firm entering the textile industry is likely to take its design cues from established firms, much as a new entrant to the aerospace industry will look around to see how other aerospace firms are organized.

Thus, while an organization has a very wide choice of design, in practice its choice is considerably circumscribed by the environment in which it functions, its technology, size, type, function, the abilities and beliefs of its management, the goals of management, cultural values. (See Figure 7–1.)

Causation

Unless management knows what organizational means are appropriate for what strategic ends, and what consequences follow from an organizational choice, it can hardly choose a sensible design for the organization. This is the province of organization theory. Organization theory has to provide answers to questions such as the following:

1 What organizational consequences follow when the organization undertakes a major change, such as the installation of a computer-based information system, divisionalization, or organization development à la the managerial grid of Blake and Mouton? Leavitt has argued that the organization's goals, structure, technology, and members are related in such a way that change in any one will trigger a complex chain of events that ultimately will affect the other three as well.[5] We need more precise predictions of these effects. In other words, what we need is a body of laws that link together environment, style, goals, structure, technology, and behavior.

2 What organizational structure and strategy are best geared to achieving a goal like high profitability? A high rate of growth? A high level of morale? A high degree of collaboration among personnel? Psychologically healthy organizational members?

In the succeeding chapters we will attempt to build up a body of knowledge that provides at least tentative answers to these questions.

In Summary

Management is the designer of organizations, but design is subject to pressure from workers, white-collar staff, customers, suppliers, owners of the organization, and a number of other groups. In other words, not all the features of an organization's design reflect management's preferences. The subject matter of design consists of people, organizational structure, technology, goals, management style, and the organizational environment. These elements differ, however, in the extent to which they can be altered by management and the speed with which they can be altered. The range of choice in design is vast. But, practically, choice is limited by a number of factors such as the need to adapt to the nature of the organization's situation (its size, technology, purpose, external environment, etc.), the goals of the organization, the properties and preferences of management itself, and the dominant cultural values. To be able to design organizations effectively, we need a body of knowledge that links desired goals and the organizational means by which they are achieved, as well as a body of knowledge that predicts for us what consequences to expect from given organizational changes. The development of such a body of knowledge is the primary goal of this book.

We turn next to a model of organizational functioning that can help us get started on the road to developing this body of knowledge. The model is a broad framework for organizational analysis and theory-building. It is not a tight system of concepts, assumptions, and hypothesis. We will flesh out this model in succeeding chapters with specific, empirically testable hypotheses.

A MODEL OF ORGANIZATIONAL FUNCTIONING

Introduction

In previous chapters we discussed several aspects of organizations. Many of the ideas and empirical findings discussed in these chapters can help us develop a coherent model of how organizations function. This model in turn can guide our exposition of a body of theory that can underpin the practical work of designing organizations. Some major conclusions from previous chapters are:

> **1** The organization is powerfully influenced by the nature of its environment and the events taking place in its environment. As we saw in Chapter 2, economists have long argued that the price and output decisions of a firm are determined by demand and supply conditions in its markets. Sociologists such as Parsons have pointed to the organization's need to maintain legitimacy in the society in which it operates. Both economic and cultural forces, then, are likely to affect the way the organization functions. The contingency and systems theorists (Chapter 6), too, have stressed the dependence of the organization on its environment. Thus the external environment of the organization is likely to be a powerful molder of organizational structure and operations.
>
> **2** The sociological penchant for studying how societies and institutions change and evolve (Chapter 3) has provided an awareness that

time is an important variable affecting organizations. Thus, the age of an organization may be a notable determinant of aspects of its functioning. The economist's concern for the scale of operations and the many consequences of economies of scale, which we explored in Chapter 2 suggest that the size of the organization may be an important independent variable affecting the organization. In fact, research findings (reported in Chapter 4) indicate that size is a major determinant of organizational structure. The kinds of functions the organization performs in society—that is, the type of organization it is (a key concern of sociologists)—is also likely to affect the design of the organization. Clearly, a commercial manufacturer of mass-produced cars is likely to have an organizational design different from that of a purveyor of customized health service. Thus, size, age, the type of business the organization is in are likely to be key variables shaping it; we may for convenience call them "demographic variables."

3 The style and philosophy of key decision makers or top management may have far-reaching consequences for the organization. We noted in Chapter 2 the concern of political scientists with ideologies and the polities they give rise to. In Chapter 5, when reviewing the human relations orientation, we noted the strategic importance of the style of supervision—whether, for example, it is participative or autocratic. Clearly, therefore, a model of how organizations function must take into account the values and goals of those at the helm of affairs in the organization. These are likely to have far-reaching implications for the design of the organization.

4 Organizational structure, workflow, and technology are the means by which the organization pursues its goals. In Chapter 4 we reviewed two major schools of organization theory, the bureaucracy school founded by Max Weber and the principles of management school founded by Henri Fayol. The principal focus of both these schools has been the structure of the organization. Other researchers reviewed in Chapter 6, principally Woodward and Perrow, have firmly established technology as a key variable in organizational design. The work of the Carnegie "bounded rationality" theorists, reviewed in Chapter 5, suggests that workflow, or the sequencing of performance program, is another key element in the functioning of organizations. Thus the work of a great many researchers and theorists impels us to include organizational structure, workflow, and technology as elements of our model.

5 Organizations consist of people. As we noted in Chapter 3 and again in Chapter 5, human motivation, perception, and attitudes profoundly affect the functioning of organizations. Whether the members of an or-

ganization are motivated or alienated, cooperate or fight with one another, are creative and innovative or staid and conservative must surely play a part in the way the organization operates. Thus, dimensions of human behavior should be included in a model of organizational functioning.

6 In Chapter 6, while reviewing the systems orientation in organization theory, we noted that an organization is a living system with a built-in homeostatic mechanism. This implies that organizations continually adjust their functioning in order to stay viable. If a firm makes a loss, its management will take administrative and other steps to try to minimize the loss in the next period and perhaps even to make a profit. Thus, how the organization performs with respect to its goals needs to be included in a model of organizational functioning.

7 As was pointed out in Chapter 6, the organization is a *system* of interconnected parts. The environment, demographic variables, the style and goals of management, organizational structure, technology, workflow, behavioral variables, and organizational performance are not isolated but interconnected. A change in one is likely to have consequences for the rest. However, as the contingency theorists have argued, certain elements are likely to have more profound effects on the organization than others. Thus, a model of organizational functioning must recognize not only the interconnectedness of organizational element but also the principal *directionality* of the relationships. For example, the bulk of the evidence gathered to date indicates that task environmental and demographic variables influence organizational structure rather than vice versa (see the review of the contingency orientation in Chapter 6).

The foregoing, as well as the author's beliefs about how organizations operate, prompt the model of organizational functioning shown in Figure 7–2 and described below.

Description of the Model

The model postulates relationships among five classes of variables—namely, situational, strategic, structural, behavioral, and performance variables. The *situational* or contextual variables cover external environmental and what may be called demographic variables. They represent the situation or context within which an organization functions. They are the primary source of constraint, contingencies, opportunities, and threats faced by the organization as a unit. They represent the field of forces that over the long run profoundly shape the inner workings of the organization.

FIGURE 7–2
A Model of Organizational Functioning

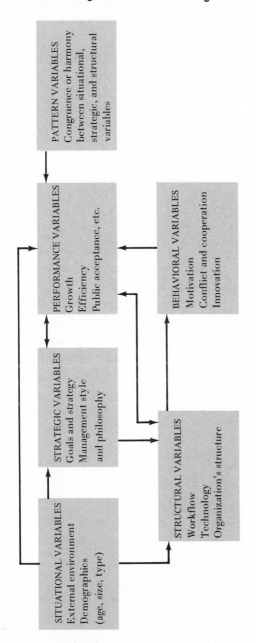

The external environment is the set of events, information, constraints, opportunities, threats, or contingencies that originates *outside* the organization. It is the set that has relevance for the resources that the organization acquires from outside its boundaries and for the products or services it exports to keep viable. The external environment may be analyzed in terms of its *properties*, such as whether it is stable or dynamic, homogeneous or heterogeneous, and so on.[6] Or it may be analyzed in terms of its principal components, such as the type of economic system and market structure the organization is operating in, the nature of society, the political system regulating the organization, and the like.[7]

The so-called demographic variables are the principal ways a population of *organizations* may be meaningfully classified. The chief ones are organizational size, age, nature of ownership (or who the principal beneficiaries of the organization are), and the nature of output (products versus services). These are treated as situational or contextual variables because, although they profoundly affect the organization, they can be changed through managerial action only with great difficulty.

The *strategic* variables consist of the organization's goals, top management ideology and style, and organizational strategy for survival and growth. In management literature they are called "policy variables." These are deemed strategic because they are manipulable to a degree and because changes in them can have long-term and major consequences for the organization. As Parsons has pointed out, they commit the organization as a whole to a course of action. The rest of the organization takes its cues from them.[8] For example, if a government gave up the goals of free trade and pursued instead the goal of national self-sufficiency, as Germany did with the rise of Hitler, it would have major consequences throughout the government. If General Motors gave up its ideology of decentralization of operations, that too would have profound and long-term consequences for the

FIGURE 7–3
Some Strategic Variables

Low performance aspirations	$\longleftrightarrow$	High performance aspirations for the organization as a whole
A conservative management philosophy	$\longleftrightarrow$	An entrepreneurial, risk-taking management philosophy
A "satisficing" management philosophy	$\longleftrightarrow$	An "optimizing," comprehensive planning management philosophy
A nonparticipative management philosophy	$\longleftrightarrow$	A participative management philosophy
A mechanistic, structure-oriented management philosophy	$\longleftrightarrow$	An organic, flexibility-oriented management philosophy
A coercive, authoritarian management philosophy	$\longleftrightarrow$	A noncoercive management philosophy

entire organization. Figure 7–3 shows some strategic variables. Typically, they are the preserve of the top management of organizations. Some of the dimensions are orientations towards the external environment, such as the risk-taking orientation. Others are administrative orientations, such as the organic or the participative orientation.

The *structural* variables are the ones that form the skeleton of the organization, so to speak. They describe the durable arrangements and formally sanctioned relationships in the organization by which the repetitive work of the organization gets done. The superstructure of the organization —the way people are grouped into departments in the organization—is one dimension of structure. The infrastructure of the organization—the system of controls and authority relationships, staff functions, formalization of communications, various performance programs and operating procedures —is another dimension. The superstructure and infrastructure of organizations serve a number of functions, such as the reduction of uncertainty, differentiation of activities, and coordination and integration of activities. Technology and the system of programs making up the organization's workflow also constitute structural variables, for they represent the durable arrangement of the flow of organizational work.* Figure 7–4 shows some of the dimensions of structure.

The *behavioral* variables describe the actual behavior that takes place in organizations as their rank and file struggle to meet their own needs as well as the organization's demands on them. Some organizations evince a great deal of conflict between different individuals and groups in the organization; some exhibit considerable cooperation. Similarly, morale and job satisfaction will be high in some organizations and lower in others. In some organizations there is much innovation; in others very little; in others even resistance to invention. In some, members tend to exhibit highly mo-

* Some researchers treat technology as a situational rather than a structural variable. It probably is both. In some industries, technology is pretty well fixed. (An example is the batch processing of chemicals.) In these industries it is proper to regard it as a situational variable. In many other industries, however, management has a choice as to the type of technology that is best for the organization. In the printing industry, for example, various technologies are in use. A firm that wants to offer a complete product line is likely to employ a different machinery than one that wants to offer a narrowly specialized product line. Thus, for many, perhaps most, organizations, the technology they employ is an outcome of strategic decisions its management makes with regard to what market segments it wants to serve. Also the relative costs of factors of production vary from society to society and affect the relative use of factors of production in the technology employed. A steel firm in China is likely to be much more labor intensive than one in the United States. For these reasons, technology is not regarded as a situational or contextual variable in this model.

FIGURE 7–4
Some Structural Variables

Few, invariant programs constitute the work flow	⟷	Multiple and variable programs constitute the workflow
A highly labor-intensive technology of operations	⟷	A highly automated, capital-intensive technology of operations
Technology of operations oriented to production of customized goods or services	⟷	Mass-production oriented technology of operations
Simple infrastructure (few sophisticated controls and specialists and a simple hierarchy)	⟷	Complex and elaborate infrastructure of controls, specialists, and authority relationships
Functionally departmentalized superstructure	⟷	Divisionalized superstructure

tivated behavior; in others they may be much less motivated or even show signs of alienation. Just as the structural variables represent the formal, stable part of the functioning of the organization, the behavioral variables constitute the nonformal, dynamic elements in the functioning of the organization.

The *performance* variables represent dimensions in terms of which the organization's performance is evaluated by the key decision makers within, sometimes outside, the organization. The more common performance variables are: efficiency (profitability), rate of growth (positive or negative), and degree of market or community acceptance. Organizational performance is usually assessed in reference to some standards. Past performance of the organization and the performance of comparable organizations are the usual sources of these standards.

The Relationship Between Variables

The model (Figure 7–2) assumes that situational variables affect strategic and structural variables. For example, as Burns and Stalker have shown, a dynamic environment tends to inculcate an ideology of flexibility, looseness, open communications, and situational expertise in the top management.[9] This ideology enables it to cope with the novel and complex problems such an environment generates. In a study by Dill of two Norwegian firms, the one in the more turbulent environment had a stronger tradition of managerial autonomy.[10] In a study of British firms by Pugh and his associates, size, a demographic variable, was associated with a number of structural aspects like decentralization, formalization, and specialization.[11] It is well known that oligopolistic firms in the United States (oligopoly being a situational condition) maintain large legal departments (an aspect of structure) because of the antitrust laws (an aspect of the political environment).

The model shows that the situational variables, in addition to affecting strategic and structural variables, also affect performance variables. Short of very poor management a firm in a rapidly growing industry can scarcely fail to grow. The research of industrial economists indicates that firms in less competitive industries earn higher profits than firms in highly competitive industries.[12] The research of Roos, Schermerhorn, and Roos, Jr., indicates that the performance of hospitals on such criteria as the occupancy rate, total expenses per bed, or percentage with accreditation is related to such demographic properties as size and ownership.[13] Thus, favorable situational variables can aid performance just as unfavorable ones can hurt it.

The model indicates that strategic variables affect structural variables. The goals and strategy of management translate into the design of the means (structure) by which they are to be achieved. For example, the management of Litton Industries set rapid growth as a major goal. This translated into a strategy of vigorous conglomerate diversification, which in turn resulted in the organization's adopting a divisionalized structure. Ideology of management, too, can be a powerful shaper of organizational structure. In a large, paternalistically managed consumer products firm, following the sale of the firm by its aging owner to an aggressive conglomerate, the ideology changed from paternalism to profitability and growth at all costs. The organization changed from a functionally departmentalized mode to a divisionalized mode, and the incentive system changed from one of promoting and paying on the basis of seniority to promoting and paying exclusively on the basis of performance.

The model further postulates that structural variables—technology, workflow, departmentalization, hierarchy, controls—affect behavioral variables, notably motivation, conflict, cooperation, and innovation. There is widespread belief to this effect, and research, too, points to it. It is widely believed that automation and standardization of work cause worker disaffection. Argyris has argued persuasively, on the basis of his research, that structural properties such as departmentalization, hierarchy, and controls frustrate the needs for autonomy and growth of those who work in organizations.[14] Steiner has listed a number of structural conditions, such as decentralization, open communications, suggestion systems, and heterogeneous personnel policy, that may be necessary for creative behavior in organizations.[15]

The model hypothesizes that besides situational variables, strategic, structural, and behavioral variables also affect the performance of the organization. If the organization's strategy is bold and expansive, then, given a congenial business situation, the organization is likely to perform better than if in the same circumstances the organization pursues a cautious strategy. Similarly, an organizational structure or technology that is appropriate to the business of the organization is likely to deliver better results than a structure or a technology that is inappropriate to the organization's business situation. We have already reviewed the work of Lawrence and Lorsch in Chapter 6, which indicates that an organization whose structure has a degree of differentiation and integration that is appropriate to the nature of the organization's task environment tends to be a relatively high performing organization.[16] It also seems plausible that high levels of motivation and innovative behavior are likely to be associated with superior organizational performance, just as alienation, excessive conflict, and resistance to innovation are likely to be associated with relatively poor organizational performance.

While each of situational, strategic, structural, and behavioral variables may affect performance independently, in appropriate combinations they may affect organizational performance to an even greater extent. These appropriate combinations may be called "pattern variables." Thus, the *combination* of a dynamic business environment, a risk-taking top management philosophy, a flexible organizational structure with a strong information and control system, and high levels of motivation and readiness to accept innovation on the part of the organizational rank and file may more surely lead to superior organization performance than any of the foregoing in isolation. The model hypothesizes that combinations or patterns such as the foregoing are powerful determinants of organizational performance.

Finally, the model postulates that performance, or rather a comparison of performance with the previously set targets, leads to a reappraisal of those variables that are within the control of management. Strategic variables and structural variables are amenable to managerial modifications, certainly more so than contextual variables and behavioral variables. For most organizations it is very difficult to change the properties of the environment, size, age, nature of business, and the like, except over the long term. Similarly, the direct modification of human behavior is very difficult. Management exhortations for quarreling groups to start cooperating usually cut little ice. Unless one is a Gandhi or a Mao Tse-tung, a manager's order to subordinates to work harder, cooperate, innovate, and make prompt and wise decisions is just so much noise. On the other hand, targets can be reset, management style and philosophy can be reconditioned, strategy can be modified, and structural changes such as decentralization and reorganization can be wrought more easily.

Some Properties of the Model

Causality. In Figure 7–2 causality is shown, for the most part, as unidirectional. For example, the situational variables are shown as influencing the strategic variables, but not vice versa, and the strategic variables are shown as influencing the structural variables, but not vice versa. This is a simplification. In real life, causality often runs in both directions. Thus, the strategic variables affect the situational variables, too. As an example, if the goal of management is stability, and management style is conservative, these may result in the organization's eventually getting into stable markets. But the influence of the strategic variables on situational variables is postulated to be weaker, at least in the short run, than the influence of the situational variables on the strategic variables. Hence the arrow is shown to go from the situational variables to the strategic variables, rather than vice versa. In other words, the arrows in the figure show the direction of *net* influence.

Determinism. The arrows in Figure 7–2 indicate lines of influence. For example, the situational and performance variables *influence* strategic variables; they do not completely determine the strategic variables. All organizational research to date indicates that relationships between variables are stochastic or probabilistic in nature, not exact or deterministic. For example, a dynamic environment increases the *probability* that the management style will be organic; but there may be the odd organization that quite successfully copes with a dynamic environment by being mechanistic. The organization world is enormously complex. Many, many forces shape organizations. There is no push-button way of forging organizations. One can say only that if certain changes are made in, say, the situational variables, specific changes become more probable in strategic and structural variables.

Organizational level. Another important point that needs to be made about the model in Figure 7–2 is that it applies to all the levels of an organization. It applies to the overall organization, but it applies also to any department or division of this organization that shows the characteristics of an organization as listed in Chapter 1. The only difference is that the remainder of the organization constitutes a large chunk of the so-called external environment or context of this department or division. Thus, the external environment of the firm is its competitors, the laws of the land, and so on; the external environment of, say, the manufacturing department of this firm includes the competition it is facing with other corporate departments over the allocation of funds, the corporate policies that are a part of its legal environment, and so on. What this implies for organizational analysis is that if we wish to study the entire organization, we must study its highest levels first. What we find at its highest levels becomes a datum in the study of the next highest level, and this process, carried far enough, gives us a much fuller understanding of the functioning of all the levels of an organization. As a corollary, if we wish to study a part of an organization, such as a department or a division that has the properties of an organization, we should apply the model to the larger entity of which the smaller one is a part, perhaps broadly rather than in detail, and use the insights we gain there for a more intensive application of the model to the entity we are primarily interested in.

Domain of organization theory. The model outlines this author's perception of the domain of organization theory—namely, that it is the systematic study of the relationships between situational, strategic, structural, behavioral, and performance variables. It also indicates the author's perception of what the most fruitful areas of research and theorizing are. These are the relationships between situational variables on the one hand and strategic, structural, and performance variables on the other, the relationships between strategic and structural variables, between structural and behavioral, behavioral and performance, performance and strategic, and performance and structural variables.

The model does *not* embrace all possible variables that affect organizations. For example, it omits variables relating to the physical properties of organizations or their geographical locations. These may well be important. But the research and conceptual base is lacking at present to integrate these into organization theory.

Taken as a whole, the model incorporates especially the systems and the contingency viewpoints. The organization is viewed as a system of interacting parts, open to the environment and shaped by situational variables. The model, as will be shown in later chapters, also emphasizes the principle of equifinality or multiple ways of reaching the same goal even when the situational conditions are the same or quite similar. For example, the work of several researchers suggests that as an organization grows, it tends to become more bureaucratic to retain efficiency. But some organizations may instead become more flexible as they grow larger, especially if they believe in decentralization. In other words, the same stimulus, increase in size, may give rise not just to one organizational response, bureaucratization, as contingency theory tends to emphasize, but to two or more modal responses that may sometimes even be quite contradictory.

Organizational analysis. The model indicates, not only what the most fruitful areas for organizational theorizing are, but what the most important variables are in the analysis of how a particular organization functions.

Organizational design implications. In the following chapters, within the guidelines provided by the model, a body of hypotheses about organizations has been set out. These propositions have been made on the basis of research results and/or informed speculation. This body of hypotheses serves as the basis for suggestions about the design of organizations. For example, if on sensible grounds the use of sophisticated controls is postulated to co-vary with the decentralization of decision-making, then one feasible design is relatively extensive use of sophisticated controls *and* relatively extensive decentralization; another is relatively little use of sophisticated controls *and* centralization; a third is moderate use of sophisticated controls *and* moderate decentralization. At the very least, organization theory helps to narrow the search for feasible designs. In the foregoing example, it rules out as impractical or harmful the combination of great centralization and extensive use of sophisticated controls as well as great decentralization of authority without a sophisticated control system.

By way of illustration, in the Appendix to this chapter the facts concerning a paper-converting company are presented and then analyzed in terms of the model outlined in this chapter.

SUMMARY

Drawing on the broth of ideas about organizations outlined in the earlier chapters, we have developed a model of organizational functioning. The model indicates relationships between situational, strategic, structural, behavioral, and performance variables. The relationships are probablistic in nature, not deterministic. In the following chapters, the relationships are set out in the form of propositions, which are then the bases for suggestions about organizational design.

The model incorporates the systems and the contingency frameworks. It emphasizes the principle of equifinality. It helps us identify those configurations of situational, strategic, structural, and behavioral variables that are associated with superior organizational performance.

The model can be applied not only to an entire organization but to a unit in the organization (an "embedded" organization) that has the properties of an organization as listed in Chapter 1. The Appendix to this chapter describes a firm in terms of this model.

Like all other models of organizational functioning, this model is only a highly simplified version of an extremely complex reality. It is useful to the extent that it provides a framework for a systematic development of organization theory and of notions about organizational design.

In the next chapter we examine the demographic characteristics of organizations—their age, size, ownership, nature of business, and the like. These are important situational variables.

SUGGESTED READINGS

Harold J. Leavitt, *Managerial Psychology*, 3rd ed. (Chicago: The University of Chicago Press, 1972). In Part IV of the book, Leavitt describes some of the relationships between structure, technology, people, goals, and environment.

Jay Lorsch, and Paul Lawrence, eds., *Studies in Organization Design* (Homewood, Ill.: Irwin-Dorsey, 1970). The book outlines the Lawrence and Lorsch view of organizational design and describes several empirical studies.

QUESTIONS FOR ANALYSIS

1 Take a look at an organization you are familiar with, such as your church, or the school you attend, or a firm in which you work. Try to remember as many facts as you can about how it has been functioning during the past year or two. Use the model outlined in the chapter (Figure 7–2) to see more clearly the relations among these facts.

2 Sequence the events reported in the following short case.[17] How good is the fit between the sequence of events and the model outlined in Figure 7–2? Do you notice any significant gaps in information in the case? Would you care to make any recommendations to Mr. Pierce?

THE ROSE COMPANY

Mr. James Pierce had recently received word of his appointment as general manager of the Jackson Plant, one of the older established units of the Rose Company. As such, Mr. Pierce was to be responsible for the management and administration at the Jackson Plant of all functions and personnel except sales.

Both top management and Mr. Pierce realized that there were several unique features about his new assignment. Mr. Pierce decided to assess his new situation and relationships before undertaking his assignment. He was personally acquainted with the home office executives, but had met few of the Jackson personnel. This case contains some of his reflections regarding the new assignment.

The Rose Company conducted marketing activities throughout the United States and in certain foreign countries. These activities were directed from the home office by a vice president in charge of sales.

Manufacturing operations and certain other departments were under the supervision and control of a senior vice president. These are shown in Exhibit 1. For many years the company had operated a highly centralized functional type of manufacturing organization. There was no general manager at any plant; each of the departments in a plant reported on a line basis to its functional counterpart at the home office. For instance, the industrial relations manager of a particular plant reported to the vice president in charge of industrial relations at the home office, and the plant controller to the vice president-controller, and so on.

Mr. Pierce stated that in the opinion of the top management the record of the Jackson Plant had not been satisfactory for several years. The Rose Company board had recently approved the erection of a new plant in a different part of the city and the use of new methods of production. Lower costs of processing and a reduced manpower requirement at the new plant were expected. Reduction of costs and improved quality of products were needed to maintain competitive leadership and gain some slight product advantage. The proposed combination of methods of manufacturing and mixing materials had not been tried elsewhere in the company. Some features would be entirely new to employees.

EXHIBIT 1
The Rose Company
Old Organization

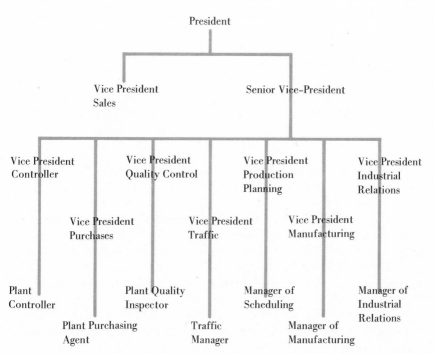

EXHIBIT 2
The Rose Company
New Organization

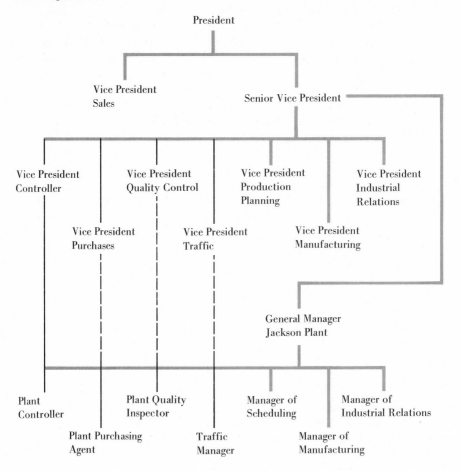

According to Mr. Pierce the top management of the Rose Company was beginning to question the advisability of the central control of manufacturing operations. The officers decided to test the value of a decentralized operation in connection with the Jackson Plant. They apparently believed that a general management representative at Jackson was needed if the new experiment in manufacturing methods and the required rebuilding of the organization were to succeed.

Prior to the new assignment Mr. Pierce had been an accounting executive in the controller's department of the company. From independent sources the casewriter learned that Mr. Pierce had demonstrated analytical ability and general administrative capacity. He was generally liked by people. From top management's point of view he had an essential toughness described as an ability to see anything important through. By some he was regarded as the company's efficiency expert. Others thought he was a perfectionist and aggressive in reaching the goals that had been set. Mr. Pierce was aware of these opinions about his personal behavior.

Mr. Pierce summarized his problem in part as follows:

I am going into a situation involving a large number of changes. I will have a new plant, new methods and processes; but most of all I will be dealing with a set of changed relationships. Heretofore all the heads of departments in the plant reported to their functional counterparts in the home office. Now they will report to me. I am a complete stranger and in addition this is my first assignment in a major "line" job. The men will know this.

When I was called into the senior vice president's office to be informed of my new assignment he asked me to talk with each of the functional members of his staff. The vice presidents in charge of production planning, manufacturing, and industrial relations said they were going to issue all headquarters instructions to me as plant manager and they were going to cut off their connections with their counterparts in my plant. The other home office executives admitted their functional counterparts would report to me in line capacity. They should obey my orders and I would be responsible for their pay and promotion. But these executives proposed to follow the common practice of many companies of maintaining a dotted line or functional relationship with these men. I realize that these two different patterns of home office plant relationships will create real administrative problems for me.

Exhibit 2 shows the organization relationships as defined in these conferences.

Footnotes to Chapter Seven

1 Alfred Chandler, *Strategy and Structure.*
2 T. Burns and G. M. Stalker, *The Management of Innovation.*
3 Rensis Likert, *New Patterns of Management,* Ch. 4.
4 Jay Lorsch and Paul Lawrence, *Studies in Organization Design,* Ch. 4.
5 Harold Leavitt, *Managerial Psychology,* Ch. 24.
6 For example, as J. D. Thompson has done in *Organizations in Action.*
7 An example is the Farmer and Richman model for the comparative study of management. See R. N. Farmer and Barry M. Richman, "A Model for Research in Comparative Management."
8 Talcott Parsons, "Suggestions for a Sociological Approach to the Theory of Organizations."
9 Burns and Stalker, *op. cit.*
10 William Dill, "Environment As an Influence on Managerial Autonomy."
11 D. S. Pugh et al., "The Context of Organizational Structures."
12 F. M. Scherer, *Industrial Market Structure and Economic Performance,* pp. 183–86.
13 Noralou Roos, John Schermerhorn, and Leslie Roos, Jr., "Hospital Performance: Analyzing Power and Goals."
14 Chris Argyris, *Personality and Organizations.* See also Lyman Porter and E. E. Lawler III, "Properties of Organization Structure in Relation to Job Attitudes and Job Behavior."

[15] Gary Steiner, ed., *The Creative Organization*, pp. 16–18.

[16] Paul Lawrence and Jay Lorsch, *Organization and Environment*.

[17] C. Roland Christensen, Kenneth R. Andrews, and Joseph L. Bower, *Business Policy: Text and Cases*, pp. 777–81.

[18] The author is indebted to Mr. Stephen Bennett for supplying the facts of the case. Names have been disguised.

Appendix to Chapter 7

Garrett Converted Papers

A. FACTS[18]

History and business. Garrett Converted Papers, a private company, produces both coated and printed papers products. The company started operations in 1946 and was located in the basement of a factory in the east end of Boston. During its early years, Garrett concentrated on the production of gummed papers. In 1952, having outgrown their basement premises, management decided to move to larger facilities on Belmount Street. Here the business took root and developed from a firm specializing in gummed papers to one with a great diversity of product lines. Garrett serves the intermediate market between raw and fine papers. Some of its products include price tickets for supermarkets, electrostatic copying paper, crepe paper, beer bottle labels, and specially treated wrapping paper sold to large paper producers. In 1969–70, Garrett began exporting their products, and at the present time they are supplying customers in the United Kingdom, Australia, Italy, South Africa, Venezuela, Japan, Ireland, and Canada.

Environment. Garrett forms part of "a close knit, friendly industry." This can best be illustrated by a quote from Bill Garrett, Vice President, Sales, "I like to keep in contact with my opposite number in our competitors' company. In that way if anything unexpected comes up, we can deal with it quickly and in an equitable manner." Intraindustry coordination, although strictly with respect to prices and production, has tended to deteriorate in the last few years, due to the difficulty in obtaining resource inputs. The conditions in the pulp and paper industry (supplier to paper converting firms) are mainly responsible for this shortage, and Garrett spends a good deal of its resources in the search for supplies: "Everybody at the top level will help in getting supplies from all over—from China to Finland," says Bill Garrett.

Inflation has also had its effects on Garrett. "No one questions or challenges price increases anymore," says President George Garrett. "This was something not tolerated a few years ago, but now everybody is doing it and getting away with it." The frequent upward pressure on prices has increased the need for coordination of industry members. However, this has been offset in part by the rapid growth in the demand of converted paper products, and Garrett's management feels that this growth will accelerate in the future, varying directly with the decrease in the use of polyvinyl chloride and other plastic oil derivatives.

Thus management has a favorable outlook on its environment, and it feels confident that it can maintain its 20 percent yearly growth rate. It also feels that Garrett's need for a research and development program is minimal at this time. In its present lines the production technology requirements are not very complex, and the addition to capacity wrought by more complex machinery would be out of proportion to its capital cost. Technology, however, plays a larger role in the demand by other industries for Garrett's products. The development of electrostatic copying papers, telex rolls, and electronic computer papers were products that added greatly to Garrett's sales.

Management perceives the social and political environment to have deleterious effects on the labor supply. Striking a confidential air, the president said, "If I were your age I would not bother working; instead I'd be taking it easy collecting unemployment insurance." In a more serious tone he told the interviewers that there was something basically wrong with the lack of motivation in young people today and that his company had to rely to a large extent on immigrant workers.

Garrett's small size precludes it from having any political leverage. However, it is subject to government legislation concerning the business sector. Management for the most part viewed this legislation favorably and did not express any overt dissatisfaction with it.

Organization demographics. Garrett Converted Papers is a closely held private company. Garrett maintains a staff of about 240 employees. There are 200 unionized workers and 10 supervisors on the shop floor, with about 30 persons involved in office work. It can be classified as a small firm with assets totaling $13 million. It has annual sales of $15 million. It is about 30 years old. It may best be classified as a producer-goods firm, since its products are used as inputs for other products. Coated papers make up 52 percent of its sales, gummed papers 31 percent, and printed papers 17 percent. A wide variety of consumer-goods industries and other industries use its products for wrapping, labeling, and related purposes.

"Garrett Converted Papers is a progressive and diversified corporation. . . . it is number one in the New England paper gumming industry." This statement made by Mr. M. Dodd, Vice President, Research and Development, gives a fairly accurate estimate of the position Garrett holds in the local paper-converting industry. It can claim more than 40 percent New England market share in at least six of its twelve major product lines. In fact management is now in a position to drop product lines that do not meet their targeted rates of return.

Although Garrett is small by absolute standards, it is at a point now where the president is losing substantial control of operating activities. Upper management is faced with the problem of how to delegate authority in a rational manner, and because all the top executives are also part owners this is an especially difficult task for Garrett Converted. The V.P. Research and Development stated it this way, "We want people who will fit into the organization, yet our organization is too small to hire a full time personnel officer. This places heavy demands on our time."

During its nearly thirty years of existence Garrett Converted has been able to build up contacts throughout the international paper-coating industry. This has helped somewhat the search for qualified personnel. One director said that he personally knew every president and most vice presidents of paper-converting companies in Europe, North America, and Japan. Garrett, in fact, has been able to attract two of its directors from outside the country, thus building up a more international management team.

Goals. At its inception the goals of Garrett Converted Papers were simple. In the words of its founder and president, they were "to provide a living for my brother and myself."

Garrett Converted is controlled by four director managers, the president having principal and controlling interest. Unity in decision-making is facilitated because of this unity in interest. The basic goal of Garrett's management is capital accumulation. The researchers were told that the only true entrepreneur was he who "ploughed back" all his profits into the firm and took only a meager salary for himself. Management feels that the best way to increase its capital assets is by maximizing both profits and growth. But due to the oligopolistic structure of Garrett's industry, price-cost margins and relative sales volumes in existing product lines are held fairly constant. Thus the raising-profits-through-rapid-growth formula is found to be most actively used in the development of new, and the modification of existing, product lines.

The following incident gives some idea of the goal conflicts at Garrett. In 1970, Garrett had the opportunity to buy out a small paper-converting firm. From the sales standpoint, the purchase would allow it to go into new product lines and to increase its production capacity in a very short time. The sales department was particularly interested in new product lines because its percentage of the old product markets was fixed by a tacit agreement with its competitors. New products meant higher sales volume, and higher sales volume meant profits. The administrative side of the organization did not see such a rosy picture. There were definite advantages (tax savings, new patents, some of the new firm's capital equipment, which would be difficult to purchase secondhand on the open market). However, many disadvantages were also foreseen. For example, to get the acquisition going, many experienced men would have to be taken from the present operations. Who would take their place? With the increased size of operations (spatially separated), could management keep proper control? How much work and money did revamping the acquisition's capital equipment involve? Could the financial resources be found to do this without overextending the firm? And, finally, how would the other firms in the industry react to such a takeover?

Although the sales and the administration people had the same goal in mind, the means for achieving it were at odds. Sales was willing to take the risk, but administration and production sought stability. Finally a compromise decision was reached. The new plant would be bought and used as a pilot plant for the development of new product lines. After a time, the employees and equipment at the pilot plant would be brought to Garrett's main premises and housed in a new extension being built.

Garrett's growth-oriented goal has had its impact on other areas of the firm's operations. In its early days, the president spent much time in the general process of production. Management was in close touch with the workers, and the two groups had common goals. But as the firm began to grow, the workers became more interested in monetary rewards and less interested in the quality of the products and the general workflow. This, of course, had a depressing effect on motivation. The researchers were told that in the early days, an employee could plan his own schedule and would often work many hours overtime without pay to complete it. However, currently the employee would not even finish the work on the machine when the shift bell sounded. And now all scheduling is done by the administration.

Management style. The styles within the administration/production section and the sales section are different. Sales is characterized by an entrepreneurial, bold style, and the personnel have some operating autonomy. Although major decisions are centralized, each individual member of the department is free to make decisions "on the spot" if the situation calls for it. As the vice president of sales said, "Each of my salesmen is a prima donna." The sales management is free to set its own goals (within reason), and it can draw freely on a fair amount of the company's resources.

With this operating power, the managers are free to pursue new markets and allow their individual salesmen much freedom of action without worrying too much about cost constraints. The sales department goes after growth. In contrast is the administrative/plant section headed by the president and the vice president for research and development. The types of constraint and opportunity faced by this part of the firm make for a more adaptive style of management. In other words, they take the environment as given and try to work within its constraints. Overall, Garrett has passed on from a purely entrepreneurial firm to one where decisions are made and resources built up adaptively, then expended in a typically entrepreneurial fashion. An example of this is the new addition to plant outlined in the previous section. Also, Garrett is not yet highly bureaucratized—the decision-making rules senior management uses are not yet very formalized.

At the lower level of management (the shop floor) the researchers were told by all three supervisors, "We don't like to push people, we use a low key approach towards our employees." This suggests a human relations approach. However, they received a somewhat different picture from the workers: "My supervisor is a nice guy, but if I don't do my job he's going to give me hell." As is clearly evident, this is the classic carrot and stick method, but it works at Garrett, and upper management applauds anything that works.

Structural variables. The company policy has changed from receiving orders and then filling them to producing a fixed number of units of a product per month and then selling from inventories. In other words, the company has shifted from a policy of custom production to one of standardized mass production. This sometimes leads to delays in filling orders, but, given the increasing size of the plant, this seems to be quite reasonable. The change in policy has led to some real economies on both the production and the sales sides of the firm. For example, the operation of scheduling workloads can be carried out on a monthly instead of a daily basis. This leads to substantial savings in set-up costs and in scrap. The marketing position is best summed up by the vice president for sales: "Instead of our looking for customers, customers come to us." This has led sales to adopt a more passive and cheaper promotional approach as opposed to their former "hard sell" doctrine.

At Garrett Converted there are not many managerial levels. Besides the top four management positions covering administration and production, R and D, finance, and sales there are no other areas in which autonomous decision-making takes place. The firm is functionally organized with sales and production as the major departments. One director said that the most potent factor facilitating joint decision-making among the upper management was mutual respect. The management structure has evolved from the selection of like-minded managers, to the unity of goals of these managers, and finally to a close-knit centralized structure that satisfies the need for coordination.

The centralized, functionally departmentalized structure at Garrett implies a formal hierarchy with vertical communication channels. The methods of coordination and control at the firm are a direct result of this vertical information flow. For example, if a lag in production occurs, this information is passed on immediately from the shop floor supervisors to one of the vice presidents through the plant supervisor; the lag is analyzed, and any corrections needed are passed back to the plant supervisor for implementation.

In 1969, Garrett Converted introduced a profit-sharing program in an effort to cut production costs. Basically the plan involved the determination of standard costs of production and the sharing with the workers of any reduction in costs below the standard costs. This program has been an absolute failure, and upper management is amazed at its lack of success. "We just can't understand why these people don't want to help themselves." The plant appears to be administered in an essentially autocratic manner.

Characteristics of organization members and their behavior. The work force employed at Garrett Papers is polyglot. Of the nearly two hundred workers employed on the shop floor, there are just about equal numbers of Irish, Mexicans, Puerto Ricans, Italians, and blacks. These ethnic groups associate very little with one another and tend to group around certain processes on the work floor. For example, the Mexicans operate the gumming machines, the Italians operate the laminations, and Puerto Ricans operate the slitters.

Several of those employed are newly arrived immigrants who have not as yet learned English. This places heavy demands on the supervisors, who are required to know more than one language. Indeed, we were told by management that there are many "bright and able" young men who could be promoted but for their lack of facility in the English language.

Due to the differences in background and culture, needs tend to vary among the groups. The Italians, for example, like many of the other immigrant work groups, see their security needs fulfilled by monetary rewards. The Irish, on the other hand, want to move up.

As a result of inflation, some of Garrett's neighbors in Eastview Industrial Park have raised their wages. This hike in wages has been responsible for great discontent among Garrett's employees. It has even led to the defection of some senior workers. Management is now awakening to the fact that to retain their workers the plant's pay schedule must be revised.

From the interviews, the researchers found that management felt the monetary factor was very strong only among the new workers, where the turnover is quite high. One director said that the new employees work only to get their names on unemployment roles and then quit to take life easy. According to several of the older workers, the problem of high turnover is due primarily to the new breed who "don't seem to care about work anymore." One senior mechanic said, "You have to be born poor to want to save and many of the present generation just don't want to save; they'd rather spend a lot now and think little of the future."

Apart from the self-imposed segregation of workers along ethnic lines, there is a certain amount of segregation based on intelligence. Some jobs are reserved for the "bright employees," and these are kept apart from their fellow workers. This leads to a certain amount of jealousy, but it does not affect the workflow appreciably. Management feels that any attempts to bring the workers into the decision-making process of the firm will be totally rejected by the workers. However, as one worker put it, "It's not that we don't like the boss, but a lot of us are afraid to speak up in case we sound stupid, because most of us don't speak English too good." In addition to these frictions, there is some friction between the older and the younger workers. The former feel that the younger workers do not feel any responsibility for their jobs.

The operation at Garrett Converted Papers is by no means frictionless. There is a very visible and growing separation between management and workers. Management forms a tightly knit, highly motivated group with great internal cohesion. Likewise the workers form fairly cohesive, ethnically oriented work groups. The degree to which these two groups move in concert depends on the supervisory staff on the shop floor. In fact management relies on one man, the shop floor supervisor, to motivate and direct workers. "Bill can motivate anybody, whether its by a kick in the pants or a pat on the back. He knows what's necessary, and he makes sure the person gets the proper attention," the president said.

Performance. As an organization, Garrett appears to have been quite successful. In recent years it has grown at the rate of nearly 20 percent a year. The management's targeted rate of return on capital invested has been reached or surpassed in every year for the past five years. Garrett has achieved a leadership position in the region in several of its product lines.

B. ANALYSIS

The firm, despite some difficulties due to inflation and a weak supply position, is essentially in a benign and stable environment. Competition is by no means severe. Rapid technological change in the industries buying the company's products has expanded the company's markets. The benign and relatively stable but growing environment implies that there is not much pressure for constant adaptation, or for much market intelligence or long-range planning. Indeed, the organization has the traditional functional, departmental structure and does not appear to have a sophisticated information and planning system.

The relatively small size of the company implies a small managerial core and centralized decision-making. The private ownership of the company, and the fact that the top managers are also part owners, implies a closely integrated management team, pursuing the goal of profit and wealth maximization. The company, over its thirty-year span, has developed a stable, workable structure of standard operating procedures. The fact that it manufactures and markets standardized goods makes it easy for it to try out a performance-oriented incentive system, since in such a setup productivity is easy to measure.

The company, as it has grown in size, has found that it can reap important economies of scale by mass producing items rather than producing small lots to customer specifications as it used to do when it was small. One consequence of mass production is that it is possible to segregate the production function from the design and the marketing functions for greater efficiency, and this has bolstered the functional departmentalization in the firm.

Organizational growth has increased the distance between the top management and the workers. The personal touch is gone. As a result workers no longer identify strongly with the goals of the management. The profit-sharing plan is an attempt, impersonally, to restore identity of interests.

The organization's rather unsophisticated technology means that relatively less educated, low cost labor is employed. Since immigrants are the primary source of this kind of labor where the company is situated, it must perforce hire individuals belonging to different ethnic groups. Problems are thus created because individuals usually would prefer to work with others from the same ethnic background, and, when the different work groups may have to coordinate their activities, conflicts can occur between antagonistic ethnic groups. In addition, the diversity hampers supervision because the superior has to speak several languages and be aware of the cultural traits of several ethnic groups.

Overall, the design seems to be appropriate for a relatively small, middle-aged manufacturing company operating in a fairly stable and benign business environment. If, however, the company were to diversify into unrelated product lines, or if its markets became more turbulent, it might have to change its design. Unless the company gets divisionalized, it will not be able to diversify successfully into unrelated product lines. If its business environment becomes more turbulent and more competitive, it will have to acquire staff forecasting, market research, research and development, and planning units to secure the needed information to keep abreast of business developments. If the company grows larger the management will not be able to retain control over the operations unless it installs a sophisticated control system that sets up elaborate cost controls, quality control, audit of operations, careful budgeting, and so on. With growth will come even greater need to communicate effectively up and down the line and between work units at the same level. Some human relations training for the supervisors to facilitate communication and interaction is likely to become more and more necessary as the firm grows larger. Such training may reduce the intensity of the current personnel problems, but so long as operations are labor intensive and the needed labor is relatively low paid and unskilled, these are unlikely to go away.

"What we do depends on what we are . . . but we also are, to an extent, what we do, and we are creating ourselves continually."
Henri Bergson

The Demographic Characteristics of Organizations: Size, Age, and Type

Stuart

INTRODUCTION

What one may consider to be the demographic features of organizations—their size, age, business, and type—often have a profound effect on the structure of organizations, their management styles and strategies, and the processes animating them (see Figure 8–1). A relatively old organization, not unlike an aged person, tends to be a bit set in its ways, has a stable, recognizable structure and many standard operating procedures. A young organization, on the other hand, is likely still to be experimenting with new management philosophies and goals, with alternative organizational techniques and structures. Large organizations tend to be more bureaucratized than small organizations. The manifest function of the organization—whether it is, for example, to provide high school education or university education, serve as a general hospital or as a specialized medical unit, produce garments or produce drugs—powerfully influences the organizational choices that are made. For instance, the university is much more oriented to specialization in instruction than the high school, offers a wider variety of courses, puts greater emphasis on research, and recruits more highly trained manpower to discharge its functions. Whether a firm produces garments or

FIGURE 8–1
Scope of the Chapter

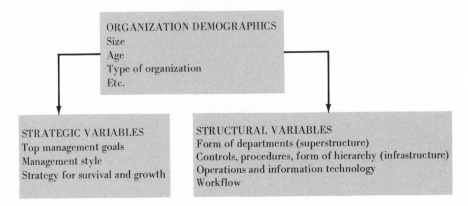

drugs implies great differences in the technology used by the firm, the kind of marketing strategy it employs, the kind of personnel it needs. The type of organization it is raises a host of implications for the organization. Whether it is a democratic institution like a municipality or a nondemocratic institution such as a prison usually means substantial differences in management philosophy, goals, and operating procedures.

SIZE OF ORGANIZATION

An Illustrative Case

The size of the organization is probably one of the most important determinants of organizational structure. Whyte's illustrative case of a growing restaurant describes graphically what happens when an organization gets progressively enlarged:

> Jones begins with a small restaurant where he dispenses short orders over the counter (Stage 1). He has two employees working for him, but there is no division of labor, and all three work together as cooks, countermen, and dishwashers.
>
> The business expands, and Jones finds it necessary to move to larger quarters and hire new employees. Here we see the beginning of the division of labor (Stage 2). He now has a staff of cooks, dishwashers, and waitresses to serve the customers over the counter or in their booths. But the staff is still small, and there is only one supervisor, Jones himself. He keeps track of everything and frequently pitches in to work when he is needed at one of the stations.

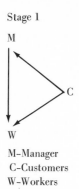

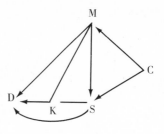

M–Manager
C–Customers
W–Workers

S–Service employees
K–Kitchen employees
D–Dishwashers

In these early stages, the restaurant is characterized by the informality of its human relations. Jones is close to all his employees. They are few enough for him to know them well, and the fact that they work together so closely forms a good basis for friendship.

There are few formal controls in evidence. The workers know what the boss expects of them, and they know what to expect of the boss. The organization rolls along in a comfortable, informal manner.

There is just one problem in Stage 2 that Jones did not have to face in Stage 1. Now, if the organization is to function smoothly, the work of waitresses, cooks, and dishwashers must be coordinated. Sometimes Jones observes that there is friction among these various workers, but he is nearly always on the spot when trouble arises so that he can step in to smooth things over. The problem, therefore, is relatively simple at this point.

The first two stages are also characterized by the close relationship between Jones and his regular customers. The regular customers are his friends. They come in to eat, but they also come in to talk with him.

Now the business continues to expand, and Jones again takes over larger quarters. No longer is he able to supervise all the work. He hires a service supervisor, a food-production supervisor, and places one of his employees in charge of the dishroom as a working supervisor. He also employs a checker to total checks for his waitresses and to see that the food is served in correct portions and style (Stage 3).

In time, he finds that he can take care of a larger number of customers if he takes one more step in the division of labor. Up to now, the cooks have been serving the food to the waitresses. When these functions are divided, both cooking and serving can proceed more efficiently. Therefore, he sets up a service pantry apart from the kitchen. The cooks can now concentrate on cooking, the runners carry food from kitchen to pantry and orders from pantry to kitchen, and the pantry girls serve the waitresses over the counter. This adds one more group of workers to be supervised, and to cope with the larger scale of the operation, he adds another level of supervision, so that there are two supervisors between him and the workers (Stage 4).

Stages 3 and 4 introduce some very significant changes in the position and activity of Tom Jones. He is no longer able to keep up such close rela-

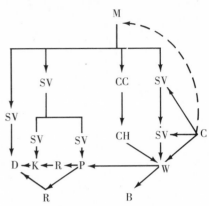

Stage 4

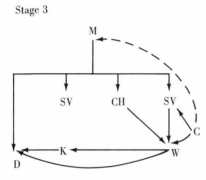

Stage 3

M—Manager
SV—Supervisor
CH—Checker
CC—Cost control supervisor
 C—Customers

W—Waitresses
B—Bartenders
P—Pantry workers
K—Kitchen workers
R—Runners
D—Dishwashers

tions with his customers. There are too many of them, and they come and go too fast.

He comes to realize that he can no longer count on personal relations with customers to build up his business. He cannot sell the good will of the restaurant directly. He must sell it through his supervisors and workers. They represent him to the customers and he must teach them to maintain the distinctive atmosphere and style which the customers find attractive. With the personal touch of the owner carrying less direct weight, he must give special attention to improving standards of food and service, so that customers who have never seen him will eat in his restaurant because "it's the best place in town."

This expansion also gives rise to new problems in the relationship between the manager and his subordinates. As the number of employees grows, Jones finds that he no longer has time to get to know them well. . . . He wonders how he can select supervisors who are capable of doing a good personnel job. He knows how to evaluate their knowledge of food production or service, but skill in human relations seems so much more difficult to measure.

When Jones was beginning, he could state his personnel problem in very simple form: How can I get the cooperation of the workers? As the organization grew, he found he had to leave that problem more and more in the hands of his supervisors. His problem was: How can I get the cooperation of my supervisors?

As the restaurant organization expanded, Jones discovered that it also moved toward standardization. When he himself worked behind the counter, he did not need to worry about elaborate financial controls. He knew his workers and he trusted them. He knew, from day-to-day experience, just about how much business he was doing, so that if the cash register was ever short, he could check up on it right away.

With a large organization, such informal controls necessarily break down. Jones had to build up a system of cost control, and the old employees had to learn new ways. . . . Increasing size required standardization of procedure, and that involved important changes in work routines and human relations. Unless these changes were made skillfully, the morale of the organization would deteriorate. Within limits, standardization was clearly necessary for business reasons, and so he faced another problem: How can I gain the benefits of standardization without losing employee morale and coopera-tion?[1]

Size and Structure

Whyte's restaurant case illustrates several effects that increasing size has on the structure of an organization:

1 As the organization grows, there is greater division of labor.

2 With continued growth coordination becomes a problem, and there-fore there is an increase in the number of levels of hierarchy.

3 With further growth, there is, besides greater division of labor, also the hiring of specialists like the cost control supervisor and the institu-tion of impersonal controls. There emerges a tendency to standardize operations.

4 With growth comes greater distance between top management and the rank and file and between top management and the clients. Morale and good will become worrisome problems. Selection of personnel be-comes particularly important to ensure that standards are maintained despite the distance between the top management and the workers.

Let us now turn to some survey evidence. In an early study, Dale surveyed American firms to discover the extent to which their managements used con-cepts from the classical management theory of Fayol and others.[2] He found that different organizational problems become salient at different levels of organizational growth. He identified seven size classes corresponding to seven stages of growth and the organizational problems that emerge at each stage. When the organization is very small, the formulation of objectives, division of work, delegation of responsibility, and accommodation of personalities are key concerns. When the organization is large, the necessity of staff functions and assistance to the line executives in making decisions become key concerns. With large organizations, the coordination of management functions, group decision-making, and decentralization become key issues.

In two studies of a sizable number of British organizations, researchers found that as the size of the organization increased, the organization tended to have greater specialization of roles and functions, greater standardization of operations through rules and procedures, greater formalization (paperwork), greater decentralization, and so on.[3]

The author's study of 103 Canadian firms confirmed many of the above findings and revealed some interesting additional ones.[4] Large firms were more divisionalized than smaller firms and were more diversified in terms of product lines. They made greater use of sophisticated controls and environment-related information gathering activities such as forecasting, research and development, and market research. They employed mass-production technologies to a greater extent.

Finally, Peter Blau studied state employment security agencies in the United States, which are responsible for administering unemployment insurance and providing public employment services througout America.[5] The data were gathered by interviewing key informants in these agencies and by perusing their records. His data suggest that as organizations grow larger, they get more differentiated along many dimensions but at decreasing rates. Some of the dimensions of organizational differentiation Blau considered were vertical differentiation—that is, the tallness of the administrative hierarchy; number of occupational positions, which can be thought of as horizontal differentiation; and spatial differentiation, or the number of local offices of a state agency.

Blau did not explain why increase in size causes the organization to get differentiated at decreasing rates. But from his basic findings he went on to derive a number of propositions. For example, if the organization gets differentiated with increase in size but at a decreasing rate, and if size is measured in terms of the number of employees, then this implies that any given work unit in the organization gets larger as the size of the organization increases. But it also implies that its size *relative* to the size of the organization declines. It also follows that the larger the organization the smaller is the percentage of total personnel that is engaged in supervisory responsibilities (administration).

The following propositions are warranted:

The larger the organization:

    the more structured and impersonal are its activities—that is, the more it emphasizes formalization of procedures and communication, and specialization of functions;

    the taller is the administrative hierarchy;

    the more diversified tend to be its activities;

    the more divisional and departmental units it possesses;

    the more the organization tends to use a sophisticated *control and information system and the more standardized and mass production oriented is its operations technology.*

Size and Strategic Variables

While the effect of size on the structure of the organization is well documented, size also has some interesting effects on strategic variables. The author's study of Canadian firms, mentioned earlier, indicated some interesting differences with respect to the management philosophy of large, medium-sized, and small firms.[6]

The management strategy of medium-sized organizations emphasizes the building up of internal and external good will toward the organization more heavily than that of large or small organizations. It also emphasizes more heavily a careful assessment of the market environment and of the long-term future. In other words, medium-sized organizations are more status conscious and more oriented to avoidance and absorption of external uncertainty, as the Carnegie theorists (Chapter 5) would call it, than large or small organizations of the same type. The behavior of the medium-sized organization, in this respect, is not too different from that of the middle-class individual! The medium-sized firm, like the latter, is caught in the crossfire between competitive sniping by small firms and the power plays of large firms. For greater adaptability, the medium-sized organization seeks greater internal cohesion and better market information. For greater security, it seeks a better market reputation.

The *administrative* strategy, as the organization grows in size, becomes increasingly one of relying on internal sources of managerial talent, on decentralization, on the use of human relations and participative management, on technocratic *systems* for increasing efficiency rather than on finding creative solutions to organizational problems through brainstorming. This, of course, makes sense given the greater resources and operating diversity and complexity of the larger organization.

Table 8–1 shows the findings from the Canadian study for large, medium-sized, and small firms.

TABLE 8–1
Size and Top Management Philosophy
(Sample: 103 Canadian Firms)

	32 large firms	Average for 37 medium-sized firms	34 small firms	Standard deviation for whole sample
Annual sales or revenues (in millions)	$369	$45	$7	$257
Nonlinear relationships with size				
Importance of high internal good will (employee morale) to top management	5.0	5.4	4.8	1.2
Importance of high external good will (public image) to top management	4.9	5.5	4.9	1.5
Importance of reliable market intelligence (market research, long-term forecasting) to top management	9.9	10.6	9.1	2.6
Linear relationships with size				
Emphasis by top management on internal rather than external recruitment of managers to fill vacancies	5.2	4.7	3.9	1.3
Human relations and participative decision-making oriented top management style	46.4	45.7	40.3	8.9
Emphasis by top management on decentralization of decision-making	5.1	4.9	3.9	1.4
Importance to top management of operating efficiency-raising activities such as operations research, sophisticated management control and information system, and management training and development	14.5	13.6	11.1	3.7
Importance to top management of brainstorming for finding novel solutions to problems	2.6	3.7	4.1	1.6

NOTE: To dampen the great variability in the sizes of firms, their annual sales were subjected to a logarithmic transformation. The three size classes were formed on the assumption of a lognormal distribution of annual sales.

We propose that:

The larger the organization,
> *the more its management adopts an administrative strategy built around decentralization of decision-making authority, human relations and participative management, and a systematic, technocratic response to problems rather than a creative, brainstorming one.*

*As the organization grows in size,
its management's concern for internal and external acceptance and legitimacy initially rises and then falls.*

stop

AGE OF THE ORGANIZATION

Introduction

Like people, organizations show the characteristics of age. Old organizations
find their niche in the world. They learn to cope with their environment as
well as with the needs and idiosyncracies of their members. They reduce to
a routine the solution of most of their operating problems. They also become
conservative, as old folk do. They often resist innovations. Here is a version
of how Arthur Guinness Son and Company, a well-known brewery, has operated over the centuries. The example is an extreme one, but it is illustrative of the behavior of old, tradition-bound organizations.

The first Arthur Guinness took, on the 31st December, 1759, a 9000-year
lease of an existing small brewery in Dublin. At that time, and for many
years after, they brewed ale and stout or porter, as it was then called. I
would say that the first milestone in the road that has led to our success was
the decision to concentrate on one product. There is an entry in one of the
old brewing books that reads as follows: "Today, April 22nd 1799, was
brewed the last ale brew." Since then we have brewed nothing but stout or
porter. That is unique among brewers. The decision was taken when the
founder was an old man and his son had already begun to take a large part
in the business. Whoever made the decision, it was a stroke of genius.

The second and similar vital decision is not so easy to pinpoint. It was
probably never a single definite decision, but became the invariable policy.
This was the restriction of the Guinness activities—or rather those of brewing branch—to brewing alone. In spite of many other activities of the first
Arthur, the second Arthur and his son were only brewers. Moreover, nothing in the nature of either vertical or horizontal trustification was attempted.

It is usual for breweries to own their own maltings. The Guinness policy
on the other hand has been to malt only a small proportion of their requirements—just enough to give them a clear insight into all the problems of
barley and malt.

Guinness have never owned their retail outlets. This policy, while natural
in the early days of their history, was later a decision reached, and over
and over again confirmed, after the closest consideration. All this is part
and parcel of that singling out of the objective which has throughout
characterized the direction of this great business by successive members of
the Guinness family, which I would add has in my experience been a characteristic of some of the most successful businessmen I have known. If then

I were asked the chief reason, in so far as one can be dogmatic in such a matter, for the success of Guinness, I would say without hesitation that it has been due to the singleness of purpose. . . .[7]

The young organization is quite a contrast to the grandfatherly old organization. It is likely to be imbued with a missionary zeal, but it may not be very clear as to exactly what it is so zealous about. Everything is tentative, makeshift, changing. There is more chaos than order, and adaptation is the key phrase. One president of a successful firm of architects, speaking to the author about the early days of his firm, put the matter thus:

> Well, G. and I just felt that it was a damned shame imaginative projects were being turned down at H. And so we decided to start out. G. proposed to sell his summer cottage and put the proceeds at our disposal—which turned out to be $1,500! But anyway, we got going. Sometimes we worked all night. And of course we doubled as architects and managers. We hadn't the foggiest idea about accounting procedures. At the end of the year we had $2,000 left in our bank account. That was our first year profit, we thought. We found out otherwise when we went to the bank for a loan. . . . It was an exhausting but exhilarating first year . . . we were surprised to be still in business. . . .

Age and Organizational Change

The common assertion that old organizations resist change more than young organizations do is perhaps a simplification. Starbuck has suggested that old as well as young organizations resist changes in their task structures—that is, in the programs that constitute the means by which the organizations achieve their goals—because they upset routines and tend to redistribute power. But old organizations tend to resist changes in the social relations within them, while young organizations tend to resist changes in their goals. On the other hand, young organizations support, or at least do not strongly resist, changes in the social structure, while old organizations support or do not strongly resist, changes in organizational goals.[8]

Starbuck grounds these speculations in the assumptions he makes about the kind of commitment members of an organization feel. In young organizations, particularly young voluntary organizations such as newly formed partnerships, unions, clubs, and the like, members feel a special commitment to the goals of the organization. Idealism, after all, is often the moving force in the formation of new organizations. So changes in goals are strongly resisted. But lasting friendships at work have not been formed yet, and so changes in social relations are not particularly resisted. In old organizations, lasting friendships have already developed, and so changes in social relationships or social structure are resisted. On the other hand, over the years members generally develop a commitment to the organization itself, and/or develop strong vested interests in its continuance, and therefore are likely to countenance changes in its goals that help it survive or grow. Indeed, the survival of the organization is viewed as so important that even when the organization's central mission or goal becomes inoperative, the organization's members, rather than folding it up, go in search of new goals that will justify the existence of the organization. This happens quite often. Citizens' welfare groups that spring up in an emergency or a natural calamity often outlive the calamity because of the fun members have had in working together. The Townsend Movement, although originally a liberal political movement, adopted a program of merchandising health foods and vitamins, and an emphasis on social functions, when faced with loss of members and financial disaster.

We propose that:

As organizations grow older,
> *their goals become more flexible and their social and task structures less flexible.*

Some Survey Evidence

Let us now turn to some survey evidence. In the author's Canadian study, it was found, as may be expected, that the age of the firm and its size were fairly strongly correlated.[9] After all, those young organizations that do survive normally grow larger as they mature. To examine what age alone does to an organization, the effect of size was eliminated by computing the correlations of age with a number of other variables, holding size constant. Thus, what follows is an account of the effect of age on the organization, controlling for the effects of size.

The most interesting findings were as follows:

1 As organizations grow older, they seek or find themselves in safer, more predictable, more stagnant, and less variable environments—they tend to find a niche in a less turbulent part of the environment. Alternatively, as organizations grow older, their familiarity with their environment increases, so they tend to view a given environment as less turbulent or unpredictable than younger organizations would view the same environment.

2 Older organizations tend to scale down their goals, particularly their

profit goals. This is consistent with Starbuck's suggestion that as organizations grow older, their commitment to their central goals declines.[10]

3 Older organizations tend to adopt a conservative corporate philosophy. For example, they emphasize job security rather than up-or-out personnel policy. They tend to rely more on internally generated funds to finance their investments than on external finance (e.g., borrowing from banks). They rather strongly avoid high-risk–high-return investments in favor of moderate-risk–modest-return investments. And to a lesser extent, they tend to emphasize internal recruitment of personnel to staff supervisory and managerial positions than external recruitment of such personnel.

4 As a consequence, perhaps, of being in a relatively stable environment, having relatively modest goals, and pursuing conservative, risk-aversive policies, aging organizations see less need for brainstorming than younger organizations. (Brainstorming is a technique for generating novel solutions to complex problems.)

We propose that:

The older the organization,
> *the more it will tend to be in a relatively stable environment;*
> *the lower will be its aspirations; and*
> *the more conservative will be its philosophy and policies.*

Industry Traditions and Current Organizational Practices

The Canadian study also revealed some interesting nonlinear relationships (Table 8–2). Most middle-aged firms in the sample were founded between 40 and 60 years ago, during the heyday of mass-production technology and severe cyclical fluctuations. The old organizations in the sample were founded 60 to 180 years ago, in an age of small-scale, customized production. The youthful organizations in the sample were founded, in general, between 5 and 20 years ago, during a time when marketing and distribution had come to be regarded as keys to firm success. It is at least plausible that besides current situational pressures, the cultural values that shaped the organization early in its life may still be influencing the present structure and operations of the organization.

It is interesting that the middle-aged firms tend to emphasize recourse to hierarchy and the formalization of decision-making authority less than the

TABLE 8–2

Nonlinear Relationships Between Organizational Age and Organizational Variables
(Sample: 103 Canadian Firms)

	22 old firms	Average for		Standard deviation for whole sample
		42 middle-aged firms	39 youthful firms	
Age since founding (in years)	120	52	15	48
Use of custom technology	3.0	2.0	2.7	1.6
The use of hierarchical formal authority in resolving disputes	4.5	4.2	4.8	1.1
Importance to top management of formalizing decision-making authority	5.1	4.1	4.4	1.5
Top management philosophy of tough bargaining with unions rather than of friendly cooperation	5.0	4.2	4.5	1.1

NOTE: The three age classes were formed on the assumption that the age distribution of firms is normal.

old or the youthful firms. The military model of rigid hierarchical differentiation was the vogue during the last century when many of the older firms in the sample were formed. For young firms, hierarchy and formalization of authority are mechanisms for imposing some order on the organizational chaos. Also, it is interesting to note that the old firms believe in tough bargaining with unions to a greater degree than either the middle-aged or youthful firms. Again, the anti-union biases of the last century may be a factor contributing to the management philosophy of the old firms.

Indeed, Stinchcombe has suggested strongly that organizations tend to retain the traditions of the age during which their early forms appeared. For example, hotels and lodging as an industry predates the Industrial Revolution. When that industry was first founded, the typical pattern was that of a family business with an owner-manager running it. Even today, roughly 20 percent of the work force in this industry consists of self-employed and family workers. By way of contrast, Stinchcombe found no industry founded after the onset of the nineteenth century, except the automobile repairs industry, in which this percentage is higher than 6 percent.[11] Is this because somehow the *traditions* of the hotel industry are so strong that they persist even today? Or is it because the *nature* of the hotel business is such (small costs of entry, possibility of gainfully employing surplus family labor, etc.) that

FIGURE 8–2
Forces Shaping the Organization over Time

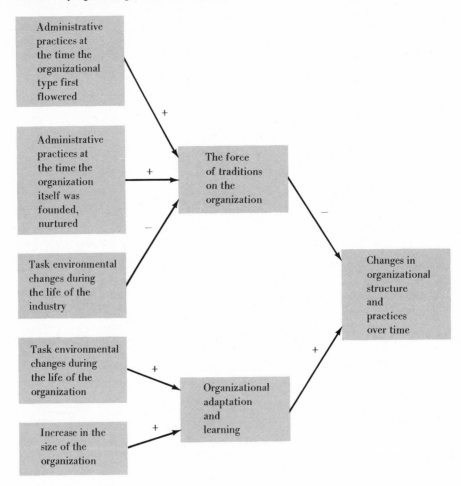

despite the efflux of centuries, the structure of the typical hotel's organization is in important ways similar to that of the hotels of that century in which the hotel industry had its first flowering? The answer probably is that both assertions are partly right. In industries whose task environment or technologies have not changed appreciably over the ages, such as the beer-brewing industry, traditions are sanctified, but perhaps in part because they make good economic sense even today. It is doubtful whether traditions could survive if major changes took place in the industry's task environment. Figure 8–2 shows graphically the various forces at work shaping the organization over time.

We propose that:

The older the industry,
>   the stronger is the force of traditions in the industry.

The more turbulent the task environment of the industry (its markets, technology, etc.),
>   the weaker is the force of traditions in the industry.

TYPE OF ORGANIZATION

Introduction

The business of the organization often affects its philosophy, the goals it pursues, the organization's structure and policies, and also its technology. A service organization like a hospital is organized on a different ideological basis than, say, a business firm. A cooperative society, which may be called a mutual benefit organization, has, generally speaking, an ideology and structure that are different from either a hospital's or a firm's.

There are many different ways of typifying organizations. The typology developed by Blau and Scott is well known; what is more, at least some empirical work has been done to examine its validity. We examine it in some detail.

Classification by Whom the Organization Benefits

Blau and Scott classify organization by *whom the organization is set up to benefit*. Thus, business firms are set up to benefit their *owners*. A wide class of organizations such as unions, fraternities, cooperatives, and clubs are set up to benefit their *members*. Blau and Scott call them "mutual benefit organizations." Another class consists of organizations, called "service organizations," that are set up to benefit their *clients*. Examples are insurance companies, welfare agencies, private schools. Finally, what Blau and Scott call "commonweal organizations" are set up to serve the whole *society*, such as governmental departments or fund-raising agencies.[12]

Some comments need to be made about this typology. First, it is absurd to think that any organization benefits only those it is set up to benefit. A business firm is set up to realize profits for the owners. But its functioning benefits many others, including its employees, its customers, and its suppliers. This is true of service organizations and other types of organization, too. A government department is set up to provide services to society. But it employs a great many people, and if it functions well its performance redounds to the credit of the politicians and administrators who set it up. A typology such as the Blau and Scott typology is thus only a starting point in classifying organizations. Indeed, it would make more sense to say that organizations *vary* in the extent to which they are business oriented, the extent to which they serve society, the extent to which they benefit their members, and the extent to which they serve their clientele. Thus, an advertising agency or an insurance company not only may be very business or profit oriented but may have a very strong orientation toward serving its clients. Not only may a hospital be very service oriented; it may also have a strong orientation toward realizing at least some surplus over its expenditures. It may be best to locate individual organizations on the dimensions of Figure 8–3.

Blau and Scott discuss some of the crucial concerns of each organizational type. Business firms, because of their emphasis on profits, are greatly concerned over operating *efficiency*—"the achievement of maximum gain at minimum cost in order to further survival and growth in competition with other organizations."[13] The crucial concern of mutual benefit associations is that of maintaining *their members' control* over the organizations' activities and policies. The problem is that of maintaining internal democracy in the face of the apathy and ignorance of members and attempts by vested interests to attain control. Mutual benefit organizations, such as unions and cooperatives are often large. In addition, they are often in conflict with other powerful organizations. As a consequence, members tend to leave the affairs of the organization to the leadership, and an oligarchy tends to develop.[14]

The crucial concern of service organizations is that of *providing professional services* to their clients. Since, often, the client is ignorant in the professional's area and the professional is, therefore, in a position to exploit the trust relationship, there are strong pressures to institute a code of conduct to regulate the actions of the professional. In other words, professional organizations, such as the American Bar Association, develop to ensure that the conduct of professionals in service organizations will be ethical. *Public accountability* is the crucial concern of commonweal organizations—that is, organizations set up to benefit the public at large. This is because these commonweal organizations are generally either publicly funded, such as government departments are, or state supported, as state universities and even many private universities are. Public accountability forces organizations to be concerned as much about procedures as about performance, since they live in the glare of public scrutiny. Often it is very difficult to measure

FIGURE 8–3
Organizational Location on Orientation to Benefit Dimensions

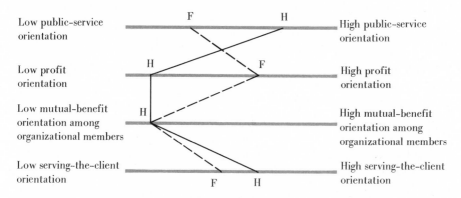

NOTE: The orientation profiles of a hypothetical hospital H and a hypothetical firm F are illustrated above on dimensions based on the Blau and Scott typology.

their performance unambiguously (in the absence of wars, how does one measure the performance of the army?). This strengthens the focus on procedures, since these at least are observable, and conformity with them is capable of being evaluated. As a result, a fairly common fate of commonweal organizations is a bureaucracy. Sometimes the bureaucracy develops dysfunctional features. Its ultimate objectives may get supplanted by the means of achieving them. There may be a loss of direction, loss of flexibility, and loss of innovation.

We make the following propositions:

The more profit or gain oriented is the organization,
the more it views operating efficiency as a critical concern.

The more the organization is oriented to mutual benefit for its members,
particularly if it is large and in an adversary situation with other organizations,
the more oligarchic its management tends to be.

The greater the orientation of the organization to serving its clients,
the more use it makes of professionals and
the more it tends to adopt the norms of the professional organization,
such as a code of ethical professional conduct, operating autonomy
for professionals, and situational expertise rather than position in
hierarchy as the decisive factor in decision-making.

*The stronger the orientation of the organization to serving the general public,
the more it is subject to the pressure of public accountability and
the more bureaucratic it tends to become.*

In a study by Hall, Haas, and Johnson, an attempt was made to apply
the Blau and Scott typology to 75 assorted American organizations.[15] The
authors examined a number of characteristics of these organizations. They
found that organizations classified as mutual benefit organizations tended to
be the least complex of the lot. Most complex, in the sense of carrying on
many activities, having many divisions and subdivisions, and having a large
number of levels in the hierarchy, were service and business organizations.
A significantly higher percentage of commonweal organizations were classified as highly centralized and highly formalized (in terms of who had what
authority and in terms of emphasis on written communications) than mutual
benefit, service, or business organizations. When it is remembered that most
government-operated organizations tend to be commonweal organizations
and vice versa, the researchers' findings suggest that governmental organizations tend to be more centralized and more bureaucratic than other types
of organization.

Another interesting finding was that the ease of assessing how far the
organization achieved its goals varied quite a lot among the different types
of organization. For example, business firms were judged to be able to assess
goal achievement substantially more easily than service organizations and
also more easily than the mutual benefit and commonweal organizations.
This fact is of considerable importance in the functioning of organizations.

If performance is measurable, faster remedial action can be taken when
performance has fallen. If it is not easy to measure, an early diagnosis of
poor performance will be unlikely, and remedial action will be taken only
after a great deal of deterioration of performance. Thus, organizations
whose performance is measurable tend to maintain their equilibrium (in
performance) much better than organizations whose performance is difficult
to measure.

On the other hand, measurable goals tend to displace goals whose achievement is difficult to measure. Organizations whose goals are more easy to
measure will tend to follow these rather specific goals and tend to ignore or
devalue other important but difficult to measure goals that they may have.
Profit is not the only goal of business firms. But it is a measurable goal, and
so it is often pursued in preference to such other corporate goals as public
image, social service, and employee job satisfaction. Universities and schools
usually enunciate as their primary goals educating their students and helping them to fully develop their potential. But those are difficult to measure.
Consequently, they fasten on the measurable to evaluate themselves: the

average starting salary of their graduates for example, in the case of universities. This kind of substitution of goals often drains the organization of much of its "moral" appeal, and the commitment of the members of the organization degenerates from one of strong identification to a calculative commitment and even to alienation.

Two other findings in the Hall, Haas, and Johnson study are of interest. Organizations classified as business organizations reportedly experienced more severe competition, and they also reported being subject to greater governmental control and regulation, than other types of organization (excluding governmental agencies). Presumably, firms are subject to greater governmental regulation than other nongovernmental organizations because they may be perceived to be relatively less imbued with the spirit of social welfare. Also, when the outputs of an organization are readily identifiable and carry price tags, they invite comparison with those of other similar organizations by customers, thus initiating competition among such organizations.

The study by Hall, Haas, and Johnson suffers from many methodological and other shortcomings.[16] But it does point up some of the similarities and differences among different types of organization. The differences seem to be the sharpest between business organizations and other organizations. Generally speaking, the goals and outputs of business organizations are more readily measurable than those of other organizations, and business organizations tend to be more subject to severe competition and governmental control than other nongovernmental organizations. Organizationally, mutual benefit organizations like cooperatives, unions, and professional associations tend to be less centralized and less bureaucratized than commonweal organizations such as the post office and governmental agencies and departments.[17]

We propose that:

The more measurable the performance of an organization,
> *the more stable tends to be the performance of the organization,*
>> *other things, such as the nature of the environment, being equal.*

Given a mix of measurable and relatively difficult to measure goals, the former will tend to displace the latter as the primary operating goals of an organization.

The more profit or gain oriented an organization and
the less it is commonweal oriented,
> *the more it tends to be subject to governmental surveillance and regulation.*

The more measurable the outputs and goals of an organization and

the more profit or gain oriented it is,
   the more it is likely to be subject to competitive pressures.

Classification by Nature of Output

Another basis for classifying organizations is by the nature of their output. The question here is: Is the organization geared primarily to producing goods, as manufacturing firms are, or is it geared primarily to producing or offering services, as banks, hospitals, universities, and government agencies are?* The importance of the distinction lies in the fact that *generally speaking* it is possible to automate the production of goods to a much greater degree than the production of services. The latter generally is a labor-intensive process. In addition, there is, generally, a qualitative difference in the transactions with its customers of the goods-producing organization and the service-producing organization. There is much greater face-to-face contact between the service organization and its clients than there is between the goods-producing organization and its clients.

Several consequences follow from these two key differences between service organizations and goods organizations. First, the possibility of extensively using machinery to produce goods, and thereby cutting costs, usually means the dominance of machine over man (work tends to be machine paced). Since increase in mechanization is always a possibility, the situation is more threatening for the workers in goods-producing organizations than in service organizations. Worker-management conflicts tend to be more severe in goods-producing organizations than in service organizations, and militant unionism tends to be more common in the former.

A second consequence of the greater automation of factory-type organizations is the pressure for growth and full utilization of capacity. Automation and mechanization usually imply large economies of scale—that is, the larger the plant the lower, up to some point, are the unit costs, provided the plant is fully utilized. For example, ingot steel plants of less than a million-ton capacity are not very competitive. Also, because plants are engineered that way, large excess capacities can confront the growing organization. As an example, if a steel firm can sell 1.5 million tons of ingot steel, and its present capacity is 1 million tons, it will think seriously of acquiring another million tons of capacity because of potential cost savings

---

* In actuality, there are quite a few organizations whose outputs are *both* products and services. Restaurants and hotels produce food as well as services. Machinery manufacturers not only sell goods but offer after-sales service.

and will have to give careful thought to how to market that additional ½ million tons. These pressures for growth and full utilization of capacity are less acute for service organizations. One consequence of the pressure for full utilization of capacity is an attempt at vertical integration by manufacturing organizations to secure greater control over the market as well as resources or inputs.

Third, service organizations have much more intense interpersonal transactions with their clients than goods organizations. Since people have all sorts of idiosyncrasy, it often becomes very hard indeed for the personnel of service organizations to deal with their clientele. The doctor, the lawyer, the accountant, the architect, not to mention the insurance salesman and the bank teller, all must develop a special ability to adapt to the large range of customer requirements. As the data from the author's study of Canadian firms showed, this diversity in the requirements of customers tends to beget a marketing orientation, a tendency to use custom rather than mass, standardized output technologies, a tendency to have an "open" organization (that is, permit open channels of communication), and a tendency to decentralize decision-making. It also tends to beget a "people first" or "service to the customers" orientation or ideology and a corresponding incentive system that rewards ability to serve the client effectively.

Thus, other things being equal:

The more the organization is geared to the production of goods rather than services,
    the greater is the mechanization of operations, and
    the lower is the extent of face-to-face transactions with the organization's customers.

The more the organization is geared to the production of goods rather than services,
    the more sensitive, other things being equal, are the relations between management and workers, and
    the greater is the pressure for growth, full utilization of capacity, and vertical integration.

The more the organization is geared to the production of services rather than goods,
    the more of a "service to the client" ideology does it hold,
    the more oriented it is to customized operations, and
    the more decentralized and organically managed it is.

Different Classes of Goods Manufacturer

The goods-producing organizations can be classified further into those that produce *consumer durable goods,* such as cars and television sets; *consumer nondurable* goods, like processed foods and clothing; *producer goods,* like steel, cement, chemicals and fibers that get used up in the production of consumer or capital goods; and *capital goods,* like machinery, ships, aeroplanes, and buildings, that are the means of further production.

The demand for consumer durable goods tends, typically, to be *cyclical* (because of the need to replace a durable good such as a car every few years) and *income elastic* (that is, quite sensitive to changes in the level of income of a society). The key problem of organizations producing consumer durable goods is to develop a productive capacity that can meet peak demand but in a recession does not overly penalize the organization for having excess capacity. These organizations are usually geared to mass production with very mechanized means. To control the flow of production and assure low cost, standard quality output, they tend to get vertically integrated and employ a sophisticated control and information system. To support mass production, these organizations engage in national and even international distribution networks.

The organizations producing nondurable goods, particularly goods of common usage, tend to have more *even demand patterns* than organizations producing durable goods. Also, the goods are more perishable, less bulky, and more subject to competition because relatively low capital costs make it possible for many organizations to enter a market. Effective advertising, packaging, and marketing are the key problems of these organizations, as well, of course, as efficient manufacture, for they tend to face severe price as well as marketing competition.

The demand for producer goods—that is, goods that are in turn incorporated into further goods—is a *derived* demand; it depends on the demand for those "further goods." If the producer good is used primarily in the manufacture of a nondurable good, its demand will be stable like that of the nondurable good in which it is incorporated. Thus, how production is organized will depend on the nature of the demand for the producer good. In general, the producer goods organizations will need to make only limited marketing efforts since their clients are primarily other organizations rather than consumers. But they often are research and development oriented in an effort to discover new uses for their products and to cheapen the cost of production. The wider the range of products in which a particular producer good is used, the larger and more stable tends to be the demand for it.

Capital goods are relatively very *expensive* (a ship can cost several million dollars, and so can a coke oven plant), and commonly they are produced to the *specifications of customers*, which usually are other organizations. Price, delivery, performance, and after-sales service are the critical competitive issues among the producers of capital goods. They tend to be very capital intensive, large, custom-production oriented organizations and to have large research and development establishments to develop more sophisticated machines and products. These organizations typically make a sale before they have manufactured the product, while the other types discussed above typically sell from inventory. They are therefore rather risky ventures, and as examples of Rolls Royce and General Dynamics show, can make vast losses. These organizations often subcontract good chunks of the product they have contracted to supply, partly to reduce risk and partly because of the difficulty of assembling all the capacities needed to produce the product under one roof. Since each product tends to be unique, the project form of organization with its matrix structure is common. (An organization has a matrix structure when its members are located in functional departments as well as being assigned to individual projects. An electrical engineer, for example, may belong to the electrical engineering department, and he may be assigned simultaneously to the development of electronic equipment for a company client.)

Table 8–3 shows the differences among organizations that produce durable consumer goods, nondurable consumer goods, producer goods, and capital goods.

We propose that:

The more the organization is geared to the production of goods that can be sold from inventory,

    the greater is its management's concern with operating efficiency and a wide distribution network;
    the more standardized are the organization's operations; and
    the more vertically integrated does the organization strive to be.

The more the organization is oriented to selling goods prior to their manufacture,

    the more it is characterized by project groups and a matrix structure.

Classes of Service Organization

Banks, insurance companies, advertising agencies, unions, political parties, religious organizations, hospitals, schools, and government agencies are all service organizations—they are in the business of providing services. These

TABLE 8–3
Classes of Goods Manufacturer and Their Organizational Characteristics

Nature of product	Dominant technology	Characteristics of demand and costs	Management concerns and organizational design
Consumer durable (e.g., automobiles)	Mass production, assembly line	Cyclical demand, income elastic demand; high fixed costs. Somewhat naive customers	Periodic excess capacity; need to diversify product lines; emphasis on operating efficiency; standardization creates apathy in workers; use of controls; wide distribution network; vertical integration; long-term planning; accent on product differentiation and aggressive marketing; divisionalization
Consumer nondurable (e.g., clothing, processed foods)	Small batch to mass production	Usually stable demand; fixed costs can vary a great deal; generally, high labor and material costs. Somewhat naive customers	Competition because of easy entry into the industry; focus on marketing, packaging, advertising, and cost control
Producer goods (e.g., steel, cement, cotton yarn, meat, industrial chemicals)	Batch production or continuous process production; highly capital intensive technology	Demand dependent on the nature of products in which used; buyers mostly other organizations; generally, high fixed costs and high materials costs	Worry of severe price competition because the product is homogeneous; research and development of new uses of the product; emphasis on operating efficiency
Capital goods (e.g., various kinds of machinery, ships, planes, weapons systems)	Custom production—that is, production to buyer specifications	Cyclical demand, often subject to strong political influences; sophisticated buyers, mostly other organizations	Risk due to sales prior to production; delivery, performance, price, after-sales service key competitive issues; project management and matrix structure

can be firms, commonweal organizations, service organizations, or mutual benefit organizations, and their characteristics will tend to be what we have proposed for these types of organization.

There are some fundamental differences between service organizations that are dominated by professionals and those that are not.[18] When operations are technically complex, service organizations tend to be dominated by professionals. Examples are public accounting firms, hospitals, universities, engineering and design departments of firms, and so on. When work is not very technically complex, they tend to be dominated by administrators and nonprofessional managers. Hall's work suggests that professional-dominated organizations tend to be characterized by an ideology of autonomy and decentralization, a sense of moral calling to the profession, belief in self-regulation, belief in service to the public and especially to the clients, and the acceptance of codes of ethics promulgated by associations of professionals. Bureaucratic values such as a rigid hierarchy of authority and an emphasis on rigid application of rules and regulations and standard operating procedures do not go well with professional values.[19] Rather opposite conditions prevail in organizations whose operations do not call for high technical expertise. In other words, they tend to subscribe strongly to bureaucratic values.

The various organizational properties associated with the different dimensions of service organizations are summarized in Table 8–4.

OWNERSHIP

Organizations can be publicly or privately owned. Publicly owned organizations either are owned or funded by the public at large through the government or are owned broadly, such as corporations whose shares are listed on stock exchanges.

Generally speaking, public organizations have a higher visibility, and therefore their managements behave as if they have a high public accountability. This, of course, tends to make them quite bureaucratic. Private organizations are generally smaller and less visible; and therefore they tend to be less bureaucratic, and their managements feel a lesser concern about public accountability.

It has been argued that private ownership organizations are likely to be more efficient than public organizations because in the former the owners tend to be the managers, or at least the owners can wield effective supervision over the managers. On the other hand, others have argued that owners are not necessarily good managers, and that for professional quality management, owners should *not* be managers.[20]

TABLE 8—4
Dimensions of Service Organizations and Their Organizational Properties

Service organization dimensions	Organizational design
Profit orientation (e.g., firms)	Emphasis on operating efficiency, productivity, and marketing
Commonweal orientation (e.g., government bureaus, jails)	Highly bureaucratic structure and functioning
Service to clients orientation (e.g., public accounting and law firms)	Use of professionals; norms of professional organization (see fifth item below)
Mutual benefit orientation (e.g., cooperative societies, labor unions)	Centralized, oligarchic, management, especially if the organization is large and in an adversary position with other organizations
Dominance of professionals (e.g., associations of professionals, hospitals, universities)	Emphasis on technical competence; strong service to public (especially to clients) orientation; belief in self-regulation by professionals rather than hierarchical regulation, autonomy at work, decentralized decision-making, etc.; conflict with norms of efficiency
Dominance of administrative or nonprofessional managers (e.g., restaurants, trading firms)	Centralization of decision-making; strong emphasis on hierarchical relationships, standard operating procedures, efficiency

Actually, research evidence presents a mixed picture. In studies of privately owned and publicly owned firms that were matched for type of industry, two studies showed that the privately owned firms outperformed the publicly owned firms. However, in one of them, it was also found that when privately owned firms changed over to public ownership, their performance improved! In a study of a restaurant chain, it was found that the branches operated by franchisee-owners achieved higher performance than those operated by hired managers, and, indeed, there was a tendency for performance to improve when a branch previously managed by a hired manager was turned over to a franchisee-owner.[21] In a study of sugar factories in India, no notable differences in performance were found between cooperatively owned factories and privately owned factories.[22] Clearly, ownership per se is not a decisive influence on performance, although in certain specific situations it may make a difference. For example, when larger resources and wider managerial talents are needed, as when a small organization is on the verge of becoming a big one, a change from private to public ownership may be useful. If technology is simple and the environment relatively noncomplex, private ownership may yield better dividends because the owners *can* keep an eye on operations. Under opposite conditions it may be better to be a public organization with a professional management team.

SUMMARY, PROPOSITIONS, AND IMPLICATIONS FOR ORGANIZATIONAL DESIGN

Summary

In this chapter we have tried to show how demographic factors affect organizations. We noted particularly the effects of size, age, type, and ownership of organization on organizational structure and management philosophy.

Increasing size, generally speaking, has the effect of making the organization more bureaucratic, more marked by specialization and division of labor, and more technocratic. Medium-sized organizations tend to want to absorb and avoid uncertainty more than very large or very small organizations of their type.

As the organization grows older, it tends to get more conservative and more risk aversive, and also more structured. However, its goals become more flexible. The structure and style an organization has at a particular moment depend, not only on its present size, age, type of business, and ownership, but also on its history and on the traditions in its industry.

There are many ways of classifying organizations. One way is by asking, "Whom does the organization benefit?" A second way is by asking what kinds of outputs (goods or services) organizations produce and, if goods, whether they are consumer durable, consumer nondurable, producer, or capital goods. There can be many other ways of classifying organizations. Each classificatory scheme yields valuable organizational predictions. At the same time, it should be noted that every scheme of classification requires organizations to be pigeonholed into one of a number of mutually exclusive classes. In reality, however, most organizations tend to have the properties of several of the classes, though they may have more of the properties of one class than of the others. In fact, quite often, there is a wide variation in the extent to which organizations of a certain type exhibit the properties that characterize their type. There are commonweal, community controlled, as well as profit-oriented privately owned hospitals. This is no less true of other types such as schools and firms.

Propositions

The following propositions have been advanced:

1. The larger the organization,

> the more structured and impersonal are its activities (that is, the more it emphasizes formalization of procedures and communication and specialization of functions);
>
> the taller is the administrative hierarchy;
>
> the more diversified tend to be its activities;
>
> the more divisional and departmental units it possesses;
>
> the more the organization tends to use a *sophisticated* control and information system;
>
> the more standardized and mass production oriented is its operations technology.

2. The larger the organization,

> the more its management adopts an administrative strategy built around decentralization of decision-making authority, human relations and participative management, and a systematic, technocratic response to problems rather than a creative brainstorming one.

3. As the organization grows in size,

> its management's concern for internal and external acceptance and legitimacy initially rises and then falls.

4. As organizations grow older

> their goals become more flexible and their social and task structures less flexible.

5. The older the organization,

> the more it will tend to be in a relatively stable environment;
>
> the lower will be its aspirations; and
>
> the more conservative will be its philosophy and policies.

6. The older the industry,

> the stronger is the force of traditions in the industry.

7. The more turbulent the task environment of the industry (its markets, technology, etc.),

> the weaker is the force of traditions in the industry.

8. The more profit or gain oriented is the organization,

> the more it views operating efficiency as a critical concern.

9. The more the organization is oriented to mutual benefit for its members, particularly if it is large and in an adversary situation with other organizations,

> the more oligarchic its management tends to be.

10. The greater the orientation of the organization to serving its clients,

> the more use it makes of professionals and
> the more it tends to adopt the norms of the professional organization, such as a code of ethical professional conduct, operating autonomy for professionals, and situational expertise rather than position in hierarchy as the decisive factor in decision-making.

11. The stronger the orientation of the organization to serving the general public,

> the more it is subject to the pressure of public accountability and
> the more bureaucratic it tends to become.

12. The more measurable the performance of an organization,

> the more stable tends to be the performance of the organization, other things, such as the nature of the environment being equal.

13. Given a mix of measurable and relatively difficult to measure goals, the former will tend to displace the latter as the primary operating goals of an organization.

14. The more profit or gain oriented an organization *and* the less it is commonweal oriented,

> the more it tends to be subject to governmental surveillance and regulation.

15. The more measurable the outputs and goals of an organization *and* the more profit or gain oriented it is,

> the more it is likely to be subject to competitive pressures.

16. The more the organization is geared to the production of goods rather than services,

> the greater is the mechanization of operations, and
> the lower is the extent of face-to-face transactions with the organization's customers.

17. The more the organization is geared to the production of goods rather than services,

  the more sensitive, other things being equal, are the relations between management and workers, and

  the greater is the pressure for growth, full utilization of capacity and vertical integration.

18. The more the organization is geared to the production of services rather than goods,

  the more of a "service to the client" ideology it holds,

  the more oriented it is to marketing and customized operations and

  the more decentralized and organically managed it is.

19. The more the organization is geared to the production of goods that can be sold from inventory,

  the greater is its management's concern with operating efficiency and a wide distribution network;

  the more standardized are the organization's operations; and

  the more vertically integrated does the organization strive to be.

20. The more the organization is oriented to selling goods prior to their manufacture,

  the more it is characterized by project groups and a matrix structure.

Implications for Organizational Design

We have examined the possible effects of size, age, and type of organization on the way organizations get shaped. It is well to remember some of the imperatives these pose for the organization.

For example, as an organization grows larger, it must expect to get more bureaucratized, more differentiated through role specialization and extensive departmentalization; it must expect to be decentralized; and it must also expect to use a sophisticated control system. Failure to do all of these will, under normal circumstances, result in poor performance by its members and poor coordination of its operations. At the same time, the designer must remember that these very acts, necessary as they may be, are likely to result in a considerably more impersonal organization. This impersonality will cause internal morale problems and difficulties with the organization's customers. The designer can counteract these by having smaller work groups, by encouraging more participative decision-making, and by training those members of the organization that come into contact with the public in public and human relations. The knowledge of what to expect as an organization grows larger can help the designer take remedial action. As a corollary, a small organization, other things being equal, need not have a bureaucratized, differentiated, technocratized, decentralized structure. Many large organizations, among them corporations and governments, make the mistake of encumbering their small offspring (small subsidiaries, small local agencies, etc.) with the kind of structure that is appropriate to their massive parents. Since different parts of an organization differ in the size of their operations, sometimes to a great extent, it may make sense to have somewhat different structures for the different parts. Naturally, if such a structural differentiation is permitted, the designer must make sure that the activities of the organization as a whole are properly integrated through planning, controls, or otherwise.

As an organization grows older it is very likely to develop a body of practices and precedents that will stand in the way of innovation. The organization will also acquire a great deal of familiarity with its environment. Both these forces are likely to make it conservative. Conservatism is not necessarily bad provided the organization continues to aspire to high performance, continues to look for and create growth opportunities, and retains an ability to adapt flexibly to changing circumstances. So long as the designer remembers this, he can take appropriate steps. For example, a periodic review of the management philosophy and the assessment of its relevance in the current context can be institutionalized. A policy of actively seeking "fresh blood" can be adopted. A tradition of rewarding members with ideas and initiative can be inculcated. A permanent group can be set up in the organization to monitor the environment and identify growth opportunities. Knowing what will happen as an organization grows older can enable the designer or designers to do much to prevent the hardening of organizational arteries.

We noted the many consequences associated with the type that an organization is. Whether it is profit oriented or oriented to serving society, whether it is a manufacturing organization or a service organization, has major consequences. For instance, whether the performance of the organization is readily evaluated or not has enormous consequences for the production, planning, and control systems in the organization. The performance of profit oriented manufacturing organizations is relatively easy to measure, and therefore they are able to employ sophisticated production, planning, and control systems. Commonweal service organizations like universities suffer from the disability of not being able to measure their performance accurately and early, and they therefore find it difficult to employ sophisticated techniques of planning, control, and production. But again, being aware of this, the designer or designers can take remedial steps, such as initiating cost-benefit analyses of current and proposed programs, a better information-gathering system, deliberate use of greater technical expertise in planning operations, and so on. Just because the nature of the organization favors amateurish or seat-of-the-pants type of management does not mean that that is what the organization should have. On the other side of the coin, firms often get too obsessed with the measurable, like short-term profits, and neglect the relatively nonquantifiable goals like morale and public image. Here again, the designer or designers can take remedial action by institutionalizing a consideration of these goals in all major decisions and by setting up programs to measure how well the organization is doing on these intangible goals.

SUGGESTED READINGS

Chs. 2 and 4 in Richard H. Hall, *Organizations* (Englewood Cliffs, N. J.: Prentice-Hall, 1972). Chapter 2 describes various typologies and the components of a classificatory system. Chapter 4 describes the various definitions of size, its various correlates, and the impact of size on the individual, on the organization, and on society.

William H. Starbuck, "Organizational Growth and Development" in James March, ed., *Handbook of Organizations* (Chicago: Rand McNally, 1965). This is a review article on organizational growth and maturation.

QUESTIONS FOR ANALYSIS

1 What makes an organization grow bigger? What forces may keep it small?

2 Why are there over 4 million small organizations in North America and only a few thousand big ones?

3 Read "Growth at Shamrock," particularly pp. 152–154, in the book of cases by Wegner and Sayles.[23] If the Board of Directors of the company hired you as a consultant to advise it on the design of the Shamrock organization, what advice would you give?

4 Here are some facts about the Lord Jim High School in Montreal. What organizational design would be appropriate for it? (Adapted from a report by Mark Hubscher, Nick Riehle, Lise Rocheleau, and Anthony Stelliou, prepared under the author's supervision.)

Lord Jim High School is affiliated with the Protestant School Board of Greater Montreal, and the School Board, in turn, is part of the Department of Education of the Province of Quebec. The school was built to serve the immigrant children around the St. Lawrence–St. Urbain area whose popu-

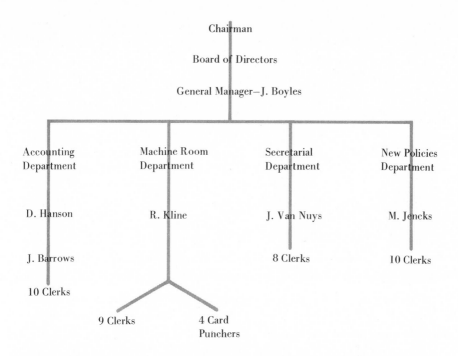

Chairman

Board of Directors

General Manager—J. Boyles

Accounting Department	Machine Room Department	Secretarial Department	New Policies Department
D. Hanson	R. Kline	J. Van Nuys	M. Jencks
J. Barrows		8 Clerks	10 Clerks
10 Clerks			

9 Clerks   4 Card Punchers

lation at that time was primarily Jewish. Today, the school serves the same purpose with students also coming from the Park Extension area. The only major difference is that the school's population is now 82% Greek.

Lord Jim is one of 22 high schools under the Protestant School Board of Greater Montreal. Lord Jim is an old and relatively small school in comparison to other schools on the Island of Montreal. The school is 63 years old and presently serves about 680 students. Furthermore, there are 53 employees—2 administrators, 5 department heads who also teach, 44 teachers, a 2-member secretarial staff, and 3 superintendents. Because Lord Jim is classified by the Protestant School Board as an inner city school,* it has a lower teacher to student ratio than most schools.

Lord Jim lacks many facilities. At present it does not have an auditorium nor an athletic field. The school is fighting for a million dollar budget in order to add facilities.

Lord Jim seems to be concerned primarily with the moral and technical socialization of youth through education. To quote the Vice Principal: "I feel that the prime function of the school should be acculturation. In other words to make it easier for the kids to fit into the dominant culture." The means used are somewhat coercive: "They (the students) appreciate some semblance of order and this is what they are looking for. They are caught

* The term inner city school is not clearly defined. The definition by the administration is a school with a lower student to teacher ratio than most other schools. Another definition by a Montreal Teachers Association Representative was a school whose academic achievement was lower than the norm.

in the crunch between the license in this society and the extreme pressure their parents put on them. If they could find some half-way system for them to fit into, that would make them feel more secure."

The administration tends to feel that some of the teachers are not really as professional at their jobs as they should be. The administration has tried to use some coercion. This has caused some conflicts between the administration and the teachers. As stated by the Vice-Principal: "The teachers are quite militant here. They have a strong sense of their rights and are very quick to pick up any infringement of their rights. They insist on being treated as professionals which means that you don't impose rules and regulations on them. You expect them to be professional. Yet," he adds, "they sometimes fail to live up to these expectations.

5 How do hospitals differ from universities?

6 What qualitative changes, if any, has the organization of the government undergone in the last hundred years?

7 Suppose there are two hotels, both of about equal size. One gets 80 percent of its revenues from room rent and 20 percent from the bar and dining room. The other gets 20 percent of its revenues from room rent and 80 percent from the bar and dining room. What organizational differences would you expect between the two hotels?

8 What organizational differences would you expect between a department store like Eaton's or Macy's and a diversified manufacturing firm such as Westinghouse that manufactures many items sold in department stores?

Footnotes to Chapter 8

1 W. F. Whyte, *Organizational Behavior: Theory and Application*, pp. 571–77.
2 Ernest Dale, *Planning and Developing the Company Organization Structure.*
3 See John Child and Roger Mansfield, "Technology, Size, and Organization Structure," pp. 369–93, for a description of the two studies.
4 See Appendix A to this book for a description of the sample, method of data collection, and operational definitions of variables.
5 See Peter Blau, "A Formal Theory of Differentiation in Organizations," pp. 201–18.
6 See Appendix A for details.
7 R. S. Edwards and H. Townsend, "The Growth of Firms," pp. 240–41.
8 W. H. Starbuck, "Organizational Growth and Development," pp. 473–77.
9 See Appendix A for a description of the study.
10 Starbuck, *op. cit.*
11 Arthur Stinchcombe, "Social Structure and Organizations," p. 158.
12 Peter Blau and Richard Scott, *Formal Organizations*, Ch. 2.
13 *Ibid.*, p. 49.
14 See R. Michels, *Political Parties*, tr. 1949, especially his discussion of the iron law of oligarchy.
15 Richard H. Hall, J. Eugene Haas, and Norman J. Johnson, "An Examination of the Blau-Scott and Etzioni Typologies." They also categorized their 75 organiza-

tions as utilitarian, normative, and coercive, applying the Etzioni typology based on the means of control used to regulate the organizational rank and file (see Amitai Etzioni, *Modern Organizations*, Ch. 6).

[16] See Peter D. Weldon, "An Examination of the Blau-Scott and Etzioni Typologies: A Critique," for a critique of the Hall, Haas, and Johnson paper.

[17] For detailed studies of the many institutional forms, such as firms, hospitals, unions, public bureaucracies, local governments, see James March, ed., *Handbook of Organizations*.

[18] See Etzioni, *op. cit.*, Ch. 8; and Richard H. Hall, "Professionalization and Bureaucratization."

[19] *Ibid.*, p. 102.

[20] F. M. Scherer, *Industrial Market Structure and Economic Performance*, pp. 30–31. Weber considered the separation of ownership from control as one of the key properties of the bureaucracy as an ideal organizational form—see Max Weber, *The Theory of Social and Economic Organizations*, tr. 1947.

[21] See Scherer, *op. cit.*, pp. 34–36, for a description of these studies.

[22] Jai Ghorpade, "Organizational Ownership Patterns and Efficiency: A Case Study of Private and Cooperative Sugar Factories in South India."

[23] R. Wegner and L. Sayles, *Cases in Organizational and Administrative Behavior*, pp. 152–54.

*"There is a force that drives us on and yet we are
the force and sometimes have controlled it."*
Paul Engle

The External
Environment
of Organizations

Start

INTRODUCTION

Environmental Pressure

In Chapter 6 we reviewed work of the systems theorists and the contingency
theorists. We noted the view of the systems theorists that the organization
is in a symbiotic relationship with the environment, taking from it the
inputs needed for its operations, and exporting to it the outputs of goods
and services needed by the environment. We also noted the view of the contingency theorists that differences in the properties of the task environment
cause differences in the way organizations are designed. In this chapter we
explore in some detail the way the _external_ environment affects the strategic
and structural aspects of organizations. We should remember, however, that
for "embedded" organizations—that is, organizations such as departments or
divisions that are parts of a larger organization—the parent organization
may form a substantial chunk of the external environment.

The environment is a source of many different kinds of pressure on the
organization. Here is an example:

L. M. Barren Company is a well-known manufacturer of surgical sutures. L. M. Barren pioneered the development of needled suture combinations from their invention in 1921, under the trademark Eyless. In the postwar 1940's there developed a much greater interest in Eyless needled sutures for all types of exacting surgery, with the result that about sixty different styles and sizes of needles were developed, and the sales became a significant part of the total L. M. Barren volume.

Competition from other suture manufacturers increased during the postwar period, which kept prices for these products frozen at their introductory levels.

From 1921 until two years ago, all Eyless needles used by L. M. Barren were produced to its specifications by the Trent Company of Trent, Connecticut. Trent is an important producer of textile needles, and one of its engineers originally devised the Eyless type needle and sold his patent rights to L. M. Barren in 1921. Since L. M. Barren had no facilities for metal working in this exacting field, it developed its needles in cooperation with Trent over this long period. Since Trent was the only major supplier of Eyless type needles in the United States during most of this time, and the patent had expired, Trent has been selling such needles to all suture manufacturers, including L. M. Barren competitors.

L. M. Barren management became uneasy about this situation three years ago when, due to a strike at Trent, L. M. Barren had a lasting and serious back-order situation. Trent then raised prices to L. M. Barren to the level charged smaller suture manufacturers and showed an increasing tendency to make all developments available to any customer. At the same time, L. M. Barren's chief competitor developed another source for surgical needles which had some superior characteristics that Trent could not match.

Two years ago, L. M. Barren encouraged the Allen Company of Allentown, Pennsylvania, to produce surgical needles following Barren specifications, in order to provide price competition and more incentive for product development to Trent. A year later it became apparent that this strategy was successful since better needles at lower prices were being obtained from both Allen and Trent.

At the same time, it was clear that needle products were gaining a steadily larger share of the market. Yet, profit margins on these products were still below par, and this was steadily shrinking the company profit despite the increasing over-all volume. An attempt to increase the prices of needled sutures was thwarted by the major competitor, who was anxious to gain volume in this growing segment of the market.

As a result, L. M. Barren management induced another textile needle producer, the Hack Company of Hackensack, New Jersey, to produce suture needles. Hack is long on automation and competitive pricing but somewhat short on quality. The immediate effect of Hack as a third supplier was to again reduce prices from Trent and also Allen as anticipated. However, several new problems shortly developed to plague Barren management:

1 The major competitor developed several improvements in needle quality which neither Trent, Allen, nor Hack could match without extensive expenditure of time and money.

2 The variation in production processes used by the three needle suppliers increased Barren's costs in set-up time, inspection, and scrap.

3 Trent, the only full-line producer of all sixty models of Barren's Eyeless needles, indicated that it was going to increase its prices 20 percent on all of the short-run, low-volume items, which it solely produced, and further served notice that it would cease producing surgical needles if it were not assured regular volume of 600,000 needles monthly.[1]

The case describes in rich detail the constraints, contingencies, opportunities, and problems the environment presented to L. M. Barren Company. A *constraint* is something the organization has to live with, such as depressed prices or legal minimum-wage requirements. A *contingency* is a probable (but not certain) future event that could seriously affect the working of an organization, such as a strike, price war, or change in government import policy. An *opportunity* is a *potentially* gainful situation that must, however, be recognized and exploited, such as export possibilities that became available to American corporations once the embargo against trade with China was relaxed. A *problem* is a current event that unfavorably affects the organization's performance, such as a breakdown of equipment. In Barren's case, many constraints, contingencies, problems, and opportunities are identifiable:

1 The initial constraint of monopsony, or a single supplier.

2 The constraint of price competition, "which kept prices for these products frozen at their introductory levels."

3 The disruption of supplies due to a prolonged strike at Trent. Thus, a future strike at the supplier's facilities is a serious contingency.

4 The major supplier withdrew the preferential pricing for L. M. Barren and raised prices. Future changes in the special prices offered to Barren is therefore an important contingency.

5 The major competitor neutralized L. M. Barren's attempts to raise prices. This, too, could happen again.

6 The major competitor came out with a better product. In the future, product improvement by the competitor is a contingency.

7 The production costs of L. M. Barren increased because of the "variation in production processes used by the three needle suppliers." This is a current problem.

8 The opportunity of making the Allen Company, and later on the Hack Company, the alternate suppliers of needles. This led to successive decreases in needle prices.

Thus, the environment is a source of many pressures. Environmental pressures on organizations vary considerably. Some organizations are subject to a great many pressures; others either are not subject to many pressures or are able to insulate themselves quite effectively from environmental pressures. The environment, too, is not immune from the pressures that the organization exerts on it. Marketing activities, such as an advertising campaign, political lobbying, attempts to form a trade association, vertical integration, diversification of activities, and so on are organizational attempts to influence the environment or to insulate the organization from some of the unfavorable aspects of the environment. The organization and its environment do have a symbiotic relationship. But they also form a mutual pressure system—both exchange gifts, and both often also exchange blows! Figure 9–1 shows the various types of organization-environment relationship.

In Figure 9–1, the dominated organizations are those that are more or less at the mercy of their environments in respect of the terms on which they get their inputs and the terms on which they are able to export their outputs to their environments. Most organizations find themselves in this condition. A few organizations have a relative parity with their environments. Very few indeed are able to dominate their environments—that is to say, secure inputs from their environments and export outputs to them

FIGURE 9–1

The Relative Power of the Environment and the Organization

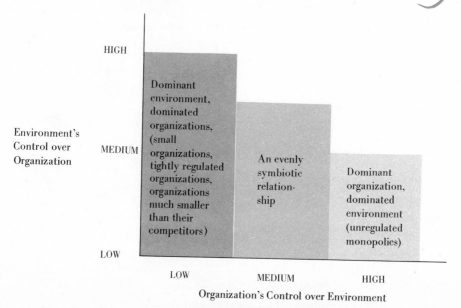

on the organization's terms. Unregulated monopolies and totalitarian governments are perhaps the only organizations that come close to having such overwhelming power over their environment.

Environmental Information and Organizational Adaptation

We noted earlier that the environment is a source of constraints, contingencies, problems, and opportunities that affect the terms on which the organization transacts business with its environment. The organization, however, is unlikely to adapt effectively to these without reliable information. If reliable information about business expansion and contraction, technological change, changes in legislation, and the like is not available to the organization, it cannot plan effective responses to them. The establishment of forecasting units, market research activity, participation in trade associations, and staff meetings to discuss the environment are the usual organizational responses to the need to have better quality information about the environment. Naturally, organizations facing several crucial contingencies about which reliable information is needed are likely to make these organizational responses to a greater degree than those that face only a few. Figure 9–2 shows the key role of environmental information in the way the environment affects the organization. At any given time, the information coming from the environment is filtered and processed through the mechanisms developed by the organization for this purpose. These may range from tuning in to the business grapevine to deploying highly trained forecasters and market researchers. The filtered information reaches key decision makers. If it is of acceptable quality and reliability, decisions will be taken that affect the organization's strategy and structure. If it is not, the information-gathering and -processing mechanisms may get modified. If the organization's goals or strategy are modified, it may result in changes in the information-gathering and -processing mechanisms utilized by the organization. As an example, the management of a private hospital was perplexed about some of the implications of proposed legislation affecting the delivery of medical care to the community by private hospitals. The hospital grapevine indicated conflicting implications. The management called in a consultant. The consultant was able to clarify the implications. On the basis of this new understanding of the proposed legislation, the hospital decided to fight the legislation. It decided upon a strategy of forming an association of private hospitals. As a consequence it set up a task force to gather information about where other hospitals stood on the issue and to canvass support for an association of all the private hospitals in the area.

FIGURE 9–2
Information As a Linkage Between the Environment and the Organization

External environment	Information-gathering and -processing mechanisms of the organization	Quality and reliability of environmental information available to decision makers	Effect on organizational strategic and structural variables
Constraints (e.g., the law, social norms, the "facts" of economic life) Contingencies (e.g., likely changes in government policies, entry of new competitors, technological change, recession) Opportunities (e.g., the emergence of new markets, the invention of new techniques or products, the availability of new sources of supply) Problems (e.g., strikes, excess capacity, rise in price of supplies)	Business grapevine Forecasting Market research Sharing of information by managers Participation in trade associations Etc.	How certain is it that the economy will grow at x percent next year? Are the effects of the proposed new legislation clearly understood? Is the competitor's invention known and understood in detail? Etc.	On goals On management philosophy On strategy for survival and growth On departmental structure On controls, procedures, etc. On technology On workflow

Thus, how the environment affects the organization depends on two crucial factors: the kind and quality of environmental information reaching decision makers and the interpretation and use of the information by them. How the information is interpreted and used depends in turn on the goals and attitudes of the decision makers. In the example of the proposed government legislation, the response of one private hospital was to fight it; that of another was to accept it as being in the public interest despite the best efforts of the militant hospital to persuade it to the contrary. No doubt the goals and attitudes of decision makers are influenced by their organization's environment; but they are seldom determined wholly by the environment. Thus it is that in the same industry one often finds different organizational designs, although perhaps the range of variation is not as great as that between organizations in sharply differing industries. Kaiser Aluminum and Alcoa are both large aluminum-producing corporations. Yet, often in the past, when Kaiser has been aggressive and entrepreneurial, Alcoa has been relatively conservative in its responses to developments affecting the aluminum industry. Often, the U.S. Senate has seemed to respond dovishly, while the U.S. House of Representatives responded hawkishly to presumably the same information concerning international political developments.

The Anatomy of the Environment

In Chapter 6, we encountered several ways of analyzing the task environment. Thompson proposed that the environment could be viewed as stable or shifting and homogeneous or heterogeneous.[2] Lawrence and Lorsch proposed that it could be viewed as highly differentiated or relatively uniform, in terms of the uncertainty surrounding the major parts of the organization.[3] Perrow suggested that it could be viewed as easily analyzable or not easily analyzable, and also as one requiring many exceptions to standard procedures or few such exceptions to be made in responding to environmental stimuli.[4]

But there are many other ways of viewing the environment. The author proposed in his doctoral dissertation that the environment be measured in terms of how uncertain or complex it is, how hostile or stressful it is, and how heterogeneous it is.[5] Several management writers have analyzed the environment of a corporation in terms of the pressure groups seeking to influence the policies of the corporation. Farmer and Hogue identify these as the public, stockholders, creditors, managers, employees, suppliers, the trade, consumers, and governments.[6] Farmer and Richman, two scholars in the comparative management field, prefer to break the environment down into four components: economic, legal-political, sociological, and educational.[7] Cyert and MacCrimmon prefer to distinguish between the macro aspects of the environment (particularly the economic environment, such as periods of boom and recession for the economy as a whole), an intermediate level of the environment (the organization's industry), and a micro aspect (the organization's immediate suppliers, competitors, and customers).[8]

Thus, the organization's environment has been analyzed in a bewildering variety of ways. Broadly speaking, however, it has been analyzed in terms of (a) its perceived *properties* and (b) its *components*. As a field of forces it may be turbulent or stable, hostile or benevolent, heterogeneous or homogeneous, complex or simple, constraining or constraint free, dominating or controllable, and so on. In terms of its components, one may distinguish among the organization's economic, cultural, and legal-political environments. Both of these are valid perspectives and may indeed be fruitfully combined in assessing the pressures the environment exerts on the organization. Beyond that, it is important to be aware, not only of the pressures the environment exerts on the organization, but of how these pressures are *interpreted* by key decision makers in the organization. If industry demand falls off, most business firms will cut back their production. But the pessimistic may expect a deep depression and shelve all capital expenditure plans, while the optimistic may aggressively seek to invest in other areas and diversify their operations.

To keep the discussion of environment within decent limits, our preference is to focus attention on five properties of the environment—namely, turbulence or dynamism, hostility, heterogeneity, restrictiveness, and technical complexity—and to identify the components of the environment that cause the environment to be perceived as dynamic, hostile, and so forth.

ATTRIBUTES OF THE EXTERNAL ENVIRONMENT

Five attributes of the external environment are likely to have substantial impacts on organizational strategic and structural variables. These are: turbulence of the environment, hostility of the environment, diversity of the environment, technical complexity of the environment, and restrictiveness of the environment.

Turbulence

A dynamic, unpredictable, expanding, fluctuating environment is a turbulent environment. It is an environment marked by changes. It is an environment in which the information received by the organization is often contradictory. The best estimates that management can make of the future are really only "guesstimates" and get obsolete fairly quickly since the environment often takes unpredictable turns. It is an environment in which the ability to take calculated risks in the face of uncertainty is vital. It is an environment that attracts entrepreneurs.

The opposite of a turbulent environment is a stable environment. What little change occurs is highly predictable. The information about the environment is easy to get and generally fairly reliable. It is an environment in which the ability to take calculated risks in the face of uncertainty is seldom exercised. It is an environment that attracts risk averters and conservatives.

Very many phenomena can cause the environment to be perceived as turbulent. Technological change is one of them. If the industry is bombarded with new products and/or new operating processes, as electronics and aerospace have been for a while, the environment would be perceived as turbulent.[9] A highly competitive environment in which organizations compete not only on the basis of price but on the basis of advertising and promotion, product quality, after-sales service and in which they compete also for raw materials, other inputs and technical manpower is likely to be viewed as turbulent because of the intense, many-sided, and continuous chains of competitive thrusts and parries. An environment in which there are large cyclical or other swings of economic activity and a rapidly growing industry, too, is likely to be viewed as turbulent.[10] Rapid sociocultural change, as in North America during the past decade, rapid change in the needs of the organization's clientele, or unpredictable shifts in government policies can also lead the decision makers to perceive the environment as turbulent. The more of these components that occur together, the stronger, of course, will be the inference about the degree of turbulence. It should be remembered that environmental turbulence is a variable that ranges all the way from complete stability to total instability and that many organizations operate in neither very stable nor very turbulent environments but rather in moderately dynamic environments.

The organization is shaped in important ways by environmental turbulence. A highly turbulent environment is rich in growth opportunities as well as in problems and contingencies. A highly turbulent environment is a challenging environment because of this blend of uncertainty and opportunity. It tends to attract entrepreneurs and risk takers, much as a highly stable environment attracts conservatives and seekers after the status quo.[11] Beyond this, the more turbulent the environment, the more importance management must attach to seeking information about crucial prospective changes in the environment through careful forecasting, market research, and the like. The management may also try to insulate the organization from the external turbulence to the extent it can through devices like vertical integration. A good deal of administrative flexibility is needed to cope with high turbulence. An organic management style is likely to evolve, marked by free and open channels of communication, informality, a loose administrative structure, and the like. At the same time, continual readjustment of operating plans is likely to lead to friction between interdependent departments. Rather opposite are likely to be the consequences of high stability in the environment.[12]

We propose that:

The more turbulent the external environment,

> *the more strategically important to management are uncertainty absorption and avoidance mechanisms like market research, forecasting, advertising, vertical integration;*
> *the more risk-taking and organic is the top management style; and*
> *the greater is interdepartmental conflict.*

Hostility

A hostile environment is one that is risky, stressful, and dominating. The opposite of a hostile environment is a benign environment, which is safe, rich in profitable opportunities, and manipulable or controllable by the organization. A hostile environment is a frustrating environment. A benign environment is an encouraging environment. The environment faced by the Nixon administration immediately upon his reelection was relatively benign; a year later it was very hostile.

A number of happenings in the environment can lead to the inference that the environment is hostile. Industries in which there is severe price competition tend to be perceived as hostile because even a small cut in prices can amount to large losses for the organizations in the industry. Once a firm starts cutting prices, others must follow suit, and there is little an individual organization can do about it.[13] An analog to low prices for nonbusiness organizations is stringent budgets. When state-supported hospitals or universities cannot get more money out of the government despite an urgent need for more funds, then a reasonable inference of hostility can be drawn. On the other hand, when they can get as much money as they want, then the opposite inference is warranted. Arbitrary and harsh laws, or government actions such as threats of nationalization and punitive taxes can also lead to an inference of hostility. On the other hand, minimal legal harassment, various tax breaks, and a comfortable working relationship with the government are likely to lead to the perception of the environment as benign. Organizations whose activities have high community acceptance and support, such as the Catholic Church had for many centuries, are likely to consider their environment as benign. Those that find that the community has turned against them—that is, those whose legitimacy is being questioned —are likely to consider their environment as hostile.

If the organization experiences hostility on a number of important fronts, it will tend to regard the environment as quite hostile. If it does not experience hostility on crucial fronts, it will tend to regard the environment as not hostile. If it experiences hostility on some fronts but acceptance or ease of maneuver on others, it is likely to regard its environment as moderately hostile. For example, if price competition is severe but very many tax breaks are available, the environment is likely to be perceived as moderately hostile. If price competition is severe and government actions are unhelpful, it is likely to be perceived as quite hostile. If there is little price competition and the government is very helpful, the environment is likely to be perceived as quite benign. Obviously, there is no simple formula for identifying the degree of hostility; judgment has to be exercised in weighing the various factors.

A number of studies have suggested that the organizational response to a crisis arising from events in the environment leads to a centralization of power. For example, Janowitz reported that as a military situation took on aspects of a crisis, officers tended to claim that new problems were outside their jurisdiction and therefore required directives from higher authorities.[14] Pruitt found that the increase in danger to U.S. objectives correlated with both an increase in the coordination required for tackling the threat and also with a rise in the level of approval of orders.[15]

The Canadian study by the author supported these findings only partially. The data suggested that as the level of environmental hostility rises from a low level to a moderate level, there is a sharp rise in authoritarianism in management—orders tend to get issued without those affected being consulted, management uses threats to secure compliance, managers seek to resolve their disagreements on the basis of might rather than right, and so on. However, this authoritarianism wanes somewhat as the degree of hostility increases from a moderate to a high level. This may be because by then nonconformists are weeded out or softened up. Also, the perception of the difficult situation the organization is in percolates down to the rank and file, and since organizational survival is at stake, less force is needed to elicit their cooperation.

The Canadian study also suggested that as environmental hostility increases from a relatively low level to a modest level, there is a pruning of expensive staff activities like market research, research and development, long-range planning. However, as the degree of hostility continues to increase, there is a sharp increase in these activities. In other words, the initial management reaction may be one of getting rid of the dead wood and the organizational slack. If the environment continues to deteriorate once staff services are streamlined, the organization may well increase its investment in them in order better to understand environmental forces.

The data suggested that as environmental hostility increases (a) the organization moves away from customized, high unit cost operations and toward more standardized products and production operations, presumably to cut costs and (b) there is a perceptible drop in the use of human relations for securing employee cooperation for organizational decisions and changes, perhaps because tender-hearted supervisors are not seen as capable of pushing through needed draconian measures.

We propose that:

As the hostility of the external environment increases,

> *there is initially an increase in the coercive authoritarian orientation of top management and then a decrease in it, and*
>
> *there is an initial decrease in the investment in staff-based sophisticated information-generating and -processing activities and then an increase in them.*

As environmental hostility increases,

> *the outputs and operations of the organization become more standardized, and*
>
> *the practice of "human relations" for securing the cooperation of personnel decreases.*

Diversity

An environment is diverse or heterogeneous if the organization's clientele or markets have variegated characteristics and needs. For example, the customers of car dealers or dry cleaners have fairly similar needs. On the other hand, those of department stores exhibit a great variety of needs. Typically, but not exclusively, diversified organizations tend to have highly variegated environments. Large organizations also tend to have a diverse environment because they tend to have a wide variety of outputs.[16]

Organizations functioning in a variegated environment of necessity get differentiated. That is, they must develop separate homogeneous structures to deal with each major, distinctive element of their environment.[17] A firm with operations in North America and also in Asia will find the conditions so different in these two continents that it will be forced to set up (at least) one organizational structure, possibly a division, to look after its American business interests and another to look after its Asian business interests. The needed managerial talent is different, tactics and product market strategies are likely to be different, and the customs and mores of the people working for the firm in the two continents are likely to be different. Similarly, universities set up separate organizational structures to offer their various degree programs, and hospitals set up different structures to offer various distinctive medical facilities.

But this internal differentiation creates problems of coordination, waste, and duplication. To achieve operating efficiency, the central administration is likely to (a) utilize a sophisticated control and information system to keep track of the environment, operations, and performance of the subunits and (b) institute throughout the organization those standard operating procedures that seem to work well in a variety of situations. In addition, for securing cooperation of the subunits, it is likely to institute a participative style of management.[18] Thus:

The more heterogeneous the external environment,
> *the greater is the internal differentiation in the structure of the organization, and*
> *the more the organization seeks integration through a sophisticated control and information system, standard operating procedures, and a participatory style of management at top levels of the organization.*

There is another sense in which the environment is diverse. If the environment of the different *subsystems* in the organization—such as the production, the marketing, and the design subsystems—are very diverse, then, too, the environment may be said to be diverse. Let us call this a *differentiated* environment, in distinction from a heterogeneous environment, for the latter refers to the variety in the organization's markets for its products or services. As Lawrence and Lorsch have argued, an organization with a differentiated task environment is likely to be differentiated in terms of a number of attributes, such as norms about interpersonal behavior, departmental goals, structuring of activities, and time span of feedback from the environment.[19] Such an organization needs, for effective functioning, to be integrated by complex means like special liaison personnel that share the values of interfacing departments.

We propose that:

The more differentiated the task environment of the various subsystems of the organization—that is, the greater the differences in the task environments of the major parts of the organization
> *the more internally differentiated is the organization, and*
> *the more it must resort to complex modes for keeping its operations coordinated or integrated.*

Technical Complexity

An environment is technically complex when the information needed for making strategic decisions is technically highly sophisticated. The technology employed in the industry is such that unless decision makers have a sound grasp of its pitfalls and potential, they are liable to make serious errors. Techniques that are rapidly developing, as in aerospace, pharmaceuticals, electronics, and nuclear power, or technologies that are extremely capital intensive and automated, as in the case of chemicals and oil-refining, call for a high order of technical expertise in management for making investment and pricing decisions.[20]

The data from the Canadian study indicated that firms that view their environment as highly complex tend to have managements that are strongly oriented to long-term planning and optimal utilization of resources through the use of management science techniques because they must be managed by technocrats. These firms tend to have sophisticated management control and information systems, and their operations tend to be highly automated and computerized. On the other hand, firms in relatively noncomplex environments tend to have seat-of-the-pants judgments oriented managements, relatively much less sophisticated information and control systems, and much less automated and computerized operations technology.[21]

We propose that:

The more technologically complex the external environment,

> *the more its top management adopts an optimization- and planning-oriented style;*
>
> *the more sophisticated and complex is the organization's control and information system; and*
>
> *the more automated and computerized are its operations.*

Restrictiveness

A restrictive environment is one in which the organization must operate under many constraints. These constraints may be legal, such as the legal restraints governing prices charged by utilities.[22] They may be political in nature. For example, in developing countries representatives of the government often sit on the boards of directors to monitor the behavior of firms in which the government has invested substantial funds. Socialized undertakings, such as the Canadian Broadcasting Corporation, operate under a glare of parliamentary scrutiny and must watch very carefully the political consequences of their actions. They must take care not to offend political sensibilities of the ruling party or the opposition. Organizations may also be subjected to economic constraints, such as the tradition of price leadership in an industry, or the scarcity of certain crucial inputs, or restraints on the undertaking of certain activities. There can also be many cultural constraints, such as a taboo on discrimination based on race or sex, a taboo on certain personnel practices. For example, in Japan employment with a corporation tends to be a life-long affair. The firing of personnel in a business downturn, quite common in North America, is taboo there.

A restrictive environment is a complex environment, because decision-making, especially the formulation of strategy, must carefully take into account the many constraints such an environment imposes on the organization. This is especially so where the organization has high performance aspirations but has difficulty achieving them because of these constraints. The Bell Telephone Company of Canada, a regulated monopoly, has the problem of planning the expansion of its plant so precisely that several years from now, when the plant becomes operational, the return at the price then allowed is no less than the one permitted, but also no more.

A restrictive environment begets a need for a good deal of careful planning and controlling of operations and a fact- and research-based scientific approach to decision-making. This is especially true where the restrictions are largely legal in nature and imposed on the organization because of its monopoly nature or because it serves vital public interests. In the author's Canadian study, it was found that the degree of restrictiveness of environment was significantly correlated with a planning- and optimization-oriented top management style. It was also significantly correlated with the degree of sophistication of the organization's control and information system, but this was no longer so when optimization orientation was controlled for. In other words, the relationship was restrictiveness of environment ⟶ optimization orientation ⟶ sophistication of control and information system.

Firms that perceived their environment as highly restrictive because of the many legal, political, and economic constraints they had to contend with, as well as firms that perceived their environment as relatively free from constraints, tended to have less coercive top managements than firms that viewed their environment as moderately constraining. Apparently, when there are few constraints, there may be little need for management to be coercive. As constraints increase the traditional patterns of decision-making may need to be changed drastically by top management fiat in order to take into account the new constraints. However, the organization is simultaneously getting technically trained staff and installing a sound control system to deal more effectively with the constraints. If constraints should continue to increase, decision-making then relies increasingly on technocratic advice rather than on power plays by managers. In other words, organizations in highly constraining environments must rely on systems rather than on personal power to ensure that constraints are not violated and operations are efficient.

We propose that:

The more restrictive the external environment,
> *the more planning- and optimization-oriented is the style of top management.*

As the external environment becomes more restrictive,
> *there is at first an increase and then a decrease in the coercive orientation of top management.*

Environment As a Configuration of Forces

We have taken each attribute of the environment and sketched some major organizational consequences of variation in it. Needless to say, in designing an organization, all the attributes must be considered simultaneously. The environment is not merely relatively turbulent or stable, but also relatively restrictive or unconstraining, hostile or benign, technologically complex or simple, heterogeneous or homogeneous. The environment of an organization is a particular *configuration* of the specific degrees of each of these characteristics. For example, one fairly common environmental configuration in the Canadian study was high turbulence and hostility with low to moderate heterogeneity, restrictiveness, and technical complexity. Another was low turbulence and hostility with fair to high levels of heterogeneity, restrictiveness, and technical complexity.

The point to note is that quite commonly the different aspects of the environment may point to contradictory design implications. As an example, an organization may be operating in a technically highly complex environment that is, however, low in restrictiveness. The environment of an electronics firm is an example. Technical complexity implies a planning- and optimization-oriented management style, while low restrictiveness implies a seat-of-the-pants style. What kind of top management style should the organization have? A quick answer is that it should have the selectivity to roll with the punches: employ sophisticated management techniques in dealing with the environment's technological complexity, but take advantage of its lack of constraints by also inculcating intuitive judgment, and identify good rules of thumb and the like implied in good seat-of-the-pants management. If the environment were to be technologically complex and restrictive, a much greater reliance on sophisticated controls and information systems, technically sophisticated research on and analysis of strategic problems, and reliance on highly trained managerial personnel would be called for. If the environment were to be technically simple and unrestrictive, a much greater emphasis on seat-of-the-pants methods of making decisions would be required. Guidelines such as these cannot be reduced to neat mathematical formulas, for the phenomena under discussion are inherently qualitative and not at all easy to measure. But such guidelines can at least prevent gross errors, such as the imposition of a uniform managerial practice on all the divisions of a diversified corporation or on all the departments of a government or on all the faculties of a university.

Managerial Interpretation of Environment

Organizations are not machines. They adapt to their external environment primarily through the efforts of a *human* agency—their managements. This human agency may misperceive the environment, distort reality, react emotionally to it. One management may interpret the same environment quite differently from another management. It is important, therefore, to take into account the way the management of an organization *perceives* the external environment and the organizational consequences of this perception.

The study of Canadian firms afforded a striking example of different interpretations managements often make of the same or similar environments. For the sample as a whole, as we should expect, the senior management of the firms tended to view competitive pressure as dynamic. The firms in the top half of profit performance, however, viewed any *increase* in competitive pressure as leading to a less constraining, a more diverse, a more variable, and a more expansionary environment. The firms in the bottom half of profit performance, on the other hand, saw an increase in competitive pressure as implying a more constraining environment. As a consequence, perhaps, the aspirations of the high profit group with respect to corporate goals tended to rise much more strongly with any increase in competitive pressure than those of the low profit group. Clearly, the human agency designing high profit firms was responding much more optimistically to competitive pressures than the one in low profit firms. It was perceiving opportunities that the other was not. It also was perceiving quite accurately the diversity and variability of competitive pressures—the measure of competitive pressure encompassed price, product, and marketing competitive pressures as well as competition for inputs and specialized technical manpower. It is worth bearing in mind that the data did not show that the environment of high profit firms was perceived to be more diverse, more expansionary, more variable, and less constraining than that of the low profit firms. The data showed that as *competitive pressure increased,* there was a tendency for high profit firms to perceive their environment as more diverse, more expansionary, and so on.

The Assessment of Environment

The external environment is a powerful shaper of the organization. But unlike the organizational demographics that were reviewed in the preceding chapter, it is a rather difficult influence to assess. Some questions that can help such an assessment are:

1 What is the nature of the society or the community the organization is operating in? Is it an economically developed or underdeveloped society? Is it governed by a democratic government or a totalitarian government? Is it a planned economy or a free enterprise economy or a mixed economy?

2 What is the nature of the industry the organization is operating in? Is it competitive or not? Is there much innovation taking place in it? Is it an expanding industry? Are there severe business fluctuations in it? Is the technology employed in it highly sophisticated? Is it subject to many legal constraints? Is the industry marked by great diversity in the demands or needs of the customers?

3 What is the nature of the organization's particular situation? Is it a powerless organization within its industry or a dominant member of it? Is it an embedded organization that is closely regulated by the parent organization, or is it quite autonomous? If it is an embedded organization, how severely is it competing (for funds, etc.) with other organizations embedded in the parent organization? Is it subject to some special pressures and disabilities, such as those arising from a disadvantageous location, or from inexperience due to its relative youth, or from difficult access to the market because of its being relatively unknown? Or is it the beneficiary of some special advantages such as those that come from a particularly favorable location, a great deal of experience with its markets, a good reputation? Does the organization produce a great diversity of outputs or relatively homogeneous outputs?

These questions can lead to a realistic assessment of *how* turbulent, hostile, diverse, technologically complex, and restrictive the organization's environment is.

Here is an example of the assessment of the external situation of J. B.

Company, a successful independent, medium-sized firm in the business of retailing expensive furniture and home furnishings.[23]

1 The firm operates in a large North American metropolis.

2 Since it has a relatively high-income clientele, it is not much subject to business fluctuations that affect the rest of the furniture industry. Its target market is the top 4 percent of the city population in terms of income levels. However, the firm has begun to penetrate the well-to-do blue-collar market, and this segment of the market is, relatively, highly income elastic—in other words, susceptible to fluctuations in general economic conditions.

3 There is some uncertainty about deliveries from the firm's European suppliers.

4 The home furnishings industry has been a growing industry during recent years. It is not a very research and development oriented industry, but it does experience a fairly high rate of innovation of new products.

5 There is not much competitive pressure on the firm. It is an old and well-respected firm. It bought off a major competitor a few years ago. It is located in a well-to-do part of the city, but one that is not as expensive as the location of its competitors downtown in terms of rent and parking facilities. As its president said, the present location is "50 percent closer to 90 percent of our market."

6 The firm imports most of its products from outside the country, so import duties and transportation sharply raise its costs. The skilled craftsmen and special wood materials are simply not available locally.

Based on the above, the external environment may be assessed as follows:

Turbulence: Low to moderate. Low business fluctuations, little competitive pressure make for low turbulence. Growth in industry and some innovation of new products raise turbulence somewhat.

Hostility: Low. The firm is in a monopolistic niche of the market due to its market segment, favorable location, and reputation.

Diversity: Low to moderate. Predominantly a single market segment. Also, the large volume of semi-custom manufacture implies a very close and continuing interdependence between marketing and manufacturing and therefore a low degree of environmental differentiation.

FIGURE 9-3

The Environmental Profile of an Organization and Its Design Implications

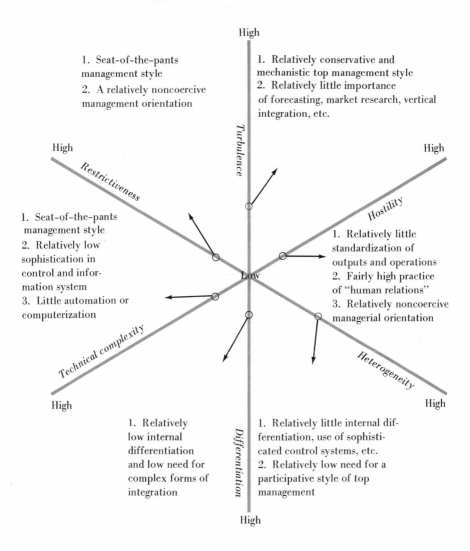

embody a labor intensive technology. Little research and development.

Restrictiveness: Low. No serious legal, political, economic, or cultural restraints.

From this analysis it may readily be inferred (see Figure 9–3) that the style of top management is likely to be only slightly risk taking, quite seat-of-the-pants, not much oriented to participative management, and non-coercive, but with a good deal of emphasis on human relations. The actual style was in agreement with these predictions except that the degree of an optimizing, planning orientation was a little higher than predicted because the owner-manager was an M.B.A. from a prestigious business school whose academic program strongly supports managerial professionalism.

SUMMARY, PROPOSITIONS, AND IMPLICATIONS FOR ORGANIZATIONAL DESIGN

Summary

The organization and its external environment constitute a symbiotic as well as a mutual pressure system. The environment is the source of most of the inputs needed by the organization to keep it going; but it also relies on the organization to supply it with some of the inputs it needs to keep operating. The environment is the source of many pressures through the constraints, contingencies, opportunities, and problems it poses for the organization. The organization, too, tries to impose its will on the environment through such devices as building monopoloid coalitions with other organizations, marketing activities, public relations, diversification, and vertical integration. In responding to the environment as well as in trying to influence it, the organization acquires a distinctive strategy and structure.

The external environment has been analyzed in terms of its legal, political, economic, and cultural components and further analyzed by macrosocial, industry, and micro levels. It has also been analyzed in terms of its attributes. In the chapter, five attributes of the organization's environment—namely, turbulence, hostility, diversity, technological complexity, and restrictiveness—have been discussed, along with the environmental factors or components that should be taken into account in making inferences about the organization's environment in terms of these attributes. The realistic assessment of the environment in terms of fairly abstract attributes is difficult. A good deal of judgment needs to be exercised, especially when its different aspects point to contradictory design implications. An illustrative example of its assessment is provided.

Propositions

1. The more turbulent the external environment,
   > the more strategically important to management are uncertainty absorption and avoidance mechanisms like market research, forecasting, advertising, vertical integration;
   > the more risk-taking and organic is the top management style; and
   > the greater is interdepartmental conflict.

2. As the hostility of the external environment increases,

> there is initially an increase in the coercive authoritarian orientation of top management and then a decrease in it, and
>
> there is an initial decrease in the investment in staff-based, sophisticated information-generating and -processing activities and then an increase in them.

3. As environmental hostility increases,

> the outputs and operations of the organization become more standardized, and
>
> the practice of "human relations" for securing the cooperation of personnel decreases.

4. The more heterogeneous the external environment,

> the greater is the internal differentiation in the structure of the organization, and
>
> the more the organization seeks integration through employing a sophisticated control and information system, standard operating procedures, and a participatory style of management at top levels of the organization,

5. The more *differentiated* the task environment of the various subsystems of the organization—that is, the greater the differences in the task environments of the major parts of the organization—

> the more internally differentiated is the organization, and
>
> the more it must resort to complex modes for keeping its operations coordinated or integrated.

6. The more technologically complex the external environment,

> the more its top management adopts an optimization- and planning-oriented style;
>
> the more sophisticated and complex is the organization's control and information system; and
>
> the more automated and computerized are its operations.

7. The more restrictive the external environment,

> the more planning- and optimization-oriented is the style of top management.

8. As the external environment becomes more restrictive,

> there is at first an increase and then a decrease in the coercive orientation of top management.

Implications for Organizational Design

Identifying the properties of an organization's environment is a crucial step in the business of consciously designing it. The preceding propositions, then, can provide clues for a workable design (we have left for later chapters the question of designs that are not merely workable but also highly effective). For example, whether a firm in a given type of business is functioning in Russia, India, or the United States can make for a fair degree of difference in its design. In Russia the government is totalitarian, and the environment is highly restrictive. Planning at the organizational level is strongly emphasized and indeed necessary to synchronize the organization's activities with those of the Soviet government. The same firm in India would have to be designed somewhat differently. Industry technology is likely to be much less capital intensive and sophisticated because labor is cheap. In a mixed economy with socialistic leanings, the environment for a private firm is often fairly hostile and restrictive. A somewhat coercive, authoritarian management is in the cards. Also, managers with an elastic conscience may need to be hired to obtain various governmental licenses; fewer technocrats may be needed because the technology is not very advanced; production-oriented managers may be needed because in the scarcity-ridden Indian economy, marketing is not a key function; and so on. In the United States, with its relatively highly turbulent environment, the firm would have to be risk taking and marketing oriented. It would also have to hire employee-oriented, participative managers because firms in the United States tend to be larger and more diversified than elsewhere and also because, in this affluent society, higher order needs such as those for autonomy and self-actualization are active. Besides, high wage rates and a mass market imply that a highly capital intensive, sophisticated, automated technology may be the norm in its industry, so the top management style would be strongly optimization and planning oriented, and the top management would favor the installation of a sophisticated control and information system.

Finally, it is necessary to remember that many organizations are embedded in larger organizations. These embedded organizations have an interface with differing external environments. They are subject to two sets of environmental pressures, pressures from their own environments and pressures from those that affect the organizational system in which they are embedded. Their design should, therefore, reflect both types of pressure.

Although in this chapter we have reviewed the *external* environment's effect on the organization, one may quite reasonably extend the analysis to a part or subsystem of an organization that has the properties of an organization. For example, one can justifiably consider the production subsystem's external environment to include the rest of the firm, particularly the marketing, engineering, purchasing, and research subsystems. The way the production subsystem should be designed then depends in good measure

FIGURE 9–4
Task-Environment-Based Design for the Organizational System

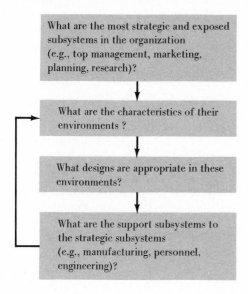

on the properties of this environment, and the propositions developed in this chapter may come in handy in designing the production subsystem.

Generally, therefore, the process of designing the whole organization is one of applying these propositions to the organization's subsystems, starting from the most strategic and exposed subsystem, such as the top management subsystem, and moving progressively to the consideration of the environments and designs of successively less strategic subsystems. Figure 9–4 shows the design strategy.

STOP

SUGGESTED READINGS

John Child, "Organizational Structure, Environment, and Performance: The Role of Strategic Choice," *Sociology* (Jan. 1972), pp. 2–22.

F. E. Emery and E. L. Trist, "The Causal Texture of Organizational Environments," *Human Relations,* No. 18 (1965).

Pradip N. Khandwalla, "Environment and Its Impact on the Organization," *International Studies of Management and Organization,* (Fall 1972), pp. 297–313.

QUESTIONS FOR ANALYSIS

1 Here is a story from *Time* magazine on Pan American Airways, the giant

American airline.[24] In what ways has Pan Am been affected by its environment? How is it seeking to influence its environment?

The long, stormy letdown of Pan American World Airways has been as visible as a thunderhead, and just as ominous. Pressed by soaring fuel costs and shrinking transatlantic passenger loads, Pan Am lost $18.4 million last year, despite a stringent cost-cutting program imposed by Chairman William T. Seawell: 8,000 of 40,000 employees have been fired. By July of this year, matters were even worse. Losses were running in the $30 million range, and Pan Am and TWA, a line with even greater first-half losses but lesser troubles overall, had appealed to the Civil Aeronautics Board for federal subsidies of around $265 million for 1974 alone. In August, a desperate Pan Am declared it needed an immediate $10.1 million-a-month subsidy just to keep going, and insisted that it be retroactive to April. The Department of Transportation, worried and bewildered by the plight of the nation's largest overseas carrier, began pressing earlier this month for merger between Pan Am and TWA, a marriage that neither line really wants.

Cut competition. Last week, with still not a cent of federal money in hand, Pan Am laid out its case in a detailed, hard-hitting and far-reaching brief to the CAB. The carrier reiterated its need for a "temporary" subsidy, but went much further. What really is needed, said Pan Am, is a more sweeping, permanent solution. The airline proposed a major rethinking of U.S. overseas air policy, with the aim of eliminating head-on competition between itself and TWA, nipping potential new overseas competition from U.S. carriers before it even gets started, and securing the firm backing of the Government in the private carriers' losing battle against other nations' heavily subsidized, state-run airlines.

Specifically, Pan Am called for routes to more European "gateway" cities in the U.S. (Atlanta, Cleveland, Houston, Dallas/Fort Worth, Tampa) to help counterbalance TWA's strong domestic network. It also sought permission to trade off certain overseas runs with TWA, leaving London as the only major city served by both carriers, and urged the CAB to reject pending applications by National and six other airlines for overseas services. Pan Am called too for even higher transatlantic fares, already up 25% between New York and London this year alone and scheduled to go up 10% more in November. "Drastic action," concluded Pan Am, "is desperately needed."

On paper, at least, the airline sounded like the arrogant, politically potent Pan Am of yesteryear. Pan Am haughtily refers to its desired subsidy as a "national interest payment." But does it have a case for subsidy by any name? Should taxpayers in, say, Tulsa, Des Moines and Wichita (who do not see Pan Am aircraft at local airports) be called upon to keep Pan Am flying? Or should Pan Am simply be allowed to die, its profitable routes parceled out among other carriers and its unprofitable ones dropped?

Some Congressmen think so. In the Department of Transportation, the feeling is that even if the CAB authorizes a subsidy, Congress will not fund it because it is tired of being asked to bail out private companies in the manner of Penn Central, Lockheed and Grumman. Wisconsin's influential Democratic Senator William Proxmire, a longtime foe of subsidies to business, is adamant against any aid to Pan Am beyond possible increases in fares. He bristles at the thought of turning Pan Am into "the nation's largest welfare recipient."

But Pan Am backs up its plea with a convincing array of arguments. It assuredly is not crying wolf: the threat to survival is real. The line owes some $300 million to banks led by New York's First National City. The thrust of the airline's argument is that its problems are not of its own making. Fuel costs alone have more than tripled since last October, from 11¢ to 35¢ per gal. on the average and even higher in some places; fully 94% of Pan Am's fuel is bought out of reach of any U.S. price controls. Pan Am's transatlantic passenger volume, badly hurt by withering purchasing power in the face of worldwide inflation, is down 23% this year.

Through it all, Pan Am has been forced to fly lightly loaded, fuel-guzzling 707s and 747s to distant places mandated by its CAB certificates, while at the same time competing with some 30 state-owned foreign carriers in a vastly overserved transatlantic market. In 1972, for example, those 30 airlines competed for 8.4 million passengers while only three carriers competed for the 1.9 million passengers in the New York-Los Angeles-San Francisco market. The line has been forced, too, into paying exorbitant landing fees ($4,200 in Sydney for a 747, v. $178 in Los Angeles) that currently total around $40 million, up 15% from last year.

Unique case. The Pan Am council of the Air Line Pilots Association, which is siding firmly with management and urging members to write Congressmen, sounds an ironic note: the U.S. Government actually pays Pan Am (and other U.S. lines) less than half what it pays foreign carriers to fly the mail, a loss to Pan Am of around $35 million annually. Pan Am pioneered many worldwide routes that later were taken from its exclusive domain as its political power waned during the Johnson and Nixon years. Nixon, for example, awarded the Miami-London run to National Airlines after Pan Am tested it at great expense during the 1950s and 1960s.

The clinching argument is that Pan Am, even in its present battered condition, brings in some $400 million a year to help right the U.S. balance of payments. Should the line go under, much—or most—of that money would go to subsidized foreign carriers. Subsidies to private companies are inherently unpalatable, but Pan Am is a truly unique case. It is a private airline with no important domestic operations, competing internationally against lines that are in effect arms of governments. As such, Pan Am deserves special treatment.

2 The following is the profile of the environment of a company in the computer services field. Its business hitherto has been to design computer-based "hardware" and "software" systems for engineering-oriented companies. What would be the likely organizational design for this company?

Demographics: Small size, young, public company, produces services
Society: Canada, early 1970's
Industry: Data processing
Environmental turbulence: High
Environmental hostility: High
Diversity of environment: High
Differentiation in the environments of major departments of the company: Moderate
Technological complexity of environment: High
Complexity due to social, political, economic constraints: Low

3 Here is the environmental profile of a sizable manufacturer of cotton textiles. What should be the design of its organization? What should be the design of its manufacturing subsystem?

Demographics: Medium-sized, middle-aged, public company, manufacturing
Society: India, early 1970's
Industry: Textiles
Industry growth rate: Low
R and D orientation of industry: Moderate
Industry size fluctuation: Low
Rate of innovation of new processes and products in industry, and competitive pressure from marketing, product, price competition and from competition for acquiring needed raw materials and technical personnel: Moderate
Governmental regulations for import, export, expansion of capacity, etc.: Stringent
Diversification of products: Moderate, all within the cotton textile segment of the industry

Footnotes to Chapter Nine

[1] William H. Newman, *Cases for Administrative Action*, pp. 13–15.
[2] J. D. Thompson, *Organizations in Action*, Ch. 6.
[3] P. Lawrence and J. Lorsch, *Organization and Its Environment*.
[4] Charles Perrow, *Organizational Analysis*.
[5] P. N. Khandwalla, "The Effect of the Environment on the Organizational Structure of Firms."
[6] R. N. Farmer and D. Hogue, *Corporate Social Responsibility*, Ch. 24.
[7] R. N. Farmer and Barry M. Richman, "A Model for Research in Comparative Management."
[8] R. M. Cyert and K. R. MacCrimmon, "Organizations."

[9] In the author's study of 103 Canadian firms, the correlation between environmental turbulence as rated by senior executives with rated innovation of new products and processes was .31. See Appendix A for operational definitions and a description of the Canadian study.

[10] In the author's study of Canadian firms, environmental turbulence was correlated .44 with rated competitive pressure on the firm from price, marketing, product competition, and competition for technical manpower and for inputs; it was correlated .44 with cyclical fluctuations in the firm's industry and .20 with the growth rate of the firm's industry.

[11] In the Canadian study, the correlation between environmental turbulence and a risk-taking management style was .50. Since environmental stability was defined to be the opposite of turbulence and conservatism the opposite of risk taking, the correlation between environmental stability and conservatism was also .50.

[12] In the author's Canadian study, the correlations between environmental turbulence and (a) marketing orientation; (b) the importance of vertical integration; and (c) interdepartmental conflict were .30, .26, and .25, respectively. The correlation between turbulence and organic style was not significant, but the research of Burns and Stalker reviewed in Ch. 6 indicates that organic values in management are likely to be associated with turbulence in the environment and mechanistic values with stability.

[13] In the author's Canadian study, the correlation between environmental hostility and (a) price competition, (b) firm's breakeven point, and (c) the firm's profitability were .25, .28, and −.29, respectively.

[14] M. Janowitz, *Sociology and the Military Establishment*.

[15] D. G. Pruitt, "Problem Solving in the Department of State."

[16] In the Canadian study, the correlation between environmental diversity and size of the firm was .31. The correlation between firm size and diversification by the firm of its products or services was .38.

[17] In the Canadian study, the correlation of environmental diversity with the extent to which the firm was divisionalized was .29, and with the diversity of technologies employed in the firm was .26.

[18] In the Canadian study, the correlations of environmental diversity with the extent to which the firm's information and control system was sophisticated, with the institution of standard operating procedures, and with a participatory style of top management were, respectively, .31, .31, and .30.

[19] See Lawrence and Lorsch, *op. cit.* See also Ch. 6 of the present book.

[20] In the Canadian study, the technological complexity of the environment was correlated .39, .18, and .45, respectively, with the degree to which the firm's industry was research and development oriented, with the labor productivity in the industry (a crude measure of automation), and with the degree to which the firm's operations were automated and computerized.

[21] In the Canadian study, technological complexity was correlated significantly with planning and optimization orientation in top management, sophistication of the control and information system employed by management, and the automation of operations technology. The relationships of environmental technological complexity with the use by the firm of a sophisticated control and information system and the use of an automated and computerized operations technology remained significant even after controlling for the optimization orientation of top management style with which both were significantly correlated.

[22] In the author's Canadian study, the correlation between the perceived restrictiveness of the environment and the rating of government regulations as blocking the firm's growth was .50.

[23] Based on a case study by C. Royce, F. Haigis, C. McCleary, and J. Chapman, students at McGill University.

[24] *Time* (Sept. 23, 1974), p. 63.

"It is not enough to take steps which may some day lead to a goal; each step must be itself a goal and a step likewise."
Goethe

The Goals of Organizations

stant

INTRODUCTION

In this chapter we examine the goals of the organization. Organizational goals are the objectives that the organization as a whole is trying to achieve, such as seeking a certain rate of return on investment or attempting to capture a majority of the seats in the legislature. We explore a number of questions related to organizational goals: (a) How are organizational goals formed? (b) What consequences do they have once they are established? (c) What factors affect how high the organization's goals are? (d) What consequences follow from high aspirations with respect to organizational goals?

In terms of the model outlined in Chapter 7, the relationships explored in this chapter are outlined in Figure 10–1.

THE FORMATION OF ORGANIZATIONAL GOALS

Do Organizations Have Goals?

Do organizations have goals? Some may argue that only individuals can have goals, but most people, if asked, would say that organizations do have

FIGURE 10–1
Relationships Explored in This Chapter

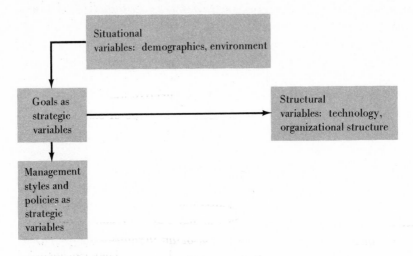

goals. They are liable to expostulate: "Don't the Republicans say that they want to capture the Congress? Doesn't G.M. say that it wants to sell cars and make money? Don't the Weightwatchers want people to reduce and Alcoholics Anonymous to stop them being drunks?" In other words, whether or not organizations can be said technically to have goals, they often behave as if they are pursuing some goal or goals.

Stated Goals

The goals of organizations do often get formally stated. For example, the constitution of an undergraduate management society states:

> The purpose of the M.U.S. is to represent undergraduates in the Faculty of Management at McGill University taking courses leading to the degree of Bachelor of Commerce. Furthermore, the M.U.S. is to act as the official body of, and to control matters concerning the above mentioned students, in the best interests of the undergraduate body as a whole and to the credit of McGill University.

Note the formality and broad scope of the language. No mention is made of precisely what the "best interests" are and how they are to be served, or how any conflict between the students' best interests and those of the university are to be reconciled. Also, there is an "apple pie and motherhood" flavor to the language. Indeed, this kind of formal language, broad scope, vagueness or lack of operational definitions of key goals, and the expression of noble sentiments is very widespread. Why should this be the case?

There are several good reasons. The nobly stated formal goals of organizations help to make the activities of organizations legitimate in the eyes of "society"—more particularly, in the eyes of the law, the government, the "establishment," those who are powerful watchdogs of ethical, "socially responsible" conduct and major purveyors of resources. It is doubtful whether a company that publicly stated that its objective was to defraud its customers would be allowed to operate. The wide scope of stated goals enables the organization to do extraordinary things in an emergency or to take advantage of opportunities. Many a corporate memorandum of association declares that the company is formed to undertake a long list of activities. Usually, however, the entrepreneurs have only one or two of these in mind at the time they start the company, but they list many other activities—just in case an opportunity comes along. Formally stated objectives have a symbolic function for the members of the organization, serving to differentiate their organization from other organizations. They can identify with the noble sentiments expressed through some of the goals. They can legitimate their personally preferred action proposals in terms of the organization's (vaguely) stated goals. Every weapons system developed in the many nooks and crannies of the Pentagon has been defended by its progenitors in the name of national security.

Operating Goals

But just because the goals of the organization are documented does not mean that everybody in the organization accepts all of them and tries to achieve them. The *operating* goals of the organization are the ones that attract the lion's share of the organization's resources and the attention of its key decision makers. They may or may not be the same as the documented goals. However, they are liable to be *consistent* with the documented goals if for no other reason than to maintain an aura of legitimacy. Certainly, the goals operating much lower down in the organization have very little direct connection with the stated goals—or, for that matter, with the operating goals of top management. The goal of the janitor is keeping the floor acceptably clean, not profit maximization, growth, good corporate citizenship, or maximizing the customer's welfare.

There is evidence that the operating goals of the organization sometimes deviate strikingly from the stated goals. For example, in a study of certain juvenile correctional institutions, the publicly stated goal was the rehabilitation of the delinquents. However, in practice, the emphasis was more on keeping the delinquents out of mischief than on professional treatment. It would therefore be reasonable to infer that the *operating* goal of these institutions was custodial rather than correctional.[1] In another study of workshops for the rehabilitation of the blind, it was found that once these workshops began to compete with other workshops hiring nonblind persons, the service motive fell by the wayside, and the criterion became one of hiring competent workers regardless of whether they were blind or not.[2]

In organizational analysis, the crucial question therefore is, not what the stated goals of the organization are, but, rather, what are its operating goals. Let us now see how operating goals get formed.

The Forces Shaping Operating Goals

Stated goals are fixed; operating goals are much more dynamic and change on account of a number of factors. The two major sets of factors are (a) external pressures and (b) internal pressures.

Thompson and McEwen have suggested that the goals of the organization are affected by the kinds of relations an organization has with other organizations (or individuals) in its environment.[3] With some organizations these relations may be *competitive*, as when two firms compete for patronage or two faculties compete for the same body of students. Three other types of relations are *bargaining* relationships, such as price bargaining between a firm and its suppliers; *cooptive* relationships, such as when a financially threatened firm coopts representatives of its bankers on to its board of directors to keep the support of the bankers; and *coalitional* relationships, such as two organizations agreeing to form a partnership to exploit a new market or to lobby the government for preferential treatment.

These various relationships shape operating goals by making the achievement of some goals more feasible than that of others. Often, firms experiencing fierce competition may effectively give up the goal of making profits and adopt one of mere survival. When an organization coopts outside forces into its decision-making structure, inevitably the goals of these forces influence the operating goals of the organization. One of the functions of the Tennessee Valley Authority was to assist small and poor farmers. The wealthier landed interests felt threatened and mounted powerful political opposition to the T.V.A. on the grounds of its being "socialistic." The T.V.A. had to coopt these interests onto its board to survive, and once they got onto the T.V.A.'s board of directors, they successfully got T.V.A. to ease off its programs for helping poor and small farmers.[4]

As far as internal pressures are concerned, these arise from the conflicting goals of different pressure groups within the organization. Owners of a firm want the firm to make more profit and allocate it to them. Workers want a larger share of the profits allocated to *them* instead in the forms of bonuses, higher wages, perquisites, and the like. Managers want higher salaries and larger staffs. Professionals, such as engineers and scientists, not only want more money, but want more influence in decision-making and want the firm to demonstrate a greater commitment to quality of products or services than merely to a pursuit of profits.[5] The Carnegie theorists (reviewed in Chapter 5) have developed an elaborate theory of how conflicts between these various factions influence the operating goals of the organization.

The Carnegie View of Goal Formation

Cyert and March have argued persuasively that goal conflict among different groups is the general organizational condition, especially in sizable monopolistic organizations, and that the organization's operating goals emerge from this conflict.[6] Their arguments may be summarized as follows:

Whatever are the stated goals of an organization, its operating goals are the goals of the coalition of members currently ruling it. These operating goals may be opposed by other coalitions in the organization. Coalitions are formed by members agreeing to swap "side payments" with one another. These side payments may be financial in character. For example, one basis of a coalition may be managers agreeing among themselves to hike their salaries by 10 percent in view of "inflation" and "past abstinence." They may be in the form of policy adjustments. For example, the marketing people may support a greater R and D effort by the organization in return for the R and D people's support for a greater marketing orientation. There may be other kinds of side payment, too, involving the exercise of discretionary authority, perquisites, privileges, and so on. The character of the budget of the organization and the allocation of responsibilities within the organization indicate what coalition is ruling the organization and what the current operating goals and priorities are.

But, Cyert and March argue, organizational goals in practice are relatively stable over time, while coalitions tend to be unstable. The reason organizational goals are relatively stable is the existence of precedents. The continuation of past practices and activities tends not to be questioned and generally does not enter into the bargaining process among members of a ruling coalition. People tend to take past practices for granted. On the other hand, the coalition itself can be upset by numerous events. It is held together by the expectation of the individuals constituting it that their aspirations will be satisfied through the coalition. But the environment may change. Experience with the working of the coalition can revise expectations. New opportunities or threats may visit individual members of the coalition. These events will lead to fresh bargaining and possibly to a different coalition of individuals with possibly altered goals. Thus, the actual goals that an organization is observed to be pursuing is some function of its past goals and practices acting as precedents and of the aspirations of the current ruling coalition.

Cyert and March point to the fact that organizational members, by and large, devote only a limited amount of attention to goals. Most of the time they are engrossed in their particular tasks. One consequence of this limited attention to goals is that an organization can pursue conflicting goals: it will pursue one goal at one time (or in one part of the organization) and another at some other time (or in some other part of the organization). For example, in the U.S. Government, during the same administration, swings of policies have been observed from those supporting a free market economy to those supporting a controlled economy, from those supporting racial integration to those supporting the opposite. One explanation is that the free market policy or the racial integration policy is pushed through by a coalition of organizational members while those in the opposite camp are not looking, so to speak, and the process is subsequently reversed when exponents of a controlled economy or racial segregation begin to get exercised over the drift of policy.

Limited attention to goals also implies that members of an organization do not ordinarily press their demands simultaneously. If students demanded better or "more relevant" teaching, professors demanded higher salaries and better research facilities, and the support staff demanded shorter working hours, all simultaneously, a faculty would quickly grind to a halt. But the chances are that students press their demands when the professors and the support staff are engrossed in their work, and the latter actively pursue their demands when the students are on vacation, and so the organization has a chance to attend to demands more or less one at a time.

Conflict over goals is dampened by organizational slack. Due to limited information and other factors, organizations often "pay" (in the broad sense of the term) more money, power, perquisites, and autonomy than they need to pay to keep members in the organization. In good times, of course, the slack is higher, and different factions within the organization can pursue their own goals without getting in one another's way. In bad times, slack is squeezed out by cost cutting and the like, but this permits the goals essential for the survival of the ruling coalition to be pursued.

In sum, Cyert and March argue that (a) there is widespread conflict over organizational goals among key factions of any organization, but (b) organizations generally function successfully despite this conflict thanks to processes such as coalition-building, respect for precedents, side payments, limited attention to goals, task specialization, sequential attention to goals, and organizational slack. The net result is that there is usually a good deal of stability in the general *direction* in which the organization is proceeding—that is, there is a good deal of stability in its operating goals—but these goals are constantly subjected to *marginal* adjustments.

Variation in the Consensus on Organizational Goals

Further research may well find that this is a generally valid view of organizations. However, we still have to account for the variation in goal consensus among organizational decision makers. After all, there are organizations where the disagreement on goals is extreme—the Democratic party at the time of George McGovern's nomination as the party's presidential candidate in 1972 was an example of this type of disagreement. There are also organizations with a great deal of goal consensus—the coalition British government during much of the Second World War was an example of this condition. What accounts for this variation?

First of all, to the extent that an organization carefully preselects members so that their values and goals for the organization coincide with those of the ruling coalition—as in the case of the Communist party and the Catholic Church—there will be less goal conflict than there will be where no screening is employed. Similarly, the more an organization tries to indoctrinate its members in the official philosophy, and the more ruthlessly it weeds out deviants, the less goal conflict and the more goal consensus there will be. The more functional specialization there is in an organization (this is the usual case as size of an organization increases), the more goal conflict the organization tends to have. The more threatening the environment, the more the organization's survival is at stake, the more its members will tend to submerge conflict over lesser goals, a phenomenon widely observed in governments as well as other types of organization when they are faced with a crisis.[7] The greater the perception of interdependence in solving mutual, job-related problems, the greater is the potential for conflict over goals, since each party in an interdependent situation will try to get the others to fit in with its goals and plans. But with greater interdependence comes more frequent interaction. This interaction may lead each to a better understanding of the others' goals, possibly to a greater appreciation of the validity of the others' goals; and if the interdependent parties work out a way of jointly solving their problems, the result may be less goal conflict. The more optimization and planning oriented the prevailing ideology in the organization, the more the emphasis will be on establishing priorities through rational discourse among decision makers. And, while this process may not eliminate conflict over purely personal goals, it is likely to minimize conflict over what the decision makers deem as appropriate organizational goals. Finally, ambiguity in the criteria by which organizational performance is to be evaluated is likely to increase goal conflict. Many professors in a university will agree that research is an important goal of the university; but since research cannot be evaluated as unambiguously as, say, profits, there tends to be a great deal of disagreement on what kind of research the academics should be doing. Many in democratic governments will agree that one important goal of government is to serve the citizen. But since this cannot be defined clearly, these governments tend to be rife with disputes about what are appropriate citizen welfare goals.

No very solid evidence exists to substantiate the preceding speculations, but it seems worth proposing that:

The more careful the selection, training, and indoctrination of organizational members;
the more the organization's survival is at stake;
the more frequent and collaborative the interactions between key organizational groups;
the stronger the ideology of optimization and planning, and the less ambiguous the criteria by which organizational performance can be evaluated;
the greater is consensus on the operating goals of the organization.

The larger the organization and
the more differentiated its activities,
the greater is conflict within the organization as to its operating goals.

VARIETY OF OPERATING GOALS

Hitherto, we have tried to distinguish between the stated goals of the organization and its operating goals. We have explained that operating goals emerge from the organization's interaction with its environment and from the play of conflicting forces within the organization. We have discussed the factors that make for a consensus on operating goals and those that stimulate conflicts about operating goals. Now we examine the *variety* of goals that organizations pursue.

Perrow has proposed that the goals of the organization can be classified into five types.[8] Serving social needs is one type of goal, for unless the organization can fulfill some social need or needs, it cannot survive. A second class of goals concerns what the outputs of the organization ought to be. A third class of goals concerns the preferences of the managers about what kind of an institution the organization should be and what kind of performance it should be striving to attain. These are system goals. A fourth class of goals are product-characteristic goals—that is, goals or preferences about the quality and other features of the organization's outputs. Finally, there are derived goals—that is, goals that the organization pursues because of its power or surplus resources or to protect and further its primary goals. Each of these different categories of goals reflects the interests and concerns of a pressure group—society at large, clients, managers, owners, and others—that influence the organization's operating goals.

Serving social needs. Parsons has advanced the view that organizations seek legitimacy in the eyes of society, for without such legitimacy they would not be able to survive.[9] Without such legitimacy, organizations would not generally be able to get the resources they need from society, nor would they be able to export their outputs to society. The bankrupt organization and the illegal bootlegging operation are examples of organizations with little social legitimacy.

The problem with this view is that "society" is an abstraction; it is not an entity with fairly clear objectives, and it does not in any centrally coordinated fashion go about getting its needs met. It is individuals, organized groups, and organizations in society that have needs, often very conflicting needs. Thus, legitimacy of the goals of organizations is a matter of legitimacy in the eyes of the institutions and individuals in a society. Goals that are legitimate for one section of a society may not be legitimate from the point of view of other segments of that society. From the point of view of a large segment of North American society, the goals of the Mafia are not legitimate. But the Mafia survives because its activities are acceptable to many gamblers, drug pushers, prostitutes, corrupt businessmen, policemen, politicians and the like. The goals of the Communist party are legitimate for the small minority of Americans that subscribe to its ideology; they are not legitimate for the American political right and not legitimate to many members of the American center either. Investigating what functions an organization serves in society may give some idea of what goals the organization should rationally be pursuing to maintain its legitimacy, but this enterprise may not be very fruitful since what society needs is subject to such varied interpretations that almost any activity can be rationalized as legitimate.

Output goals. Output goals are the organization's preferences for the kinds of output it should have, such as consumer goods or producer goods, specialized medical care facilities or general medical care facilities. Output goals stem from the basic questions: "What business is the organization in? What business should it be in?" These questions are the cornerstones of much literature in the area of business policy.[10]

The broad choices before any organization are to produce goods or services, with or without the profit motive. Goods may be consumer durable, consumer nondurable, producer, or capital goods, and services may be rendered by professionals with sophisticated training (as in universities, hospitals, public accounting firms) or by vocationally trained people (as in barber shops, clearing and forwarding agents). We have sketched the organizational consequences of these choices in Chapter 8 (see especially Tables 8–3 and 8–4).

A key output goal is not only what business to be in, but *how many* businesses to be in. That is to say, the organization must decide how much *diversification* of its outputs it wants, and what kind of diversification it should attempt. Diversification is fueled by a number of concerns: spreading of risks, opportunistic growth, fuller utilization of productive and distributive capacity, wider career opportunities for personnel, and so forth. Diversification helps to cancel out one product's failure with the success of the rest. Diversification also provides the organization with a wider set of opportunities for growth due to familiarity with a number of markets. It often permits fuller utilization of capacity. By diversifying into summer and continuing education programs, universities have been able to utilize their fixtures and their staff more fully. Organizations with established national or international channels of distribution often take up additional products that can be marketed through these channels at relatively little extra cost. A diversified organization offers its personnel, especially managers and white-collar staff, opportunities not only for vertical mobility but also for horizontal mobility. A marketing executive can move readily from a job involving the marketing of toys to the marketing of, say, home appliances, if he or she is a member of an organization that markets both.

Diversification is broadly of two types: concentric or related diversification and conglomerate unrelated diversification.[11] In concentric diversification, the more common type of diversification, the organization enters activities that are somehow related to its current outputs. For example, a textiles manufacturer may undertake the production of bleaching chemicals, or a shoe manufacturer may undertake the production of socks. One common form of concentric diversification is vertical integration. For example, the Curtis organization, when it published the *Saturday Evening Post,* owned not only publishing facilities, but also printing facilities, paper-making facilities, and even sources of wood.[12] In this form of concentric diversification, the attempt is to acquire facilities that produce and distribute not only the final products, but also several of the inputs that go into the final products. In the conglomerate form of diversification, the organization's goal is to enter totally unrelated activities, provided they are profitable. Litton Industries is one of the better known conglomerates, with interests ranging from real estate to electronics.

The Canadian study by the author afforded some idea of the conditions under which diversification becomes an important goal, and the conditions under which the organization prefers to pursue concentric and conglomerate diversification. Diversification assumed particular importance for management in a turbulent, especially a cyclically fluctuating, environment. This was also true of the importance of vertical integration (a form of concentric diversification) to top management. In addition, vertical integration assumed importance when there was considerable competition in the industry for securing raw materials, and the environment was generally quite hostile. There was also some tendency for larger firms to be more interested in vertical integration than smaller firms, presumably because larger organizations command the resources needed to engage in vertical integration and can utilize plant capacities large enough to realize economies of scale. Conglomerate diversification (diversification into unrelated lines) was pursued especially when the organization's main industry experienced severe cyclical fluctuations, and also in "high technology" environments, that is, environments with considerable technological sophistication.[13]

Cyclically fluctuating and "high technology" industries are generally oligopolistic, and oligopolies generally succeed in securing some control of the pricing and output decisions of member organizations.[14] It is likely that aside from spreading risks in a fluctuating industry, conglomerate diversification helps the organization escape from the straitjacket of price and output controls imposed by the oligopoly. Vertical integration, aside from helping the organization secure greater control over essential supplies and channels of distribution, offers the organization some cost advantage over the nonintegrated members of the oligopoly, and so may be important as a competitive tool that does not violate the (usually nonformal) price and output controls in the industry.

Diversification (especially of a conglomerate type) became an important top management goal also when the top management was entrepreneurial and risk taking. Conversely, when top management was conservative, diversification was not generally considered important. To some extent this is understandable because we noted in Chapter 9 that top management tends to be risk taking in a turbulent environment and conservative in a static environment, and we noted a few paragraphs back that diversification assumes importance when the organization is operating in a turbulent environment. The relationship between a risk-taking management orientation and importance of diversification held after controlling for the effects of environmental turbulence, so that a risk-taking orientation, regardless of the turbulence in the environment, makes the top management reach for diversification (of the conglomerate kind).[15] This, of course, makes sense, since considerable risks are involved in venturing into relatively unfamiliar businesses, risks that are unlikely to be taken without a strong risk-taking orientation in top management.

A well-known consequence of diversification is divisionalization.[16] In divisionalization, complementary staff and facilities are grouped under executives responsible for the overall results (say, profits) of the units under their charges. But the form of divisionalization may vary somewhat depending on the form of diversification. For example, product divisions are very likely if diversification is of the conglomerate type. In other words, under the latter type, division heads have responsibility for a product or service regardless of where it is marketed. If, however, diversification is of the concentric type, such that the outputs of the organization are somehow linked through common production or distribution facilities, then joint planning and coordination of production and/or marketing of these related products becomes important, and full-scale product divisionalization becomes difficult. Since centralized management of many products is not feasible or efficient, some kind of divisionalization is necessary. Large, concentrically diversified organizations often use territorial or area divisionalization. In this form, area managers have the responsibility for the profitable production and marketing of the organization's products in their respective regions. Area divisionalization is especially used if the products are, by and large, in the maturity phase of their life cycles. For example, in a study of multinational corporations, Stopford and Wells found that multinationals with mature product lines tended to resort to area divisionalization, whereas multinationals with products involving much research and development (and thus modification) tended to resort to product divisionalization.[17]

Besides divisionalization, diversification has other consequences. A wider *variety* of professionals and managers, not to mention operatives, enter the organization and share power with the management. The role of the chief executive changes from one that involves intimate knowledge of one business to one requiring superficial knowledge of many businesses. The executive's role becomes one of a strategist rather than that of a coordinator. Top management can no longer rely on personal supervision but must rely on a sophisticated control and information system to monitor the multifarious activities, especially if diversification is of the concentric or vertical integration type requiring close coordination of production and marketing activities. Extensive communication and consultation become critical concerns, and increasingly management becomes participative and committee-based. Much strategic planning must be done to enter new businesses in the future, ease out of unprofitable ventures, and so forth. In short, diversification wreaks a profound change in the structure and culture of the organization.[18]

We propose that:

The more turbulent the external environment, especially the more it fluctuates cyclically,

> *the greater is the importance of diversification and vertical integration to top management.*

The more subject the organization is to oligopolistic or other controls over the pricing and output of its principal products,

> *the greater is the importance of diversification and vertical integration to top management.*

The greater the uncertainty about crucial inputs and crucial channels of distribution,

> *the greater is the importance of vertical integration to top management.*

The larger the organization,

> *the greater is the feasibility and importance of vertical integration to top management.*

The more risk taking and entrepreneurial the style of top management,

> *the greater is the importance of diversification to top management.*

The more diversified the organization,

> *the more divisionalized is the organization's structure;*
> *the more differentiated is the organization's culture;*
> *the more sophisticated is the control, information and planning system of the organization;*
> *the more participatory is the style of top management.*

The more concentric the diversification, or the more vertically integrated the organization,

> *the greater is the delegation of authority by the chief executive;*
> *the more sophisticated is the control, information, and planning system of the organization.*

The output goals of organizations are not static. They are liable to enlargement and elaboration in response to the desire for growth and for spreading risks and in response to unexpected opportunities or contingencies. The National Foundation for Infantile Paralysis was set up to combat polio and to do research that would lead to control of the dread disease. After this goal was accomplished through the discovery of the Salk vaccine, instead of folding up the organization decided to continue its activities by enlarging its scope to include all childhood diseases.[19]

Changes in the output goals of organizations can have large implications. For example, the principal output goal of police departments is crime prevention and detection. But increasingly, police departments are called upon to perform additional services, such as providing emergency health facilities, breaking up family quarrels, and so on. As Perrow points out, because of this diversity in output goals, "the selection and training of a 'peace' officer becomes more difficult as are supervisory practices, promotion criteria, resource allotment, and the like."[20] If output goals should multiply, the organization often suffers from goal conflicts. Hospitals sometimes take on research activities, and these can create severe problems. For example, should doctors be allowed to try out expensive new drugs on patients as part of a research effort to determine how effective they are? But that may mean taking chances with the lives of patients. Should the hospital go in for expensive new equipment that can help research on esoteric, rare diseases at the expense of equipment that is needed to treat the common ailments? In addition to goal conflicts, organizational units set up to achieve different goals may drift apart in norms and values and have difficulty communicating with one another. The arts faculty of a university commonly has communications problems with the science faculty. In cases where one output goal is replaced by another, fairly dramatic changes in technology and organizational structure may need to be made to achieve the new goal.

System goals. System goals are the preferences of the organization's owners and managers about *the mode of operation* of the organization and about the nature of its *performance.* In the next chapter we will review several styles of management. For example, the risk-taking style has growth as its dominant objective and entrepreneurial, risk-taking decision-making as the *modus operandi.* One can think of an organization heavily using the risk-taking style as having these system goals. On the other side of the coin, an organization heavily using the conservative style may be said to have a strong preference for stability and cautious adjustment to changing situations. Other common system goals are democracy, participative decision-making, technocratic decision-making aimed at the selection of "optimal" alternatives, profit maximization, an ideologically pure organization, and so on. Here is Mao Tse-tung outlining a system goal for the Communist party of China:

In the sphere of theory, destroy the roots of ultra-democracy. First, it should be pointed out that the danger of ultra-democracy lies in the fact that it damages or even completely wrecks the Party organization and weakens or even completely undermines the Party's fighting capacity, rendering the Party incapable of fulfilling its fighting tasks and thereby causing the defeat of the revolution. Next, it should be pointed out that the source of ultra-democracy consists in the petty bourgeoisie's individualistic aversion to discipline. When this characteristic is brought into the Party, it develops into ultra-democratic ideas politically and organizationally. These ideas are utterly incompatible with the fighting tasks of the proletariat.[21]

As another example, here is the system goal of Indian Head Mills:

As expressed by the president, the goal is not to produce textiles, let alone to manufacture products of particular quality, variety, or novelty. Nor is growth the goal. According to the policy manual prepared by the president, "the objective of this company is to increase the intrinsic value of the common stock". . . . The manual then explains that the company is in the business *not* "to grow bigger for the sake of size, nor to become more diversified, nor to make the most or best of anything, nor to provide jobs, have the most modern plants, the happiest customers, lead in new product development, or to achieve any other status which has no relationship to the economic use of capital.

Any or all of these may be, from time to time, a means to our objective, but means and ends must never be confused. Indian Head Mills is in business solely to improve the inherent value of the common stockholders' equity in the company!"[22]

Notice that system goals are really the goals of *upper* level management for the organization. In large organizations it is not unusual for lower level participants in organizations to have very different system goals. However, it is the upper level management, because of the hierarchical nature of power and authority in organizations, that generally calls the tune, and so their system goals are generally likely to have much more pervasive an influence on the functioning of organizations than those of lower level organizational members.

What are the system goals of different types of organization? We do not have research findings for hospitals, parties, or many other types, but we do have some for firms. A layman is likely to consider profit maximization, or a variant such as the maximization of the value of its share capital, as *the* system goal of firms, certainly of upper management. Research evidence suggests a more complex picture. In a study by Dent, the chief executives or their deputies of 145 business establishments were asked, "What are the aims of top management in your company?" Only 36 percent began by mentioning making money, profits, or a living as a goal of their management. About 21 percent started off with provision of a good product and public service as an aim, and 12 percent with growth as an aim. But these percentages just refer to the goal that was spontaneously mentioned first. More revealing perhaps are the percentages of managers who mentioned a goal among the first three they enunciated. Making profits was among the first three aims mentioned by only 52 percent of the managers. The provision of a good product and public service, and providing for the welfare of the employees were fairly close seconds at 39 percent each.[23]

In the author's study of 103 Canadian firms, the respondents (mostly one or two senior or top executives of each firm) rated the importance to their top management of high, above-industry-average performances on five goals —namely, profitability, growth, liquidity, employee morale, and public image.[24] On 7-point scales in which 1 was equivalent to moderate importance and 7 was equivalent to extreme importance, with 4 as equal to quite important, the average rating for profitability was highest at 5.4, with good public image and employee morale coming second at 5.1 each. Growth was fourth at 4.8, and liquidity was lowest at 4.3.

Both the Dent study and the author's study confirm the great importance of profitability as a system goal of firms. Both also confirm that it is *not* a preeminent goal, that goals like good public image, public service, and employee morale are quite important system goals, too. In a cross-cultural study by England and Mee, profit maximization was rated fourth overall, third by U.S. managers, fourth by Japanese managers, and fifth by Korean managers. Overall, high productivity, organizational growth, and organizational efficiency were rated as more important, and organizational stability, industry leadership, employee welfare, and social welfare as less important, system goals.[25]

Generally speaking, a sizable organization *must* have several system goals. Ultimately, any sizable organization is run by a coalition of several individuals, not all of whom share the same needs. These multiple needs seek legitimate means of fulfillment. No one goal is likely to fulfill multiple needs. Thus organizations, generally speaking, should have multiple system goals to maintain intact the coalition that runs the organization. If universities energetically pursued only research, they would lose most of their students and a good portion of their faculty. If hospitals proscribed research and concentrated only on treating patients, they might lose many of their bright, young doctors who are interested in research. If a political party emphasized only one goal, it could rapidly lose electoral support to those with more inclusive goal sets. While no organization can pursue too many goals and remain effective, equally truly few organizations of any size can pursue just one goal and survive.

Product-characteristic goals. Product-characteristic goals of the organization are goals with respect to the quality of the organization's goods or services. Such goals as an emphasis on quality rather than on the quantity of the organization's products or services, their variety, styling, availability, uniqueness, innovativeness, and so on are product-characteristic goals. These goals are often quite complex. Sometimes they are purely tactical, as when Henry Ford mass produced the Model-T to cater to the need of Americans for a standardized, inexpensive but individualized means of transport, or when the German Volkswagenwerk produced the beetle to cater to a similar market in post-Second World War Germany. At times they are a part of the sustaining ideology of the organization, as perhaps is the case of Daimler-Benz, the makers of Mercedes cars. High quality of the product is a goal in itself, an orientation this company shares with Harvard University, Oxbridge, and Rolls Royce.

> A glimpse of an organization with a product goal of quality is provided by the *Fortune* story of "Daimler-Benz: Quality über Alles" . . . the firm built the world's first practical automobile and has been building quality cars in small numbers for over 75 years. The chief engineer of the company described the 75-year-old tradition as "constant experimentation, concentration on new developments, and continuous improvement." This has meant that the Mercedes has incorporated, as standard equipment, all significant innovations as soon as they appear, whether the public demands them or not and without regard to the increase in the cost of the car. For example, Daimler-Benz introduced such innovations as four-wheel suspension, fuel injection, and joint rear swing axle long before they were adopted by other manufacturers. The company is dominated by engineers and has an adequate pool of skilled labor. Its workers have lived and worked for generations in the German towns where the cars are produced, and they take a fierce pride in the skilled craftsmanship. . . . Daimler-Benz has always built automobiles to the tastes of the engineers whether the public likes it or not.[26]

The product-characteristic goals of an organization are in part a species of its system goals, for they reflect the ideological preferences of its management. In part, they are also its output goals, since they represent the organization's assessment of what its clients want. When the management of Magnavox says that it is in the business of producing high quality electronic equipment, it is in a sense expressing its preference for the production, not just of electronic consumer goods, but of high quality, distinctive electronic consumer goods. At the same time, it probably also represents a hard-headed, profitable market strategy.

The author's study of Canadian firms indicated some interesting reasons why organizations adopt a high quality, high price orientation rather than a standard quality, standard or low price orientation. Those firms that had a high quality, high price orientation tended to operate in a fluctuating industry, presumably because in such an industry reputation for quality may be an important stabilizing influence for the firm, and also because the affluent customers of such an industry would be less prone to booms and busts. These firms also tended to operate in an environment the firm could control and manipulate. Conversely, a high quality, high price reputation enabled the firms to secure monopolistic niches in their respective industries. Also, those firms that regarded acquiring and maintaining a good public image as an important goal tended to have a high quality, high price orientation. On the other hand, firms that operated in a nonfluctuating industry, and in a dominating environment tended to adopt a standard quality, standard or low price orientation, as did firms that did not regard a good public image as an important goal.

The Canadian study suggested that whether an organization has a high quality, high price orientation or not apparently has some important organizational consequences. For one thing, organizations that are oriented to standard quality and low price are likely also to employ a mass-production oriented technology, while organizations oriented to high quality and high price are prone to employ a more customized production technology. For example, public schools tend to be oriented to producing "standardized" students, while private, high cost, high tuition schools tend to be oriented to producing individualistic students. The former employ large classes, standardized instructional technology, and a uniform reward system. The latter tend to have lower student-teacher ratios, customized instructional technology, and a reward system tailored to the learning needs of the student. As the Mercedes-Benz example indicates, production of high quality products or services involves a fair degree of engineering or design activities. Thus, the high quality, high price organization tends to be characterized by special task forces and teams for coordinating the various functions involved in designing high quality products or services.[27]

We propose that:

The more fluctuating the size of the market,
>   *the more the organization is motivated to find a stable niche by competing on the basis of the quality of its outputs.*

The more the environment is under the control of the organization,
> *the more it tends to compete on the basis of the quality of its outputs and the less on the basis of their economy.*

The more the organization competes on the basis of quality rather than the economy of its outputs,
> *the more its technology tends to get oriented to custom-built production;*
>
> *the more importance design-type activities acquire, and the more use the organization tends to make of task forces for design and coordination purposes.*

Derived goals. Derived goals are the subsidiary uses to which the organization puts the power or resources it generates while seeking its primary goals. For example, profitable corporations often enter the field of philanthropy by donating large sums to museums, universities and other bastions of the imperishable. They also often seek (illegally at times) to influence political decision-making by lobbying legislatures and bankrolling candidates for political office. In recent years, churches in the United States, for long in the business of saving souls, have tried to use their influence over their parishioners to promote libertarian causes like civil rights for minorities. Many corporations have provided "leadership" in "community rebuilding" (clearing the ghettoes), a goal that becomes particularly conspicuous in good times.

There may be many reasons prompting organizations to have derived goals. An organization may develop subsidiary goals because these are seen as means by which it can more effectively achieve its primary goals. Organizations that bankroll candidates for political office appear to do so for clearly perceived self-interest. An organization may also develop subsidiary goals in the glow of success, much as a wealthy man is likely to wax benevolent once the millions accumulate in his tills. Organizations also develop derived goals because as they grow larger they tend to get decentralized, and so individual executives feel freer to pursue their own goals rather than the goals of the organization. This happens fairly frequently in large bureaucracies, where department and division heads often pursue pet projects that are only tangentially related to the primary goals of the organization.

We propose that:

The greater the surplus resources of an organization—that is, the greater the organizational slack—
> *the more secondary or derived goals does it pursue.*

The more differentiated and decentralized the organization,
the more secondary goals it pursues.

The different categories of goal we have reviewed are expectations about what the organization should strive for on the part of the public at large, the organization's clientele, and its management and owners. These goals may not, of course, be identical. From the point of view of society, taking care of the sick and the wounded in the community served by a hospital probably constitutes the goal of that hospital. While the administrators and the senior medical staff of the hospital—its management—may acknowledge this goal, their goals for the hospital will be more specific. They may like to emphasize economy, especially in administering expensive drugs to indigent patients. They may prefer to combine research with ministering to the patients. They may like to make decisions informally. They may like to build up the reputation of the hospital by acquiring the most advanced (if infrequently used) equipment. From the point of view of society, the function of political parties is to maintain a healthy democracy. From the point of view of the clientele or supporters of a political party, the latter's goal is to try and enact a legislative program that the supporters like. From the point of view of the management of that political party, the goal may be to capture power so that senior party cadres may be able to enjoy the plums of political office. Clearly, since an organization cannot survive without the support of society, its clientele, and its management, the expectations of these for the organization act as constraints subject to which much of the decision-making and resource allocation within the organization takes place.

Indeed, Herbert Simon has suggested that a fruitful way of identifying the operating goals of the organization is to identify the *constraints* under which decision makers operate, many of which arise from the variety of goals that the organization must pursue to keep its various pressure groups pacified.[28] Some of these constraints initiate search for alternatives, some are used to test or assess the alternatives generated. These constraints may be organizationally imposed through formal orders and rules or through informal norms and "suggestions" of the powerful. They may also be purely internal to the decision maker—that is, they may reflect his personal aspirations, preferences, and norms. Thus, if we wish to understand what the operating goals of the chief executive of an organization are, it may be better to rephrase the question as: "What are the constraints under which he makes the kind of decision he does make?" This question will lead us to a discussion of the environment within which the organization operates (a major source of search-initiating constraints); the past practices of the organization (a major source of evaluative constraints); the financial condition of the organization; the preferences of the chief's colleagues; his own preferences and needs; and his perception of what the clients of the organization want, of what "society" will put up with, of what the owners will applaud, and so on.

CONSEQUENCES OF OPERATING GOALS

We have reviewed so far the process by which operating goals get formed in the organization and the variety of operating goals. Now we examine what happens when a goal is adopted by the ruling coalition in the organization and comes to be accepted as legitimate by the rest of the organization. We also examine the determinants of the performance level of the goal, the organizational consequences of variation in performance level, what happens when the organization tries to accomplish a number of goals rather than only a few goals, and the consequences of incompatibility among the goals the organization pursues.

Goal-Means Hierarchies

A major consequence of the adoption of a goal is that it gets elaborated into a goal-means hierarchy. The firm's goal of earning a profit gets translated into the objectives of earning a certain rate of return on investment. This goal in turn translates into more detailed profit goals per product, market share goals, investment goals, production goals, and others, right down to the budget for janitorial services and the job specifications for janitor. Each step of this ladder, whose highest rung is a certain rate of return and whose lowest is the detailed job descriptions of operatives, is both a means for achieving a goal higher in the hierarchy and a goal of those immediately lower down in the hierarchy. The advertising budget of x million dollars is the means by which a certain market share is expected to be achieved. It is also the target expenditure of the firm's media executives. Thus, the roles that organizational members play are shaped by the goal-means hierarchies operating in the organization. The following diagram (Figure 10–2) illustrates two goal-means chains or hierarchies of a firm. Each goal-means hierarchy is a pyramid of programs—one goal can branch out into innumerable means chains.

This bifurcation of superordinate goals and means is, of course, both an advantage and a disadvantage. Since goals are not shared, the members of the organization need not be anxious about the relevance of their actions to such superordinate goals as profit maximization or good corporate citizenship. Good old Joe in the safety and maintenance department is con-

FIGURE 10–2
The Goal-Means Hierarchies of Toys, Inc.

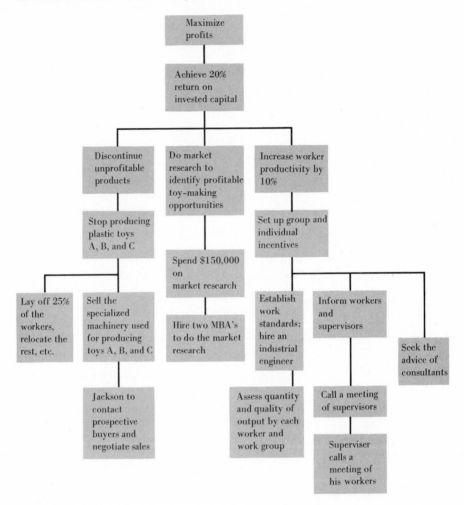

cerned about the maintenance checks on the lathes, not about the eventual effects of this on the public image of the corporation and the price of its share on the stock exchange. On the other hand, Joe also tends to identify less and less with the overall objectives of the corporation and often does things that may in fact be inconsistent with these goals, such as insisting on a tight maintenance checks schedule that holds up emergency production for a customer. Goal-means hierarchies simplify the roles that organizational

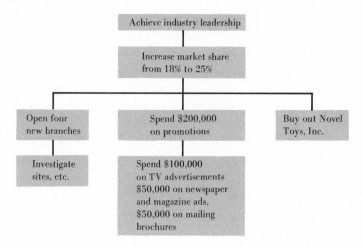

members have to play; but they also often lead to suboptimization and sometimes also to anomic, "irresponsible" behavior on the part of members, as when students riot in protest against poor facilities, not knowing or not caring about the financial constraints under which a college may be operating.

Determinants of Performance Aspiration
Levels of Goals

Some organizational goals, such as survival, are either/or goals. Others, such as market share, profitability, public image, employee morale, are capable of variation. A school may set as its target a 60 percent rather than a 50 percent success rate in matriculation examinations. An employment agency may set a target of finding jobs for 80 percent of applicants rather than 60 percent. What factors determine the level at which such goals will be set?

Two factors are likely to induce high performance aspirations. One is the buoyancy of the environment. If high performance is easy to come by, aspirations will tend to be high. Research on the level of aspirations of individuals has shown that the higher the past achievement on a goal, the higher is the target for the next period, and the lower the past success, the lower is the target.[29] Thus, it is quite obvious that the human agency managing organizations is likely to feel optimistic in an expansionary environment in which previous targets have been met relatively easily and to feel pessimistic in an environment in which high performance has not been feasible.

The other factor is the challenge in the environment. If the environment is highly challenging, as in a competitive industry, that is to say, if organizational performance depends on the initiative and competence of managers, then, through a process of selective reinforcement of boldness, initiative, competence, high achievement motivation, and commitment to organizational rather than personal goals, individuals with such qualities will rise to key management positions in organizations operating in such an environment, and the organization's aspirations with respect to major goals will tend to be high. A competitive environment will also tend to make the commitment to organizational goals more durable through the intermittent (rather than continuous) reinforcement of organizational policies.[30] On the other hand, if the environment is noncompetitive, high achievers will tend not to be attracted to the organization, and the performance aspirations of the latter will tend to be low.

In the Canadian study, the level of top management's corporate aspirations was measured by summing the scores of the importance accorded by top management to high, above average performance by the firm on five corporate goals—namely, profitability, growth, liquidity, employee morale, and public relations or image.[31] As Table 10–1 shows, these aspirations

TABLE 10–1
Environment and Top Management Aspirations
(Sample: 103 Canadian Firms)

	Rated importance of high performance on corporate goals
Mean for whole sample	24.7
Standard deviation for whole sample	4.4
Mean for firms in high growth rate industries	27.2
Mean for firms in moderate growth rate industries	24.5
Mean for firms in low growth rate industries	23.7
Mean for firms reporting high competitive pressure	26.0
Mean for firms reporting moderate competitive pressure	24.8
Mean for firms reporting low competitive pressure	23.1
Mean for the 10 firms in high growth *and* high competitive pressure environment	28.4
Mean for the 6 firms in moderate growth *and* moderate competitive pressure environment	24.7
Mean for the 18 firms in low growth *and* low competitive pressure environment	22.2

were substantially higher for firms in high growth, buoyant environments than for firms in low growth, static environments. Similarly, they were higher for firms in highly competitive environments marked by change, challenge, and intermittent reinforcement of corporate policies than in noncompetitive environments marked by stability, lack of challenge, and nonintermittent reinforcement of corporate policies. They were *much* higher for firms in buoyant *as well as* changing, challenging environments than for firms in static, *as well as* unchallenging environments.

We propose that:

The more buoyant the environment,
> *the higher will be the organization's performance aspirations with respect to operating goals.*

The more competitive and challenging the environment,
> *the higher will be the organization's performance aspirations with respect to operating goals.*

Consequences of High Aspirations with Respect to Individual Goals

In a previous section we discussed goal-means hierarchies. The notion is that each goal is the apex of several layers of means or programs aimed at attaining the goal. Logically, therefore, if an organization has high aspirations with regard to a goal, all the means utilized to attain targeted performance on that goal will acquire strategic importance: the organization gears up to meet the target. Structures and processes that facilitate achievement of the target will tend to be retained and strengthened or, if not in existence, introduced. Those that impede achievement of the target will tend to be discarded or de-emphasized. The *value* of the internal resources of the organization—be they in the form of labor, capital, technical know-how, or management ability—is strongly determined by the goal or goals being pursued.

The organizational consequences of high performance aspirations vary somewhat from goal to goal. Let us assume that the goals of all organizations consist of at least the following: profit maximization (or in the case of nonprofit organizations, minimization of deficits), growth, solvency, good morale of organizational members, and public acceptability and good will (a striving after social legitimacy and acceptance). Table 10–2 shows the *covariation* between the degree of importance to top management of relatively high performance on each of these five goals and a number of strategic and structural variables.

TABLE 10–2

Correlations Between Goal Importance and Strategic and Structural Variables (Sample: 103 Canadian Firms)

	Profitability (minimization of deficits)	Growth in size	Liquidity (solvency)	Morale of employees	Public image (social acceptance)
Planning- and optimization-oriented management style				.35	.26
Strategic importance as perceived by management of:					
Management information and control systems	.29	.24			
Job design and job enrichment				.52	.23
Management training	.22			.48	.32
Formulation of corporate strategy	.31	.30		.27	
Participative, human-relations oriented management style	.20			.45	.20
Corporate policies:					
A policy of decentralizing operations decisions	.22			.33	
A high risk, high return rather than a safe, risk aversive, investment policy	.29				—.20
A policy of above industry average promotion of organization's products or services	—.21				.22
External rather than internal recruitment of senior and middle level managers				—.24	
An up-or-out personnel policy rather than one of offering job security to employees	.19				—.20
Diversification of organizational products or services	.29				
Divisionalization	.35				

NOTE: Only "product moment" correlations significant at the 5 percent level or less are reported.

The table shows that as high profitability becomes a more salient goal, a number of activities assume greater importance. These are related chiefly to diversification of the organization's outputs, decentralization of authority, formulation of corporate strategy, divisionalization (a form of decentralization), and control and coordination of activities. Also, the management becomes more venturesome and also somewhat more participative. The increasing salience of growth and solvency does not have a comparable organizational impact. However, an increase in the importance of morale and social acceptance does have several consequences, although somewhat different from those mentioned above. Concern with employee morale and social acceptance, the hallmark of conscientious, possibly also social-status conscious management, appears to be associated with a technocratic as well as a participative management style.[32] Activities that are popular with employees, such as job enrichment and management training, also acquire importance as management becomes more aware of its responsibilities toward its subordinates and toward society.

Salience of employee morale and profitability tends to push the organization toward a policy of decentralization. But the *raison d'être* is different. When employee morale is a key goal, decentralization is seen as a way of satisfying the needs of junior and middle managers for autonomy and responsibility. When profitability is a key goal, decentralization is a part of a wider strategy of diversification of the products or services offered by the organization and the attendant divisionalization, the latter aimed at spurring performance through greater competition among managers.

Notice, however, the opposite directions in which the organization is pushed when profitability as well as social acceptability assume key importance. Profitability pulls the organization toward a more risk-taking investment policy; social acceptability toward a safe investment policy. Profitability pulls the organization toward a frugal promotion and advertising policy; social acceptability toward an extravagant promotion and advertising policy. Profitability impels the organization to follow an aggressive, performance-oriented personnel policy; social acceptability argues for a "softer" job-security oriented personnel policy. The data show the contrary forces set in motion within the organization when the organization sets out to please both its owners and the society in which it operates.

We propose that:

As between major organizational goals, high aspirations with respect to employee morale push the management to adopt a participative, human-relations oriented style and to emphasize human resources development activities more than other goals do.

As between major organizational goals, high aspirations with respect to profitability impels the management to emphasize a sophisticated management information and control system, risk taking, diversification of products or services, and divisionalization more than other goals do.

The more strongly held are the goals of profitability and social acceptance or public image,

> *the more the organization is pulled in opposite directions with respect to investment, personnel, and product promotion policies.*

Consequences of High Aspirations with Respect to Many Goals

How does an organization that has several goals (as most organizations do) *and* has high aspirations with regard to all (or most) of them respond? First of all, management is likely to feel a strong need for *professional* management of those resources that are perceived to be the common means for the achievement of these goals, such as capital, managerial skills, technical staff, staff cooperation. These are likely to be found in short supply, and the organization is likely to engage in rationing and *planning* activities. It is also likely to engage in activities aimed at *enhancing the productive value* of whatever crucial resources are available. For example, it may institute management training programs to update management skills, install sophisticated incentive schemes to raise the motivation of organizational members, and hire operations researchers to improve the efficiency of operations. It is likely to aim at a better *coordination* of programs to prevent duplication, waste, and conflict and at more collaborative relations between superiors and subordinates through the practice of human relations and participative management. It is likely to seek a clearer formulation of organizational *strategy* and the structure by which the performance targets are to be achieved. The pursuit of high performance on multiple goals raises the complexity of organizational decision-making and resource allocation, and it enlarges the area of actual or potential conflict; inevitably, the organizational response is an attempt at better planning, more complex coordination, more "professional" management.[33]

We propose that:

The higher the performance goals of the management of an organization,

> *the more planning, optimization oriented and participative is the style of top management;*
>
> *the greater is the attention paid to activities designed to raise the efficiency of organizational resources;*
>
> *the greater is the effort at coordinating the organization's activities; and*
>
> *the more sophisticated is the organization's control and information system.*

SUMMARY, PROPOSITIONS, AND IMPLICATIONS
FOR ORGANIZATIONAL DESIGN

Summary

While organizations commonly state their goals, their operating goals, which have greater relevance for organization theory, sometimes deviate strikingly from publicly stated goals. External pressures in the shape of competitive, bargaining, cooptational, and coalitional relations with other organizations shape the operating goals by stressing the feasibility (or lack of it) of various courses of action. Conflicting pressures from various groups within the organization also shape the operating goals. Despite these internal conflicts the operating goals retain a fair degree of stability because of a number of organizational processes such as selective and limited attention to goals, organizational slack, respect for precedents, and side payments by members of the ruling coalition to buy off recalcitrants.

The degree of consensus on operative goals is subject to a number of factors such as selection and indoctrination of members, the existence of threats to the organization's security, professional management norms, and the measurability of performance.

Organizations pursue a variety of goals, chiefly the goal of securing and maintaining social legitimacy, output goals, system goals, product-characteristic goals, and derived goals. These goals represent the concerns of a number of pressure groups associated with the organization. They act as constraints on decision-making in the organization.

A major consequence of an organizational goal is that it gets amplified into a goal-means chain. This limits the responsibility of members but also limits their involvement with the organization's major goals.

Performance aspirations with respect to organizational goals are affected by the buoyancy and competitive challenge in the environment. The consequences of high aspirations are a professionalization of management as the organization struggles to achieve high levels of performance on each of several goals. However, this can push the organization into incompatible policies.

Propositions

The following propositions were developed in the chapter:

1. The more careful the selection, training, and indoctrination of organizational members;

   the more the organization's survival is at stake;

   the more frequent and collaborative the interactions between key organizational groups;

the stronger the ideology of optimization and planning, and
the less ambiguous the criteria by which organizational performance
can be evaluated;
   the greater is consensus on the operating goals of the organization.

2. The larger the organization, and
the more differentiated its activities,
   the greater is conflict within the organization as to its operating
   goals.

3. The more turbulent the external environment, especially the more it
fluctuates cyclically,
   the greater is the importance of diversification and vertical integration to top management.

4. The more subject the organization is to oligopolistic or other controls
over the pricing and output of its principal products,
   the greater is the importance of diversification and vertical integration to top management.

5. The greater the uncertainty about crucial inputs and crucial channels
of distribution,
   the greater is the importance of vertical integration to top management.

6. The larger the organization,
   the greater is the feasibility and importance of vertical integration to top management.

7. The more risk taking and entrepreneurial the style of top management,
   the greater is the importance of diversification to top management.

8. The more diversified the organization,
   the more divisionalized is the organization's structure;
   the more differentiated is the organization's culture;
   the more sophisticated is the control, information, and planning
   system of the organization;
   the more participatory is the style of top management.

9. The more concentric the diversification, or the more vertically integrated the organization,

the greater is the delegation of authority by the chief executive;
the more sophisticated is the control, information, and planning
system of the organization.

10. The more fluctuating the size of the market,
  the more the organization is motivated to find a stable niche by
  competing on the basis of the quality of its outputs.

11. The more the environment is under the control of the organization,
  the more it tends to compete on the basis of the quality of its
  outputs and the less on the basis of their economy.

12. The more the organization competes on the basis of quality rather than
  the economy of its outputs,
  the more its technology tends to get oriented to custom-built
  production;
  the more importance design-type activities acquire, and
  the more use the organization tends to make of task forces for
  design and coordination purposes.

13. The greater the surplus resources of an organization—that is, the greater
  the organizational slack—
  the more secondary or derived goals does it pursue.

14. The more differentiated and decentralized the organization,
  the more secondary goals it pursues.

15. The more buoyant the environment,
  the higher will be the organization's performance aspirations
  with respect to operating goals.

16. The more competitive and challenging the environment,
  the higher will be the organization's performance aspirations
  with respect to operating goals.

17. As between major organizational goals, high aspirations with respect to
  employee morale push the management to adopt a participative,
  human relations oriented style and to emphasize human resources development activities more than other goals do.

18. As between major organizational goals, high aspirations with respect to
  profitability impels the management to emphasize a sophisticated man-

agement information and control system, risk taking, diversification of products or services, and divisionalization more than other goals do.

19. The more strongly held are the goals of profitability and social acceptance or public image,

>the more the organization is pulled in opposite directions with respect to investment, personnel, and product promotion policies.

20. The higher the performance goals of the management of an organization,

>the more planning, optimization oriented and participative is the style of top management;

>the greater is the attention paid to activities designed to raise the efficiency of organizational resources;

>the greater is the effort at coordinating the organization's activities; and

>the more sophisticated is the organization's control and information system.

Implications for Organizational Design

What are the implications for the design of organizations? One obvious implication is that it is not enough to think of what goals an organization should have; it is also necessary to think through the means necessary to achieve them and then to design the organization appropriately to achieve them. A second implication is that the designer(s) must attend not only to performance goals such as profitability or growth but to other kinds of goal, particularly to preferences about how the organization must operate —for example, whether mechanistically or organically. Another implication is that in any sizable organization there are several pressure groups, and therefore it is unrealistic to pursue a single goal such as profit maximization, because it will satisfy very few. Too many goals spoil the broth, so to speak, but too few goals may also affect the viability of the management as a cohesive group. If, then, an organization must pursue several goals, the designer(s) must make provision for the rationing, planning, coordinative, and problem-solving mechanisms necessary to pursue several goals simultaneously. The designer(s) must be prepared to professionalize management if the organization pursues several goals, particularly if it sets itself high performance targets on them. Not only that, but the maintenance of a viable managerial coalition becomes a vital need in pursuing several high performance targets. The designer(s) must be prepared to take steps to keep goal conflicts among key members of the organization within bounds by designing appropriate selection and training procedures. This is a tricky job. Too much uniformity in the organizational goals and aspirations of members of the ruling coalition can be deadly in terms of seeking fresh growth opportunities and creative problem solving. Too much diversity is likely to produce immense coordination problems. Judgment combined with the knowledge of what consequences to expect from various combinations of goals and aspirations is needed to produce an effective organizational design.

SUGGESTED READINGS

Ch. 3 in Richard M. Cyert and James G. March, *A Behavioral Theory of the Firm* (Englewood Cliffs, N. J.: Prentice-Hall, 1963).

Ch. 5 in Charles Perrow, *Organizational Analysis: a Sociological View* (Belmont, Calif.: Wadsworth, 1970).

Herbert Simon, "On the Concept of Organizational Goal," *Administrative Science Quarterly*, Vol. 9, No. 1 (June 1964), pp. 1–22.

QUESTIONS FOR ANALYSIS

Stop

1 Consider the social, output, system, product-characteristic, and derived goals discussed in the chapter. How do they differ for the C.I.A., the General Motors Corporation, the United Nations, and Harvard University? What organizational differences do these differences in goals imply?

2 Here is the goal profile of two large merchandising corporations. What design would be appropriate for each?

	Corporation A	*Corporation B*
Importance of above average profitability	Low	High
Importance of above average growth rate	High	High
Importance of above average liquidity	Medium	Medium
Importance of above average employee morale	Low	High
Importance of excellent public image	Low	High

3 Here is a story that appeared in *Time* magazine.[34] What goal conflicts are tearing the Lutheran Church-Missouri Synod apart? Why are the goal conflicts so acute? What are the organizational consequences of the goal conflicts? What do you recommend be done?

Lutherans at War

"The Lutheran Church-Missouri Synod we have known is dead. The institution that has given us life is no more. Its structures are hopelessly corrupt. Its leadership is morally bankrupt. Its rank-and-file members have chosen to ignore and overlook evil."

Wearing flowing white ecclesiastical robes, the Rev. John Tietjen, leader of the Missouri Synod's breakaway liberal faction, delivered that bitter eulogy last week from a pulpit set up in an auditorium at the O'Hara Inn near Chicago. It was what his 1,600 listeners wanted to hear. They were members of Evangelical Lutherans in Mission (E.L.I.M.), a dissident group that has been warring openly with the conservative hierarchy of the 2.8 million-member denomination. Tietjen's lament for the church underlined the fact that the Missouri Synod's conservative leadership is now firmly in command.

For more than a year, the Missouri Synod has been torn by an ever deepening division between the church's conservatives, who hew to a strictly literal interpretation of the Bible, and its moderate liberals, who more readily use modern methods of biblical criticism and tend to view some supposedly historical passages (the Garden of Eden story, for example) as religious myth. At the Synod's convention in New Orleans last year, the conservatives consolidated their hold on the denomination by returning the Rev. Jacob A. O. ("Jack") Preus to the church's presidency and winning a majority on the board of its keystone theological school, Concordia Seminary of St. Louis.

Last January, the Concordia board suspended John Tietjen as the seminary's president on charges that included the fostering of heresy (*Time,* Feb. 4). The action incited a wholesale student and faculty rebellion and prompted the rebels to establish a liberal-oriented Seminary in Exile (Seminex) that almost stripped the official seminary of teachers and students. Evangelical Lutherans in Mission, founded a year ago, has become the organizational voice of the dissidents and the funding channel for the breakaway seminary.

But instead of reeling from the dissidents' vigorous challenge, the Synod's conservatives have recovered remarkably. This week, as registration begins at Concordia, no fewer than 170 full-time students are expected to enroll in the standard master of divinity program, along with 20 other graduate students; that total is well above the most optimistic predictions after the split last winter, even though far below the 650 enrolled before the controversy began. Acting President Ralph A. Bohlmann, who has been Preus' theological aide-de-camp, has fielded a full-time faculty of 18 (compared with four last spring). Meanwhile, the Missouri Synod's other official theological school, Concordia Seminary of Springfield, Ill., has an aggressive new president, the Rev. Robert D. Preus—Jack's brother and a conservative with impressive intellectual credentials. It also has its biggest incoming class (118) in years. All this suggests a strong allegiance to old-line traditionalism, even among younger Lutherans.

Nonetheless, the liberals' Seminex, which continues to use the classrooms of the Society of Jesus at St. Louis University and those of the United Church of Christ's Eden Seminary, is holding its own. Nearly all of last year's under-classmen will return, as well as 70 newcomers, for a total enrollment of 408. Though the conservatives pressured congregations against accepting Seminex's 124 May graduates, 77 have already been placed in church work (only 21, however, have thus far been ordained). As for E.L.I.M., though it claims heavy clerical backing (1,827 members out of 5,100 North American clergy), financial support comes from only 296 of the Missouri Synod's 6,100 parishes. Still, it is enough: after subsidizing Seminex's first semester last spring, E.L.I.M. ended the fiscal year with a surplus of $230,000.

At last week's Chicago meeting, E.L.I.M. delegates generally agreed to stay and fight within the church rather than break with it in open schism—at least until conservatives actively move to throw them out. Respected Church Historian Martin Marty—a board member of E.L.I.M.—argued that before that could happen, the detested conservative leadership might simply fall apart, largely because of its inherent divisiveness. "I don't believe the two official seminaries will survive," he says. "They will have to combine. The financial devastation will start showing soon. Careers are gone, families are divided. Any congregation that gets active in this situation is destroyed."

The conservatives, of course, take an opposite view, especially in the wake of Concordia's astonishing rebound. Seminex, predicts Church President Preus, "will wither away in a couple of years." Preus dismisses talk of any actual schism. "E.L.I.M. is mainly a clergy movement," he observes. "There will not be any split, primarily because the lay people are not cranked up." Moreover, Preus insists, he is not going to do anything "to stir things up further." With the conservatives' firm grip on the seminaries, "there's no reason for heresy hunts in the parishes."

Footnotes to Chapter Ten

[1] M. N. Zald, "Comparative Analysis and Measurement of Organizational Goals: The Case of Correctional Institutions for Delinquents."

[2] Robert A. Scott, "The Factory As a Social Service Organization: Goal Displacement in Workshops for the Blind."

[3] J. D. Thompson and W. J. McEwen, "Organizational Goals and Environment: Goal Setting as an Interaction Process."

[4] Selznick, *T.V.A. and the Grass Roots.*

[5] See Robert D. Joyce, *Encounters in Organizational Behavior,* pp. 212–15, for a very good illustration of goal conflict.

[6] R. M. Cyert and James March, *A Behavioral Theory of the Firm,* Ch. 3.

[7] For an experimental demonstration of this, see Muzafer Sherif, "Experiments in Group Conflict."

[8] Charles Perrow, *Organizational Analysis: A Sociological View,* Ch. 5.

[9] Talcott Parsons, *Structure and Process in Modern Societies.*

[10] See Igor Ansoff, *Corporate Strategy.*

[11] For a detailed classification of different types of diversification, see Richard P. Rumelt, *Strategy, Structure, and Economic Performance,* pp. 52–57.

[12] See the case study of *The Saturday Evening Post* in C. Roland Christensen, Kenneth R. Andrews, and Joseph L. Bower, *Business Policy,* 3rd edition.

¹³ The importance to top management of (a) diversification and (b) vertical integration were correlated .20 and .26, respectively, with environmental turbulence and .30 and .31, respectively, with extent of cyclical fluctuation in industry. Importance of vertical integration was correlated .26 with industry competition for raw materials, .19 with environmental hostility, and .20 with firm size. The top management's commitment to a policy of *conglomerate* diversification was correlated .23 with extent of cyclical fluctuations in industry and .28 with technological sophistication of environment.

¹⁴ For evidence that cyclically fluctuating and "high technology" industries tend to be oligopolistic, see F. M. Scherer, *Industrial Market Structure and Economic Performance,* especially Chapters 13 and 15.

¹⁵ The risk taking orientation of top management was correlated .30 and .28, respectively, with the strategic importance of diversification to top management and commitment to conglomerate diversification.

¹⁶ See Alfred Chandler, *Strategy and Structure.* In the Canadian study, the extent of diversification was correlated .60 with the extent of divisionalization of the organization.

¹⁷ See John M. Stopford and Louis T. Wells, Jr., *Managing the Multinational Enterprise,* Chapter 3, especially Table 3–4 on p. 42.

¹⁸ In the Canadian study, extent of diversification was correlated .33 with the sophistication of the organization's control and information system, .26 with the participative orientation of top management, and correlated .19 with the planning-and-optimization orientation of top management. Extent of vertical integration was correlated .25 with the sophistication of the control and information system, .22 with delegation of authority to subordinates by the chief executive, and .21 with the planning-and-optimization orientation of top management.

¹⁹ David L. Sills, *The Volunteers.*

²⁰ Perrow, *op. cit.,* p. 138.

²¹ From Quotations from Chairman Mao Tse-tung, pp. 163–64.

²² See Perrow, *op. cit.,* pp. 163–64.

²³ J. K. Dent, "Organizational Correlates of the Goals of Business Managements."

²⁴ See Appendix A for a description of the author's study of Canadian firms.

²⁵ George England and Raymond Mee, "Organizational Goals and Expected Behavior Among American, Japanese, and Korean Managers."

²⁶ Perrow, *op. cit.,* pp. 168–69.

²⁷ The relationship between a high quality, high price orientation and (a) fluctuation in the size of the industry and (b) the controllability of the environment remained significant at the 5 percent level in the Canadian study even after controlling for the effects of the other environmental variable. The relationship between high quality, high price orientation and management preference for customizing output, and the relationship between high quality, high price orientation and the use of task forces for securing better coordination between the different personnel in an organization, were statistically significant at the 5 percent level even after controlling for the effects of each other and the two environmental variables.

²⁸ Herbert Simon, "On the Concept of Organizational Goal."

²⁹ Kurt Lewin, et al., "Level of Aspiration."

³⁰ B. F. Skinner, *Science and Human Behavior.*

³¹ See Appendix A for details.

³² The covariation between the importance to management of a good public image and a participatory as well as a technocratic top management style clearly indi-

cates the high social status of "professional" management. The covariation between the importance to management of high employee morale and a participative orientation is not surprising—participative management, after all, is widely believed to be a motivational device. The covariation between the importance of morale and a technocratic orientation may be not only because employee morale may be furthered by the top management espousing modernity and professionalism but also because a rank and file committed to the organization is indispensable if sophisticated management practices are to be implemented successfully.

[33] In the Canadian study, performance aspirations with respect to five major corporate goals was correlated .31 and .29, respectively, with the participative and optimization-and-planning orientations of top management; .34, .32, .37, .32, and .36 with the strategic importance to top management, respectively, of formulation of corporate strategy, a sophisticated incentive system for all employees, training of managers, job design and job enrichment, and formalization of decision-making authority; and .27, .29, and .30, respectively, with the use of hierarchy, liaison personnel, and a sophisticated control and information system for coordination purposes.

[34] *Time* (Sept. 9, 1974), pp. 54–55.

11

"Style is the perfection of a point of view."
Richard Eberhart

The Style
of Top
Management

Start

INTRODUCTION

The Scope of the Chapter

In this chapter we discuss a very important strategic variable, the ideology and style of the organization's top management. This strategic variable is central to the practical work of designing organizations, for generally speaking, what the top management prefers gets carried into organizational practice. We touched briefly on the style of management in the preceding chapter while discussing the system goals of organizations. Here we discuss five dimensions of management ideology and style—namely, beliefs about risk taking, about the usefulness of planning and scientific management, about participation in decision-making, about administrative flexibility, and about the efficacy of coercion. Styles of top management are defined to be various combinations of these dimensions. We outline some styles of management, and then distinguish between some effective and some less effective ways of combining these dimensions. In the eighth and ninth chapters, we described some of the situational influences on the style of management. In Chapter 10 we explored the relationships between operating goals, performance aspira-

392

tions, and the style of management. In this chapter, we draw upon these earlier discussions and develop a more in-depth view of top management style.

Ideology and Style

Every organization has a top management—that is, a group of individuals who, either because of their formal position or expertise or political or other power, have a major say in the making of the *strategic,* long-term decisions of the organization. The formally designated officers of an organization, be it a union or a firm, a club or a government, are the obvious members of management. Sometimes, however, a person may have an honorific title but wield little power. State governors in the United States are powerful members of the top management of their state governments. In India they are ceremonial heads of state governments, the chief executive being the chief minister and not the governor. So one has to go behind mere titles to determine whether particular individuals are members of the top management or not. Sometimes untitled persons may wield considerable management power. In Communist countries, the party functionary who is habitually asked for his views whenever the management is contemplating major decisions is a nonofficial member of the management.

The members of the top management tend to develop what may best be described as an *ideology.* As Krech, Crutchfield, and Ballachey point out, the ideology of a group consists of common beliefs, common values, and common norms.[1] For management groups, assumptions or beliefs about people, particularly the members of the organization, are important aspects of their ideology. Other key elements of ideology are the goals of the organization or its mission, as well as norms about what means of achieving these goals are proper and what are not. Shared values such as order, efficiency, service, innovation, dominance, conservatism, democracy, and self-fulfillment are additional elements of management ideology. Ideology represents the system goals of management, which were discussed briefly in the preceding chapter. It represents the management view of the good, the true, and the beautiful for the organization.

Management ideologies develop for a number of reasons. One very important reason is the interaction among the members of management in solving organizational problems. During this interaction, individuals communicate their norms, beliefs, and values, drawing on their experience to justify them. The fact of interdependence and the necessity of maintaining power against the claims of other pressure groups, such as workers and shareholders in the case of firms, strengthens the need for a common, cementing management ideology. A number of other forces also contribute to the top management group's having a shared ideology: managerial training and apprenticeship, the punishment of deviants, the screening of potential candidates for top management membership for "congeniality," imitation of the powerful managers by the less powerful, and so forth.

Ideology should not be equated with dogmatism. Some ideologies are dogmatic and actively oppose other beliefs. But a management may also adopt a fairly liberal ideology, especially the view that heterogeneity of values and beliefs is desirable for reaching more creative solutions, and it may use its powers to protect this heterogeneity. Some university faculties frown upon retaining their doctoral graduates as faculty members, to prevent "inbreeding." The democratic ideology is explicitly pluralistic and representationally oriented. Nor are ideologies static. They change with the infusion of new members, new experiences, and new ideas. In the British government, every few years major ideological changes take place as a Conservative government is succeeded by a Labour government with its socialistic ideology.

Management ideology is important because it plays many important organizational functions. First of all, it gives a focus and a coherence to organizational activities—it gives rise to what one may call the "style of management." When making decisions, managers learn to ask, "Is this consistent with our philosophy?" Not that every managerial act is consistent with the management ideology—pragmatism, after all, is supposed to be the soul of management—but ideology usually is at least one input, often a powerful input, into management decision-making. If an ideology is strongly held, most acts tend to be legitimated by reference to their ideological inspiration, not unlike Chinese achievements in rocket and nuclear technology and other fields being attributed to the inspiration of Mao's little red book. Ideology often creates or redefines operational goals. In firms that have adopted humanistic ideologies, such as the set of assumptions about human nature that constitute McGregor's Theory Y, profit may still be the most important goal, but investment in the organization's human resources may become a powerful subgoal. As the personnel director of a product group at TRW, Inc. (an electronics and space firm bitten by the bug of behavioral-science oriented techniques), put it, "Our goal is to impact [sic] every one of 9,000 production operators and each of their foremen in the Components Group with the team improvement program."[2]

If ideology is the invisible network of values, beliefs, and norms, management style is its visible, operating manifestation. For example, if the management ideology in a firm is conservative, it will translate into a cautious approach to many issues. Need new products really be developed? Must the current equipment that has given good service for the past ten years really be changed? Aren't management training and operations research just passing fads? As anyone connected with a university quickly finds out, the democratic ideology of these august bodies translates into a style that seeks its principal validation in counting the number of committees! In many a government bureau, a passion for the values of order, efficiency, structure, and the like implies a management style of documenting everything and referring to some holy book of rules for every action.

An Illustrative Case

The following account of the chief executive of Aerojet-General Corporation dramatically illustrates the strategic role of the top management's ideology and style in shaping an organization.

> Plenty of aerospace companies have run into trouble in recent years, but California-based Aerojet-General Corp. seemed in danger of disappearing from sight altogether. Sales shriveled year after year, from a peak of $703-million in 1963 to only $271-million in 1971, and the company lost $10.2-million in 1967.
>
> The big reason, of course, was the steady drop in government orders for the rocket engines that are the backbone of Aerojet's business. But to some industry observers an over-centralized and heavy-handed management that failed to explore potential new markets was equally to blame.
>
> That was before 52-year-old Jack H. Vollbrecht took over. Vollbrecht, a former executive at ITT and Dresser Industries, went to Aerojet in 1969 when officials at General Tire & Rubber Co., which has long controlled Aerojet and last fall bought it outright, decided the slump had lasted long enough. . . .
>
> As a president, Vollbrecht has imposed a management on Aerojet that combines a heavy dose of independence at the operating level with a strong distaste for computers, memos, and paperwork. . . .
>
> *Tough on failure.* Vollbrecht's medicine seems to be working. Last year, earnings climbed to $13-million, double the figure for 1971, and record profits of more than $17-million seem likely for 1973. More important, Aerojet seems on the way to making diversification work—a goal of most aerospace companies, but one that few have achieved. A number of profitless businesses were sold off, and it has moved into some promising new areas. Aerojet's defense business accounts for 50% of sales against 90% four years ago. . . .
>
> When Vollbrecht arrived, Aerojet's structure was monolithic. His first act was to split Aerojet into 13 operating companies, each based on a product line for which it was made totally responsible. At each company

Vollbrecht named a "natural leader"—all but one from inside Aerojet—as president, and instructed each: "You tell us what to do with this business. We won't tell you. If you're wrong, we'll replace you." . . .

Vollbrecht then set up a planning system. A refinement of "management by objectives," his "management by commitment" not only requires managers to set their own goals but emphasizes the consequences of their success or failure in meeting them.

It is a hard-nosed system that is tough on failure, and Vollbrecht is the first to admit it. Three of Aerojet's 13 original company presidents lost their jobs when performance failed to measure up. To Vollbrecht that is not a bad batting average. He says the system is no deathtrap for managers because he does not condemn them for all errors, only unexplainable ones.

"You simply have to make your subordinates realize they have a firm commitment," he says, "Otherwise, there is a fuzzy relationship." And Vollbrecht uses the carrot as well as the stick. The cash bonus plan he established generously rewards subsidiary presidents who perform and offers little to those who do not.

Acceptance was far from automatic at first. Operating managers had grown so accustomed to a central authority that for a long time they could not believe their autonomy was real. To drive home the point, Vollbrecht literally refused to talk to them for a while. Even now he normally gives advice only when asked "so they know the decisions are theirs." . . .

The one tight link to management is the list of "commitments" that each subsidiary prepares annually. Every fall, each company draws up a set of goals to which it commits itself for the coming year, ranging from the contracts it plans to win the acquisitions it intends to make. Forecasts of production schedules, sales, and earnings are all part of the package. And to make sure the commitments are up to an acceptable minimum, a corporate executive is assigned to help each subsidiary prepare its report.

Once the report is in, a subsidiary president is remarkably on his own. His progress is assessed at quarterly meetings with corporate management, but other than that his only normal reporting duty is a brief flash report to Vollbrecht each month before the books are closed, laying out the unit's estimated sales and profits. The reports, says Vollbrecht, are mainly for the benefit of the managers who write them. "It is more important that they know what is happening than that I know," he says. "The reports are good discipline". . . .

Fewer memos. Vollbrecht himself detests reports and insists on dealing with his managers in person. So he spends much of his time roaming around Aerojet's subsidiaries. "A guy can only manage people face to face," he says. "If you do that, you don't need paperwork."

Vollbrecht decided early in the game that one way to cut down on reports was to eliminate the tools of report writing. He promptly ripped out Aerojet's big central management computer—at an annual saving of $4-million —and forbid subsidiaries to acquire their own. Computers used in management simply relay raw data, Vollbrecht says. "I want the judgment of the man who originates the data". . . .

Once Aerojet's new structure and management styles were set, Vollbrecht turned his attention to weeding out "silly" operations. . . .

Reshaping success. Each operating president was asked what he wanted to dump. Taking their suggestions, Vollbrecht shut down or sold off such operations as a structural materials division, a nuclear fuel research project, and a night-vision equipment unit. . . .

The Vollbrecht axe fell on research and development, too. He ended what he calls "the debilitating management practice" of centrally funded R & D. Vollbrecht, in fact, dismisses most R & D as merely "a tool used to maintain engineering organizations." Subsidiaries were ordered to pay for their own R & D. "You'd be surprised how many nutty ideas stopped coming up," he says.

Trimming away. Vollbrecht built his management philosophy largely from his experience at Dresser Industries. Vollbrecht recalls that his boss there, Donald H. Larmee, and Bud Fabian, former president of Dresser, "pounded my head into the wall, sent me into the field and made me do things." Adds Vollbrecht: "I was blessed with those two guys. I've also worked with guys who are stifling in their approach. I could see how much more you got out of people when you show them you rely on them". . . .

The company wants to stay in the rocket engine business, but contracts are much harder to come by than in the early 1960s when Aerojet churned out engines for Titan, Minuteman, and Polaris missiles. The Polaris program is over and Minuteman production has been substantially curtailed.

To broaden its base, Vollbrecht is pushing Aerojet into new kinds of business. Subsidiary managers are under standing orders, in fact, to determine how their companies can survive without any of the business they already have. "I suspect we spend more time on that than anything else," says Vollbrecht. . . .

Looking ahead. Aerojet has made six acquisitions since Vollbrecht's arrival, the largest of which he engineered himself. But most of the acquisitions were discovered by operating managers, who negotiated the deals themselves. . . .

Some aerospace executives outside Aerojet think the company may indeed have found its proper path. "They sagged while looking for the right leadership," says one competitor. "My feeling is they have it now and that morale is on the upswing."

The improved morale, Vollbrecht says, derives from a feeling of trust he thinks he has built between headquarters and operating managers. "Whenever there is doubt over granting freedom or tightening the reins," he says, "we err on the side of freedom."[3]

We can summarize the top management style and strategy at Aerojet as follows:

1 An aggressive performance and growth orientation.

2 Individual rather than group decision-making.

3 Strong planning orientation and a strong emphasis on administrative flexibility. Aversion to bureaucratization.

4 Decentralization of growth-related and operating decisions combined with fair but ruthless performance appraisal of operating executives and product lines.

5 Diversification of product lines to reduce the risks of being in a highly politically sensitive industry.

Notice, too, that the management style is not just a matter of Vollbrecht's personality. The style makes sense given the environmental and demographic factors of Aerojet—a large company that had passed through the trauma of seeing its size cut by two-thirds; a highly unstable, politically determined size of the market; and a dynamic, competitive, differentiated, innovative industry with a highly sophisticated technology. Notice, too, the pervasive influence of the style of top management on the structure and functioning of the company.

Dimensions of Top Management Style

We can think of top management style as having several dimensions or elements. The work of Burns and Stalker suggests that the degree of flexibility is one dimension.[4] In other words, management ideology and operating style may be characterized by rigidity (mechanistic style) or flexibility (organic style). Likert's work indicates that another dimension may be the degree to which decision-making is participative, ranging from highly individualistic to highly participative and group oriented.[5] His work as well as that of McGregor and Cyert and March suggests that another dimension may be the degree to which the management style is coercive.[6] Lindblom has contrasted what he calls an analytical, rational-comprehensive, planning-oriented mode of decision-making with a seat-of-the-pants-judgments oriented mode.[7] Thus, another dimension of management style is how technocratic, long-term oriented, and optimal-efficiency oriented management is. Mintzberg, besides identifying the planning dimension, has identified two other modes of decision-making: the entrepreneurial, risk-taking mode and the cautious, conservative mode.[8] Thus, whether decision-making is risk aversive or risk taking, stability oriented or growth oriented, is another dimension. Figure 11–1 shows the different dimensions of management style. Note that the risk-taking and the optimization dimensions are more

FIGURE 11–1

Dimensions of Top Management Style

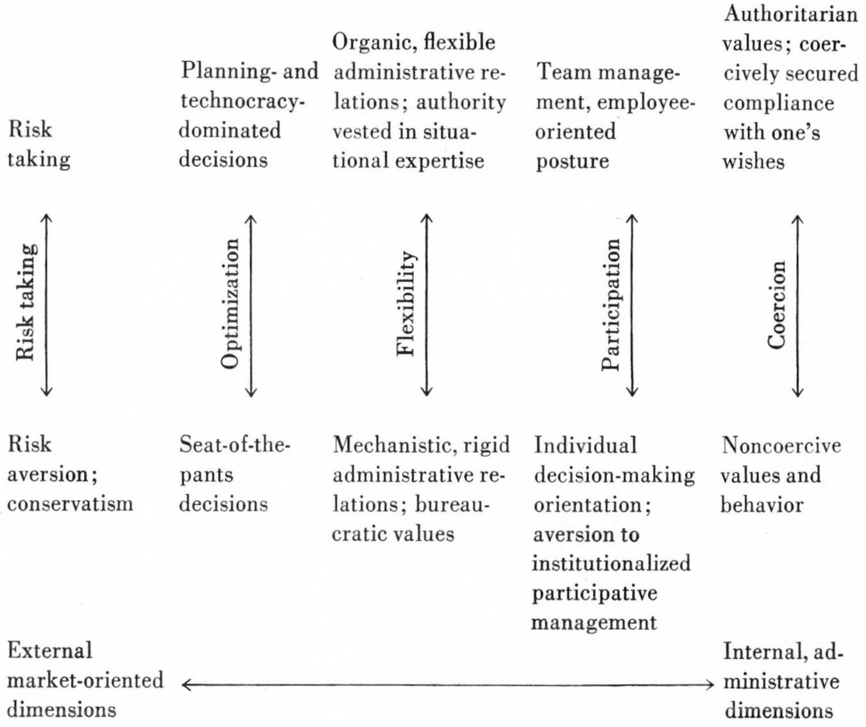

Risk taking	Planning- and technocracy-dominated decisions	Organic, flexible administrative relations; authority vested in situational expertise	Team management, employee-oriented posture	Authoritarian values; coercively secured compliance with one's wishes
↑ Risk taking ↓	↑ Optimization ↓	↑ Flexibility ↓	↑ Participation ↓	↑ Coercion ↓
Risk aversion; conservatism	Seat-of-the-pants decisions	Mechanistic, rigid administrative relations; bureaucratic values	Individual decision-making orientation; aversion to institutionalized participative management	Noncoercive values and behavior

External market-oriented dimensions ←——————————————→ Internal, administrative dimensions

externally oriented behavioral dimensions of style than the other three; flexibility, participation and coercion are more internally directed, administrative dimensions of management style. The profile of an organization's top management on these dimensions constitutes its style and a first approximation to the organization's strategy for growth and survival.

In this chapter, first we discuss in some depth each of these dimensions of management style, and then we take a look at some combinations of these dimensions.

Stop

DETERMINANTS OF STYLE DIMENSIONS

Risk Taking

Some individuals are risk takers and some are risk averters; some are cautious and some are daring; some believe in slow adaptation and some in constant change. Similarly, some organizations—which after all are assemblages of individuals—demonstrate a risk-taking, enterpreneurial, innovation-centered orientation, and some others demonstrate a cautiously adaptive, conservative orientation. While both accept change, the former's tolerance for it is much greater than the latter's. One believes in quantum changes; the other in incremental changes.

The differences between the two modes are anchored in different ideologies. The ideology of the conservative management emphasizes stability, evolutionary rather than revolutionary change, a view that the status quo is good unless proven otherwise. Why rock the boat, the conservative asks. In this troubled world change often produces unforeseen and undesirable consequences, he asserts; we can see only so far ahead, so let us take care of our todays and the tomorrows will take care of themselves. Rather opposite are the assumptions of the risk-taking manager. No risk no gain, says he. You cannot grow, he feels, unless you seek out opportunities—opportunities do not come on a platter. Besides, what fun is life if you don't change and innovate. If everybody loved the status quo, we would still be back in the Stone Age, he is liable to say.

Here is a description of Saint Gobain, the great French glass and chemical company, that illustrates well the conservative mode:

> The most trenchant description of La Compagnie de Saint Gobain came from its chairman some years ago during an intramural debate over the architecture of a prospective headquarters building. An adviser had been pressing Baron Hély d'Oissel, then head of the company, to make the design modern and exciting. Abandon the plans for a traditional stone facade, he was urged; instead combine glass and aluminum to express a spirit of youthful elan. The appeal fell on deaf ears. "Saint Gobain," said the chairman, as though intoning a corporate litany, "is an old lady."
>
> Such a characterization may seem ill suited to a great international enterprise, the world's third-largest manufacturer of glass, and Europe's biggest . . . . Yet Saint Gobain is currently wrestling with the universal corporate problem of change; only in its case the problem has been enormously—and fascinatingly—complicated by three centuries of tradition, obligation, and success. Consider the magnitude of some of the challenges now facing the enterprise.
>
> Here is a company run by sexagenarians on the verge of retirement, with no second echelon trained to take over.
>
> Here is a company steeped in the cartel's tradition of fixing prices and allocating quantities—used to distributing glass rather than selling it—now coming into a market where salesmen will hold the keys to success.
>
> Here is a company accustomed to the glacial movement of glass technology suddenly confronted by a radical British development in the manufacture of plate, long the queen of Saint Gobain's line; this is bound to bring new, powerful competition flooding in upon it.
>
> The generally low estate of glass technology, prevalent throughout the

industry on both sides of the Atlantic, gave rise to precious little in the way of invention—that is, until January, 1959, when Pilkington unveiled its revolutionary float-glass process.

The second great area of change confronting Saint Gobain is in the merchandising of glass. Here the forces at work are again new approaches and new competition, and they are putting the company under heavy pressure both at home and in world markets . . . .

"The company has never emphasized sales; production has always been king," declared a top executive.

"The salesmen are just production people who've been thrown out of the plants for blowing the fuses. The sales service manager at all our plate plants is called *le chef de magasin,* the head of the warehouse! The production manager is really in charge of sales: it's he who decides how much glass the customer is going to get and when, or if he's to get any at all . . . . I know an American plant that changed its product six times in one hour, or once every ten minutes. But at Saint Gobain changes take weeks or months. Changes are too much trouble for the production manager. We haven't been selling glass, we've been distributing it."

The days are also past for Saint Gobain's self-delusion that it has enough managerial manpower. For many years it had an almost suicidal policy of not hiring anybody. The result is that the company is now confronted with a "lost generation" of management. To be sure, there are a number of extremely able men in the organization . . . . But no mere list of able executives can disguise gaping holes in the corporate leadership. Besides, all the top people will reach the retirement age of sixty-five within five years' time, yet there is no second echelon of experienced men ready to take their places. Instead, the next group is composed of executives in their early forties, who have not been prepared for the succession. . . .

Aggravating the problem is a somnolent board of directors. . . . "Some directors are in their eighties, and one who always comes to important meetings can't even stay awake. I turned to address myself to him, and there he was, fast asleep. Yet the chairman won't do a thing without the board. He has to carry them with him to get things done."

Saint Gobain is also hamstrung by another tradition, that of not allowing foreigners a place in the top management in Paris. . . .

. . . changes at Saint Gobain are likely to be neither rapid nor revolutionary: the company will simply evolve. It took two hundred and seventy-one years to get rid of the *direction collegiale,* the executive council of directors, which very nearly ruined the company by trying to run it as if a board of directors could handle day-to-day management problems.

So, Saint Gobain will remain something of "an old lady." . . . There will be evolution instead of revolution because, to a degree incomprehensible to Americans, Saint Gobain must move through a veritable jungle of blood ties and corporate ties while carrying the dead weight of dozens of intracompany empires and three centuries of tradition.[9]

Notice the faith in evolutionary change, the reliance on true and tried products, the weight of traditions and customs. What situational factors account for this conservatism? Age and size are certainly factors. So is the recruitment of top management from the French aristocracy. So is the hitherto oligopolistic and noninnovative character of the glass industry. Contrast the description of Saint Gobain with that of the highly entrepreneurial Litton Industries:

> Litton is . . . a legend in its own land, and the reasons for its glamor are simple. One is plain money. According to President Roy Ash, there are shareholders in Litton who have seen $3 of investment grow to $100 in a decade . . . fiscal year 1967 sales were some 56 times those of 1957, with profits up by 39 times after tax. . . .
>
> "We sub-define technologies and go for frontier technologies more than static ones," says Ash. "For instance, Litton is not doing anything about chemistry. Where technical innovation can be expected to continue at a rapid rate, we're interested. If you can't innovate, we're not interested. . . . We got started in power tubes for radar" (this was in 1953) "where the key is chemistry and metallurgy, but the end-output is measured in electronics—a technology on which Litton rather obviously has a heavy emphasis."
>
> "The basic theme," says Ash, "is converting the technical developments of the day into commercial products". . . .
>
> "We founded Litton," says Ash, "on the theory that the end is to match technological innovation with equal skills by management, marketing and finance. An engineer thinks in one-onlies, never thinks in aggregates. The marketing man cannot afford this. The management has to integrate all the factors." There are certain basic rules to this billion-dollar game. First, since "almost all new products have their first application in military uses, we always want at least 25% of our business in defence and space" (and currently get approximately a third). Second, Litton is wholly uninterested in situations like competing with IBM in large-scale data-processing— "you don't run a race you are destined to lose"; however, this has not prevented Litton from entering races, against the aerospace giants in inertial navigation, NCR is cash registers or IBM in electric typewriters, where it saw a chance of winning from far behind. Third "we beg, borrow or steal technology from those who have it, or we pick a narrow range."
>
> The fourth rule is that "in the big fields we are talking about resources. Take inertial navigation. On this one product, R & D came to $300-million." The fifth key ("one critical leg of our philosophy") is that "typically all new product lines start with a lab oriented fellow. He may well succeed, but is just beginning. It takes more money to finance success than failure. So many people are not prepared to realize this." . . . although "we do allow mistakes—you have to if you want to run a company this way," Litton is no place for the manager who can't succeed in business and doesn't really try.

. . . The main lesson of Litton actually has rather little to do with the technological cornucopia aspect of its legend. Many companies command wide spreads of technology. But how many shop relentlessly for corporate buys (and make doubly sure they are sound ones) as a deliberate means of growth in new or existing markets; apply extremely strict financial disciplines as a matter of course to all divisions, both as a means of control and of planning expansion; accept and practice the idea that a large group's central organization should be minimal, concerned almost exclusively with both control and direction; grasp the fact that the point of technology is to produce products for the widest possible markets and organize; and recognize that it is the job of the manager, not the technologist, to extract the best results in commercial terms from innovation?[10]

Note the reliance on research and development, aggressive expansion, diversification, risk taking, far out ventures, aversion to overstaffing, and tight control. As in the case of Saint Gobain, so in the case of Litton, situational factors play a part: a youthful, American management that started out in an industry with a very dynamic and also very sophisticated technology.

In the author's Canadian study, several scales were utilized to measure the firm's risk-taking orientation.[11] A low total score indicated an essentially adaptive and conservative management orientation toward its task environment, while a high score indicated an essentially entrepreneurial, growth- and innovation-minded, competitive, risk-taking external orientation (see Figure 11–2). In Chapter 9 we noted that a turbulent environment, marked by growth, fluctuation, change, and uncertainty, was strongly correlated with risk taking, while a stable environment was strongly correlated with

FIGURE 11–2
Risk Taking Orientation of Top Management in the Author's Canadian Study

HIGH RISK-TAKING ORIENTATION	CONSERVATIVE, RISK-AVOIDANCE ORIENTATION
Entrepreneurial, risk-taking, growth-oriented decision-making	Cautious, pragmatic, stability-oriented decision-making
Emphasis on research and development, technological leadership, innovations	Emphasis on the marketing of true and tried products and avoidance of R and D
Proclivity to high risk, high return investments	Proclivity to low risk, average return investments
External financing of investments	Internal financing of investments
Competitive, "undo-the-rivals" philosophy	Philosophy of cooperative coexistence with rivals

risk aversion and conservatism. In Chapter 8 we noted that old organizations tend to have substantially more conservative managements than young ones.

Optimization

Two great adversary orientations have been the seat-of-the-pants, "satisficing" mode and the technocratic, planning, "optimizing" mode.* The former emphasizes experience, the application of rules of thumb, the here and now, common sense, the consensus of "experts," intuitive judgment, and a bird-in-the-hand-is-worth-two-in-the-bush philosophy. The planning mode emphasizes formal expertise, the long-term future, careful investigation of problem areas and opportunities, and careful consideration of the costs and benefits of various alternatives to enable the organization to make "optimal" choices. The ideological roots of the seat-of-the-pants mode lie in the aversion to "new fangled" techniques and technocrats. Most of the practitioners of this mode have succeeded by relying on their common sense, intuition, and experience. So why should they get dependent on the "pointy-headed" types that speak an incomprehensible technical jargon and cost a fortune to maintain? The ideology of the planners is radically different. The planner distrusts common sense much as the scientist disdains it. Common sense tells us that the earth is flat and the moon is larger than the stars. It is science that corrects the delusions of common perception. Also, experience is useful, but if you rely solely on it you would learn things after years that you learn in months through proper, scientific training. The planner believes fervently in thinking ahead, anticipating problems, and systematically investigating problems and opportunities, because, he will argue, that is the only way to navigate the organization safely through the highly complex currents of the environment and optimally achieve the organization's objectives.

To the planner management is a science, and it is imperative that in reaching a solution all the assumptions be made explicit, all the major alternatives be considered consciously, and as far as possible the demonstrably *optimal solution* be picked. To the seat-of-the-pants "satisficer," scientific analysis may be acceptable in dealing with relatively trivial problems like how to manage the inventory and how to set up the assembly line, but impossible and irrelevant in making complex policy decisions. In making

* "Satisficing" is a term used widely by the Carnegie theorists (Ch. 5). It means the tendency to pick the first available alternative that meets with one's often vaguely thought-out criteria for picking a solution. "Optimization," in contrast, is the tendency to specify carefully the criteria that should govern choice and to find through systematic search the *best* solution rather than merely an acceptable one.

such decisions, he feels, it usually is impossible to demonstrate that the choice or decision one makes is optimal to the goals of the organization. Rather, the realistic test is whether "experts" agree, for whatever reasons, that the decision is a good one. It is the nod of the wise that is the clincher. Charles Lindblom has called the satisficing mode the method of successive limited comparisons or "muddling through." He has called the planning mode the rational-comprehensive method.[12]

Robert McNamara, the former president of Ford Motor Company and the Secretary of Defense under Presidents Kennedy and Johnson, transformed intuitive seat-of-the-pants decision-making at the Department of Defense (D.O.D.) into highly planning- and optimization-oriented decision-making. Here is an account of what he did that illustrates beautifully the optimization orientation in action:

> Prior to his (Secretary McNamara's) regime the Army, Navy, and Air Force budgeted rather independently, coordinating hardly at all with each other's programs. What McNamara instituted was planning by missions. Key missions were identified, for example, a nuclear retaliation mission, a "hotspot response" mission requiring high-capacity airlift of police-type forces, and others. Strategic elements and their supporting expenditures were assembled into a complete five-year plan by what have been popularly termed "mission program packages." A mission package plan thus often had elements from the Army, the Navy, the Air Force, and several supporting staff groups such as development and procurement.
>
> The Secretary's staff determined the needs of each of the several missions. These studies resulted in a number of highly significant moves. In mid-1961, the 1962 plan as originally submitted was hurriedly rebudgeted. Investigation had clearly revealed inadequate air- and sea-lift forces, badly in need of supplement. Nuclear retaliation capabilities were modified with greater dependence on stationary missiles, eliminating B-70s and Minutemen on railroad cars, and the Army received substantially more money for "limited" warfare. McNamara also challenged the tendency toward unilateral service plans, which had imbalances in the allocated resources for a given mission, rather than unified D.O.D. plans.
>
> In short, introduction of the missions concept in the D.O.D. led quickly to many important changes—billion-dollar changes, as measured by their impact on various parts of the budget.
>
> The Pentagon was allotting insufficient time for strategy studies—studies of what each area of the military was trying to accomplish. At budget time each year, there was a distinct tendency for the service head to allot enormous sums for continuation of present commitments, without proper analysis of the country's changing needs. His plans then were assembled in a relatively short period of time in order to meet budget deadlines, thus compounding any difficulties.
>
> To correct this situation, McNamara and Charles J. Hitch, his Assistant

Secretary-Comptroller, created the position of Deputy Assistant Secretary for Programming. This executive's function is the institution and maintenance of a "running" five-year program budget which will completely reflect all strategic decisions and all projected expenditures. This program budget may be updated monthly through a managerial system, created by Hitch, which allows proposals for program changes to pass through a prescribed set of review and approval steps and be inserted into the "running" five-year plan . . . .

Within three weeks after Robert McNamara assumed his D.O.D. duties, he produced what are popularly called his "seventy-six trombones." These were a long list of questions, often beginning with *why*. Why are you doing this? Why can it not be done in a more effective way? Why are the boundaries of certain programs set as they now are? He assigned responsibility for each question and asked for answers within three weeks. These were important fundamental questions, and from their answers he concluded that changes were urgently needed. For instance:

There was inadequate use of cost-benefit analysis as a basis for measurement of weapons systems alternatives. Service leadership did not really know the total cost of supporting a B-70. The Polaris submarine, in fact, proved far cheaper to maintain for the same unit of retaliation effectiveness. Prior to this point, the Pentagon had conducted few, if any, studies for cost comparison of alternatives . . . .

What impact have these changes had on D.O.D. operations? Study of strategic questions followed by the asking of new ones has kept Department people thinking and responding with adequate programs. Part of the McNamara technique is to write out questions and to insist on written answers. He maintains on his desk a black looseleaf notebook containing an annual list of over 100 questions on basic issues. Each February the questions identified by him and other line or staff executives are assigned to various advisers. The answers are due by the end of the summer, at which time they become the basis for changes in the five-year program budget.

Many of the questions require complex study. Consequently, McNamara assigns them to a unique study group, Dr. Enthoven's Systems Analysis Department. Dr. Enthoven has characterized the workings of the Pentagon technique as follows:

"It can best be described as a continuing dialogue between the policymaker and the systems analyst, in which the policymaker (McNamara) asks for alternative solutions to his problems, while the analyst attempts to clarify the conceptual framework in which the decisions must be made, to define alternative possible objectives and criteria, and to explore in as clear as possible (and quantitatively) the cost and effectiveness of alternative courses of action . . . ."

In numerous cases, the financial implications of program decisions were also poorly determined. For instance, the Chiefs of Staff authorized development of major weapons systems and yet had not projected the total cost of development beyond a year. Further, they had not predetermined how much it would cost to operate these weapons over an extended period of time. Too frequently a poorly conceived project consumed gigantic expenditures. Because of circumstances like these, the Dyna-Soar and Skybolt projects were canceled.

Under McNamara, the D.O.D. set up a formalized system of cost-benefit analysis by groups not allied with any branch of the military but positioned organizationally near the Secretary of Defense. This step has helped ensure that failures like Dyna-Soar and Skybolt will not happen again. . . .

As is well known, PERT was developed by the combined forces of the Navy Special Projects Office, Lockheed, and Booz, Allen and Hamilton. The application for which it was designed was the planning and control of what is familiarly known as the Polaris Project in 1958. Through the use of PERT, the efforts of many hundreds of contractors and many thousands of subcontractors were coordinated so effectively that the missile was operational two years ahead of the original schedule. Since then the transfer to business has been so complete that the application of the majority of PERT-like systems is now in nongovernmental work. . . .

When McNamara assumed command of the D.O.D., he felt that there was an excessive number of committee meetings and reports which tended to delay decisions on program changes. Consequently, a specially designed strategy decision room was created under the management of the Office of Programming, which is also in charge of maintaining the running five-year plan . . . .

The military and NASA have created complex decision centers using advanced electronic display equipment, but these facilities are designed for the deployment of *already allocated* resources. Decision environment rooms for resolving strategy questions have substantially different requirements. For instance, the information displayed is usually required on an *ad hoc* basis for single, not repeated, use in determining the best allocation of *new* resources.[13]

Smalter and Ruggles summarize the lessons of the planning orientation at the D.O.D. for top management of all organizations committed to growth and efficiency:

1. Top management's primary job in any enterprise is the allocation of limited resources—for selected mission purposes, in proper dimensions of time—for the furtherance of specified objectives.

2. Management should integrate one-year budgeting with long-range planning in a scheduled annual cycle.

3. Management should apply operations-research or systems-analysis principles of mathematical analysis to complex strategy questions.

4. Systematic program analysis and planning can best be accomplished through use of logical, sequenced steps of approach.

5. Logic or task-sequence network diagrams should be used in planning, implementing, and monitoring complex projects.

HIGH OPTIMIZATION ORIENTATION	←————————→	HIGH "SATISFICING," LOW OPTIMIZATION ORIENTATION

A strong planning orientation, systematic search for opportunities, systematic assessment of alternatives, much emphasis on long-term profit maximization and efficient achievement of organizational objectives

Strategic importance of forecasting future sales, technology, etc. and of operations research, market research, and long-term planning of goals and investments

Great reliance on specialized, technically trained line and staff personnel

Heavy reliance on formal management training programs

Little strategic importance of long-term planning, forecasting, market research, operations research, etc.

Great reliance on personnel with experience and common sense in decision-making

Heavy reliance on apprenticeship, "learning by hard knocks"

6. Decision-making centers are useful devices for expediting, review or approval of programs in complex organizations.[14]

In the author's Canadian study, several scales were utilized to derive a measure of the extent to which the management was optimization oriented. Figure 11–3 shows what a high score on optimization meant and what a low score on optimization indicated.

The data indicated that the optimization mode was, independently and statistically, significantly associated with firms in restrictive and technologically complex environments (see Propositions 6 and 7 of Chapter 9). Conversely, the seat-of-the-pants mode was associated with firms in technologically unsophisticated and nonrestrictive environments. The data also indicated an independent positive association between the degree of optimization orientation and research and development activity in the firm's industry.

The findings, of course, make sense. If the environment is technologically complex, as in the aerospace or pharmaceutical industries, the organization must hire technically trained personnel to survive. If the industry is R and D oriented, as the electronics, drug, or aerospace industries are, costs of innovation are high, and there is a considerable time lag between a discovery and its commercial exploitation. The organization must hire scientists and technicians to do research and/or to understand the latest scientific developments or innovations in the industry, and also to think ahead to the future.

If the environment is highly restrictive because there are many economic, legal, or social constraints, the inevitable implication is that the organization must get the help of technically trained personnel like lawyers, accountants, economists, and statisticians to make sure that the constraints are not violated. For example, in oligopolistic industries in the United States such as the automobile and oil industries, firms employ large staffs of lawyers to make sure that their acquisitions or mergers do not violate the antitrust laws. In regulated industries such as public utilities (electricity, telephone, rail transportation), careful planning and careful selection of investments is absolutely necessary. Since the rates firms can charge are normally regulated by the government, very close attention must be paid to cost control and the level of operations. What the data suggest is that policy issues that elicit a seat-of-the-pants approach in environments not especially rich in sophisticated constraints and contingencies will tend to elicit a planning approach in environments rich in *sophisticated,* highly complex contingencies and constraints.

Flexibility and Situational Expertise

In Chapter 6 we reviewed two styles of management, the organic and the mechanistic. The organic style is associated with flexibility and authority derived from situational expertise. The mechanistic style is associated with bureaucratic values and rigidity. Here is an account of a mechanistically managed rayon plant, employing a fairly sophisticated but stable technology:

> The system of management within the factory was quite explicitly devised to keep production and production conditions stable. With this as the underlying principle, the system defined what information or instructions arrived at any one position in the hierarchy, what information or instructions might leave it, and their destination. Such definition was a matter of fixed, clear, and precise routine. Similarly, each working position in the hierarchy had its authority, information, and technical competence specified once for all. Moreover, since each position below the General Manager's in the hierarchy was specialized in all three features of authority, technique, and information, and nobody was empowered to act outside defined limits, all departures from stable conditions were swiftly reported upwards, and, so far as the works were concerned, the General Manager existed as the fountainhead of all information about commercial and other conditions affecting the affairs of the factory (as against technique). Such changes as did occur, therefore, were inaugurated at the top. There was, accordingly, a fairly stringent authoritarian character about the conduct of superiors to their

subordinates, an authoritarianism which was accepted as reasonable, and did not in the least interfere with sociable friendliness on an equal footing on the many occasions on which members of the staff met each other outside work in the small town in which the works was located. It was perfectly possible, that is, for members of the firm to accept instruction and command as appropriate to work relationships, but to isolate these relationships from what went on outside.[15]

Contrast the foregoing account of a firm in an industry with a relatively stable technology with this account of one in an industry (the electronics industry) that was experiencing a great deal of technological change:

> Beyond this point, in the electronics industry proper, one begins to meet concerns in which organization is thought of primarily in terms of the communication system; there is often a deliberate attempt to avoid specifying individual tasks, and to forbid any dependence on the management hierarchy as a structure of defined functions and authority. The head of one concern, at the beginning of the first interview, attacked the idea of the organization chart as inapplicable in his concern and as a dangerous method of thinking about the working of industrial management. The first requirement of a management, according to him, was that it should make the fullest use of the capacities of its members; any individual's job should be as little defined as possible, so that it will "shape itself" to his special abilities and initiative.
>
> In this concern insistence on the least possible specification for managerial positions was much more in evidence than any devices for ensuring adequate interaction within the system. This did occur, but as a consequence of a set of conditions rather than of prescription by top management. Written communication inside the factory was actively discouraged. Most important of all, however, was the need of each individual manager for interaction with others, in order to get his own tasks and functions defined, in the absence of specification from above. When the position of product engineer was created, for example, the first incumbents said they had to "find out" what they had to do, and what authority and resources they could command to do it.
>
> In fact, this process of "finding out" about one's job proved to be unending. Their roles were continually defined and redefined in connection with specific tasks and as members of specific co-operative groups. This happened through a perpetual sequence of encounters with laboratory chiefs, with design engineers who had worked on the equipment the product engineers were responsible for getting made, with draughtsmen, with the works manager, with the foremen in charge of the production shops they had to use, with rate-fixers, buyers, and operatives. In every single case they, whose only commission was "to see the job through," had to determine their part and that of the others through complex, though often brief, negotiations in which the relevant information and technical knowledge

possessed by them would have to be declared, and that possessed by others ascertained.

The disruptive effects of this preoccupation were countered by a general awareness of the common purpose of the concern's attitudes. While this awareness was sporadic and partial for many members of the firm, it was an essential factor in, for example, the ability of the "product engineers" to perform their tasks, dependent as they were on the co-operation of persons and groups who carried on the basic interpretative processes of the concern. Indeed, discussion of the common purposes of the organization featured largely in the conversation of cabals and extra-mural groups existing among managers.[16]

In the author's Canadian study, several scales were utilized to derive a measure of how organic the top management's operating mode was. The higher the score on this measure the more it was oriented to an organic style; the lower the score, the more the top management was oriented to a mechanistic style (see Figure 11–4). It should be emphasized that an organic *top* management style does not preclude a high degree of bureaucratization lower down in the organization; nor does a mechanistic top management style imply that no organic segments will be found at lower levels. Organizations, particularly sizable organizations, often exhibit a great deal of variation in styles of management in their different parts.[17]

FIGURE 11–4
Organic and Mechanistic Top Management Styles in the Author's Canadian Study

ORGANIC TOP MANAGEMENT STYLE ⟵⟶	MECHANISTIC TOP MANAGEMENT STYLE
Open channels of communication; free flow of information throughout the organization	Highly structured channels of communication and highly restricted flow of information
Managers' operating styles allowed to vary freely	Uniform managerial style insisted upon
Authority for making decisions rooted in situational expertise	Authority for making decisions rooted in formal line managers
Free adaptation by the organization to changing circumstances	Insistence on holding fast to true and tried management principles despite changes in business conditions
Emphasis on getting things done rather than on following formally laid out procedures	Personnel to follow formally laid down procedures
Loose, informal control; emphasis on norm of cooperation	Tight control of operations through sophisticated control systems
On-job behavior permitted to be shaped by the requirements of the situation and personality of the individual doing the job	On-job behavior to conform to job descriptions

There was some, but not very strong, support for the observation of Burns and Stalker that changing market and technological conditions tend to breed the organic style.[18] A high rate of innovation of new products and processes in the firm's industry was modestly associated with the use of the organic mode. Conversely, the mechanistic mode was modestly associated with a low rate of innovation.

The relationship of the organic mode to various features of the environment was found to be fairly strong for the firms in the top half in terms of performance. These were the firms that were relatively high performers not only in terms of profits but in terms of stability of profits and the growth rate of sales or revenues. Two particularly interesting associations are worth noting. For high performers, the intensity and variety of competitive pressures on the firm were associated fairly strongly with the use of the organic mode. Conversely, the lower the competitive pressure the more the firm tended to be managed mechanistically. For the low performers the association between the two was negligible. Similarly, the more heterogeneous the firm's environment, the more the high performance firm tended to be managed organically, and, conversely, the more homogeneous the environment the more mechanistic it tended to be. Here, too, the association for the lower performers was negligible and in fact was in the opposite direction. The data suggest that where pressures on the top management are intense, diverse, and constantly changing, flexibility *ought* to be an important element of management style.

We propose that:

The more intense, diverse, and shifting the pressures on the organization's top management,
>   *the greater is the need for flexibility and an organic top management style.*

Coercion

"Power tends to corrupt and absolute power corrupts absolutely," wrote Lord Acton. There is a possible Nero in the gentlest human creature that walks, someone else once said. But if power can corrupt, to many its exercise is quite delightful. It is better, says a Spanish proverb, to be the head of a mouse than the tail of a lion. Besides, as a Frenchman, Roger de Bussy-Rabutin said, God is usually on the side of the big battalions.

Coercion is an undeniable fact of organizational life; to many political scientists it is the central fact of organizational life. The use of the coercive mode is as old as communal living by man. It is an aggressive, arbitrary, dominance-seeking mode. Its psychological roots are probably in the need for power over others and in the authoritarian personality. Its ideological base is the rationale that some men are somehow superior to others and therefore must have power over the latter for their own good. The divine right of kings is one manifestation of this ideology. Another is the faith in the efficacy of force as a means of solving problems. As many a Marxist has argued, the power to make a revolution grows out of the barrel of a gun.

In contemporary organizations, the authoritarian ideology has generally waned partly because of the democratic temper of the times and partly because people in modern societies have a wide choice as far as membership in organizations is concerned. Authoritarianism frustrates the individual's need for autonomy, and since this need becomes particularly active in a libertarian culture, there are severe limits on the extent to which authoritarianism can be practiced before members of an organization leave it en masse. One of the last bastions of authoritarianism is the school classroom, but even here, what with parent-teacher associations, student ratings, and the prohibition of corporal punishment, it can no longer flourish in its pristine purity. Here is a description of the autocratic new manager of the industrial engineering department of a beer producer:

> Reeves held a department meeting in which he stated his work rules and philosophy: "Only Seniors are to report to me. All reports that leave this department will be under my name. All contacts with upper management are to be made through me. Until the job is done, you are expected to work without overtime compensation. Gentlemen, the I.E. department is the most important department in this firm. We must work as a team, and, above all, maintain good public relations. . . ."
>
> Then, in rapid-fire order, Reeves discharged a couple of men and hired Bill Francis, Mall Cobb, Ralph Ryan, Ned Sutton, and Bob Latt. In doing so, Reeves changed the whole department. Ray was shifted from John to Carl. Ray was angry because he had quit his job at ConCan to get out of packaging, and now he was being put back into it. John was angry because Reeves had taken his experienced man away and given him a Junior. The hiring of Latt upset John and Carl because they thought that Bob was too young to hold a Senior's position. John expressed the belief that the role of the Senior was being downgraded . . . .
>
> A few weeks later, Reeves announced to the department that too much time was being wasted and that from then on there would be no more coffee breaks because the men had abused this privilege. He reasoned that he and Saunders didn't take breaks, and the men themselves shouldn't either.[19]

In authoritarian organizations, decisions are made on the basis much more of might than of right. Consequently, in organizations in which such a mode is much in evidence, there is a continuous and intense struggle for power. Here is a story of one such struggle at the highest levels of the U.S. government:

Whiplashed by the embargo and leaping oil prices, President Nixon last December set up what became the Federal Energy Administration to centralize U.S. energy policymaking. The centralization lasted little longer than the crisis. Almost as soon as last winter's gasoline lines disappeared, the question of who should coordinate energy policy began to breed baroque rivalries—and now, with the Ford Administration in control, three potent Washington figures are scrapping for leadership. They are:

Interior Secretary Rogers C. B. Morton. A longtime Republican Party professional, Morton was overshadowed during the Nixon presidency, but has reemerged as a power under Ford. Before FEA was created, energy problems tended to gravitate toward Interior.

Treasury Secretary William Simon. The unchallenged energy czar when he headed FEA through its first five months, Simon supposedly relinquished the job when he moved to Treasury. But he thinks energy problems are primarily economic and that he should play a major role in both areas.

FEA Administrator John Sawhill. Once Simon's protege, Sawhill is energy chief in name but has been unable to establish his pre-eminence in fact. One reason: alone among the three, he lacks Cabinet rank. He inherited an agency exhausted by Simon's punishing pace and bereft of the public attention it commanded during the oil shortage. Nonetheless, he has tried to act, in the words of one energy official, "like the crisis is still on and he is Bill Simon."

Much more is at stake in the battle than personal power. With international oil prices likely to stay high for a long time, the U.S., as Ford has noted, must accelerate Project Independence to develop alternate sources of energy—but the effort needs an undisputed leader. A more pressing question—how long to maintain price controls on domestically produced oil—is also hanging fire. Morton and Simon last week advocated a quick start on phasing out the controls. Sawhill, who administers the controls, insists that rapid decontrol would be inflationary.

Meanwhile, the brew bubbles. Morton's Interior Department has griped that Sawhill's FEA is duplicating Interior's contingency planning to deal with a possible coal strike this fall. Sawhill has complained to Presidential Aide Kenneth Rush that Simon was virtually building a parallel operation to FEA, mostly by hiring ex-FEA staffers. When Rush suggested to Simon that this was not quite proper, Simon blew up and said that only White House Chief of Staff Alexander Haig could call him off, which Haig did not do. In another incident, Simon's and Sawhill's staffs got into a spirited argument over which of the men should sign a letter about natural-gas policy to be sent to the Senate Commerce Committee. They compromised by agreeing that both should sign—and then got into another brouhaha over whether Simon should sign as Secretary of the Treasury or chairman of the energy committee, which would have lent weight to that body. Sawhill wanted Simon to sign as Treasury Secretary, and he got his way.

Some odd alliances have been struck. Simon and Budget Boss Roy Ash have been vying for the loudest voice in overall economic policy, but they have occasionally joined forces to attack Sawhill. Says one Administration official: "When Sawhill criticized Mobil's take-over of Marcor, they (Simon and Ash) crawled all over him." Sawhill had rather mildly observed that he had justified high oil-company profits to the public as necessary to encourage more petroleum exploration and production, and that Mobil had complicated his job by using some of its profits to bid for control of Marcor, a giant retailer.

Morton and Sawhill, despite their differences over decontrol of oil prices, have formed an entente of sorts, apparently in order to neutralize Simon. Both Morton and Sawhill would like to see the creation of a Department of Energy and Natural Resources, which would replace both Interior and the FEA and also take over certain functions of the Commerce Department and the Atomic Energy Commission. The proposal is said to have some chance of congressional approval next year. At this point Morton appears most likely to become the nation's No. 1 energy figure, whether or not such a department is approved, but as head of it he would be more firmly entrenched: Sawhill would get the FEA apparatus made permanent as part of the new structure. But Washingtonologists warn that nothing is predictable in the shadowy corridors of energy power.[20]

A coercive value system legitimizes the *frequent* resort to force, not only by rivals and by superiors, but by subordinates in their conflicts with their superiors. Joint problem solving and persuasion tend to be utilized less frequently than bargaining, political gamesmanship, and the naked exercise of power in resolving conflict between factions.

In the Canadian study, coercive orientation was measured by aggregating the ratings on several scales. One scale measured the use of threats by management in accomplishing organizational changes. Another measured the extent to which senior managers were observed to resort to "forcing" or seeking dominance in attempting to resolve their disagreements. A third scale measured the extent to which the management failed to explain to those affected why organizational changes were being made. A fourth scale measured the extent to which outside experts were asked to investigate problems and propose changes. Asking in outsiders is often a symptom of grave internal conflict. Also, it can be a powerful weapon in the hands of the decision maker. He can claim neutrality and yet selectively and ruthlessly implement the recommendations of the outside experts. For the organization

HIGHLY
COERCIVE ⟵————————————⟶ NONCOERCIVE
ORIENTATION   ORIENTATION

Organizational changes instituted without explanations, and issuing of threats to subordinates for noncompliance	Explanation of organizational changes to those affected by them
Resolution of disagreements between senior managers on the basis of might is right	Organizational changes instituted without issuing threats
Investigation of organizational problems by outside experts	Disagreements resolved on basis other than might is right
Institution of arbitration procedures	Absence of arbitration procedures

member, having to confront unknown but powerful outsiders is usually a traumatic experience. A fifth scale was a measure of the extent to which arbitration procedures were used in settling disputes. Arbitration procedures are a symptom of the autocratic mode. Also, the resolution of conflicts is not on the basis of agreement or trade-off but on the basis of the superior authority and power of the arbitrator. Also arbitration procedures make authoritarianism more palatable by seemingly providing the relatively weak some protection from the whims of the relatively strong. See Figure 11–5 for a graphic version of the coercive orientation.

In Chapter 9 we noted that a coercive orientation increases at first and then declines (a) as environmental hostility increases and (b) as the environment becomes more restrictive (Propositions 2 and 8 of Chapter 9). The data from the author's Canadian study also indicated that a coercive orientation in top management was far commoner in a relatively stagnant environment—that is, an environment with, for example, stagnant or shrinking markets—than in an expanding environment. This may be because a stagnant environment is not rich in challenges and problems, and so motivation, involvement, creative solutions, collaboration, and the like are not perceived as key conditions of organizational survival. Instead, for daily operations obedience to superiors is perceived as necessary and sufficient for efficiency. Also, a stagnant environment makes difficult the achievement of corporate goals like high profits and growth. In other words, it is a frustrating environment and may translate into low pay levels for the organizational rank and file and feelings of insecurity and discontent within the top management. These in turn lead to deep cleavages within the organization and to the use of force to maintain coordination.

We propose that:

The more stagnant the organization's markets,
*   the more coercive is the orientation of the organization's top manage-*
*   ment.*

Participation

In Chapter 4 we reviewed two related movements in organization theory, the human relations orientation initiated by Mayo and the human resources movement initiated by Argyris and McGregor. Though these differ somewhat, their common theme is a deep concern for the individual's needs and the primacy of the group in the operations of the organization. The central idea is that it is ethical as well as efficient for the individual member of the organization to participate in the shaping of those events that affect him vitally, such as the work he does, his objectives, the way his performance is evaluated, and so on. The building up of esprit de corps in work groups through participative, employee-oriented decision-making is seen to be a highly productive exercise.

The participative mode should be distinguished from the practice of democracy. In both, the relatively powerless individuals get some say in the making of decisions that affect them or their constituents. However, the democratic mode is based on giving a say to conflicting interest groups, and the hope is that the decisions will result in the greatest good of the greatest number of people rather than that of everyone. It is also a system with formal checks and balances to minimize the abuse of the minority by the majority and of one part of the organizational system by another. In the participative mode on the other hand, the hoped for result is *consensus*. Influence over decisions is not necessarily formalized into one vote per person. Most important, the output of the system is expected to be beneficial to both the organization and the individuals comprising it. The differences between the participative mode and the democratic system are traceable to their place of origin: the participative mode took root in industrial organizations, where it was important to secure the wholehearted cooperation of employees in achieving corporate goals; the democratic system took root in political organizations such as the government, where it was important to give representation to the different geographical areas because of the diversity of their needs and cultural practices.

One ideological base of the participative, human relations mode is the notion that all individuals have an ego need. They crave to be considered important, to feel that they are worth something. If one can so arrange relationships in an organization that the individuals feel *supported* in their endeavors, it may be possible to secure their commitment to the goals of the organization. Likert's principle of supportive relationships states the requirement well:

> The leadership and other processes of the organization must be such as to ensure a maximum probability that in all interactions and all relationships with the organization each member will, in the light of his background, values, and expectations, view the experience as supportive and one which builds and maintains his sense of personal worth and importance.[21]

Another aspect of the participative mode's ideology is the notion that cooperation is better than competition, and warm, friendly relations among organizational members are more desirable than mutual hostility and suspicion. This is best achieved by power equalization, in sharp contrast to the power struggles characteristic of the coercive mode. In other words, in the participative mode, the normal power, status, and authority differences between supervisors and subordinates are deliberately muted, while in the coercive mode they are deliberately accentuated. Team-building and consensual group decision-making are a third element of the participative mode. Frank, open confrontation of issues and feelings and stress on working constructively with one another is a fourth element of the participative mode that has particularly been stressed by the human resources movement.

Here is an example of a team of postal supervisors, carrier examiners, finance personnel, and a trainer-consultant (Mr. Saxbe) attempting to learn to be a more effectively functioning group. It illustrates well the different elements of the participative mode:

WRIGLEY: Well, so far we've agreed to eliminate numbers 1, 2, and 4 as problems this group would like to work to improve. Now then, let's take a straw vote on the remaining problems. How many would like to work on number 3, *How to prevent mis-sent mail to direct firm holdouts?*
(*counts raised hands*)
One . . . two . . . three . . . and I make four.
How about *Better internal communication?*
(*counts hands*)
One . . . two. Okay, reducing absenteeism?
One . . . two.
HERNANDEZ: Hey, who didn't vote?
EVANS: Saxbe and Cline
SAXBE: The facilitator has no vote.
MCCLEARY: (*smiling*) Stand up and be counted, Mrs. Cline.

CLINE: I hesitated because I think they are all very interesting problems and I'll go along with the majority.

HERNANDEZ: Well, that settles it . . . we'll work on mis-sent mail . . . .

EVANS: (*upset*) Now wait a second! If we've been assembled to meet here four hours each week for eight weeks, I think we should tackle a really big problem like communication. Lord knows we need better communication!

LOWELL: I agree with Mr. Evans. Communication is a terribly important problem.

WRIGLEY: But, as stated, it's so vague. How do we begin to go about attacking the problem?

HERNANDEZ: It's like the weather. You can talk about it all you want but nobody's going to be able to do much about it.

SMITH: That's for sure!

FISHER (*irritated*) Let's get on with it! We're not getting anywhere.

HERNANDEZ: Majority rules. We'll work on mis-sent mail.

SAXBE: (*breaking in on group discussion*) Since our purpose here is to better understand the nature of leadership and group process methods as well as solving particular Postal Service problems, I feel I am justified in intervening at this point. Behavioral scientists agree that the majority vote, or so-called democratic process, is generally better for obtaining personal decision commitment than, say, autocratic choice of the leader . . . .

HERNANDEZ: That's what I just said . . . majority rules . . . we'll work on mis-sent . . . .

SAXBE: (*interrupting Hernandez*) But majority rule, although a reasonable expedient for the sake of time, is not always the best way . . . .

BLACKMAN: What other way is there?

SAXBE: Consensus. Although procedurally slower at first, it can often prove to be better than majority rule.

BLACKMAN: I don't see the difference.

SAXBE: Consensus is a working through of differences to ultimately arrive at a decision, whereas the democratic vote has a tendency to arbitrarily cut off all objections, reasonable or not, at a fixed point in time. This can, often, suppress further involvement or commitment by someone whose views have been overruled or denied expression.

SMITH: Good grief! You mean we have to get *everyone* to agree before we move on? We'll be as deadlocked as a hung jury!

BLACKMAN: Exactly what are the implications of consensus to group progress, Mr. Saxbe?

SAXBE: Not nearly as bad as I have apparently made it appear. Your straw vote was procedurally sound. It showed where the majority stands on the issue. My only concern is that the minority should not now be arbitrarily shut off.

FISHER: You mean we keep talking until Evans wins us over to *his* point of view?

SAXBE: Not necessarily, although that could happen. We're not severely time limited. I prefer to see consensus within the group before moving on than to have us work on a democratically chosen problem and not have the full and active support of several persons.

WRIGLEY: I'm a little confused. What should we do next? What is my role as the leader?

SAXBE: I'd ask the group what they think.

WRIGLEY: Okay. (*to group*) Where do we go from here?

LOWELL: I still stand with Mr. Smith, but I do see that we will have some difficulty addressing ourselves to a problem as complex and vague as communication unless we break it down in some way. I suggest we ask our two members who voted for *reducing absenteeism* for their comments.

WRIGLEY: Good idea. Who voted for working on the absenteeism problem? (*McCleary and Blackman raise hands*)

MCCLEARY: Let's not fight, team. (*smiling*) I voted for absenteeism because I see it as a big problem. However, at the large mail processing and distribution center, absenteeism could be job related . . . that is, somehow tied in with carelessness and poor motivation. If I have to make a choice between the two, I lean toward working on the problem of mis-sent mail. (*pause*) Even in discussing that problem I'll still get in some shots at the absenteeism problem. (*general laughter*)

WRIGLEY: I think you're right, McCleary. I have a feeling that excessive absenteeism may well be a symptom of low job motivation. (*momentary silence*)

BLACKMAN: Well, I voted for absenteeism as well. I lean toward taking communication as our problem but it really is too vague as we've stated it up to this point. We'd really have to break it down.

HERNANDEZ: Hey! If we're going to take one aspect of improving communication, why not tie it in with the mis-sent mail problem? Maybe the clerks don't fully understand the implications when they don't "stick" mail correctly? Maybe we have to communicate better or give them better instruction or training. Maybe mis-sent mail involves communication.

CLINE: That's a good idea Mr. Hernandez. I'll go along with that and support the mis-sent mail problem.

BLACKMAN: (*smiling*) I wouldn't want it to get around that I actually agreed on something with Hernandez (*a few chuckles*) but he does have a point. I'll go along with mis-sent mail.

WRIGLEY: All right, that makes seven who support the idea of working on the problem of mis-sent mail.

LOWELL: I really have no objections either, except that as a Customer Service Representative I have no knowledge of operations at the mail processing and distribution centers. I don't feel I will be able to contribute very much.

WRIGLEY: That's not really true, Mrs. Lowell. Some of us are too close to the problem and may not be able to see the forest for the trees. You can check our thinking by asking questions and by offering fresh and unbiased ideas.

LOWELL: You make my role sound very important, Mr. Wrigley. I'm glad we made you the leader. (*general laughter*) I only hope I don't ask too many dumb questions.

HERNANDEZ: (*emphatically*) There is no such thing as a dumb question. Right, Mr. Saxbe?

SAXBE: Right.

(*momentary silence*)

FISHER: Well, what do you say, Mr. Evans? You going to join us?

EVANS: The group has my support. I'm sorry if I was divisive and held up progress. It's just that I feel so strongly about the communications problem . . . .

WRIGLEY: Not at all, Evans. All of us share your general sentiments.

MCCLEARY: Hey, Evans, you can still get your shots in . . . like I'm going to.

WRIGLEY: (*summarizing*) It appears then that we have indeed reached a consensus that this group will work on the problem of mis-sent mail to direct firm holdouts.

LOWELL: Mr. Saxbe, is this what you meant by working through differences in arriving at a decision?

SAXBE: Essentially. It took a few minutes longer but the group is now more likely to make better progress from this point forward . . . and with everyone's active support.

CLINE: I think we really work well together.

SAXBE: You do. (*winking*) For all practical purposes I might as well go home.

FISHER: I'll buy that! I'd like to go home too.[22]

In the Canadian study, ten scales were summed to measure the extent to which top management was participative and human-relations oriented. Of these, three scales measured the extent to which top management decisions were participatively made rather than made individualistically by the formally responsible executives. Two scales measured the extent to which human relations were used, respectively, to effect organizational changes and to achieve better cooperation and coordination in the organization. One scale measured the extent to which management sought to involve personnel affected by a possible organizational change in all the phases of the organizational change by means of participative, consensus-seeking, democratic decision-making. Two scales measured the strategic importance top management accorded, respectively, to participative management at middle and senior management levels and to management by objectives, a form of participation in decision-making at middle and junior levels of management popularized by Peter Drucker and Douglas McGregor. The ninth scale measured the extent to which the corporate philosophy emphasized group- or committee-oriented, consensus-seeking, participative decision-making rather than individualistic decision-making by the formally responsible executive. The tenth scale measured the extent to which behavioral science techniques such as the managerial grid and sensitivity training were employed in the organization to foster a climate of mutual trust and collaboration among managers.

In the management literature, participation is often posed as an alternative to authoritarianism. But it should be remembered that in measures of participation, a low value does not always mean a coercive orientation. It can imply *individualistic* decision-making by the formally responsible executives; and this may be autocratic and arbitrary, or it may be in accordance with established policies and rules and consistent with the formal authority of the individual making the decision. It also implies an aversion to *institutionalized* participative management, which then results in low participative decision-making and low use of behavioral science techniques. Also, just as low participation does not necessarily imply high coercion, high participation does not necessarily imply low coercion. Political institutions often are founded on participatory, democratic philosophy but are rife with coercive practices. The opposite to consensual decision-making can be technocratic decision-making, bureaucratic decision-making, laissez-faire decision-making, as well, of course, as arbitrary decision-making. Similarly, group consensus is not the only alternative to arbitrariness and coercion. For the meaning of high and low values of the participative mode as employed in the Canadian study, see Figure 11–6.

The study suggested that firm size and environmental diversity were inde-

FIGURE 11–6
The Participative Mode in the Canadian Study

PARTICIPATIVE MODE ←——————→	NONPARTICIPATIVE MODE
Consensus-oriented team decision-making at the level of top management	Decision-making by formally responsible executives at top management levels
Use of human relations in effecting organizational changes and securing better cooperation from employees	Lack of emphasis on human relations, participative management, and organization development
Involvement of personnel in organizational changes affecting them	
Strategic importance to top management of participative management at middle management levels and of management by objectives	
The use of organization development, of techniques like sensitivity training and managerial grid	

TABLE 11–1
Situational Determinants of the Dimensions of Management Style

Situation	Style dimensions		Situation
Stable environment; old age of organization	Conservatism ⟷	Risk taking; entrepreneurship	Turbulent environment; youth
Constraint-free, technically unsophisticated, non-R and D oriented environment	"Satisficing" seat-of-the-pants judgments ⟷	Optimization of performance; long-term planning; technocracy	Constraining, technically sophisticated, R and D oriented environment (complex environment)
Noninnovative, noncompetitive, homogeneous environment	Rigidity; formal authority; mechanistic mode ⟷	Flexibility; situational expertise; organic mode	Innovation-rich, competitive, heterogeneous environment
Expanding environment; either very restrictive or unrestrictive, and very hostile or benign environment	Not oriented to dominance; nonauthoritarian ⟷	Power- and dominance-oriented; coercive	Stagnant or shrinking environment; moderately hostile and restrictive environment
Homogeneous environment; small size of organization	Nonparticipative; nonhuman relations oriented ⟷	Participative; human-relations oriented	Heterogeneous environment; large size of organization

pendently associated with the use of the participative mode at top management levels.[23] A large organization, as was noted in Chapter 8, is more differentiated than a small one, and so is an organization that has diversified outputs or operates in a diverse environment. Participation affords a ready way to integrate the organization by building up an esprit de corps. Also, large organizations and organizations in diverse environment tend to be more technocratic than small organizations and organizations operating in homogeneous environments (see Chapters 8 and 9), and participation in recent decades has become, at least in North America, an important element of "professional" management.

We have reviewed each of five dimensions of management style—namely, risk taking, optimization, flexibility, coercion, and participation. Table 11–1 summarizes our discussion of their determinants.

STYLES OF MANAGEMENT

Corporate Management Styles

Management styles are different *combinations* of various dimensions, such as risk taking, optimization, participation, flexibility, and coercion. Table 11–2 describes the management styles of two corporations of comparable size in the Canadian study, with annual sales of about $40 million each. The first is in the construction and associated equipment distribution and manufacturing business; the second is a bakery.

As the table shows, the bakery's top management is conservative, seat-of-the-pants judgments oriented, organic but coercive. The top management of the equipment company is seat-of-the-pants judgments oriented and organic too. But it is risk taking and nonauthoritarian.

Each organization's management has, of course, a unique management style—that is, a unique combination of risk taking, optimization, flexibility, participation, and coercion. However, some managements are likely to be more similar to one another than to other managements. In order to see the major management styles, cluster analysis was performed on the Canadian data.[24] Table 11–3 shows the principal styles that were identified.

There was a clear tendency for several of these styles to be shaped by the situation in which the organization operated, although the relationship between the situation and the style did not appear to be deterministic. For example, we would expect the risk-taking organic style to flourish in a turbulent environment. Six of the 8 firms utilizing this style operated in a highly turbulent environment, 1 in a moderately turbulent environment, and only 1 in a stable environment. We would expect that the professional style, which heavily accents planning, optimization, and participation, would be

TABLE 11–2
The Top Management Style of an Equipment Manufacturer and Distributor and a Bakery

	Equipment company	Bakery
Risk taking, entrepreneurship	High	Low
Optimization, planning, technocracy	Low	Low
Flexibility, situational expertise, organic management	High	High
Participative, human relations orientation	Low	Medium
Coercive, authoritarian orientation	Low	High

TABLE 11–3
Management Style Clusters
(Sample: 103 Canadian Firms)

Style	Description
Risk taking organic (8 firms) *risk*	Highly risk taking and organic; but also fairly seat-of-the-pants judgments oriented, noncoercive and, nonparticipative
Conservative organic (9 firms) *conservative org*	High on conservatism and flexibility; fairly seat-of-the-pants and participative; and moderately coercive
Professional (16 firms) *pro*	High on optimization and participation; low on coercion; moderately organic and risk taking
Quasi-professional (22 firms) *Quasi pro*	High on optimization and low on flexibility orientations; fairly risk taking, participative, and coercive
Anti-professional (13 firms) *Anti pro aut o*	Highly seat-of-the-pants, nonparticipative, coercive; fairly risk taking; moderately organic
Golden mean (27 firms) *Golden mean*	Moderate orientation with respect to optimization, flexibility, participation, and coercion; somewhat conservative orientation
Conservative laissez-faire (8 firms)	Highly conservative, nonparticipative, and noncoercive; fairly seat-of-the-pants; moderately flexible

found in heterogeneous, technologically complex, or restrictive environments. Nine of the 16 professionally oriented firms operated in heterogeneous environments and only 2 in homogeneous environments; 9 in technologically sophisticated environments but 5 also in technologically unsophisticated environments; 11 in restrictive environments and only 3 in nonrestrictive environments.[25]

The data require a reconciliation of the contingency and the systems views of organizational design that we discussed in Chapter 6. Both views emphasize the importance of situational, environmental factors in shaping organizations. However, the contingency orientation tends to identify a dominant or unique response to each contingency posed by the environment. The equifinality principle of systems theory admits the possibility of several feasible responses to the contingency. In the Canadian study, even in highly specific situations, there was evidence of more than one strategic response by management. For example, the top managements of medium-sized firms experiencing low competitive pressures tended to be either very optimization oriented *or* very seat-of-the-pants judgments oriented, either very mechanistic *or* very organic, either very coercive *or* quite low on coercion. The top managements of medium-sized firms subjected to heavy competitive pressures tended to be either very conservative *or* very risk taking, and very participative *or* quite nonparticipative. (See Appendix A of this book for the operating definition of competitive pressure; size was measured by taking the logarithm of the firm's annual sales.) The Canadian data suggest the following proposition:

Given the situational factors, the choice among management styles is circumscribed but not eliminated. ~~situation inf not controls~~

The Design of Top Management Style

We do not live in a world in which whatever exists is the best that is possible. The possibility of improvement is all too palpable. What, then, could be particularly effective combinations of the dimensions of management style?

1. We might speculate that wherever there is a strong risk-taking orientation there ought to be an organic orientation. This is because risk-taking managements usually seize opportunities and make commitments of resources before fully understanding precisely what actions need to be taken. Unless management is flexible, the organization will not be able to adapt itself to the evolving situation. A highly coercive orientation may be helpful when there is considerable internal resistance to rapid and major changes implied by entrepreneurial decisions, for the advantage lies in *quick* adaptation to the evolving situation. On the other hand, if the rank-and-file is committed to such changes, little or no coercion may be needed. The data from the Canadian study indicated that of the 17 firms that were highly risk taking, at least moderately flexible, and either very coercive or noncoercive, 14, or 82 percent, were in the high performance group consisting of the firms scoring in the top half of an index of performance based on the long-range profitability, growth rate, and stability of profits of the firm.[26] On the other hand, of the 6 firms that were strongly risk taking but were low on flexibility, only 2, or 33 percent, were in the high performance group.

2. Just as a combination of flexibility and risk taking is a useful one, the combination of risk avoidance or conservatism, inflexibility, and nonauthoritarianism is also likely to be a useful one. This is because, when management is conservative, the advantage lies in *efficiently* producing *true and tried* products or services. Since efficiency lies in standardizing procedures

and the like, conservatism and a mechanistic mode make good bedfellows. When the organization is highly structured and impersonally controlled by systems of procedures, there is little need for authoritarianism. In fact, the arbitrary exercise of power can only create needless anxiety and can throw a spanner in the works. The Canadian study showed that of 22 firms that were highly conservative, and *at least* moderately mechanistic and noncoercive, 14, or 64 percent, were in the high performance group. On the other hand, of the 14 firms whose top managements were highly conservative but also strongly organic or coercive, only 3 firms (21 percent) were in the high performance group.

3. Whenever the management is strongly technocratic, with a strong commitment to planning and optimal utilization of resources, we should expect a participative orientation to be helpful. This is because a technocratic management relies on highly trained specialists. Unless the needs of these specialists for participation in decision-making are met, they are likely to be quite dissatisfied. With such an extensive use of staff specialists, staff-line and staff-staff conflicts are likely to be common unless headed off by a collaborative climate and good human relations. The chief danger of technocracy is the tunnel vision and selective perception of experts. Open communications, participation, human relations, sensitivity training, and the like represent the necessary investment in human resources to overcome this deficiency. In the Canadian study, the top managements of 23 firms had a strong optimization orientation and also a strongly participative orientation. Of these, as many as 16, or 70 percent, were in the high performance group. On the other hand, of the 15 firms with a strongly optimizing orientation but *not* a strongly participative orientation, only 6, or 40 percent, were in the high performance group.

4. If the management is oriented to making seat-of-the-pants judgments, then it relies on its intuition and familiarity with the business situation rather than on experts and technically trained specialists. Thus, a large investment in human resources that a participative orientation implies is not called for. We have noted earlier that seat-of-the-pants decisions are feasible in relatively noncomplex situations. In such situations, risks of alternatives can be calculated relatively reliably without help from experts like statisticians, economists, and forecasters. Also, what distinguishes an organization from the herd in such an environment is risk taking and entrepreneurship. Thus, a combination of seat-of-the-pants, nonparticipative, and risk-taking orientations is a useful one. In the Canadian study, of the 13 firms whose top managements had a strongly seat-of-the-pants orientation and *at least* a moderately nonparticipative and risk-taking orientation, 7, or 54 percent, were high performers. On the other hand, of the 14 firms whose top manage-

no part

TABLE 11–4
Some Effective and Less Effective Combinations of Top Management Orientations
(Sample: 103 Canadian Firms)

Style combination	Number of firms	Percentage of high performers
Strong risk taking, moderate to strong flexibility, *and* highly coercive or noncoercive orientation	17	82
Strong risk taking, but mechanistic orientation	6	33
Strong optimization *and* participation	23	70
Strong optimization but weak or moderate participation	15	40
Strongly conservative, moderately or strongly mechanistic, *and* moderately or weakly coercive orientation	22	64
Strongly conservative, but highly flexible or coercive orientation	14	21
Strongly seat-of the-pants orientation *and* an at least moderately nonparticipative and risk-taking orientation	13	54
Strongly seat-of-the-pants orientation but either a highly conservative or a highly participative orientation	14	43

ments had a strongly seat-of-the-pants orientation but also a strongly participative or nonrisk-taking orientation, only 6, or 43 percent, were high performers.

Table 11–4 summarizes the above data.

We propose that:

If the orientation of the top management is risk taking and entrepreneurial, it should also be at least moderately organic, and coercive in proportion to internal resistance to change, for superior performance on key organizational goals.

If the orientation of the top management is risk aversive and conservative, it should also be at least moderately mechanistic and noncoercive for superior performance on key organizational goals.

If the orientation of the top management is highly optimization and planning oriented,

> *it should also be strongly participative for superior organizational performance on key organizational goals.*

If the orientation of the top management is highly seat-of-the-pants and non-technocratic,

> *it should also be at least moderately risk taking and nonparticipative for superior organizational performance on key organizational goals.*

Remembering that the risk-taking orientation is commonly found when the organization operates in a turbulent (but not necessarily complex) environment, and the planning and participative orientations are commonly found when the organization operates in a technologically complex, constraining, or heterogeneous environment (but not necessarily a turbulent environment), we propose that:

The more turbulent the organization's environment,

> *the more the top management style should reflect risk taking and organic values, with coercion proportionate to internal resistance to change, for superior performance on key organizational goals.*

The more stable or static the organization's environment,

> *the more the top management style should reflect conservative, mechanistic and nonauthoritarian values for superior performance on key organizational goals.*

The more complex the environment, as judged by its heterogeneity, technological sophistication, and restrictiveness,

> *the more optimization oriented and participative should the top management style be for superior performance on key organizational goals.*

The more simple the environment, as judged by its homogeneity, lack of technological sophistication, and lack of constraints,

> *the more seat-of-the-pants judgments oriented, nonparticipative, and risk taking should the top management style be for superior performance on key organizational goals.*

Table 11–5 shows the support for these propositions from the Canadian study.

TABLE 11–5
External Environment and Effective Designs of Top Management Style
(Sample: 103 Canadian Firms)

	Total number of firms	Number of high performance firms	
		Number	Percentage
Firms in moderately to highly turbulent environments	64	32	50
Firms in moderately to highly turbulent environments with highly risk-taking managements	21	15	71
Firms in moderately to highly turbulent environments that were highly risk-taking, *at least* moderately organic, and highly coercive or noncoercive	13	11	85
Firms in highly stable or static environments	39	22	56
Firms in highly stable or static environments with *at least* moderately conservative top managements	31	17	55
Firms in highly stable or static environments with *at least* moderately conservative, mechanistic, *and* noncoercive top managements	17	12	71
Firms in *at least* moderately heterogeneous, technologically sophisticated, *and* restrictive environments (complex environments)	27	17	63
Firms in complex environments as above, and top management with *at least* moderately high optimization orientation and a strongly participative orientation	11	8	73
Firms in *at least* moderately homogeneous, technologically unsophisticated, *and* nonrestrictive environments (simple environments)	35	14	40
Firms in simple environments with *at least* moderately seat-of-the-pants managements, low participative orientation, and high risk-taking orientation	6	6	100

Concluding Comments

We have developed a number of important ideas in this chapter. These are:
   1. The values and beliefs of top management are critically important in

the design of organizations. They affect vitally the structure, functioning, and performance of the organization.

2. There are many dimensions to management style. Especially important are those of risk taking, optimization, participation, flexibility, and coercion. Much literature on the subject focuses on only one or two of these dimensions. Thus, when Likert and his followers admonish management to be participatory and organic, they do not indicate whether management should be technocratic or not and risk taking or conservative. When the votaries of formal planning and management science techniques prescribe the optimization orientation as the right one, they fail to indicate whether management should be conservative or organic, coercive or noncoercive. And so it goes. It is obvious that any such one-sided focus on aspects of management style must lead to serious design deficiencies.

all equal

3. The style of management is in good measure a response to the stimuli in the environment. This is in marked contrast to much of the earlier literature on management style that simply ignored the question of the circumstances in which a particular mode of management was feasible.

4. Even though situational variables limit the choice of management style, they do not eliminate choice. In several situations, more than one management style is feasible. This implies considerable freedom in the practical design of organizations. For example, if long-term planning and risk taking are alternative feasible responses in a hostile environment, the designer can help management pick the one that is closer to their current practices.

5. There is no ideal management style, certainly not in all circumstances. It is misleading to suggest, as many writers have, that participation, planning, a scientific management orientation, and risk taking are "good" and that coercion, nonparticipation, seat-of-the-pants management, and conservatism are "bad." Each of the latter in the right circumstances and combined appropriately with other dimensions can provide results comparable to those of the former. Improperly combined and in the wrong circumstances, participation and the other "good" management practices can yield pretty poor results. This means that instead of proselytizing management into the current ideological fad, it makes more sense to build on the strongest proclivity of top management. For example, if it is seat-of-the-pants (much maligned in the management literature), then the sensible thing to do is not to brainwash management into an optimizing mode but to increase the risk taking and limit the participatory orientation of top management.

seat of pants good in its place

All in all, the foregoing ideas represent quite a revolution in management thought and organization theory.

SUMMARY, PROPOSITIONS, AND IMPLICATIONS FOR ORGANIZATIONAL DESIGN

Summary

The top management's operating style and its supporting ideology is a strategic variable of the highest importance. The top management's style is largely a combination of several modes or orientations, chief among which are risk taking, planning and optimization, flexibility and situational expertise, participation and human relations, and coercion. The opposite poles of these modes are conservatism, seat-of-the-pants judgments, administrative structuring and rigidity, nonparticipation, and nonauthoritarianism.

Contextual variables like size, age, type of business, and properties of the environment partially determine what mode is likely to be accentuated. A number of top management styles that represent combinations of these modes were identified.

The data cited in the chapter suggest that while the context within which the organization operates makes the use of certain styles or certain elements of these styles more probable, for viability the top management has a wide choice of management styles and survival strategies. However, certain combinations of orientations seem to be more effective than others.

Propositions

1. The more intense, diverse, and shifting the pressures on the organization's top management,

    the greater is the need for flexibility and an organic top management orientation.

2. The more stagnant the organization's markets,

    the more coercive is the orientation of the organization's top management.

3. Given the situational factors, the choice among management styles is circumscribed but not eliminated.

4. If the orientation of the top management is risk taking and entrepreneurial,

    it should also be at least moderately organic, and coercive in proportion to internal resistance to change, for superior performance on key organizational goals.

5. If the orientation of the top management is risk aversive and conservative,

> it should also be at least moderately mechanistic and noncoercive for superior performance on key organizational goals.

6. If the orientation of the top management is highly optimization and planning oriented,

> it should also be strongly participative for superior organizational performance on key organizational goals.

7. If the orientation of the top management is highly seat-of-the-pants and nontechnocratic,

> it should also be at least moderately risk taking and nonparticipative for superior organizational performance on key organizational goals.

8. The more turbulent the organization's environment,

> the more the top management style should reflect risk taking and organic values, with coercion proportionate to internal resistance to change, for superior performance on key organizational goals.

9. The more stable or static the organization's environment,

> the more the top management style should reflect conservative, mechanistic *and* nonauthoritarian values for superior performance on key organizational goals.

10. The more complex the environment, as judged by its heterogeneity, technological sophistication, and restrictiveness,

> the more optimization oriented *and* participative should the top management style be for superior performance on key organizational goals.

11. The more simple the environment, as judged by its homogeneity, lack of technological sophistication, and lack of constraints,

> the more seat-of-the-pants judgments oriented, nonparticipative, *and* risk taking should the top management style be for superior performance on key organizational goals.

Implications for Organizational Design

Knowledge, it has been said, is power. The propositions listed above describe likely—but not inevitable—relationships among a variety of variables.

Knowledge of what is likely to happen to an organization can lead to several consequences. If the designer likes what is probable, he can make it happen more efficiently and more painlessly. If he does not like any part or all of what is likely to happen, he can think up some alternatives and take remedial action. It is one of the purposes of science to provide explanations for phenomena and make predictions so that human beings using this knowledge can design better systems. A third consequence is that the designer avoids breaking his head over the improbable or the impossible.

Consider the following scenario. A new administrator is placed in charge of a moribund agency of the government to put life into its operations and bring out innovative, new services that will meet the needs of a highly dynamic social milieu. The Department of Health, Education, and Welfare in the United States might serve as a good enough example. What should the new administrator do?

Clearly, the top administrator needs to use an innovative, risk-taking mode of operations. If he is sensible, he will do so. But will he also put equal emphasis on inculcating flexibility, authority located in situational expertise, open communications, emphasis on getting the job done even if it means bureaucratic procedures are disregarded? Will he get himself and his subordinates to use power to get things done, push through unpopular decisions, crush opposition from the diehards? If *any* of these are not sufficiently emphasized, the chances are that the agency will falter, possibly quite badly. A one-thing-at-a-time approach is common among administrators. Such an approach may not work here. The attack on established ways of doing things needs to be mounted simultaneously and systematically on several fronts. The strategy needs to be thought through and expeditiously implemented. Notice that the administrator needs to know, not only that risk taking, flexibility, and coercion need to be key elements of the top management style, but also that optimization and participation are, *at this phase of the agency's renewal,* clearly of secondary importance and may well be postponed or given only a limited attention.

On the other hand, once the innovations are put into effect, the agency's top management style *needs to shift. Efficient* execution is important. Given a high enough diversity in the agency's operations, a high enough technical complexity in its operations, and major political, legal, and economic constraints under which the agency operates, a strongly optimizing *and* participative orientation is highly necessary. The context has changed. The strategic importance of risk taking, flexibility and situational authority, and the use of coercion must relatively wane; that of participation, planning, and technocracy must wax. The more this happens in a *synchronized* fashion, the better for organizational performance.

For the designer, it is important to know the structural and processual implications of the choice of a top management style (a system goal), so that the top management philosophy is translated into organizational practice. Organizational structure is the set of durable and legitimate arrangements within the organization for securing the goals of the organization. We will examine structural variables in greater detail in Chapters 12 and 13, but for the moment we note that they consist of three distinctive mechanisms: those that reduce external and internal uncertainty (such as an information and control system) so that the planning of organizational moves becomes possible; those that enable the organization to carry out a large variety of necessary activities (such as through division of labor, specialization, departmentalization, and a hierarchical differentiation of authority and responsibility); and those that enable the organization to coordinate and integrate its diverse activities (such as by means of a hierarchy of authority, standard operating procedures, planning and control).

Thus, for example, if the top management orientation is risk taking, external as well as internal uncertainty will sought to be reduced by a number of mechanisms: reliance on the judgment of intuitive decision makers; systematic tapping of the business grapevine for present and future developments; cultivation of contacts that can give early information about profitable future developments; early commitment to major, bold moves so that the rest of the organization experiences certainty about the future course of action. Division of labor, functional specialization, departmentalization, and the hierarchical differentiation of power and authority are the usual means by which organizations seek to achieve the needed differentiation of their activities. In risk-taking organizations, the hierarchical or vertical differentiation of power and authority is likely to be particularly pronounced: the lower managerial ranks are likely to be concerned mainly with routine matters and the implementation of strategic decisions taken by the top management group. The goal of rapid growth, and the power, prestige, and charisma of the top management are likely to be important mechanisms of integration of the organization's activities, over and above the normal integrative mechanisms of hierarchy, controls, and standard operating and conflict resolution procedures.

Table 11–6 indicates the uncertainty reduction, differentiation, and integration mechanisms likely to be distinctively associated with the top management orientation discussed in this chapter. Since the actual style of top management is a combination of these orientations, the table enables one to identify at a glance the structural mechanisms associated with a particular style of management. For example, if the style of top management is to be "professional," characterized by high optimization and participative orientations and a low coercive orientation, then it is likely that an information system based on sophisticated forecasting, market research, and manage-

TABLE 11–6
Structural Mechanisms Associated with Top Management Orientations

Top Management Orientations	Uncertainty Reduction Mechanisms	Differentiation Mechanisms	Integration Mechanisms
Risk taking	Intuitive judgments of top management decision makers supplemented *selected* by grapevine, informal contacts, and a formal information system. Early commitment to a course of action creates a sense of certainty despite the objective uncertainty about the outcomes.	Delegation of authority to junior managers for routine decisions and for implementing the details of top level decisions. Strong vertical differentiation of power and authority and responsibility. *del*	Goal of rapid growth dominates the organization's operations. Charismatic personality of key decision makers. *Growth oriented*
Conservatism	Considerable attention to the actions and pronouncements of industry leaders, industry associations, government policy pronouncements. Reliance on industry grapevine.	No particularly distinctive differentiation mechanisms.	Widely shared conservatism and adherence to traditional modes of solving problems and resolving conflicts. Selection of conservative personnel. Socialization of organizational members into respect for organizational traditions. *screen*
Technocratic	A sophisticated market research and forecasting-based information system. Management training to handle complex information and complex information technology.	High levels of functional specialization; separation of line and staff functions; high levels of decentralization.	Sophisticated strategic and tactical planning, budgeting, and control. Socialization into managerial professionalism.

Seat-of-the-pants	Interpretation of external and internal information on the basis of rules of thumb learned through long experience. Reliance on grapevine, field experience, informal contacts, consensual validation.	No particularly distinctive differentiation mechanisms.	Hierarchy; consensual validation of what the key problems are and what to do about them; reliance on rules of thumb that have worked in the past in resolving conflicts and ensuring coordination. Management-is-an-art socialization.
Coercive	Internal uncertainty is reduced by weeding out deviants and malcontents.	Especially noticeable differentiation between members of the ruling coalition and others.	Personal rather than systemic control of hiring, firing, and promotion to secure a high level of compliance with orders of key decision makers. Socialization into obedience.
Participative	Exchange of information during group decision-making. Group analysis of problem areas.	No particularly distinctive mechanisms.	Commitment to a course of action participatively decided upon; peer pressure ensuring compliance with group decisions. Human relations training and socialization.
Mechanistic	Formal and structured channels of communication and information.	Division of labor, functional specialization, and vertical differentiation of authority especially marked.	Standard operating procedures, formal job descriptions to ensure "efficient" performance. Internalization of sound management "principles."
Organic	Multiple and "open" channels of communication and information lead to widely shared awareness of key problem areas and sources of information and expertise.	"Natural" rather than formal division of labor, specialization. Operating autonomy for individuals. Differentiation is constantly shifting because of the norms of situational authority.	Shared norms of cooperation. Widespread awareness of organizational objectives due to "open" communication channels. Integration provided by commitment to achieve challenging tasks requiring cooperation of interdependent personnel.

ment controls plus exchange of information during group or committee meetings will be specially important uncertainty reduction mechanisms. Weeding out deviants and malcontents will *not* be a significant feature of the mechanisms for reducing internal uncertainty. A high degree of functional specialization, separation of line and staff functions, and decentralization will be significant differentiation mechanisms. Sophisticated strategic and tactical planning and control, commitment secured through participative decision-making, and compliance with group decisions through peer group pressure will be the distinctive integrative mechanisms. Arbitrary, personalized hiring, firing, and promotion will *not* be a significant mechanism for ensuring "cooperation" with top management decisions.

SUGGESTED READINGS

Rensis Likert, "A Comparative View of Organizations," Chapter 14 in *New Patterns of Management* (New York: McGraw-Hill, 1961).

Henry Mintzberg, "Strategy Making in Three Modes," *California Management Review*, Vol. 16, No. 2 (Winter issue, 1973), pp. 44–53.

Robert Hay and Ed Gray, "Social Responsibilities of Business Managers," *Academy of Management Journal*, Vol. 17, No. 1 (March 1974), pp. 135–43.

Roger Harrison, "Understanding Your Organization's Character," *Harvard Business Review*, May–June 1972, pp. 119–28.

Joseph O. Eastlack, Jr. and Philip R. McDonald, "CEO's Role in Corporate Growth," *Harvard Business Review*, May–June 1970, pp. 150–63.

QUESTIONS FOR ANALYSIS

1 Here are the profiles of several banking executives done by *Business Week*.[27] Identify and evaluate their ideologies and management styles.

Reese: An oldtimer with new ideas

At 64, Addison H. Reese, a chairman of NCNB Corp. of Charlotte, N.C., hardly qualifies as one of the new bankers. But that has not kept him from making the holding company that owns North Carolina National Bank into a glittering success.

Deposits jumped to $2.5 billion at midyear, putting NCNB ahead of its not-so-friendly rival, Wachovia Corp. of Winston-Salem. First-half profits were up 25% to $13.2 million, on top of a 22% gain in 1972. Its return on common equity in 1972 was an impressive 19%, and its stock commands the highest price/earnings ratio—an impressive 24—of any major bank holding company.

The holding company was created four years ago—earlier than most, and Reese has been pushing into new fields ever since: insurance sales, mortgage banking, investment management, a real estate investment trust.

Last year, it opened a branch in London in a bid for more international banking business. As a bank, of course, it can operate only in North Carolina. As a holding company, it can—and does—operate over a much broader area.

"Perhaps of even greater significance," says Reese, "is the development of managerial capabilities at various levels, and this is certainly the thing I have personally been more interested in than anything else. Starting more than 10 years ago, we had a fairly intense effort in the recruitment and development of the brightest young men we could find. This covers all the major colleges and universities—from Harvard to Florida. It started 13 years ago and obviously at this point is making handsome returns."

NCNB's management team is filled with some very bright young men. The top job, when Reese retires late this year, will almost certainly go to Thomas I. Storrs, the bank's 55-year-old president. But the real fight in Charlotte these days is over who will succeed Storrs, and there are three contestants: William H. Dougherty, Jr., 42, who is vice-chairman of the holding company; Luther H. Hodges, Jr., 37, son of the former Commerce Secretary; and Hugh L. McColl, Jr., 38, who is vice-chairman of the bank,

Internal growth. Meanwhile, the pace of diversification will probably slow at NCNB. In the next five years, says Reese, "I see a more gradual development and extension of activities in the one-bank holding company area. By that I mean I see a more dynamic internal growth than in going out and acquiring new companies—more attention to the development of the business we are already in, rather than extension into areas we are not presently in."

But Reese certainly does not think the revolution in banking is nearing an end. "I look for continued change in the whole commercial banking system," he says. "Some changes proposed by the President's Hunt Commission (the Administration's proposals for changes in the financial system have just gone to Congress) will be adopted in the next five years, and these will have a right profound effect on banking generally. I think it is the banks that are best prepared from the standpoint of personnel and management that will be able to take advantage of these developments, and for the banks not prepared it will be a setback."

The betting in Charlotte—and on Wall Street—is that NCNB is one of the institutions best prepared to take advantage of whatever comes along.

Rockwell: Enter banking's technocrat

"Bankers are in a unique position to pick the brains of customers and adopt the best management ideas we see for ourselves," says George B. Rockwell, 47, president and chief executive officer of State Street Boston Financial Corp., the holding company that controls Boston's venerable State Street Bank and Trust Co.

Rockwell is an example of the new breed of banking technocrats, men who have been imported to infuse new techniques and technologies into the industry. Rockwell brought a lot of new ideas from his old job as salesman with International Business Machines Corp. when he came to SSB in 1963 to head its computer operations. "IBM taught me how to plan," says Rockwell.

Today, with Rockwell calling the shots from the top, the bank has $1.5-billion in assets, and it bristles with incentive systems and forecasting techniques keyed to computer methods that might puzzle old-line bankers but are the everyday stuff of banking to SSB's increasingly young crew of officers and managers.

Despite his background, Rockwell notes that in his recruiting he does not try to go after computer specialists. Instead, he aims for broad-gauged MBA's, who he feels can quickly pick up the more esoteric wrinkles of finance on the job. Besides, he notes, MBA's seem to absorb just enough modeling know-how in school to enable them to come up with the bank's most useful computer models, usually within five years of joining the bank.

"These young people have really helped us massage our future more comprehensively," says Rockwell in the jargon on his first career.

"We're very big on setting goals around here," he says. "Managers like to know what's expected of them."

He spends much of his time trying to identify new services that fit into holding company legislation and so far says he has come up with more than 100. Among other things, SSB opened its own equipment-leasing operation two years ago and last May used stock to buy a mortgage banking concern.

Rockwell is convinced, he says, that the coming computerized era of electronic banking will put a personal touch back into the business, because machines that cough up cash anytime at the flash of a plastic card will free customers from the "prove you're you" glares of human tellers that seem frozen into the present system.

Bunting: He's created a model conglomerate

John R. Bunting is the feisty maverick of banking—the one-time Federal Reserve economist who took the nation's oldest commercial bank, First Pennsylvania Banking & Trust Co. of Philadelphia, and turned it into the very model of a financial conglomerate that the new banking is all about.

Some fellow bankers may not like him very much, but for a long time the 48-year-old Bunting was the darling of Wall Street analysts and investors. Only this year has First Pennsylvania's p/e begun to slip, with investors disturbed by the poor showing of its mortgage banking business. But earnings for First Pennsylvania Corp., the holding company that now owns the bank, were up 13% in the first half of 1973, after an 11% gain in 1972.

Bunting, chairman of the bank since 1972, recalls that when he became president five years ago, he found its image "even stodgier than banking's."

Since then, what admirers call Bunting's dynamism and imagination, and critics call his "showmanship," has been apparent in original and often controversial borrowing and lending innovations. That, and his highly visible community involvement, have given First Pennsylvania the new identity he sought for it—and made Bunting one of the country's best-known bankers.

A new personality. In the process, First Pennsylvania's assets have nearly doubled to $4.6-billion, and deposits have increased by 55%. Its return on invested capital (14%) and on common equity (17%) in 1972 were the highest for any major banking company.

Bunting recalls that when he came to the bank in 1964, it had no distinctive personality. He says: "The bank was trying to be a replica of one of the New York giants. That's all wrong. We have to be a different kind of institution. We have to have some identity."

Bunting's first chance came almost immediately after he was named president in late 1968. He dropped the bank's prime rate $\frac{1}{4}$ of a point under the established $6\frac{1}{2}$%, and by the time the rest of the industry belatedly followed a couple of weeks later, Bunting had proved his point. "We could pick up $40-million to $50-million in new loan business every week we were ahead," he recalls.

Since then, First Pennsylvania has led four other prime rate moves. "We have used changes in the prime—moving deliberately ahead of the other banks—to achieve an identity as a commercial leader," he explains.

Banking "specials." During the 1969–70 credit crunch, Bunting again moved ahead of the others, creating a retail "mini-note" sold in $100 denominations for 30-month maturities. At $7\frac{1}{4}$%, First Pennsylvania was able to sell $20-million worth in 11 days.

And just two months ago, with the lifting of the interest rate ceiling on savings, Bunting brought out its "inflation fighter," a four-year certificate of deposit whose interest rate moves with the consumer price index up to a 10% high. First Pennsylvania gained attention as well as about $6-million a day in deposits until federal limitations stayed its sale after 15 days.

During his five-year tenure, Bunting has redirected the bank's activities from its generally unprofitable consumer lending orientation to commercial lending, which today accounts for 66% of its loans.

Meanwhile, Bunting has pushed First Pennsylvania's horizons beyond the state's borders. This fall, the bank will be opening its first U.S. representative office—in Chicago—to be followed by four others in the next two years. Overseas, in 1972 First Pennsylvania bought a 41.6% interest in the First International Bank of Israel—Israel's fourth largest.

2 Here is a story on Texas Instruments. Identify the ideology and style of its corporate management, and explain why it is the way it is.

Texas Instruments, Inc., the Dallas-based semiconductor maker, has a long history of tinkering with the human element in the management equation, and its painstakingly structured job enrichment and team-planning programs have had their effect. Sales at TI have risen at a compounded rate of 30% annually for 20 years, to $943-million last year. Increased employee productivity clearly is one of the reasons.

"Nobody ever gets an ulcer from working strenuously at things they like," says TI president and chief executive officer Mark Shepherd, Jr., who admits that he himself, motivated by the Depression, is strongly oriented to the work ethic. "We've found that if you get people involved, they'll set tougher goals for themselves than you would dare do. And have fun doing it."

Some TI managers and professionals view the pace as more of a grind than a joy, but the company's ploy of hiking productivity by letting individuals set their own goals seems to have worked far more often than not.

Now TI is pioneering some new personnel approaches, aimed at production workers and top executives alike. There is, for example, an experiment in psychoanalyzing employees. Once management learns what turns an employee on to his job, he can be treated as an individual instead of a faceless member of the herd.

Room at the top. Another experiment, which has the blessings of management right up to Chairman Patrick Haggerty, prescribes the early retirement of most executive vice-presidents, by age 55, to make room for younger men. The retired executives are pacified by getting a chance at a new kind of job called officer of the board. Another policy lays down new rules for the directors themselves.

All this is just part of TI's continuing concern with maximizing the effectiveness of the individual employee. For three years the company has been focusing even more attention than usual on this effort with a program aimed at getting the most out of employees and capital resources. Called "People and Asset Effectiveness," the results have been phenomenal.

Net sales per employee rose from $14,600 in 1970 to $18,500 in 1972, while after-tax profits went from $510 to $870. Return on assets per person shot up from 5.6% to 10.1% over the three years.

The People and Asset Effectiveness program was devised to force TI planners to think hard about employees right down to the woman on the assembly line—and about their ability and willingness to produce.

Shooting high. And TI management expects the program to keep paying off. By the late 1970s, sales billed per person are expected to rise from this year's $18,500 to $30,000. Similarly, the goal for profits produced by each employee is $1,500 to $1,800 by that time, compared to last year's $878. That level of after-tax profits would result in a return on assets of 10% to 12%. Now the strategy is to move "diagonally," increasing assets and productivity, toward the 1980s and TI's stated goal of $3-billion in annual sales.

In pursuit of its goals, TI has unleashed a whole array of acronym-laced programs dealing with planning, control, and "people effectiveness." Many of them put TI's computer capabilities to work. A system called "dynamic line balancing" allows a foreman in TI's semiconductor and printed circuit-board assembly areas to simulate manpower requirements under different conditions. As a result, productivity in some areas has jumped 50%, and the average improvement is 20%.

Increased automation has helped, of course. To eliminate tedious assembly operations at the microscopic level, engineers designed a time-saving system to weld tiny gold wires to terminals on silicon chips about one-tenth of an inch square. Now the operator positions only one wire on a chip and 14 other wires are placed by the computer.

Synergism. But automation accounts for only part of the improvement, says Fredrick C. Ochsner, vice-president and director of corporate personnel. "It is a whole bunch of things acting synergistically," he says. It's the attitudes, the team improvement programs, the campus environment, the open-door management policy, the non-structured pecking order. It's the unified goal approach—with everybody looking at his own piece of that goal."

Nor do these programs affect only lower-echelon workers. This spring, Chairman Haggerty announced the new rules calling for early retirement of executive vice-presidents. Retirement for the company's chairman and president will be compulsory at 62, a policy that will affect Haggerty first, since he reaches that age in March, 1976. The idea is to open opportunities for young managers who might otherwise leave TI for other jobs. In the past 18 months alone, two vice-presidents left to become presidents of other companies.

"I'm 50," says Shepherd. "Let's take the bright guy who is 30. He looks up, sees that Shepherd isn't going anywhere for another 15 years and decides he'll go somewhere else."

If Haggerty, Shepherd, and the three current vice-presidents served until the old retirement age of 65, there would be just three vacancies allowing promotions to those posts in the next 15 years. With the new policy, there are likely to be at least seven.

TI plans to continue using the talents of its early retiring executives, too. According to Haggerty, they will be prime candidates for a unique kind of TI post, officer of the board, which means they will function in much the same way as outside directors. That will require a change in work style, but not much change in pay. An executive vice-president retiring at 55, for example, will receive 85% of the amount to which he would have been entitled at 65, had he worked to that age, based on his last five years of service.

No escape. Not even board members escape the company's meticulous rule-making. Officers of the board, who include all the outside directors as well as some with a TI background, must work at least 25 to 30 days a year on company business, but no longer than 110 to 125 days, to assure sufficient time to develop "meaningful activities other than with TI."

At lower levels, TI shows signs of institutionalizing a growing appreciation that today's worker is an individual. Charles L. Hughes, director of personnel and organizational development at TI, warned in an article for the HARVARD BUSINESS REVIEW that companies "must develop existentially managed organizations that truly accept and respect people with differing values."

To start TI down this road, Hughes collected questionnaires from about 600 employees of the company and tentatively divided them into six categories based on how they perceive the world around them.

One category, the "tribalistic," includes those who respond to strong leadership, who can be happy and dedicated if shown genuine care and concern. The "existential" group, on the other hand, is comprised for the most part of employees who will do a job only if it is meaningful. While perhaps contentious, the existential employee is usually the brainiest and most creative. Other types are "egocentric" (entrepreneurial); conformist (tradition-oriented); "manipulative" (achievement oriented); and "sociocentric" (socially oriented).

There is considerable disagreement at TI over how the findings should be used. Hughes believes that ultimately the research will influence TI's selection and placement procedures, producing a more flexible organization. An existential worker, for example, will be given an existential supervisor. Others say that kind of use of the data is premature. "I just don't want to start putting people in different colored boxes," says Ochsner.

Not all TI's 60,000 employees are happy with its emphasis on the work ethic, however much it is tailored to the modern worker. An electrician who has frequently been called on to work up to 60 hours a week for long stretches grumbles about the extra work even though it means overtime pay. And he is luckier than some. Many professionals who are on straight salary are expected to work grueling schedules. And the company has a tendency to move some professional employees around at will. One Dallas-based electrical engineer, ordered at 3:30 P.M. to report to the company's Sherman, Tex. plant the next morning for reassignment, promptly resigned.

On the whole, though, the personnel experiments seem to be working. TI has been trying out new methods to increase productivity and worker satisfaction since the early 1950s, when the company began its version of work simplification. Most supervisors and thousands of workers have been through the program, which involves a joint effort to study a problem and work through basic steps to a solution.

Ochsner is unwilling to say which of the programs has contributed most to TI's productivity gains. The key, he says, is flexibility. Some programs work well with one manager or supervisor or group of workers, some work well with others.

What makes it work, says Ochsner, is simple. "There are two things in life that people want," he explains. "They want to achieve and they want to be loved. And if you provide an atmosphere where these things can occur with a minimum amount of structure in the work flow, you are going to get what you want." [28]

Footnotes to Chapter 11

[1] D. Krech, R. Crutchfield, and E. Ballachey, *Individual in Society*, p. 402.
[2] See H. Rush, *Behavioral Science*, p. 154.
[3] Excerpted from *Business Week* (Sept. 22, 1973), pp. 72–79.

[4] T. Burns and G. M. Stalker, *The Management of Innovation.*

[5] Rensis Likert, *New Patterns of Management.*

[6] Douglas McGregor, *The Human Side of Enterprise;* R. M. Cyert and James March, *A Behavioral Theory of the Firm.*

[7] Charles Lindblom, "The Science of 'Muddling Through.' "

[8] Henry Mintzberg, "Strategy Making in Three Modes."

[9] Excerpted from R. A. Smith's "At Saint Gobain, the First 300 Years Were the Easiest."

[10] Excerpted from R. Heller's "The Legend of Litton."

[11] See Appendix A for a description of the author's study of Canadian firms.

[12] Lindblom, *op. cit.*

[13] Excerpted from D. J. Smalter and R. L. Ruggles, Jr., "Six Business Lessons from the Pentagon."

[14] *Ibid.*

[15] From Burns and Stalker, *op. cit.,* pp. 82–83.

[16] *Ibid.,* pp. 92–94.

[17] See Paul R. Lawrence and Jay Lorsch, *Organization and Its Environment,* for evidence of such variation; also Richard H. Hall, "Intraorganizational Structural Variation: Application of the Bureaucratic Model."

[18] Burns and Stalker, *op. cit.*

[19] Excerpted from R. Wegner and L. Sayles, *Cases in Organizational and Administrative Behavior,* pp. 191–92.

[20] Excerpted from *Time* (Sept. 23, 1974).

[21] Likert, *op. cit.,* p. 103.

[22] Excerpted from Robert D. Joyce, *Encounters in Organizational Behavior,* pp. 54–57.

[23] See Proposition 2 in Ch. 8 and Proposition 4 in Ch. 9.

[24] Ward's method was employed in doing the cluster analysis. Seven clusters were extracted. See J. H. Ward, Jr., "Hierarchical Grouping to Optimize an Objective Function."

[25] Five of the professionally managed firms operated in environments that were neither very homogenous nor very heterogenous; 2 in environments that were only moderately technologically sophisticated; and 2 in only moderately restrictive environments. For the purpose of this analysis, the environmental variables were trichotomized into high, medium, and low categories. For operational definitions, see Appendix A of this book.

[26] For the purpose of analysis, each style and performance dimension was trichotomized into high, medium, and low categories. For developing an index of performance, the high, medium, low categories for profitability, growth rate of revenues, and stability of profits were given values of 3, 2, and 1, respectively, and summed. The resulting distribution was divided into the high performance group (52% of the total sample) and the low performance group (48% of the sample). See Appendix A of this book for details.

[27] *Business Week* (Sept. 15, 1973).

[28] *Ibid.* (Sept. 29, 1973).

12

"It is good that one machine can do the work of
fifty ordinary men. No machine, however, can do
the work of one extraordinary man."
Tehyi Hsieh

Workflow
and Technology

Start

INTRODUCTION

In this chapter we examine the workflow of the organization, the technology
of its operations, and information technology. Workflow is the way programs, activities, and events in the input-process-output cycle of the organization are *sequenced*. Operations technology is the *role* of *mechanical* aids
in transforming inputs to the workflow into the outputs of the workflow.
Information technology is the role that mechanical aids play in transforming
informational inputs into informational outputs. These three are discussed
together in this chapter because of their intimate relationship. The work
that goes on in an organization powerfully influences decisions regarding the
kind of equipment that is needed for its efficient execution. In turn, the kind
of equipment that is used in an organization affects the flow of work in an
organization. The flow of work and the use of mechanical aids generates
information and the need for certain kinds of information, and it therefore
affects decisions regarding the acquisition of information-processing aids.
The use of information-processing equipment in turn affects the flow of
work in the organization and sometimes also the use of mechanical equip-

446

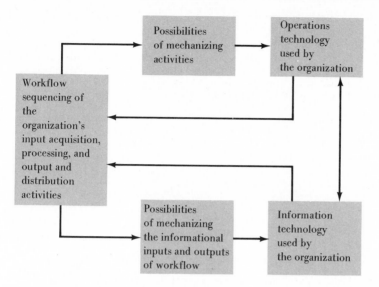

ment. Figure 12–1 shows the interrelationships between workflow, operations technology, and information technology.

Imagine, for example, an oil refinery. Its basic workflow consists of getting crude oil, processing or refining this crude oil into petrochemical products, and then arranging its distribution. The processes of acquisition of crude oil may give rise to pressure to automate the ordering of supplies and therefore induce the organization to go for a computerized inventory control system. The processes of refining the crude oil into petrochemical products will not be possible without the acquisition of sophisticated fractionating equipment. This equipment is hard to operate without a computerized production-scheduling system and a computerized quality control system. The acquisition of production machinery and information technology may in turn lead to a reassessment of the sequencing of activities for greater efficiency. The processes involved in distribution may induce the organization to acquire mechanized delivery systems, and to install computerized distribution systems. These in turn may powerfully affect the sequencing of distribution activities.

Workflow, or the sequencing of the organization's activities, is, of course, vitally affected by certain strategic decisions, such as what goals to pursue. For example, an exclusive pursuit of efficiency may lead to one workflow design, characterized perhaps by extreme specialization and structuring of activities. The goal of high employee morale on the other hand, may lead to a different workflow, characterized perhaps by teamwork, job enrichment,

FIGURE 12–2
Relationships Explored in This Chapter

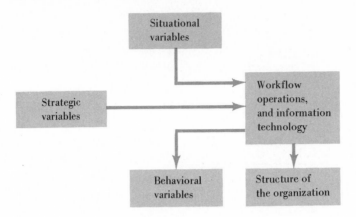

job rotation, and the like. The production workflow at most General Motors plants, oriented very heavily to efficiency, contrasts rather dramatically with the production workflow at Sweden's Volvo plants, which are oriented much more to involving workers in their work.

Besides strategic goal decisions, the demographic and environmental variables also are likely to affect workflow, operations technology, and information technology. Whether the organization is a manufacturing organization or a service organization, and what type of manufacturing or service organization, will clearly affect the workflow and technology of the organization. Pressure from the environment also may affect these. In Chapter 9 we noted that environmental hostility tends to force the organization to standardize its operations. This, of course, is likely to translate into substantial changes in the workflow, operations technology, and information technology of the organization. Figure 12–2 shows the broad relationships explored in this chapter and what this chapter contributes to the model described in Chapter 7.

THE NATURE AND DIMENSIONS OF WORKFLOW

The Nature of Workflow

We noted earlier that workflow is the way programs and activities are sequenced. Very broadly speaking, the workflow of every organization consists of the acquisition of inputs, the processing of these inputs, and the exit of outputs. For example, a school takes in students, processes them through classes, and then exits them as graduates of the educational program. Similarly, a hospital takes in patients, treats them, and sends them out, hopefully healthier. A manufacturer takes in raw materials, processes them, and then markets the finished products. Inputs may consist of raw materials, data, cash, services, or even humans with certain capabilities. Processing is generally through labor and machinery. Outputs may consist of finished products, information, credit, services, or humans with certified added capabilities.

Since each of these three stages in the workflow repeats itself over and over again, each stage tends to get programmed. Each stage gets elaborated, too, for greater efficiency and comes to consist of its own three stages (Figure 12–3), each of which may get further programmed and elaborated. An example of the structuring and elaboration of organizational workflows is the flow chart for the receipt and execution of sales orders in the industrial division of a paper-converting company (Figure 12–4).

Equally detailed programs or flow charts can easily be constructed for each of the nine steps listed in Figure 12–4. In other words, the organization's workflow is in reality the linking together of a series of more limited workflows, or programs. The principle commonly involved in the linking together of programs is one of "maximizing" the productivity of work—work outputs are directed to those points in the organization where their marginal value is *known* to be highest. Thus, after the order is received, material is not directly issued. The order is first checked by the sales manager to determine whether the order is worth accepting and by the order, planning, and scheduling departments to minimize the cost of servicing the order.

Each program in a workflow may be triggered by a cue, such as the receipt of an order or the breakdown of a machine. The program may then be executed by one or more individuals with or without the aid of machinery or tools. The point to note is that the execution of a program generally involves fairly specific, *formal role behavior* on the part of the individuals entrusted with the job. In other words, the program elicits organizational goal-directed rather than personal goal-directed behaviors. On receiving an order a sales manager does not wander off to chat with his cronies; he either holds it for further correspondence or inquiry or puts on it the stamp of his approval and passes it on to the order department for execution. In this way, the organizational workflow and the programs constituting it powerfully regulate and coordinate human behavior in organizations. It is in this sense that the workflow is the organization's structure in motion.

Quite commonly, organizations have several parallel workflows that may, however, be linked at some strategic points. For example, in a commercial broadcasting station, there are typically two major workflows. One involves

FIGURE 12–3
Elaboration of Organizational Workflow

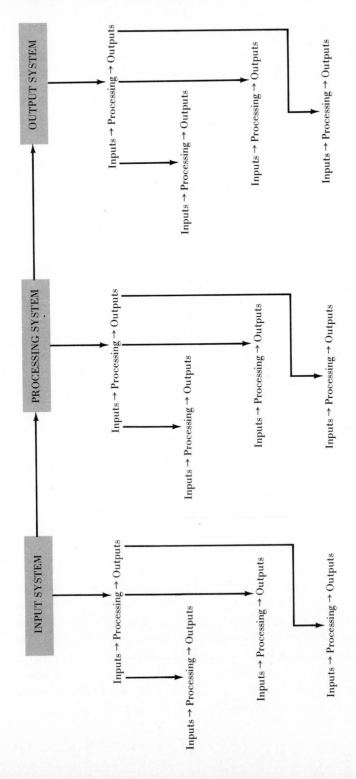

FIGURE 12–4

Flow Chart of an Industrial Products Division

1. Receive order
   Order is time stamped
2. Order checked by sales manager
   a. And held for correspondence or
   b. Passed to order department
3. Order checked by order department
   a. If repeat order, check is made for old work ticket. If new order, quotation is pulled.
   b. Work ticket is typed with copies as follows:

   Billing copy   Accounting department
   Factory copy ⎫
   Control copy ⎪
   Planning copy ⎬   Planning department
   Packing slip ⎭
   Customer's copy   Customer
   Two salesmen's copies ⎫
   Sales department copy ⎭   Sales department

4. Planning prepares layout
   a. Layout of specifications is made on ticket
   b. Ticket is dittoed, master copy retained, other copies to all appropriate foremen
   c. Layout to running inventory for material requisitions
   d. Control copy is registered, forwarded to shipping
   e. Master layout, material requisition slip, packing slip, wrapper, and factory copy to scheduling
5. Scheduling
   a. Finds spot for order in daily schedule for machines which is returned to planning
   b. Forwards material requisition to warehouse at appropriate time
   c. Forwards wrapper and contents to machine at appropriate time
6. Material is issued
7. Factory copy and wrapper are sent to accounting for billing after shipment
8. Inventory records adjusted
9. Planning makes out backlog report for order department

SOURCE: Edward Bowman and Robert Fetter, *Analysis for Production Management* (Homewood, Ill.: Irwin, 1961), p. 467.

the design of broadcasting programs; the other involves the getting of business and the production of commercials. Figure 12–5 shows the simplified workflow of one such Montreal station. In the diagram, the programming director is the hub of the workflow related to the design of programs. The commercial director is the hub of the workflow related to the securing of and production of commercials. Note that the two workflows are linked together at the level of the two directors and at the point where the traffic department that schedules commercials must get together with the disc

FIGURE 12–5
Workflow of a Broadcasting Station

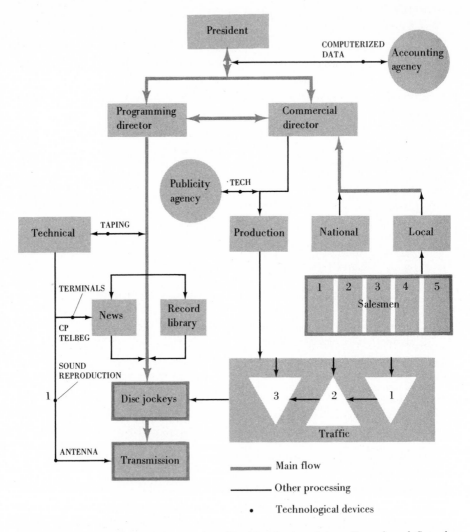

SOURCE: From a study by Messrs. Arthur, Krivicky, Lorion, Orban, Renaud, and Savard, McGill students.

jockeys for broadcasting the right commercial with the right program. The figure also shows where technology or mechanical devices intervene in the workflow.

Besides the flow of activities, the flow of information and communication and the flow of decisions are other aspects of the workflow that need to be borne in mind. The communication flow is a subspecies of workflow. Transmission of information within the organization is akin to the flow of activities. Indeed, in most formally designed organizations, each activity gives rise to several bits of information that are then transmitted to appropriate administrators and eventually stored in files, in the computer, or simply in human memory. Information and action are indissolubly linked in organizations. One gives rise to the other and vice versa. The flow of neither is random. Indeed, without a deliberate channeling of both, the organization would operate chaotically.

But while organizations of any size do have formally structured work and information flows, they commonly have *nonformal* patterns of activities ("socializing") and information flows ("grapevine"). Indeed, it has been alleged by several students of human relations in organizations that these nonformal flows take place precisely because of the excessive structuring of formal workflows and the excessive channeling of information flows.[1] The actual activity that goes on in organizations is a function of the formal and nonformal work and information flows. Unfortunately, at this point we have little systematic knowledge of how these flows mesh together and what effects this produces.

There is also a vertical aspect of workflow that is worth noting—the flow of decisions. In most organizations, the actual work flows from department to department, and we may consider this the horizontal aspect of workflow. But decisions flow from top levels to lower levels, from the level of the board of directors of a firm regarding the profit and growth goals for the year down through the intervening levels to lower levels where operating decisions about how much and what to produce and how to sell it are taken. This is the vertical aspect of workflow.

Workflow Dimensions and Administrative Consequences

It is difficult to generalize about the entire workflow of an organization. If the organization is at least moderately large, there are too many variations in its workflow. The workflow in some parts, such as in manufacturing, may be highly routinized. In other parts, such as in design departments or in policy-making units at the top of the organization, it is likely to involve a good deal of problem solving and decision-making, and the routine aspect of the workflow may be relatively minimal. Thus, for analyzing the effects of the workflow on organizational structure, it is best to consider the workflow as varying in different parts of the organization, and to consider the administrative consequences of its *local* variations.

Based on the work of March and Simon discussed in Chapter 5 and of Thompson and Perrow discussed in Chapter 6, we identify the following dimensions of workflow:[2]

1. *Complexity*. At one extreme there are workflows that involve very *little* analysis and problem solving by the associated personnel. At the other extreme are workflows that require a great deal of analysis and problem solving. In a hospital, the workflow in a first aid ward is a good example of *relatively* low complexity; the workflow in an intensive care unit is an example of relatively great complexity. In a firm, the long-term planning and policy formulation unit has a much more complex workflow than the short-term planning unit. The administrative implication of complexity is that the unit must be organically managed, since no one person is likely to have all the expertise for solving problems, and that it must have access to much expertise to carry out technical analysis. A fair amount of teamwork may be needed to solve complex problems.

2. *Variability*. At one extreme are workflows that have an invariant sequence of steps. At the other extreme are workflows whose modus operandi can vary a great deal because of the great variation at the input and the output ends. A job shop is a good example of variable workflow. A mass production unit is a good example of an invariant workflow. In between are workflows that involve a limited number of contingencies. The associated personnel deal with these by standardizing the procedures required to be followed in the event of each contingency. The workflow of the internal audit unit in an organization is of this type, and so is the workflow of many government bureaus.

High variability implies many contingencies. For efficient operations it becomes necessary to devise many rules, each set of rules to be applied in a particular contingency. It also implies that the associated personnel are likely to need equipment and human resources that can be combined flexibly to meet different task contingencies. Many contingencies also imply that advance planning of operations is quite difficult. More or less opposite administrative implications flow from low variability.

3. *Interdependence*. The workflow may consist of highly interdependent performance programs, as in the case of the operating unit in a hospital. The different functions performed by the surgeon, the assistants, the nurses, and so on must be highly synchronized for successful surgery. They need not be integrated that intensively by the medical research unit of a hospital. Coordination and advance planning and scheduling are a key requirement when a great deal of integration or interdependence is needed among the various performance programs constituting the workflow. When the required integration is low, not only is there little need for advance planning and scheduling, but considerable decentralization of operating authority becomes possible. But that makes it difficult to monitor the direction in which the organizational segment is going. The tendency, then, is to set up *overall* controls that monitor overall performance. In a typical research unit there may be little

interdependence among researchers' work. The research unit may, however, try and monitor its performance by computing every year an index of research ideas taken up for development by the corporation.

The three dimensions of the workflow and their administrative consequences are shown in Table 12–1. It is worth stressing that the more homogeneous is the segment of the organizational workflow under consideration,

TABLE 12–1
Dimensions of the Workflow and
Their Administrative and Technological Consequences

Dimension	*Characterization and consequences*	
Invariance	Workflow has invariant pro-⟷grams	Highly variable programs in the workflow
	Consequences: Few contingencies, few rules, advance planning of operations	*Consequences:* Many contingencies, many rules, needed capability for flexibly combining resources, difficulty in advance planning of operations, contingency planning, need for sophisticated information technology
Complexity	Workflow is characterized by⟷little search, analysis, and problem solving	Workflow is characterized by a great deal of search, analysis, and problem solving
	Consequences: Little discretionary decision-making, limited involvement of the rank and file in problem solving, mechanistic management, low power of specialists and high power of line managers, extensive mechanization of operations	*Consequences:* Much discretionary decision-making, intensive involvement of the associated rank and file in problem solving, participative decision-making, organic management, substantial power of specialists, need for sophisticated information technology
Program interdependence	Low interdependence among⟷the programs constituting the workflow	High interdependence among the programs constituting the workflow
	Consequences: Little need for advance planning of operations or for their centralized coordination, substantial autonomy for the operating personnel, use of global controls for monitoring the outputs of the workflow	*Consequences:* Strong need for advance planning of operations and their central coordination, possible desirability of automation of operations, need for sophisticated information technology

The Nature and Dimensions of Workflow **455**

the more accurate are likely to be the predictions of administrative and technological consequences for the work units associated with that segment.

The Determinants of Workflow

What factors determine whether the workflow will be invariant or variable, complex or noncomplex, characterized by highly interdependent or independent programs? Unfortunately, there is little research evidence to guide us in answering these questions. We may speculate, however, that:

1 Organizations (or organizational segments) in stable environments will have invariant workflows, while those in turbulent, dynamic environments will have variable workflows.

2 Organizations in technologically complex *and* turbulent environments will have complex workflows, while those in technologically noncomplex *and* stable environments will have noncomplex workflows. Much design and problem-solving activity is needed to navigate a complex *and* turbulent environment.

3 Organizations having diverse outputs or operating in diverse environments will have workflows characterized by considerable independence of programs, while those having homogeneous outputs or operating in homogeneous environments will have workflows characterized by much interdependence of programs.

Workflow and the Power of Administrative Units

The power of a work unit is likely to depend on how strategic its location is in the workflow of the organization. The work of Hinings, Hickson, Pennings, and Schneck gives us insights about what factors influence the relative power of work units.[3] They focused on the structural sources of power rather than on any personalistic, charismatic sources. They studied the engineering, marketing, production, and accounting units of each of seven manufacturing organizations operating in North America. Their work suggests the following determinants of the relative power of work units:

1 Nonsubstitutability: the less the work of a unit can be substituted by other units, the more power it has.

2 Workflow pervasiveness: the more interconnected the work of a

work unit is with that of other work units in the organization, the greater is its power relative to other work units.

3 Workflow immediacy: the greater the speed and intensity with which the workflow of a unit affects the *final* outputs of an organization, the greater is its power.

4 Coping with uncertainty: the more effectively a work unit copes with the uncertainties it or the organization as a whole faces, the greater power it has, since the easier it is for work units dependent on it to operate effectively.

Hinings and his associates found that especially powerful work units had relatively high scores on all the determinants of power. They judged coping with uncertainty to be the most important source of power, followed by workflow immediacy and nonsubstitutability. They found pervasiveness to be the least important source of a work unit's power.

We propose that:

The more strategic the location of a department or a work unit in the work-flow of an organization, as judged by how well it copes with task uncertainties, the swiftness with which its actions affect the organization's outputs, the nonsubstitutability of its functions, and the pervasiveness of its work connections with other departments,
the greater is its power.

MEANING AND IMPORTANCE OF TECHNOLOGY

In its root, the word "technology" literally means "the measure or design of *method* of performance." In the organizational context we limit its meaning to "the *role* of *mechanical* aids in the workflow." When we talk of technology, we have in mind machinery and plant, laboratory apparatus, mechanical communication aids like the telephone, electronic data-processing equipment, and so forth, as well as the role they play in the work that gets done in the organization. Of these, operations technology and information technology, particularly the computer, have received a fair amount of attention from organizational researchers. We have already reviewed the work of Joan Woodward, James Thompson, and Charles Perrow in Chapter 6, three researchers who have done the most to make technology a central concern of organization theory.[4]

Technology can be thought of as a structural variable because, directly and durably, it shapes human relationships within the organization. The machine, whether it be a computer or an assembly-line plant or oil-fractionating equipment, is often a very expensive and also a very prolific factor of production. Organizations often find it more economical to rearrange their human operatives in response to the installation of a major piece of machinery than vice versa. Subject to some sort of innovation, the men-machine and men-men relationships stemming from such machinery become a permanent feature of the functioning of the organization. In other words, they become part of organizational structure.

Technology has been held to have profound consequences for organizations. Rightly or wrongly, the single greatest fear of blue-collars workers all over the world is automation, the substitution of mechanical devices for labor. Another major concern is job satisfaction: in some quarters, technology is synonymous with boredom on the job. As a number of researchers have tried to show, technology also affects the structure of the organization in many different ways. In this chapter we examine in greater detail some of these multiple consequences, first of operations technology and then of information technology.

DIMENSIONS OF OPERATIONS TECHNOLOGY

The Role of Operations Technology

Operations technology plays several roles in the activities of an organization. It not only transforms inputs into outputs, but it automates the process—that is, it substitutes machinery for human labor—and it helps in the standardization of the organization's outputs. These roles, however, can vary from organization to organization. In some organizations, such as service organizations, there may be minimal automation of operations, which thus remain mostly manual. In certain types of manufacturing organization, on the other hand, such as in oil refining, the technology may be instrumental in greatly automating the operations. In some organizations, such as car-making firms, the operations technology is geared to mass production and standardization. In printeries, it is geared to executing jobs to the specifications of customers.

These varying roles that operations technology plays, of automating operations and standardizing outputs, can be thought of as *dimensions* of operations technology. In other words, the operations technology of an organization can be described usefully by locating it on the dimensions depicted in Table 12–2. Different organizations are likely to show different profiles or designs of operations technology, if an attempt is made to depict them in diagrams of the type shown in the table. The designs of the opera-

TABLE 12–2
Dimensions of Operations Technology

	Technological spectrum	
Automation of operations	Highly labor-intensive, non-automated operations tech- ⟷ nology	Highly capital-intensive, automated operations technology
Standardization of outputs	Highly custom-output oriented operations technology ⟷	Highly standardized-production oriented operations technology

tions technologies of a car manufacturer, a telephone switching-equipment producer, and an employment agency are shown in Figure 12–6 for illustrative purposes.

It is worth stressing again that we are discussing the role of *mechanical* aids utilized in the work of the organization. The analysis of technology to follow makes most sense for organizations or parts of organizations whose operations are considerably mechanized (even if the machinery used is quite labor intensive) and least sense for those whose operations involve little or minimal use of mechanical aids. A telephone exchange in a little developed country is mechanized even if the machinery is far more labor intensive as compared to the computerized telephone exchanges in highly developed countries. A family-planning unit, on the other hand, probably uses little machinery beyond telephones and typewriters. It really has no operations *technology* worth speaking of, although it has a mode of operating and a workflow. Such an organization's (or part of an organization's) technology is not particularly subject to the conclusions drawn from the analysis in this section.*

It is also worth remembering that different parts of a sizable organization may sometimes use quite different operations technologies. In such a case it may make more sense to examine the operations technology in each distinct part and study its consequences for that part rather than try to aggregate the diverse technologies and their administrative and behavioral consequences.

* A rough and ready method for determining the relevance of operations technology in the design of an organization is to compute the value added, where this is feasible, that can be attributed to mechanical aids or machinery. If this value added is a significant percentage of the total value added by the organization, then its operations technology is worth analyzing. If the value added by machinery, etc., is relatively negligible, the operations technology of the organization is likely to have a negligible effect on the organization. *Value added* by the organization is the total value of its sales less outside purchases.

FIGURE 12–6
Dimensions of the Operations Technology of Three Organizations

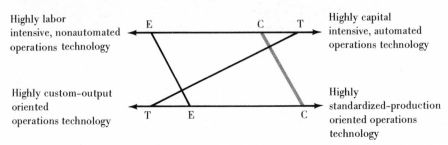

NOTE: E = Employment agency (single line)
C = Car manufacturer (double line)
T = Telephone switching-equipment producer (heavy line)

Capital Intensity–Labor Intensity Dimension

Capital intensity denotes the ratio of the contributions of plant, machinery, and mechanical aids to those made by human labor in the operations of an organization (or part of an organization). Labor intensity is simply the opposite of capital intensity. Examples of capital intensive and labor intensive technologies are easy to find. The production of chemicals is highly capital intensive; in contrast, the production of lumber and wood products is substantially more labor intensive. Wages to operatives account for less than a sixth of the value added by manufacture in the chemicals industry; they account for nearly half of the value added by manufacture in the lumber and wood products industry.[5] The treatment of patients in hospitals and clinics is relatively far more labor intensive than the operations of an oil refinery. This, of course, does not mean that modern hospitals do not use equipment extensively. But, whereas some of the more highly capital intensive industries invest over a million dollars per operative, in dairies, garment-manufacturing firms, hospitals, and universities, for example, the capital investment is often only a few thousand dollars per operative. On the other hand, capital intensity of technologies differs greatly across cultures. There may be steel plants in China that are less capital intensive than dairies in North America. Thus, to assess the capital intensity of an organization's technology relative to others one must bear in mind the society in which the organization is functioning.

A number of situational variables affect the capital intensity of the technology of an organization. Across societies and industries, the general wage level accounts significantly for differences in the capital intensity of the technologies employed by similar types of organization. For example, both wage rates and capital intensity are two to three times higher in the United States as compared to Great Britain in a number of manufacturing industries such as steel, automobiles, machinery, and paper. The higher the wage level, the stronger is likely to be the tendency to substitute capital for labor. The converse, however, is also true. In societies in which machinery is abundantly used, the marginal productivity of labor, and therefore the wage rate, tends to be higher than in those that use little machinery.

Within a society, the level of technological complexity of an industry is likely to affect the capital intensity of the operations technology of organizations operating in it; generally speaking, sophisticated operations are not possible without expensive machinery. In the Canadian study by the author the extent of the reported automation of the operations of firms was strongly correlated with the degree to which their external environment was perceived to be technologically sophisticated and complex and the degree to which the organization's industry was research and development oriented.[6]

We propose that:

The higher the wage rate of operations personnel in a society or an industry, the more capital intensive is the operations technology employed by organizations functioning in that society or industry, and vice versa.

The more technologically sophisticated and complex the industry, the more capital intensive is the operations technology of the organizations functioning in that industry.

How does the capital intensity of technology affect the organization? Capital intensity is generally associated with automation and the displacement of labor by machinery. Because of the widespread fear of automation, we may expect organizations to get militantly unionized as their technologies get more capital intensive unless steps are taken to protect jobs.

Increasing capital intensity may also have other human consequences. Here is a description of the consequences of automation in a steel mill:

After World War II a large American steel corporation decided to install one or more automatic seamless pipe mills "to make a better product more cheaply" and to solve the typical manufacturing problem of "sharper competition in an era of rising costs." They solved the problem—and in the process created, almost without knowing it, a wholly new working world for the men and supervisors affected. What happened in this mill is a story that, in many respects, may be happening over and over again in American industry.

The work environment of this new mill is quite unlike the old, where physical labor and manual control of tool and product prevailed. The complex system of conveyers and moving tables which now take the product through its complete work-flow cycle is wholly automatic, characterized by electric eyes, timing devices, limit switches, rotary controls, and so forth. The top operators are partly technicians, partly coordinators of operations. The furnace discharger has a mixed job, half of it consisting of watching truly automatic equipment, the other half of manually operating levers and buttons. Jobs like the bar inserter's and the stripper's are wholly automatic, performed by machinery without the operator's lifting a hand; but they must watch and, if anything goes wrong, intervene with manual correction.

Here are typical comments from hourly workers:

"I'd rather have to work hard for eight hours than to do nothing physical but have to be tense for eight hours, the way I do now."

"On my old job . . . my muscles got tired. I went home and rested a bit and my muscles were no longer tired. On this new automatic mill, your muscles don't get tired, but you keep on thinking, even when you go home."

The fact that technology is replacing muscular fatigue with increased tension or mental effort is one of the most striking parts of the story—but only one part. In many other ways the unique demands on the human personality imposed by automation are affecting the working lives of both manager and worker in the modern factory.

But what about the impact of technology on the range of human relationships? Individuals function not just as individuals but as members of social groups. Does automation tend to destroy or create a more cohesive work community within the mill with a sense of common interest between its members?

Group Cohesiveness. It was clear from our study that the advent of automatic equipment neither destroyed nor weakened primary work groups as represented by the three hot mill crews. Their internal structure was transformed, but as social units within a larger mill society they remained cohesive and strong. Most members of the mill crews had made or were likely in the future to make work careers out of pipe making. This was a life investment, in other words, and as they put it: "We actually spend more time together than with our own family." In fact, the crew members spent more time with the automatic machines than with any living or nonliving object in their lives (including their automobiles)!

In the seamless pipe mill the forces for social and functional unity were clearly triumphing toward the end of the period of our study. By that time, for example, all or nearly all production and nonproduction workers were sharing in an incentive based on the output of the entire mill. This condition corresponded to the men's wishes and to the nature of the productive process. Finally, although there were many ups and downs in the quantity and quality of worker-supervisor relations, the potential for functional—and friendly—relationships was being realized toward the end of our study.

Joint Problem Solving. The most striking evidence of the desire on the part of the workers to become integrated into a bona fide work community was their continuing eagerness to share in the solution of production problems.

For instance, we asked: "If you were boss, what would you do to make this a better mill?" The two most important answers as measured by frequency and emotion were (a) "better relations with supervision" and (b) "the chance to help solve mill problems." It was obvious that the two ideas were connected in the men's thinking. Moreover, they were talking about something much more intimate, meaningful, and continuous than a "suggestion box." In effect they were saying:

"Each one of us knows more about his own job than anyone else—including management. Besides being individuals, we are members of a closely knit work team, which also tells us important things about this mill and its product. We work at making seamless pipe eight hours a day and expect to do so the rest of our working lives. For these reasons the mill as a work community is as much our mill as management's. Why shouldn't we be asked, then, to contribute our brains and our imagination—as well as our muscle—to the solution of mill problems?"

In short, automation accents the interdependence of all the elements in a plant—men, machinery, maintenance, and management—in achieving uninterrupted production: and interdependence implies participation.[7]

Thus, increasing capital intensity of an organization's technology tends to push lower level members of an organization in different directions: toward greater militancy to protect jobs; toward greater desire for growth, power, self-actualization, autonomy, participation in decision-making, and so on. The current popularity of job enrichment, human relations, and participative or team management may be seen as management's response to these forces in organizations employing capital intensive technologies. Capital intensive technology tends to require in its train a more sophisticated incentive system, a system that relies on the activation of a wide range of human motivations.

The other major effect of employing a more capital intensive technology is that the organization must hire more professionals and skilled personnel. Capital intensive technologies are technically highly complex and generally require highly skilled, often professionally trained staff to work the technology and the associated control system. For example, the electrical equipment industry employs more than double the percentage of professional and skilled personnel employed by labor intensive industries like apparel manufacture and lumber and wood products manufacture.[8] In the author's study of Canadian firms, there was a significant correlation between the degree of reported automation of the firm's technology and the use of various sophisticated staff services and controls.

This professionalization in organizations employing capital intensive technologies has implications for superior-subordinate relations. The professional tends to get his work direction mainly from his training and the nature of the task he is performing. The supervisor is there not so much to direct work or police it as to ensure coordination among technical personnel and to help out subordinates should problems develop. Thus, in organizations employing capital intensive technologies, at the operating levels the relations between the supervisor and the subordinates tend to be egalitarian and organic.

We propose that:

The more capital intensive the operations technology of an organization gets, the more active become the operatives' needs for job security, growth, self-actualization, power, autonomy, and participation in decision-making.

The more capital intensive the organization's operations technology gets, the more sophisticated become the organization's control and incentive system, the more professionalized does its work force get, and the more organic and participative is supervision at the operating levels.

Customized Output—Standardized Mass Output Dimension

One can array technologies along a continuum of how standardized their output is. At one extreme there are organizations (or parts of organizations) that design and produce unique products or services. Many organizations of professionals—clinics, job shops, research labs, consulting engineering firms, architects, and accountants, to name a few—approximate this type. Somewhat in the intermediate range are organizations whose outputs are substantially standardized but also partly differentiated in response to somewhat differentiated customer needs. Universities at the undergraduate level fall into this genre as do banks, insurance companies, and a number of other manufacturing and service organizations. At the far end of the mass, standardized production scale are organizations such as chemical plants, automobile assembly lines, and steel plants, which may have a number of lines of products or services but which strive to produce rather uniform outputs within each such line.

Generally speaking, it is relatively easy to routinize the workflows associated with standardized, mass production technologies. The following is a brief description of the workflow at an assembly line plant of a car manufacturer. It shows how carefully sequenced the various activities in such a plant tend to be.

> The production line is split into four major categories. The first in the series is called the Body Shop. Here, the major components of the body shell (e.g., fenders, roof, etc.) are assembled through the use of highly sophisticated welding machinery. The next step is the Paint Shop. We should initially note that painting is accomplished on a level above the rest of the assembly line. First the cars are dipped in a series of baths in preparation for the final painting. As is the case in the Body Shop, painting operations are highly automated. From there, the shell descends to the Trim and Hardware Department where such fixtures as carpeting, seats, windows, door handles and miscellaneous decorations are installed. These operations are more labor intensive than the two previous ones. The last major department is called either Chassis or Final Assembly, the latter being more appropriate to (the car's) unibody construction. This last operation includes the insertion, from below, of the complete power train, suspension, wheels, etc. Quality checks are made all along the line and the cars undergo various tests after Final Assembly. Any defects are corrected at this stage.[9]

It is commonly believed that the workflow of custom technology organizations is more difficult to routinize because of the greater diversity and unpredictability of the jobs such organizations are called on to perform. However, many such organizations are in fact able to program their workflows to a surprisingly high degree. Typically, they limit the diversity of jobs they are willing to take, and then they work out fairly detailed workflows for the majority of the situations they are likely to be confronted with.[10]

In Chapter 8 (proposition 1) we noted that large organizations tend to be more standardized, mass-output oriented than smaller ones. In Chapter 9 (proposition 3) we noted that as the external environment gets more hostile, there is a tendency for the organization to get more standardized-output oriented. The Canadian study indicated (Chapter 10, proposition 12) that organizations competing on the basis of quality rather than price tended to be custom-output oriented, presumably the better to meet the needs of well-heeled customers and thereby build up a profitable clientele for the organization. The study also indicated that organizations whose top managements considered diversification of the organization's activities as strategically important tended to be more custom-output oriented, presumably the better to serve a large number of partially different market segments.[11]

We propose that:

The greater the importance of diversification to top management,
*   the less oriented the organization's technology is to standardized,*
*   mass outputs and the more oriented it is to customized outputs.*

There are enormous economies in mass producing standardized outputs. And yet many organizations prefer to produce nonstandardized outputs because of the highly differentiated nature of demand for their outputs. To remain viable a hospital simply cannot treat every patient identically. Thus, while the logic of operating efficiency calls for standardized mass production, the logic of differentiated needs of customers often argues in the direction of customization. Sometimes these two opposite pulls can create a very difficult situation for an organization. In the late 1960's an international business machines manufacturing company was in trouble because its marketing personnel insisted on accommodating very particular needs of their clients, in effect forcing the manufacturing department to customize production. The company dominated the industry, but its profitability was dismal.

A major consequence of employing a standardized mass production technology is the need to ensure the steady availability of inputs and disposal of outputs. If supplies of inputs are unreliable, the plant would be forced to operate at uneven loads, and this would imply less than the optimal cost performance. On the other hand, if essential supplies are assured, and if the organization's products or services can be marketed in a predictable way, highly efficient production planning becomes possible. Thus, there is considerable pressure for such organizations to integrate vertically—that is, to acquire control or ownership of crucial inputs and output channels. Steel and oil-refining firms, for example, typically integrate vertically by acquiring ownership of the relevant mineral deposits and by trying to distribute their main products (such as steel and petroleum) through depots, dealers, branches, and the like. The automobile firms are well known for their dealer organizations (forward integration). Not so well known is the tendency of some of the large automobile firms, such as General Motors, to *partially* integrate backwards into the ownership of facilities for producing key parts, components, and even raw materials. This enables them to have considerable control over their principal supplies, and during a recession they can keep their own supplying facilities fully loaded, shifting the blow of the recession onto their external suppliers. Vertical integration in custom technology firms is quite difficult because of the great diversity of their inputs and outputs; if they tried vertical integration, they would be saddled with huge excess capacities and inventories. Subcontracting is usually a more feasible strategy for them.

There is empirical support for the relationship between mass production technology and vertical integration by the organization. In two studies by the author, one of U.S. manufacturing firms and the other of Canadian firms, there was a substantial positive association between the degree to which the firm was mass-production oriented and the degree to which it was vertically integrated. Obversely, custom-production oriented firms tended to be not vertically integrated.[12]

Vertical integration brings some consequences. Since the range of the organization's activities expands, it becomes less feasible to centralize decision-making at the top, and therefore the organization gets formally decentralized. To coordinate and control more effectively the operations that are decentralized, the organization tends to set up a sophisticated information and control system. Thus, those firms that employ a mass, standardized production technology also tend to be vertically integrated, decentralized, and controlled through a sophisticated information and control system.

Another organizational consequence of the custom–standardized output dimension is worth noting. An organization with a standardized mass output technology is likely to have routinized its operations. Such routinization makes possible considerable division of labor and elaborate departmentalization. When the organization is custom-output oriented, high levels of routinization, specialization, and departmentalization become somewhat difficult. Flexibility in the organizational structure becomes very important in order to employ the same men and equipment in a variety of combinations. Consequently, organizations employing custom technology tend to be more informal and organic than organizations employing a standard output technology. Where the nature of the organization's output requires high levels of technical specialization, such as in aerospace firms, the organization tends to develop a matrix structure (discussed in the next chapter) in which specialists are formally assigned to technical functional departments but spend substantial amounts of time working on projects as members of interfunctional teams.

Over the years assembly line technology, a form of mass production technology, has got a bad name for causing boredom on the job.[13] There is little question that when work is standardized and routinized it can get quite boring. Also, in firms employing assembly line technology, because the work is machine paced, the worker may experience a loss of control over his work and thus slump into passivity.[14] However, at lower organizational levels, intellectually unexciting work is the practice in non-mass output organizations as well. The ward boys, the laboratory technicians, the secretaries, the sweepers, even when they may be working in custom type organizations, do not noticeably wax eloquent about the intellectual challenge of their jobs. One must be careful in apportioning blame for worker alienation to a specific technology. While specialization, monotony, and passivity may be the lot of most operatives in assembly line organizations, specialization characterizes most operators of non-assembly line technologies as well. The latter's work may be a little more varied, but not necessarily more interesting or less routinized.

Actually, even in an assembly line plant, appropriate management practices can lead to fairly high levels of morale. When hourly workers at a Canadian car-manufacturing plant were asked whether they found their work interesting, 65 percent agreed or strongly agreed that they did, and 28 percent disagreed or strongly disagreed (compare these, however, with scores of 82 percent and 16 percent for salaried employees).[15] At this plant, a climate of open and frank communication between supervisors and operatives seemed to be a factor in the relatively high levels of job satisfaction expressed by the operatives.

We propose that:

The more the operations technology of an organization is geared to standardized mass outputs of goods or services,

> *the more vertically integrated and decentralized the organization tends to become and the more sophisticated is its control and information system;*
> *the more rigidly departmentalized and structured are its activities; and*
> *the more attention management needs to pay to human relations to maintain a given level of morale among operatives.*

Information Technology

Ever since organizations first arose, their managements have striven to get regular and reliable information. Information is needed for a variety of purposes—for control and coordination of current activities, for planning future moves, for innovating. As civilization has grown more complex, the organization's task environment and the organization's internal operations have grown more complex, too. The need for information has grown proportionately.

In parts of Africa today drums are a major means for communicating information over distances. The ancient Egyptian government used to keep its records on papyrus leaves, and the Babylonian government kept its on stone tablets. The advent of printing facilitated far more complex organizational activities than those of these venerable organizations. Today the vast business of the governmental organization or of the modern corporation would be all but impossible without prodigiously powerful instruments for recording, storing, and processing information. Of these instruments the electronic computer is, of course, the most formidable. Other information technology machines are accounting machines, telex equipment, filing systems, typewriters, telephones, dictaphones. Their impact on the organization, however, pales in comparison to the apparent impact of the computer.

Information technology bears a close resemblance to operations technology. It incorporates a substantial mechanical component. Like operations technology, it embodies an input-throughout (or process)-output cycle, but with information as the input and the output. The computer, as a machine, is highly capital intensive, capable of highly customized production of data, capable, when appropriately programmed, of transforming data to a very great extent. Let us examine in some depth the effect this versatile machine has had on the organization.

The Computer and the Organization

The computer has fascinated many organization researchers and thinkers. Much as God may be admiring—perhaps fearing—the brilliance of His human creations, many humans are awed by the versatility and computational power of this mechanical counterpart of the human brain. A powerful computer can compute in a minute what a thousand accountants may take a year to compute. What is more, computers have been programmed to solve complex problems, compose fugues, play chess, and perform a variety of tasks that can do justice to a first-rate mind. Researchers have been able to program a computer to develop in a few hours many of the theorems that Russell and Whitehead developed after years of laborious work.[16]

Simon claimed that in a few years it would be possible, in principle, to computerize practically all operations (other than purely manual operations), including decision-making.[17] He cautioned, however, that just because this becomes possible does not mean that in fact operations will get almost totally computerized. Whether organizations computerize their operations, and to what extent, will depend on the comparative advantage of the computer vis-à-vis humans in particular operations. For example, if computer time is utilized for inventory control and production scheduling more productively than for long-range policy information, and human capabilities show a reverse *relative* advantage, then even if, in terms of cost, the computer is superior to humans in both production scheduling and policy formulation, the chances are that the computer will specialize in production scheduling and humans in policy formulation (the argument was long ago developed by economists into the doctrine of comparative advantage to explain trade between nations).

In the 1950's and 1960's a number of sometimes quite contradictory predictions were made concerning the impact of the computer on the organization. There was no dispute about the likely automation of many accounting and clerical jobs. Given the vast computational ability of the computer, most management researchers concluded that whatever requires measurement and number manipulation would be computerized. The bone of contention was what effect the computer would have on managerial decision-making, particularly on whether decision-making would be centralized or decentralized. Some felt that since middle level managers make relatively structured decisions (ordering of inventories, scheduling of production, selection of media for advertising and promotion, approving minor capital expenditures, etc.), their jobs essentially would be eliminated because the computer would be able to make these decisions much faster and more consistently and logically, or at least that the middle manager's job would become more structured since he would become a prisoner of the information provided by the computer.[18] Some others felt that, on the contrary, middle managers would be able to sit back and think "big" for a change, that in effect they would take on more and more the roles of the top managers, and they would be able to delegate many of their present chores to lower level assistants.[19] Some felt that the computer would have essentially no impact on middle or top management,[20] while a few felt that the computer would facilitate centralization of decision-making if that is the top management philosophy but could equally facilitate decentralization should that be its philosophy.[21] To assess these contradictory predictions, given the rapidly changing nature of computer technology, the difficulty of assessing the relative advantage of the computer vis-à-vis the human in different kinds of work, and the versatility of the computer, let us turn to research evidence.

An article by Charles Hoffer provides an admirable summary of research findings, his own and those of several others.[22]

1. Computer applications have led to drastic changes at the middle management level (supervisory to executive junior grade). Many jobs have been either combined or eliminated.

    EDP has systematized and standardized formal information flow and also has seemed to dam up the upward and downward flow of information through both formal and informal channels.

    As more and more operations are programmed, the power and status of new computer personnel have been expanded, while the functions of other departments have been undercut, and the authority of their managers truncated.

EDP stimulates two distinct kinds of recentralization—one type referring to the integration of specific functions, the other involving regrouping of entire units of the operation and causing sweeping changes of the external structure as well.[23]

2. While EDP has undoubtedly eliminated a vast amount of monotonous, detailed administrative work, there has been no accompanying reduction in the need for middle managers. Actually, EDP has made the middle manager's job more complex.

The centralization of activities has not been accompanied by an elimination of managerial positions. On the contrary, EDP and the new activities have resulted in the addition of over 50 middle management positions in the companies studied.[24]

3. The nature and magnitude of the EDP impact is basically governed by the computer technology and the management attitude toward the use of the technology.

Drastic changes (centralization of the decision-making process and reduction in the number of middle management jobs) have not occurred to date in the companies studied during the early period of industrial experience with EDP.[25]

4. Top management does not seem to use the computer directly for decision-making.

The use of the computer by middle management permits top management to:
  Make some decisions at an earlier date.
  Gain time in which to consider some decisions.
  Consider more thorough analysis of some situations.
  Review several courses of action on many problems.
  Examine analyses of the impact that recommended courses of action will have on the problem or opportunity identified.
  Obtain additional information from middle managers concerning problems, opportunities, and promising alternatives before making decisions.[26]

Hoffer also reports the results of his own in-depth research on two firms, one of which was a division of a corporation with divisional sales of $200 million, and another a firm with sales of $8 million a year.[27] His major findings for the two companies are:

1 At the functional level (marketing, production, and other functional departments), as well as at those operating levels which processed a

large amount of *quantitative* data, new roles related to data processing were created, such as the positions of data-processing manager, programmers, and systems analysts. Some hierarchical reorganization of units also took place.

2 In those operating levels that processed a great deal of *quantitative* data, there was a substantial increase in personnel efficiency, as measured by the ratio of number of staff in the operating unit to total firm sales.

3 At the top functional level—that is, at the level of the heads of functional departments—there was some delegation of decision-making authority to subordinates and a tendency to pay greater attention to the planning of operations. At the operating levels, the quality of decisions tended to improve, and some decisions were programmed into the computer.

4 Managers at the top functional level were able to devote more time to examining ways to improve systems and operating procedures, and at those operating levels where not much quantitative data was processed, managers were better able to direct attention to areas where efforts would be most productive.

5 At the general management level (topmost management level), managers were able to ask for more detailed back-up statistics on problems. At the top functional levels quantitative measures of the performance of operations level personnel and units improved in both content and accuracy. At the operating levels quantitative measures of the performance of employees, distributors, suppliers, and so on similarly improved.

Hoffer's study suggests that the computer has had maximum impact on those top functional units and operating units that process a lot of quantitative data, somewhat more limited impact on those top functional units and operating units that do not process much quantitative data, and minimal impact on the topmost or general management. The impact, in general, was positive in the sense that the *quality* of decision-making improved, the time perspective of managers got enlarged, control and evaluation became more precise, and so on.

The data in the author's Canadian study indicated that the use of EDP by the firm was significantly and independently correlated (a) with the size of the organization; (b) with the extent to which the organization used a large distribution network of branches, dealers, and the like; (c) with the technological sophistication of the environment; (d) with the restrictiveness of the environment; and (e) with delegation of authority by the chief executive.

We propose that:

The larger the organization;
the wider its distribution network;
the more technologically complex its external environment; and
the more restrictive the environment,
> *the more extensively does the organization use an electronic data processing system.*

The greater the use of an electronic data processing system,
> *the more it facilitates decentralization, and*
> *the more it permits quicker and more integrated decision-making.*

The more quantifiable the informational inputs or outputs of a department,
> *the greater is the impact of the computer on the administrative structure of the department in terms of increased power of EDP specialists, reorganization of the workflow, and greater complexity in the job of the departmental manager.*

SUMMARY, PROPOSITIONS, AND IMPLICATIONS FOR ORGANIZATIONAL DESIGN

Summary

Workflow is the sequencing of the organization's activities from the receipt of inputs through the processing of these inputs to the export of the outputs to the environment. It is the organization's structure in motion. Technology is the role of the mechanical aids used in transforming inputs into outputs. Two broad kinds of technology are the production or operations technology and information-processing technology. Workflow, operations technology, and information technology are intimately related. The overall workflow of an organization gets elaborated into smaller, less comprehensive workflows. Along with the flow of activities there is an information flow and a decision flow. Three dimensions of a workflow are complexity, variability of its constituent programs, and interdependence of the constituent programs. Important administrative consequences are associated with these dimensions, as shown in Table 12–1. It is useful to remember that different segments of the organizational workflow may vary greatly from one another in terms of these dimensions, thus creating differences in related administrative structures. Those departments that have a strategic position in the workflow wield substantial power in the organization.

Technology, where machinery is widely used, has many organizational consequences, such as the fear of automation, job dissatisfaction, the awakening of various needs, and effect on organizational structure.

The major dimensions of operations technology are the extent to which it is oriented to standardized production of outputs rather than custom production and the extent to which organizational operations are capital intensive rather than labor intensive. Since large organizations employ several technologies, in such organizations it may be useful to identify these technologies and assess their local administrative consequences.

Information technology is similar to operations technology, except that the former processes information, while the latter processes goods or services. The computer dominates contemporary information technology.

There has been considerable speculation on the impact of the computer on organizations and their managements, as well as some research. The available research indicates that the computer has less impact at the topmost management level than at those operating levels that make great use of quantifiable data. Generally speaking, its impact is positive in the sense that the quality of operating decisions tends to improve, the time perspective of managers gets enlarged, and control and evaluation become more precise.

Propositions

1. The more strategic the location of a department or a work unit in the workflow of an organization—as judged by how well it copes with task uncertainties, the swiftness with which its actions affect the organization's outputs, the nonsubstitutability of its functions, and the pervasiveness of its work connections with other departments—
   the greater is its power.

2. The higher the wage rate of operations personnel in a society or an industry,
   the more capital intensive is the operations technology employed by organizations functioning in that society or industry, and vice versa.

3. The more technologically sophisticated and complex the industry,
   the more capital intensive is the operations technology of the organizations functioning in that industry.

4. The more capital intensive the operations technology of an organization gets,
   the more active become the operatives' needs for job security, growth, self-actualization, power, autonomy, and participation in decision-making.

5. The more capital intensive the organization's operations technology gets,

> the more sophisticated become the organization's control and incentive system;
>
> the more professionalized its work force gets; and
>
> the more organic and participative is supervision at the operating levels.

6. The greater the importance of diversification to top management,

> the less oriented the organization's technology is to standardized mass outputs and the more oriented it is to customized outputs.

7. The more the operations technology of an organization is geared to standardized mass outputs of goods or services,

> the more vertically integrated and decentralized the organization tends to become and the more sophisticated is its control and information system;
>
> the more rigidly departmentalized and structured are its activities; and
>
> the more attention needs to be paid by management to human relations to maintain a given level of morale among operatives.

8. The larger the organization;
   the wider its distribution network;
   the more technologically complex its external environment; and
   the more restrictive the environment,

> the more extensively does the organization use an electronic data processing system.

9. The greater the use of an electronic data processing system,

> the more it facilitates decentralization, and
>
> the more it permits quicker and more integrated decision-making.

10. The more quantifiable the informational inputs or outputs of a department,

> the greater is the impact of the computer on the administrative structure of the department in terms of increased power of EDP specialists, reorganization of the workflow, and greater complexity in the job of the departmental manager.

Implications for Organizational Design

The interrelationships between workflow, operations technology, and information technology provide plenty of grist for the mill of the organizational designer. The problem is one of so designing the operating system of the organization that all necessary activities are properly sequenced, operations are efficiently discharged, the flow of information is commensurate with the flow of activities, decisions are synchronized with the flow of activities, *and* this whole operating system is acceptable to the operating personnel.[28] Hopefully, by formally stating the likely consequences of alternative actions, such as making the operations technology more capital intensive or more custom oriented, or making greater use of the computer, we make the task of the organizational designer a more manageable one.

The option for the designer is either to let nature take its course as suggested by theory, or to make the probable happen more efficiently and with less organizational trauma, or to take steps to *prevent* what is probable. If an organization has decided to go in for more capital intensive equipment, the designer can decide to let the operations people adapt to the situation incrementally and in a fire-fighting manner. The *eventual* results are likely to be higher wage levels, possible staff retrenchment, union militancy, hiring of more technically trained personnel, greater pressure for participative decision-making at operating levels, and so on. These may come about after a long time and many crises. On the other hand, knowing what is likely to occur, the designer can institute a training program to update the technical skills of operatives, a program to make the supervisors more participatively oriented, a review of wage and salary classifications to bring them into line with new realities. If the designer does not like the idea of increasing union militancy, he may try to prevent this by getting the union leadership involved in the planning of change.

SUGGESTED READINGS

Eliot Chapple and Leonard Sayles, "The Workflow As the Basis of Organizational Design," in D. Hampton, C. Summer, and R. Weber, *Organizational Behavior and the Practice of Management* (Glenview, Ill.: Scott, Foresman, 1968).

Charles Hoffer, "Emerging EDP Pattern," *Harvard Business Review* (March-April 1970).

P. N. Khandwalla, "Mass Output Orientation of Operations Technology and Organizational Structure," *Administrative Science Quarterly* (March 1974).

QUESTIONS FOR ANALYSIS

1 Here are technological and other data on two corporations. What designs are appropriate for them?

	Corporation X	Corporation Y
Size	Medium	Medium
Industry	Printing	Chemicals
Mass production orientation	Medium	High
Automation of operations technology	Low	High
Use of electronic data processing	High	High

2 Here are technological and other data on two corporations in service industries. What designs are appropriate for them? What designs would be appropriate if they were two government welfare agencies rather than two corporations?

	Corporation M	Corporation N
Size	Medium	Medium
Industry	Banking	Merchandising
Standardized operations	Moderate	Moderate
Automation of operations	High	Low
Use of EDP	High	Low

3 Read the "Pioneer company (A) Part 2" case in the book by Dalton, Lawrence, and Lorsch (pp. 175–182).[29] Analyze the technology and workflow of the company. What organizational design would be appropriate?

4 Here is a description of the workflow in the inventory control unit of the Collins Card Company, a large American greeting-card manufacturing company. The company manufactures about a million cards a day, ranging in price from about two cents to a dollar. Production includes cards for birthdays, Christmas, New Year, Valentine's Day, and so forth. Identify the main performance programs in the workflow. Flowchart the different activities to the extent possible. Analyze the workflow and indicate what organizational design is most appropriate for the inventory control unit.

When orders for everyday cards are received, they first go to the credit department, and then to shipping, and then to production planning where they are entered on record cards. Monthly, the sales for each card are entered on the manufacturing record cards in the production control department and are deducted from a running total of stock on hand. From the running total the time when it is necessary to rerun can be seen. As a double check there is a red stock control ticket inserted in the pile of boxes at the return point. When this is uncovered, it is sent to production planning.

The rerun point is first set on the basis of estimated sales, allowing enough so that the stock will not run out during the rerun time. This rerun point is then adjusted according to actual volume of sales.

From 8 to 10 weeks are usually allowed for rerun time, although it may actually take less time than this for manufacture. The management chooses the right time to reorder during this period, thus avoiding conflicts with other lines.

Among the everyday cards are some cards that are "proven sellers," those cards which if kept in the sales line more than one year will keep up roughly the same sales volume. There are 160 models of birthday cards that are considered proven sellers. Since birthdays occur throughout the year, the sales for these proven seller birthday cards is just about a constant. Collins Card tries to maintain a minimum base inventory that will cover this constant demand and still keep setup costs on reruns at a minimum. The company adds a 30-day card supply to the basic inventory stock to serve as a safety factor. Exhibit 3 is a summary of production data for Card 1923, a proven birthday seller.

The seasonal cards are shown to dealers about 9 months or more before the date for which the cards were designed. By this showing date the original run of cards has to be furnished so as to have cards available for sampling. This initial run is about 60 per cent of the estimated sales of the card. After the line has been out for about 30 days, the sales are analyzed to determine how much should be rerun. By comparing past sales performances at this time, and knowing from experience the number of each type of card that will probably be sold, the management claims that they can predict the sales of each card within about 2 per cent.

Exhibit 3
Card No. 1923 (Two-Color)

1. Sales—about $100,000 worth of cards were sold to dealers last year
2. Unit cost—2.25 cents
3. Sales price to dealer—5 cents
4. Retail price—10 cents
5. Annual carrying charge: on stock in general: about 4 per cent of amount of sales to dealers, according to company estimates
6. Setup charges
   a. Material: $80/color/plate
   b. There are 16-card patterns/plate
   c. Concurrent expenses setup time, $5.00
7. Opportunity cost of capital—10 per cent

The cards are broken down into two basic types: good sellers which will be rerun in amounts greater than that necessary to satisfy the demand for the year, and the poorer cards which will either not be rerun or rerun in small enough amounts so that they will definitely run out. The cards that are left over will be resampled the next year if enough are left to make it worth while. If some of the poorer selling cards are left over, they are scrapped. In any case, if the original run of cards or the first rerun is not sold by the end of the second year, it is discarded.

The poorer cards demand constant management attention so that no cards are left over after the period in which they were designed to be sold. Management likes to keep these cards in stock until the end of the ordering period, since they like to have the full number of cards in the line at all times. However, any cards that are left at the end of the period are completely valueless. Top management feels that it is much more important to avoid this financial loss than to take care of the slight loss in good will that might come about from removing cards from the line early.

The stock of cards is constantly watched, and the salesmen are notified so that, in the ideal case, they will remove the card from their line exactly when the stock of cards runs out. If the card that has been ordered by a dealer is out of stock, most dealers allow a similar card to be substituted, but about 10 per cent of the orders are lost.

The management has to decide on the proper time to notify salesmen that a poor seller is being pulled from the line. This means that the management must decide on the proper lead stock necessary for notifying the salesmen. This is done so that the company will be able to supply the cards that the salesmen sell while the "pull" notification is being mailed to them. When they call the card out too early, any left unsold will probably be lost, unless there is time to put the card back into some salesmen's lines. If the notification goes out too late, the salesmen will oversell the supply of this card, and the company will have to substitute in the order. As mentioned earlier, not being able to supply a card results in about a 10 per cent loss in orders. If the proper lead stock has been determined, the company will have just enough cards to fill the orders taken, while the order was being mailed to the salesmen. This lead stock is also supposed to have a safety allowance for the salesman who forgets to pull the card from his line after he receives the notification.

If the management feels that they can dispose of more of these poor cards, they order a rerun. The actual amount of printing rejects for a rerun is hard to predict, but the reruns can be made small enough so that the company is almost sure to run out of the poorer cards at the end of a particular selling period.

The good selling seasonal cards are much easier to manage. There is very little penalty for holding cards over. They are only stored for a few months more than a new line made for the next year. This is due to the fact mentioned above that the cards are manufactured about a year early so that some can be available for sampling. Storage costs are about 12 per cent of the cost price per year, and the extra storage time is about 2 months. The management says that about 95 per cent of the carryover is salable. This 5 per cent that is not salable is mostly made up of some of the poorer cards that are left over.

At the beginning of a season the management has to decide on the amount to be rerun and added to the holdover stock in preparation for the new sales season. Again, management feels that they lose 10 per cent of their orders by not having a particular card in stock when an order comes in. Management also wants to have some kind of a safety factor so that if the demand is larger than they had originally planned, they will have enough cards ready.

The company feels that the preseasonal reruns and original runs on these good seasonal sellers should be as big as possible. Of course there is always some chance that the card will not sell this season which prevents them from making the printing runs too large. One factor that tends to make runs as high as possible is that if they carry over enough to last for a while the next year, then the company can wait until the second year rerun to make more. This means that they can cut down on future storage time and eliminate the setup costs for one printing. Since the cards are not shipped until after the orders have been taken, in fact quite a bit after, if they have enough cards to sample for the next year, there is no reason to run more and store them.[30]

Footnotes to Chapter Twelve

[1] See Raymond E. Miles, *Theories of Management*, Ch. 6, for a discussion of non-formal communication flows.

[2] James March and Herbert Simon, *Organizations*; J. D. Thompson, *Organizations in Action*; Charles Perrow, *Organizational Analysis: A Sociological View*.

[3] Chris Hinings, et al., "Structural Conditions of Intraorganizational Power."

[4] See Joan Woodward, *Management and Technology*, and its expanded version, *Industrial Organization: Theory and Practice*.

[5] U.S. Dept. of Commerce, *Census of Manufactures, 1967*, p. 28.

[6] See Appendix A for a description of the author's study of Canadian firms.

[7] C. W. Walker, "Life in the Automatic Factory."

[8] U.S. Dept. of Commerce, *Census of Manufactures, 1967*, p. 165.

[9] From a study by Messrs. Baer, Case, Charland, Grenier, and Kerr, all McGill University M.B.A. students.

[10] For an example of the workflow of a custom manufacturer, see Edward Bowman and Robert Fetter, *Analysis for Production Management*, pp. 509–19.

[11] The correlation of each of environmental hostility, high quality high price (rather than standard quality and low price) orientation, image, organizational size, and strategic importance of diversification with the mass, standardized production orientation of the firm's operations technology was statistically significant even after controlling for the effects of the three other independent variables.

[12] See P. N. Khandwalla, "Mass Output Orientation of Operations Technology and Organizational Structure."

[13] See C. R. Walker and R. H. Guest, *The Man on the Assembly Line*.

[14] Robert Blauner, "Work Satisfaction and Industrial Trends in Modern Society."

[15] From a report by Messrs. Baer, Case, Charland, Grenier, and Kerr.

[16] See Julian Feldman and Edward A. Feigenbaum, *Computers and Thought*.

[17] Herbert Simon, *The New Science of Management Decision*.

[18] Harold Leavitt and T. Whisler, "Management in the 1980's."

[19] Melvin Aushen, "The Manager and the Black Box."

[20] John Dearden, "Computers: No Impact on Divisional Control."

[21] John F. Burlingame, "Information Technology and Decentralization."

[22] Charles Hoffer, "Emerging EDP Pattern."

[23] Ida Hoos, "When the Computer Takes Over the Office."

[24] Donald Shaul, "What's Really Ahead for Middle Management?"

[25] Hak Chong Lee, "The Impact of Electronic Data Processing upon Patterns of Business Organization and Administration."

[26] Rodney H. Brady, "Computers in Top Management Decision Making."

[27] Hoffer, *op. cit.*

[28] See Eliot D. Chapple and Leonard R. Sayles, "The Workflow As the Basis of Organizational Design," for some useful suggestions, particularly their suggestion that the workflow should be very carefully identified and that the design of the organization's structure should be based on the flow of work in such a way as to minimize costs of coordination.

[29] G. W. Dalton, Paul R. Lawrence, and Jay Lorsch, *Organizational Structure and Design*, pp. 175–77.

[30] Edward Bowman and Robert Fetter, *Analysis for Production Management*, pp. 522–26.

13

The Structure
of Organizations

Start

DEFINITION AND FUNCTIONS OF ORGANIZATIONAL STRUCTURE

Structure is the more or less permanent arrangement of the parts of a whole. Organizational structure is the network of *durable* and *formally sanctioned* organizational *arrangements* and *relationships.** Durable relationships between individuals in the organization, between individuals and machines, and between work groups are all elements of organizational structure. Permanent arrangements about who reports to whom, how an organizational participant is expected to communicate with other participants, what functions he is to perform, and what rules and procedures link together the activities of organizational members are parts of organizational structure. What rewards and sanctions influence the relationships of members with one another and with the mechanical devices employed by the organization, how members are grouped together, what relationships link subordinates to their superiors, line personnel to staff personnel, and so forth, are other common aspects of structure.

What writers on bureaucracy such as Weber call the hierarchy of au-

---

* The actual behavior of the members of an organization may often deviate from these officially sanctioned or prescribed arrangements and relationships.

482

thority, formal intermember communications, specialization of functions, and specification of rules and procedures are elements of organizational structure. What students of classical management theory such as Urwick call the organization chart, forms of departmentalization, and the span of control are also elements of organization structure. What the administrative decision-making theorists such as Simon call performance programs are also elements of structure. In every case, however, the element of structure is a formally sanctioned relationship. It is, or is intended to be, durable. And it is, or is intended to be, an appropriate *administrative* means by which the organization goes about achieving the purposes for which it is set up.

Organizational structure performs three major functions. First of all, it affords the organization the mechanisms with which to *reduce* external and internal *uncertainty*. The forecasting, research, and planning units in the organization help it to reduce external uncertainty. The control units help it to reduce uncertainty arising out of variable, unpredictable, random human or mechanical behavior within the organization. Next, it enables the organization to undertake a wide *variety* of activities through devices such as departmentalization, specialization, division of labor, and delegation of authority. Finally, it enables the organization to keep its activities *coordinated,* to pursue goals, to have a focus in the midst of diversity. Hierarchy, formal committees, information system are all aspects of the structure that facilitate the integration of organizational activities.

In this chapter we discuss two aspects of organizational structure, the highly visible superstructure, or departmentalization, and the less visible network of controls, procedures, authority relationships, specialization, and the like that may be called the organization's infrastructure. We discuss why each is an important subject of study; what situational, strategic, and technological forces determine the form of each in an organization; and what are some of their behavioral implications. Figure 13–1 lays out the terrain of this chapter.

THE SUPERSTRUCTURE OF ORGANIZATIONS

Importance

The superstructure of an organization is the way it is departmentalized—that is, the way its personnel are grouped into different departments, divisions, or sections. The superstructure also describes how these departments are *related* to one another. It is important because it tells us at a glance how the organization is *geared* to meet its tasks. A firm that has a production, a

FIGURE 13-1
The Coverage of This Chapter

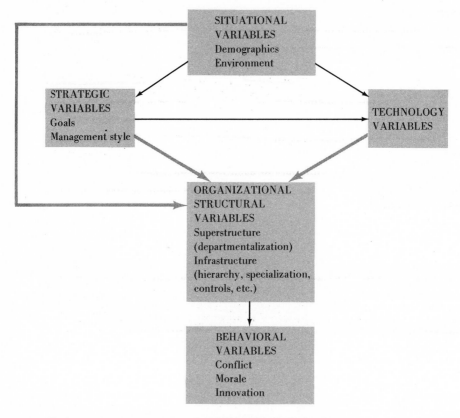

NOTE: The heavier lines represent the relationships explored in this chapter.

marketing, a finance, a personnel, and an engineering vice president report-ing to the president is evidently geared differently to running its business than another firm in the same industry in which divisional heads report to the president. The superstructure tells us how *differentiated* the organization is—that is, how elaborately specialized its activities are that involve groups of people. One firm may have a marketing department, a sales department, and a distribution department. Another may have only one omnibus mar-keting department. The superstructure may also indicate some of the princi-pal ways in which the organization's operations are *integrated* or coordinated. For example, the superstructure may indicate whether top level coordina-tion is by formally designated executives or through committees of top level executives. The superstructure also tells us what different arrangements the organization may have for reducing environmental *uncertainty*—whether for example, the organization has attempted to reduce this uncertainty through vertical integration, through setting up research, forecasting, and planning units. The superstructure tells us which groups, because of their proximity to the top levels of management, have *strategic* importance and which do not because they report to lower management levels. In short, the superstructure in good measure represents the top management's *administrative* strategy.

The superstructure is commonly depicted pictorially by the organizational chart.[1] Consider the following organizational chart of a brewery (Figure 13–2). The chart is given for the first three levels of the management, and for an additional level in respect of "Production." Notice that the top management considers personnel, production, marketing, and finance as the four key functional areas. Members of each functional department, as shown for the production department, are in turn further grouped into more specialized sections. Members of each section may, in turn, be allocated to even more specialized groups. Notice also that in its production operations, the organization is not very vertically integrated—there is no indication that the firm owns its own barley fields or has facilities for manufacturing its own bottles and cans. The existence of seven departments under production suggests that at least that function is fairly highly differentiated. Since the organization chart does not show any top level committees, the integration of operations seems primarily to be through the "boss." The absence of specialized staff departments reporting at high management levels suggests that staff activities are not of great strategic importance in this firm. Contrast this chart with the superstructure of a giant maker of cars as shown in

FIGURE 13–2
The Organizational Chart of a Brewery

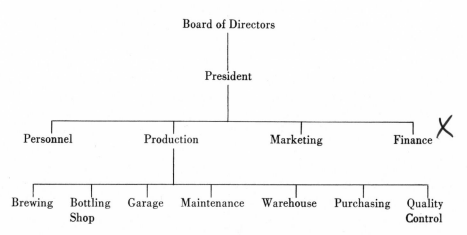

FIGURE 13–3
The Organizational Chart of an Automobile Producer

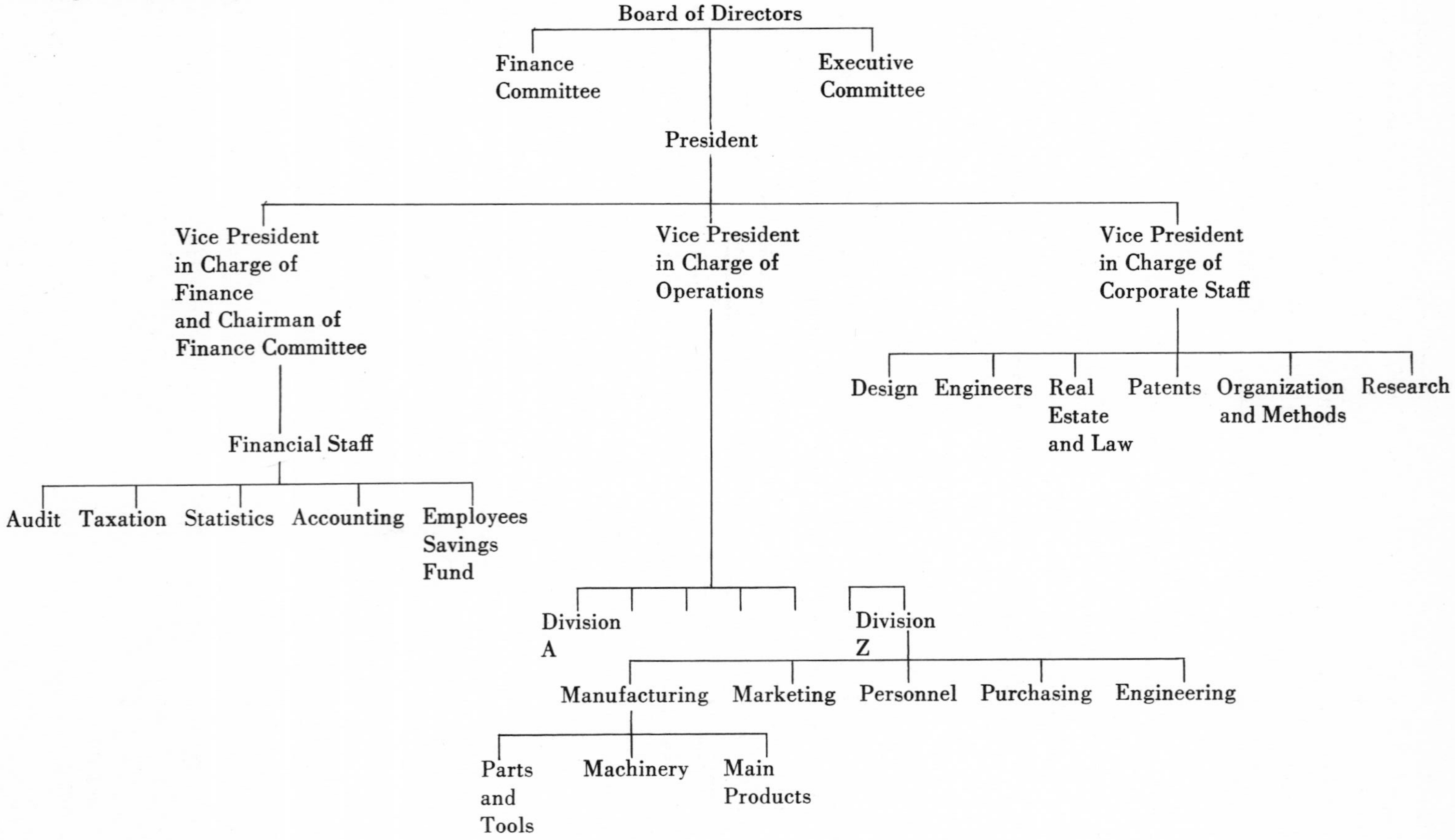

its organizational chart (Figure 13–3). It shows an organization vastly more complex and differentiated, highly divisionalized, powerfully oriented to finance, operating efficiency, and technical staff expertise, an organization that relies heavily on top level committees to integrate its operations, an organization that, as shown in its typical Z division, is highly vertically integrated.

Factors Affecting Groupings of Personnel

What factors influence the way people are grouped together in organizations —that is, allocated to departments, divisions, or sections? Thompson suggests that organizations strive to minimize the costs of coordinating their activities.[2] He further suggests that coordination costs are maximum when two individuals (or groups) are reciprocally dependent, as when the output of one becomes the input of another *and* vice versa. When this is the case the two need to communicate very frequently. Each must dovetail his activity carefully with that of the other. A common example is that of people involved in designing a product such as a television set. The electrical engineers determine in theoretical terms what the overall system will be like. The mechanical engineers try to fit the components together, and these components in turn have to fit the cabinet designed by other engineers. Engineers involved with automation design the machinery which makes the printed circuits and attaches the tubes to it, while industrial engineers determine the efficient techniques by which the set will be manufactured. However, all of these engineers must constantly interact because modifications by one will require modifications by all the others. A change in the cabinet, for instance, may require adjustments by every other section, and the adjustments by the latter may trigger further adjustments all around.

Thompson argues that to minimize coordination costs, organizations tend first to group together individuals or groups that are reciprocally dependent. Next, they tend to group together individuals some of whom are dependent on the rest but not vice versa. That is, they group serially or sequentially dependent individuals with those on whom they are dependent for their inputs, such as assembly line crews. Finally, they group together individuals who are only indirectly dependent on one another ("pooled" interdependence). For example, in a secretarial pool, the work secretaries perform may not be directly related. However, by its very nature, if one secretary is absent or busy, the others have to pick up any new work that comes into the pool.

While Thompson highlights the nature of interdependence among organizational participants as a major factor affecting departmentalization, there are other rationales, too, for grouping people. One is the span of control or supervision. There are limits on the number of individuals a supervisor can effectively supervise directly. These limits, of course, vary depending on the nature of the tasks performed by the subordinates, the intensity of required interaction between the boss and the subordinates, and so on. But, clearly, if a person is supervising ten individuals effectively, doubling that number may drastically reduce the quality of supervision. Thus, several sections of individuals performing similar work may have to be formed to retain an adequate quality of supervision.

Ease of supervision is a factor in grouping together individuals who perform the same type of work. If accountants (or for that matter any other group of specialists) were scattered randomly throughout the organization, their immediate supervisors would not have the expertise to provide competent supervision. By putting all the accountants together in the accounting department under the chief accountant, the organization is able to assure itself of a reasonably high degree of control over their activities.

Moreover, birds of a feather often like to flock together. If, in a brewery, bottlers were mixed together with market researchers, since they have little in common, morale and communication would probably fall. Bottlers are more likely to get along well with other bottlers, much as market researchers are likely to prefer the company of other market researchers. Thus, morale is an important reason why people doing similar things are grouped together.

Putting together individuals performing similar technical functions is beneficial from another point of view, too. It makes it easier for the rest of the organization to gain access to their specialized skills. This is a particularly important rationale for grouping together staff or service personnel having specialized skills whose services are needed widely throughout the organization. Examples are the personnel department, the computer services department, the plant maintenance department, guidance and counseling services in universities and schools, and various medical laboratories in hospitals. In fact, the more diversified the demand for the services of specialists of a type, the more likely they are to be grouped together.

Thus, a number of forces influence departmentalization in an organization. The most important considerations revolve around the need for coordination, ease of supervision, the social needs of individuals, and access to specialists.

We propose that:

The greater the reciprocal interdependence between personnel;
the greater their serial dependence; and
the greater their pooled interdependence,
     the greater is the probability of their being grouped together.

488   *The Structure of Organizations*

As between the three forms of dependence,

1. *reciprocal interdependence will be the strongest factor in grouping together individuals;*
2. *serial dependence the next strongest; and*
3. *pooled interdependence the weakest.*

The greater the ratio of subordinates doing a particular kind of work to their supervisors (beyond what is considered the optimal span of control for that kind of work),

the greater will be the pressure to increase the number of departments or groupings of personnel doing the same type of work.

The more specialized the tasks performed by individuals,

the more likely they are to be grouped together by areas of specialization to permit effective supervision.

The greater the similarity in the kind of work performed by individuals and in their norms and values related to work and to interpersonal relations,

the greater the probability of their being grouped together for maintaining morale.

The more diversified the demand for a service within an organization,

the more likely it is that individuals providing that service will be grouped together to facilitate access to them.

The preceding propositions suggest that while reciprocal interdependence is often a powerful force for grouping complementary personnel (such as different types of engineer engaged in designing a product, or the different types of personnel assembled under one roof to permit a corporate division to function autonomously), ease of supervision, ease of access, and morale are equally powerful factors in the grouping together of individuals performing similar tasks. These forces are the bases for different forms of departmentalization, notably the divisional form, the functional form, and the matrix form.

Forms of Departmentalization

Two major forms and one hybrid form have been identified in the literature. They are, respectively, the functional form, the divisional form, and the matrix structure.

Functional form. In the functional form the governing principle is that all personnel that can contribute to the accomplishment of a specific function are located together. Thus, in a manufacturing corporation that is functionally departmentalized, all personnel concerned with the marketing function —such as sales and media persons, marketing and sales managers, market researchers, etc.—are grouped together. Similarly, all personnel concerned with manufacturing operations are grouped together in the manufacturing department, all personnel engaged in personnel administration are located in the personnel department, and so forth. The simplified organizational chart of a brewery in Figure 13–2 shows what a functionally departmentalized organization looks like.

Firms are not the only users of functional departmentalization. Every variety of organization utilizes it. The following abbreviated organizational chart of a hospital (Figure 13–4) shows extensive use of the principle of grouping by functional specialization.

In the previous section we noted some of the reasons why personnel doing similar work tend to be grouped together (e.g., better organization-wide access to specialized personnel, ease of supervision, better morale). However, functional departmentalization tends to accentuate the need for coordination. Each functionally specialized department tends to develop its own culture, its own "lingo," its own goals and preferred ways of operating. Friction tends to develop wherever one specialized department interfaces with another. Often, disagreements that originate lower down in the hierarchies of two departments must be funneled up all the way to the common boss of the two departments before they are resolved.

To take an illustration: in a functionally organized electronics-goods manufacturing firm, the engineers were very competent but interested more in the elegance of design than the profitable marketability of their products. The manufacturing department wanted designs of products that would be

FIGURE 13–4
The Organizational Chart of Montreal General Hospital Center

easy to mass produce. The engineers often delayed giving designs to manufacturing for several months while working out the niceties of their blueprints. The manufacturing vice-president complained bitterly to the executive vice-president about this, saying that design engineers fiddled while the company got burned through lost orders and expensive and hurried retooling. Eventually, the executive vice-president had to step in to resolve the conflict.

Even in the absence of these kinds of disagreement, coordination between functional departments is a difficult matter and is often performed by a committee consisting of the representatives of the interfacing departments. For example, in a company functionally organized producing many products, one commonly finds product committees. These are committees on which the marketing, the engineering, and the production personnel responsible for each of the major products or product lines are represented. The function of these committees is to coordinate the engineering, manufacturing, and marketing requirements of these products. Another common coordinative device is, of course, the common boss of the interfacing departments. But this can overload the common boss and slow down coordination. Planning is a powerful alternative coordination device. By thinking ahead what the operating requirements are likely to be, given the organization's goals, abrasive interfaces can be forestalled, and the whole workflow can be made smoother. But this is possible only if the future unfolds as expected. If unforeseen contingencies or exigencies crop up, the need for coordination between interfacing departments again becomes urgent. Interfaces can also be made smoother by developing standard operating procedures for use whenever usual coordination problems arise. Finally, communications and human relations training can be useful in securing better coordination.

We propose that:

The more extensive the functional departmentalization in an organization, the greater is the possibility of conflict among the personnel of interfacing departments.

The greater the interface between functionally organized departments, the greater is the need for coordinative mechanisms such as planning, standard operating procedures, committees, a common boss, and communications and human relations training.

Divisionalization. Divisionalization is an alternative way of grouping organizational members by aggregating all the specialists needed to produce a given product or service. For example, if a firm markets three distinct prod-

FIGURE 13–5
Organizational Chart of Rest Easy Furniture Company, Inc.

ucts, it may set up three self-contained divisional profit centers, one for each product. Within each division all the needed manufacturing, engineering, marketing, and other manpower and facilities are assembled. The principle here is one of assembling within one department individuals with complementary but diverse expertise rather than similar expertise. Figure 13–5 is an abbreviated organizational chart of a fairly large furniture-making company organized this way.

This principle of assembling diverse personnel to create more or less self-sufficient units, which in corporate management circles is called "divisionalization," is used by many nonprofit organizations as well. The different faculties of the university, each replete with its own administrators, teaching staff, secretaries, and students, is an example of the same principle at work. Although these faculties are, by and large, not profit-oriented bodies, they resemble corporate divisions in the degree of autonomy they enjoy.

There are different kinds of divisionalization. Divisionalization by product or service line is the most common among large corporations. But many corporations also set up fairly autonomous, self-sufficient divisions to serve distinct territories, and sometimes even to serve particularly important customers with special needs. For example, national railway lines, such as the Canadian National Railways, set up territorial divisions such as the Atlantic Division, the Midwest Division, the Pacific Division. Aerospace firms and electrical equipment manufacturers often set up an autonomous division to serve the government's defense and related needs because of the special needs of the government and the special procedures that have to be followed in dealing with the government.

The difference between functional departmentalization and divisionalization often tends to be overstated. An organization that is divisionalized at one management level usually is functionally departmentalized at the next (see Figure 13–3 for illustration). True, some organizations, such as General Motors, tend to push the idea of self-sufficient units farther down than others, but very quickly, the functional departmentalization principle asserts itself. Indeed, upon observing the largest organizations one is struck by the pervasive influence of this principle. Though strategically important, the divisional principle is far less widely used than the functional specialization principle in grouping organizational members.

The division is an illustration of grouping complementary, interdependent personnel. Because of its self-sufficiency, its head has a relatively high degree of autonomy. Many advantages have been claimed by advocates of division-alization.[3] It shortens lines of communication between interdependent personnel. It makes planning and coordination easier and, particularly, facilitates quick adaptation to environmental changes. Since the divisional head is the head of a more or less independent firm, he is motivated to high performance, particularly because he is, in a corporate context, evaluated by how profitable his division is rather than by how the division goes about doing its business. If an organization has many divisions, it is possible to compare performances, and invest more resources in profitable divisions and withdraw resources from unprofitable ones. Divisionalization also affords valuable top management training and experience to middle level executives, since they are responsible for running what amounts to a firm. Thus, divisionalization is a built-in device for management training and a continuous source of top flight executives with general management skills. As Chandler has argued, divisionalization was an indispensable structural change that many diversifying American corporations had to adopt to continue their growth.

Growth through diversification into several lines increased the number and complexity of both operational and entrepreneurial activities even more than a world-wide expansion of one line. The problems of obtaining materials and supplies, of manufacturing and of marketing a number of product lines for different types of customers or in different parts of the world made the tasks of departmental headquarters exceedingly difficult to administer systematically and rationally. The coordination of product flow through the several departments proved even more formidable. Appraisal came to involve not only a constant intelligent analysis of the operating performance in the different economic functions, including engineering and research as well as production, distribution, transportation, the procurement of supplies, and finance, but the making of these appraisals in several very different industries or lines of business. Long-term strategic planning not only called for decisions and action concerning the future use of existing facilities, personnel, and funds, and the development of new resources in the company's current lines, but also involved decisions on entering into new lines of products and dropping or curtailing old ones.

By placing an increasing intolerable strain on existing administrative structures, territorial expansion and to a much greater extent product diversification brought the multidivisional form. . . .[4]

But divisionalization is not without problems. Often it results in duplication of staff and facilities. Each division likes to have its own accountants, statisticians, organization developers, personnel men, forecasters, market researchers, computer services, research labs, and the like. However, these may not be fully utilized at all times, in which case considerable excess staff is being employed by the organization as a whole. At other times, particularly during recessions, since divisions are assessed in terms of performance criteria like profitability, they may skimp on needed quality staff in order to save on expenses, and this may have deleterious effects in the long run. Thus, if times are good, divisionalization may encourage empire building and result in excessive staff; in bad times not enough quality staff may be employed by the individual divisions.

In view of this, many divisionalized organizations have evolved an organizational structure with centralized staff functions. Typically, personnel services, financial services, research and development, and the like are substantially withdrawn from divisional management and concentrated at the organizational headquarters. The divisions avail themselves of these services as and when they need them. The headquarters can usually maintain a wider variety of staff and also probably a higher quality of staff, than any individual division can. The General Motors Corporation under Sloan developed this idea to great perfection. Figure 13–3 is also an example of this.

Another problem with divisionalization is competition among the organizations' divisions. If their markets are not overlapping, there may be no serious damage to the organization as a whole. If their markets overlap, however, the divisions may end up competing with one another as much as with other firms. This has been alleged with divisions of corporations like General Motors and Ford Motor Company. Should this be the case, there is considerable pressure on the top management to restrain interdivisional competition by parceling out markets, sometimes even centralizing some of the production or other facilities. In its pristine form divisionalization works best when an organization's markets (or business) are clearly severable into nonoverlapping parts, as in the case of the many different faculties of a university, and the many different product lines of a conglomerate.

We propose that:

The more divisionalized the organization,
   the more centralized tend to be the staff functions commonly used by
   all the divisions.

The more divisionalized the organization,
> *the better is intradivisional coordination but the more intense is interdivisional rivalry.*

3 *Matrix structure* A third principle of grouping organizational members is that of multiple membership. This is an old principle—the interdepartmental committee or task force is the classic example. Typically the organizational member is a member of two units, one of which is a more or less permanent posting, the second being usually a temporary unit. This idea has been given the fancy name of *matrix structure*. As a principle it is being applied widely in organizations such as engineering-oriented firms that do business in the form of a number of distinctive projects. In these firms, technical personnel are located in the appropriate functional departments but are then assigned to one or more projects. On completion of these projects, they revert back to their respective departments, until the next assignment to a project. Typically these projects require the use of personnel from a number of technical disciplines, so they are really like miniature but temporary divisions and strive for self-sufficiency at least in technical manpower.[5] Thus the so-called matrix structure is a combination of the principle of specialized departments with the principle of self-sufficient, more or less autonomous units or divisions, in situations where a number of temporary divisions or autonomous units need to be created. An internal document describes the matrix or project structure in operation at the TRW Systems Group of TRW, Inc., a division dedicated to the use of very sophisticated technologies in the development of earth satellites, landing modules, and the like.

> TRW Systems is in the business of application of advanced technology. The company's organization has been expressly planned for effective performance of the projects that comprise our business and for flexibility for future shifts in this business.
>
> The hardware work that we do is awarded by our customers in bid packages that usually involve a number of technical fields and integration of hardware from these into a single end item. We have several hundred of these projects in operation at a time. They range in people assigned from three or four to several hundred. Most of the projects are small—only a few fall in the "large hardware projects" category we are mainly concerned with here.
>
> From the standpoint of personnel and physical resources, it is most efficient to organize by specialized groups or technologies. To stay competitive, these groups must be large enough to obtain and fully utilize expensive special equipment and highly specialized personnel. If each project had its own staff and equipment, duplication would result, resource utilization would be

low, and the cost high; it might also be difficult to retain the highest caliber of technical specialists. Our customers get lowest cost and top performance by organization and specialty.

For these reasons, the company has been organized into units of individual technical and staff specialties. Each customer's needs call for a different combination of these capabilities.

A way of matching these customers' needs to the TRW organization elements that can meet them is necessary. The project system performs this function.

In the project system, a project office is set up for each customer program. The project office reports to a company manager of appropriate rank in the organization with cognizance in the technical area of the project. The over-all project organization is similar for each project. The project manager has over-all management responsibility for all project activities and directs the activities through the project office and substructure described in the following. The project office is the central location for all project-wide activities such as project schedule, cost and performance control; system planning, system engineering, and system integration; and contract and major subcontract management. Assistant project managers are appointed for these activities as warranted by project scope.

The total project effort is divided into subprojects according to the technical specialty involved, thus matching the TRW Systems' basic organization structure. Each subproject has a subproject manager who takes project direction from an assistant project manager. The subproject manager is responsible for performance in his specialty area to the supervisor of the organizational element that will perform the subproject work. The subproject manager is the bridge between the project office and this organizational element. The members of the next subordinate level of management in that organization take project direction from him. The work is further subdivided and performed within their organizations.[6]

The dynamics of human interaction in a matrix structure are fascinating. Rush reports in his study of TRW Systems:

In an organization like TRW, when getting a job done cuts across departmental boundaries, contact with a large number of other people is a way of life . . . because of the necessity for interaction of a technical and personal nature, the team approach is viewed as the most manageable system. Since the teams comprise a heterogeneous group of technical specialties and individuals, conflict is understandable enough. . . .

As one executive expressed it, ". . . groups and individuals in TRW derive the necessary discipline from the job itself and the preciseness of the technological and support specialties required to get that job done effectively. We focus on the problem and organize ourselves to solve that particular problem."

Because people are encouraged to do things "a different way," and because the company has designed a system in which a man's responsibility emerges from the job to be done, he must obtain the cooperation of others over whom he has little traditional, direct authority. . . . "Making the matrix organization really work can be difficult and frustrating; we attempt to reduce the difficulties by encouraging openness and cooperation," comments a training specialist. "If openness exists, a man can devote his time and energies to the real job of making an effective organization, instead of politicking and empire building which dissipate energy and drain off effort that ought to be used constructively on the job."[7]

It is obvious that in a matrix structure, the ability to work as a member of a team is very important. Interpersonal conflict is frequent because of the heterogeneity of team members. Unless conflict is brought into the open and managed constructively, the teams are likely to flounder in a morass of bitter feelings. Participative decision-making and heavy investment by the organization in the development of its human resources (organizational development, team building, interpersonal competence, human relations training and the like) become necessary.

Equally important is flexibility. While a matrix organization requires a reasonably high level of administrative support to allow project teams to operate freely without having to worry about administrative details, the ability of each team to seek the organizational form most appropriate to the project each is handling is of strategic importance. In other words, in some projects a great deal of specialization, structuring of activities and jobs, and the like may be necessary; in others, of a more creative kind, much greater flexibility and situational expertise may be in order. In fact, in the same project different management styles may be appropriate at different phases of the project: a free form style at the initial period, followed in the later phases perhaps by a technocratic-participative style. Thus, given the great variety in the projects that a matrix organization has to handle, an organic management ideology and style is a necessity.

We propose that:

> *The more an organization's superstructure resembles a matrix organization, the more organic, participatory, human-relations oriented, and technocratic tend to be the management style and ideology at the operating levels of the organization.*

Task Environment and the Form of Departmentalization

Jay Galbraith has argued that each of the three departmental forms—functional, divisional, and matrix—is appropriate in different task environmental conditions. He lists several factors that affect the choice of the form.[8]

The more diverse the product lines of the organization and the range of services it offers, the greater, he argues, is the pressure to move toward a divisional (or, as he puts it, a product) structure. This is because "when product lines become diverse, it becomes difficult for the general managers and functional managers to maintain knowledge in all areas; the amount of information they must handle exceeds their capacity to absorb it."[9] There is support for this argument. In the author's study of over 100 Canadian firms, the extent to which the firm's activities and product lines were diversified was correlated strongly with the extent to which it was divisionalized. Similarly, the extent of dissimilarity in the firm's markets was fairly strongly correlated with the extent to which the firm was divisionalized.[10]

Galbraith argues that the faster the rate of *new* product (or service) introduction, the more unfamiliar are the tasks being performed. "Managers are, therefore, less able to make precise estimates concerning resource allocations, schedules, and priorities. During the process of new product introduction, these same decisions are made repeatedly. The decisions concern trade-offs among engineering, manufacturing, and marketing. This means there must be greater product influence in the decision process."[11] In other words, if product innovation in an organization is rapid, there is likely to be pressure for divisionalization.

The tighter the operating schedule and the greater the interdependence between different personnel, the more frequent will be occasions for joint problem solving and decision-making among manufacturing, design, and marketing personnel, and therefore the greater, according to Galbraith, will be the need for "product influence" in decision-making. In other words, a tight integration in the organization's operating schedule will tend to push the organization toward divisionalization.

The more sophisticated the technology of operations, the greater is the need for expertise in technical specialties such as different branches of engineering, manufacturing, market research, and the like. Galbraith argues that this strengthens the tendency for functional departmentalization because of the more economical use of variegated and high quality staff that this form allows.

Large economies of scale favor the functional form, because in the latter the manufacturing operations can be centralized in one relatively large plant. Such an option is not available if the organization has many self-sufficient divisions, each with its own manufacturing capabilities. Thus, when unit costs can be decreased appreciably by having a larger plant, as for example in the manufacture of steel and aluminum, there will be a pressure toward the functional form.

Since most plants have an optimum size beyond which there is no further decrease in unit costs, if the organization is very large, it can have economies of scale *and* divisionalization. For example, there are considerable economies of scale in the manufacture of cars. But if a firm manufactures 3 million cars and an optimum size plant need have a capacity of no more than 300,000, then the firm can, without loss of economies of scale, set up as many as 10 divisions. G.M. and Ford are, of course, good examples of this. In the author's study of Canadian firms, firm size and divisionalization were strongly correlated.

We propose that:

The greater the diversity in the product lines or services offered by an organization;
the faster the rate of introduction of new product lines or services by the organization;
the tighter the operating schedule;
the greater the needed interdependence between diverse personnel; and
the larger the organization,
  the more divisionalized it will tend to be.

The more sophisticated the technology of operations and
the larger the economies of scale,
  the more functionally departmentalized the organization will tend to be.

The more customized and varied the products or services provided to the organization's clientele,
the faster the rate of innovation or introduction of new products, projects, or services by the organization;
the tighter the operating schedule; and
the more sophisticated the technology of operations,
  the more the organization will tend to develop a matrix project structure provided the economies of scale are not large.

The Types and Determinants of Work Unit Structures

Hitherto, we have examined three overall forms of departmentalization—the functional, the divisional, and the matrix. But within an overall departmental form or any combination of departmental forms, one may find a great variety in the structures of work units. Work units are small departments or sections embedded within larger departments. The work of Van de Ven and Delbecq points to a number of interesting types of work unit structure.[12] As they put it, depending on how complex and how variegated

FIGURE 13–6
Different Types of Work Unit Structures Described by Van de Ven and Delbecq

		"System" mode	"Service" mode	"Group" mode
COMPLEXITY OF WORK UNIT'S TASKS	*Very difficult, complex tasks*	Specialist system unit (e.g., intensive care unit)	Intensive service unit (e.g., a graduate faculty unit)	Development group unit (e.g., a product development unit)
	Moderately complex tasks	Technical system unit (e.g., a computer-programming unit)	Technical service unit (e.g., a sales unit)	Design group unit (e.g., a product redesign unit)
	Relatively simple tasks	Routine system unit (e.g., an assembly line unit)	Routine service unit (e.g., a secretarial pool)	
		Uniformly performed tasks	*Moderately programmed tasks*	*Novel or variable tasks*

VARIABILITY OF WORK UNIT'S TASKS

or discretionary a work unit's tasks are, a work unit may operate in the "system" mode, or the "service" mode, or the "group" mode. Figure 13–6 shows their different work unit types.

A work unit operates in a "system" mode if its operations are uniform enough to be planned out in advance and if the element of discretion in its performance programs is relatively low because the available technology indicates the "optimal" way of doing things. Work then can be reduced to a system. Of course, the required personnel can range all the way from relatively unskilled to highly skilled. The mechanical assembly line unit in an automobile factory is perhaps a good example of a *routine* system unit involving relatively unskilled personnel. On the other hand, intensive care nursing units are probably good examples of *specialist* system units employing very highly trained personnel. In between these two are the *technical* system units such as computer programming units.

When a work unit's tasks are labor intensive and fairly variegated, and when a fair degree of discretion must be exercised by its personnel, the "service" mode is operative. Discretion may have to be exercised because available technology is unable to specify precisely the best way to perform the tasks. Typically, personnel apply appropriate solutions after analyzing the tasks, and the work performed by the different members is not strongly interrelated or interdependent. Depending on the level of complexity of the tasks, there will be routine, technical, or intensive service units. The secretarial pool and the security guards unit are likely examples of *routine* service units. Various departmental units of a high school's faculty and the sales units of a corporation are examples of *technical* service units. Graduate school departmental faculty units, staff consulting units, homicide investigation units of the police force are good examples of *intensive* or specialist service units.

The "group" mode is operative when a work unit's tasks vary considerably from time to time and the level of complexity is at least fairly high. In other words, tasks tend to be novel, and no one person has all the needed expertise. The group mode is characterized by teams to analyze, diagnose, design, or develop. As Van de Ven and Delbecq point out,

> Typically, tasks undertaken by group-mode work units are temporary and center on the solution to specific problems; the structure is flexible and is adapted to the unique requirements of each task. . . . Unit members are highly interdependent. . . . Decisions on tasks are made collegially and individual discretion is subject to guidelines set forth by the team. The role of the unit supervisor in a group mode is primarily that of a group coordinator and team leader.[13]

A research group designing an experiment to test a theory and teams to redesign products are examples of design group units. Teams working on radically new products or programs are examples of the more complex development group units.

Van de Ven and Delbecq examined a large number of work units in the field offices of an American state employment security agency. On the basis of their examination of the performance programs of these work units, they assigned each work unit to one of the types in Figure 13–6. Then they secured data on the complexity or difficulty and variability of the tasks of the work units as perceived by their members. Table 13–1 reproduces the scores for the six types of work unit for which they report the data. The data are in general agreement with the predictions of the researchers about the kinds of task each work unit type is likely to have.

Using the term "department" in its generic sense to include any grouping of people within an organization, we propose that:

The more complex the tasks of a department,
> *the higher is the technical level of the personnel employed in the department.*

The more novel the tasks,
> *the more varied and discretionary are the procedures employed in the department, and the more organic are the superior–subordinate and peer relations within it.*

TABLE 13–1

Task Difficulty and Task Variability Scores of Six Types of Work Units
(Sample: 120 Work Units in an American State Employment Agency)

| | AVERAGE SCORE OF | |
	Task difficulty or complexity	Task variability
Routine system	2.2	2.8
Technical system	3.8	4.2
Routine service	2.9	4.6
Technical service	4.4	6.2
Intensive service	6.0	7.3
Design group	6.0	8.2

SOURCE: Based on Andrew Van de Ven and André Delbecq, "A Task Contingent Model of Work Unit Structure," *Administrative Science Quarterly*, Vol. 19 (1974), pp. 183–197.

THE INFRASTRUCTURE OF ORGANIZATIONS

The Importance of Infrastructure

If departments are the highly visible superstructure of an organization, the administrative structure—who has what authority, how formalized communications are, the extent of division of labor and specialization, what controls and rules are employed to monitor performance—is the less visible but equally important infrastructure of organizations. It is the nuts and bolts of the organizational machine—to the extent that the organization is a machine.

The infrastructure enables the organization to engage in a number of very disparate activities *and* to keep them coordinated. Division of labor, specialization of functions, delegation of authority, differences in the standard operating procedures in different parts of the organization, all aspects of infrastructure, make possible the needed organizational differentiation without which a complex entity like an organization simply cannot function. But just as the equally highly differentiated human system needs central coordinative organs like the nervous system and the brain, so does the differentiated organization need hierarchy, management controls, performance evaluation, and an information network—all aspects of infrastructure, to keep its operations integrated. By furnishing mechanisms of control and coordination, the infrastructure reduces internal uncertainty in the organization. Because the performance-related behavior of individuals and groups is made reliable through the infrastructure, coordination between the acts of dozens, hundreds, sometimes thousands of individuals, all playing their little or big roles, becomes possible. The stupendous scale of operations of the modern organization—as compared to that of an individual or a group—is possible because of the staid but durable focus provided by the infrastructure for an organization's diverse activities.

As organizations grow older they learn to do their work more efficiently. This learning gets embedded in their structures, particularly in their formalized procedures. In many hospitals, the patient who has come for treatment for the first time is required to fill out a form before being admitted. This may appear at the time to be just a lot of red tape, but it really isn't. The time utilized in acquiring the form is well spent, because during subsequent visits the patient can be processed quickly, thanks to the form. Thus, organizational structure, at least in intent, is designed to make human behavior not only more predictable but also more efficient.

Infrastructure is important for another reason too. It is a powerful mechanism for both frustrating and fulfilling the wants of members. The literature on organizational behavior abounds with scare tales of what organizational structure does to the human spirit. Undoubtedly, by channeling human behavior, organization structure frustrates several needs. One simply cannot barge into the president's office whenever one feels like doing so, nor can one stop working any time one feels like reading *Playboy*—not at least outside the academia! Structure constrains behavior, sometimes quite painfully. But structure also often facilitates the satisfaction of needs. The university researcher would be lost without the able support of a secretary and the administrative staff. The doctor could scarcely do an effective job in a hospital without the contingent of nurses, administrators, and others to take care of the chores. It is true that structure, especially a badly designed infrastructure, can impede initiative and creativity. It is equally true that without an appropriate structure the vast job of transforming a bright idea into reality is unlikely to be accomplished.

Elements of Infrastructure

Recall that organizational structure is the set of durable and formally sanctioned relationships and arrangements designed to reduce internal and external uncertainty, permit the organization to engage in a variety of tasks, and yet secure for it a high degree of coordination among these tasks so that it achieves its goals efficiently. Logically, therefore, the elements of infrastructure are:

1. The control and information system of the organization, whose primary function is to reduce internal and external uncertainty for decision makers.

2. Delegation of authority, division of labor, specialization of functions,

FIGURE 13–7
Dimensions of Infrastructure

Uncertainty reduction function

| Simple, seat-of-the-pants; little formal forecasting, planning, research, internal monitoring, and so on | Control and information system (C.I.S.) ⟷ | Highly sophisticated, comprehensive, technocratic; much sophisticated forecasting, planning, market research, monitoring of internal activities, and so on |

Differentiation function

| Little delegation of authority for making decisions to lower administrative levels | Delegation of authority ⟷ | Much delegation of authority for making decisions to lower administrative levels |
| Very limited division of labor and specialization of functions; limited standardization and formalization | Division of labor, specialization, standardization, and formalization ⟷ | Very elaborate division of labor and specialization of functions; extensive standardization of activities, and their codification and documentation |

Integration function

| A "flat" hierarchy, designed for "management by exception" | Hierarchy ⟷ | A "tall" hierarchy to permit close supervision and effective coordination at the top levels of the organization |
| Little use of committees to coordinate activities | Committees ⟷ | Extensive use of committees to coordinate activities |

and standardization of procedures and activities so that the myriad different tasks in the organization are performed effectively.

3. Hierarchy of authority and the use of committees to keep the myriad activities coordinated and focused on the main goals of the organization.

Figure 13–7 outlines the dimensions of the infrastructure. Needless to say, the dimensions shown in the figure are neither as independent nor as specialized in the organizational functions they perform as they might superficially seem. For example, the control and information system is designed primarily to reduce uncertainty confronting decision makers. But quite clearly, the control part of it can and often does serve a secondary function —that of keeping the organization's activities coordinated by providing norms of performance to the different parts of the organization. Not only that, by providing significant information quickly to key decision makers, the control and information system increases their willingness to delegate more authority and permit more specialization—that is, it facilitates differentiation. Similarly, division of labor and specialization primarily facilitate organizational differentiation. But as the sociologist Emile Durkheim argued, this increases a sense of interdependence and therefore fosters an organic unity in a collectivity.[14] In other words, it facilitates integration. So, while for analytical purposes we may classify elements of the infrastructure by the primary functions they are supposed to perform, we should recognize that most of them also have important secondary functions.

Let us take a look at these several dimensions of the infrastructure.

Control and Information System (C.I.S.)

Meaning and importance. Decision makers in all organizations need to have information about their environments and about the state of affairs within the organization so that they can respond more effectively to changes in the environment and exercise some control over internal operations. However, they may elect to gather this information and exercise this control in a rudimentary way or with the help of a sophisticated and complex *system* involving the utilization of experts and sophisticated information-processing equipment.

Control and information system (C.I.S.) is a very important element of organizational structure. To begin with, organizations with a sophisticated C.I.S. employ many more specialists, relatively, than those with little sophistication in their C.I.S. In organizations with a simple C.I.S., experience and power of the line manager are ascendant. The organization with a sophisticated C.I.S. is likely to experience more line-staff conflicts than the one with a simple C.I.S.; in the former, managers can easily find themselves in a disquieting situation: they have the authority to make a decision, but should they, for however important a purpose, ignore the informed advice of a staff specialist that later proves to be right, they would be in trouble with their superiors.

The sophisticated C.I.S. organization, other things being equal, has higher administrative overheads than the less sophisticated C.I.S. organization because the former hires salaried staff specialists, institutes formal procedures and controls that have to be manned by salaried technicians and clerical personnel, and so on. One consequence of this is that in businesses where the profit margins are thin and risk is high, the sophisticated C.I.S. organization is at a disadvantage. In Chile, for instance, during the Allende socialist interlude, U.S. subsidiaries that were previously doing better than local companies in the same business began to show a poorer performance.

One of the reasons was that the corporate sector was squeezed hard by price and employment controls and rampant inflation, and while the local firms with their simple organizational structures and lower fixed costs could adapt quickly to this exigency, the U.S. subsidiaries with their expensive, complex structures and C.I.S. modeled on their parent companies, could not, and so fared poorly. The U.S. corporate liners were ill-designed to navigate the turbulence in the Chilean teacup!

If high administrative overheads is the cost of a sophisticated C.I.S., the ability to tackle complex technical or marketing problems is its principal benefit. A sophisticated C.I.S. organization can throw into its battle for growth a regiment of market researchers, statisticians, forecasters, operations researchers, and management trainers. It can make "optimal" use of computer facilities. It can establish standards, procedures, and controls that enable the organization to use a highly complex technology efficiently. It can take on problems and opportunities well beyond the capability of the simple organization.

Determinants of the sophistication of C.I.S. In the author's study of over 100 Canadian firms, sophistication of C.I.S. was measured by aggregating a large number of scales. Over half of these scales measured the usage of sophisticated management controls for monitoring internal operations. The controls included quality control of operations, internal audit, personnel evaluation, establishment of the standard costs of operations and analysis of cost variations from these standards, the use of accounting ratios to analyze operations, break-even analysis, establishment of cost centers, control of inventories through the use of operations research techniques, sophisticated assessment of prospective investments in terms of the rates of return expected, and more. Other scales forming part of C.I.S. measured the extent to which the organization engaged in staff-type activities designed to secure vital environmental information. These included market and technology forecasting, market research, research and development, electronic data processing, long-term planning and capital budgeting. Figure 13–8 shows the independent determinants of C.I.S. revealed by the Canadian study. Each of the situational variables was found to be significantly related with C.I.S. even after partialing out the effects of the other situational variables indicated in the figure. The strategic variable (professional management style) was strongly related to C.I.S., and the correlation remained significant even after controlling for the effects of the situational variables.

What Figure 13–8 suggests is that sophistication in C.I.S. is the organization's response to a number of environmental pressures and the ideological preferences of top management. Diverse, complex, competitive, and innovative environments create severe coping problems. *Sophisticated* control of

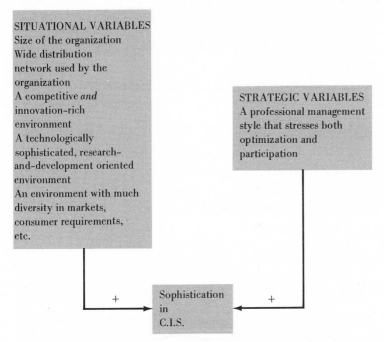

NOTE: The plus sign indicates that the relationship is positive; that is, an increase (or decrease) in one is associated with an increase (or decrease) in the other.

operations that permits management to take prompt remedial action without jeopardizing the creativity and initiative at the operating levels so badly needed in such environments becomes important. Not only that, the organization must institute a number of sophisticated and complex activities (a) to *monitor* the developments in the environment (forecasting, market research) and (b) to enlarge the organization's capacity to *respond* to these developments (through long-term planning). Large organizations tend to get very differentiated and to get involved in a variety of markets and activities, so they need sophisticated C.I.S. Their large resources, of course, permit them to acquire it. It is not much of a surprise that professionalism in management, regardless of size or nature of environment, impels the organization to adopt a sophisticated C.I.S.

We propose that:

The more competitive and innovation rich the environment;

the more technologically sophisticated and complex the environment;
the more diverse the environment;
the larger the organization; and
the wider its distribution network,
> *the more sophisticated and comprehensive is the control and information system employed in the organization.*

The more professional the orientation of the top management—that is, the more it stresses both optimization and participation—
> *the more sophisticated and comprehensive is the control and information system employed in the organization.*

Decentralization

Meaning and importance. In management literature decentralization connotes several different, though related things. Decentralization can mean dispersal of capacities or facilities, as when a bank opens a large number of branches to get closer to its customers or when a firm's research staff is distributed among its different divisions. More commonly, however, decentralization means the delegation of authority for making decisions by a group or an individual to another group or to other individuals who are usually lower in rank.[16] Thus, in corporations the board of directors may delegate authority to the chief executive to make all operating decisions as well as capital budgeting decisions up to some magnitude. The chief executive in turn may delegate to management committees or to individual subordinates the job of making a number of operating decisions related to marketing, production, finance, personnel, and the like. The relevant question in assessing this form of decentralization is: What is the management level at which specific types of decision are actually taken, even if they are rubber-stamped at higher levels?

Decentralization should be distinguished from participative decision-making. For example, all capital budgeting decisions in Firm A may be made participatively at the top management level by a management committee consisting of the president and the executive vice-presidents. In Firm B, however, most capital budgeting decisions are made by division heads individually who are merely vice-presidents. In the case of Firm A, capital budgeting decisions are centralized but made participatively. In Firm B, they are decentralized but made nonparticipatively.

Many advantages—and some disadvantages—have been claimed for decentralization. Decentralization has been considered a powerful motivator of subordinates because it satisfies their higher order needs for power, autonomy, more meaningful and responsible work, and so on. It has also been claimed to make the organization more flexible and to enable it to respond more rapidly to local contingencies than a centralized organization can. It frees top management from the drudgery of relatively routine decisions so that they can devote attention to strategic, nonrecurring, novel problems. The opponents of decentralization have claimed that it creates too many vested interests, breeds resistance to organization-wide changes, and, therefore, makes the organization vulnerable in a crisis.[17] Obviously, for organizational designers to make a sensible choice about the extent to which their organizations should be decentralized they need to be aware of the circumstances in which decentralization is badly needed and those in which it is not.

Determinants of decentralization. In the so-called Aston studies of organizational structure, it was found that the more the activities of an organization were formalized and structured through rules and the like, the more decentralized its authority structure was.[18] Child expresses well the implications of these findings:

> within certain limits imposed by the organization's operating situation, managers appear to have a choice between: (a) maintaining control directly by confining decisions to fairly senior levels. This economizes on the need for systems or procedures and paperwork and reduces the overhead of indirect specialist personnel to operate and maintain the systems, or (b) maintaining control indirectly by relying on the use of procedures, paper records, and on the employment of expert specialists to take decisions at lower levels. . . .[19]

Thus, for controlling their members' behavior, organizations have a choice of relying on an impersonal *system* or relying on *personal* supervision by managers. Blau and Schoenherr, too, in a study of American employment security agencies, found that "the restraints imposed by formalized procedures encourage the development of a less centralized authority structure that permits more flexible decision making."[20] In a study of 79 mostly medium-sized U.S. manufacturing firms, the author found a strong relationship between the extent of decentralization of top level decision-making by the chief executive of the firms and the use of sophisticated management controls in the firm.[21] In the author's Canadian study, too, the decentralization of authority by the chief executive was highly significantly correlated with the sophistication of the control and information system.

Several studies indicate that large organizations are more decentralized than small organizations.[22] Since large organizations carry on many diverse activities, those at the top must of necessity distinguish between urgent, strategically important tasks and the more routine, tactical tasks. The latter tend to be delegated, resulting in a substantial decentralization of decision-making authority, which is reinforced even further by the fact that large organizations tend to use sophisticated C.I.S.

The author's study of U.S. manufacturing firms offered clues about additional determinants of decentralization of authority at the top management level.[23] The data from the study suggested that, at least for highly profitable firms, organizations subsisting in a competitive environment tend to be more decentralized at top levels of management than organizations subsisting in a relatively noncompetitive environment. The data also suggested that competition faced by an organization has the effect of making the chief executive delegate authority more selectively. In a competitive environment the chief executive has the tendency to decentralize decision-making in such areas as marketing strategy, product development, and pricing, more than in such other decision areas as capital budgeting and acquisitions. In a noncompetitive environment, the chief executive is likely to delegate or not delegate authority more or less equally in different areas.

The Canadian study revealed the strong influence of top management ideology and goals on decentralization. Even after controlling for the effects of the size of the organization and the competitive pressure on the firm, participation as an aspect of management style was significantly correlated with the degree to which the chief executive had delegated decision-making authority to subordinates. This of course makes good sense. Participatory ideology jibes with decentralization of authority. But, in addition, in situations in which decentralization is a necessity (large size, competitive pressures), participation supplies the integration to offset the differentiation that decentralization causes. In addition, decentralization was correlated with the importance to top management of profitability as well as of employee morale.

The foregoing results suggest that decentralization is an important part of an overall administrative strategy whose chief elements are management concern about efficiency *as well as* about the morale of the organization's employees. As a tool, decentralization offers a neat synergy between the organization's performance aspirations and the needs of its middle and lower level managers. It is also a tool that enhances the adaptive capacity of different parts of the organization. But it exposes the organization to the risk of a lack of coordination among the activities of managers. Apparently, participative management, human relations, and C.I.S. are utilized by the organization, partly at least, to ensure proper coordination among managers who have considerable discretionary authority.

In Chapter 8 we noted that in organizations of professionals (such as hospitals, educational institutions, research labs) that have strong professional norms, or strong norms about service to clients, operating authority tends typically to be decentralized. The assumption is generally made that professionals know best what needs to be done in situations that fall within their area of competence. Their conduct is subject to control not so much by supervisors or by a sophisticated, formal control system as by the professional *norms* they have internalized and the opinion of their colleagues. Operating decentralization is especially in evidence when the tasks to be performed are rather nonstandardized, variable, custom tasks.

We propose that:

The more comprehensive and sophisticated the control and information system,

       the more decentralized is decision-making in the organization.

The larger the organization,
the greater the competitive pressure on the organization, and
the more participative the top management ideology,

       the greater is decentralization of authority at upper levels of management.

The higher the performance aspirations of top management with respect to morale of personnel as well as efficiency,

       the more conspicuous are a participative ideology, a sophisticated control and information system, and decentralization as jointly utilized elements of the top management's administrative strategy.

The more an organization resembles an organization of professionals that have internalized professional norms,

       the more decentralized is the authority for making operating decisions, especially if the tasks to be performed are relatively variable and nonstandardized.

Specialization, Standardization, and Formalization of Activities

Meaning and importance. Like decentralization, the *primary* function of division of labor and specialization in organizations is to permit a great variety of activities to be executed *efficiently*. Standardization of activities is linked closely to specialization, for standardizing them makes their execution more efficient. Besides, even an untrained employee can quickly master activities once they are standardized and codified. Thus, specialization (including division of labor), standardization, and formalization (documentation) are closely interrelated—and very necessary in enabling the organization to pursue a great diversity of activities and goals.

The Aston group has studied the relationship between these variables and their determinants. In their study of nearly fifty organizations in the Birmingham area of England, they found that functional specialization, role specialization, standardization, and formalization were quite strongly correlated.[24] Their work bears closer scrutiny.

As the Aston group measured it, *functional specialization* is the degree to which several activities common to all work organizations are each performed, more or less full time, by someone or some group of people, with that function and no other, who is not in the line chain of command. Thus, functional specialization measures the extent to which the organization undertakes staff public relations and advertising, sales and service, transport, training, buying and stock control, accounts, production control, design and development, organization and methods, market research, and other similar activities.

Role specialization is the extent to which specialist roles exist within each of the activities considered in functional specialization. For example, in the activity called public relations and advertising, one organization may designate a publicity staff role, a public relations role, a customer relations role, a display role, a publicity by product role, and an overseas relations role; another may designate only one or two roles. The first organization would therefore have greater role specialization in the public relations and advertising area. Role specialization in a number of areas was summed to determine the extent to which the organization had role specialization.

Standardization is the extent to which each of several organizational activities is subject to standard procedures and rules. For example, is stock taking done daily, weekly, quarterly, semi-annually, yearly, or never? Is work study performed for all direct workers, operatives, and clerks? Or only for direct workers and operatives? Or only for direct workers? Or not at all? Is promotion handled on the basis of internal advertisement and selection? Or on the basis of grade plus qualification? Or on an ad hoc "as needed" basis? Though the measure has some obvious weaknesses, it probably is a fair measure of the depth of routinization in an organization.

Formalization in the Aston studies is the extent to which procedures, rules, instructions, and communications are formalized—that is, reduced to writing. For example, are contracts of employment with the organization in writing? Is there an official organizational chart? Are there written job descriptions? Are there memo forms? Are minutes of meetings kept? Are there work assessment records?

Functional specialization, role specialization, standardization, and formalization were highly intercorrelated and in data analysis formed the principal constituents of a factor. The authors called this factor "structuring of activities." The more functional and role specialization, standardization, and formalization an organization had, the more structured its activities were deemed to be.

We have said that the primary function of specialization, standardization, and formalization is to allow the organization to carry on many activities efficiently. But the secondary function of these activities is to knit together the diverse activities of the organization, particularly through programs that link together activities. Overall, the structuring of activities gives a great deal of stability and predictability to whatever goes on in organizations. Some of the costs, however, are inflexibility and red tape.

Determinants of the structuring of activities. In the Aston study, the size of the organization was most strongly correlated with the factor of the structuring of activities. Three other contextual variables were also significantly correlated with this factor. One was the size of the organization's parent organization (the Aston researchers do not indicate what procedure they followed for independent organizations in their sample.) The second was what the authors call "workflow integration," a composite measure of how rigid the workflow is, how automated it is, how interdependent the different segments of it are, and so on. By way of an example, an assembly line operation would tend to score higher on the workflow-integration measure than a job shop. The third was the extent of recognition given to trade unions by the organization's management. This ranged from no recognition to full recognition given plus facilities for regular union meetings on the organization's premises and the recognition of a works convenor to represent all the unions that have members in the organization.

The strong relationship between size and structuring of activities is not surprising. Increasing size usually implies a wider range of organizational activities and tasks. This necessitates a greater division of labor and specialization of functions and a greater use of formally documented standard operating procedures.

The larger the parent organization, the more bureaucratized it is likely to be, and if it chooses to impose its mode of operation on the dependent organization, the latter's activities are likely to get highly structured, too. Organizations that recognize trade unions are generally under considerable pressure to formalize wage contracts and work procedures, and this is likely to lead to a more elaborately structured organization. Conversely, overly structured organizations, by making work meaningless, may invite unionization by alienating the workers. Workflow integration, too, is likely to impel the firm toward more elaborate structuring of activities. The planning and execution of highly interdependent and integrated work schedules would be virtually impossible without standardization, documented work schedules, specialist planners and schedulers of operations, and so on.

We propose that:

The larger the organization,
the more unionized it is, and
the more integrated and automated its workflow is,
> *the more structured its activities are likely to be.*

The larger the organization in which an organization is embedded, and
the less autonomous the latter is,
> *the more structured its activities are likely to be.*

Hierarchy

Meaning and importance. An important element of structure is hierarchy. Consider two organizations with five members each, one of which is minimally hierarchical and the other maximally hierarchical (Figure 13–9).

Notice that in the "tall" organization there are five levels in all versus only two in the "flat" organization. The *horizontal* span of control—that is, the average number of persons reporting directly to a supervisor—is one in the "tall" organization and four in the "flat" organization. The *vertical* span of control—that is, the number of management levels in the organization—is five in the "tall" one and two in the "flat" organization. Clearly, if we hold the number of organizational members constant, the larger the number of management levels (that is, the larger the *vertical* span of control), the lower is the average *horizontal* span of control, and vice versa.

FIGURE 13–9
"Tall" and "Flat" Hierarchies

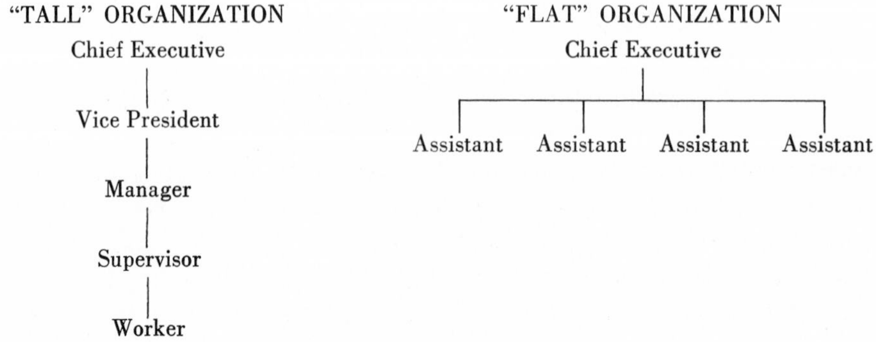

"TALL" ORGANIZATION   "FLAT" ORGANIZATION

Chief Executive

Vice President

Manager

Supervisor

Worker

Chief Executive

Assistant   Assistant   Assistant   Assistant

Hierarchy is primarily an integrative device. It is an important mechanism for coordinating the diverse work of subordinates, for keeping them focused on achieving the organization's goals. It is a mechanism for resolving disputes between underlings and a mechanism for setting up the goal-means hierarchies we talked about in Chapter 10.

But hierarchy is also a special way of dividing up work. The upper levels of management deal with relatively nonroutine, unstructured, complex problems and make strategic decisions. They make decisions that have long-term or far-reaching consequences for the organization, such as deciding whether or not to invest resources in research and development, whether to diversify operations or concentrate operations in a single industry, whether or not to expand capacity. The lower levels of management deal generally with much more routine, structured, relatively simple, and tactical, or short-term problems, such as how large a batch should be run on the production line, whether a customer should be granted credit or not, what educational qualifications should be specified in recruiting supervisors or staff. The taller the hierarchy, the sharper is the differentiation between the kinds of work performed at upper and at lower levels. This is, of course, of great significance because power, status, and earnings are generally all tied to how strategic are the decisions that an executive is making. In other words, in "tall" hierarchies one is likely to find much greater differentials between high and low management levels than in flat organizations of the same type and size.

The other side of the vertical span coin is the horizontal span of control. If the vertical span tells us how differentiated the organization is in terms of strategic versus short-term decision-making, the horizontal span indicates the range of the work performed by each subordinate. If ten individuals report to a supervisor, the work each performs is likely to cover a narrower range of activities than if only five individuals report to a supervisor. Since the vertical span is inversely related to the horizontal span, this implies that in a *given* organization, increasing the number of levels of supervision (tantamount to decreasing the horizontal span of control) implies not only an increase in differentiation in decision-making but also an increase in the range of activities performed by each subordinate.

The vertical span of control has implications for the upward and downward flow of communications. In "tall" organizations, information originating in the lower reaches of the organization (such as regarding worker resentment of new work rules) has to travel many levels before it reaches the ears of those who have the appropriate authority to respond to it. As in the game of whisper, the journey from person to person distorts the information, besides taking a good deal of time. Argyris, for example, reports how supervisors in a plant selectively communicated information upward, tending to minimize problems, to emphasize successes, and to transmit unsavory information about others in the organization.[25] Similarly, information originating at upper management levels, such as a decision to automate the plant or close down a product line, winds its way slowly down the hierarchy, and when it reaches the lower levels, it is so larded with the selective perceptions of the intervening human filters as to be almost unrecognizable. Blau reports how, in an employment agency, directives from the top got adjusted, elaborated, and redefined as they passed to the lower levels.[26] Thus, the taller the hierarchy, the slower and less accurate is the two-way vertical flow of information.

The horizontal span of control has implications for the looseness or tightness of supervision as well as for the access subordinates have to their supervisor. Given the kind of work a group is doing, should the group leader have ten subordinates, the chances are that he is not going to have the time to supervise them as closely as if he had only five of them. Of course, one should not assume that just because a supervisor has five subordinates he in fact supervises them more closely than if he had ten. If he believes in giving a lot of autonomy to his subordinates, he may supervise them as loosely when he has five as when he had ten. The number of subordinates simply gives an upper limit to how much supervision each subordinate will, on an average, receive.

The obverse of the potential for tight supervision is the potential access to the superior. Students in a class of fifty are likely less to be able to reach their professor for individual guidance than students in a class of ten. Here again, one must not assume that simply because the horizontal span of control is small the subordinates individually in fact have more actual interaction with their boss than were the span of control larger. A small horizontal span of control simply makes it *possible* for subordinates to have access to their supervisor if they want it and if the superior allows it. Likewise, a small span implies a small work group and therefore facilitates frequent interactions between group members. Research evidence suggests that small groups tend to be more cohesive and exhibit a higher level of morale than large groups.[27]

The designer of organizations is caught in a dilemma. A small horizontal span of control may result in cohesive work groups; but it may at the same time overload each subordinate, lead to too tight a supervision, and distort vertical communications due to a long hierarchy. A large span of control may result in greater autonomy for the individual and may enable a rapid and accurate flow of vertical communication; but it may lead to poorly supervised work groups and to small cliques within each work group. Let us turn to research findings to identify the conditions under which the horizontal span of control should be large or small.

Determinants of span of control. 1. A number of studies suggest that the larger the organization the larger tends to be the horizontal span of control, especially of the chief executive.[28] This may be because as size increases the organization tends to develop a more sophisticated information and control system, making possible an increasing degree of management by exception. Since a system geared to management by exception obviates the need for close supervision of subordinates, it facilitates a larger span of horizontal control. Thus, as an organization grows larger, the number of managerial personnel tends to grow at a decreasing rate. However, staff involved in the information-gathering and control functions may grow at an increasing rate, offsetting most of the economies resulting from an increasing horizontal span of control.[29]

2. Jon Udell studied the determinants of the span of control of the chief marketing executive of a sizable sample of firms.[30] He analyzed his data through correlational, partial correlational, and regression techniques. The only consistent finding was that the more similar the tasks performed by subordinates, the larger was the executive's span of control. This is analogous to saying that a professor of a class in which every student does identical work can handle more students than one in which instruction, assignments, and testing are individualized.

3. Where the work subordinates perform is highly routinized, the span of control of the supervisor tends to be large. Woodward found that the span of control of the first line supervisor (the lowest level of management) was larger in firms employing mass production and assembly line technologies than in firms employing custom *or* continuous process technologies.[31]

In custom technology, because each product or service is, for the most part, unique, work can be routinized only to a limited extent. In continuous process technology, such as that employed in oil refining, while work is usually heavily automated, the operative has important monitoring responsibilities toward the machine—it must frequently be adjusted in the light of the readings on the various dials and gauges, and so the work is not very routinized. The operative may frequently need to consult the supervisor. In mass production, assembly line technology, on the other hand, work is generally extremely routinized, and there is extreme division of labor (e.g., one worker does nothing but turn the screws, another does nothing but rivet pipes together, etc.). The role of the superior is more that of an overseer of operations than that of an expert or a guide to subordinates. It is likely, therefore, that in organizations or parts of organizations in which work is heavily routinized, the average span of control will be large, other things being equal.

Woodward's data also indicate that the span of control tends to be substantially larger at the lowest management level than at the top management level. The median span of control of the chief executive was 4, 7, and 10, respectively, in custom technology firms, large batch and mass production firms, and process production firms. The average span of control of the first line supervisor was about 22, 48, and 13, respectively, in these firms.[32] Since work tends to be more routinized the lower the level of management, these findings, too, support the contention that the more routinized the work performed by subordinates the larger is their number reporting to a supervisor. An implication of the above is that in parts of the organization interfacing with a changing, complex environment, the span of control will tend to be small because of the continuous influx of relatively novel and complex problems. The subordinates need to interact frequently with one another and with their superior. In the author's study of Canadian firms, there was a marked tendency for executives of firms under intense competitive pressure to report recourse to their boss for settling conflicts and the like. Presumably, this would translate into a relatively small span of control to facilitate greater interaction between the boss and the subordinates.

We propose that:

The stronger the formal control and information system in the organization (or part of the organization),
the larger is the horizontal span of control and the shorter the length of the hierarchy.

The greater the similarity in the work performed by subordinates,
the larger is the horizontal span of control.

The more routinized, less complex, and less interdependent the activities of subordinates,
the larger is the horizontal span of control.

These propositions indicate that if spans of control vary in an organization, they do so because parts of an organization differ in the extent to which their activities are standardized and controlled. The key factor is the required degree of interaction with the superior. Where this is high, as it often is at the top level of management, the span of control is small; where it is low, as on the factory floor, the span tends to be large.

Committees

Meaning and importance. A committee is a group of people specifically designated to perform a managerial act.[33] Committees are ubiquitous in modern organizations, be they universities or corporations, hospitals or legislatures. Except for small organizations, modern organizations seem to find committees an inexorably alluring device, despite the common joke that a camel is a horse designed by a committee. Why is this so?

First of all, committees have important coordinating, integrative functions. Committee meetings are the occasions for an exchange of information on current and future problems and for some sort of coordinated planning of steps that need to be taken in meeting these problems.

But committees also serve a number of other functions. They have a democratic format and therefore often create a feeling among members of participation in decision-making. They also permit the satisfaction of important social needs—organizational members busy in their individual niches get an opportunity to renew their acquaintances in the committee. But while coordination, problem solving, participation, and socializing are some of the positive functions committees are designed to perform, sometimes they are also used to bury controversial or embarrassing issues. Committees are notorious for being slow. Embarrassing issues can safely be dumped by assigning "blue ribbon," "impartial" committees or commissions to investigate them. Public memory being short, even if the committee were to come out with startling conclusions, the impact might be relatively light.

Unfortunately, little systematic empirical work appears to have been done on committees or the determinants of their utilization. Organizations with strong participatory ideologies seem to have a particular affinity for them because the committee is perceived as a more participative, less arbitrary means for making decisions than the exercise of authority by an individual. Parts of the organization where coordination among specialized personnel is vital because of their interdependence are also often rife with committees.

SUMMARY, PROPOSITIONS, AND IMPLICATIONS FOR ORGANIZATIONAL DESIGN

Summary

We have examined what we have called the superstructure of organizations (the way individuals are grouped together into sections, teams, divisions, and departments) and the infrastructure of organizations (control and information system, decentralization, structuring of activities, the hierarchy, and committees). It should not be forgotten that these represent the *durable* and *formally* sanctioned relationships of organizational members with one another, with roles, procedures, technology, and so on. Words like "specialization" or "decentralization" are abstractions. What lies behind them is a certain molding of human behavior, the creation of certain role expectations.

Organizational structure is the structuring or molding of *human* activities (as distinct from mechanical activities) in the organization.

The various elements of organizational structure perform a number of functions—chiefly, reduction of external and internal uncertainty confronting decision makers, the efficient undertaking of a multitude of activities, and proper coordination of these activities so that the organization can achieve its objectives. While all elements of structure fulfill these functions, they vary considerably in the extent to which one or the other function is primary.

A variety of forces shape the structure of the organization. Some of these forces are external, such as competition, technology, diversity of markets and customers, and some are internal, such as operations technology and values and beliefs of the more powerful members of the organization. Generally speaking, organizations in dynamic, heterogeneous, competitive environments tend to be structurally more complex than organizations in relatively static, homogeneous, noncompetitive environments. Size and complex technology also make for structural complexity—that is, for greater structuring and for greater sophistication in control and information systems. Similar factors affect two other important facets of organizational structure—namely, decentralization of authority and the hierarchy of authority. Decentralization is an important element of the administrative strategies of those top managements that stress efficiency as well as morale, and its effectiveness depends on the simultaneous use of a number of integrative mechanisms. The horizontal and vertical spans of control have significant implications for superior-subordinate interactions, vertical communication, and the like.

Propositions

1. The greater the reciprocal interdependence between personnel;
   the greater their serial dependence; and
   the greater their pooled interdependence,
        the greater is the probability of their being grouped together.

2. As between the three forms of interdependence,
        reciprocal interdependence will be the strongest factor in grouping
           together individuals;
        serial interdependence will be the next strongest; and
        pooled interdependence will be the weakest.

3. The greater the ratio of subordinates doing a particular kind of work to
        their supervisors (beyond what is considered the optimal span of
        control for that kind of work),
            the greater will be the pressure to increase the number of departments or groupings of personnel doing the same type of work.

4. The more specialized the tasks performed by individuals,

> the more likely they are to be grouped together by areas of specialization to permit effective supervision.

5. The greater the similarity in the kind of work performed by individuals and in their norms and values related to work and to interpersonal relations,

> the greater the probability of their being grouped together for maintaining morale.

6. The more diversified the demand for a service within an organization,

> the more likely it is that individuals providing that service will be grouped together to facilitate access to them.

7. The more extensive the functional departmentalization in an organization,

> the greater is the possibility of conflict between the personnel of interfacing departments.

8. The greater the interface between functionally organized departments,

> the greater is the need for coordinative mechanisms such as planning, standard operating procedures, committees, a common boss, and communications and human relations training.

9. The more divisionalized the organization,

> the more centralized tend to be the staff functions commonly used by all the divisions.

10. The more divisionalized the organization,

> the better is intradivisional coordination, but the more intense is interdivisional rivalry.

11. The more an organization's superstructure resembles a matrix organization,

> the more organic, participatory, human-relations oriented, and technocratic tend to be the management style and ideology at the *operating* levels of the organization.

12. The greater the diversity in the product lines or services offered by an organization;
the faster the rate of introduction of new product lines or services by the organization;
the tighter the operating schedule;
the greater the needed interdependence between diverse personnel; and
the larger the organization,

> the more divisionalized it will tend to be.

13. The more sophisticated the technology of operations and
the larger the economies of scale,
> the more functionally departmentalized the organization will
> tend to be.

14. The more customized and varied the products or services provided to
the organization's clientele,
the faster the rate of innovation or introduction of new products, projects, or services by the organization;
the tighter the operating schedule; *and*
the more sophisticated the technology of operations;
> the more the organization will tend to develop a matrix, project
> structure *provided* the economies of scale are not large.

15. The more complex the tasks of a department,
> the higher is the technical level of the personnel employed in the
> department.

16. The more novel the tasks,
> the more varied and discretionary are the procedures employed
> in the department, and the more organic are the superior–
> subordinate and peer relations within it.

17. The more competitive and innovation rich the environment;
the more technologically sophisticated and complex the environment;
the more diverse the environment;
the larger the organization; and
the wider its distribution network,
> the more sophisticated and comprehensive is the control and
> information system employed in the organization.

18. The more professional the orientation of the top management—that is,
the more it stresses both optimization and participation—
> the more sophisticated and comprehensive is the control and information system employed in the organization.

19. The more comprehensive and sophisticated the control and information
system,
> the more decentralized is decision-making in the organization.

20. The larger the organization;
the greater the competitive pressure on the organization; and
the more participative the top management ideology,
> the greater is decentralization of authority at upper levels of
> management.

21. The higher the performance aspirations of top management with respect to morale of personnel as well as efficiency,

  the more conspicuous are a participative ideology, a sophisticated control and information system, and decentralization as jointly utilized elements of the top management's administrative strategy.

22. The more an organization resembles an organization of professionals that have internalized professional norms,

  the more decentralized is the authority for making operating decisions, especially if the tasks to be performed are relatively variable and nonstandardized.

23. The larger the organization;
the more unionized it is; and
the more integrated and automated its workflow is,

  the more structured its activities are likely to be.

24. The larger the organization in which an organization is embedded and the less autonomous the latter is,

  the more structured its activities are likely to be.

25. The stronger the formal control and information system in the organization (or part of the organization),

  the larger is the horizontal span of control and the shorter is the length of the hierarchy.

26. The greater the similarity in the work performed by subordinates, the larger is the horizontal span of control.

27. The more routinized, less complex, and less interdependent the activities of subordinates,

  the larger is the horizontal span of control.

Implications for Organizational Design

The designing of an organization's structure is a highly complex task. There is no one best structural design. If, however, the designer is aware of the demands that the organization's environment and technology make on the organization, and the costs and benefits of the structural alternatives, the chances are that the organization will not be saddled with a faulty design.

For example, forming departments is in many ways useful. It makes for better control of organizational members' activities; it gives easier access to organizational specialists; it makes for better coordination of activities within a group; and so on. But departmentalization can also lead to suboptimization, interdepartmental conflicts, and other problems. By observing the type of task environment an organization has, the designer can so departmentalize the organization as to accent the benefits and minimize the costs. If the organization's environment is very heterogenous, the designer can certainly do better by divisionalizing the organization than by functionally departmentalizing it, at least at senior administrative levels. If the environment is technologically very dynamic, the designer can opt for a matrix structure and thereby make the organization's operations more effective, given the circumstances.

The designer has a choice between centralization and a simple structure on the one hand and decentralization and a complex structure on the other. Centralization can make for quick, but not necessarily for the locally most sensible or timely, decisions. Decentralization can facilitate decisions that are locally sensible and timely, because of the familiarity of the persons making them with local situations, but it does not necessarily foster the speedy top level decisions needed in a crisis. Besides, decentralization requires a complex and expensive infrastructure to make it work effectively. Again, an awareness of the circumstances under which one or the other makes sense can be very helpful to the designer. The author's study of U.S. manufacturing firms suggests that firms that are decentralized and have a complex structure show a superior profit performance *provided* they are in a highly competitive, contingency-rich environment. On the other hand, firms that tend to be relatively centralized and have a simple structure show a superior profit performance provided they are in a modestly competitive or a noncompetitive environment.[34] Clearly, therefore, the designer can avoid serious problems for the organization by paying attention to the task environment and selecting the combination of decentralization and structural complexity that is most apt in that environment.

As to the shape of the organizational hierarchy, too, the designer has a choice. Suppose that a "flat" organization with wide horizontal spans of control is preferred. Vertical communication may be faster that way, and managers and workers may possibly experience greater autonomy. But the cost may be in inadequate interaction between supervisors and their subordinates, in loose supervisory control, and possibly in the formation of little cliques among subordinates. On the other hand the designer can opt for a "tall" organization with narrow spans of control. This way, more supervisory control over activities can be had, and work groups, being smaller, may get more cohesive; but the cost may be slow and distorted vertical communication and large status and power differentials between the top level managers and those at the bottom.

Here, too, the designer is between Scylla and Charybdis. But here, too, organization theory comes in handy. By looking to the type of work that organizational members are performing, the designer can help the organization make sensible choices about the shape of the hierarchy: narrow in those parts of the organization in which considerable interaction between supervisor and subordinates is required to get the job done, and wide in parts where, through standardization or sophisticated controls or otherwise, the need for this kind of interaction is not very great.

stop

SUGGESTED READINGS

Peter Blau, "A Formal Theory of Differentiation in Organizations," *American Sociological Review*, Vol. 35, No. 2 (1970), pp. 201–18.

John Child, "Organization Structure and Strategies of Control: A Replication of the Aston Study," *Administrative Science Quarterly*, Vol. 17 (1972), pp. 163–77.

Pp. 1–16 and 266–309 in Gene W. Dalton, Paul R. Lawrence, and Jay Lorsch, *Organizational Structure and Design* (Homewood, Ill.: Irwin and Dorsey, 1970).

Jay Galbraith, *Designing Complex Organizations* (Reading, Mass.: Addison-Wesley, 1973).

P. N. Khandwalla, "Viable and Effective Organizational Designs of Firms," *Academy of Management Journal*, Vol. 16, No. 3 (Sept., 1973), pp. 481–95.

QUESTIONS FOR ANALYSIS

1 In what circumstances would you recommend the following organizational structure?

Departmentalization:	Divisional at upper management levels; functional below the divisional level Central staff groups
Sophistication of C.I.S.:	High
Decentralization of authority:	High
Vertical span of control:	Large
Horizontal span of control:	Varies considerably in different parts of the organization

How would the circumstances have to change for you to recommend a matrix departmental structure? How would they have to change for you to recommend a functional departmental structure?

2 Given below is the structural design of a firm. What changes would you recommend if (a) the size were to increase; (b) competitive pressure were to increase; or (c) the organization, a press and a publishing company, were to automate its operations?

Divisionalization:	Low
Use of sophisticated management controls:	Low
Staff service units such as for forecasting, planning, or market research:	Low
Delegation of authority by the chief executive:	Moderate

3 Can you think of circumstances under which you would recommend a larger horizontal span of control at top management levels than at much lower management levels?

4 Here are the key situational and strategic facts about a foreign subsidiary of a worldwide Japanese conglomerate:

    a. Total annual sales of around $20 million. Total managerial and clerical staff of about 30.

    b. Trading operations only. Markets a great variety of sophisticated products of the conglomerate, notably those not commonly available in the host country.

    c. Environment is viewed by top managers as fairly turbulent, not very hostile, quite heterogeneous, fairly complex technologically, and only moderately constraining.

    d. Very high performance aspirations on the part of the management of the subsidiary, particularly with regard to profitability growth and liquidity. Very high consensus about these goals among the managers.

The structure of the organization has the following characteristics:

    a. Highly divisionalized (see organizational chart).

    b. A highly sophisticated control and information system. The subsidiary receives a flood of telex messages everyday from the headquarters in Tokyo as well as from the worldwide network of fellow subsidiaries. There is very tight profit control.

    c. Great decentralization of decision-making authority. Division managers have authority to enter into contracts worth up to $2 million without consulting the general manager of the subsidiary.

    d. Substantial structuring of activities. Considerable specialization of functions and roles and standardization of buying, selling and financing procedures. Some formal description of roles; a good deal of paperwork with regard to buying and selling contracts, employment of host country personnel, and all monetary transactions.

    e. A relatively flat hierarchy (see organizational chart).

    f. A single management committee consisting of the general manager, an assistant, and the seven division heads. Meets once every two weeks.

Critique the organizational structure of this subsidiary.

5 Read the case on the Wall Street counseling and brokerage firm of Harwick, Smyth, and Blanchard, as presented by Dalton, Lawrence, and Lorsch

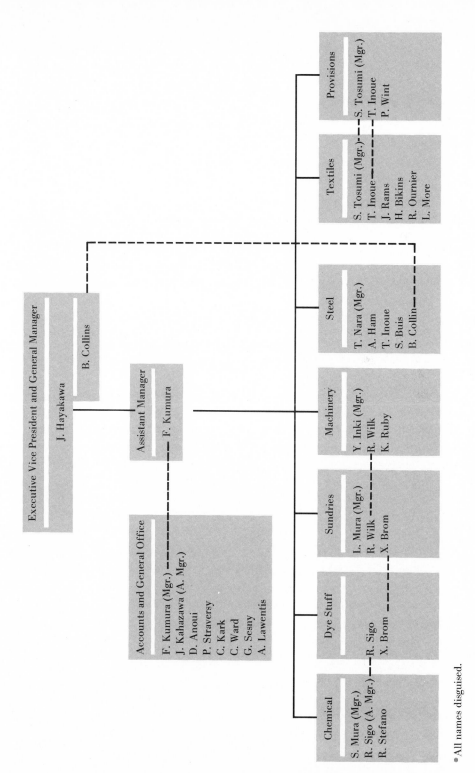

Executive Vice President and General Manager
J. Hayakawa
B. Collins

Assistant Manager
F. Kumura

Accounts and General Office
F. Kumura (Mgr.)
J. Kahazawa (A. Mgr.)
D. Anoui
P. Straversy
C. Kark
C. Ward
G. Sesny
A. Lawentis

Chemical
S. Mura (Mgr.)
R. Sigo (A. Mgr.)
R. Stefano

Dye Stuff
R. Sigo
X. Brom

Sundries
L. Mura (Mgr.)
R. Wilk
X. Brom

Machinery
Y. Inki (Mgr.)
R. Wilk
K. Ruby

Steel
T. Nara (Mgr.)
A. Ham
T. Inoue
S. Buis
B. Collin

Textiles
S. Tosumi (Mgr.)
T. Inoue
J. Rams
H. Bikins
R. Ourmier
L. More

Provisions
S. Tosumi (Mgr.)
T. Inoue
P. Wint

*All names disguised.

in *Organizational Structure and Design* (Homewood, Ill.: Irwin-Dorsey, 1970), pp. 134–38. Critique the organizational structure of Harwick, Smyth, and Blanchard, Inc. Would the present structure remain if the company continued to grow rapidly? If Wall Street were to hit a long period of slump? Do you expect any administrative differences among the research work units shown in Exhibit 5 of the case?

6 What kind of organizational structure would make sense were you to start a medium-sized printing plant? Were you to head a small electronics parts division of a multinational corporation?

Footnotes to Chapter 13

[1] See Ernest Dale, *Planning and Developing the Company Organization Structure*, for different kinds of organizational chart. Also see Robert Stieglitz, "What's Not on the Organization Chart," for a discussion of what the organizational chart shows and what it fails to show, such as the degree of responsibility and authority, status or importance, lines of communication, the "informal" organization, etc.

[2] J. D. Thompson, *Organizations in Action.*

[3] See W. H. Newman, C. F. Summer, and E. K. Warren, *The Process of Management*, 3rd ed., pp. 56–61, for advantages and disadvantages of divisionalization in firms (profit decentralization).

[4] Alfred Chandler, *Strategy and Structure*, p. 44.

[5] For an excellent study of the many aspects of the matrix organization at work at N.A.S.A., see Leonard Sayles and Alfred Chandler, *Managing Large Systems.*

[6] H. Rush, *Behavioral Science: Concepts and Management Application*, pp. 158–59.

[7] *Ibid.*

[8] Jay Galbraith, "Matrix Organization Designs: How to Combine Functional and Project Forms."

[9] *Ibid.*

[10] See Appendix A to this book for a description of the author's study of Canadian firms.

[11] Galbraith, *op. cit.*

[12] Andrew Van de Ven and André Delbecq, "A Task Contingent Model of Work Unit Structure."

[13] *Ibid.*, p. 188.

[14] See Emile Durkheim, *The Division of Labor in Society*, tr. G. Simpson.

[15] See Appendix A for the operational definition of C.I.S.

[16] For the many measure of decentralization, see T. Whisler, et al., "Centralization of Organizational Control: An Empirical Study of Its Meaning and Measurement."

[17] For advantages and disadvantages of decentralization, see Richard B. Heflebower, "Observations on Decentralization in Large Enterprises."

[18] See Pugh, et al., "The Context of Organizational Structures"; for a replication of the Aston studies, see John Child, "Organization Structure and Strategies of Control."

[19] John Child, "More Myths of Management Education?"

[20] Peter Blau and Richard Schoenherr, *The Structure of Organizations*, p. 121.

[21] P. N. Khandwalla, "Viable and Effective Organizational Designs of Firms."

[22] Pugh, et al., *op. cit.;* and John Child and Roger Mansfield, "Technology, Size, and Organization Structure."

[23] P. N. Khandwalla, "The Effect of Competition on the Structure of Top Management Control," and "Viable and Effective Organizational Designs of Firms."

[24] Pugh, et al., *op. cit.*

[25] Chris Argyris, *Executive Leadership*, pp. 44–48.

[26] Peter Blau, "The Dynamics of Bureaucracy."

[27] George Strauss and Leonard Sayles, *Personnel: The Human Problems of Management*, p. 376.

[28] See W. H. Starbuck, "Organizational Growth and Development," pp. 500–501.

[29] Peter Blau, "A Formal Theory of Differentiation in Organizations."

[30] John Udell, "An Empirical Test of Hypotheses Relating to Span of Control," pp. 420–39.

[31] Joan Woodward, *Industrial Organization: Theory and Practice*, p. 62.

[32] *Ibid.,* pp. 52–53 and 62.

[33] Newman, Summer, and Warren, *op. cit.*, p. 94. Also see Robert F. Bales, "In Conference," for some practical suggestions about the use of committees.

[34] Khandwalla, "Viable and Effective Organizational Designs," *op. cit.*

"*Right conduct can never be promoted by ignorance or hindered by knowledge.*"
Bertrand Russell

The Design of Human Behavior in Organizations

start at 541

INTRODUCTION

In this chapter we deal with the design of the behavior of individuals and groups in the organization. The study and modification of human behavior in organizations has come to be termed "behavioral science" or "organizational behavior." While behavioral scientists have focused rather exclusively on the modification of behavior through an important but relatively narrow set of means—primarily participative decision-making, job enrichment, various forms of sensitivity training, and the like—we take into account a wider range of means by which human behavior can be shaped, including modifications of organizational structure and technology, of the organization's goals and ideology, and even of its environmental and demographic properties. Figure 14–1 outlines the scope of this chapter.

The designer can alter the structure of the organization. For example, it can be changed from one of functional departmentalization to a divisional form. Or, the shape of the hierarchy can be altered and the degree of specialization, formalization, or decentralization, increased or decreased. By changing the way people are grouped together, or by changing the access individuals have to decision makers, or by changing the mix of the types

530

of people in the organization, major changes could be produced in the motivation to remain with the organization and the motivation to "produce."

These dimensions of behavior can also be affected by altering the organization's technology and the tasks performed in the organization. Time and motion study, human engineering, operations research, electronic data processing, job enrichment, rationalization, and the like are methods by which tasks performed by individuals can be altered, thereby altering motivation, interaction between individuals, and other aspects of behavior.

A third strategy for molding human behavior is by going to work directly on individuals. By changing selection procedures, or by changing the way personnel are trained, "socialized," and rewarded or punished, or by improving communications through human relations type programs, or by engaging in "organizational development," the designer can usually hope to have a powerful impact on human behavior.

A fourth strategy for designing human behavior is one of modifying organizational goals. We noted in Chapter 10 that top level goals translate into a number of goal-means hierarchies. If a firm changes its profit goal from one of a 10 percent return on investment to one of a 20 percent return on investment, substantial changes may follow, not only in the tasks performed in the organization (e.g., the addition of a market research function), but in the way the tasks are performed (e.g., greater pressure from superiors to "produce"). Inevitably, these changes will affect human behavior in the organization.

A fifth strategy is one of changing the environment of the organization or its mission or type. If a private company is changed into a public company, a local political party into a national political party, or a purely health care hospital into a teaching-cum-research hospital, powerful forces are set into motion that alter patterns of human behavior. Similarly, when an organization shifts its product line or line of services and thus places itself in a much more dynamic or competitive environment, powerful forces are set into motion that affect human behavior in the organization.

This business of shaping behavior is not, of course, a push-button job. Human beings have minds of their own. They have learned habits over the years that often are hard to change. They sometimes band together to thwart the designs of the designer. On top of these, the strategies we listed above are not mutually exclusive. As Harold Leavitt has pointed out, one strategy, such as that of a structural change, can trigger many anticipated as well as unanticipated changes in tasks, techniques, the system of rewards and punishments, and the like, which in turn affect each other and human behavior.[1]

The field of organizational behavior is simply not yet sufficiently sophisticated to be able to predict all these ramifications with a reasonable de-

FIGURE 14–1
The Design of Behavior in Organizations

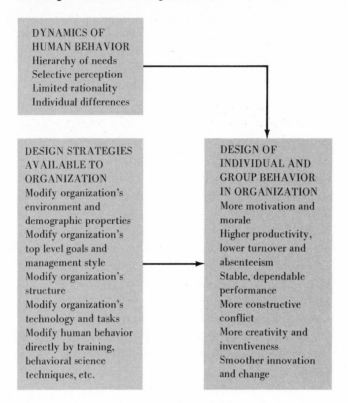

gree of accuracy. Thus, the organizational designer must tread with care, treat these strategies merely as starting points, carefully and periodically evaluate the feedback from design actions, and adjust strategies in the light of this feedback.

Incidentally, the unwary may think that when we talk of "the designer," we have in mind some technocrat at the hub of the organization manipulating people with invisible strings. Nothing of the kind. There is nothing in our perspective to preclude the widest possible participation by organizational members in the work of designing their organization, as in a kibbutz or a cooperative. On the other hand, neither does it preclude the design function's being discharged by a small clique of powerful top level executives or technocrats. The question we pursue is: Whether the designer is a team of top level executives or a large number of individuals representing different constituencies in the organization, such as a legislative body, given what we know about organizational behavior, how would the designing unit proceed to shape organizational behavior to reach ends it considers worthwhile?

THE DESIGN OF MOTIVATION AND MORALE

The Nature of Motivation and Morale

Motivation on the job, from the point of view of the organization, is the intensity of *desire* on the part of its personnel to seek *additional rewards* through job-related activities. These rewards may be pecuniary in nature, such as earnings and perquisites; they may relate to a desire for job security; they may relate to how interesting and challenging the work is or to the prospects for personal growth; and so on. Morale is the extent to which personnel are *satisfied* with their jobs, with their colleagues and supervisors, with the organization they belong to. Generally speaking, high motivation and high job satisfaction are both desirable from the point of view of the organization, but for somewhat different reasons. Highly motivated personnel make it easier for the organization to raise productivity, institute innovations, and ride out crises. Alienated or indifferent personnel make it more difficult for the organization to do so. Highly satisfied personnel may or may not be motivated to be highly productive, but they are more likely to want to remain with the organization than dissatisfied personnel. Research evidence does not indicate a link between job satisfaction and productivity, but it does indicate that satisfied personnel tend to exhibit lower absenteeism and turnover rates than dissatisfied personnel and probably identify more with their organization than do dissatisfied personnel.[2]

The difference between the psychological states of motivation and satisfaction is crucial. Motivated individuals aggressively look for ways to achieve a goal. They are people in an alert, searching, problem-solving frame of mind. Satisfied individuals, on the other hand, have a psychological investment in the status quo, for the status quo is the source of their feelings of satisfaction. Satisfaction is a condition that *dampens* or freezes activity, search, receptivity to new ideas, problem solving; motivation is a condition that *activates* these. Dissatisfaction is thwarted motivation. It too can spur search behavior, but commonly search for another job or for ways to get even with the source of dissatisfaction. If the organization can respond creatively to dissatisfaction, so that personnel can realistically expect to better their lot by working for the organization's goals, dissatisfaction can be turned into motivation. For tasks that require change, innovation, search, and problem solving, high motivation in the personnel performing them is desirable, but not high satisfaction, for the latter may be lethal. For repetitive tasks, satisfied personnel are desirable; too highly motivated personnel may destabilize operations through tinkering with the routine.

In any theorizing about motivation and job satisfaction, one must take into account Maslow's theory of human motivation. It predicts that as lower order needs (physiological, security, etc.) get satisfied, the aspiration level with respect to the satisfaction of lower order needs falls and that for the higher order needs (social, achievement, self-actualization, etc.) rises.[3] Hall and Nougaim's research evidence indicates that there is a tendency for greater satisfaction of lower order needs to be accompanied by heightened aspirations with respect to needs higher in the hierarchy but that there is, however, no decrease in the aspiration level for lower order needs. Indeed the latter tend to rise also. For example, in their data, reported satisfaction of safety needs of management trainees was correlated .26 with its current reported strength, and the satisfaction with respect to achievement and esteem needs was correlated .54 with the current strength of these needs.[4] These findings are in accord with experimental work on the level of aspiration. This work suggests that as achievement on a goal increases (decreases), the aspiration level with respect to goal attainment goes up (down), too.[5] Thus, if getting job security is a goal of an employee, securing some job security will whet the appetite for more. Similarly, if a man wants to have an interesting job and gets one that is more interesting than the previous one, he will now want an even more interesting job. It is likely, of course, that this process of rising aspirations with respect to needs that are being satisfied is subject to what the economists call diminishing marginal utility (satiety).

We propose that:

The higher the job satisfaction with respect to needs lower in Maslow's hierarchy of needs,
> *the higher, subject to satiety, is motivation to achieve a higher level of satisfaction of these needs, and*
> *the higher also is motivation with respect to needs higher in the hierarchy.*

The higher the job satisfaction of personnel,
> *the lower is their absenteeism and turnover, and*
> *the higher is their loyalty to the organization.*

The higher the job motivation of personnel,
> *the greater is the proclivity to high productivity and the acceptance of innovations that can lead to high productivity.*

Organizational Strategies for Raising Morale and Motivation

A number of strategies are available to the organization for influencing the morale and motivation of personnel.

Environment. In Chapter 10 we noted that a buoyant and challenging environment—a combination of high growth and high competitive pressure—sharply raises the performance aspirations of top management. A design implication of this is that the tasks performed by work units and departments might be so arranged that *their* managements get highly motivated. Growth in the size of units can be made probable by the organization diversifying its activities and trying to grow rapidly. The element of competition may be provided by tying the resources and rewards each unit gets to its performance on explicit criteria, and letting the units compete with one another for these resources. Permitting unchecked competition between departments may not, of course, be either feasible or desirable, especially if their activities are interdependent. But among units whose activities are not highly interdependent, this may be possible and desirable. Divisionalization is, indeed, one such administrative arrangement that corporations commonly engage in.

We propose that:

The more buoyant and challenging the task environment of departments within an organization—that is, the higher the rate of growth in their activities and *the more subject they are to competitive pressures—*
the higher is the level of motivation of their managers.

Size. Porter's study of the relationship between the size of the organization and managerial morale revealed some intriguing findings.[6] Porter found that deficiency in the satisfaction of several needs was higher in the small company at higher levels of management as compared to the large company, while at lower management levels, the advantage was with the smaller company.

For example, the average *need deficiency score* (computed by subtracting the reported extent to which a manager's need was met from what was desired by him to be met) for *upper-middle* managers in the largest organizations in respect of the feeling of self-esteem was .71. Need deficiency was higher, at 1.26, for upper-middle managers in the smallest firms. For the same class of managers, the average need deficiency score for opportunity to participate in setting of goals, determining methods and procedures was .75 for managers in the largest firms; it was 1.32 for managers in the smallest firms.

On the other hand, on the dimensions "prestige inside company associated with the manager's position," "authority connected with the manager's position," "opportunity to participate in the setting of goals," and "feeling of self-fulfillment," the need deficiency scores of the *lower level* managers of medium-sized companies were notably smaller than those of the lower level managers of the largest companies.

Talacchi found, in a study of 93 manufacturing and nonmanufacturing organizations, a fairly strong negative relationship between the size of the organization and the level of satisfaction of employees (including managers).[7] This finding is consistent with Porter's findings that the level of need deficiency is lower at lower management levels in smaller organizations as compared to large organizations. After all, the bulk of employees in any organization tend to be lower level supervisors and blue-collar personnel.

The findings suggest that upper level managers are happier in large organizations than in small ones, while lower level managers are happier in small organizations than in large ones.

There may be several reasons for these intriguing findings. The large firm tends to be more decentralized at the upper levels—that is, upper level managers in large firms tend to have greater operating and decision-making autonomy than upper level managers in small organizations. The large firm also offers better auxiliary services to decision makers than the small firm, services such as electronic data processing, market research, systematic forecasting, and systematic evaluation of investment proposals. The large organization also is less vulnerable to environmental exigencies than the small firm, and so can offer greater job security to its managers. On the other hand, in the small firm, upper level managers are often glorified assistants to the chief executive, and in making decisions must often shift for themselves as best they can in the relative absence of staff specialists to help with advice and information. At the lower management levels, the large organization, with its standard operating procedures, extensive functional specialization, a tall hierarchy, and impersonality, is a less appetizing place to work in terms of higher order needs such as self-esteem, autonomy, and self-actualization, than the less impersonal, less bureaucratized smaller organization.

Research evidence suggesting that morale is higher in small work *groups* than in large ones[8] may be combined with Porter's findings to suggest that in large organizations at lower managerial as well as at staff and blue-collar levels, one way of raising morale is to lower the size of the work groups, while in smaller organizations, a way of raising morale at upper management levels is to lower the size of the work groups at that level and increase the manager's operating authority, autonomy, and participation in goal setting relevant to his position—in other words, have more of what Drucker has called management by objectives.[9]

On the strength of the above studies, we propose that:

The larger the organization,
> *the greater is the distance between senior management and the lower level personnel, and so the lower tends to be the morale of blue-collar, clerical, and lower management personnel.*

The larger the organization,

> *the greater is the lateral and vertical mobility of managers, and the greater is the support staff to help them in problem solving, and so, the higher tends to be the morale of the upper level managers.*

Top management goals. Another force tending to raise the strategic importance of motivation and morale is high performance aspirations on the part of top management. The data from the author's Canadian study suggest that high performance aspirations are associated not only with the importance accorded to sophisticated personnel incentive systems but with the importance accorded to other motivational tools like job enrichment, participative management, management by objectives (advocated by Drucker and McGregor), and the like.[10] High performance aspirations of top management cannot be realized unless a great many decision makers, workers, and staff members are highly motivated. If these high performance aspirations can be communicated to the rank and file, and if the rank and file can identify with them, as has occasionally been attempted with success in China and Russia, then the motivational level of the organization's membership could be raised substantially.

We propose that:

The higher the performance aspirations of managers,

> *the more attention they are likely to pay to motivational tools like incentive systems, job enrichment, participative management, and management by objectives.*

Management ideology. Likert documents a good deal of research that suggests a link between employee-oriented, participative supervision and high morale among subordinates.[11] He presents data from a large public utility, in which he makes a comparison of the perceptions of supervisors by workers in work groups with favorable job attitudes with those of workers in work groups with unfavorable job attitudes.

The biggest differences between the perceptions of workers in the two groups seem to lie in whether the supervisor recommends promotions, transfers, pay increases or not; whether he informs the men as to what is happening in the company or not; whether he keeps them posted on how well they are doing or not; whether he hears complaints and grievances or not; whether he is seen as treating employees as humans or tools, whether he supports his men or not; whether he takes interest in them or not. In other words, groups whose supervisors are perceived as practicing good human relations tend to have workers with favorable job-related attitudes, and those perceived as flouting good human relations tend to have dissatisfied workers. One must, however, be cautious in interpreting these findings. Is it the cooperative attitudes and behavior of the subordinates that lead the superior to show concern and support for them, or is it the supervisor's concern and support for subordinates that leads them to have favorable attitudes toward their jobs? Perhaps the causal arrow goes both ways, that is, the superior and the subordinates reinforce each others' behavior and attitudes, aided perhaps by the work group's high productivity due to superior technology and staff support systems.

We propose that:

The more participative and employee oriented the supervision,
the higher is the morale of subordinates, and possibly vice versa.

Structure and technology. Research evidence indicates that organizational structure is a major determinant of job satisfaction. In a review article, Porter and Lawler concluded that job satisfaction increases at each higher level in the organization.[12] This would argue for flattening somewhat the organizational hierarchy as a way of increasing job satisfaction. They also concluded that supervisory positions, are more satisfying to the incumbents than advisory positions. This would argue for expanding promotion opportunities within the staff by developing a parallel hierarchy for staff personnel. In other words, for improving the morale of line personnel it may be desirable to flatten the line hierarchy somewhat; for improving the job satisfaction of staff personnel, it may be desirable to *lengthen* the staff hierarchy somewhat. This may be accomplished by increasing the span of control of line managers and decreasing that of the staff managers.

Porter and Lawler's article also concludes, on the basis of the evidence of several studies, that the smaller the work unit the higher is the job satisfaction of its members. This is consistent with the findings in social psychological research that indicate that the smaller the group's size the higher is the morale in the group.[13]

Beyond these strategies for altering the environment, goals, management style, and organizational structure, alteration of technology and workflow offers another tool for improving motivation and morale. The work of Herzberg and his associates indicates that job enrichment may be a fairly powerful tool for increasing job satisfaction.[14] The following excerpt from *Time* magazine provides an interesting example of how the technology and workflow may be changed to increase job satisfaction:

Volvo's Valhalla
To Henry Ford, patron saint of mass production, the new Volvo plant in

Kalmar, Sweden, would seem curious indeed. It looks more like a giant repair shop than an auto factory. . . . But the most puzzling question in Ford's mind would be: What happened to the assembly line?

Busy interest. The answer is that it has been changed beyond recognition as part of an attack on an international labor problem: the growing dislike that today's young, comparatively well-educated workers have shown for tedious, repetitive factory jobs. In the U.S. and other countries, that attitude is reflected in heavy absenteeism and high turnover among factory work forces, poor-quality production and occasional strikes by workers desperate to get away from the line for a while. Volvo's system at Kalmar is attracting worldwide attention as an imaginative effort to set up a factory that will keep workers interested while busy.

Instead of a clanking, high-speed conveyor line, the Kalmar plant uses 250 "carriers"—18-ft. long computer-guided platforms that glide silently over the concrete floor. Each carrier delivers the frame for a single Volvo 264 to each of the plant's 25 work teams. The teams consist of 15 to 25 workers who are responsible for a certain aspect of assembly; one team, for example, will install the car's electrical system and another will work on the interior finish.

The teams organize themselves as they wish and work at the speed they choose. While a worker on a conventional assembly line might spend his entire shift mounting one license-plate lamp after another, every member of a Kalmar work team may work at one time or another on all parts of the electrical system—from tail lights to turn signals, head lamps, horn, fuse box and part of the electronically controlled fuel-injection system. The only requirement is that every team meet its production goal for a shift. As long as cars roll out on schedule, workers are free to take coffee breaks when they please or to refresh themselves in comfortable lounges equipped with kitchens and saunas.

The new plant cost $23 million, about 10% more than a conventional factory of the same capacity. It includes the most up-to-date devices to monitor production and promote quality control. At each team's work station, for example, a computer-connected television screen projects figures comparing the team's production goal with the number of assemblies it has actually completed. On top of the screen a yellow light flashes if the team is behind schedule; a green light comes on when it is ahead. So far, the plant is only turning out 56 cars a day, but by 1975 the company hopes to achieve annual production of 30,000 cars.[15]

Research evidence indicates that not only the Herzberg motivators but many of the so-called hygiene factors, such as pay level, congenial supervision, and friendly co-workers, are correlated with job satisfaction.[16]

We propose that:

*The fewer the number of levels in the line hierarchy (i.e., the flatter the
line hierarchy), and*

*the more numerous the number of levels in the staff hierarchy (i.e., the
taller the staff hierarchy),*

> *the higher is likely to be the morale of the line and staff personnel,
> respectively.*

The smaller the work unit,
> *the higher is morale.*

*The more interesting the work, the greater the chances for promotion, the
higher the pay, and the more congenial the supervision and the co-workers,
the higher is morale.*

The various strategies for raising morale and motivation are summarized
in Table 14–1.

TABLE 14–1
Strategies for Raising Motivation and Morale

Strategies for raising motivation	*Strategies for raising morale (job satisfaction)*
Create a buoyant and challenging environment for managers of work units by facilitating their rapid growth *and* by increasing competition among them	In large organizations, lower the size of the work unit at lower managerial as well as at staff and blue-collar levels to increase job satisfaction at those levels
Raise performance aspirations of managers so that they get more interested in tools for motivating subordinates	In relatively small organizations, lower the size of the work group at upper management levels, and increase the senior managers' operating authority and participation in decision-making to increase the job satisfaction of senior managers
	Inculcate a participatory, employee-oriented ideology and practice by supervisors through human relations training
	Flatten the line hierarchy to increase satisfaction of ego needs of supervisors; elongate the generally flat staff hierarchy to increase the satisfaction of ego needs of staff
	Improve both "motivation" and "hygiene" factors

THE DESIGN OF INTERUNIT CONFLICT AND COOPERATION

Introduction

The organization is a system of cooperative, interdependent behaviors. No one individual can perform all of the organization's tasks. Division of labor and specialization necessarily imply that individuals and groups must cooperate with one another to get tasks accomplished. As a Malay proverb has it, clapping with one hand does not any sound produce. Complex tasks such as planning and budgeting in firms, or patient care in hospitals, or the running of political campaigns by political parties would be impossible without a great deal of cooperation between personnel. In sizable organizations, assuring a reasonable degree of cooperation between personnel is a major problem for the organizational designer.

But if cooperative behavior is a necessity, conflict in organizations is inevitable. In the rain shadow of human ambitions and organizational arrangements lies the fascinating panorama of conflict: conflict within the individual; conflict between individuals; conflict between the individual and the work group or the organization; conflict between work groups; conflict between organizations. But conflict is not all arid and destructive. A number of organizational writers have noted the constructive aspects of conflict, especially the possibility that conflict can stimulate search for creative solutions.[17] As Robert Browning said, "When the fight begins within himself, a man's worth something." This is often true also of fights between individuals and groups. The task of the designer is to try to arrange organizational matters so that conflict is constructive, not destructive.

Interunit Conflicts and Their Causes

Conflicts between one individual and another or other individuals, as between one group or department and another or other groups or departments, are interunit conflicts. March and Simon indicate four outcomes of this form of conflict: problem-solving behavior, persuasion, bargaining, and political behavior.[18] In problem solving, the conflicting units seek the most effective means for reaching agreed upon goals. In persuasion, each unit tries to persuade the other unit to accept its goals as legitimate. Once goals are agreed upon, it becomes relatively easy to find the most effective means for reaching them. In bargaining, goal conflict is explicit and recognized, but there is some agreement as to the procedures that may legitimately be employed for resolving the conflict. The run-of-the-mill union-management conflict is of this type. In politics (at least as March and Simon use the term), there is total disagreement not only on goals but on the means by which the conflict may be resolved. Anything goes, and the conflict is marred by sabotage, back-stabbing, spying, and so on. Problem-solving behavior is, from the organizational standpoint, obviously the most desirable outcome and political behavior the least. It is necessary to understand the nature of organizational conflict and how it can be shaped to maximize the former and minimize the latter.

According to March and Simon, three factors significantly affect interunit conflicts. Interdependence, or, as they call it, felt need on the part of organizational units for joint decision-making, is one major contributor. Differences in the goals of the units in conflict is a second major contributor. And differences in the perception of the conflict situation by the units is a third major contributor. Each of these three in turn is determined by other factors. Let us briefly examine each factor, its causes, and the conflict resolution mechanisms available to the organizational designer that are appropriate to each.

Interdependence. Organizational units (be they individuals or groups or departments) are often dependent on one another in a variety of ways. Let us illustrate the various forms of dependency by examining the relations between a production crew and a maintenance crew that services the machines used by the production crew. First of all, if the maintenance crew does not maintain the machines properly, the production unit's output will suffer due to frequent machine breakdowns. The service provided by the maintenance crew is an input into the outputs produced by the production group. This is serial, one-way dependence. If the production crew misuses the machines so that they break down frequently, the record of the maintenance crew will look bad. In other words, the latter, too, is partially dependent on the behavior of the production crew. Thus, in reality, the relationship is one of reciprocal dependence. Both crews get their budget from the budget of the production department. In other words, there is a pool of resources from which both draw, so one unit cannot draw too much without affecting the share going to the other group. Thompson calls this pooled dependence.[19] Finally, there may be a more directly competitive interdependence between the two groups for organizational prestige and power. For example, if the heads of the two groups are in the running for the job of the production manager who is about to retire, one group's gain through its boss being appointed to the post will be perceived by the other group as a loss. Thus, there can be a highly competitive relationship between the two groups as well.

Clearly, any of these four forms of interdependence can sour relations between the two crews. Indifferent performance by the maintenance crew could make the production crew unhappy; abuse of the machines by the production crew, perhaps in retaliation, could upset the maintenance crew. A cut in the budget of the production department could mean that one or both groups' requests for additional men or equipment are turned down, making both unhappy, possibly with each other as well. And if the job of the production manager is offered to the boss of one of the two crews, the other group is likely to feel resentful and afraid of being discriminated against.

The very functioning of organizations, with their elaborate division of labor and specialization, is such that various forms of dependence between units are inevitable. This means that interunit conflicts due to interdependence are likely to be frequent. Advanced programming and planning of the work schedules of interdependent units—we may call this the "depersonalization of their interface"—is a frequent device for reducing the frequency of these conflicts. For example, rather than leave the frequency of maintenance to the discretion of the maintenance crew, a system may be put in force that requires machines to be serviced every second Tuesday of each month during a predetermined time. This system could be devised on the basis of past experience, possibly with the help of industrial engineers and operations researchers.

In many cases, interunit conflict due to interdependent work schedules can be reduced by providing for buffers or inventories. In a manufacturing organization, for example, the output of each production unit in an assembly line or process operation could go into an inventory rather than directly on to the next process. This way the inventory absorbs any fluctuations in the outputs of prior units.

Joint payoffs or incentives are a third way of reducing interunit conflicts. Here the interdependent units get a joint bonus for the successful completion of the whole job. Thus, the maintenance crew and the production crew both could be given a bonus if the volume of production lost through machine breakdown during a given period is less than some "normal" quantity. Joint payoffs simply increase the motivation of the interdependent units to collaborate better. Collaboration can be improved also through a training program designed to educate the interdependent units in the mutuality of their interests and the possibility of synergetic benefits through cooperation. Programs such as those of the Blake and Mouton managerial grid are examples.[20]

Putting interdependent units under a common boss is the age-old way of reducing interunit conflict. More often than not, it is a way of suppressing conflict, because in the event of a dispute what usually happens is that the common boss steps in and decides what is to be done. The conflict is temporarily out of sight—but hardly out of mind.

Finally, participatory, joint decision-making is another common conflict resolution device. The ubiquitous committee of the representatives of the warring units is the usual form of joint decision-making. Seldom does a committee resolve conflicts without some prerequisites, in particular an atmosphere of mutual trust and good will and the possibility of a solution that can benefit all the parties to a dispute. Without these, committees become elaborate façades for temporarily covering up conflicts or for postponing coming to grips with them.

Thus, a number of strategies are available to the organizational designer for containing interunit conflict that stems from interdependence. Some are technocratic in nature, such as trying to build frictionless workflow systems through the use of the computer, buffer stocks, and operations research techniques. Some involve structural arrangements, such as placing interdependent units under one boss or forming a committee of their representatives to coordinate the activities of these units. Some attempt to alter the motivation to collaborate through joint payoff schemes. Others work on the ability to collaborate, such as the intergroup collaboration programs of the Blake and Mouton managerial grid.

Without some form of interdependence, conflict between organizational units is likely to be either nonexistent or quite muted. But if there is a condition of interdependence, and in addition the units have conflicting goals and/or perceptions, the level of conflict is likely to be very intense. Interdependence creates a *potential* for conflict that is often *precipitated* by cleavages in goals and in the perception of the conflict situation.

Goal and perception differences. Organizational realities are such that goal and perception differences between organizational units are often inevitable. Our view of the organizational world is heavily dependent on the kind of job we have, the kind of training we have, the kind of information we get, the opinions of our immediate colleagues, and so on. Any sizable organization is considerably differentiated through a lengthy hierarchy, predetermined channels of communication, division of labor, specialization of functions, and a substantial contrast in the authority and obligations of those who make decisions and those who carry them out. No wonder then that individuals and groups within an organization differ considerably as to their goals and their perceptions of problems and relationships. Goal and perception differences are even sharper when the overall goals of the organization are fuzzy ("profit maximization," "service to society," "education," "taking care of the health needs of the community," "maintenance of law and order"). As in some ink-blot test, organizational units project their own concerns and priorities onto vaguely enunciated goals.

Here is an example of perceptual differences that arise for a variety of reasons—differences in training, differing perceptions of what is a proper way of working, even simple errors of perception. In this example, a group of machinist trainees, considered above average in intelligence and craftsmanship, were temporarily withdrawn from the training program and asked to help out in a warehouse. The case writer interviewed Yarby, the shipping foreman of the warehouse, and Nelson, a spokesman for the machinists, with whom Yarby was having trouble getting along. Here is his report of the comments of the two men concerning several situations in which the two did not see eye to eye.

YARBY: I noticed cigarettes lying on the pallets a few times. I told them not to smoke in the boxcars. I think they were smoking a good part of the day whenever I wasn't there.

NELSON: After loading a skid in the boxcar, another fellow has to truck the skid away and bring in a new skid. We have to wait while the guy does those things, so I smoked a cigarette on the dock—which was permissible. As soon as another skid is brought in I put my cigarette on the load of pallets on the dock because I would still have a few drags left when the next load was finished. The foreman made an issue over it because of the fire hazard. Naturally I knew there was a little hazard, but I told him I had my eyes on it. I still didn't go out and put it out just because it might cause a fire.

YARBY: I called the roll, and Nelson came in late. I told him to check with the timekeeper. He came after me five minutes later and said, "Do you expect me to wait around here like this when I could be doing something more valuable back in school?" I told him again that he would have to check with the timekeeper.

NELSON: I came in late and I said good morning, but he (Yarby) didn't answer. I figured he was busy, so I excused it. I think he definitely had an I'm-too-busy-for-you attitude. He told me, "You see the timekeeper so he can check you in." I stood there a few minutes, and the timekeeper didn't come around. I noticed Yarby at the RR dock and he wasn't busy. I told him I'd like to go back to the school area because I thought it was foolish just to wait and miss school . . . .

YARBY: The men were tossing the cartons. I told them "Don't toss the cartons, just place them." I came back fifteen minutes later, and they were doing the same thing. This time I gave them a direct order and said that I wasn't kidding. I guess I had a nasty look on my face, and I meant it. It was indicative of the type of work they were doing.

NELSON: There was a big space between the dock and the RR car. It was dangerous to keep walking across the space. We figured out a way of making a sort of fire line and handing the cartons out easier and faster than we could do the regular way. It was also safer because we didn't have to walk across that space. Yarby said we were throwing the cartons, but we really weren't. He made us go back to the old way, and we couldn't understand why . . . .[21]

Or, consider this vignette from Melville Dalton's classic study of staff-line conflicts in three industrial plants:

> Explaining the relatively few cases in which his staff had succeeded in "selling ideas" to the line, an assistant staff head remarked, "We're always in hot water with these old guys on the line. You can't tell them a damned thing. They're bull-headed as hell! Most of the time we offer a suggestion its either laughed at or not considered at all. The same idea in the mouth of some old codger on the line'd get a round of applause. They treat us like kids."
>
> Line officers in these plants often referred to staff personnel (especially members of the auditing, production planning, industrial engineering, and industrial relations staffs) as "college punks," "slide rules," "crackpots," "pretty boys," and "chair-warmers."

Summarizing his observations, Dalton had this to say:

> the struggles between line and staff organizations were attributable mainly to (1) functional differences between the two groups; (2) differentials in the ages, formal education, potential occupational ceilings, and status group affiliations of members of the two groups (the staff officers being younger, having more education but lower occupational potential, and forming a prestige-oriented group with distinctive dress and recreational tastes); (3) need of the staff groups to justify their existence; (4) fear in the line that staff bodies by their expansion, and well financed research activities, would undermine line authority; and (5) the fact that aspirants to higher staff offices could gain promotion only through approval of influential line executives.[22]

Dalton's analysis of the underlying reasons for staff-line conflicts applies not only to staff-line conflicts but, in the main, to many other forms of organizational conflicts as well, such as union-management conflicts, conflicts between functional departments, and conflicts between lower level management and upper level management.

Organizations usually attempt to resolve conflicts arising from goal and perception differences in much the same way they try to resolve conflicts that arise from interdependence. Thus, they try to employ planning and operations research techniques, form committees, put conflicting units under the same boss, set up joint incentive schemes, and so forth. These sometimes work but often do not because of the *emotional barriers* against collaboration that differences in goals and perceptions of reality have created. Deep-seated negative stereotypes ("the line managers are bull-headed," "the staff boys are crackpots") do not vanish simply because the boss so ordains, or because the new computer-based techniques seemingly make the interaction

impersonal, or because now there is a committee to look after the grievances, or because arbitration procedures are set up. To overcome the emotional barriers to collaboration, behavioral scientists have developed some
powerful techniques aimed primarily at restoring realism and rationality in
the way units in conflict *perceive* one another. Here is a description of one
such technique that has been applied in many situations of intergroup conflict in industrial settings:

> First, the leadership or membership of the two groups are brought to-
> gether. They are asked to concur that it would be desirable as a common
> purpose to reduce some of the tension and frustration that exists and to
> see if there are ways of finding mechanisms for getting more production
> and more collaboration through joint effort and understanding. This is the
> only requirement for commitment at the beginning of the meeting.
>
> The two groups are then sent to separate locations and asked to think
> about and develop a list which defines their attitudes about the other group—
> what is it about the other group's functioning and activities that exasperates
> them or gives them trouble. They are not to try for consensus, but just note
> their feelings and attitudes about the other group.
>
> A second task is to develop another list of their speculations about what
> the other group is writing about them right now. Then the two groups are
> brought together—Group A reports its attitudes and feelings toward Group
> B, and Group B does the same with Group A. There is no discussion between
> the groups. Group A then reports its list of what it thought Group B would
> write about them, and Group B does the same with Group A.
>
> The groups return to their separate locations to react to this shared infor-
> mation and to produce a list of issues which should have the priority atten-
> tion of both groups. During this second team meeting, most teams find that
> a number of the issues on their first list were misunderstandings which were
> cleared up merely by sharing the information. They are usually also able
> to reduce the list, from the large number of items on the first list, to the
> most relevant issues to be worked.
>
> The two groups then meet and compare their lists of issues. They make
> one list out of these, set priorities and agenda, and go to work in much the
> same way as described in the previous illustrations.
>
> It has been found repeatedly that in a relatively short period of time, an
> activity of this kind makes it possible for two groups in an organization to
> move toward considerable change in their relationship and their work effec-
> tiveness. Typically they produce an action plan which continues over time
> and assures reduction of the inappropriate competition.[23]

Notice the psychological mechanisms involved in this technique:

1. An initial public recognition of interdependence and common fate, and
a public commitment to an attempt at improving collaboration.

2. The accepting of a common purpose or superordinate goal. As Sherif's

research indicates, making a superordinate goal salient activates powerful cooperative impulses in groups in conflict.[24]

3. The expression of hostile feelings toward another group and that, too, in the legitimate setting of a reconciliation exercise. This expression of feelings alone would have some cathartic benefit.

4. An attempt at empathizing by thinking of what the other group is feeling. This exercise would create at least some sympathetic understanding of the other group's behavior and perceptions.

5. An exchange of information.

6. A situation in which each group can see how ludicrous or ill-founded some of their suspicions and assumptions have been about the other group. This can be an unfreezing experience, for if one has been so wrong in respect of specific beliefs, might one not be wrong in respect of many other beliefs about the other group? Might one not have been unfairly judging the other group?

7. An experience of insight into the motivations and behaviors of the members of the other group, a dawning of "understanding," and a feeling of euphoria at discovering that the members of the other group are human after all, and not at all the minions of the Devil.

8. The focusing of the energies of both groups into a plan of action with specific targets. For people who have gone through the trauma of a deadend conflict, there is nothing more relaxing, more uplifting, more energizing than a feeling that the problem is about to be "licked" through specific, step-by-step behaviors. It is the appearance of a solution that is important. The eventual solution may have little resemblance to this initial solution, but psychologically this initial solution powerfully mobilizes constructive and cooperative behavior. Kissinger's initial success in the Middle East may well be attributable to his ability to get the Arabs and the Israelis (a) to see each other as humans and (b) to *experience* a possible solution to their seemingly interminable conflict.

Figure 14–2 presents a summary of interunit conflict and the strategies available to the designer to minimize destructive conflict and improve coordination and collaboration.

Contextual and Strategic Determinants of the Use of Coordinative Mechanisms

We looked at some frequent causes of interunit conflict: interdependence, goal differences, and perception differences, especially when exacerbated by emotional stereotyping. We also noted some common administrative responses to interunit conflicts. Let us now examine the circumstances that elicit these coordination and conflict resolution responses. Table 14–2 shows

FIGURE 14–2
A Model of Interunit Conflict and Design of Coordination

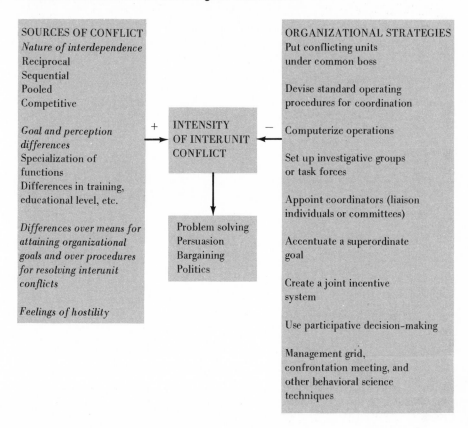

SOURCES OF CONFLICT
Nature of interdependence
Reciprocal
Sequential
Pooled
Competitive

Goal and perception
differences
Specialization of
functions
Differences in training,
educational level, etc.

Differences over means for
attaining organizational
goals and over procedures
for resolving interunit
conflicts

Feelings of hostility

+ → INTENSITY
OF INTERUNIT
CONFLICT ← −

Problem solving
Persuasion
Bargaining
Politics

ORGANIZATIONAL STRATEGIES
Put conflicting units
under common boss

Devise standard operating
procedures for coordination

Computerize operations

Set up investigative groups
or task forces

Appoint coordinators (liaison
individuals or committees)

Accentuate a superordinate
goal

Create a joint incentive
system

Use participative decision–making

Management grid,
confrontation meeting, and
other behavioral science
techniques

NOTE: The plus sign implies a positive relationship (a change in one leads to a change in the other in the same direction). The negative sign implies that a change in one leads to a change in the other direction in the opposite direction.

some of the more common coordination and conflict resolution strategies and their major situational and strategic correlates.

The table suggests that a complex environment—marked by constraints, sophisticated technology, research and development, and so on—tends to encourage the use of task forces, human relations training, and behavioral science techniques as coordinative, conflict-management devices. An environment marked by intense and many-sided competition tends to encourage a recourse to hierarchy for settling disputes, and a fluctuating environment a recourse to liaison personnel for the same purpose. A heterogeneous environment, like a complex environment, seems to encourage the organization to use task forces—but also standards and procedures. Large size seems to impel the organization to use human relations. Since large organizations

TABLE 14–2
**Correlates of the Use of Common Coordination and Conflict Resolution Strategies
(Sample: 103 Canadian Firms)**

Coordinative mechanisms	Situational correlates	Strategic, top management correlates
The use of *hierarchical authority*—heads of groups in dispute refer disputes to the executive with authority over both	Intense and many-sided competitive pressure on the firm	High performance aspirations
Standards and procedures—clear standards of job performance and detailed procedures for getting tasks accomplished, designed to minimize jurisdictional conflicts; explicit procedures for what to do in the event of disagreement between work groups	Heterogeneous environment	Professional orientation;* mechanistic orientation
Human relations training for managers to make them understand better their colleagues and subordinates and to help them communicate more effectively with them	Legally and economically constraining environment; large size of the organization; a nonhostile environment	Professional orientation
Behavioral science techniques like confrontation meetings, sensitivity training, or managerial grid type programs designed to raise the level of interpersonal competence and to create a climate of mutual trust and collaboration	A technologically sophisticated, research and development oriented environment	Professional orientation
Task forces or *ad hoc* committees whose objective is to examine a dispute and seek a solution that is optimal for the organization as a whole	Research and development oriented environment; legally and economically constraining environment; heterogeneous environment	
Liaison personnel—individuals or groups whose primary function is to act in a liaison or mediating capacity between groups in a conflict	Variable, fluctuating environment	High performance aspirations

* Equally strong emphasis on participatory and optimization values (see Ch. 11).

NOTE: For each coordinative mechanism, only those situational correlates are shown that were independently and statistically significantly correlated with the co-ordinative mechanism in question. Only those strategic correlates are shown that were statistically significantly correlated with the coordinative mechanism despite controlling for the effects of situational and other strategic variables.

commonly have diverse environments, the data suggest that operating diversity instigates the organization to utilize a number of integrative coordinative devices such as task forces, standards and procedures, and human relations training.

The table also indicates that a professional orientation in top management that emphasizes participative decision-making as well as planning and optimization (see Chapter 11) seems to induce the use of several different kinds of coordinative mechanism: the mechanistic one of standards and procedures alongside the expected one of human relations training and behavioral science techniques. On the other hand, a traditionally inclined top management, strongly nonparticipatory and seat-of-the-pants in its orientation, is likely to rely on far fewer coordinative mechanisms. High performance aspirations seem to induce the organization to employ two coordinative mechanisms—namely, hierarchical authority and the use of liaison personnel.

We propose that:

The greater the interdependence between organizational units
the more specialized their functions and
the greater the differences between their personnel in terms of goals, the
means for achieving goals, and the procedures for resolving disagreements,
the greater is likely to be the intensity of conflict between them.

The more restrictive, diverse, or technologically complex the environment
the more professionally oriented the top management style (including an
emphasis on participation and optimization) and
the higher the aspirations of the top management with respect to organizational goals,
the greater is the variety of coordinative mechanisms employed in
the organization.

THE DESIGN OF INVENTIVE AND INNOVATIVE BEHAVIOR

Invention and Innovation

In the organizational context, "invention" is the act of *creating* something novel *and* useful; "innovation" is the process of developing the invention so that it can be put to practical use.[25] Either can relate, not only to new products, services, or technical processes, but to new structural arrangements (such as the matrix structure), new ideologies and management styles (such as the organic style), and new ways of problem solving (such as through brainstorming). The discovery in some research laboratory that laser beams can trigger a fusion reaction is an invention. The development and marketing by an electronics firm of a process that allows the commercial production of electricity using this discovery is an innovation. Computation by electronic means is an invention. Gearing up an organization for the commercial production and marketing of computers is an innovation. The identification and measurement of a need for achievement in human beings is an invention. The development of a training program to raise and consolidate this need in managers is an innovation. Invention is the gift of genius, innovation that of management.

Invention is often the work of individuals (although it is being increasingly institutionalized in research laboratories). Innovation is a cooperative effort of dozens, sometimes hundreds and thousands of individuals and groups. Both are indispensable to human progress. (One estimate puts the contribution of invention and innovation to raising living standards in the United States as greater than that of capital accumulation.)[26] But the consensus of experts is that the design of the two processes in organizations has to be quite different.

The Design of Inventive Behavior

Invention is largely the handiwork of gifted, creative individuals. These may be towering geniuses like Einstein, Edison, Buckminster Fuller, Freud, and Marconi. More commonly, they are the humbler men in research laboratories, advertising agencies, architectural firms, and the like. A lot of psychological research suggests that gifted, creative individuals are rather different from ordinary people.[27] They have a richer and far more bizarre fantasy life. For example, here is the response of a child with a very high IQ score (a measure of intelligence), but not much creativity, to a Thematic Apperception Test picture:

> This is a story of counterfeiters. The man with the hat is the printer. The other man is the big boss. They are in danger of being captured by the police. They want to get out of the house. The police will arrive too late. The man and the evidence will be gone.[28]

Contrast this rather staid story with its projection of an escape wish with this story by a highly creative child:

> The man in the foreground is the leader of a counterfeiting ring. They have abducted the older man in the background. The older man is an excellent artist. They have kidnapped him so that they can force him to engrave the plates. He is very reluctant but they threaten to harm his wife

and children so he gives in. But he draws George Washington cross-eyed and the counterfeiters are captured and he is released.[29]

Note the exuberant imagination, the humor, the element of surprise, the rich if "wild" associative thinking. The creative individual is not only highly imaginative; he is also a very independent and strong-willed individual. He is highly motivated by an intrinsic interest in what he is doing rather than by the rewards associated with the task. He is difficult to control and difficult to please. He has a questing mind that likes to rock the boat. The way to his heart is by giving him a lot of autonomy and challenging tasks.

How should the organization be designed so as to raise the probability of attracting and retaining creative, inventive individuals? Steiner draws the outlines of such an organization. He lists the characteristics of creative persons and then speculates about the characteristics an organization must possess to accommodate creative individuals.[30]

In Table 14–3, one can readily see the fit between the attributes of the creative, inventive individual and those of the creative, inventive organization. Notice the likely structural attributes of a creative organization: decentralization, enough structuring of routine activities so that the creators are free to create, and separate units for generating ideas and evaluating ideas. Notice also the contextual and strategic determinants of creative behavior: the organization being an autonomous decision-making unit; the organization having unusual goals; heterogeneous personnel policy; selection and promotion on merit only; an innovating, risk-taking orientation; an organic, flexibility-oriented management ideology.

Brainstorming is an important management tool for generating novel solutions for complex problems.* The importance accorded to it by top management indicates at the least the desire to be a creative, inventive policy-making unit. The study of Canadian firms by the author indicates the following:

1. Brainstorming is more important to the management of relatively young, small firms than to the management of older, larger firms.

2. Managements of firms in rapidly growing industries and of organizations in industries with a high rate of process and product innovation regard brainstorming as more important than the managements of firms in low growth or low rate of innovation industries.

3. The riskier the firm's external environment, the more the management

---

* Osborn popularized the term "brainstorming." The essential idea of the technique is (a) to structure a problem; (b) to indulge in an uninhibited search for solutions, however bizarre they may seem; (c) to separate the phase of idea generation and solution finding from the phase of critically evaluating ideas and solutions. See A. F. Osborn, *Applied Imagination*, 3rd ed.

TABLE 14–3
The Creative Individual and the Creative Organization

The creative individual	The creative organization
Conceptual fluency—is able to produce a large number of ideas quickly	Has idea men; maintains open channels of communication; uses *ad hoc* devices like suggestion systems, brainstorming; idea units absolved of other responsibilities; encourages contact with outside sources
Originality—generates unusual ideas	Follows heterogeneous personnel policy; includes marginal, unusual types; assigns nonspecialists to problems; allows eccentricity
Separates source from content in evaluating information; is motivated by interest in problem and follows wherever it leads	Has objective, fact-founded approach; evaluates ideas on their merits, not on status of originator; uses *ad hoc* approaches like anonymous communications and blind votes; selects and promotes on merit only
Suspends judgment — avoids early commitment, spending more time in analysis and exploration	Lacks excessive financial, material commitment to products and policies; invests in basic research; flexible long-range planning; experiments with new ideas rather than prejudging on "rational" grounds —everything gets a chance
Less authoritarian — has relativistic view of life	Is more decentralized and diversified; has administrative slack, time and resources to absorb errors; follows risk-taking ethos, tolerating and expecting to take chances
Accepts own impulses — playful, undisciplined exploration	Is not run as a "tight ship"; employees have fun; allows freedom to choose and pursue problems; gives freedom to discuss ideas
Independence of judgment; less conformity; deviant—sees self as different	Is organizationally autonomous; has original and different objectives; is not trying to be another X
Rich, "bizarre" fantasy life and superior reality orientation and controls	Establishes security of routine, allows innovation— "philistines" provide stable, secure environment that allows "creators" to roam; has separate units or occasions for generating vs. evaluating ideas— separates creative from productive functions

SOURCE: Based on Gary Steiner, ed., *Creative Organization* (Chicago: University of Chicago Press, 1965).

regards brainstorming as important. The safer the environment, the less importance is accorded to brainstorming.

4. Managements with high performance aspirations, especially the ones that attach a great deal of importance to above industry average growth,

regard brainstorming as more important than managements with low performance aspirations.

The data suggest that in changing environments that *require* of the organization frequent and major adjustments to stay alive or grow, creative behavior is likely to assume strategic importance. Old and large organizations also may have dynamic environments. But if they have learned to cope successfully with change through minor adaptations of their standard operating procedures, they are unlikely to regard creative behavior as strategically important. The data also indicate that high performance aspirations are likely to breed dissatisfaction with the status quo and thereby elevate the strategic importance of creative behavior.

We propose that:

The more dynamic the external environment and *the more vulnerable the organization to changes in the environment, as well as the higher the performance aspirations of the organization's top management, the more likely is the organization's management to aspire to be creative.*

The higher the strategic importance of creativity to top management, the more likely to constitute the key design elements of the organization are decentralization, an organic, "open" organization, the hiring and promotion of creative, nonconformist personnel, and an ideology of risk taking and innovation.

It should be noted that the above propositions apply to organizations as well as to "embedded" organizations—policy-making units, research laboratories, advertising departments, design units, and so forth.

The Design of Innovation

As Mohr has defined the term, innovation is "the successful introduction into an applied situation of means or ends that are new to that situation."[31] Innovation is the successful bringing into use of an invention. The invention may or may not originate in an organization. But if that organization successfully uses that invention, as when an American automobile manufacturer successfully adopts the rotary engine invented in Germany, or an Indian firm successfully adopts a management training system designed in the United States, then that organization has innovated.

Let us first see what the process of innovation is like. The following story of how the invention of a photographic printing process became the innovation of the plastic printing plate at Du Pont illustrates well the complexities of the process:

E. I. du Pont's decision to go into large-scale production of plastic printing plates marks the end of one phase of a story that has been running almost a dozen years. It's a story with desperate moments and last-minute discoveries and tough decisions and frayed tempers. Yet it's the same kind of story that has occurred over and over again at du Pont and will be repeated many times in the future. . . .

Du Pont's pattern of new products development is rooted in the over-all task it has charged itself with—"to come out with entirely new products." Dycril meets this qualification easily. The traditional way of making a letter-press printing plate for a long press run is to take a mold of lead type and engravings, and then make a copy of it by casting or electro plating. In contrast, Dycril turns to the photographic approach used in photo-engravings and offset printing plates. The Dycril plastic plate is exposed to light through a photo negative of the material to be printed; ultraviolet light hardens the part of the plate it hits, leaving a relief image when the unexposed part is washed away chemically. The advantage of the new process is the speed with which a finished plate can be made and the ease with which complicated designs can be used. . . .

Fundamental research is done by all 11 of the manufacturing departments at du Pont, but it is the special interest of the Central Research Dept., a staff operation servicing all departments. . . .

Dr. Paul Salzberg, department head, and five of his key lieutenants sort out the written proposals submitted by the company's researchers for new lines of investigation, O.K. those which promise to be "really scientifically new" . . . .

A project is initially a one-man operation and is intentionally vague. When Dr. Louis Plambeck, Jr., began work on what turned out to be the plastic printing plate, for instance, all he knew was that he was interested in seeing how light could be used to form images by processes other than those used in photography. Du Pont held patents arising from some work done in this area, which is called photopolymerization, in the early 1940s. These provided a point of departure for printing plate project. . . .

In just about a year, Plambeck had narrowed his field of investigation down to the idea of making a printing plate. He was able to take a liquid, expose it to a pattern of ultraviolet light. The liquid hardened where the light hit it, and, when the rest of the solution was washed away with a solvent, a raised relief of the light pattern remained. When this point had been reached the fundamental research stage was over.

Salzberg's job now was to sell an operating department on underwriting further—"applied"—research, done either in his laboratories or in the department's own lab. In this case, the selling job was easy. Photo Products was excited about the new printing idea, decided to pick up further bills and let Plambeck continue with the research.

The applied research stage is the long one. As one du Pont man put it, "the hardest work lies between the invention and the invoice." . . .

At the same time, Plambeck was giving private demonstrations of the process. The first enthusiasm came from personnel at du Pont's own printing plant in Philadelphia. Chicago Lakeside Press & Intertype Corp., maker of phototype-setting equipment, and, later, the Philadelphia Inquirer, also were impressed.

By the end of 1951, the technique had been developed to the point where a small brochure was prepared on the plastic plates for the du Pont board, showing how the process could handle different kinds of copy. . . . The plate held up—and the bulk of the research work was transferred to the departmental labs. Central Research continued to iron out bugs in the plate, while Photo Products worked on techniques to manufacture it. . . .

Then the general manager of the Photo Products Dept. made a decision that might have spelled the end of the product right there—he said he would not market the process in a liquid state or with a flammable solvent.

The project went back to Central Research. Plambeck, now with two other men working with him, then developed a putty-like form and finally, by 1953, arrived at his first solid-layer photopolymer printing plate. What was essentially the present product was in hand by 1955.

By this time the departmental sales division, responsible for all market research and product testing, had begun to get ready for the product. Men experienced in the printing industry were added to the payroll, and on their recommendations minor alterations were made in the plate. . . .

Finally, in May, 1957, the company was ready to announce publicly the development of a light-sensitive plastic printing plate. . . .

Field results were promising. The technique was first demonstrated to the industry at large—to some 2,700 paid attendees at a letterpress forum in New York—in September, 1958. By then an option had been taken on a plant site, and the department was just about ready to ask top management approval to roll ahead with the product. . . . Then one worry—fanned by a reaction at the letterpress forum—stopped the project cold.

The worry was price.

The manufacturing process then used required that the plate be sold for about $10 a sq. ft., and even with quantity production, the price seemed unlikely to go far below that. That was just too high, John M. Clark, manager of the Photo Products Dept. decided; he sent the production men and laboratory experts back to work to come up with a new production process. If they couldn't come up with one, he said, the light-sensitive printing plate would die right then. There were a lot of hurt feelings and angry thoughts. . . .

There was another problem to be tackled, too. The plate was then being made by a batch method which limited its size. This hadn't been of much importance when development began, because the size was adequate for flatbed presses. But printers kept putting more and more of their work on high-speed presses, using cylindrical plates; these needed bigger plates to operate at maximum efficiency.

It took about a year, but du Pont engineers managed to replace the batch method of making the plates with a "more-or-less continuous flow" process which licked both the size and price problems. . . .

With these problems overcome, the only step left was to ask the executive committee and the finance committee for more than $1 million to build a plant. Approval came early this year. . . .[32]

Note the long time and the large amount of resources it took for the invention to fructify into an innovation. As someone put it well, "the hardest work lies between the invention and the invoice." Note also other aspects of the process of innovation: the frequent need to obtain management support; the numerous marketing, financial, and other evaluations of the product; the complex planning and coordination of the various phases.

Innovation is a chancy business. Not all good ideas automatically become innovations. Though the principle of the steam engine was discovered nearly 2,000 years ago, the commercial use of steam engines had to await a Thomas Watts and an industrializing England. The experience at du Pont of the fate of inventions is instructive:

Not all prospective new products get the go-ahead for commercial production on the first trip to the executive and finance committees. Some are sent back for more research work to have specific bugs eliminated. Some products have made four trips to the committees before getting approval. Others have died on the way. And some requests have been rejected for reasons not connected with the quality of the product itself. Some du Pont executives even remember one case where the committees turned thumbs down because there weren't enough manufacturers in the field—the company didn't want to court anti-trust trouble. . . .

Few projects, however, die at this level—most that fail to make the marketplace are killed off much earlier. Sometimes even when the fundamental research has been promising. Salzberg has a hard time drumming up the departmental sponsorship necessary for further investigation. . . .

Sometimes no department will give the go-ahead. Then Central Research simply patents the discovery and waits. In the mid-1930s some polyurethanes were made in the lab, but none of the operating departments would spend any money to work further on them. Suddenly a dozen years later, upholstery foams turned out to be a hot item in the chemical industry, and the polyurethane patents were dust off and carried on into applied research. But with a 17-year patent limit, the company tries to keep shelf time to a minimum.

Sometimes a department will drop a project in mid-stream. . . .

Getting to the field test stage or even into commercial production is no guarantee of success for a product idea. . . .

Even orlon—with a $25-million expenditure before commercial production began—came within a hair's breadth of being a flop. Artificial fibers can be made either in filament form—squeezed out in long strands—or in short staple lengths, which are then treated like cotton or wool natural staples. Orlon was conceived by du Pont as a filament fiber for industrial textiles. But it never managed to catch on. Only the success of the orlon staple plant, opened a year later to produce the fiber for clothing textiles, saved the day.[33]

The du Pont experience points to several interesting elements of the design of innovation. These are:

1 There must be *perception* of the need for an innovation by key decision makers.

2 Innovation is or can be an expensive business, not only in the amount of money needed, but also in terms of managerial time, the time of specialists, space, and so on. Substantial *resources* are needed for successful innovations.

3 Innovation is not merely an economic process, it is also a political process. Those in favor of an innovation cannot rely simply on their good intentions and the rationality of their position. They must build a base of support for the innovation—that is, build a *coalition* of the influential to put through the innovation.

4 For an organization to be continually innovative, its *management* needs to develop an activist ideology, professionalism, strong planning and control skills, and an ability to be (or to be able to utilize) effective change agents.

Let us briefly discuss these elements.

Perception of need. The awareness of the problems confronting an organization and the awareness of the means by which they can be solved are key ingredients in the design of innovation. This points to the necessity of a reasonably sophisticated control and information system. The control system yields information about the internal problems of the organization. The information system tells management what inventions and developments are available and provides it with a diagnosis of the present and the future.

The importance of a good control and information system is underscored by the fact that most inventions originate outside the organization, and there are substantial time lags between the appearance of an invention and its utilization.[34] To be able to utilize inventions originating outside the organization promptly, the management of an organization clearly needs to be aware of them and their potential usefulness to the organization. In the author's study of Canadian firms, managerial philosophy of stressing innovation, technological leadership, and research was correlated quite strongly with the employment of a sophisticated control and information system.

The need for innovation is likely to be felt more acutely in certain kinds of environment than in others. In the author's study of Canadian firms, it was found that management tended to subscribe to a philosophy of innovations, research, and technological leadership in a turbulent environment. It tended to subscribe to a philosophy of marketing true and tried products and the avoidance of research and development in a stable environment. Similarly, an innovation-oriented philosophy was markedly present in firms in technologically sophisticated environments and a conservative, innovation-avoiding philosophy characterized firms in technologically unsophisticated environments.

Resources. Substantial financial, administrative, and professional resources are needed to put through innovations. Walker's study of innovative legislation by the states of the United States strongly suggests that those states that have had high per capita incomes, degree of industrialization, and urbanization, and therefore large tax bases, have been legislatively more activist than states with low per capita incomes, industrialization, and urbanization.[35] Mohr found that the progressiveness of the health departments in North America was significantly correlated with the expenditures of these departments.[36] Stinchcombe has suggested that what he considered as "progressive" firms had a higher proportion of professionals among their top operatives than "stagnant" firms.[37] Hill and Harbison have shown that industrial firms that innovated extensively between 1947 and 1955 also increased their employment of professionals during that period.[38] In Browning's study of two departments in a state government, the more innovative department was far more "professionalized"—for example, the more innovative department subscribed to 105 professional journals (the less innovative department, 11) and sent its personnel to 91 out-of-state professional meetings (the less innovative department, 5).[39]

Coalition. Innovation is generally a highly *political* process and requires considerable political ability on the part of those trying to innovate. Innovation often treads on the vested interests of many in the organization. The power and status of some may be devalued by an innovation; that of some others may be enhanced. Coalition-building skills need to be in abundance in those invested with the responsibility for the innovation. In centralized organizations the support of the chief executive needs to be developed, while in decentralized organizations the support of one's immediate boss and one's colleagues and subordinates needs to be cultivated. This is especially true for innovations that require a substantial commitment of the organization's resources.

Shepard has distinguished between innovation-resisting and innovation-supporting organizations.[40] In innovation-supporting organizations, since the climate is supportive of innovation, political coalition-building skills are less essential. But in innovation-resisting, bureaucratic, or tradition-bound organizations, political tactics are particularly needed to get others, especially those in senior management, to accept the changes that attend upon an innovation. Major changes may be too threatening. In innovation-resisting organizations, either the innovation may have to be concealed initially, or it may have to be put forward as a minor improvement or presented as "the" solution to a current crisis. In fact, research suggests that in innovation-resisting organizations, crises provide the most frequent occasions for innovation.[41] Once the organizational commitment is secured, once the camel's head, so to speak, is inside the tent, the process of innovation is likely to go smoother. This appears to be a favorite tactic of government administrators: to get appropriations for a new system or program by grossly underestimating its cost and grossly overestimating the benefits. Once substantial resources are committed to the program or system, the legislature has little choice but to keep on funding the system, even though the costs are rapidly escalated. The B-1 bomber system, initially supposed to cost just a "few" billion dollars, in 1975 was estimated to cost nearly $20-billion, a figure way above cost escalation due simply to inflation.

Management. An activist managerial ideology; professional management orientation; managerial skills at planning, coordination, and control; and the ability to be effective agents of change are the crucial managerial ingredients in the design of innovation.

As for the action orientation of management, Mohr's work on local health departments in four U.S. states and Ontario suggests that innovation is associated with the extent to which the chief executive's *ideology* is innovation oriented.[42] Two measures of innovation—first, the adoption of new health care programs by the local health department and, second, the resources devoted to nontraditional program areas during 1960–64 by the local health department ("progressive programming")—were both fairly strongly associated with the chief health officer's score on a composite measure of activism and liberal ideology. The relationship held even when the size of the community served by the department was controlled for. Activism in this study meant "the health officer's perception of the extent to which the role of local health officer requires interaction with others, especially outside the health department, to obtain ideas, support, approval, and resources for departmental programs." Public health ideology in the study meant "the health officer's opinion regarding the scope of services that should properly be offered by the local public health agency (as distinguished from local private and voluntary enterprise) in nontraditional public health program areas." That is to say, the larger the scope of public health programs as perceived by the health officer, the more liberal and activist the health officer's ideology was considered to be.

In the Canadian study of the author, a managerial philosophy of research, innovations, and securing technological leadership was quite strongly correlated with a professional management orientation that stressed both participation and optimization. We have noted before that a managerial philosophy of innovations was also strongly correlated with the employment of a sophisticated control and information system. The case study of du Pont cited earlier shows graphically the extent of careful planning, control, and coordination that is needed in the successful management of innovations.

The management of innovation and innovative behavior is not quite the same as the management of inventive behavior. Certainly, innovation implies change in the status quo, and therefore a certain amount of flexibility, openness, and the like in the organization are needed.[43] However, the task situation in an innovation is more structured than in an invention. Often the experience of others who have adopted the invention is available, and that cuts down greatly the search processes needed for a successful innovation. Even when an invention originates within an organization, for example when the research and development department of a pharmaceutical firm synthesizes a new drug, the structuring of the task situation is considerable—the uses and potential clientele of the invention are reasonably well known to management, and the past experience with the current product or service or process that the invention displaces generally gives good guidance as to what to do to bring the invention to fruition. As Shepard points out, for implementing an innovation quite distinctive managerial qualities are needed: "singleness of purpose, functional division of labor, responsibility and authority, discipline, the drawing of internal communication boundaries, and so on."[44]

All innovations involve organizational changes. The management of organizational change has become a key focus of behavioral scientists. Bennis has listed several types of change program.[45] Most of these, such as the exposition and propagation of knowledge and information about a problem, or scholarly consultation, or staff programs, have a rationalistic and technocratic bias. Knowledge is assumed to be power. But, as Bennis usefully points out, "Knowledge *about* something does *not* lead automatically to intelligent action. Intelligent action requires commitment. . . ." In other words, it is not enough for change agents to focus only on the technical aspects of the innovation. It is necessary to take into account the very human fears and anxieties innovation commonly provokes.

562 *The Design of Human Behavior in Organizations*

Another problem is that many of these programs emphasize the role of the individual and do not take adequate cognizance of organizational realities. "It may be that *role corrupts*. . . . In any event, there is no guarantee that placing certain types of people in management . . . leads to more effective action. Scientists act like administrators when they gain power. And graduates of human relations training programs tend to act like non-alumni shortly after their return to their organizational base."[46]

Bennis argues that the management of change and innovation is a *professional* activity. It requires change agents (be they managers, in-house behavioral scientists, or outside consultants) to have the following goals and the ability to achieve these goals:

> Improve interpersonal competence of managers.
> Effect a change in values so that human factors and feelings come to be considered legitimate.
> Develop increased understanding among and within working groups to reduce tensions.
> Develop "team management."
> Develop better methods of "conflict resolution" than suppression, denial, and the use of unprincipled power.
> View the organization as an organic system of relationships marked by mutual trust, interdependence, multigroup membership, shared responsibility, and conflict resolution through training or problem solving.[47]

He feels that change agents can effectively facilitate organizational changes and innovations through the use of laboratory sensitivity training programs. These aim at creating a better self-insight in the participants and at a greater awareness of interpersonal and group processes. It can also be facilitated through the change agents playing the role of consultants. For example, "Argyris as consultant, confronts the group with their behavior toward him as an analogue of their behavior vis-à-vis their own subordinates." Third, applied research also can facilitate organizational change.

> Most methods of research application collect information and report it. Generally, the relationship ends there. In the survey-feedback approach, as developed . . . at the University of Michigan's Institute for Social Research, this is only the beginning. Data are reported in "feedback" meetings where subjects become clients and have a chance to review the findings, test them against their own experience, and even ask the researchers to test some of their hypotheses. . . . (R)esearch results serve to activate involvement and participation in the planning, collection, analysis, and interpretation of more data.[48]

We propose that:

The more turbulent the external environment, and

the more technologically sophisticated the external environment,
> *the more innovation-supportive is the top management philosophy.*

The more innovation-supportive the top management philosophy,
> *the more professional tends to be its orientation, and*
> *the more sophisticated tends to be the control and information system employed by the organization.*

The more innovation-supportive and activist the top management philosophy, and
the greater the resources available to the organization,
> *the greater is the rate of innovation in the organization.*

The more innovation-resisting the organization,
> *the greater are the requirements for building coalitions to push through innovations, and*
> *the greater is the need for political abilities in those sponsoring the innovations.*

SUMMARY, PROPOSITIONS, AND IMPLICATIONS FOR ORGANIZATIONAL DESIGN

Summary

In this chapter we have examined several dimensions of organizational behavior: motivation and morale, cooperation and conflict, and invention and innovation. We have identified the many strategies available to the designer in attempts to mold human behavior in organizations: the modification of situational variables such as the nature of the external environment and type of business, that of strategic variables like goals and ideology of top management, and that of structural and technological variables. We have also identified some of the techniques available for doing so, especially techniques developed by behavioral scientists for motivating personnel, for resolving conflicts and fostering cooperation, for creative problem solving, and for effecting innovations and the organizational changes they imply.

Propositions

1. The higher the job satisfaction with respect to needs lower in Maslow's hierarchy of needs, then
> the higher, subject to satiety, is motivation to achieve a higher level of satisfaction of these needs, and
> the higher also is motivation with respect to needs higher in the hierarchy.

2. The higher the job satisfaction of personnel,
>   the lower is absenteeism and turnover, and
>   the higher is loyalty to the organization.

3. The higher the job motivation of personnel,
>   the greater is the proclivity to high productivity and the acceptance of innovations that can lead to high productivity.

4. The more buoyant and challenging the task environment of departments within an organization—that is, the higher the rate of growth in their activities *and* the more subject they are to competitive pressures—
>   the higher is the level of motivation of their managers.

5. The larger the organization,
>   the lower is the distance between senior management and the lower level personnel, and so the lower tends to be the morale of blue-collar, clerical, and lower management personnel.

6. The larger the organization,
>   the greater is the lateral and vertical mobility of managers, the greater is the support staff to help them in problem solving, and so, the higher tends to be the morale of the upper level managers.

7. The higher the performance aspirations of managers,
>   the more attention they are likely to pay to motivational tools like incentive systems, job enrichment, participative management, and management by objectives.

8. The more participative and employee oriented the supervision,
>   the higher is the morale of subordinates, and possibly vice versa.

9. The fewer the number of levels in the line hierarchy (*i.e.*, the flatter the line hierarchy), and
the more numerous the number of levels in the staff hierarchy (*i.e.*, the taller the staff hierarchy),
>   the higher is likely to be the morale of the line and staff personnel, respectively.

10. The smaller the work unit,
>   the higher is morale.

11. The more interesting the work, the greater the chances for promotion, the higher the pay, and the more congenial the supervision and the co-workers,
    the higher is morale.

12. The greater the interdependence between organizational units;
    the more specialized their functions; and
    the greater the differences between their personnel in terms of goals, the means for achieving goals, and the procedures for resolving disagreements,
    the greater is likely to be the intensity of conflict between them.

13. The more restrictive, diverse, or technologically complex the environment;
    the more professionally oriented the top management style (including an emphasis on participation and optimization); and
    the higher the aspirations of the top management with respect to organizational goals,
    the greater is the variety of coordinative mechanisms employed in the organization.

14. The more dynamic the external environment *and* the more vulnerable the organization to changes in the environment, as well as
    the higher the performance aspirations of the organization's top management,
    the more likely is the organization's management to aspire to be creative.

15. The higher the strategic importance of creativity to top management,
    the more likely to constitute the key design elements of the organization are decentralization, an organic "open" organization, the hiring and promotion of creative, nonconformist personnel, and an ideology of risk taking and innovation.

16. The more turbulent the external environment, and
    the more technologically sophisticated the external environment,
    the more innovation-supportive is the top management philosophy.

17. The more innovation-supportive the top management philosophy,
    the more professional tends to be its orientation, and
    the more sophisticated tends to be the control and information system employed by the organization.

18. The more innovation-supportive and activist the top management philosophy, and

    the greater the resources available to the organization,

        the greater is the rate of innovation in the organization.

19. The more innovation-resisting the organization,

        the greater are the requirements for building coalitions to push through innovations, and

        the greater is the need for political abilities in those sponsoring the innovations.

Implications for Organizational Design

Again we affirm that the molding of human behavior is not a push-button job because human beings react, sometimes in quite unanticipated ways, to attempts to change their behavior. Nor should it be misunderstood that attempts to shape human behavior need be only in the interests of the managerial or technocratic cliques that often preside over organizations. The work of organizational design can be the prerogative of the few for the benefit of the few, or it can be widely shared and for the benefit of the many in the organization. In either case a body of knowledge is needed to guide decision-making. It is this body of knowledge that this book has attempted to sketch out.

But having said this, it is perhaps worth saying that *how* behavioral change is attempted—by full participation of those in whom change is desired, or by the fiat of the dictator, the bureaucrat, or the technocrat—may have major implications for the magnitude of change, the durability of change, and the predictability of change. As our earlier quote from Bennis indicated, many of the nonparticipative modes of organizational change—and behavioral change is a species of organizational change—do not often elicit the *commitment* of the targets of change to the required changes. The cost, therefore, is a large organizational effort devoted to external, administrative regulation and supervision to ensure the continuance of altered patterns of behavior. On the other hand, the participative mode, too, though it commonly elicits commitment, and a fairly durable one at that, has its costs. It often is slower in achieving results, and because change is at the discretion of the targets of change, it may go in directions not anticipated by, sometimes not liked by, the agents of change. Obviously, therefore, there is no best *process* of changing or designing human behavior in organizations. The designer must choose the process, bearing in mind how great and how durable a change is wanted, how certain the designer wants to be that the change is in the desired directions, and how quickly the change is needed.

SUGGESTED READINGS

Warren Bennis, "Theory and Method in Applying Behavioral Science to Planned Organizational Change," *Applied Behavioral Science*, Vol. 1 (1965), pp. 337–60.

Daniel Katz, "The Motivational Basis of Organizational Behavior," *Behavioral Science* (1964), pp. 131–46.

Lawrence Mohr, "Determinants of Innovation in Organization," *American Political Science Review*, Vol. 63 (1969), pp. 111–26.

Lyman Porter and Edward E. Lawler III, "Properties of Organization Structure Related to Job Attitudes and Job Behavior," *Psychological Bulletin*, Vol. 64, No. 1 (1965), pp. 23–51.

Pp. 1–24 in Gary Steiner, ed., *The Creative Organization*, (Chicago: University of Chicago Press, 1965).

James M. Utterback, "The Process of Technological Innovation Within the Firm," *Academy of Management Journal*, Vol. 12 (1971), pp. 75–88.

Richard E. Walton and John M. Dutton, "The Management of Interdepartmental Conflict: A Model and Review," *Administrative Science Quarterly*, Vol. 14 (1969), pp. 73–84.

QUESTIONS FOR ANALYSIS

1 In the following short case, what design options does Latimer have?

Lewis Latimer, Supervisor of Special Test Operations, has a motivational problem created by organizational structure and work rules. The problem is a familiar one to many managers in business and industry even if the titles here are different. Let Lew Latimer explain:

"My problem is easy to explain but beyond me in terms of solution. I'm a supervisor at an electronics company which manufactures desk top electronic calculators. I head a group of about twenty special electrical test technicians. These men don't test parts on the assembly line but conduct special electrical tests on completed units as directed by management. We do such things as:

1. Conduct systems tests on field failure units.
2. Conduct on-going reliability testing.
3. Conduct experimental testing for engineering.
4. Conduct special customer product testing (e.g., units for special applications).

"My men are electronics specialists typically, with military electronics background or are graduates of electronic trade schools. Some have certificates of completion from junior colleges which specialize in the sciences. We train the men we hire on the use of our test equipment and procedures but require practical electronic test experience as an employment prerequisite.

"The company currently has three technician classifications. They are:

Technician C *Trainee.* (Six months maximum.)

Technician B *Equipment Test Technician.* Familiar with all usual systems tests. Can perform all tests without assistance other than use of test manuals. (Up to four years.)

Technician A *Senior Equipment Test Technician.* Must perform all functions of Technician B plus be able to calibrate test equipment and write test specifications. (No limit.)

"Most men are hired as Technician C, which is considered an entry level position. If they learn their job well, they are promoted to Technician B at the end of six months. Technician B carries a higher pay scale and a limit of four years that the classification can be maintained. The purpose of this is to force a man to qualify for a broader range of responsibility. The same is true for Technician A. Most men qualify for Technician A in about three years.

"So, in my department, the majority of men are now in the top pay classification. It breaks out like this:

Technician C	1 man
Technician B	5 men
Technician A	14 men
Total	20 men

"We're a young company in a fast moving industry. We make a good, reliable line of calculators, and most of our employees are proud of their products and the company. This has certainly been true of my technicians. You couldn't find a more highly motivated bunch of guys anywhere in the company.

"In recent months attitudes have begun to change. Several of the men have soured on the company and their jobs, after they reached the top of the pay scale for Technician A. For them, there's no place to go in the company and they know it.

"It's beginning to show up in their work too. A few of the men are taking a much more casual attitude toward their work than they used to . . . the old team spirit is really gone. When five o'clock comes the whole area is deserted. And these are guys that I used to have to chase home each evening.

"I talked to Frank Duncan about the problem. Frank is my boss and the Director of Operations at our facility. I suggested that the most promising persons in the Technician A category should be allowed to move to the Junior Engineer classification. But Frank didn't care much for this solution. He said that all engineering classifications should be used only for professionals (he means college graduates), and that if we opened this classification to non-professionals (he means my technicians), morale problems will develop in other areas.

"Duncan said he would consider a Super-Grade classification for out-standing men in the Technician A category, and asked me to write a new job description for this classification.

"For the moment I'm going along with that approach for lack of anything better, but I feel it is a short-range solution and the problem will be back in a year or so."[49]

2 Read the case "Operations research stubs its toe in retailing" from the book by Wegner and Sayles.[50] Diagnose the behavioral problems of the Operations Research Department. What design options would you like to explore? What recommendations do you have for the process by which the department and its personnel should act as agents of innovation in the company?

3 Read the case "Conflict at sea" from Wegner and Sayles.[51] It describes interunit conflict at sea. What organizational design do you recommend for the ship that would minimize such conflicts and elicit the required degree of cooperation between the personnel?

Footnotes to Chapter Fourteen

[1] Harold Leavitt, "Applied Organizational Change in Industry."
[2] A. H. Brayfield and W. H. Crockett, "Employee Attitudes and Employee Per-formance."
[3] Abraham Maslow, *Motivation and Personality*, Ch. 5.
[4] Douglas Hall and Khalil Nougaim. "An Examination of Maslow's Need Hier-archy in an Organizational Setting."
[5] Kurt Lewin, "The Psychology of Success and Failure."
[6] Lyman Porter, "Job Attitudes in Management: IV. Perceived Deficiencies in Need Fulfillment as a Function of Size of Company.
[7] S. Talacchi, "Organization Size, Individual Attitudes and Behavior: An Empirical Study."
[8] J. C. Worthy, "Organization Structure and Employee Morale"; George Strauss and Leonard Sayles, *Personnel: The Human Problems of Management*, p. 376.
[9] Peter Drucker, *The Practice of Management*.
[10] See Appendix A to this book for a description of this study.
[11] Rensis Likert, *New Patterns in Management*, pp. 16–17.
[12] Lyman Porter and E. E. Lawler III, "Properties of Organization Structure in Relation to Job Attitudes and Job Behavior."
[13] See Strauss and Sayles, *op. cit.*, for a summary view that emerges from these studies.
[14] See Nathan King, "Classification and Evaluation of the Two-Factor Theory of Job Satisfaction," for a critical review of the relevant evidence.
[15] *Time* (Sept. 16, 1974), pp. 78–79.
[16] See King, *op. cit.*
[17] See especially Mary Parker Follett, "Constructive Conflict."
[18] James March and Herbert Simon, *Organizations*, pp. 121–29.

19 See J. D. Thompson's *Organizations in Action*, pp. 54–55, for a discussion of reciprocal, sequential, and pooled interdependence.

20 See R. R. Blake and J. Mouton, *The Management Grid*, pp. 270–73.

21 See R. Wegner and Leonard Sayles, *Cases in Organizational and Administrative Behavior*, pp. 50–57, for the full case.

22 M. Dalton, "Conflicts Between Staff and Line Managerial Officers."

23 Richard Beckhard, *Organizational Development: Strategies and Models*, pp. 34–35.

24 Muzafer Sherif, "Experiments in Group Conflict."

25 J. M. Utterback, "The Process of Technological Innovation Within the Firm."

26 See Paul A. Samuelson, *Economics*, p. 720.

27 See Frank Barron, *Creative Persons and Creative Process*, for a summary of this research.

28 J. W. Getzels and P. O. Jackson, *Creativity and Intelligence*, p. 107.

29 *Ibid.*

30 Gary Steiner, ed., *Creative Organization*, pp. 16–18.

31 Lawrence B. Mohr, "Determinants of Innovation in Organization," p. 111.

32 *Business Week* (Feb. 20, 1960), pp. 105–107.

33 *Ibid.*

34 Utterback, *op. cit.*

35 J. Walker, "The Diffusion of Innovations Among the American States."

36 Mohr, *op. cit.*

37 Arthur Stinchcombe, "The Sociology of Organization and the Theory of the Firm."

38 S. E. Hill and F. Harbison, *Manpower and Innovation in American Industry*.

39 Rufus Browning, "Innovative and Non-innovative Decision Processes in Government Budgeting."

40 Herbert Shepard, "Innovation-Resisting and Innovation-Producing Organizations."

41 James Q. Wilson, "Innovation in Organization: Notes Toward a Theory."

42 Mohr, *op. cit.*

43 See T. Burns and G. M. Stalker, *The Management of Innovation*.

44 Shepard, *op. cit.*

45 Warren Bennis, "Theory and Method in Applying Behavioral Science to Planned Organizational Change."

46 *Ibid.*

47 *Ibid.*

48 *Ibid.*

49 Robert D. Joyce, *Encounters in Organizational Behavior*, pp. 148–50.

50 Wegner and Sayles, *op. cit.*, pp. 20–23.

51 *Ibid.*, pp. 39–41.

The Design of Inventive and Innovative Behavior **571**

15

The Design of Organizational Performance

THE CONCEPT OF PERFORMANCE

What the organization *as a collectivity* succeeds in achieving is organizational performance. It is not the performance of an individual or a group but the net result of the combined efforts of all individuals and groups in the organization that is the subject of this chapter. Needless to say, in discussing organizational performance, we have in mind not only independent organizations but also embedded ones, such as departments and divisions that have the properties of an organization.

Organizational performance is, of course, the *summum bonum* of organizational design. The whole point of designing an organization is to improve its performance. But performance is important not only as a "dependent," end-result-of-design variable but as a change-initiating, "independent" variable. As our model in Chapter 7 indicates, situational, strategic, structural, behavioral, and pattern variables affect organizational performance. In turn the relative performance of the organization—that is, the performance of the organization in relation to its targets or its rivals—can initiate important changes in its strategic and structural variables, and sometimes also in its situational and behavioral variables.

572

"Organizational performance" is as ambiguous a term as "organizational goal." Since it is difficult to define exactly what the goals of an organization are (Chapter 10), so it is difficult to determine how well the organization has performed. In assessing organizational performance we are forced to ask the question: Performance from whose viewpoint? Take, for example, a firm. From society's viewpoint, efficient production of products or services needed by society may be said to be the goal of the firm, and so the firm should be evaluated in terms of whether it does this or not. From the point of view of the owners of the firm, profitability and growth rate in earnings may be the criteria for assessing performance. From the point of view of the employees of the firm, the firm's performance may be assessed in terms of its prestige in the community and in terms of how well it treats its employees. From the point of view of the firm's customers, courteous service, prompt delivery, a good product, and a competitive price may be the criteria in terms of which the firm's performance is assessed.

In Chapter 10 we noted that management must take into account the various expectations of society, customers, employees, and owners in planning its strategy. These expectations serve as constraints subject to which top managers make decisions. Thus, as a first cut at the problem, we may assume that the top management's goals reflect these constraints, and therefore we may accept the top management's goals as the criteria in terms of which the organization's performance may be assessed. Also, as an agency that has the greatest control over the organization's strategy and structure, the top management's assessment of the organization's performance is likely to be critical in initiating organizational changes. At the same time, it needs to be borne in mind that management may not give as much *weight* to the needs of society or to those of the organization's employees or suppliers as one might wish. It is entirely possible, therefore, that by changing the weights given to various criteria, one may come to different conclusions about how an organization has performed and what the consequences of its performance are likely to be. For the present, however, we will live with the assumption that management's criteria for assessing organizational performance adequately reflect the concerns of society, employees, suppliers, customers.[1] In the next section, we examine how different classes of variables affect the performance of the organization.

PERFORMANCE AND ORGANIZATIONAL VARIABLES

Demographic Variables and Organizational Performance

There is some evidence that demographic variables such as age, size, type of business, and nature of ownership affect organizational performance by affecting the goals of the organization. Roos, Schermerhorn, and Roos, Jr., studied three types of American hospital that deliver short-term health care.[2] The three types were: (a) State and local government *public* hospitals, owned and operated by municipalities, counties, or states and oriented to the delivery of health care to the public at large living in their vicinity. (b) Voluntary, nonprofit *community*-supported hospitals that are usually tax exempt but commonly raise the bulk of their revenues from community fund drives. They are generally controlled by a board of trustees drawn from the elite of the communities they serve. (c) Proprietary, for-profit *private* hospitals that really are business firms with professional medical norms. There are presumably some goal differences between these three types. Supposedly, the public hospitals are oriented to giving free access to all patients including indigent patients, to a lesser extent to economy and efficiency, and last to quality of care. The community hospitals supposedly emphasize quality care most and efficiency least, since they must build up good will in the community they service. The private hospitals supposedly emphasize efficiency most and access least and, contrary to the beliefs of the researchers, quality quite heavily, in order to build up a wealthy clientele. Table 15–1 summarizes the actual performance of these three types on a number of measures of efficiency, access, and quality.

No one type of hospital comes off best on all the criteria of performance. The community hospital, sensitive to the needs of the community it services, generally comes out best in occupancy rate and accreditation. The public hospital, usually quite large and sensitive to legislative outcries about costs, generally comes out best on expenses per bed, more a measure of economy than efficiency, and on the number of emergency visits per hospital. The private hospital, generally relatively small, catering to the well-to-do and without a captive clientele, does fairly well on occupancy rate and number of clinic visits per hospital. This latter could well be construed as a measure of thoroughness of care—that is, as a quality measure. The Roos study suggests that demographic factors—the type of organization, the nature of ownership, possibly size—may importantly affect the performance of the organization via affecting the *goals* of the administration.

Whether, however, demographic variables directly affect performance is far from clear. A study of cooperative and privately owned sugar factories in India did not reveal any notable differences in their performance, despite the presumption of greater profit orientation on the part of privately owned factories.[3] There is only weak evidence that privately owned firms out-perform public firms in the same line of business.[4] In the author's study of over 100 Canadian firms, the age of the firm, a demographic variable, was significantly negatively correlated with the rate of growth of its revenues.[5] The reason for this may be that the older a firm gets, the more of its products

TABLE 15–1
The Best Performing Types of Hospitals for Different Hospital Sizes on Selected Criteria of Efficiency, Access, and Quality of Care

	SIZE CLASSES						
Measure of performance	*Very small (25–49 beds)*	*Small (50–99 beds)*	*Medium small (100–199 beds)*	*Medium (200–299 beds)*	*Medium large (300–399 beds)*	*Large (400–499 beds) (No private hospitals)*	*Very large (500 beds and over)*
Efficiency and economy measures							
Occupancy rate	Private	Community and private	Community	Community	Community	Community	Community
Total expenses per bed	Public	Public	Public	Public	Community	Public	Public
Access measures							
Number of emergency visits per hospital	Public	All three about equal	Public	Public	Public	Public	Public
Number of clinic visits per hospital	Private	Private	Community	Public	Public	Public	Public
Quality measures							
Percentage with accreditation	Community	Community	Community	Community	Community	Community and public	Community

SOURCE: Adapted from Noralou P. Roos, John R. Schermerhorn, and Leslie Roos, Jr., "Hospital Performance: Analyzing Power and Goals," *Journal of Health and Social Behavior*, Vol. 15 (1974), Table 3.

or services tend to have reached the maturity phase of the product or service life cycle, and therefore the slower tends to be the firm's growth rate. In this study, the size of the organization was uncorrelated with any measure of performance. This is an interesting finding, for it suggests that the various economies of scale, particularly those of production and distribution, tend to be offset by various diseconomies, such as large administrative overheads, poor coordination, and the like.

The evidence suggests the following proposition:

The effect of demographic variables on organizational performance is stronger when the goals of the organization are affected by demographic variables than when goals are not affected by demographic variables.

Environmental Variables and Organizational Performance

Economic theory indicates that monopolies are likely to earn fatter profits than firms in competitive industries. There is some evidence that the degree of monopoly power is at least modestly associated with profitability. In several studies it was found that concentrated industries tend to have higher profit rates and more stable profits than less concentrated industries.[6] Industry concentration means the share of market of the largest firms in the industry. The higher it is, the more concentrated the industry is, the easier it is for the leading firms to coordinate their pricing and other policies (that is, behave like a monopoly), and so the higher and less volatile are the industry profits.

The author's study of 103 Canadian firms indicated that firms in high growth rate industries tended to perform substantially better than firms in low growth rate industries. The performance of the firms was assessed in terms of an index of objective performance in which its long-term profitability, growth rate of revenues, and stability of profits were equally weighted. Long-term profitability is generally regarded as a measure of efficiency, stability as a measure of risklessness, and growth as a measure of dynamism. These three are probably the most commonly utilized criteria for assessing corporate performance. In addition, firms reporting a hostile environment tended to show a lower objective performance than firms reporting a nonhostile or munificent environment. Both these findings, though not surprising, show that the external environment can affect the performance of the organization, regardless, within limits, of the strategy and structure of the organization.

We propose that:

*Regardless, within limits, of the strategy and structure of the organization,
the more buoyant and/or benign the external environment,
the higher is organizational performance.*

In the Canadian study, an attempt was made to develop an index of relative performance in terms of the goals and concerns of top management. The ratings of how well the firm had done on five goals in comparison with the industry average or principal rivals were aggregated for this purpose.[7] The five goals were profitability, growth, employee morale, solvency, and public good will, reflecting managerial concern with the expectations of shareholders, employees, creditors, suppliers, and clients, as well as of managers themselves. It was found that the perceived rate of innovation in the firm's industry, an environmental measure, was fairly strongly correlated with this subjective index of relative performance of the firm. It should be remembered that the rate of innovation as measured was weighted by the strategic importance accorded to it by the top management. Thus, where the rate of innovation of new products and processes was high *and* management accorded it a great deal of importance, the firm's performance relative to its rivals was perceived to be, and probably was, high. Where the rate of innovation was low, or, when high, was de-emphasized by the top management, the relative performance was perceived to be, and probably was, low. The findings suggest that an innovation-rich environment creates an objective necessity for the organization to be innovative. If the management *sees* this necessity and responds to it, the performance of the firm is likely to be relatively higher than that of rivals whose managements fail to see this necessity.

Strategic Variables and Organizational Performances

Regardless of the situation the organization is in, can management improve the performance of the organization through a better strategy and management ideology? Systematic research on the point so far permits a tentative "yes." Let us briefly review the evidence. The work of Thune and House, Ansoff and his associates, the author, and Negandhi and Prasad are the principal sources of this evidence.

Thune and House. Thune and House studied the performance of 17 matched pairs of firms in 6 industries over a period of 7 years to determine whether long-range planning pays off or not.[8] The firms were matched for size, growth rate, and industry, but not for product line. The firms were fairly large, with sales of over $75 million each. In each pair, throughout the period of the study, one firm had a formal planning system, while the other did not. Firms were deemed to have a formal planning system if (a) they specified their corporate strategy and goals for at least three years into the future *and* (b) they developed specific operating procedures and programs for achieving these goals. If neither condition was met, the firm was deemed to be a nonplanner. Thune and House found that though the pairs were matched initially for size and growth rate, the planners significantly outperformed the nonplanners. Indeed they surpassed their own performance before adopting planning, in terms of financial criteria like growth in earnings per share. With Herold, Thune and House tracked the performance of 5 of these pairs for 4 more years.[9] They also found that the planners outperformed the nonplanners.

Planning is partly a top management ideology and partly a set of techniques, such as forecasting, capital budgeting, goal setting, and the like. Thus, the studies of Thune and House and Herold indicate that a managerial ideology of planning and optimization, when translated into a planning-oriented organizational structure may improve organizational performance.

Ansoff, Avner, Brandenberg, Portner, and Radosevich. These authors did a questionnaire study of 93 U.S. firms designed to investigate the impact of planning on the success of acquisitions.[10] Only those firms were studied that had made at least two acquisitions separated by a year or less, had a preceding four-year period without any acquisitions, and another two-year post-acquisition period. They concluded that the planners outperformed the nonplanners on objective criteria like earnings per share growth, sales growth rate, and stock price growth. However, there was little difference between the two groups in the subjective evaluation of the performance of the firms by their managements. This study, too, tends to support the findings of Thune and House and Herold.

Khandwalla. In the author's study of Canadian firms, the optimization dimension of top management ideology, in which values supportive of comprehensive planning predominate, was uncorrelated with the objective index of performance based on the actual profitability, growth rate, and earnings stability of the firm.[11] It was modestly correlated with the index of subjectively rated performance *relative* to the firm's rivals. This last finding is in accord with those just discussed.

A participative management ideology, it has been suggested, improves organizational performance, by increasing the motivation of members of the organization to work for the organization.[12] In the author's study of

Canadian firms, the participative ideology of top management was uncorrelated with the objective index of performance, but it was fairly strongly correlated with the subjective index of performance relative to rivals.[13] Here, too, it seems probable that the participative management organization confers a comparative advantage on the organization vis-à-vis its nonparticipative rivals. The Canadian study also indicated that the coercive ideology was significantly and independently negatively correlated with the subjective index of relative performance but uncorrelated with the index of objective performance.[14]

It stands to reason that organizations whose managements are oriented to optimization, planning *and* participation—a style that in Chapter 11 we have termed the "professional style of management"—possess a significant comparative advantage over those of their rivals whose managements are nonparticipative *and* oriented to seat-of-the-pants methods. In the author's study of Canadian firms, as Table 15–2 shows, 43 percent of the firms with

TABLE 15–2
Top Management Style and Absolute and Relative Performance of the Firm (Sample: 103 Canadian Firms)

	Performance relative to industry average as assessed by corporate management			Performance on objective performance index	
	High	*Middle*	*Low*	*High (top half)*	*Low (bottom half)*
1. Firms with a strongly participative and optimization oriented corporate philosophy (highly professional management style) (23 firms)	43%	39%	18%	70%	30%
2. Firms with a nonparticipative *and* seat-of-the-pants oriented corporate philosophy (traditional management style) (18 firms)	22	28	50	56	44
3. Firms with a strongly risk-taking *and* organic top management style (13 firms)	69	8	23	77	23
4. Firms with a strongly conservative *and* mechanistic top management style (11 firms)	28	36	36	64	36

NOTE: Although 1 and 2 are mutually exclusive groups of firms, as are 3 and 4, a few firms in 1 or 2 may be found in 3 or 4 and vice versa.

a professional management style rated themselves as doing better than the average performance of firms in their industries, while only 18 percent rated themselves as doing poorly compared to the industry average. By way of contrast, only 22 percent of the firms with a traditional style of management—low on both participation and on planning and optimization—rated themselves as doing better than the industry average, and 50 percent rated themselves as doing worse than the average corporate performance in their industries.[15] At the same time, as the table shows, while professionalism significantly improved corporate performance in relative as well as absolute terms, its absence did not depress it below the average for the entire sample of 103 firms in *absolute* terms, though it depressed it in *relative* terms.

This suggests that while traditionally managed firms do not perform badly on the average in terms of objective criteria, they *could* improve their performance *relative* to their rivals by changing over to a professional style. Since the professional style dominates the traditional style on both relative and absolute indexes of performance, it is, *in general,* the more desirable style, *unless* special circumstances (such as a noncomplex environment) warrant otherwise.

In Chapter 11 we noted that risk taking and administrative flexibility were a desirable combination and so was an association of conservatism and administrative structuring. As Table 15–2 shows, the firms practicing a risk-taking and organic management style as well as those practicing a conservative and mechanistic style performed better than average on the objective index.[16] On the relative index, however, the performance of the risk-taking organic firms was much stronger. This suggests that while the conservative mechanistic firms generally do well enough, they could improve their performance *relative* to their rivals if they switched to a risk-taking organic style. But one must be cautious here. The data relate to *surviving* firms. Many an entrepreneurial firm disappears because its risky decisions turn out to be ill-advised or because of sheer bad luck. On the other hand, sudden deaths are perhaps not so frequent among conservatively managed organizations. Hence, the superior performance that risk taking and administrative flexibility offer must be discounted appropriately by the possibly heightened organizational mortality. Also, of course, as we noted in Chapter 11, a conservative mechanistic style may be much more appropriate than a risk-taking organic style in a nonturbulent environment.

Negandhi and Prasad. Other evidence of the relationship of managerial philosophy with organizational performance comes from the work of Negandhi and Prasad.[17] Their study was a cross-cultural one, encompassing U.S. subsidiaries and matching local firms in a number of developing countries. They and their associates gathered data by interviewing executives of the selected firms. The data are most completely available for 15 U.S. subsidiaries and 15 local Indian firms operating in the same industries as the U.S. subsidiaries. The data indicate that the index of management effectiveness, a measure of organizational performance, was strongly correlated with a measure of progressiveness in management philosophy and also with the resulting progressive organizational practices. The probable causal sequence is shown below.

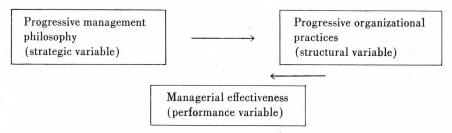

The progressiveness of management philosophy was measured by assessing the top management's concern for each of several groups. These groups were: the firm's employees, consumers, distributors, suppliers, and stockholders, as well as the government and the community at large. The greater the concern professed by the top management, the more progressive the management philosophy was deemed to be.[18] The progressiveness of organizational practices was assessed by aggregating the scores on three subsidiary indexes. One was an index of how decentralized decision-making was. On closer examination, this index appears more to measure committee or joint or participative decision-making at the top levels of management than delegation of authority by the chief executive to his subordinates. The second was an index of how progressive were the personnel practices. This index appeared to measure whether such things as manpower planning, employee selection, training, appraisal, and compensation were formally instituted or not. The third was an index of progressive management processes. It included factors such as long-range planning, budgeting and resource allocation, standard or objective setting, cost control, quality control, equipment maintenance, and superiors' confidence in their subordinates. The more of these were done formally and systematically, the more progressive management processes were deemed to be. Finally, managerial effectiveness was measured by assessing whether the organization attracted high level manpower, whether this manpower was utilized for policy making and planning, how high employee morale, turnover, and absenteeism were, whether interpersonal and intergroup relations appeared to be cooperative or not, whether the executives appeared to attach importance to overall organizational objectives or merely departmental objectives, and whether the organization effectively adapted to its external environment.[19]

A few comments need to be made about the Negandhi and Prasad findings. First of all, the vast majority of the firms in their sample of 30 appeared to be utilizing technologies that are quite sophisticated compared to the average Indian firm. Eight of their firms were pharmaceutical firms; 14 others manufactured heavy engineering goods and metals, heavy machine tools, elevators, typewriters, automobile tires, electrical bulbs, and sewing machines. The rest of the 8 firms produced soft drinks, canned products, soaps, and cosmetics. On the basis of our arguments in Chapter 11 and Chapter 13, we should expect firms operating in technologically sophisticated environments to be adopting a professional or "progressive" management style and a complex organizational structure marked by decentralization and a sophisticated control and information system. This appears to be the case for the firms studied by Negandhi and Prasad, so their findings lend support to, or at least do not contradict, a contingency view of organizational design. At the same time, it should be borne in mind, that the data gathered by Negandhi and Prasad were their interpretations of their impressions of what was being told to them by a few executives of these firms. In other words, the data are highly impressionistic. Their attempts to gather "hard" performance data like profitability were not very successful, and indeed, their feeling was that in the "sellers' market" conditions prevailing in India, the firm's profitability should more meaningfully be attributed to the monopoly power wielded by these firms than to management philosophy or organizational practices.[20]

The following propositions may be made:

The more optimization and planning oriented, or participative, or progressive, or professional the top management's orientation relative to that of the organization's rivals,
> *the higher tends to be the performance of the organization relative to that of these rivals.*

The more risk taking and organic the top management's orientation relative to that of the organization's rivals,
> *the higher tends to be the performance of the organization relative to that of these rivals.*

Unless contra-indicated by the nature of the organization's task environment, the more professional the style of top management,
> *the higher is the organization's performance.*

Unless contra-indicated by the nature of the organization's task environment, the more risk taking and organic the style of top management,
> *the higher is the organization's performance, but the higher also are the chances of its mortality.*

Structural Variables and Organizational Performance

Structural variables include the organization's workflow, operations and information technology, the form of departmentalization, the shape of the hierarchy, the control and information system, decentralization, and so on. They are the durable means by which the organization seeks to achieve its goals. In a study of 79 U.S. manufacturing firms, the author found that *none* of a large number of structural variables, such as the use of controls, staff services, decentralization of authority by the chief executive, divisionalization, functional departmentalization, vertical integration, and team decision-making at the top was significantly correlated with long-run profitability.[21] However, in the author's study of Canadian firms, the delegation of authority by the chief executive was significantly but modestly correlated with the indexes of objective as well as subjectively rated relative performance. The extent to which the firm employed a wide distribution network was also correlated significantly with the two indexes. In addition, the extent to which the organization employed a sophisticated control and information system was modestly correlated with the subjective but not the objective index of performance. However, the correlations of delegation of authority and sophistication of control and information system with the subjective index did not remain significant when participative and optimization dimensions of top management style were controlled for.

There is substantial evidence, reviewed later under the section on pattern variables, that suggests that structural variables *in association with* situational variables affect the performance of the organization. The evidence for their independent impact on organizational performance is, as we have seen, somewhat thin.

Thus, we propose that:

Individual structural variables in and of themselves—that is, with situational and strategic variables controlled for—tend not to affect organizational performance strongly.

Behavioral Variables and Organizational Performance

Behavioral variables, reviewed in Chapter 14, are dimensions of the behavior of the organizational rank and file, like motivation and morale, cooperation and conflict, creativity, conformity, innovation, and the quality of leadership.* Two studies, one by Bowers and Seashore and the other by

* Notice the distinction between leadership and style of management. Leadership relates to the *abilities* and *interpersonal behavior* of an *individual* with authority vis-à-vis his or her subordinates. Style of management is the operating *philosophy* of the top management *group* and covers not only supervisor–subordinate relations but also the organization's *strategy* for growth and survival.

Paul Mott, indicate the range of behavioral variables that may be related to organizational performance.

Bowers and Seashore. Bowers and Seashore examined the style of leadership as a predictor of organizational effectiveness.[22] They prefer the term "effectiveness" to "performance," since it combines performance on tasks performed by the organization with the job satisfaction of its personnel. In their study of 40 agencies of a large, geographically dispersed U.S. life insurance company, they identified, through factor analysis of 70 measures of agency performance, 7 factors of performance. The ones that appear to have some face validity as performance measures were the factors of business growth, business costs per unit of new business, business volume, and manpower turnover. Curiously, they left out an obviously important performance measure: profitability!

Bowers and Seashore argue, on the basis of a review of many past conceptualizations, that leadership may best be thought of as having four elements: the *support* the leader extends to group members (friendliness, willingness to make changes, etc.); the degree to which the leader facilitates interactions between group members through, for example, group decision-making (*interaction facilitation*); the degree to which the leader facilitates the work of the group members through planning, scheduling, and the like (*work facilitation*); and the degree to which the leader emphasizes achievement of group goals (*goal emphasis*). These dimensions are elaborations of the well-known human relations view, discussed in Chapter 5, that leadership should be both task and employee oriented. Among the four performance factors mentioned earlier, unit business costs was the most strongly correlated (negatively) with these dimensions of leader behavior. In other words, unit costs of new business tended to be lower in agencies in which the leader was perceived by the respondent members of the agency as supportive, emphasizing agency goals, and facilitating work and interpersonal interactions. They tended to be higher under opposite conditions. Bowers and Seashore indicated that nonleadership variables, too, were associated with performance measures, in many cases more frequently than leadership variables, but they did not report what these nonleadership variables were and what their relationships with performance measures were like.

Thus, while Bowers and Seashore hint at nonbehavioral explanations for differences in the performance of the agencies, clearly they accent behavioral explanations—to the extent that their measures of managerial leadership describe the actual behavior of supervisors in the agencies.

Mott. Paul Mott studied the performance of the administrative units within a potpourri of nonbusiness service organizations.[23] His research venues included community general hospitals, the offices of administration of NASA, the U.S. State Department, the financial management office of the Department of Housing, Education and Welfare, and a mental hospital in Pennsylvania. Mott prefers the term "organizational effectiveness" to "performance." His concept of organizational effectiveness has three components.[24] The first is productivity (quantity of production, quality, and efficiency of production). The second component is the adaptability of the organization. This involves the degree to which the organization anticipates problems and develops timely solutions and the degree to which the organization stays abreast of new technologies and methods relevant to its activities. The third component, a minor one in actual operationalization, is flexibility, or the organization's ability to cope with unpredictable overloads. The three components turned out to be quite highly interrelated.

In Mott's study, the productivity, adaptability, and flexibility of each administrative unit was rated subjectively by its members. The ratings were aggregated to derive the members' estimate of the unit's effectiveness. The scores of the members were averaged to secure the index of effectiveness of the administrative unit. Generally, this effectiveness index was in fairly good agreement with the assessment of effectiveness by others in the organization having dealings with the administrative units in question, such as the top management and directors of other administrative units. However, no objective assessment of unit effectiveness in terms of hard data was attempted.

Unfortunately, when it came to other variables, Mott appears to have failed to follow a similar procedure of averaging the ratings of all the respondents from a unit. Hence, it is not clear whether his unit of analysis is the individual or the administrative unit. Subject to this qualification, his data, when assessed for uniformity of findings across several research sites, appear to show that the *effectiveness* of the administrative unit *varies* with:

1. The clarity of the objectives of the administrative unit (as seen by its members).

2. The effectiveness with which the various tasks undertaken in the unit are integrated.

3. The ease with which personnel doing related work can exchange ideas and information.

4. The extent to which people doing related work avoid creating problems for one another.

5. The effectiveness with which coordination problems between personnel doing related work are handled.

6. The proportion of personnel perceived as competent to do the unit's work.

7. The extent to which the needs of personnel, especially for personally challenging work; rational, fair, known norms of work; and competent and fair supervision are met.

8. The degree to which the supervisor is perceived to be effective.[25]

In addition, the findings suggested that at lower levels, or in administrative units with highly structured tasks, the technical and planning skills of the supervisor ("work facilitation" in the terminology of Bowers and Seashore) are considered by personnel as contributing to the unit's effectiveness. At higher levels of the organization, or in administrative units with relatively unstructured, variable tasks, besides technical and planning skills, a great many other supervisory skills are seen by personnel to contribute to the effectiveness of the unit. These are administrative skills, human relations skills, openness to employee influences in decisions, willingness to stand up for subordinates with the supervisor's own supervisor, and others.[26] The lower the level of anxiety felt by the supervisor, the more capable he seemed to be of exhibiting these skills and characteristics.

The wide-ranging study of Mott suggests, as the above list shows, that a number of behavioral factors affect performance. Some of them represent effective *leadership*, such as the effectiveness with which the various tasks undertaken in the unit are integrated; the effectiveness with which coordination problems between personnel doing related work are handled; the extent to which the needs of the personnel for personally challenging work, rational and fair norms of work, and competent and fair supervision are met; and the degree to which the supervisor is perceived to be effective. Some others represent effective *colleagueship*, such as the extent to which people doing related work avoid creating problems for one another and the ease with which personnel doing related work can exchange ideas and information. Some of them represent both effective leadership and *subordinacy*, such as the pains taken by the leader to communicate clearly the unit's objectives to the subordinates and the efforts of the latter to understand them clearly; the hiring of competent personnel; and competent discharge of responsibilities by personnel.

Notice the situational factors affecting effective leadership. When the unit's tasks are highly structured, the task-related competence of the supervisor is all important. When the tasks are variable or unstructured, *both* human relations skills and task-related competence become crucial. This is something of an advance over the human relations view that task and employee-oriented leadership is, generally speaking, beneficial in all circumstances. In neither study are we certain that the work units did in fact have the characteristics of full-fledged organizations, although this is more likely to be the case with respect to the insurance agencies studied by Bowers and Seashore. Subject to this caveat, it is worth proposing that:

The more the formal leadership has task-structuring, planning, control, and coordination skills in those parts of the organization in which tasks are relatively structured,
  the higher is organizational performance.

The more the formal leadership has task as well as human relations competence in those parts of the organization in which tasks are relatively novel or variable,
  the higher is organizational performance.

The more effective the leadership;
the greater the interpersonal and intergroup collaboration;
the more technically competent the rank and file; and
the more highly motivated the rank and file,
  the higher is organizational performance.

Pattern Variables and Organizational Performance

Research suggests that *combinations* of situational and strategic and situational and structural variables are often more effective in raising organizational performance than any one of these sets of variables acting alone. These combinations may be termed pattern variables. Studies by Lawrence and Lorsch, Child, and the author indicate some of the pattern variables associated with superior organizational performance.

Lawrence and Lorsch. Lawrence and Lorsch studied 10 firms in 3 industries —6 in the plastics industry and 2 each in the container and the packaged food industries.[27] The plastics industry was chosen because of the diversity and dynamism of its environment; the other two because of the relatively greater stability of their environments. In each industry, Lawrence and Lorsch identified high performing and low performing organizations. They failed, however, to give any data about the performance of the 10 firms.

Lawrence and Lorsch found that the high performing organizations were differentiated and integrated in *proportion* to the diversity of the task environments of their three major departments—namely, production, research, and marketing. The degree of differentiation and integration of the low performers was not generally related as well to the diversity of their major department's task environments. By differentiation, Lawrence and Lorsch had such things in mind as differences between departments in decision-making and planning horizons, interpersonal differences (formal relations in one department versus informal relations in another), differing orientations to the programming of activities (detailed programming versus loose, organic sequencing of activities), and the like. By integration Lawrence and Lorsch meant the quality of collaboration between interdependent departments. This quality, when it was in proportion to the degree of diversity in the task environments of the organization's departments, was particularly crucial for high performance, Lawrence and Lorsch concluded. Collaboration was secured by several means. Coordination secured by liaison personnel was especially important. Liaison personnel were individuals or groups assigned the task of coordinating the activities of interdependent departments that were experiencing difficulties in working together. The liaison personnel that shared the norms of the departments in conflict or had norms midway between those of these departments, seemed to be particularly effective. Also of importance was the level at which coordination took place. The closer it was to the areas experiencing conflict, the more effective it was. Resolution of conflict was also facilitated when managers confronted their differences with other executives rather than evaded them or suppressed them by superior force or tried to smoothe them away. For example, a confronting style may be epitomized by the aphorism "Only by digging and digging is the truth discovered." Evasion may be epitomized by "It is easier to refrain than to retreat from a quarrel." Suppression may be epitomized by "If you cannot make a man think as you do, make him do as you think." Smoothing things may be characterized as "Kill your enemies with kindness."

The Lawrence and Lorsch explanation for their interesting findings is worth noting. When an organization's major departments confront very different task environments, especially with respect to the degree of uncertainty and the time span of feedback about departmental performance, it is obvious that these departments cannot possibly be identically designed. Their structures and the behaviors taking place in them must be quite different. Thus, diversity in the task environments of the organization's major departments (as a situational condition) *must* be matched by a corresponding differentiation in the structures and functioning of the departments (a structural condition). But since the departments *must* coordinate their activities for achieving the goals of the organization, the more differentiated they are, the more intense and complex must be the attempts to integrate their activities (another structural condition). On the other hand, when the task environments of an organization's major departments are rather similar in major respects, these departments need not be designed very differently, and consequently intensive and complex modes of coordination are not called for. Not only is an organization that has a level of differentiation and integration proportionate to the degree of differentiation in its environment likely to show better performance, but people working in such an organization are also likely to experience stronger feelings of competence in coping with their jobs, than in an organization in which the degrees of differentiation and integration are out of joint with the degree of environmental differentiation.[28]

Khandwalla. Two studies by the author, one of 79 middle-sized U.S. manufacturing firms and another of 103 Canadian manufacturing and service firms turned up some interesting combinations of situational and structural variables and situational and strategic variables associated with high organizational performance.

In the study of 79 U.S. firms, the performance measure was the long-term profitability of the firm, secured by averaging the highest and the lowest before tax returns on net worth during the five years preceding the study.[29] The data were gathered during 1968 and 1969 through a questionnaire addressed to presidents of corporations in a wide variety of manufacturing industries. A number of organizational variables were considered. These were categorized into three classes of variables. The first class was uncertainty reduction variables (vertical integration, and staff market intelligence and uncertainty absorption services like R and D, use of electronic data processing, long-term forecasting and planning, etc.). The second class of variables was the differentiation variables—namely, decentralization of authority by the chief executive, divisionalization, and functional departmentalization. The third class of variables was called integration or coordination variables and consisted of participative or team decision-making at the top levels of management, and the extent of use of sophisticated management controls.

It was hypothesized that while all organizations face some uncertainty in their technoeconomic environments, some face more of it than others. Hence, the greater this uncertainty—that is, the broader the range of issues about which the organization's decision makers experience uncertainty—the more use the organization will make of uncertainty reduction devices. Once the key areas of uncertainty are identified, the organization will get differentiated to respond more appropriately to each area of uncertainty. To keep its activities coordinated, the differentiated organization will invest considerable resources in integration activities. Thus, the greater the technoeconomic uncertainty (operationalized in that study as perceived competition and technological change), the greater the use of all of uncertainty reduction, differentiation, and integration devices. Since these are developed by the organization in response to variations in technoeconomic uncertainty, the use of uncertainty reduction, differentiation, and integration devices would tend to co-vary.

The key findings relating to performance were the following:

1. None of the several measures of uncertainty reduction, differentiation, or integration was associated with profitability. Since these are popular management tools, this tended to question their usefulness in isolation.

2. The degree of *covariation* between the three classes of variables was a predictor of profitability. The data suggested that if the firm had to employ any of these to a substantial degree it would have to employ the others to approximately the same degree to become more profitable. Conversely, if it had reason to avoid using any of these to any major extent, then perhaps it was better off avoiding the use of the others, too. Thus, a certain specific *pattern* of relationships between elements of organizational structure, not the individual elements of structure, was a predictor of performance.

3. The two measures of technoeconomic uncertainty, competition and technological change, had substantially higher positive correlations with the three classes of variables when only the relatively highly profitable firms were considered (there were 38 of them, each earning over a 12 percent return on net worth). The average correlation of competition with the three classes of variables was .29 for this group of high profit firms; it was .03 for the remaining group of 41 low profit firms. The average correlation of technological change with the three classes of variables was .20 for the high profit group; and .10 for the low profit group. An implication of this finding is that in technoeconomic environments high in uncertainty, it is necessary for the organization to employ uncertainty reduction, differentiation, and integration mechanisms to a considerable extent. On the other hand, in technoeconomic environments low in uncertainty, it is better for the organization to avoid any significant use of these. This finding suggests strongly that patterns of relationship between situational and structural variables can substantially affect organizational performance.

In the Canadian study, the sample was somewhat different. The average size was over twice the average size of the firms in the U.S. study. The proportion of "public" firms—that is, firms listed on the stock exchange—was higher. While the American sample consisted only of manufacturing firms, about a third of the firms in the Canadian study were trading and service firms. Appendix A to this book fully describes the Canadian study. The bulk of the data were gathered in 1972–73.

None of the strategic variables considered in Chapters 10 and 11 was, in isolation, associated with the objective performance index. The strategic variables considered in these chapters were the top management's performance aspirations, a risk-taking versus a conservative orientation, an optimizing and planning versus a seat-of-the-pants decisions orientation, an organic versus mechanistic administrative orientation, a participative orientation, and a coercive orientation. But these variables, when appropriately combined in response to environmental pressures, seemed to evoke a high organizational performance. In Chapter 11 we presented some of the evidence of the effect of pattern variables on organizational performance. Briefly, the principal findings were:

1. In highly turbulent, dynamic, changing environments a risk-taking and organic management style with coercion proportionate to internal resistance to change tended to be associated with high organizational performance.

2. In highly stable environments, a conservative, mechanistic, noncoercive management style tended to be associated with high organizational performance.

3. In complex environments, marked by constraints, technological sophistication, a variety of markets, and so on, a professional management style with an emphasis on participation, optimization, and planning tended to be associated with high organizational performance.

4. In relatively noncomplex environments—that is, in environments without much diversity, constraints, and technological sophistication—a seat-of-the-pants, unparticipative, and risk-taking management style tended to be associated with high organizational performance.

Beyond these findings, the Canadian data revealed some interesting effective and ineffective responses to a hostile environment. A hostile environment is interesting for the simple reason that success, almost by definition, is hard to come by, while failure is easy. In a nonhostile or munificent environment, the organization can make even random responses and probably still muddle along. But in a hostile environment the organization's strategy must be carefully designed. Table 15–3 shows some effective and ineffective responses to a hostile environment. For this purpose, firms scoring in the top third of the distribution of reported environmental hostility were selected. Since environmental hostility and environmental turbulence were correlated, the firms whose reported environment was highly turbulent (top third of the distribution of environmental turbulence) were eliminated from consideration in order to see more clearly the responses to a hostile environment. Thus the sample studied consisted of 27 firms in a highly hostile but not very turbulent environment.

The table shows, as we should expect, that only 33 percent of the firms operating in a hostile but not very turbulent environment were high performers on the objective index of performance, well below the 52 percent score for the whole sample of 103 firms. However, two effective responses were (a) a professional one of emphasizing optimization and planning *as*

TABLE 15–3

High and Low Performance Responses to Hostile (but Not Very Turbulent) Environment (Sample: Canadian Firms Scoring in the Top Third of the Distribution of Environmental Hostility)

	Total number of firms	*Number of high performers*	
		Number	*Percentage*
1. Firms in a hostile environment (but not a very turbulent environment)	27	9	33
2. Firms in the above environment with a professional management orientation (heavy emphasis on participation and planning and optimization) *and/or* a risk-taking and moderately to strongly organic and coercive orientation	9	6	67
3. Firms in the above environment with a conservative and moderately to strongly seat-of-the-pants and coercive orientation	5	1	20
4. Firms in the above environment with a moderately conservative, coercive, and organic style	6	1	17
5. Firms in the above environment with an optimization- and planning-oriented and mechanistic style	5	1	20

NOTE: Groups 2, 3, 4 and 5 are mutually exclusive, except that groups 2 and 4 share a high performance firm and groups 2 and 5 a low performance firm.

well as participation; and/or (b) an entrepreneurial one of risk-taking, flexibility in administration, *and* authoritarianism. This is further evidence of what the systems theorists call equifinality. The reasons for the effectiveness of these two alternative responses are not far to seek. Faced with external hostility, one may effectively use experts to gauge the present and future situation and plan proper responses and at the same time try to build a cohesive management team through a participatory philosophy to hold the front against external enemies. Or one may go in for bold, risky moves, keep the administration flexible so as to respond creatively and expeditiously to the evolving situation, and use whatever force is needed to implement the risky decisions.

The table also shows some other responses that are associated with *low* performance. For example, one response is one of extreme caution, a good deal of seat-of-the-pants decisions, and internal coercion, probably indicative of a demoralized and paranoid management. Another ineffective response is the naive technocratic mechanistic one of optimization orientation and administrative structuring. The vital ingredient of participation is missing. Without it, in a hostile environment in which frustrations are frequent, technocracy and administrative structuring tend to degenerate into a faction-ridden polity of alienated members.

Child. Child studied 82 British companies in 6 industries: electronics, pharmaceuticals, chocolates and sweets, newspapers, advertising, and insurance.[30] He and his associates interviewed the senior executives and specialists of each firm and followed this up with a questionnaire directed to the senior and departmental managers of 78 of these firms. The two main performance measures employed by him were the growth rate of the firm's sales and the ratio of its net income (before depreciation) to sales. The latter measure is somewhat unsatisfactory because it tends to overstate the profitability of companies with plants that are expensive relative to their size, such as those of the manufacturing companies in the sample.

Child's major findings are:

1. The faster growing companies in a *variable* environment had *less formalized* organizational structures than slow growing companies. Variability of the environment was assessed in terms of how far the sales of the firm's industry fluctuated around the long-term growth trend and also in terms of the proportion of industry sales devoted to research and development. The second measure of variability may confound the unit cost of innovation with environmental variability through innovation. For example, the advertising industry is highly innovative, but the unit *cost* of innovation is very low compared to, say, the electronics industry, which spends heavily on research and development because the average cost of an innovation in it is much higher.

If we assume that the faster growing companies in a variable, possibly turbulent environment secured their high growth through entrepreneurship and a risk-taking strategy, then Child's data suggest that organizations that combine risk taking with low administrative structure (a relatively highly organic management) tend to be high performers. As indicated earlier, this is, of course, precisely what the author found in his study of Canadian firms.

2. In "less variable" environments, the faster growing companies had more formalized organizational structures than the slower growing companies. As measured by Child, low variability could mean low turbulence, or a lower rate of innovation, or a lower technological sophistication of the environment. Thus, Child's "less variable" environment may be a stable environment or a simple environment, or both a stable and a simple en-

vironment (the "less variable" firms in Child's sample belonged to the chocolates and sweets industry, newspaper industry, and the insurance industry).

It may be recalled that in the Canadian study, the conservative, mechanistic, noncoercive style was associated with high performance in a stable environment; and a seat-of-the-pants, unparticipative, risk-taking style was associated with high performance in a simple environment. Child's data suggest that the faster growing companies in "less variable" environments were more mechanistic and possibly more risk taking than the slower growing companies. There is, therefore, some (but not complete) consistency between his findings and the author's.

3. Those firms operating in a *"less variable"* environment in which decision-making authority was *selectively delegated* (a good deal of delegation in the production area, a good deal of centralization in purchasing and in making and authorizing expenditures) tended to be higher performers.

4. The more profitable firms in a *variable* environment tended to *centralize* decision-making in a number of areas (including marketing and pricing strategy and labor disputes), more so than the less profitable ones. This is consistent with a possibly entrepreneurial orientation of the managements of the more successful firms.

5. As *size* increased, the high performers tended to get formally *structured* and bureaucratized (in Weber's sense of the term) to a higher degree than low performance firms. Particularly noticeable was the standardization of procedures and role formalization with respect to financial and accounting matters, production methods, personnel matters, and so forth. The difference in the rate of bureaucratization with respect to increasing size was sharpest between the high performers and the low performers in a stable environment. The findings suggest that a mechanistic ideology and a bureaucratic structure are particularly appropriate to a sizable organization in a stable environment.

We propose that:

The more appropriate the top management strategy and the organizational structure are to the nature of the organization's situation—that is, the better the fit between situational, strategic, and structural factors— the higher is organizational performance.

In a hostile environment, other things being equal, the more the top management style stresses optimization and participation, or risk taking, flexibility, and coercion, or all of these, the higher is organizational performance.

The more evenly developed the uncertainty reduction, differentiation, and integrative mechanisms,

> *the higher is organizational performance.*

The broader the range of task-related uncertainties confronted by the organization,

> *the more highly need to be developed the uncertainty reduction, differentiation, and integrative mechanisms for superior organizational performance.*

The larger the organization, the more it should have formal role and functional specialization and standardization of procedures—that is, the more bureaucratic should be its structure—for superior organizational performance, especially in a stable environment.

The greater the variety in the task environments of major parts of the organization,

> *the greater should be the permitted differentiation in the structures of these parts and in the attitudes and values of their respective personnel, and the greater should be the effort devoted to integrating the operations of these parts, for superior organizational performance.*

Concluding Comments

A very wide range of variables seems to be associated with organizational performance. However, some caveats are in order:

1 The studies that we have reviewed are cross-sectional, not longitudinal. That is to say, measurements of the situational, strategic, structural, behavioral, and performance variables, as the case may be, are taken at a point of time rather than over a period of time. In longitudinal studies it may be possible to see more clearly what causes what. In laboratory studies it is possible to see this very clearly. Unfortunately, longitudinal and laboratory studies of *organizational* performance are conspicuous by their absence. In cross-sectional studies, the problem is that if there is an observed association between two variables, we cannot be sure of the direction of the causal arrow. For example, suppose that a participatory style of management is found to be correlated with organizational performance. Several interpretations are

possible: (a) participation raises performance and its absence causes a decline in performance; (b) performance raises participation and its lowering causes a lowering of participation; (c) both mutually cause each other, such as disease and physical debility; (d) both are caused simultaneously by a common cause; (e) the observed association is purely a chance event. Now the organization theorist, when confronted by a finding from a cross-sectional study, must select an interpretation to put on the data based on the theorist's own theoretical orientation or prior knowledge or plain common sense. But the choice of interpretation may quite possibly be wrong. This possibility *must* be borne in mind. This possibility makes all our theorizing about design tentative, subject to revision as and when additional studies are reported.

2 Different researchers have used different measures of performance. Findings that are relevant to one measure of performance, may not be relevant if the measure of performance is changed. If we find a design that is associated with high levels of profitability, what is the assurance that such a design will also be consistent with high levels of social responsibility on the part of the organization? We have assumed that management, in pursuing its goals, bears in mind the expectations of customers, suppliers, the public and so on. But, while no organization can survive or prosper without at least *some* regard for these expectations, surely there is a fairly wide latitude in what *weight* the management gives to these expectations. This, too, is a source of uncertainty in making use of research findings for the practical work of designing organizations.

3 The data base is disproportionately corporate. This is, of course, understandable, because corporate performance is easier to measure and has been more widely measured than the performance of other types of organization. There are undeniable institutional differences between corporations and other organizational types. Can findings based on corporate performance be meaningfully applied to hospitals? To charitable trusts? To cooperative societies? Our presumption is that they can be because, while *institutional* goals may differ, the behaviorally more relevant *managerial* goals may be quite similar. Managers of cooperative societies may not strive to make profits, but they may strive for efficiency, which in the context of cooperatives is behaviorally equivalent. Also, other evidence suggests that *relationships* between variables apply across different types of organization. For example, in corporations as well as public bureaucracies it has been found that as size of the organization increases, the organization tends to have more and more of the features of a bureaucrcy.[31] The relationship between employee oriented leadership and work group morale has been found in a very wide variety of organizations.[32] Thus, if these relationships hold despite superficial institutional differences, why should findings pertaining to performance of one type of organization not reasonably be expected to be sustained in other types? Yet this is a question that ultimately can be settled only through further research. In the meanwhile we must learn to live with the present ambiguities of research findings.

4. We have no guarantee that findings that may be relevant today will stay relevant in the future. Can we assume that the relationship between a pattern variable and organizational performance, even if well-confirmed today, will persist in the changed conditions of tomorrow? Here again, our presumption is that while the magnitudes of variables may change over time, their underlying relationships do not. Thus, it may well be that business environments in general will become even more turbulent in the future. If our current finding is that an entrepreneurial style is appropriate to a turbulent environment and a conservative style to a stable environment for high organizational performance, can this finding be of any use in the far more turbulent future? The answer is probably "yes." On the average, the organizations of the future should be more entrepreneurial than those of today. But even in the future, there will be *variation* in the degree of turbulence facing different organizations. Those in the more turbulent environments of the day will have to be more entrepreneurial than those operating in the less turbulent environments of the day. Or, to put it the other way, the latter will have to be more conservatively managed than the former.

THE EFFECT OF ORGANIZATIONAL PERFORMANCE ON THE ORGANIZATION

Research by social and industrial psychologists has suggested that the performance of a group has important behavioral consequences for the group. The losing group generally feels demoralized and may even break apart over fault-finding and internal bickering. The winning group feels happy and smug and stands pat on its current strategy.[33] Organizations are not, of course, groups, but they are powerfully influenced by groups, especially the top management group. So, somewhat similar responses by organizations are not unlikely. Here we are in a blind area, for little systematic, empirical work has been published on the question. But some informed speculation may not be amiss.

Winning and Its Consequences

Let us suppose that the organization has "won"—that is, has performed very well compared to its rivals. What is more, the management expects to continue to win. There would then be little incentive on *its* part to change the organization's strategy, or structure, or the behavior of its rank and file. But a very important consequence of the organization's "winning" may be that the aspirations of the organizational rank and file to share in the "loot" will rise rapidly. *This* may have important consequences for strategic, structural, and behavioral variables. The top management and other groups in the organization are likely to bargain with one another for a share of what the Carnegie theorists (Chapter 5) have labeled organizational slack. The bargaining is likely to involve not only monetary resources but power and the content of policy. In general, we may expect the internal administrative strategy to become more participative. Some of this participativeness may be an attempt to buy off the lower level members of the organization. Some of it may be due to generosity induced by good times. Some of it may be because the management now has the time to devote attention to the development of the organization's human resources and feels that in the long run these are its greatest asset.

A more benign participatory strategy may in turn have several structural consequences. One may be greater formal decentralization of authority. Another may be the formal institution of supervisory training in human relations and participative management. A third may be the redesign of operations technology to make jobs less boring. In addition, good times may induce the top management to sanction prestigious if dubiously economical "growth" projects such as heavy image-building marketing, the installation of the latest computer or other gadgetry, and the setting up of prestigious research and planning staff units. Superficially at least, this may imply a more professional orientation. In an earlier section we have advanced the proposition that a professional management style leads to a superior organizational performance vis-à-vis the organization's competitors. It is possible that the reverse may also be true, that superior organizational performance leads to a participatory and planning-oriented top management style. In fact the causal arrow may go both ways, in that a professional style may lead to superior organizational performance, which in turn may reinforce a professional style. Indeed, one can quite generally argue that whenever we find strong associations between organizational strategy and organizational performance, there are likely to be mutually reinforcing mechanisms at work. Thus, the Canadian data showed that 69 percent of the firms that had a risk-taking and organic style reported performing better than their rivals, while only 23 percent reported doing relatively poorly. Certainly it is plausible to argue that taking risks and flexibly implementing risky decisions is a good formula for success, especially if the rivals do not take risks or, if they do, execute their decisions mechanistically. But one could also argue that success is likely to increase managerial boldness and risk taking. Successful innovations and risky ventures are likely to whet the appetite for more, and success is also likely to reduce pressures for rigidity and increase those for a permissive, loose organizational climate.

And yet, we can sometimes indicate which way the causal arrow may be *stronger*—that is whether superior performance is the *primary* stimulus and management strategy largely the effect, or management strategy is the primary stimulus and performance largely the effect. If performance is the primary stimulus, causing the organization to adopt participation, optimization, risk taking, and flexibility, then we would expect those organizations that have done much better than their rivals to show high levels of *all* four in tandem.

Table 15–4 shows the percentage of 32 relatively successful Canadian firms that had respectively highly participative, optimizing, risk-taking, organic, professional, and entrepreneurial orientations. These firms scored in the top third of the distribution of the *relative* index of performance. It is true that over two-fifths of these firms reported being highly participative, highly planning and optimization oriented, highly risk taking, and highly organic—*but* not the same two fifths! In fact, only 9 percent of the firms reported high levels of all four of these at the same time. Even if we assume that high performance reinforces either a professional orientation *or* an entrepreneurial orientation, then also only about a fifth each reported respectively the professional orientation (but not the entrepreneurial orientation) and the entrepreneurial orientation (but not the professional orientation). When we remember that 69 percent of all the firms practicing an entrepreneurial style reported doing better than their rivals and 43 percent of all the firms practicing a professional style reported doing better than their rivals (see Table 15–2), then one has to accept that management strategy is likely to be the primary cause of superior performance, although one may readily concede that superior performance quite strongly reinforces whatever strategy has initiated success.

"Losing" and Its Consequences

Now let us suppose that the organization has lost—that is, its performance has been below the standard for its reference group. If the loss is a bad one,

TABLE 15-4

The Effect of Relative Success on Organizational Strategy

(Sample: 32 Firms Reporting Superior Performance to Rivals from a Total Sample of 103 Canadian Firms)

	Percentage of high success firms
1. Participation	
Highly participative top management style	47
Nonparticipative top management style	28
2. Optimization	
Highly planning and optimizing orientation	41
Seat-of-the-pants, low planning and optimization orientation	19
3. Risk taking	
High risk-taking orientation	44
Conservative, low risk-taking orientation	37
4. Flexibility	
Organic orientation	44
Mechanistic, low organic orientation	16
5. Professional orientation (high participation and optimization)	31
6. Entrepreneurial orientation (risk taking and flexibility)	28
7. Professional and entrepreneurial orientation	9

NOTE: In each of 1, 2, 3, and 4 above, the residual percentages are firms scoring in the middle third of the distribution of the respective variables.

there will be intense frustration in the ranks of the top management. The tension may be relieved if the management either finds environmental or organizational scapegoats and displaces its resentment or faces up to the problem and seeks rationally to improve matters. If the scapegoating is the chosen alternative, as it probably more commonly is, the chances are that the rank and file are going to be in for a rough time. The internal strategy is likely to get more coercive. A good deal of arbitrary and authoritarian managerial behavior is likely. Established procedures, structures, and precedents are likely to be summarily upset. Firing and psychological executions are likely. In an increasingly bitter atmosphere, countervailing forces are likely to gather momentum. Unionization is likely, or if unions already exist, union activity is likely to get more militant. Organizational politics are likely to get rougher as expedient coalitions are formed to "get" or "get even with" real or imaginary organizational enemies. Participation is likely to suffer gravely, for where there is no trust or confidence in the abilities of others, decisions are hardly likely to be made on a consensual basis. The outer *forms* of participation might remain, but the participative spirit is likely to vanish.

Not much can be said about the external strategy of the organization. The shock of a really bad loss can have unpredictable consequences. It can make some organizations super-cautious, others willing to gamble their all to regain their position. A good many may be too shocked to change at all. Some may lose faith in all planning and technocracy. Others may blindly seek their salvation in it. Again, many may simply be too paralyzed to change one way or the other.

Specifically, we may expect "losing" organizations to get more coercive and less participative and to perceive their environment as inimical. Table 15–5 provides support for these expectations. Out of 32 firms that reported scoring in the lowest third of the index of performance relative to that of competitors, half reported a low participative orientation, about half thought their environment was hostile, and nearly two fifths reported a highly coercive orientation.

The interesting question is: Did relatively low performance cause low levels of participation, high levels of coercion, and the perception of the environment as hostile? Or, is it the other way around? In other words, was relatively low performance caused by environmental hostility, low participation, and a coercive top management orientation? If relatively low per-

TABLE 15–5
Organizational Performance and Organizational Strategy
(Sample: 32 Canadian Firms Scoring in the Bottom Third of the Distribution of the Relative Index of Performance)

	Percentage of low success firms
1. Participation	
High participation orientation of top management	22
Low participation orientation of top management	50
2. Coercion	
Highly coercive orientation of top management	37
Noncoercion orientation of top management	12
3. Environmental Hostility	
Perception of the environment as very hostile	47
Perception of the environment as benign, not hostile	25
4. Low participation, high coercion orientation of top management	19
5. Perception of the environment as very hostile, low participation, high coercion orientation	9

NOTE: The residual percentages in 1, 2, and 3 above are, respectively, moderately participative firms, moderately coercive firms, and firms reporting a moderately hostile environment.

formance causes low participation, high coercion, and perception of the environment as being hostile, we should expect a large number of low performers to be low on participation *and* high on coercion *and* high on environmental hostility. However, only 9 percent of the relatively low performers satisfied this prediction (see Table 15–5). On the other hand, of the four firms that reported being in a hostile environment *and* were non-participative *and* were highly coercive, 3 (or 75 percent) reported doing poorly compared to the industry average, and the remaining one reported doing about average. Thus, our conclusion is that low performance relative to competitors probably causes participation to fall, coercion to rise, and the environment to be perceived as more hostile; but equally, or more probably, these three and possibly other situational and strategic factors also cause a fall in the organization's performance relative to its rivals.

The all too rare rational managerial response to a bad loss is likely to involve a good deal of analysis of why the loss occurred, the forecasting of the future state of affairs, and the mapping out of a careful strategy of recuperation. As we have noted in discussing the effective responses to environmental hostility, the top management may elect either professionalism or entrepreneurship (or both). If it elects to go the professional route, it will institute *administrative* innovations like good research, planning, forecasting, and control systems. It will concentrate on building a cohesive management team and a loyal and motivated force of employees to execute its comprehensive, well-planned strategy of recuperation. If it elects the entrepreneurial route, it will search for innovative new *products or services* that it can market and thereby recoup its lost position. For doing this speedily, it will insist on loosening up the administrative structure (organic management) and may take recourse to a certain amount of authoritarianism to get past vested interests and resistance to change.

We propose that:

The stronger the association between an organizational strategy and organizational performance,
    the more likely it is that the two act as causes of one another.

The higher the performance of the organization relative to its rivals,
    the more participative, optimization oriented, risk taking, and/or organic its top management style is likely to get, the particular path of development being dictated by reinforcement provided by the environment in the shape of continuing good performance.

The lower the organization's performance relative to rivals, the more desirable is an entrepreneurial and/or a professional top management style.

SUMMARY, PROPOSITIONS, AND IMPLICATIONS
FOR ORGANIZATIONAL DESIGN

Summary

A wide range of studies suggests that a number of variables affect organizational performance. Several situational, strategic, structural, behavioral, and pattern variables have been shown to affect organizational performance. Organizational performance has been assessed in terms of the goals of the organization's top management, on the assumption that the top management must take into account the expectations of the key influencers of the organization's viability and prosperity.

Several caveats need to be borne in mind in assessing the reported studies. They are cross-sectional, and hence it is difficult to say whether performance is caused by situational, strategic, structural, behavioral, or pattern variables or whether performance causes changes in these variables, or both. Also, different researchers have used different measures of performance. Design that is effective from the point of view of one measure of performance may not necessarily be effective as regards other measures of performance. The studies of performance are disproportionately those of firms. One must apply with care findings about one type of organization to other types. It is an open question whether contemporary research findings will be relevant in the future.

Just as performance is affected by a host of variables, the assessment of performance in turn may affect the strategy, structure, and functioning of organizations. Whenever a strong association is found between organizational performance and strategic variables, it is likely that strategy is a cause of and also is caused by performance. It is likely that *relatively* high performance causes the organization's management to become more participative, optimization oriented, risk taking, and organic, although the reverse is likely to be even truer. Relatively low performance may impel the organization's management to get more coercive, less participative, and more paranoid about the external environment.

Propositions

1. The effect of demographic variables on organizational performance is stronger when the goals of the organization are affected by demographic variables than when goals are not affected by demographic variables.

2. Regardless, within limits, of the strategy and structure of the organization, the more buoyant and/or benign the external environment, the higher is organizational performance.

3. The more optimization and planning oriented, or participative, or progressive, or professional the top management's orientation *relative* to that of the organization's rivals,
    the higher tends to be the performance of the organization *relative* to that of these rivals.

4. The more risk taking and organic the top management's orientation *relative* to that of the organization's rivals,
    the higher tends to be the performance of the organization *relative* to that of these rivals.

5. Unless contra-indicated by the nature of the organization's task environment, the more professional the style of top management,
    the higher is the organization's performance.

6. Unless contra-indicated by the nature of the organization's task environment, the more risk taking and organic the style of top management,
    the higher is the organization's performance, but the higher also are the chances of its mortality.

7. Individual structural variables in and of themselves—that is, with situational and strategic variables controlled for—tend not to affect organizational performance strongly.

8. The more the formal leadership has task-structuring, planning, control, and coordination skills in those parts of the organization in which tasks are relatively structured,
    the higher is organizational performance.

9. The more the formal leadership has task as well as human relations competence in those parts of the organization in which tasks are relatively novel or variable,
    the higher is organizational performance.

10. The more effective the leadership;
    the greater the interpersonal and intergroup collaboration;
    the more technically competent the rank and file; and
    the more highly motivated the rank and file,
    the higher is organizational performance.

11. The more appropriate the top management strategy and the organizational structure are to the nature of the organization's situation—that is, the better the fit between situational, strategic, and structural factors—
    the higher is organizational performance.

12. In a hostile environment, other things being equal, the more the top management style stresses optimization *and* participation, or risk taking, flexibility, *and* coercion, or all of these,
    the higher is organizational performance.

13. The more evenly developed the uncertainty reduction, differentiation, and integrative mechanisms,
    the higher is organizational performance.

14. The broader the range of task-related uncertainties confronted by the organization,
    the more highly need to be developed the uncertainty reduction, differentiation, and integrative mechanisms for superior organizational performance.

15. The larger the organization, the more it should have formal role and functional specialization and standardization—that is, the more bureaucratic should be its structure—for superior organizational performance, especially in a stable environment.

16. The greater the variety in the task environments of major parts of the organization,
    the greater should be the permitted differentiation in the structures of these parts and in the attitudes and values of their respective personnel, and the greater should be the effort devoted to integrating the operations of these parts, for superior organizational performance.

17. The stronger the association between an organizational strategy and organizational performance,
    the more likely it is that the two act as causes of one another.

18. The higher the performance of the organization relative to its rivals,
    the more participative, optimization oriented, risk taking, and/or organic its top management style is likely to get, the particular path of development being dictated by reinforcement provided by the environment in the shape of continuing good performance.

19. The lower the organization's performance relative to rivals,
    the more desirable is an entrepreneurial and/or a professional top management style.

Bearing in mind the research findings reported in this chapter and in previous chapters, we suggest the following program for increasing the probability of high long-term organizational performance on goals considered key by the organization's principal decision makers:

1. Can the task environment of the organization be considered highly complex? Is there much diversity in the organization's markets? Does it have to confront many complicated legal or other constraints? Is the technology it *must* use highly complex?

2. If the answers to questions in 1 are all strongly "yes," then a professional top management style is definitely called for. Such a style emphasizes participative decision-making, humane treatment of employees, attempts to foster a collaborative organizational climate, heavy investment in the development of the organization's human resources, as well as planning, the use of modern management tools of operations research, market research, economic forecasting, and the like.

3. Can the task environment be considered turbulent? Do business or other conditions often change unpredictably, and by large magnitudes?

4. If the answers to questions in 3 are all strongly affirmative, then an entrepreneurial top management style is definitely called for. The key elements of such a style are a risk-taking, aggressively competitive, innovation-oriented business stance—coupled with a fairly high degree of administrative flexibility, organic rather than bureaucratic values, open communications, loose job definitions, authority exercised by experts in a situation rather than by the hierarchy, and authoritarianism proportionate to internal resistance to change in executing risky decisions. If the environment is turbulent as well as complex, the management style needs to incorporate the above elements plus a good deal of professionalism. If the environment is turbulent but not complex, the professionalism is much less needed.

5. Can the environment in which the organization operates be considered a hostile environment? Are there powerful forces in the environment poised to frustrate every initiative of the organization? Is survival itself at stake? Do high levels of risk attach to the organization's moves in the "market"?

6. If the answers to questions in 5 are emphatically "yes," the top management style must either be professional *or* entrepreneurial (or both). The emphasis should be either on a carefully planned, efficiency-oriented management strategy implemented by a highly cohesive, highly motivated management team; or it should be on risky, dramatic moves that take the opposition by surprise, put through forcefully but flexibly by a possibly charismatic personality at the top. Naturally, if the environment is complex as well as hostile, professionalism will be more necessary than entrepreneur-

ship. If the environment is turbulent as well as hostile, entrepreneurship will tend to prevail over professional values.

7. Is the task environment neither distinctively complex, nor turbulent, nor hostile?

8. If the answer to question 7 is "yes," then a large variety of management styles are feasible, including the professional and the entrepreneurial styles. The more effective styles are likely to be the traditional style with a strong dash of risk taking in a relatively simple environment and the conservative, mechanistic, noncoercive style in a stable environment.

9. Regardless of the organization's task environment, the top management should have a little bit more professionalism and/or entrepreneurship than the prevailing norm among the organization's rivals. Thus, if the environment is stable, the indicated top management style is the conservative, mechanistic, noncoercive one. But to do better than the rivals, the top management should be more professionalized or more entrepreneurial or both than its rivals, while basically retaining conservative, mechanistic, noncoercive values.

10. Having decided on the top management style and the business and administrative *strategy* this implies, the designer should proceed to establish the organizational *structure* that can get this strategy accomplished. If a high degree of managerial professionalism is the adopted strategy, the necessary control and information system of a high order of sophistication, the extensive decentralization of authority this facilitates, the use of a large variety of coordination and conflict resolution devices throughout the organization, units for training supervisors in participative decision-making and human relations, and the establishment of appropriate planning, budgeting, employee training and appraisal, operations and market research, and so on, units *must* be set up. If managerial professionalism is merely a variation on a basically traditional management style in order to beat the competition, these structures are needed but to a less sophisticated and smaller degree. If a high degree of entrepreneurship is the preferred strategy, then the appointment of bright, perceptive risk takers in key management positions is necessary. Another necessity is a good formal *and* non-formal information and control system, so that decisions are based on sound premises and their implementation is effectively monitored. Another necessity is to keep standard operating procedures and paperwork to the minimum, especially at higher managerial levels, in order to minimize interference with speedy execution of bold and novel moves and innovations. A third necessity may be fairly tight supervision throughout the organization, but especially at lower levels, to make sure that orders from above are faithfully and speedily carried out. Again, if entrepreneurship is merely a variation on a basically

conservative or professional or other strategy in order to do better than the competition, these structural arrangements will have to be made to a much more modest degree.

11. Organizational structure will also need to be designed in response to situational variables like the size of the organization and the type of the organization. If the organization is large, a long hierarchy, extensive delegation of authority, a good internal control system, a good deal of work specialization and division of work, the widespread use of standard operating procedures, several specialized, possibly centralized staff services, divisionalization, and so on will become necessary. These elements of structure are also likely to become necessary for public bureaucracies founded by the government and functioning under legislative scrutiny. Organizations whose outputs are standardized should be extensively functionally departmentalized for optimum efficiency and need to possess bureaucratic features like extensive use of standard operating procedures, functional specialization and division of labor, a sound control system, and a system of incentives tied to measured productivity. They also should, if their resources permit, get vertically integrated if there are uncertainties connected with the acquisition of their basic inputs and the offtake of their outputs. Organizations whose outputs are variable because they produce goods or services to the specifications of their clients should have the range of expertise and of equipment needed for this purpose. They also need to have access to other organizations to whom they can subcontract jobs that they cannot efficiently or economically undertake. They need to employ the matrix structure characterized by strong technical departments and the speedy assembling of project teams to carry through each significant customer order. They need to recruit or train technically oriented project managers who are also good at human relations, team building, planning, and liaison work with the technical departments. Organizations that are diversified should get divisionalized. The structure of these divisions should vary depending on whether their outputs are standardized or customized.

12. The structure of the organization should be appropriately differentiated in response to the diversity in the kind of work performed by its different work units or departments.

The work units with complex tasks should be highly technocratic—that is, staffed with technically qualified personnel. The work units with creative, novel, unstructured, "uncertain" tasks should be highly organic. The work units with routine tasks should be highly mechanistic but with their supervisors retaining a good deal of employee orientation. But this permitted diversity in the structures of work units should be matched by attempts to integrate their work so that interdependencies between them are properly taken care of. As far as possible, coordination should be done at the site, as it were, of the interdependency, rather than at higher levels in the administrative hierarchy. Work units that crucially influence each other's outputs should be located together under a common boss to permit coordination through rapid feedback and quick decisions. Staff whose services are demanded widely throughout the organization should be centrally located in staff units. Facilitators or liaison personnel or committees should be employed to coordinate the efforts of interdependent units that for technical or other reasons cannot be merged. In general, the greater the needed diversity in the structures of work units that at least occasionally need to work together, the greater must be the efforts at "integrating" their activities by means such as advance planning and programming of operations, locating them together under a common boss, employing special liaison personnel, confrontation and conflict resolution exercises, and so forth.

13. The organization should develop uncertainty reduction mechanisms like a market information system and vertical integration, differentiation mechanisms like functional departmentalization, decentralization, and divisionalization, and integration mechanisms like participative, team decision making and a sophisticated control system, all in tandem and in proportion to the depth and multiplicity of uncertainties in its task environment.

14. In work regions of the organization in which complex, creative, variable tasks need to be undertaken, the leaders or managers not only should be both task and employee oriented but should possess high orders of planning, coordinating, participation-inducing, human relations, and team-building skills. They also need to have the ability to coordinate their work units' activities effectively with interfacing units. The human relations, team-building, and collaborative skills will be somewhat less necessary in parts of the organization in which mainly routine tasks are undertaken. Thus, selection procedures, training, and reward systems will have to be appropriately designed to meet the need for somewhat different supervisory skills in different parts of the organization.

SUGGESTED READINGS

Paul E. Mott, *The Characteristics of Effective Organizations* (New York: Harper and Row, 1972).

John Child, "Managerial and Organizational Factors Associated with Company Performance," Parts I and II, *Journal of Management Studies*, Vol. 11, No. 3 (Oct. 1974) and Vol. 12, No. 1 (Feb. 1975).

QUESTIONS FOR ANALYSIS

1 What kind of organizational design would you think would be appropriate for the government of a highly developed country like Canada? Of a poor

country struggling to get developed like India? In your analysis take into account situational, strategic, structural, behavioral, and pattern variables, and identify your criteria of organizational performance.

2 Here is a case of an organization with an apparently declining performance. What advice would you give Mr. Millman?

In January of 1972, the Board of Directors of the Adams Corporation simultaneously announced the highest sales in the company's history, the lowest dollar after-tax profits in a twenty-year period, the retirement (for personal reasons) of its long-tenure President and Chief Executive Officer.

Founded in St. Louis in 1848, the Adams Brothers Company had long been identified as a family firm both in name and operating philosophy. Writing in a business history journal, a former family senior manager comments, "My grandfather wanted to lead a business organization with ethical standards. He wanted to produce a quality product and a quality working climate for both employees and managers. He thought the Holy Bible and the concept of family stewardship provided him with all the guidelines needed to lead his company. A belief in the fundamental goodness of mankind, in the power of fair play and in the importance of personal and corporate integrity were his trade-marks. Those traditions exist today in the nineteen sixties."

In the early 1950s, two significant corporate events occurred. First, the name of the firm was changed to the Adams Corporation. Secondly, somewhat over 50% of the corporation shares were sold by various family groups to the wider public. In 1971 all branches of the family owned or "influenced" less than one-fifth of the outstanding shares of Adams.

The Adams Corporation was widely known and respected as a manufacturer and distributor of quality, branded, consumer products for the American, Canadian and European (export) markets. Adams products were processed in four regional plants located near raw material sources,* were stored and distributed in a series of recently constructed or renovated distribution centers located in key cities throughout North America and were sold by a company sales force to thousands of retail outlets—primarily supermarkets.

In explaining the original long-term financial success of the company, a former officer commented, "Adams led the industry in the development of unique production processes that produced a quality product at a very low cost. The company has always been production-oriented and volume-oriented and it paid off for a long time. During those decades the Adams brand was all that was needed to sell our product; we didn't do anything but a little advertising. Competition was limited and our production efficiency and raw material sources enabled us to outpace the industry in sales and profit. Our strategy was to make a quality product, distribute it and sell it cheap."

* No single plant processed the full line of Adams products, but each plant processed the main items in the line.

"But that has all changed in the past 20 years," he continued. "Our three major competitors have outdistanced us in net profits and market aggressiveness. One of them—a first-class marketing group—has doubled sales and profits within the past five years. Our gross sales have increased to almost $350-million but our net profits have dropped continuously during that same period. While a consumer action group just designated us as 'best value,' we have fallen behind in marketing techniques, e.g., our packaging is just out of date."

Structurally, Adams was organized into eight major divisions; seven of these were regional sales divisions with responsibility for distribution and sales of the company's consumer products to retail stores in their area. Each regional sales division was further divided into organizational units at the state and country and/or trading area level. Each sales division was governed by a corporate price list in the selling of company products but had some leeway to meet the local competitive price developments. Each sales division was also assigned (by the home office) a quota of salesmen it could hire and was given the salary ranges within which these men could be employed. All salesmen were on a straight salary and expense reimbursement salary plan which tended to be under industry averages.

A small central accounting office accumulated sales and expense information for each of the several sales divisions on a quarterly basis and prepared the overall company financial statements. Each sales division received, without commentary, a quarterly statement showing the number of cases processed and sold for the overall division, sales revenue per case of the overall division and local expenses per case for the overall division.

Somewhat similar information was obtained from the manufacturing division. Manufacturing division accounting was complicated by variations in the cost of obtaining and processing the basic materials used in Adams' products. These variations—particularly in procurement—were largely beyond the control of that division. The accounting office did have, however, one rough external check on manufacturing division effectiveness. A crude market price for case lots goods to some large national chains did exist.

Once a quarter, the seven senior sales vice presidents met with general management in St. Louis. Typically, management discussion focused on divisional sales results and expenses control. The company's objective of being the number one largest selling line in its field, directed group attention to sales vs. budget. All knew that last year's sales targets had to be exceeded—"no matter what." The manufacturing division vice president sat in on these meetings to explain the product availability situation. Because of his St. Louis office location, he frequently talked with Mr. Jerome Adams about overall manufacturing operations and specifically about large procurement decisions.

The Adams Company had a trade reputation for being very conservative with its compensation program. All officers were on a straight salary program. An officer might expect a modest salary increase every one or two years; these increases tended to be in the thousand-dollar range regardless of divisional performance or company profit position. Salaries among the six divisional vice presidents ranged from $32,000 to $42,000 with the higher amounts going to more senior officers. Mr. Jerome Adams' salary of $48,000 was the highest in the company. There was no corporate bonus plan. A very limited stock option program was in operation, but the depressed price of Adams stock meant that few officers exercised their options.

Of considerable pride to Mr. Jerome Adams had been the corporate climate at Adams. "We take care of our family" was his oft-repeated phrase at company banquets honoring long-service employees. "We are a team and it is a team spirit that has built Adams into its leading position in this industry." No member of first line, middle or senior management could be discharged (except in cases of moral crime or dishonesty) without a personal review of his case by Mr. Adams. As a matter of fact, executive turnover at Adams was very low. Executives at all levels viewed their jobs as a lifetime career. There was no compulsory retirement plan and some managers were still active in their mid-seventies.

The operational extension of this organizational philosophy was quite evident to employees and managers. A private family trust, for over 75 years, provided emergency assistance to all members of the Adams organization. Adams led its industry in the granting of educational scholarships, in medical insurance for employees and managers, and in the encouragement of its problems and organizations.

Mr. Adams noted two positive aspects of this organizational philosophy. "We have a high percentage of long-term employees—Joe Girly, a guard at East St. Louis, completes 55 years with us this year and every one of his brothers and sisters has worked here. And it is not uncommon for a vice president to retire with a blue pin—that means 40 years of service. We have led this industry in manufacturing process innovation, quality control and value for low price for decades. I am proud of our accomplishments and this pride is shown by everyone—from janitors to directors." Industry sources noted that there was no question that Adams was number one in terms of manufacturing and logistic efficiency.

In December of 1971, the annual Adams management conference gathered over 80 of Adams' senior management in St. Louis. Most expected the usual formal routines—the announcement of 1971 results and 1972 budgets, the award of the Gold Flag to the top processing plant and sales division for exceeding targets and the award of service pins to executives. All expected the usual social good times. It was an opportunity to meet and drink with "old buddies."

After a series of task force meetings, the managers gathered in a banquet room—good naturedly referred to as "Rib Room" since a local singer "Eve" was to provide the entertainment. At the front of the room, in the usual fashion, was a dais with a long, elaborately decorated head table. Sitting at the center of that table was Mr. Jerome Adams. Following tradition, Mr. Adams' vice presidents, in order of seniority with the company, sat on his right. On his left, sat major family shareholders, corporate staff, and—a newcomer—soon to be introduced.

After awarding service pins and the "Gold Flags" of achievement, Mr. Adams announced formally what had been a corporate "secret" for several months. First, a new investing group had assumed a "control" position on the board of Adams. Secondly that Mr. Price Millman would take over as President and Chief Executive Officer of Adams immediately.

Introducing Mr. Millman, Adams pointed out the outstanding record of the firm's new president. "Price got his MBA in 1959, spent four years in control and marketing and then was named as the youngest divisional president in the history of the Tenny Corporation. In the past years, he has made his division the most profitable in Tenny and the industry leader in its field. We are fortunate to have him with us. Please give him your complete support."

In a later informal meeting with the divisional vice presidents, Mr. Millman spoke about his respect for past Adams accomplishments and the urgent need to infuse Adams with "fighting spirit" and "competitiveness." My personal and organizational philosophy are the same—the name of the game is to fight and win. I almost drowned, but I won my first swimming race at eleven years of age. That philosophy of always winning is what enabled me to build the Ajax Division into Tenny's most profitable operation. We are going to do this at Adams. I want to show progress by the June 30th Directors' meeting."

"The new owner group wants fast results. They have suggested I develop a new format for Adams' operations. They want an organizational plan that will shake this company up. Once we get that new format, gentlemen, I have but one goal—each month must be better than the last. I didn't give up a good job at Tenny to lose at Adams."[34]

3 Read the case "A new division" from Wegner and Sayles.[35] It is a case of a poorly performing new division. If approached for your advice, what would you tell the Board of Directors?

4 Take a look at the following case. Identify the situational factors confronting Complan. What strategic choices are available to Complan's top management? What strategy do you recommend? What organizational structural arrangements would be needed to implement this strategy?

In 1969 and early 1970 the computer time-sharing industry, then only four years old, was experiencing a shake-out. At a time when the stock market had shown a year of nearly steady decline and the computer software and services industries had fallen in disfavor with investors, many time-sharing companies were merging and others were falling to the wayside or being acquired on fire-sale prices.

The Time-Sharing Industry

The development and growth of the time-sharing industry was described in volume 12 of *Innovation* magazine: "Time-sharing is a special kind of service industry based on the remote manipulation of data via certain combinations of technology—computers, communications, software. This becomes a viable business largely because the technology gets attractively inexpensive to use when its essential costs are shared . . . .

"The customers use key board (e.g., teletypes) or graphic terminals linked to a central computer by telephone lines. In effect, each customer believes that the computer operates exclusively in his behalf, for certain supervisory programs within the machine analyze the demands made by various customers and interleave them" so that the response to demands by individual users optimally is given with no noticeable delay resulting from other customers' uses of the machine.

The article described the entry of some companies into the young time-sharing industry, ". . . after suitable juggling had been accomplished among potential customers, a computer supplier, and the phone company, you hired some smart programmers and whipped them like galley slaves to have the software ready on time to meld the whole affair together in an operating system . . . ."

"Technically creative people impelled most time-sharing companies. Many of them were started by programmers who were attracted by the idea of capitalizing on what they knew how to do with software—squeeze the most out of computer hardware."

The time-sharing companies soon found that operations were more complex than they had anticipated. One of the main advantages of time sharing—the immediate availability of the computer to several users simultaneously—began to haunt the time-sharing entrepreneurs. Customers could call at any time of the day or night, which was fine until too many customers called at the same time. Then the operating system—a sophisticated design of hardware and software—could answer each individual's request only after much longer response times than were desirable. If this situation occurred too frequently, customers complained and eventually discontinued using the service. On the other hand, the time-sharing company saw its machine being underutilized for portions of each day. The incremental cost of putting on new customers appeared very low, as the hardware was already there and each additional customer had only a small effect on the system's performance. The *Innovation* article described the outcome of this type of analysis: "If enough companies put enough computer time on the market based on such an incremental pricing strategy, it does not take long before the cost competition has all of them selling at below real operating costs unless their computers do run at capacity which . . . degrades service and drives customers away. Then, when people find their services aren't selling, they cut prices. This interaction becomes disastrous when there is no distinction between time-sharing services except price."

As time-sharing technology was commercially developed, many technical problems appeared. Since the technology for time sharing was much more advanced than for traditional batch-mode service and had not been completely debugged, many hardware and software problems were found only after customers began using the systems. Some problems occurred only when special circumstances, such as a unique sequence and timing of customer demands hit upon a systems design flaw. These errors were especially difficult to fix, for first the error situation had to be discovered and recreated and often little information remained after the error occurred to help discover what had actually happened. Since customers had direct access to the system, it was more vulnerable than batch operations, in which the computer was in a protected environment and was accessed only by the operator. Furthermore, the fact that several customers were using the system at any one time increased the potential damage that a systems error could cause; many users could find that midway through their session with the system it would "crash" and possibly all of the work they had done to that point would be lost and unrecoverable.

Many of the time-sharing companies' customers were not technically oriented, and the companies offered their customers little help in using the service. *Innovation* described this situation:

"Few of the companies had made any real investment in a marketing force. Many of them acquired a good peddler, knighted him with a title of vice president for marketing, paid hm $25,000 per year plus stock options, and expected him to scare up customers for the computer waiting in the back room . . . . Early in 1968 a salesman who knew little about programming could still go into a scientific research or engineering establishment and offer raw computer time on a central machine via teletype link: the client could then do as he pleased with the system. But it became more difficult to sell this way because there were lots of other customers who examined an offer of a computer and asked: But what do we do with it?

"There followed a great rush through 1968 and 1969 to produce libraries of computer application programmers . . . . After two years the great flurry of programming activity hadn't produced much of a distinction between time-sharing services after all. Almost every service, large or small, offered the same computer languages and somewhat the same kinds of programs. This similarity of services continued to depress the time-sharing market."

The programming activity had absorbed many of the resources of the companies that had gone heavily on this marketing strategy. Often, however, it became clear only after a program had been developed that it did not have as wide an application as was expected. Often the market for a program was severely limited by the fact that the program itself was technically a fine development but too sophisticated for use and too difficult to understand for more than a small number of customers.

The Time-Sharing Industry in 1970

In 1970, time-sharing companies were retrenching. Few were profitable. As a result of the several mergers in the industry, some time-sharing companies had operations in more than one city (some all across the nation).

The central computer facilities in these situations could either be one large computer with multiplexors and leased telephone lines feeding to this computer or separate computer facilities with similar programs in different cities. The choice between these two alternatives was usually made on economic determinations based upon analysis of the capital investments and operating costs, or it was de facto as a result of a merger situation.

Complan Interactive Systems

In mid-1970, Complan Interactive Systems, Inc., was formed as a new time-sharing service. The company's founders believed that if they followed the right strategy and organized properly they could profitably offer time-sharing services. Basing their strategy upon experience they had gained from observing other time-sharing companies, CIS's founders decided to differentiate themselves from the rest of the industry by offering a specialized package of programs and services to initially one specialized market. CIS's potential clients had little knowledge of computer technology but had several applications in which the use of time sharing could make a major positive impact. The company offered its clients a package which included the use of a terminal, access to the company's programs (which were designed to be both flexible in their applications and easy to use), initial instruction in the use of the system and applications programs, detailed instruction manuals, and on-going support services. CIS priced its services significantly higher than the time-sharing industry average pricing structure. The company considered its marketing area to be the United States and Canada, and it based its operations on one central computer facility.

Major Tasks

CIS believed that to be successful, it had to offer:

1. a dependable time-sharing system, which meant:
   (a) enhancing and modifying the system provided by the computer hardware manufacturer,
   (b) providing dependable operations and maintenance of the hardware and software

at   2. a reasonable (but higher than average) price,

with   3. specialized applications programs that:
   (a) met specific customer needs,
   (b) were easy to use while still being effective,
   (c) were modified and augmented as required,

and with   4. extensive customer service and training that would:
   (a) assist the customer in effectively using the service, often answering questions that were relatively simple technically;
   (b) answer occasional highly technical customer questions;
   (c) provide feedback on the customers' views of the system's performance;
   (d) provide information on additional applications and market potentials.

CIS's president felt that together with support staff, it would be necessary to assemble an organization of about 100 people. He was trying to determine what organizational arrangements would best meet his company's objectives.[36]

Footnotes to Chapter Fifteen

[1] Management's concern about society, government, customers, suppliers, employees, etc., is in point of fact a variable, as demonstrated by the research of Anant Negandhi and Benjamin S. Prasad, *Comparative Management.*

[2] Noralou P. Roos, John R. Schermerhorn, and Leslie Roos, Jr., "Hospital Performance: Analyzing Power and Goals."

[3] Jai Ghorpade, "Organizational Ownership Patterns and Efficiency."

[4] F. M. Scherer, *Industrial Market Structure and Economic Performance.*

[5] See Appendix A to this book for a description of the author's Canadian study. The age of the firm was not correlated with an objective index of performance that included profitability and stability of profits as items besides the growth rate of revenues.

[6] Scherer, *op. cit.,* pp. 183–86 and 400–402.

[7] This subjective index of relative performance had fairly high validity. It was correlated .33 with the index of objective performance.

[8] Stanley Thune and Robert House, "Where Long Range Planning Pays Off."

[9] David Herold, Stanley Thune, and Robert House, "Long Range Planning and Organizational Performance."

[10] Igor Ansoff, et al., "Does Planning Pay? The Effect of Planning on Success of Acquisitions in American Firms."

[11] See Ch. 11 and Appendix A to this book for a description and operational definition of the optimization dimension of top management style.

[12] See Rensis Likert, *New Patterns of Management.*

[13] See Ch. 11 and Appendix A to this book for a description and operational definition of the participative dimension of top management style.

[14] See Ch. 11 and Appendix A to this book for a description and operational definition of the coercive dimension of the top management style.

[15] The scores of the firms on each of participation and optimization were trichotomized. Firms that scored in the top third of the distribution of both dimensions were considered professionally managed. Those that scored in the bottom third of both dimensions were considered to be traditionally managed.

[16] See Ch. 11 and Appendix A to this book for a description and operational definition of the conservative risk-taking and mechanistic organic top management orientations. For the purpose of the data analysis reported in Table 15–2, both orientations as measured were trichotomized. The risk-taking organic firms were those that scored in the top third of each of the two orientations, while the conservative mechanistic firms were those that scored in the bottom third of the scores of the two orientations. It may be remembered that risk taking or conservatism relate to the organization's external, business-related philosophy, while organic or mechanistic modes relate to its internal, administrative orientation.

[17] Negandhi and Prasad, *op. cit.*

[18] See *ibid.,* Appendix B, for details of the operating definition of the progressiveness of management philosophy.

The Effect of Organizational Performance on the Organization **617**

[19] For operational definitions of management effectiveness and the progressiveness of organizational practices (plus the three subsidiary indexes constituting it), see *ibid.*, Appendix A.

[20] *Ibid.*, p. 147.

[21] P. N. Khandwalla, "Viable and Effective Organizational Designs of Firms."

[22] David G. Bowers and Stanley E. Seashore, "Predicting Organizational Effectiveness with a Four-Factor Theory of Leadership."

[23] Paul Mott, *The Characteristics of Effective Organizations.*

[24] *Ibid.*, pp. 20–25.

[25] *Ibid.*, pp. 72, 114, 156.

[26] *Ibid.*, p. 163.

[27] Paul Lawrence and Jay Lorsch, *Organization and Its Environment.*

[28] John A. Morse, "Organizational Characteristics and Individual Motivation."

[29] Khandwalla, *op. cit.*

[30] John Child, "Managerial and Organizational Factors Associated with Company Performance," Part I and Part II.

[31] See, for example, D. S. Pugh, D. J. Hickson, C. R. Hinings, and C. Turner, "'The Context of Organizational Structures'"; and Peter Blau, "A Formal Theory of Differentiation in Organization."

[32] See Likert, *op. cit.*

[33] See Muzafer Sherif, "Experiments in Group Conflict," for a field experimental demonstration of the structural and behavioral consequences of "winning" and "losing." Also see Aaron Lowin and James Craig, "The Influence of Level of Performance on Managerial Style: An Experimental Object-Lesson in the Ambiguity of Correlational Data," for the effect of "incompetent" performance by a subordinate on the managerial style of the supervisor.

[34] C. Roland Christensen, Kenneth R. Andrews, and Joseph L. Bower, *Business Policy: Text and Cases*, 3rd ed., pp. 814–17.

[35] R. Wegner and Leonard Sayles, *Cases in Organizational and Administrative Behavior.*

[36] Lawrence and Lorsch, *op. cit.*, pp. 73–79.

Bibliography

A

Adorno, T. W., and others. *The Authoritarian Personality.* New York: Harper, 1950.

Almond, Gabriel A., and Bingham G. Powell, Jr. *Comparative Politics.* Boston: Little, Brown, 1966.

Anshen, Melvin. "The Manager and the Black Box." *Harvard Business Review* (November–December, 1960).

Ansoff, Igor, and others. "Does Planning Pay? The Effect of Planning on Success of Acquisitions in American Firms." *Long-Range Planning* (December, 1970).

Argyris, Chris. *Executive Leadership.* New York: Harper, 1953.

——— *Integrating the Individual and the Organization.* New York: Wiley, 1964.

——— *Personality and Organization.* New York: Harper, 1956.

Asch, Solomon. "Forming Impressions of Personality." *Journal of Abnormal and Social Psychology,* Vol. 41 (1946), pp. 258–90.

——— "Studies in Independence and Conformity: A Minority of One Against a Unanimous Majority." *Psychological Monographs,* Vol. 70, No. 9 (1956).

Averitt, Robert. *The Dual Economy.* New York: Norton, 1968.

Ayllon, T., and N. H. Azrin. "The Measurement and Reinforcement of the Behavior of Psychotics." *Journal of the Experimental Analysis of Behavior,* Vol. 8 (1965), pp. 357–83.

619

B

Baker, J., and R. Schaffer. "Making Staff Consulting More Effective." *Harvard Business Review* (January–February, 1969), pp. 62–71.

Bakke, E. Wight. "Concept of the Social Organization." in M. Haire, ed. *Modern Organization Theory*. New York: Chapman and Hall, 1959.

Bales, Robert F. "In Conference." *Harvard Business Review*, Vol. 32, No. 2 (1954), pp. 44–50.

Barnard, Chester. *Functions of the Executive*. Cambridge, Mass.: Harvard University Press, 1938.

Barron, Frank. *Creative Persons and Creative Process*. New York: Holt, Rinehart and Winston, 1969.

Bass, B. M. "The Anarchist Movement and the T-Group." *Journal of Applied Behavioral Science*, Vol. 3 (1967), pp. 211–26.

Beckhard, Richard. *Organizational Development: Strategies and Models*. Reading, Mass.: Addison-Wesley, 1969.

Bennis, Warren. "Theory and Method in Applying Behavioral Science to Planned Organizational Change." *Journal of Applied Behavioral Science*, Vol. 1, No. 4 (1965), pp. 337–60.

—— *Changing Organizations*. New York: McGraw-Hill, 1966.

Blake, R. R., and J. Mouton. *The Managerial Grid*. Houston: Gulf Publishing, 1964.

—— and H. A. Shepard. *Managing Intergroup Conflict in Industry*. Houston: Gulf Publishing, 1965.

Blau, Peter. "The Dynamics of Bureaucracy." In Amitai Etzioni, ed. *A Sociological Reader on Complex Organizations*, 2nd ed. New York: Holt, Rinehart and Winston, 1969.

—— "A Formal Theory of Differentiation in Organizations." *American Sociological Review*, Vol. 35 (1970), pp. 201–18.

—— and Richard Schoenherr. *The Structure of Organizations*. New York: Basic Books, 1971.

—— and Richard Scott. *Formal Organizations*. San Francisco: Chandler, 1962.

Blauner, Robert. "Work Satisfaction and Industrial Trends in Modern Society." In W. Galerson and S. M. Lipset, eds. *Labor and Trade Unionism*. New York: Wiley, 1960.

Bonini, Charles. *Simulation of Information and Decision Systems in the Firm*. Englewood Cliffs, N. J.: Prentice-Hall, 1963.

Bowers, David G., and Stanley E. Seashore. "Predicting Organizational Effectiveness with a Four-Factor Theory of Leadership." *Administrative Science Quarterly*, Vol. 11, No. 2 (1966), pp. 238–63.

Bowman, Edward, and Robert Fetter. *Analysis for Production Management*. Homewood, Ill.: Irwin, 1961.

Brady, Rodney H. "Computers in Top Management Decision Making." *Harvard Business Review* (July–August, 1967).

Braybrooke, D., and C. Lindblom. *A Strategy of Decision*. New York: Free Press, 1963.

Brayfield, A. T., and W. H. Crockett. "Employee Attitudes and Employee Performance." *Psychological Bulletin*, Vol. 52 (1955), pp. 396–424.

Brown, Wilfred. *Explorations in Management*. London: Heinemann, 1960.

Browning, Rufus. "Innovative and Non-innovative Decision Processes in Government Budgeting." Paper read at the annual meeting of the American Political Science Association, 1963, in New York.

Burack, Elmer. *Organizational Analysis*. Hinsdale, Ill.: Dryden Press, 1975.

Burlingame, John F. "Information Technology and Decentralization." *Harvard Business Review* (November–December, 1961).

Burns, Tom, and G. M. Stalker. *The Management of Innovation*. London: Tavistock, 1961.

C

Cartwright, D. "Influence, Leadership, Control." In James March, ed. *Handbook of Organizations*. Chicago: Rand McNally, 1965.

——— and R. Lippitt. "Group Dynamics and the Individual." *International Journal of Group Therapy*, Vol. 7 (1957), pp. 86–102.

Carzo, Rocco, Jr., and John H. Yanouzas. "Effects of Flat and Tall Organization Structure." *Administrative Science Quarterly*, Vol. 14, No. 3 (1969), pp. 178–91.

Caves, Richard. *American Industry: Structure, Conduct, Performance*, 3rd ed. Englewood Cliffs, N. J.: Prentice-Hall, 1972.

Chandler, Alfred. *Strategy and Structure*. Cambridge, Mass.: M. I. T. Press, 1962.

Chapple, Eliot D., and Leonard R. Sayles. "Workflow As the Basis of Organizational Design." In D. Hampton, C. Summer, and R. Webber, eds. *Organizational Behavior and the Practice of Management*. Glenview, Ill.: Scott, Foresman, 1968.

Child, John. "Managerial and Organizational Factors Associated with Company Performance, Part I." *Journal of Management Studies*, Vol. 11, No. 3 (October, 1974).

——— "Managerial and Organizational Factors Associated with Company Performance, Part II." *Journal of Management Studies*, Vol. 12, No. 1 (February, 1975).

——— "More Myths of Management Education?" *Journal of Management Studies*, Vol. 7 (1970), pp. 376–90.

——— "Organizational Structure, Environment, and Performance: The Role of Strategic Choice." *Sociology* (January, 1972), pp. 2–22.

——— "Organization Structure and Strategies of Control: A Replication of the Aston Study." *Administrative Science Quarterly*, Vol. 17 (1972), pp. 163–77.

——— and Roger Mansfield. "Technology, Size, and Organization Structure." *Sociology*, Vol. 6 (1972), pp. 368–93.

Christensen, C. Roland, Kenneth R. Andrews, and Joseph L. Bower. *Business Policy: Text and Cases*, 3rd ed. Homewood, Ill.: Irwin, 1973.

Clarkson, G. P. E. *Portfolio Selection: A Simulation of Trust Investment*. Englewood Cliffs, N. J.: Prentice-Hall, 1962.

Cloward, R., and L. Ohlin. *Delinquency and Opportunity*. Glencoe, Ill.: Free Press, 1961.

Coch, L., and J. R. P. French, Jr. "Overcoming Resistance to Change." *Human Relations*, Vol. 1, No. 4 (1948), pp. 512–32.

Cohen, K. J., and others. "The Carnegie Tech Management Game." *Journal of Business*, Vol. 33 (1960), pp. 303–27.

Collins, B., and H. Guetzkow. *A Social Psychology of Group Processes for Decision-Making*. New York: Wiley, 1964.

Collins, O., and D. Moore. *The Organization Makers*. New York: Appleton-Century-Crofts, 1970.

Cordell, Arthur. *The Multinational Firm, Foreign Direct Investment, and Canadian Science Policy*. Ottawa: Science Council of Canada Special Study No. 22 (1971).

Crozier, Michel. *The Bureaucratic Phenomenon*. Chicago: University of Chicago Press, 1964.

——— "Cultural Determinants of Organizational Behavior." In Anant Negandhi, ed. *Modern Organizational Theory*. Kent, Ohio: Kent State University Press, 1973.

Cummings, L. L., and Donald P. Schwab. *Performance In Organizations*. Glenview, Ill.: Scott, Foresman, 1973.

Cyert, R. M., and Kalmen Cohen. *Theory of the Firm: Resource Allocation in a Market Economy*. Englewood Cliffs, N. J.: Prentice-Hall, 1965.

——— and K. R. MacCrimmon. "Organizations." In G. Lindzey and E. Aronson, eds. *The Handbook of Social Psychology*, Vol. 1. Menlo Park, Calif.: Addison-Wesley, 1969.

——— and James G. March. *A Behavioral Theory of the Firm*. Englewood Cliffs, N. J.: Prentice-Hall, 1972.

D

Dahl, Robert A. "The Concept of Power." *Behavioral Science*, Vol. 2 (1957), pp. 201–18.

——— *Polyarchy*. New Haven, Conn.: Yale University Press, 1971.

Dahrendorf, Ralf. *Class and Class Conflict in Industrial Society*. Stanford, Calif.: Stanford University Press, 1959.

Dale, Ernest. *Planning and Developing the Company Organization Structure*. Research Report No. 20. New York: American Management Association, 1952.

———, ed. *Readings in Management*. New York: McGraw-Hill, 1965.

Dalton, Gene, Paul R. Lawrence, and Larry Greiner. *Organizational Change and Development*. Homewood, Ill.: Irwin, 1970.

Dalton, G. W., Paul R. Lawrence, and Jay Lorsch. *Organizational Structure and Design*. Homewood, Ill.: Irwin, 1970.

Dalton, M. "Conflicts Between Staff and Line Managerial Officers." *American Sociological Review*, Vol. 15 (1950), pp. 342–51.

——— *Men Who Manage*. New York: Wiley, 1959.

Davis, Keith. *Human Relations at Work*, 3rd ed. New York: McGraw-Hill, 1967.

Dearborn, D. C., and Herbert Simon. "Selective Perception: A Note on the Departmental Identifications of Executives." *Sociometry*, Vol. 21 (1958), pp. 140–44.

Dearden, John. "Computers: No Impact on Divisional Control." *Harvard Business Review* (January–February, 1967).

Dent, J. K. "Organizational Correlates of the Goals of Business Managements." *Personnel Psychology*, Vol. 12 (1959), pp. 365–93.

Deutsch, Morton. "An Experimental Study of the Effects of Cooperation and Competition upon Group Processes." *Human Relations*, Vol. 2 (1949), pp. 199–232.

––– "A Theory of Cooperation and Competition." *Human Relations*, Vol. 2 (1949), pp. 129–52.

––– and R. Krauss. *Theories in Social Psychology.* New York: Basic Books, 1965.

Dill, William. "Environment As an Influence on Managerial Autonomy." *Administrative Science Quarterly*, Vol. 2 (1958), pp. 209–43.

Drucker, Peter. *Managing for Results.* New York: Harper & Row, 1964.

––– *The Practice of Management.* New York: Harper, 1954.

Dunnette, Marvin. *Personnel Selection and Placement.* Belmont, Calif.: Wadsworth, 1966.

Durkheim, Emile. *The Division of Labor in Society.* Translated by G. Simpson. Glencoe, Ill.: Free Press, 1933.

E

Edwards, R. S., and H. Townsend. "The Growth of Firms." In E. Dale, ed. *Readings in Management.* New York: McGraw-Hill, 1965.

Emery, F. E.. and E. L. Trist. "Socio-technical Systems." In C. West Churchman, and M. Verhulst, eds. *Management Sciences: Models and Techniques*, Vol. 2. London: Pergamon Press, 1960.

England, George, and Raymond Nee. "Organizational Goals and Expected Behavior Among American, Japanese, and Korean Managers." *Academy of Management Journal*, Vol. 14, No. 4 (1971), pp. 425–38.

Etzioni, Amitai. *A Comparative Analysis of Complex Organizations.* New York: Free Press of Glencoe, 1961.

––– *Modern Organizations.* Englewood Cliffs, N. J.: Prentice-Hall, 1964.

––– *A Sociological Reader on Complex Organizations*, 2nd ed. New York: Holt, Rinehart and Winston, 1969.

F

Farmer, Richard N. "Further Explorations in Comparative Management." In Anant Negandhi, ed. *Modern Organizational Theory.* Kent, Ohio: Kent State University Press, 1973.

––– and D. Hogue. *Corporate Responsibility.* Chicago: Science Research Associates, 1973.

——— and Barry M. Richman. *Comparative Management and Economic Progress.* Homewood, Ill.: Irwin, 1965.

——— "A Model for Research in Comparative Management." *California Management Review*, Vol. 7 (1964), pp. 55–68.

Fayol, Henri. *General and Industrial Management.* Translated by Constance Storrs. London: Pitman, 1949.

Feldman, Julian, and Edward A. Feigenbaum. *Computers and Thought.* New York: McGraw-Hill, 1963.

Festinger, Leon. "The Motivating Effect of Cognitive Dissonance." In G. Lindzey, ed. *Assessment of Human Motives.* New York: Holt, Rinehart and Winston, 1958.

——— *A Theory of Cognitive Dissonance.* Evanston, Ill.: Row, Peterson, 1957.

——— "A Theory of Social Comparison Processes." *Human Relations*, Vol. 7 (1954), pp. 117–40.

——— and J. Carlsmith. "Cognitive Consequences of Forced Compliance." *Journal of Abnormal and Social Psychology*, Vol. 58 (1959), pp. 203–10.

Fiedler, Frank. "A Contingency Model of Leadership Effectiveness." In L. Berkowitz, ed. *Advances in Experimental Psychology.* New York: Academic Press, 1964.

——— "Validation and Extension of the Contingency Model of Leadership Effectiveness: A Review of Empirical Findings." *Psychological Bulletin*, Vol. 76, No. 2 (1971), pp. 128–48.

Fleishman, E. "Leadership Climate, Human Relations Training, and Supervisory Behavior." In E. Fleishman, ed. *Studies in Personnel and Industrial Psychology.* Homewood, Ill.: Irwin, 1961.

Follett, Mary Parker. "Constructive Conflict." In H. C. Metcalf and L. F. Urwick, eds. *Dynamic Administration: The Collected Papers of Mary Parker Follett.* London: Pitman, 1941.

Forgy, E. W. "Cluster Analysis of Multivariate Data: Efficiency Versus Interpretability of Classification." *Biometrica*, Vol. 21 (1965), pp. 768–69.

French, J. R. P., Jr., and B. Raven. "The Bases of Social Power." In D. Cartwright, ed. *Studies in Social Power.* Ann Arbor, Mich.: University of Michigan Institute for Social Research, 1959, pp. 150–67.

G

Gagné, R. M. "Problem Solving and Thinking." In Paul Randolph Farnsworth and Quinn McNemar, eds. *Annual Review of Psychology.* Palo Alto, Calif.: Annual Reviews, 1959.

Galbraith, Jay. "Environmental and Technological Determinants of Organizational Design." In Jay Lorsch and Paul R. Lawrence, eds. *Studies in Organization Design.* Homewood, Ill.: Irwin-Dorsey, 1970, pp. 113–39.

——— "Matrix Organization Designs: How to Combine Functional and Project Forms." *Business Horizons*, Vol. 14 (1971), pp. 29–40.

——— "Organization Design: An Information Processing View." In Jay Lorsch and Paul R. Lawrence, eds. *Organization Planning: Cases and Concepts.* Homewood, Ill.: Irwin-Dorsey, 1972.

George, Claude S., Jr. *The History of Management Thought,* 2nd ed. Englewood Cliffs, N. J.: Prentice-Hall, 1972.

Getzels, J. W., and P. O. Jackson. *Creativity and Intelligence.* New York: Wiley, 1962.

Ghorpade, Jai. "Organizational Ownership Patterns and Efficiency: A Case Study of Private and Cooperative Sugar Factories in South India." *Academy of Management Journal,* Vol. 16, No. 1 (1973), pp. 138–48.

Glueck, S., and E. Glueck. *Unraveling Juvenile Delinquency.* Cambridge, Mass.: Harvard University Press, 1955.

Goffman, E. *The Presentation of Self in Everyday Life.* Garden City, L. I.: Doubleday-Anchor Books, 1959.

Gouldner, Alvin. *Patterns of Industrial Bureaucracy.* Glencoe, Ill.: Free Press, 1954.

Guetzkow, H., and P. Bowman. *Men and Hunger: A Psychological Manual for Relief Workers.* Elgin, Ill.: Brethren Press, 1946.

H

Haberstroh, Chadwick. "Organization Design and Systems Analysis." In James March, ed. *Handbook of Organizations.* Chicago: Rand McNally, 1965.

Hall, Douglas, and Khalil Nougaim. "An Examination of Maslow's Need Hierarchy in an Organizational Setting." *Organizational Behavior and Human Performance,* Vol. 3 (1967), pp. 12–35.

Hall, Richard H. "The Concept of Bureaucracy: An Empirical Assessment." *American Journal of Sociology,* Vol. 69 (1963), pp. 32–40.

——— "Intraorganizational Structural Variation: Application of the Bureaucratic Model." *Administrative Science Quarterly,* Vol. 7 (1963), pp. 295–308.

——— *Organizations.* Englewood Cliffs, N. J.: Prentice-Hall, 1972.

——— "Professionalization and Bureaucratization." *American Sociological Review,* Vol. 33 (1968), pp. 92–104.

——— J. Eugene Haas, and Norman J. Johnson. "An Examination of the Blau-Scott and Etzioni Typologies." *Administrative Science Quarterly,* Vol. 12 (June, 1967), pp. 118–39.

Halpin, A., and B. Winer. "A Factorial Study of the Leader Behavior Descriptions." In Ralph M. Stogdill and Alvin E. Coons, eds. *Leader Behavior: Its Description and Measurement.* Columbus, Ohio: Bureau of Business Research, Ohio State University, 1957.

Hampton, D., C. Summer, and R. Webber. *Organizational Behavior and the Practice of Management.* Glenview, Ill.: Scott, Foresman, 1968.

Harbison, F., and C. Myers. *Management in the Industrial World.* New York: McGraw-Hill, 1959.

Hare, A. P., E. F. Borgatta, and R. F. Bales. *Small Groups.* New York: Knopf, 1966.

Heflebower, Richard B. "Observations on Decentralization in Large Enterprises." *Journal of Industrial Economics* (November, 1960), pp. 7–22.

Heider, Fritz. "On Perception, Event Structure, and Psychological Environment." *Psychological Issues,* Vol. 1, No. 3 (1959).

Heller, R. "The Legend of Litton." *Management Today* (October, 1967), pp. 60–67.

Henry, William. "Psychodynamics of the Executive Role." *American Journal of Sociology*, Vol. 54, No. 4 (1949), pp. 286–91.

Herold, David, Stanley Thune, and Robert House. "Long Range Planning and Organizational Performance." *Academy of Management Journal*, Vol. 15, No. 1 (1972), pp. 91–104.

Herzberg, F. "One More Time: How Do You Motivate Employees?" *Harvard Business Review* (January–February, 1968).

——— *Work and the Nature of Man*. Cleveland, Ohio: World, 1966.

Hickson, D. J., D. S. Pugh, and D. C. Pheysey. "Operations Technology and Organizational Structure: An Empirical Reappraisal." *Administrative Science Quarterly*, Vol. 14 (1969), pp. 370–97.

Hill, S. E., and F. Harbison. *Manpower and Innovation in American Industry*. Princeton, N. J.: Princeton University Press, 1959.

Hinings, C. R., and others. "Structural Conditions of Intraorganizational Power." *Administrative Science Quarterly*, Vol. 19 (1974), pp. 22–44.

Hoffer, Charles. "Emerging EDP Pattern." *Harvard Business Review* (March–April, 1970).

Homans, George C. *The Human Group*. New York: Harcourt Brace Jovanovich, Inc., 1950.

——— *Social Behavior: Its Elementary Forms*. New York: Harcourt Brace Jovanovich, Inc., 1961.

Hoos, Ida. "When the Computer Takes Over the Office." *Harvard Business Review* (November–December, 1960).

Hovland, C. I., and I. L. Janis, eds. *Personality and Persuasibility*. New Haven, Conn.: Yale University Press, 1959.

I

Inkeles, Alex. *What Is Sociology?* Englewood Cliffs, N. J.: Prentice-Hall, 1964.

J

Janowitz, M. *Sociology and the Military Establishment*. New York: Russell Sage Foundation, 1959.

Jaques, Elliot. *The Changing Culture of a Factory*. New York: Dryden Press, 1952.

Jay, Anthony. *Management and Machiavelli*. New York: Holt, Rinehart and Winston, 1967.

Joyce, Robert D. *Encounters in Organizational Behavior*. New York: Pergamon Press, 1972.

K

Kahn, Robert L. "Productivity and Job Satisfaction." *Personnel Psychology*, Vol. 13 (1970), pp. 257–86.

——— and others. *Organizational Stress: Studies in Role Conflict and Ambiguity*. New York: Wiley, 1964.

Kardiner, Abram, and others. *The Psychological Frontiers of Society*. New York: Columbia University Press, 1945.

Katz, Daniel. "The Motivational Basis of Organizational Behavior." *Behavioral Science* (1964), pp. 131–46.

––– and Robert L. Kahn. "Leadership Practices in Relation to Productivity and Morale." In Dorwin Cartwright and Alvin Zander, eds. *Group Dynamics*. Evanston, Ill.: Row, Peterson, 1953.

––– *The Social Psychology of Organizations*. New York: Wiley, 1966.

Kelman, H. C. "Compliance, Identification, and Internalization: Three Processes of Attitude Change." *Journal of Conflict Resolution*, Vol. 2 (1958), pp. 51–60.

Kepner, C., and B. Tregoe. *The Rational Manager: A Systematic Approach to Problem Solving and Decision Making*. New York: McGraw-Hill, 1965.

Kerr, C., and others. "Industrialism and World Society." *Harvard Business Review*, Vol. 39 (1961), pp. 113–26.

Khandwalla, P. N. "Control System: What's Best for Your Profitability." *Canadian Business* (April, 1974), pp. 64–68.

––– "The Effect of Competition on the Structure of Top Management Control." *Academy of Management Journal*, Vol. 16, No. 2 (1973), pp. 285–95.

––– *The Effect of the Environment on the Organizational Structure of Firms*. Unpublished Ph.D. dissertation, Carnegie-Mellon University.

––– "Mass Output Orientation of Operations Technology and Organizational Structure." *Administrative Science Quarterly* (March, 1974).

––– "Viable and Effective Organizational Designs of Firms." *Academy of Management Journal*, Vol. 16, No. 3 (1973), pp. 481–95.

King, N. "Clarification and Evaluation of the Two-Factor Theory of Job Satisfaction." *Psychological Bulletin*, Vol. 74, No. 1 (1970), pp. 18–31.

Koffka, Kurt. *Principles of Gestalt Psychology*. New York: Harcourt Brace Jovanovich, Inc., 1935.

Kohler, Wolfgang. *Gestalt Psychology*. New York: Liveright, 1929.

Koontz, Harold. "The Management Theory Jungle." *Academy of Management Journal*, Vol. 7 (1961), pp. 174–83.

––– and C. O'Donnell. *Principles of Management*. New York: Knopf, 1959.

Kornhauser, Arthur, and Paul B. Sheatsly. "Questionnaire Construction and Interview Procedure." Appendix C of C. Sellitz, and others. *Research Methods in Social Relations*, rev. ed. New York: Holt, Rinehart and Winston, 1959.

Krech, D., R. Crutchfield, and E. Ballachey. *Individual in Society*. New York: McGraw-Hill, 1962.

L

Lawrence, Paul, and Jay Lorsch. *Organization and Its Environment*. Cambridge, Mass.: Harvard University Press, 1967.

Leavitt, Harold. "Applied Organizational Change in Industry." In James March, ed. *Handbook of Organizations*. Chicago: Rand McNally, 1965.

––– *Managerial Psychology*, 3rd ed. Chicago: University of Chicago Press, 1972.

——— "Some Effects of Certain Communications Patterns on Group Performance." *Journal of Abnormal Psychology*, Vol. 46 (1951), pp. 38–50.

——— and T. Whisler. "Management in the 1980's." *Harvard Business Review*
(November–December, 1958).

Lee, Hak Chong. *The Impact of Electronic Data Processing upon Patterns of
Business Organization and Administration*. Albany, N. Y.: State University
of New York at Albany, 1965.

Levenson, Bernard. "Bureaucratic Succession." In Amitai Etzioni, ed. *Complex
Organizations: A Sociological Reader*. New York: Holt, Rinehart and Winston,
1961.

Levinson, H., with Janice Molinan, and Andrew C. Spohn. *Organizational Diagnosis*. Cambridge, Mass.: Harvard University Press, 1972.

Lewin, Kurt. *Field Theory in Social Science*. New York: Harper, 1951.

——— "Group Decision and Social Change." In E. E. Maccoby, Newcomb, and
Hartley, eds. *Readings in Social Psychology*. New York: Holt, Rinehart and
Winston, 1958.

——— "The Psychology of Success and Failure." *Occupations*, Vol. 24 (1936),
pp. 926–30.

——— *Resolving Social Conflicts*. New York: Harper, 1948.

——— and others. "Level of Aspiration." In J. M. Hunt, ed. *Personality and Behavior Disorders*. New York: Ronald Press, 1944.

———, Ronald Lippitt, and R. K. White. "Patterns of Aggressive Behavior in
Experimentally Created 'Social Climates.'" *Journal of Social Psychology*, Vol.
10 (1939), pp. 271–99.

Liebenstein, Harvey. "Allocative Efficiency vs. 'X-Efficiency.'" *American Economic Review*, Vol. 56 (1966), pp. 392–415.

Lieberman, S. "The Effects of Changes in Roles on the Attitudes of Role Occupants." *Human Relations*, Vol. 9, No. 4 (1956), pp. 385–402.

Likert, Rensis. *New Patterns of Management*. New York: McGraw-Hill, 1961.

Lindblom, Charles. "The Science of 'Muddling Through.'" *Public Administration Review*, Vol. 19 (Spring, 1959), pp. 79–88.

Litwak, Eugene. "Models of Organizations Which Permit Conflict." *American
Journal of Sociology*, Vol. 67 (1961), pp. 177–84.

Loomis, Louise. *Plato*. Translated by B. Jowett. New York: Walter J. Black, 1942.

Lorsch, Jay, and Paul Lawrence, eds. *Studies in Organization Design*. Homewood, Ill.: Irwin-Dorsey, 1970.

Lorsch, Jay, and Paul Lawrence, eds. *Organizational Planning: Cases and Concepts*. Homewood, Ill.: Irwin-Dorsey, 1972.

Lowin, Aaron, and James Craig. "The Influence of Level of Performance on
Managerial Style: An Experimental Object-Lesson." *Organizational Behavior
and Human Performance*, Vol. 3 (1968), pp. 440–58.

Lupton, Tom. *Management and the Social Sciences*, 2nd ed. Baltimore, Md.: Penguin, 1971.

M

Machiavelli, Niccolo. *The Prince*. New York: Random House, 1950.

Mann, F. C. "Studying and Creating Change: A Means to Understanding Social Organization." *Research in Industrial Human Relations*. Industrial Relations Research Association, No. 17 (1957), pp. 146–47.

Mao tse-Tung. *Quotations from Chairman Mao tse-Tung*. Peking: Foreign Languages Press, 1967.

March, James, ed. *Handbook of Organizations*. Chicago: Rand McNally, 1965.

―― "The Power of Power." In David Easton, ed. *Varieties of Political Theory*. Englewood Cliffs, N. J.: Prentice-Hall, 1966.

―― and Herbert Simon. *Organizations*. New York: Wiley, 1958.

Marshall, Alfred. *Principles of Economics*, 8th ed. London: Macmillan, 1920.

Marx, Karl. *Capital: A Critical Analysis of Capitalist Production*. Edited by Frederick Engles; translated by Samuel Moore and Edward Aveling. London: Glaisher, 1920.

Maslow, Abraham. *Motivation and Personality*. New York: Harper, 1954.

Massie, J. L. *Essentials of Management*. Englewood Cliffs, N. J.: Prentice-Hall, 1971.

McClelland, David. *The Achieving Society*. New York: Van Nostrand, 1961.

―――, and others. "Obligations to Self and Society in the U.S. and Germany." *Journal of Abnormal and Social Psychology*, Vol. 56 (1958).

McGrath, Joseph E. "Toward a 'Theory of Method' for Research on Organizations." In William W. Cooper, Harold Leavitt, and Shelley, eds. *New Perspectives in Organization Research*. New York: Wiley, 1964.

McGregor, Douglas. *The Human Side of Enterprise*. New York: McGraw-Hill, 1960.

Mechanic, David. "Sources of Power of Lower Participants in Complex Organizations." *Administrative Science Quarterly*, Vol. 7, No. 3 (1962), pp. 349–64.

Melcher, Arlyn. "Strategy-making in Three Modes." *California Management Review* (Winter, 1973).

Merton, R. K., ed. *Social Theory and Social Structure*, rev. ed. Glencoe, Ill.: Free Press, 1957, especially Merton's "Patterns of Influence: Local and Cosmopolitan Influences."

Metcalf, H. C., and L. F. Urwick, eds. *Dynamic Administration: The Collected Papers of Mary Parker Follett*. London: Pitman, 1941.

Michels, R. *Political Parties*. New York: Dover, 1959.

Miles, Raymond E. *Theories of Management*. New York: McGraw-Hill, 1975.

Mintzberg, Henry. *The Nature of Managerial Work*. New York: McGraw-Hill, 1973.

―― "Strategy-making in Three Modes." *California Management Review* (Winter, 1973).

―――, Duzu Raisingham, and André Théoret. "The Structure of 'Unstructured Decisions.'" Working paper, Faculty of Management, McGill University, Montreal, 1973.

Mohr, Lawrence B. "Determinants of Innovation in Organization." *American Political Science Review*, Vol. 63 (1969), pp. 111–26.

Mooney, J. D., and Alan C. Reiley. *Onward Industry*. New York: Harper, 1931.

Morse, John J. "Organizational Characteristics and Individual Motivation." In

Jay Lorsch and Paul Lawrence, eds. *Studies in Organization Design.* Homewood, Ill.: Irwin-Dorsey, 1970.

Morse, Nancy, and E. Reimer. "The Experimental Change of a Major Organizational Variable." *Journal of Abnormal Social Psychology,* Vol. 52 (1956), pp. 120–29.

Mott, Paul. *The Characteristics of Effective Organizations.* New York: Harper & Row, 1972.

N

Negandhi, Anant. "A Model for Analyzing Organizations in Cross-Cultural Settings: A Conceptual Scheme and Some Research Findings." In Anant Negandhi, ed. *Modern Organizational Theory.* Kent, Ohio: Kent State University Press, 1973.

—— and Bernard Estafen. "A Research Model to Determine the Applicability of American Management Know-how in Different Cultures and/or Environments." *Academy of Management Journal,* Vol. 8 (1965), pp. 319–23.

—— and Benjamin S. Prasad. *Comparative Management.* New York: Appleton-Century-Crofts, 1971.

Newman, William H. *Administrative Action: The Techniques of Organization and Management,* 2nd ed. Englewood Cliffs, N. J.: Prentice-Hall, 1963.

—— *Cases for Administrative Action.* Englewood Cliffs, N. J.: Prentice-Hall, 1963.

—— Charles P. Summer, and E. K. Warren. *The Process of Management,* 3rd ed. Englewood Cliffs, N. J.: Prentice-Hall, 1972.

Nord, Walter. "Beyond the Teaching Machine: The Neglected Area of Operant Conditioning in the Theory and Practice of Management." *Organizational Behavior and Human Performance,* Vol. 4, No. 4 (1969), pp. 375–401.

Nunnally, Jim C. *Psychometric Theory.* New York: McGraw-Hill, 1967.

O

Ogburn, William. *Social Change with Respect to Culture and Original Nature.* New York: Viking, 1950.

Osborn, A. F. *Applied Imagination,* 3rd ed. New York: Scribner's, 1962.

O'Toole, James. *Work in America.* Cambridge, Mass.: M. I. T. Press, 1974.

P

Parsons, Talcott. *The Social System.* Glencoe, Ill.: Free Press, 1951.

—— *Structure and Process in Modern Societies.* New York: Free Press, 1960.

—— *The Structure of Social Action.* Glencoe, Ill.: Free Press, 1949.

—— "Suggestions for a Sociological Approach to the Theory of Organizations." *Administrative Science Quarterly,* Vol. 1 (1956), pp. 63–85.

Perrow, Charles. *Organizational Analysis: A Sociological View.* Belmont, Calif.: Wadsworth, 1970.

Pfeffer, Jeffrey. "Merger As a Response to Organizational Interdependence." *Administrative Science Quarterly,* Vol. 17 (1972), pp. 382–94.

Porter, Lyman. "Job Attitudes in Management: IV. Perceived Deficiencies in Need Fulfillment As a Function of Size of Company." *Journal of Applied Psychology*, Vol. 47 (1963), pp. 386–97.

——— and E. E. Lawler, III. "Properties of Organization Structure in Relation to Job Attitudes and Job Behavior." *Psychological Bulletin*, Vol. 64, No. 1 (1965), pp. 23–51.

Pruitt, D. G. *Problem Solving in the Department of State*. Evanston, Ill.: Northwestern University, unpublished thesis, 1961.

Pugh, D. S. "Modern Organization Theory: A Psychological and Sociological Study." *Psychological Bulletin*, Vol. 66, No. 4 (1966), pp. 235–51.

——— D. J. Hickson, and C. R. Hinings. "An Empirical Taxonomy of Structures of Work Organization." *Administrative Science Quarterly*, Vol. 14 (1969), pp. 116–26.

——— *Writers on Organizations*, 2nd ed. Baltimore, Md.: Penguin, 1971.

——— and others. "The Context of Organizational Structures." *Administrative Science Quarterly*, Vol. 14 (1969), pp. 91–114.

R

Rapaport, David, ed. *Organization and Pathology of Thought*. New York: Columbia University Press, 1959.

Ridgeway, V. F. "Dysfunctional Consequences of Performance Measurements." *Administrative Science Quarterly*, Vol. 1, No. 2 (1956), pp. 240–47.

Robbins, Lionel. *An Essay on the Nature and Significance of Economic Science*, 2nd ed. London: Macmillan, 1936.

Roethlisberger, F. J., and W. J. Dickson. *The Manager and the Worker*. Cambridge, Mass.: Harvard University Press, 1939.

Rokeach, Milton. *The Open and Closed Mind*. New York: Basic Books, 1960.

Roos, Noralou P., John R. Schermerhorn, and Leslie Roos, Jr. "Hospital Performance: Analyzing Power and Goals." *Journal of Health and Social Behavior*, Vol. 15 (1972).

Rowbottom, Ralph. *Hospital Organization: A Progress Report on the Brunel Health Services Organization Project*. London: Heinemann, 1973.

Roy, Donald. "Banana Time: Job Satisfaction and Informal Interaction." *Human Organization*, Vol. 18 (1960), pp. 158–68.

Rubenstein, Albert H., and Chadwick Haberstroh. *Some Theories of Organization*. Homewood, Ill.: Irwin-Dorsey, 1970.

Ruedi, A., and Paul Lawrence. "Organizations in Two Cultures." In Jay Lorsch and Paul Lawrence, eds. *Studies in Organization Design*. Homewood, Ill.: Irwin-Dorsey, 1970.

Rush, H. *Behavioral Science: Concepts and Management Application*. New York: National Industrial Conference Board, 1969.

S

Sales, Stephen M. "Supervisory Style and Productivity: Review and Theory." *Personnel Psychology*, Vol. 19, No. 3 (1966), pp. 275–86.

―― and James House. "Job Dissatisfaction As a Possible Risk Factor in Coronary Heart Disease." *Journal of Chronic Diseases*, Vol. 13, No. 12 (1971), pp. 261–73.

Samuel, Y., and B. Mannheim. "A Multidimensional Approach Toward a Typology of Bureaucracy." *Administrative Science Quarterly*, Vol. 15 (1970), pp. 216–28.

Samuelson, Paul. *Economics.* New York: McGraw-Hill, 1967.

Sayles, Leonard, ed. *Individualism and Big Business.* New York: McGraw-Hill, 1964.

―― and M. Chandler. *Managing Large Systems.* New York: Harper & Row, 1971.

Schachter, Stanley. "Deviation, Rejection, and Communication." *Journal of Abnormal and Social Psychology*, Vol. 46 (1951), pp. 190–207.

―― *The Psychology of Affiliation.* Stanford, Calif.: Stanford University Press, 1959.

Scheff, Thomas J. "Control Over Policy by Attendants in a Mental Hospital." *Journal of Health and Human Behavior*, Vol. 2 (1961), pp. 93–105.

Schein, Edgar. "Management Development As a Process of Influence." *Industrial Management Review* (May, 1961), pp. 59–77.

―― *Organizational Psychology.* Englewood Cliffs, N. J.: Prentice-Hall, 1961.

Scherer, F. M. *Industrial Market Structure and Economic Performance.* Chicago: Rand McNally, 1970.

Schlesinger, Jr., Arthur. "The United States Department of State." In D. Hampton, C. Summer, and R. Webber, eds. *Organizational Behavior and the Practice of Management.* Glenview, Ill.: Scott, Foresman, 1968.

Scott, J. F., and R. P. Lynton. *Three Studies in Management.* London: Routledge and Kegan Paul, 1952.

Scott, Robert A. "The Factory As a Social Service Organization; Goal Displacement in Workshops for the Blind." *Social Problems*, Vol. 15 (1957), pp. 160–65.

Scott, W. Richard. "Field Methods in the Study of Organizations." In James March, ed. *Handbook of Organizations.* Chicago: Rand McNally, 1965.

Seashore, Stanley. *Group Cohesiveness in the Industrial Group.* Ann Arbor, Mich.: Institute for Social Research, 1954.

Seiler, J. *Systems Analysis in Organizational Behavior.* Homewood, Ill.: Irwin, 1967.

Selznick, Phillip. "An Approach to a Theory of Bureaucracy." *American Sociological Review*, Vol. 8 (1943), pp. 47–54.

―― "Foundations of the Theory of Organization." *American Sociological Review*, Vol. 13 (1948), pp. 25–35.

―― *T.V.A. and the Grass Roots.* Berkeley, Calif.: University of California Press, 1949.

Shamasastry, R. *Kautilya's Arthashastra.* Translated from Sanskrit. Mysore: Sri Raghuveer Printing Press, 1956.

Shaul, Donald. "What's Really Ahead for Middle Management?" *Personnel* (November–December, 1964).

Shaw, Clifford, and others. *Delinquency Areas*. Chicago: University of Chicago Press, 1929.

Shepard, Herbert. "Innovation-Resisting and Innovation-Producing Organizations." In Lloyd A. Rowe and William B. Boise, eds. *Organizational and Managerial Innovation*. Pacific Palisades, Calif.: Goodyear, 1967.

Sherif, Muzafer. "Experiments in Group Conflict." In Werrett Wallace Charters and N. L. Gage, eds. *Readings in the Social Psychology of Education*. Boston: Allyn and Bacon, 1963.

Sills, David L. *The Volunteers*. New York: Free Press, 1957.

Simon, Herbert. *Administrative Behavior*. New York: Macmillan, 1960.

―――― *The New Science of Management Decision*. New York: Harper & Row, 1960.

―――― "On the Concept of Organizational Goal." *Science Quarterly*, Vol. 9, No. 1 (June, 1964), pp. 1–22.

Sloan, Alfred P. J. *My Years with General Motors*. New York: Sidgwick and Jackson, 1965.

Skinner, B. F. *Science and Human Behavior*. New York: Macmillan, 1963.

Smalter, D. J., and R. J. Ruggles, Jr. "Six Business Lessons from the Pentagon." *Harvard Business Review*, Vol. 44, No. 2 (March–April, 1966), pp. 64–75.

Smith, Adam. *The Wealth of Nations*. London: Routledge, 1890.

Smith, R. A. "At Saint Gobain, the First Three Hundred Years Were the Easiest." *Fortune*, Vol. 72, No. 4 (October, 1965), pp. 148–50, 188–98.

Starbuck, W. H. "Level of Aspiration." *Psychological Review*, Vol. 70 (1963), pp. 51–60.

―――― "Mathematics and Organization Theory." In James March, ed. *Handbook of Organizations*. Chicago: Rand McNally, 1965.

―――― "Organizational Growth and Development." In James March, ed. *Handbook of Organizations*. Chicago: Rand McNally, 1965.

Steiner, Gary, ed. *The Creative Organization*. Chicago: University of Chicago Press, 1965.

Stinchcombe, Arthur. "Bureaucratic and Craft Administration of Production: A Comparative Study." *Administrative Science Quarterly*, Vol. 4 (1959), pp. 168–87.

―――― "Social Structure and Organizations." In James March, ed. *Handbook of Organizations*. Chicago: Rand McNally, 1965.

―――― *The Sociology of Organization and the Theory of the Firm*. 1960.

Strauss, George. "The Personality vs. Organization Theory." In Leonard Sayles, *Individualism and Big Business*. New York: McGraw-Hill, 1963.

―――― and Leonard Sayles. *Personnel: The Human Problems of Management*. Englewood Cliffs, N. J.: Prentice-Hall, 1960.

Strum, Philippa, and Michael Shmidman. *On Studying Political Science*. Pacific Palisades, Calif.: Goodyear Publishing, 1969.

T

Talachhi, S. "Organization Size, Individual Attitudes, and Behavior: An Empirical Study." *Administrative Science Quarterly*, Vol. 5 (1960), pp. 398–420.

Tannenbaum, Arnold. *Social Psychology of the Work Organization*. Belmont, Calif.: Wadsworth, 1966.

——— and R. L. Kahn. "Organizational Control Structure: A General Descriptive Technique As Applied to Four Local Unions." *Human Relations*, Vol. 10, No. 2 (1957), pp. 127–40.

Taylor, Frederick. *The Principles of Scientific Management*. New York: Harper, 1947.

Thibaut, J. W., and H. H. Kelley. *The Social Psychology of Groups*. New York: Wiley, 1959.

Thompson, J. D. *Organizations in Action*. New York: McGraw-Hill, 1967.

——— and W. J. McEwen. "Organizational Goals and Environment: Goal Setting As an Interaction Process." *American Sociological Review*, Vol. 23 (1958), pp. 23–31.

Thune, Stanley, and Robert House. "When Long-range Planning Pays Off." *Business Horizons* (August, 1970).

Toffler, Alvin. *Future Shock*. New York: Random House, 1970.

Trist, E. L., and K. W. Bamforth. "Some Social and Psychological Consequences of the Longwall Method of Coal Mining." *Human Relations*, Vol. 4 (1952), pp. 3–38.

U

Udell, John. "An Empirical Test of Hypotheses Relating to Span of Control." *Administrative Science Quarterly* (1967–68), pp. 420–39.

Udy, S. H., Jr. " 'Bureaucracy' and 'Rationality' in Weber's Organization Theory: An Empirical Study." *American Sociological Review*, Vol. 24 (1959), pp. 791–95.

——— "The Comparative Analysis of Organizations." In James March, ed. *Handbook of Organizations*. Chicago: Rand McNally, 1965.

Urwick, L. *The Elements of Administration*. New York: Harper, 1943.

Utterback, J. M. "The Process of Technological Innovation Within the Firm." *Academy of Management Journal*, Vol. 12 (1971), pp. 75–88.

V

Van de Ven, Andrew, and André Delbecq. "A Task Contingent Model of Work Unit Structure." (June, 1974).

Von Bertalanffy, Ludwig. "General Systems Theory." In *General Systems*, the yearbook of the Society for the Advancement of General Systems Theory, Vol. 1 (1956), pp. 1–10.

Vroom, Victor. *Some Personality Determinants of the Effects of Participation*. Englewood Cliffs, N. J.: Prentice-Hall, 1960.

——— *Work and Motivation*. New York: Wiley, 1964.

W

Walker, C. R., and R. H. Guest. *The Man on the Assembly Line*. Cambridge, Mass.: Harvard University Press, 1952.

Walker, C. W. "Life in the Automatic Factory." *Harvard Business Review* (January–February, 1958), pp. 111–19.

Walker, J. "The Diffusion of Innovations Among the American States." *American Political Science Review*, Vol. 63 (1969), pp. 880–99.

Walton, R. E., and J. M. Dutton. "The Management of Interdependent Conflict: A Model and Review." *Administrative Science Quarterly*, Vol. 14 (1969), pp. 73–84.

Ward, J. H., Jr. "Hierarchical Grouping to Optimize an Objective Function." *Journal of American Statistical Association*, Vol. 58 (1963), pp. 236–45.

Weber, Max. *The Theory of Social and Economic Organizations*. Edited by Talcott Parsons; translated by Talcott Parsons and A. M. Henderson. New York: Oxford University Press, 1947.

Weick, Karl. "Laboratory Experimentation with Organizations." In James March, ed. *Handbook of Organizations*. Chicago: Rand McNally, 1965.

Wegner, R., and Leonard Sayles. *Cases in Organizational and Administrative Behavior*. Englewood Cliffs, N. J.: Prentice-Hall, 1972.

Weldon, Peter D. "An Examination of the Blau-Scott and Etzioni Typologies: A Critique." *Administrative Science Quarterly*, Vol. 17 (1972), pp. 76–78.

Wertheimer, Max. "Untersuchungen zur Lehre von der Gestalt." *Psychologische Forschung*, Vol. 4 (1923), pp. 301–50.

Whisler, T., and others. "Centralization of Organizational Control: An Empirical Study of Its Meaning and Measurement." *Journal of Business*, Vol. 40 (1967), pp. 10–26.

White, Leslie. *The Science of Culture*. New York: Farrar, Straus, 1949.

White, R., and R. Lippitt. *Autocracy in Democracy: An Experimental Inquiry*. New York: Harper & Row, 1960.

Whyte, W. F. *Human Relations in the Restaurant Industry*. New York: McGraw-Hill, 1948.

——— *Organizational Behavior: Theory and Application*. Homewood, Ill.: Irwin, 1969.

——— *The Organization Man*. New York: Simon and Schuster, 1956.

Williamson, Oliver. "A Model of Rational Managerial Behavior." In R. M. Cyert and James March, eds., *A Behavioral Theory of the Firm*. Englewood Cliffs, N. J.: Prentice-Hall, 1963.

Wilson, James Q. "Innovation in Organization: Notes Toward a Theory." In Lloyd A. Rowe and William B. Boise, eds. *Organizational and Managerial Innovation*. Pacific Palisades, Calif.: Goodyear, 1973.

Woodward, Joan. *Industrial Organization: Theory and Practice*. London: Oxford University Press, 1965.

——— *Management and Technology*. London: Her Majesty's Stationery Office, 1958.

——— *Technology and Organization*. London: Her Majesty's Printery, 1958.

Worthy, J. C. "Organization Structure and Employee Morale." *American Sociological Review*, Vol. 15 (1950), pp. 169–79.

Y

Yoshino, M. Y. *Japan's Managerial System: Tradition and Innovation*. Cambridge, Mass.: M. I. T. Press, 1968.

Z

Zald, M. N. "Comparative Analysis and Measurement of Organizational Goals: The Case of Correctional Institutions for Delinquents." *Sociological Quarterly*, Vol. 4 (1963), pp. 206–30.

Zaleznick, Abraham. "The Dynamics of Subordinacy." *Harvard Business Review* (May–June, 1965).

Appendix A
A Brief Description
of Khandwalla's
Study of Canadian Firms

SAMPLE AND METHOD

The sample consists of 103 Canadian firms. About two-thirds were manufacturing organizations, and about a third were service firms. The sample consisted mostly of public firms selected from the *Financial Post Survey of Industrials*. Initially, about 500 firms were picked randomly from those listed in the *Survey*. About 20 percent of those contacted agreed to participate, so the resulting response sample was nonrandom. However, the sample appeared to show reasonably good variation in terms of firm size, profitability, age, industry affiliation, and technology. Table A–1 provides some relevant statistics on the sample.

The data were gathered during 1972–74 through a carefully pre-tested comprehensive questionnaire.[1] The questionnaire was designed to be filled out anonymously by senior, experienced executives, and in the case of 60 percent of the firms, separate questionnaires were filled out by two or more executives. Approximately 95 percent of the respondents designated themselves as members of "topmost management" or "senior management." Informal checks with 20 firms indicated that the questionnaire was indeed nearly always completed at senior (vice president and above) management levels. In the case of those firms from which two or more questionnaires were received, the data were averaged for greater reliability.

Generally speaking, reliance on just one or two sources of information per organization is hazardous. However, in the Canadian sample information was generally sought (a) about matters of fact rather than of feelings; (b) about matters that are of particular concern to top management, such as the nature of the external environment, top management goals, top management philosophy, delegation of authority by the *chief executive*, and the like, and indeed about matters for which reliable information is available primarily only at the top management levels. If, therefore, the reliable information source in the study is primarily the top management, then it can be seen that one or two members of this group is not an unduly small sampling of opinion about what the firm's overall design is like.

TABLE A–1
Characteristics of the Sample
(N = 103)

Firm size (annual sales or revenues in millions)		
Average		$133
Standard deviation		$257
Range		$0.1 to $1,500
Firm age		
Average		49 years
Standard deviation		45 years
Range		3 years to 302 years
Profitability of firm (average before tax return on net worth)		
Average		15%
Standard deviation		12%
Range		−35% to 75%
Annual rate of growth of sales or revenues of firm during past 5 years		
Average		14%
Standard deviation		14%
Range		−12% to 100%
Industry		
Manufacturing industries		
Consumer nondurable goods industries	21%	
Consumer durable goods industries	5%	
Producer goods industries	26%	
Capital goods industries	11%	63%
Service industries		
Merchandising	9%	
Finance and investments	13%	
Utilities	5%	
Miscellaneous	10%	37%

OPERATIONAL MEASURES OF VARIABLES

The Canadian study afforded the measurement of a number of situational, strategic, structural, and performance variables. The operational measures of the more important ones are described below. Since many multiscale items consist of scales utilized in widely separated parts of the questionnaire, minor alterations, such as scale reversals, have had to be made to make it easy to see how a variable was measured. The complete instrument is reproduced at the end of this Appendix.

Demographic Variables

Size was measured in terms of the firm's total sales or revenues for the latest year. The logarithm of this figure was used to dampen the extreme variability in size and achieve a more normal distribution. Age was taken as age since the firm was founded.

Environmental Variables

Industry growth rate, research and development activity in the industry, and variability in the size of the industry were measured as shown in the following scales:

Please answer the following questions for the *industry* that accounts for the *largest* % of your sales (in other words, your principal industry).

The approximate annual growth rate during the past 5 years _____ %

Research and development activity in the industry

| Virtually no R & D in industry (e.g., bakery, publishing, real estate) | 1 2 3 4 5 6 7 | Extremely R & D oriented industry (e.g., telecommunications, space, drugs) |

How variable is the size of your industry? In other words, given the long-term trend in industry sales, how far does its size fluctuate around this trend line in a typical industry business cycle?

| Essentially no variation from the trend line (e.g., dairy products, newspapers, tobacco, rail passenger transportation | 1 2 3 4 5 6 7 | Extremely large fluctuations around the trend line (e.g., the construction industry) |

The *rate of innovation* in the firm's main industry affecting the firm was measured by using the following scales:

How *rapid* is each of the following in your main industry? Please circle the number in each scale that best approximates the actual conditions in it. If an item is not relevant to your industry, write N.A.

Rate of innovation of new or better operating *processes* used in industry

No changes in processes   1   2   3   4   5   6   7   Extremely rapid rate of
in past decade   innovation revolutioniz-
                                               ing the technology used
in industry during past decade (e.g., the electronics industry)

Rate of innovation of new or better *products (or services)* in industry

No new products in past   1   2   3   4   5   6   7   Extremely rapid rate of
decade   innovation; many, many
new products (e.g., the drug industry)

Rating on each of the two scores above was multiplied by the rating for the importance to top management of the relevant form of innovation in view of its impact on the long-term profitability or growth of the firm. These importance of innovation scales were also 7-point scales in which $1 =$ little importance; and $7 =$ extreme importance. To reduce variability and achieve a more normal distribution, the square roots of the two products were taken and aggregated. The resulting score was the rate of innovation in the industry affecting the firm.

Competitive pressure on the firm was measured by utilizing the following scales:

How *intense* is each of the following in your main industry? Please circle the number in each scale that best approximates the actual condition in it. If an item is not relevant to your industry, write N.A.

Competition for purchases or inputs (e.g., raw materials in the case of manufactures, cash in the case of banks) parts, or equipment

Negligible   1   2   3   4   5   6   7   Extremely intense (e.g.,
                                               meat packing, gas distribution)

Competition for technical manpower such as engineers, accountants, programmers

| Negligible | 1 2 3 4 5 6 7 | Extremely intense (e.g., EDP, health industry for doctors) |

Competition in promotion, advertising, selling, distribution, etc., in main industry

| Virtually none—a single seller in the market | 1 2 3 4 5 6 7 | Extremely intense (e.g., cigarettes, cars, detergents) |

Competition in the quality and variety of products or services

| Virtually none—a homogeneous product or service industry (e.g., an electric utility) | 1 2 3 4 5 6 7 | Extremely intense (e.g., the auto industry, textiles) |

Price competition in industry

| None (a monopoly) | 1 2 3 4 5 6 7 | Extremely intense, "cut throat" (e.g., discount retailing, garments) |

Corresponding to the scale for the intensity of each competition was a 7-point scale for the importance accorded to that form of competition by the top management in view of its impact on the long-term profitability and growth of the firm. In the scale, $1 =$ little importance and $7 =$ extreme importance. The ratings on the two scales for each form were multiplied and the square root of the product was taken to dampen variability. The resulting scores of competitive pressure for the five forms were aggregated to secure a measure of the competitive pressure on the firm.

The following scales were used to measure various *attributes of* the *external environment:*

How would you characterize the *external* environment within which your firm functions? In rating your environment, where relevant, please consider not only the economic, but also the social, political, and technological aspects of the environment.

1. Very homogeneous (e.g., a single, undifferentiated market and very similar customers)   1 2 3 4 5 6 7   Mixed   Very heterogeneous (e.g., a great diversity of markets, types of customers, etc.)

2. Very dynamic, changing rapidly in technical, economic, and cultural dimensions   1 2 3 4 5 6 7   Mixed   Very stable; virtually no change

3. Very safe; little threat to survival and well-being of the firm

1 2 3 4 5 6 7
Mixed

Very risky; a false step can mean the firm's undoing

4. Very unpredictable; very hard to anticipate the nature or direction of changes in the environment

1 2 3 4 5 6 7
Mixed

Very predictable; very easy to forecast the future state of affairs in the environment

5. Very rapidly expanding through the rapid expansion of old markets and the emergence of new ones

1 2 3 4 5 6 7
Mixed

Very stagnant or even shrinking markets

6. Very strong cyclical or other *periodic* fluctuation

1 2 3 4 5 6 7
Mixed

Virtually no *periodic* fluctuation

7. Rich in investment and marketing opportunities; not at all stressful

1 2 3 4 5 6 7
Mixed

Very stressful, exacting, hostile; very hard to keep afloat

8. Technologically, a very sophisticated and complex environment

1 2 3 4 5 6 7
Mixed

An environment demanding little in the way of technological sophistication

9. A dominating environment, in which your firm's initiatives count for very little against the tremendous forces of your business or political environment

1 2 3 4 5 6 7
Mixed

An environment that your firm can control and manipulate to its own advantage (e.g., a dominant firm in an industry has with little competition and few hindrances)

10. A very restrictive, constraining environment (e.g., severe legal constraints, social or economic or political constraints, such as for a regulated monopoly)

1 2 3 4 5 6 7
Mixed

A very constraint-free, unrestricted environment

Environmental *heterogeneity* was measured through scale 1 above. Ratings on scales 2, 4, 5, and 6 were aggregated for measuring environmental *turbulence* after reversing them. Ratings on 3, 7, and 9 were aggregated for measuring environmental *hostility* after reversing the number 9 scale. Environmental *technical complexity* was measured by scale 8, and environmental *restrictiveness* was measured through scale number 10. In both cases the scales were reversed for the purpose of data analysis.

Strategic Variables

Performance aspirations. The ratings on the following scales were aggregated to measure the performance aspirations of top management:

How important are the following goals to your firm's top management in making *strategic* decisions or commitments of a long-term nature?

Earning a high, above average profit	Moderately important	1 2 3 4 5 6 7 Quite important	Extremely important

Achieving a high, above average rate of growth in sales or revenue	Moderately important	1 2 3 4 5 6 7 Quite important	Extremely important

Retaining or securing high, above average liquidity and financial strength	Moderately important	1 2 3 4 5 6 7 Quite important	Extremely important

Maintaining or securing high, above average employee morale, job satisfaction, and commitment to firm's objectives	Moderately important	1 2 3 4 5 6 7 Quite important	Extremely important

Achieving or maintaining an excellent public image	Moderately important	1 2 3 4 5 6 7 Quite important	Extremely important

Orientation to diversification and vertical integration. The ratings on the following scales were taken to measure these:

An operating top management philosophy of

Concentration on a single group of related products or a single industry; great emphasis on defining one's industry and sticking to it.	1 2 3 4 5 6 7	Strong emphasis on diversification of products or services, even if it means venturing into unrelated industries

Strong avoidance of	1 2 3 4 5 6 7	Strong tendency to inte-
vertical integration		grate vertically, such as
		by acquiring raw ma-
		terial sources and pro-
		cessing facilities and/or
		by acquiring wholesal-
		ing and even retailing
		channels

Standardization orientation. The aggregated ratings on the following two scales measured:

An operating top management philosophy of

Strong emphasis on a	1 2 3 4 5 6 7	Strong emphasis on a
technology that can en-		mass-produced stan-
able the firm to offer		dardized product or ser-
products or services		vice-oriented technology
tailored to individual		
customer's needs		

High quality, high price	1 2 3 4 5 6 7	Standard quality, low or
orientation		popular price orienta-
		tion

Risk taking. The ratings on the following six scales were aggregated to secure a measure of how far top management was oriented to risk taking and entrepreneurship. The higher the score, the more risk taking was the style; the lower the score, the more conservative it was.

In top level decision-making, the use of the *entrepreneurial mode,* characterized by active search for big new opportunities; large, bold decisions despite the uncertainty of their outcomes; a charismatic decision maker at the top wielding great power; and rapid growth as the dominant organization goal.

Little resemblance to	1 2 3 4 5 6 7	Very great resemblance
style of top level deci-		to style of top level de-
sion-making in firm		cision-making in firm

In top level decision-making, the use of the *adaptive mode,* characterized by a cautious, pragmatic, one small step at a time adjustment to problems. Decisions are generally compromises between the conflicting demands of owners, unions, government, managers, customers, etc. They are made locally more often than centrally, and the primary concern is with stability and steady growth.

Very great resemblance	1 2 3 4 5 6 7	Little resemblance to
to style of top level de-		style of top level deci-
cision-making in firm		sion-making in firm

An operating top management philosophy of

Strong emphasis on the   1 2 3 4 5 6 7   Strong emphasis on re-
marketing of true and   search and development,
tried products and ser-   technological leadership,
vices and the avoidance   and innovations
of heavy research and
development costs

Strong proclivity to low   1 2 3 4 5 6 7   Strong proclivity to high
risk, moderate return   risk, high return invest-
investments (e.g., virtu-   ments (e.g., 20% R.O.I.
ally certain 10% R.O.I.   after tax with a chance
after tax)   of earning nothing

Policy of growth pri-   1 2 3 4 5 6 7   Policy of growth primarily through inter-   marily through external
nally generated funds   financing (borrowings,
(retained earnings)   capital issues, etc.)

A philosophy of cooper-   1 2 3 4 5 6 7   Very competitive, "un-
ative coexistence with   do-the-competitors" phi-
rival firms within the   losophy
limits of the law

Optimization. The ratings on the following eight scales were aggregated to derive a measure of how oriented the top management was to the optimal use of resources through planning and the use of management science methods and techniques. The higher the score, the more planning and optimization oriented it was; the lower the score, the more seat-of-the-pants judgments oriented it was.

In top level decision-making, the use of the *planning mode,* characterized by systematic search for opportunities and anticipation of problems; a systematic consideration of costs and benefits of alternatives; and a conscious attempt at integrating programs of action to achieve specified goals efficiently. The accent is on profit maximization, long-term planning, very careful screening of investments to minimize risks, and the extensive use of expertise and solid research before making decisions.

Little resemblance to   1 2 3 4 5 6 7   Very great resemblance
style of top level deci-   to style of top level de-
sion-making in firm   cision-making in firm

The strategic, long-term importance to top management of forecasting sales, customer preferences, technology, etc.

Little strategic impor-   1 2 3 4 5 6 7   Extreme strategic im-
tance   portance

The strategic, long-term importance to top management of the application of operations research techniques, such as linear programming and simulation, to operations, distribution, inventory and cash management, etc.

Little strategic impor- 1 2 3 4 5 6 7   Extreme strategic im-
tance   portance

The strategic, long-term importance to top management of market research

Little strategic impor- 1 2 3 4 5 6 7   Extreme strategic im-
tance   portance

The strategic, long-term importance to top management of planning of long-term investments and their financing (long-term capital budgeting)

Little strategic impor- 1 2 3 4 5 6 7   Extreme strategic im-
tance   portance

An operating top management philosophy of

In decision-making, 1 2 3 4 5 6 7   In decision-making
great reliance on per-   great reliance on spe-
sonnel with experience   cialized, technically
and common sense   trained line and staff
                                            personnel

A bird-in-the-hand em- 1 2 3 4 5 6 7   Emphasis on long-term
phasis on the immediate   (over 5 years) plan-
future in making man-   ning of goals and strat-
agement decisions   egy

Heavy reliance on ap- 1 2 3 4 5 6 7   Heavy reliance on for-
prenticeship "learning   mal management-train-
by hard knocks"   ing programs

Participation. The ratings on the following ten scales were aggregated to derive a measure of how participatively oriented the top management's ideology and style were:

To what extent is decision-making at top levels in your firm characterized by participative, group or democratic decision-making, in relation to the following classes of decision:

Product- or service-related decisions concerning level of operations, marketing strategy, research and development of new products or services, etc.

No participation: the 1 2 3 4 5 6 7   Decisions made by top
responsible top execu- Responsible executives management groups or
tives make the decisions discuss with others be- committees after full
using existing informa- fore deciding   discussion and attempt
tion   at reaching consensus—
                                               failing which decisions
                                               are taken by majority
                                               vote

Capital budget decisions (selection and financing of long-term investments)

No participation: the responsible top executives make the decisions using existing information   1 2 3 4 5 6 7 Responsible executives discuss with others before deciding   Decisions made by top management groups or committees after full discussion and attempt at reaching consensus— failing which decisions are taken by majority vote

Long-term strategy of growth, diversification, etc., and decisions related to changes in the firm's operating philosophy

No participation: the responsible top executives make the decisions using existing information   1 2 3 4 5 6 7 Responsible executives discuss with others before deciding   Decisions made by top management groups or committees after full discussion and attempt at reaching consensus— failing which decisions are taken by majority vote

The firm's operating management philosophy is

Strongly individualistic decision-making by the formally responsible executive   1 2 3 4 5 6 7   Strongly group or committee oriented consensus-seeking, participative decision-making

The strategic, long-term importance to top management of participative decision-making at middle and senior management levels

Little strategic importance   1 2 3 4 5 6 7   Extreme strategic importance

The strategic, long-term importance of management by objectives (goal setting by subordinates with their superiors' help)

Little strategic importance   1 2 3 4 5 6 7   Extreme strategic importance

To reduce conflict between groups in the firm, or for improving coordination, or for effective collaboration between personnel:
(a) Human relations training for managers to make them understand better their colleagues and subordinates, and to help them communicate more effectively with them

Not common at all   1 2 3 4 5 6 7   Very commonly used

(b) Behavioral science techniques like confrontation meetings, sensitivity training, managerial grid type programs, etc., designed to raise the level of interpersonal competence and maturity of managers, and to create a climate of mutual trust in which conflicts may be discussed openly and settled amicably

Not common at all   1   2   3   4   5   6   7   Very commonly used

In attempts to institute organizational changes, overcoming the resistance of personnel, and getting the required commitment for change:

(a) Train supervisors in *human relations* skills or urge them to use them so that they can ease employees' opposition to the proposed changes and possibly even get their commitment to these changes. Human relations skills involve better communications with subordinates, establishing personal relationships with them, lending a sympathetic ear to their problems, etc.

Seldom used   1   2   3   4   5   6   7   Used very commonly

(b) *Involve* fully those likely to be affected at each phase of the change process—in the articulation of the problem, gathering of pertinent information of the selected course of action—by means of participative, consensus-seeking, *democratic decision-making,* followed by feedback of results of change for group evaluation and further action

Seldom used   1   2   3   4   5   6   7   Used very commonly

Flexibility. The ratings in the following seven scales were aggregated to measure how organic, flexibility oriented was the top management style. The higher the score, the more organic it was; the lower the score, the more mechanistic it was.

An operating top management philosophy of

Highly structured channels of communication and a highly restricted access to important financial and operating information	1 2 3 4 5 6 7	Open channels of communication with important financial and operating information flowing quite freely throughout the organization
Strong insistence on a uniform managerial style throughout the firm	1 2 3 4 5 6 7	Managers' operating styles allowed to range freely from the very formal to the very informal
Strong emphasis on giving the most say in decision-making to formal line managers	1 2 3 4 5 6 7	Strong tendency to let the expert in a given situation have the most say in decision-making even if this means temporary bypassing of formal line authority

A strong emphasis on holding fast to true and tried management principles despite any changes in business conditions	1 2 3 4 5 6 7	A strong emphasis on adapting freely to changing circumstances without too much concern for past practice
Strong emphasis on always getting personnel to follow the formally laid down procedures	1 2 3 4 5 6 7	Strong emphasis on getting things done even if this means disregarding formal procedures
Tight formal control of most operations by means of sophisticated control and information systems	1 2 3 4 5 6 7	Loose, informal control; heavy dependence on informal relationships and norm of cooperation for getting work done
Strong emphasis on getting line and staff personnel to adhere closely to formal job descriptions	1 2 3 4 5 6 7	Strong tendency to let the requirements of the situation and the individual's personality define proper on-job behavior

Coercion. The ratings on the following five scales were summed to measure the coercive orientation of the top management. The higher the score, the more coercive was the style of top management.

How far within your firm do you observe senior managers using force ("Might overcomes right"; "If you cannot make a man think as you do, make him do as you think") as a mode of resolving their disagreements over personal matters and corporate issues?

Seldom used   1 2 3 4 5 6 7   Used very often

In attempting to institute organizational changes, overcome the resistance of personnel to these changes, and get their required commitment, management uses several methods:

Issue orders and implicitly or explicitly *warn* personnel of serious consequences of resisting management orders

Seldom used   1 2 3 4 5 6 7   Used very commonly

Explain *concepts* underlying the proposed changes to those involved or affected by them. In other words, provide detailed *justification* for the changes to those affected by them before or after the changes are effected.

Used very commonly   1 2 3 4 5 6 7   Seldom used

Procure the services of *outside experts,* such as consultants, to investigate the problem and propose changes

Seldom used   1 2 3 4 5 6 7   Used very commonly

For reducing conflict between different groups in the firm, or for improving coordination, or for effective collaboration between personnel, the use of *arbitration procedures:* establishment of procedures for reviewing decisions on a complaint by an aggrieved party or group, such as is common in the field of labor relations

Not common at all   1 2 3 4 5 6 7   Very commonly used

Technological Variables

The following scale was used to measure the automation and *capital intensity* of the firm's operations technology:

How automated is the technology of your operations?

Very little automation (e.g., operations of advertising agencies, auditors, architects, real estate agencies)	1 2 3 4 5 6 7	Completely automated and computerized operations (e.g., those of oil refineries, telephone exchanges)

The following scales were employed to secure a measure of how *mass production oriented* the firm's operations technology was:

To what extent are each of the following technologies used in your firm?

"Custom" technology (production or fabrication of a single unit or few units of products or services to customer specifications or needs—e.g., missile prototypes, patient care in exclusive private clinics, etc.)

Not used at all or minimally used	1 2 3 4 5 6 7	Very extensively used— over 70% of value added by operations attributable to this technology

"Small batch, job shop" technology (creation of small batches of similar units, such as fashionable dresses, tools and dies)

Not used at all or minimally used	1 2 3 4 5 6 7	Very extensively used— over 70% of value added by operations attributable to this technology

"Large batch" technology (e.g., used in manufacturing large batches of drugs and chemicals, parts, cans and bottles, counts of yarn, etc.; in universities used for instructing large batches of students in required courses)

Not used at all or mini- 1 2 3 4 5 6 7 Very extensively used—
mally used   over 70% of value added by operations attributable to this technology

"Mass production" technology (e.g., used in mass production of autos, standard textiles etc., and in computerised telephone exchanges)

Not used at all or mini- 1 2 3 4 5 6 7 Very extensively used—
mally used   over 70% of value added by operations attributable to this technology

"Continuous process" technology (e.g., used in oil refining and other automated industries, in which the output is highly standardized and mechanized and is produced continuously rather than in batches or shifts)

Not used at all or mini- 1 2 3 4 5 6 7 Very extensively used—
mally used   over 70% of value added by operations attributable to this technology

Ratings on the above five scales were given weights respectively of 1, 2, 3, 4, 5. The resulting scores for the use of the five technologies were aggregated to get a score for mass production orientation of operations technology.

The following scale measured the use of *electronic data processing* in the organization:

Not used at all   1 2 3 4 5 6 7 Covers almost all of the firm's internal and external transactions

Structural Variables

Delegation of authority. The ratings on the following scales were aggregated to derive a measure of the extent of delegation of authority by the chief executive:

To what extent has the chief executive of your firm delegated authority to others to make *each* of the following classes of decision? Please rate the *actual* rather than the merely formal delegation of authority. The delegation of authority can be to individuals or groups (e.g., committees).

Raising long-term capital to finance new investments

No delegation of au- 1 2 3 4 5 6 7 Complete delegation of
thority   authority

Development of new products/services

No delegation of au- 1 2 3 4 5 6 7 Complete delegation of
thority authority

Marketing strategy for a new product/service and changes in the marketing strategy for existing products/services

No delegation of au- 1 2 3 4 5 6 7 Complete delegation of
thority authority

The hiring and firing of senior personnel

No delegation of au- 1 2 3 4 5 6 7 Complete delegation of
thority authority

Selection of large new investments

No delegation of au- 1 2 3 4 5 6 7 Complete delegation of
thority authority

Pricing of new products and significant price changes in existing products/services

No delegation of au- 1 2 3 4 5 6 7 Complete delegation of
thority authority

Acquisition of subsidiaries or controlling interest in other firms

No delegation of au- 1 2 3 4 5 6 7 Complete delegation of
thority authority

Bargaining with personnel or their unions about wages, etc.

No delegation of au- 1 2 3 4 5 6 7 Complete delegation of
thority authority

Distributive network. The extent to which the firm's operations were geographically dispersed, a form of spatial diversification and decentralization, was measured as follows:

To what extent is "service technology" used by the firm to serve clientele through branches, dealers, etc.?

Not used at all or mini- 1 2 3 4 5 6 7 Very extensively used—
mally used over 70% of distribution accounted for by this technology

Vertical integration. This was measured by aggregating the scores on the two following scales:

To what extent is your firm vertically integrated?

Backward from operations into lease or ownership of sources of raw materials, processing of raw materials, facilities for producing spares and parts, for fabricating plant and machinery used by your firm, etc.? If your firm is purely a trading or service industry firm, write N.A.

Virtually no integra- 1 2 3 4 5 6 7 Almost fully integrated
tion backwards   backward

Forward from operations into wholesaling and retailing

Virtually no forward in- 1 2 3 4 5 6 7 Almost fully integrated
tegration   forward

Divisionalization. The degree to which the firm was divisionalized was measured by the following scale:

Would you consider yourself to be a highly divisionalized firm given your size?

No divisionalization; es- 1 2 3 4 5 6 7 Divisionalization   and
sentially a single profit   profit centers reaching
center   deep down into all of
                                               the firm's operations
                                               (e.g., G.M.)

Sophistication of control and information system. The ratings in the following scales were aggregated to measure the sophistication of the firm's control and information system:

Please rate the extent to which of the following is used or done in your firm.

Quality control of production or operations by using sampling or other techniques

Not used at all   1 2 3 4 5 6 7 Used to a very great ex-
                                             tent; applied to almost
                                             all operations

Cost control of operations by fixing standard costs and analyzing the variations of actual costs from these standards

Not used at all   1 2 3 4 5 6 7 Used to a very great ex-
                                             tent; applied to almost
                                             all operations

The computation of present values or internal rates of return for evaluating investments

Not used at all   1   2   3   4   5   6   7   Used to a very great extent; applied to almost all investment proposals

Control of inventories, cash, etc., and scheduling of operations by means of mathematical techniques like simulation, linear programming, etc.

Not used at all   1   2   3   4   5   6   7   Used to a very great extent; applied to almost all inventories and operations

Internal auditing

Not used at all   1   2   3   4   5   6   7   Used to a very great extent; covers almost all activities of firm

Systematic evaluation of managerial and senior staff personnel

Not used at all   1   2   3   4   5   6   7   Used to a very great extent; extended to almost all such personnel

Establishment of profit centers and profit targets at various levels below the top management level and in different parts of the firm (profit decentralization)

Not used at all   1   2   3   4   5   6   7   Used to a very great extent; covers almost every branch, department, and division

Establishment of cost centers for cost control of the firm's operations (in a cost center fairly detailed cost targets are developed for activities under its jurisdiction)

Not used at all   1   2   3   4   5   6   7   Used to a very great extent, from the lowest operating level to the highest

Electronic data processing

Not used at all   1   2   3   4   5   6   7   Covers almost all of the firm's internal and external transactions

Research and development and design of products or services and processes

Not done at all   1   2   3   4   5   6   7   Done to a very great extent whether in-house or under contract outside the firm

Long-term forecasting of your firm's sales and profits, and of the size and nature of its markets

| Not done at all | 1 2 3 4 5 6 7 | Done to a very great extent; detailed forecasts for next 5 years or more |

Long-term forecasting of the technology relevant to your firm's products/operations

| Not done at all | 1 2 3 4 5 6 7 | Done to a very great extent; careful, detailed forecasts for next 5 years or more |

Procedures to search for and evaluate systematically potentially profitable investments

| Not used at all | 1 2 3 4 5 6 7 | Used to a very great extent in identifying most growth opportunities |

Planning of long-term investments and their financing (long-term capital budgeting)

| Not done at all | 1 2 3 4 5 6 7 | Done to a very great extent; detailed plans for next 5 years or more |

Market research (systematic study of customer preferences, price and demand analysis of products or services)

| Not done at all | 1 2 3 4 5 6 7 | Done as a matter of course before almost all new offerings, changes, etc. |

Control of Behavior Variables

The following scales were utilized to measure the extent to which management had recourse to various conflict resolution, coordination devices:

Management often uses some or all of the following mechanisms for reducing conflict between different groups in the firm, or for improving coordination, or for effective collaboration between personnel. For example, if there are serious coordination problems between the Marketing and Operations fellows, or for the Maintenance and the Operations people, or the Credit and Sales personnel, some or all of these could be used. Please rate the usage of each of these in your firm.

Task forces or *ad hoc* committees whose objective is to examine a dispute and seek a solution that is optimal for the organization as a whole

Not common at all   1 2 3 4 5 6 7 Very commonly used

Standards and procedures: Clear standards of job performance and detailed procedures for getting tasks accomplished, designed to minimize jurisdictional and other conflicts; explicit procedures for what to do in the event of disagreement between work groups

Not common at all   1 2 3 4 5 6 7 Very commonly used

Hierarchy: Heads of groups in dispute refer disputes to the executive with authority over both

Not common at all   1 2 3 4 5 6 7 Very commonly used

Human relations training for managers to make them understand better their colleagues and subordinates and to help communicate more effectively with them

Not common at all   1 2 3 4 5 6 7 Very commonly used

Behavioral science techniques like confrontation meetings, sensitivity training, managerial grid type programs, etc., designed to raise the level of interpersonal competence and maturity of managers, and to create a climate of mutual trust in which conflicts may be discussed openly and settled amicably

Not common at all   1 2 3 4 5 6 7 Very commonly used

Liaison men: Individuals or groups whose primary function is to help resolve conflicts between organizational groups. Typically they explain to each group the other group's point of view and push for an accommodation by each side. For example, one or two senior executives experienced in marketing as well as operations are assigned the job of ironing out their differences. Or a committee of the representatives of the groups is formed to improve coordination on a continuing basis.

Not common at all   1 2 3 4 5 6 7 Very commonly used

Arbitration procedures: Establishment of procedures for reviewing decisions on a complaint by an aggrieved party or group, such as is common in the field of labor relations.

Not common at all   1 2 3 4 5 6 7 Very commonly used

Performance Variables

Index of subjective relative performance. The ratings on the following scales were summed to derive the top management's estimate of how well the firm was doing *relative* to its competitors:

Compared to your *industry's average,* or, if yours is a very diversified firm, in relation to comparable firms, how do you compare on each of the following:

Long-run level of profitability

Very low   1 2 3 4 5 6 7   Very high
                        About
                        Average

Growth rate of sales or revenues

Very low   1 2 3 4 5 6 7   Very high
                        About
                        Average

Employee morale, job satisfaction, and commitment to firm's objectives

Very low   1 2 3 4 5 6 7   Very high
                        About
                        Average

Financial strength (liquidity and ability to raise financial resources)

Very low   1 2 3 4 5 6 7   Very high
                        About
                        Average

Public image and goodwill

Very low   1 2 3 4 5 6 7   Very high
                        About
                        Average

Index of objective performance. The three constituents of this index were the firm's profitability, the stability of its profitability, and the growth rate of its sales or revenues. The figures for the highest and the lowest rates of return on net worth (before taxes) during the preceding five years reported by the respondents were averaged to secure the average profitability of the firm. The difference between the two rates was taken to be a measure of the instability of its profits (a measure of the riskiness of the firm). The figure for the average annual rate of growth of sales or revenues of the firm during the preceding five years was also elicited from the respondents. All three were in very good agreement with published information where the latter was available.

Next, each of the three distributions were trichotomized on the assumption that their underlying distributions were normal. Since the stock market generally values stability of profits more than instability, the firms in the top third of the scores of the instability of profits received a value of 1, those in the middle third a value of 2, and those with the least instability a value of 3. The firms in the top third of the distribution of profitability each received a score of 3; those in the middle third a score of 2, and those in the lowest third a score of 1. The procedure was repeated in respect to growth rate. Finally, the firm scores on profitability, stability, and growth rate were aggregated to secure an objective index of corporate performance. This ranged from a score of 3 (very low performance) to a score of 9 (very high performance). In data analysis, the scores were dichotomized into high performance and low performance categories. Firms exceeding a score of 5 on the index were categorized as high performers and others (that is, those that scored 3, 4, or 5) were categorized as low performers.

RELIABILITY AND VALIDITY OF VARIABLES

In multi-item variables, reliability or reproducibility was measured by the formula[2]

$$r_{kk} = \frac{kr_{ij}}{1 + (k-1)r_{ij}}$$

where

r_{kk} = reliability or reproducibility of a multi-item measure

k = number of items in the measure

r_{ij} = the average correlation among the items

According to Nunnally, reliabilities of .50 to .60 are quite adequate in early stages of research.[3]

In 60 firms, two senior executives completed the questionnaire. The two executives were picked by the firm's president, and he was requested to get the questionnaire completed independently. The degree of agreement (correlation) between their responses was taken to mean another form of reliability—interjudge reliability. To the extent that senior executives are experts on their firms, the degree of agreement on the information they provide is perhaps one measure also of the validity of the variables. That is, a high degree of agreement, in the absence of ambiguities in the way questions are phrased, bolsters our confidence that the variables do indeed measure what they are intended to measure. In addition, in several cases the findings in this study were consistent with previously established findings of researchers that had employed different data-gathering procedures and done research on different samples of organizations. In other words, several of the variables employed in the Canadian study had construct validity. Several findings attested to the predictive validity of the measures: the relationships between variables were what one would predict them to be.

The reliability or reproducibility and degree of agreement between pairs of senior executives from the same firm are shown in Table A–2.

Reliability of Variables in the Canadian Study

Variable	Reproducibility of multi-item variables	Correlation between responses of two executives (N = 60)	Comments
Situational variables			
Age (as reported)	N.A.	.93	Excellent agreement with published information
Size (as reported)	N.A.	.98	Excellent agreement with published information
Annual growth rate of the firm's principal industry	N.A.	.69 (N = 45)	Good agreement with published industry data
Research and development activity in the firm's industry	N.A.	.58	Fairly good agreement with published industry data. Unfortunately, published data aggregated at too gross a level.
Variability in the size of the firm's industry	N.A.	.43	Good agreement with published industry data.
Rate of innovation in the industry affecting the firm	.76	.61	Correlated with importance of brainstorming to top management. Correlated with the perception of the environment as dynamic.
Competitive pressure on the firm	.56	.61	Correlated with environmental turbulence, hostility, and heterogeneity
Environmental heterogeneity	N.A.	.60	Strongly correlated with reported diversification of the firm's products. Correlated with size of the firm.
Environmental turbulence	.58	.50	Fairly strongly correlated with rate of innovation and competitive pressure. Correlated with risk taking.
Environmental hostility	.56	.22	Significantly negatively correlated with profitability.
Environmental technological complexity	N.A.	.57	Fairly strongly correlated with R & D activity in industry. Eleven chemical, data processing, electrical equipment, and metal-producing firms scored in the top third

Variable	Reproducibility of multi-item variables	Correlation between responses of two executives (N = 60)	Comments
			of distribution; only 2 in the bottom third. Seventeen foodstuffs, merchandising, property development, and construction firms scored in the bottom third; only two in the top third.
Environmental restrictiveness	N.A.	.64	Strongly correlated with reported constraints on growth due to government regulations. Thirteen banks, trusts, and utilities scored in top third of distribution; none in the bottom third.
Strategic variables			
Performance aspirations of top management	.69	.38	Correlated with index of relative performance.
Orientation to standardization	.45	.48	
Orientation to diversification	N.A.	.35	Correlated with divisionalization. Consistent with other published findings.[a]
Orientation to vertical integration	N.A.	.61	Correlated strongly with vertical integration.
Risk taking	.53	.58	Correlated with instability of profit and growth rate of sales. Negatively correlated with age of firm.
Optimization	.80	.72	Correlated with complexity in the environment. Also with the index of performance relative to rivals. Consistent with other published findings.[b]
Participation	.85	.57	Correlated with importance of employee morale to top

Variable	Reproducibility of multi-item variables	Correlation between responses of two executives (N = 60)	Comments
			management. Correlated with perceived quality of collaboration among executives. Strongly correlated with optimization orientation. Correlated with organization size.
Flexibility	.68	.52	Correlated with rate of innovation industry. Consistent with other published findings.[c]
Coercion	.52	.49	Correlated negatively with both importance of employee morale to top management and reported quality of collaboration at senior management levels.
Technological and structural variables			
Automation of operations technology	N.A.	.29	Correlated with size of firm and technological sophistication of firm's environment.
Mass production orientation of operations technology	N.A. (not constructed on the basis of the domain sampling model)[d]	.28	Validity marred by non-applicability to some service firms. Still, correlated with size of firm.
Use of electronic data processing	N.A.	.76	Correlated with size of firm and with optimization.
Delegation of authority by chief executive	.81	.55	Correlated with firm size and sophistication of C.I.S.; consistent with other published findings.[e]
Divisionalization	N.A.	.61	Agrees we limit actual divisionalization where published data disclosed it.

Variable	Reproduci- bility of multi-item variables	Correlation between re- sponses of two execu- tives (N = 60)	Comments
Sophistication of con- trol and information system (C.I.S.)	.80	.64	Correlated with firm size. Consistent with other pub- lished findings.[f] Correlated with optimization.
Distributive network	N.A.	.67	
Vertical integration	.69	.55	Correlated with mass produc- tion orientation of technol- ogy. Consistent with other published findings.[g]
Control of behavior variables			
The use of task forces to resolve disagree- ments	N.A.	.23	Correlated with R & D activ- ity in industry.
Standards and proce- dures to minimize conflicts	N.A.	.30	Negatively correlated with flexibility. Correlated with size.
Recourse to hierarchy to settle disputes	N.A.	.28	Correlated with conflict be- tween marketing and opera- tions personnel.
Human relations train- ing to improve com- munications	N.A.	.68	Correlated with importance of employee morale to top management.
Behavioral science techniques to create a collaborative cli- mate	N.A.	.35	Correlated with technological sophistication of environment.
Liaison men to mini- mize interdepartmen- tal frictions	N.A.	.11	Correlated with conflict be- tween marketing and opera- tions personnel.
Arbitration procedures	N.A.	.36	Correlated with the use of threats by management in effecting organizational changes.
Performance Variables			
Index of subjectively rated relative per- formance	.84	.59	Fairly strongly correlated with the index of objective performance.

TABLE A–2 (Continued)

Variable	Reproducibility of multi-item variables	Correlation between responses of two executives (N = 60)	Comments
Index of objective performance	N.A. (not constructed on the basis of the domain sampling model)	.93	

[a] E.g., Alfred Chandler, *Strategy and Structure.*

[b] E.g., S. Thune and Robert House, "When Long-Range Planning Pays-Off," *Business Horizons,* August 1970.

[c] E.g., T. Burns and A. M. Stalker, *The Management of Innovation* (London: Tavistock, 1961).

[d] A multi-item variable is constructed on the basis of the domain sampling model when any particular measure is composed of a random sample of items from a hypothetical domain of items [Jim C. Nunnally, *Psychometric Theory* (New York: McGraw-Hill, 1967), p. 175]. This was not the case for the measure of mass output orientation of technology, as well as of the objective index of performance.

[e] E.g., D. S. Pugh, D. J. Hickson, C. R. Hinings, and C. Turner, "The Context of Organizational Structures," *Administrative Science Quarterly,* Vol. 14 (1969), pp. 91–114.

[f] See D. S. Pugh, D. J. Hickson, and C. R. Hinings, "An Empirical Taxonomy of Structures of Work Organizations," *Administrative Science Quarterly,* Vol. 14 (1969), pp. 116–26.

[g] P. N. Khandwalla, "Mass output orientation of operations technology and organizational structure," *Administrative Science Quarterly* (March 1974), pp. 74–97, for similar results in a study of U.S. manufacturing firms.

SIGNIFICANT INTERRELATIONS AMONG MAJOR VARIABLES

Table A–3 shows those Pearson correlations between the major variables that are significantly different from zero at a minimum of 95 percent confidence level.

TABLE A–3

Statistically Significant Pearson Correlations for the Major Variables in the Canadian Study

N = 103

	Demographic		Environmental				Strategic			
	2	*3*	*4*	*5*	*6*	*7*	*8*	*9*	*10*	*11*
Demographic variables										
1. Age of the firm	35	−28	−21	..	..	24	..	−34	..	..
2. Size of the firm (log. of sales)	..	..	..	31	..	27	..	..	..	32
Environmental variables										
3. Turbulence	..	..	33	..	..	..	22	50	19	..
4. Hostility	..	..	..	..	..	..	..	24	..	..
5. Heterogeneity	..	..	..	..	..	..	..	..	23	30
6. Technological sophistication	..	..	..	..	..	..	..	..	28	..
7. Restrictiveness	..	..	..	..	..	..	..	..	38	22
Strategic variables										
8. Performance aspirations	..	..	..	..	..	..	..	..	29	31
9. Risk taking	..	..	..	..	..	..	..	..	..	..
10. Optimization	..	..	..	..	..	..	..	..	..	54
11. Participation	..	..	..	..	..	..	..	..	..	..
12. Flexibility	..	..	..	..	..	..	..	..	..	..
13. Coercion	..	..	..	..	..	..	..	..	..	..
14. Orientation to diversification of outputs	..	..	..	..	..	..	..	..	..	..
15. Orientation to vertical integration	..	..	..	..	..	..	..	..	..	..
16. Standardization orientation	..	..	..	..	..	..	..	..	..	..
Technological variables										
17. Extent of automation	..	..	..	..	..	..	..	..	..	..
18. Mass production of orientation of technology	..	..	..	..	..	..	..	..	..	..
19. Use of electronic data processing	..	..	..	..	..	..	..	..	..	..
Structural variables										
20. Sophistication of control and information system (C.I.S.)	..	..	..	..	..	..	..	..	..	..
21. Delegation of authority by chief executive	..	..	..	..	..	..	..	..	..	..
22. Divisionalization	..	..	..	..	..	..	..	..	..	..
23. Vertical integration	..	..	..	..	..	..	..	..	..	..
24. Distributive network	..	..	..	..	..	..	..	..	..	..
Performance variables										
25. Objective index of performance	..	..	..	..	..	..	..	..	..	..
26. Index of subjectively rated relative performance	..	..	..	..	..	27	..	..	..	..

| | Strategic | | | | | Technological | | | Structural | | | | | Performance | |
	12	13	14	15	16	17	18	19	20	21	22	23	24	25	26
	..	..	..	..	..	..	..	..	..	..	..	..	..	..	..
	..	..	..	23	..	35	33	49	43	25	47	28	..	..	..
	..	..	..	..	..	..	..	..	..	..	..	20	..	..	..
	..	..	..	..	28	..	..	..	..	..	..	..	..	−28	−27
	..	−19	20	..	..	19	26	26	31	25	29	..	19	..	21
	..	..	28	..	−21	45	27	25	34	..	..	..	..	..	..
	..	..	..	..	..	30	..	36	27	..	..	..	31	21	..
	..	−19	..	..	..	..	..	..	30	22	22	..	29	19	35
	..	..	28	..	..	..	..	..	20	..	..	20	..	..	..
	−19	..	..	..	..	27	..	38	62	23	..	21	..	..	21
	..	..	25	..	..	30	25	33	56	44	20	..	21	..	36
	..	..	..	..	..	−22	..	..	..	..	..	−21	..	..	..
	..	..	..	..	..	..	..	..	..	..	..	..	..	..	27
	..	..	..	..	..	..	..	..	..	..	26	..	..	..	..
	..	..	..	..	..	21	..	..	24	19	32	57	..	..	..
	..	..	..	..	..	..	..	..	..	..	..	..	..	..	..
	..	..	..	..	..	..	45	56	43	28	..	28	20	..	..
	..	..	..	..	..	..	..	20	30	21	22	23	..	..	..
	..	..	..	..	..	..	..	..	55	40	..	27	35	22	..
	..	..	..	..	..	..	..	..	..	34	38	25	35	..	..
	..	..	..	..	..	..	..	..	..	..	..	22	23	24	19
	..	..	..	..	..	..	..	..	..	..	..	27	..	..	..
	..	..	..	..	..	..	..	..	..	..	..	..	..	..	..
	..	..	..	..	..	..	..	..	..	..	..	..	..	31	..
	..	..	..	..	..	..	..	..	..	..	..	..	..	..	33
	..	..	..	..	..	..	..	..	..	..	..	..	..	..	..

NOTE: Decimal points are omitted. For a sample size of 103, a correlation of plus or minus .19 is significant at the 5% level (both tails); ± .25 is significant at the 1% level. Only statistically significant correlations are reported in the table.

SENIOR EXECUTIVE'S QUESTIONNAIRE

This questionnaire is being administered as part of Dr. Pradip Khand-walla's study of corporate designs. The questionnaire is designed to gather information about your firm's organization structure and behavior, its environment, the nature of its industry, its policies, etc. No questions of a personal nature are asked, nor is any proprietary information requested. The questionnaire has been designed for manufacturing as well as non-manufacturing firms.

The questionnaire is to be filled out only by a senior executive who has adequate familiarity with the firm's operations and its business environment. The firm in this questionnaire means the entity of which you are a senior executive, whether it be a division, a subsidiary, or an independent corporation. All questions, unless otherwise stated, refer to this entity's operations, policies, environment, etc.

Most of the questions are rating scales. Please circle the number in each scale that seems closest to describing the reality as you perceive it. Feel free to make any additional explanatory or qualifying comments under the relevant scale. *For all scale items, 1 represents the statement on the left and 7 the statement on the right.*

Please answer all the questions, as incomplete questionnaires create severe problems in data analysis. After completing the questionnaire, please check to see that no questions are left unanswered.

The information supplied in this questionnaire will be kept in the strictest confidence, and will not be divulged to anyone except in aggregated form and for bona fide research purposes.

The main findings of this study will be made available to all participating firms. After completion, please return the questionnaire to Dr. P. N. Khandwalla, Faculty of Management, McGill University, Montreal 101, Quebec, Canada.

Name of firm:

Independent corporation, subsidiary, or division? Please underline.

Nature of business:

Size of operations: Approximate annual sales/revenues............................

                         Approximate number of employees............................

Your position in firm:
    Topmost management (........) Senior management (........)
    Middle management   (........) Other (........)

Your responsibilities (optional):

Service oriented firms (such as banks) please note: In the questionnaire, sales = gross income or revenues; product = service, manufacturing or production = principal operations of the firm (e.g., banking operations). Write N.A. where an item appears to be clearly irrelevant to your type of business.

Main Industry in Which Your Firm Operates

In this section, a number of questions are asked about your principal industry. Please name the main industries in which your firm operates and indicate the approximate share of your total sales or revenues in these industries. What is requested is not your market share in these industries, but what portion of your total sales or revenues is derived from each of them. Please identify each industry as precisely as you can (e.g., banking rather than finance; industrial chemicals rather than chemicals; construction machinery rather than machinery; life insurance rather than insurance).

	Name of Industry	% of Your Sales or Revenues
1.	---	--------------------
2.	---	--------------------
3.	---	--------------------
4.	---	--------------------
(other) 5.	---	--------------------

Please answer the following questions for the *industry* that accounts for the *largest* % of your sales (in other words, your principal industry).

1. The approximate annual growth rate during the past 5 years ....%

2. The market share of the 4 largest firms in this industry ....%

3. Are you one of these 4 firms? ....

4. Research and Development activity in the industry*

   Virtually no R & D industry (e.g., bakery, publishing, real estate)   1   2   3   4   5   6   7   Extremely R & D oriented industry (e.g., telecommunications, space, drugs)

5. How many distinct product lines or services are marketed in the industry?

   Every firm in the industry markets essentially the same product or service (e.g., electricity, flour milling, ingot steel)   1   2   3   4   5   6   7   Very great diversity of product services marketed (e.g., the pharmaceutical industry, textiles, garments)

* In this scale, as in all other scales in this questionnaire, the left hand statement is equivalent to 1, and the right hand statement is equal to 7.

6. The diversity in the requirements of the customers in your industry (in other words, the range of their demands)

Essentially, custom- 1 2 3 4 5 6 7 Very great diversity in
ers with relatively   the requirements of cus-
homogeneous re-   tomers (e.g., customers
quirements (e.g.,   of insurance companies,
customers of the tel-   furniture industry, de-
ephone industry)   partment stores, etc.)

7. How variable is the size of your industry? In other words, given the long-term trend in industry sales, how far does its size fluctuate around this trend line in a typical industry business cycle?

Essentially no varia- 1 2 3 4 5 6 7 Extremely large fluctuation from the trend   tions around the trend
line (e.g., dairy prod-   line (e.g., the construc-
ucts, newspapers, to-   tion industry)
bacco, rail passenger
transportation)

8. How *rapid* or *intense* is each of the following in your main industry? Please circle the number in each scale that best approximates the actual conditions in it. If an item is not relevant to your industry, write N.A.

Competition for pur-   Negligible   1 2 3 4 5 6 7   Extremely intense
chases or inputs (e.g.,   (e.g., meat pack-
raw materials in the   ing, gas distribu-
case of manufactur-   tion)
ers, cash in the case
of banks), parts, or
equipment

Competition for tech-   Negligible   1 2 3 4 5 6 7   Extremely intense
nical manpower such   (e.g., EDP, health
as engineers, ac-   industry for doc-
countants, program-   tors)
mers, etc.

Rate at which prod-   Negligible   1 2 3 4 5 6 7   Extremely rapid,
uts or services are   (e.g., a basic   as in some fash-
getting obsolete in the metal like   ionable goods
industry   copper)

Competition in pro-   Virtually   1 2 3 4 5 6 7   Extremely intense
motion, advertising,   none—a   (e.g., cigarettes,
etc., in main indus-   single seller   cars, detergents)
try   in the market

Rate of innovation of   No changes   1 2 3 4 5 6 7   Extremely   rapid
new or better oper-   in processes   rate of innovation,

ating processes used in industry	in past decade			revolutionizing the technology used in industry during past decade (e.g., the electronic industry)
Competition in the quality and variety of products or services	Virtually none—a homogeneous product or service industry (e.g., an electric utility)	1 2 3 4 5 6 7		Extremely intense (e.g., the auto industry, textiles)
Price competition in industry	None (e.g., a monopoly	1 2 3 4 5 6 7		Extremely intense "cut throat" (e.g., discount retailing, garments)
Rate of innovation of new or better products (or services) in industry	No new products in past decade	1 2 3 4 5 6 7		Extremely rapid rate of innovation: many, many new products (e.g., the drug industry)
Rate of increase of labor productivity in industry during recent years in the area of operations	1% or less increase a year or even declining productivity	1 2 3 4 5 6 7		Extremely rapid rate of increase— 7% or over a year
What is the average hourly wage rate of operatives in your industry?	$1.0 or less per blue collar man-hour	1 2 3 4 5 6 7	Around $4	Very high—$7.0 or over per blue collar man hour
Competition in delivery and after sales services	Virtually none (e.g., chocolates and many other perishables)	1 2 3 4 5 6 7		Extremely intense (e.g., industrial equipment)

9. How much attention does top management pay to the following characteristics of your main industry? In other words considering their impact on long-term profitability or growth, how much importance does your top management attach to these aspects?

Competition in delivery and after sales services in your main industry	Little importance	1 2 3 4 5 6 7	Extreme importance

Innovation of new or better operating processes	Little importance	1 2 3 4 5 6 7	Extreme importance
Price competition in the industry	Little importance	1 2 3 4 5 6 7	Extreme importance
Rate at which products or services are getting obsolete	Little importance	1 2 3 4 5 6 7	Extreme importance
Competition for technical manpower	Little importance	1 2 3 4 5 6 7	Extreme importance
Innovation of new or better products or services	Little importance	1 2 3 4 5 6 7	Extreme importance
Competition in promotion, advertising, selling, distribution, etc.	Little importance	1 2 3 4 5 6 7	Extreme importance
Competition for purchases or inputs (e.g. raw materials), parts, equipment	Little importance	1 2 3 4 5 6 7	Extreme importance
Competition in quality and variety of products or services	Little importance	1 2 3 4 5 6 7	Extreme importance

Technology and Operations of the Firm*

1(a). In relation to your size, how diversified do you consider your firm to be?

Essentially a single industry firm with one or two product lines or services	1 2 3 4 5 6 7 One or two industries and several product lines or services	Extremely diversified, selling in many industries with a multitude of product lines or services (e.g., General Foods, Texas Instruments)

1(b). Would you consider yourself to be a highly divisionalized firm given your size?

No divisionalization. Essentially a single profit center	1 2 3 4 5 6 7 Moderate, a few divisions or profit centers	Divisionalization and profit centers reaching deep down into all of the firm's operations (e.g., G.M.)

* Remember, firm means the division, subsidiary, or independent corporation of which you are a senior executive.

1(c). How many distinctly different product lines or services does your firm market?

Only one   1   2   3   4   5   6   7   Hundreds (e.g., a department store)

1(d). How often has your operations technology (the machine-based processes involved in your operations) undergone significant changes during the past 5 years? A significant change is one that involved some retraining of personnel, required replacement or alteration of equipment, and made a difference to the unit cost of operations.

No changes at all   1   2   3   4   5   6   7   At least 5 significant changes in last 5 years

1(e). How many new lines of products or services has your firm marketed in the past 5 years? Please exclude mere minor variations.

No new lines of products or services in past 5 years   1   2   3   4   5   6   7   Hundreds of new lines of products or services in past 5 years

1(f). In your operations, what is the required level of formal technical competence of your first line supervisors?

No training or education requirements beyond, at most, high school (e.g., supermarkets)   1   2   3   4   5   6   7   Varies considerably by functional areas   A minimum of a bachelor's degree with specialization (e.g., consulting engineering, EDP firms)

1(g). Approximately what proportion of your sales or revenues is the *value added* by your firm? By value added we mean total sales or revenues minus *outside* purchases. For example, if yours is a manufacturing firm, the value added is your total sales less purchases of raw materials, fuels, parts, etc. If yours is a bank, total revenues less the interest you pay on borrowed funds or deposits is your value added. The value added as a proportion of sales or revenues is likely to be small for purely trading firms and relatively high for vertically integrated manufacturing firms.

Value added is 10% or less of sales or revenues   1   2   3   4   5   6   7   Value added is 70% or more of sales or revenues

2. What is the percentage of your total sales/revenues accounted for by each of your 3 most important product lines (or services) in terms of annual dollar sales?

Name of Product Line (or Service)	% of Total Sales or Revenues
1. --	-----------------------
2. --	-----------------------
3. --	-----------------------

3. How similar are these product lines or services in terms of (a) the technology used to produce them and (b) their markets?

Technology   Very dis-   1 2 3 4 5 6 7   Very similar technolo-
              similar tech-   gies employed for them
              nologies em-   (e.g., all mass produced
              ployed for   with similar equipment)
              them (e.g.,
              customized
              production for
              one, mass pro-
              duction for
              another)

Markets   Very simi- 1 2 3 4 5 6 7   Very dissimilar mar-
              lar markets   kets in terms of re-
              in terms of   quired marketing strat-
              required mar-   egy, types of customers,
              keting strat-   pricing, etc. (e.g., if you
              egy, types of   are marketing all of
              customers,   soap, cement, and EDP
              pricing, etc.   systems)
              (e.g., if you are
              marketing
              men's under-
              shirts and
              shorts)

4. To what extent are each of the following techniques used in your firm?

"Custom" technology (production or fabrication of a single unit or few units of products or services to customer specifications or needs —e.g., missile prototypes, patient care in exclusive private clinics)

Not used at all   1   2   3   4   5   6   7   Very extensively used—
or   minimally   over 70% of value
used   added by operations at-
                                              tributable to this tech-
                                              nology

"Small batch, job shop" technology (creation of small batches of similar units, such as fashionable dresses, tools and dies)

Not used at all   1   2   3   4   5   6   7   Very extensively used—
or   minimally   over 70% of value
used   added by operations at-
                                              tributable to this tech-
                                              nology

"Large batch" technology (e.g., used in manufacturing large batches of drugs and chemicals, parts, cans and bottles, counts of yarn; in universities used for instructing large batches of students in required courses)

Not used at all or minimally used   1 2 3 4 5 6 7 Very extensively used— over 70% of value added by operations attributable to this technology

"Mass production" technology (e.g., used in mass production of autos, standard textiles, and in computerized telephone exchanges)

Not used at all or minimally used   1 2 3 4 5 6 7 Very extensively used— over 70% of value added by operations attributable to this technology

"Continuous process" technology (e.g., used in oil refining and other automated industries, in which the output is highly standardized and mechanized and is produced continuously rather than in batches or shifts)

Not used at all or minimally used   1 2 3 4 5 6 7 Very extensively used— over 70% of value added by operations attributable to this technology

"Service technology" used by firms to serve their widely distributed clientele through branches, dealers, etc. (e.g., used by banks, insurance companies, telephone companies, several consumer goods industries)

Not used at all or minimally used   1 2 3 4 5 6 7 Very extensively used— over 70% of distribution accounted for by this technology

5.   How automated is the technology of your operations?

Very little automation (e.g., operations of advertising agencies, auditors, architects, real estate agencies)   1 2 3 4 5 6 7 Completely automated and computerized operations (e.g., those of oil refineries, telephone exchanges)

6. At approximately what level of your normal annual sales or operating income does your firm break even (in other words make neither a profit or a loss)?

At 40%	1	2	3	4	5	6	7	At over 90% of
or less of		41%	51%	61%	71%	81%		normal sales or
normal		to	to	to	to	to		revenues
sales or		50%	60%	70%	80%	90%		
revenues								

7. Please rate the extent to which each of the following is used or done in your firm:

Quality control of production or operations by sampling or other techniques — Not used at all 1 2 3 4 5 6 7 Used to a very great extent; applied to almost all operations

Cost control of operations by fixing standard costs and analyzing the variations of actual costs from these standards — Not used at all 1 2 3 4 5 6 7 Used to a very great extent; applied to almost all operations

Flexible budgeting—that is, budgeting that takes into account variations in the level of operations — Not used at all 1 2 3 4 5 6 7 Used to a very great extent; applied to almost all budgeting

The computation of present values or internal rates of return for evaluating investments — Not used at all 1 2 3 4 5 6 7 Used to a very great extent; applied to almost all investment proposals

Control of inventories, cash, etc. and scheduling of operations by means of mathematical techniques like simulation, linear programming, etc. — Not used at all 1 2 3 4 5 6 7 Used to a very great extent; applied to almost all inventories and operations

Internal auditing	Not used at all	1 2 3 4 5 6 7	Used to a very great extent; covers almost all activities of firm
Break-even analysis or incremental cost and revenue analysis in making "make or buy" investment and/ or pricing or bidding decisions	Not used at all	1 2 3 4 5 6 7	Used to a very great extent; used in almost all such decisions
Systematic evaluation of managerial and senior staff personnel	Not used at all	1 2 3 4 5 6 7	Used to a very great extent; extended to almost all such personnel
Appraisal of the firm's performance by outside auditors (as distinguished from the usual audit by certified public accountants or chartered accountants)	Not used at all	1 2 3 4 5 6 7	Used to a very great extent; covers almost all aspects of the firm's performance and decisions
Establishment of profit centers and profit targets at various levels below the top management level and in different parts of the firm (profit decentralization)	Not used at all	1 2 3 4 5 6 7	Used to a very great extent; covers almost every branch, department, and division
Divisionalization —the establishment of relatively autonomous and self-contained di-	Not used at all	1 2 3 4 5 6 7	Used to a very great extent; the firm is almost fully divisionalized

visions for servicing different markets, groups of customers, or territories									
Establishment of cost centers for cost control of the firm's operations. In a cost center fairly detailed cost targets are developed for activities under its jurisdiction	Not used at all	1	2	3	4	5	6	7	Used to a very great extent; from the lowest operating level to the highest
Functional specialization—the grouping of persons doing the same kind of work (such as marketing, or manufacturing, or design) under one department or section head with a view to achieving greater efficiency through specialization	Not used at all	1	2	3	4	5	6	7	Used to a very great extent; from the lowest fully organized by functional areas
Electronic data processing	Not used at all	1	2	3	4	5	6	7	Covers almost all of the firm's internal and external transactions
Executive or management training and development	Not used at all	1	2	3	4	5	6	7	Done to a very great extent; extended to almost all the levels of management
Research and development and design of products or services and processes	Not done at all	1	2	3	4	5	6	7	Done to a very great extent, whether in-house or under contract outside the firm

Long-term forecasting of your firm's sales and profits and of the size and nature of its markets	Not done at all	1 2 3 4 5 6 7	Done to a very great extent; detailed forecasts for next 5 years or more
Long-term forecasting of the technology relevant to your firm's products, operations	Not done at all	1 2 3 4 5 6 7	Done to a very great extent; careful, detailed forecasts for next 5 years or more
Analysis of accounting ratios (e.g., gross profit ratios, liquidity ratios)	Not used at all	1 2 3 4 5 6 7	Used to a very great extent for analyzing and controlling operations
Procedures to search for and evaluate systematically potentially profitable investments	Not used at all	1 2 3 4 5 6 7	Used to a very great extent in identifying most growth opportunities
Planning of long-term investments and their financing (long-term capital budgeting)	Not done at all	1 2 3 4 5 6 7	Done to a very great extent; detailed plans for next 5 years or more
Market research (systematic study of customer preferences, price and demand analysis of products or services)	Not done at all	1 2 3 4 5 6 7	Done as a matter of course before almost all new offerings, changes, etc.
Human engineering and job design (scientifically matching jobs and men)	Not used at all	1 2 3 4 5 6 7	Used to a very great extent in all operating areas

| Brainstorming for novel solutions to problems. In brainstorming, the group first generates as many and varied solutions as possible before evaluating any of them for their feasibility | Not done at all | 1 2 3 4 5 6 7 | Done very frequently by executive and staff groups |

8. To what extent has the chief executive of your firm delegated authority to others to make each of the following classes of decisions? Please rate the actual rather than the merely formal delegation of authority. The delegation of authority can be to individuals or groups (e.g., committees).

| Raising long-term capital to finance new investments | No delegation of authority | 1 2 3 4 5 6 7 | Complete delegation of authority |

| Development of new products/ services | No delegation of authority | 1 2 3 4 5 6 7 | Complete delegation of authority |

| Marketing strategy for a new product/service and changes in the marketing strategy for existing products/ services | No delegation of authority | 1 2 3 4 5 6 7 | Complete delegation of authority |

| The hiring and firing of senior personnel | No delegation of authority | 1 2 3 4 5 6 7 | Complete delegation of authority |

| Periodic reviews and changes in the firm's operating, market- | No delegation of au- | 1 2 3 4 5 6 7 | Complete delegation of authority |

ing, financial,   thority
personnel, and
growth policies

Selection of large new investments	No delegation of authority	1	2	3	4	5	6	7	Complete delegation of authority

Pricing of new products and significant price changes in existing products/ services	No delegation of authority	1	2	3	4	5	6	7	Complete delegation of authority

The magnitude and direction of research into new products and/or processes	No delegation of authority	1	2	3	4	5	6	7	Complete delegation of authority

Acquisition of subsidiaries or controlling interest in other firms	No delegation of authority	1	2	3	4	5	6	7	Complete delegation of authority

Bargaining with personnel or their unions about wages, etc.	No delegation of authority	1	2	3	4	5	6	7	Complete delegation of authority

9. To what extent is your firm vertically integrated?
Backward from operations into lease or ownership of sources of raw materials, processing of raw materials, facilities for producing spares and parts, for fabricating plant and machinery used by your firm, etc. If your firm is purely a trading or service industry firm, write N.A.

Virtually no integration backward	1	2	3	4	5	6	7	Almost fully integrated backward

Forward from operations into wholesaling and retailing

Virtually no forward integration	1	2	3	4	5	6	7	Almost fully integrated forward

10. How do you rate collaboration between senior personnel in your firm, especially in responding to tough problems that competition or changes in business conditions may create for the firm?

Inadequate col-   1 2 3 4 5 6 7   Exceptionally fine collaboration   laboration; managers
                                             really work together as a
                                             team

11. To what extent is decision-making at top levels in your firm characterized by participative, group or democratic decision-making, in relation to the following classes of decision:

Product or service related decisions concerning level of operations, marketing strategy, research and development of new products or services, etc.

No participa-   1 2 3 4 5 6 7   Decisions made by top
tion; the respon-   Responsible   management groups or
sible top execu-   executives   committees after full dis-
tives make the   discuss with   cussion and attempt at
decisions using   others before   reaching consensus—
existing infor-   deciding   failing which, decisions
mation   are taken by majority
                                        vote

Capital budget decisions (selection and financing of long-term investments)

No participa-   1 2 3 4 5 6 7   Decisions made by top
tion; the respon-   Responsible   management groups or
sible top execu-   executives   committees after full dis-
tives make the   discuss with   cussion and attempt at
decisions using   others before   reaching consensus—
existing infor-   deciding   failing which, decisions
mation   are taken by majority
                                        vote

Long-term strategy of growth, diversification, etc., and decisions related to changes in the firm's operating philosophy

No participa-   1 2 3 4 5 6 7   Decisions made by top
tion; the respon-   Responsible   management groups or
sible top execu-   executives   committees after full dis-
tives make the   discuss with   cussion and attempt at
decisions using   others before   reaching consensus—
existing infor-   deciding   failing which, decisions
mation   are taken by majority
                                        vote

12a. Would a 10% price reduction by your main competitors affect the demand for your principal product or service, should you choose to stand pat?

No effect at all   1   2   3   4   5   6   7   Very drastic reduction in demand—say, of 50%

12b. What was the percentage of your total marketing expense (including sales expenses, promotion, market research, and distribution expenses) to total sales or revenues last year? ....%

13. What was the *lowest* (before tax) rate of return on net worth (i.e., on shareholders' funds, or total assets minus total liabilities) during the past 5 years? ....% If the lowest rate was a loss, please indicate the rate on net worth with a minus sign.

What was the *highest* (before tax) rate of return on net worth during this period? ....% If it was a loss, please indicate its rate with a minus sign.

14. What has been the *average* rate of growth of your sales or revenues during the past 5 years? ....%

15. How old is your firm? .... years since being first set up

Environment, Corporate Policy, Goals, Etc.

1. This question is designed to elicit from you your perception of the *operating management philosophy* of the top management of your firm, in other words the management philosophy that actually gets used in top management decision-making. Please *circle* the appropriate number. Remember, 1 represents the expression on the left-hand side and 7 represents the expression on the right-hand side, with 4 as the mid-point standing for a combination of the two ("some of both") or a mid-point along some underlying dimension.

1. Tight formal control of most operations by means of sophisticated control and information systems   1   2   3   4   5   6   7   Loose, informal control; heavy dependence on informal relationships and norm of cooperation for getting work done

           Some of both

2. Great centralization in decision-making, with most operating decisions made at the top   1   2   3   4   5   6   7   Great decentralization, with most operating decisions made at lower management levels

3. A policy offering virtually unlimited job security to employees | 1 2 3 4 5 6 7 Some of both | A strong performance-oriented up-or-out job policy

4. In decision-making, great reliance on specialized, technically trained line and staff personnel | 1 2 3 4 5 6 7 Some of both | In decision-making, great reliance on personnel with experience and common sense

5. Strong group- or committee-oriented consensus-seeking, participative decision-making | 1 2 3 4 5 6 7 Some of both | Strongly individualistic decision-making by the formally responsible executive

6. Strong emphasis on always getting personnel to follow the formally laid down procedures | 1 2 3 4 5 6 7 Some of both | Strong emphasis on getting things done even if this means disregarding formal procedures

7. A-bird-in-the hand emphasis on the immediate future in making management decisions | 1 2 3 4 5 6 7 Medium term orientation | Emphasis on long-term (over 5 years) planning of goals and strategy

8. A strongly marketing orientation | 1 2 3 4 5 6 7 Some of both | A strongly operating efficiency orientation

9. A strong emphasis on holding fast to true and tried management principles despite any changes in business conditions | 1 2 3 4 5 6 7 | A strong emphasis on adapting freely to changing circumstances without too much concern for past practice

10. Make friendly accommodation with unions or employees' representatives   1 2 3 4 5 6 7   Tough bargaining with unions or employees' representatives

11. In promoting managers, a strong emphasis on the ability to cooperate and get along well with others   1 2 3 4 5 6 7
Some of both   In promoting managers, a strong emphasis on competitiveness and capacity to out perform others

12. Strong emphasis on giving the most say in decision-making to formal line managers   1 2 3 4 5 6 7   Strong tendency to let the expert in a given situation have the most say in decision-making even if this means temporary bypassing of formal line authority

13. Policy of growth primarily through internally generated funds (retained earnings)   1 2 3 4 5 6 7
Some of both   Policy of growth primarily through external financing (borrowings, capital issues, etc.)

14. Strong emphasis on research and development, technological leadership, and innovations   1 2 3 4 5 6 7   Strong emphasis on the marketing of true and tried product or services and the avoidance of heavy research and developmental costs

15. Strong emphasis on diversification of products or services, even if it means venturing into unrelated industries   1 2 3 4 5 6 7   Concentration on a single group of related products or a single industry; great emphasis on defining one's industry and sticking to it

16. Strong tendency to integrate vertically, such as by ac-   1 2 3 4 5 6 7   Strong avoidance of vertical integration

quiring raw
material
sources and
processing fa-
cilities and/or
by acquiring
wholesaling
and even retail-
ing channels

17. Strong emphasis   1 2 3 4 5 6 7   Strong emphasis on a
on a mass pro-   Some   technology that can en-
duced, standard-   of   able the firm to offer
ized product or   both   products or services tail-
service oriented   ored to individual cus-
technology   tomer's needs

18. Strong reliance   1 2 3 4 5 6 7   Strong reliance on for-
on task forces or   Varies   mal line managers for
project teams   from   executing new projects,
for executing   project   innovations, and im-
new projects, in-   to project   provements in operations
novations, and
improvements
in operations

19. Managers' op-   1 2 3 4 5 6 7   Strong insistence on a
erating styles   uniform managerial
allowed to range   style throughout the
freely from the   firm
very formal to
the very informal

20. Very competi-   1 2 3 4 5 6 7   A philosophy of co-
tive, "undo-the-   operative coexistence
competitors"   with rival firms within
philosophy   the limits of the law

21. Strong empha-   1 2 3 4 5 6 7   Strong emphasis on
sis on growth   Some   growth through the
through acquisi-   of   building of new plants
tions and/or   both   and facilities
mergers

Please remember, what is wanted is not what management philosophy you
would prefer for the firm, but the one that actually gets used in your firm.

22. Strong emphasis   1 2 3 4 5 6 7   Strong   emphasis   on
on profitability   Some   sales growth and market
and liquidity   of   share
                     both

23. Strong emphasis 1 2 3 4 5 6 7 Strong tendency to let
    on getting line   Some   the requirements of the
    and staff person-   of   situation and the indi-
    nel to adhere   both   vidual's personality de-
    closely to for-   fine proper on-job be-
    mal job descrip-   havior
    tions

24. Heavy reliance 1 2 3 4 5 6 7 Heavy reliance on ap-
    on formal man-   Some   prenticeship, "learning
    agement train-   of   by hard knocks"
    ing programs   both

25. Strong empha- 1 2 3 4 5 6 7 A strongly conservative
    sis on acquiring   policy towards changing
    the latest, most   equipment or acquiring
    sophisticated   new equipment
    plant, machin-
    ery, or equip-
    ment

26. Open channels 1 2 3 4 5 6 7 Highly structured chan-
    of communica-   nels of communication
    tion, with im-   and a highly restricted
    portant finan-   access to important fi-
    cial and operat-   nancial and operating
    ing information   information
    flowing quite
    freely through-
    out the organ-
    ization

27. Strong procliv- 1 2 3 4 5 6 7 Strong proclivity toward
    ity toward high   Some   low risk, moderate re-
    risk, high return   of   turn investments (e.g.,
    investment (e.g.,   both   virtually certain 10%
    20% R.O.I.   R.O.I. after tax)
    after tax with a
    chance of earn-
    ing nothing)

28. Heavy advertis- 1 2 3 4 5 6 7 Low advertising and
    ing and promo-   Varies for   promotion compared to
    tion compared   different   industry average
    to industry   products;
    average   average

29. High quality, 1 2 3 4 5 6 7 Standard quality, low or
    high price   popular price orienta-
    orientation   tion

30. In structuring
or modifying
the organiza-
tion, heavy em-
phasis on initia-
tive, quick
adaptation to
local situation
(as in division-
alization and
profit decen-
tralization)

1 2 3 4 5 6 7
Some
of
both

In structuring or modi-
fying the organization,
heavy emphasis on effi-
ciency through special-
ization and on overall
coordination at the top
(as in departmentaliza-
tion by functional areas
such as marketing, per-
sonnel, production, etc.)

31. Recruitment
mostly from
within company
to fill middle and
senior manage-
ment positions

1 2 3 4 5 6 7
Some
of
both

Recruitment mostly from
outside company to fill
middle and senior man-
agement positions

2. How would you characterize the *external* environment within which
your firm functions? In rating your environment, please consider,
where relevant, not only the economic but also the social, political, and
technological aspects of the environment.

1. Very homo-
geneous (e.g., a
single, undiffer-
entiated market
and very similar
customers)

1 2 3 4 5 6 7
Mixed

Very heterogeneous
(e.g., a great diversity
of markets, types of cus-
tomers, etc.)

2. Very dynamic,
changing rap-
idly in technical,
economic, and
cultural dimen-
sions

1 2 3 4 5 6 7
Mixed

Very stable; virtually no
change

3. Very safe; little
threat to sur-
vival and well
being of the firm

1 2 3 4 5 6 7
Mixed

Very risky; a false step
can mean the firm's un-
doing

4. Very unpredict-
able; very hard
to anticipate the
nature or direc-
tion of changes
in the environ-
ment

1 2 3 4 5 6 7
Mixed

Very predictable; very
easy to forecast the fu-
ture state of affairs in
the environment

5. Very rapidly expanding through the rapid expansion of old markets and the emergence of new ones

   1 2 3 4 5 6 7
       Mixed

Very stagnant, or even shrinking markets

6. Very strong cyclical or other *periodic* fluctuation

   1 2 3 4 5 6 7
       Mixed

Virtually no *periodic* fluctuation

7. Rich in investment and marketing opportunities; not at all stressful

   1 2 3 4 5 6 7
       Mixed

Very stressful, exacting, hostile; very hard to keep afloat

8. Technologically, a very sophisticated and complex environment

   1 2 3 4 5 6 7
       Mixed

An environment demanding little in the way of technological sophistication

9. A dominating environment, in which your firm's initiatives count for very little against the tremendous forces of your business or political environment

   1 2 3 4 5 6 7
       Mixed

An environment that your firm can control and manipulate to its own advantage (e.g., dominant firm in an industry has one with little competition and few hindrances)

10. A very restrictive, constraining environment (e.g., severe legal constraints, social or economic or political constraints, such as for a regulated monopoly)

   1 2 3 4 5 6 7
       Mixed

A very constraint-free, unrestricted environment

3. Compared to your *industry's average*—or if yours is a very diversified firm, in relation to comparable firms—how do you compare on each of the following?

Long-run level of profitability   Very low 1 2 3 4 5 6 7 Very high
About average

Growth rate of sales or revenues   Very low 1 2 3 4 5 6 7 Very high
About average

Employee morale, job satisfaction, and commitment to firm's objectives   Very low 1 2 3 4 5 6 7 Very high
About average

Financial strength (liquidity and ability to raise financial resources)   Very low 1 2 3 4 5 6 7 Very high
About average

Public image and goodwill   Very low 1 2 3 4 5 6 7 Very high
About average

4. How far within your firm do you observe senior managers using each of the following modes of resolving their disagreements over personal matters and corporate issues?

1. Compromise ("You scratch my back and I'll scratch yours"; "A fair exchange brings no quarrel")   Seldom used   1 2 3 4 5 6 7 Used very often
Moderately used

2. Smoothing things over ("Kill your enemies with kindness"; "soft words win hard hearts")   Seldom used   1 2 3 4 5 6 7 Used very often
Moderately used

3. Forcing ("Might overcomes right"; "If you cannot make a man think as you do, make him do as you think")   Seldom used   1 2 3 4 5 6 7 Used very often
Moderately used

4. Confronting dif-   Seldom   1 2 3 4 5 6 7   Used very often
   ferences ("By   used   Moderately used
   digging and dig-
   ging, the truth is
   discovered"; "A
   question must be
   decided by knowl-
   edge and not by
   numbers")

5. Nonengagement   Seldom   1 2 3 4 5 6 7   Used very often
   ("It is easier to   used   Moderately used
   refrain than to re-
   treat from a quar-
   rel"; "Don't stir
   up a hornets'
   nest"

5. Three key areas of a firm often have conflicts with one another. One is Marketing; another is Operations; and the third is R & D and Design. Please rate the extent of conflict between pairs of these in your firm: If any item is irrelevant to your firm, write N.A. For manufacturing firms, Operations covers production-related activities.

Marketing and   No con-   Strong disagree-
Operations   flicts   1 2 3 4 5 6 7   ments between
                                               Marketing and
                                               Operations per-
                                               sonnel

R & D and Design   No con-   Strong disagree-
and Marketing   flicts   1 2 3 4 5 6 7   ments between
                                               R & D and Design
                                               personnel and Mar-
                                               keting personnel

Operations and   No con-   Strong disagree-
R & D and Design   flicts   1 2 3 4 5 6 7   ments between
                                               Operations per-
                                               sonnel and R & D
                                               and Design per-
                                               sonnel

6. How important are the following goals to your firm's top management in making *strategic* decisions, or commitments of a long-term nature?

1. Earning a high,   Moderately 1 2 3 4 5 6 7   Extremely
   above average   important   Quite   important
   profit   important

2. Achieving a high, above average rate of growth in sales or revenues

	Moderately important	1	2	3	4 quite important	5	6	7	Extremely important

3. Retaining or securing high, above average liquidity and financial strength

	Moderately important	1	2	3	4 quite important	5	6	7	Extremely important

4. Maintaining or securing high, above average employee morale, job satisfaction, and commitment to firm's objectives

	Moderately important	1	2	3	4 quite important	5	6	7	Extremely important

5. Achieving or maintaining an excellent public image

	Moderately important	1	2	3	4 quite important	5	6	7	Extremely important

7. What are the main constraints or bottlenecks affecting the growth of your firm? Please rate the extent to which each of the following operates to slow down your sales/revenue growth:

Insufficient capital (e.g., inadequate retention of earnings, high interest rates)

	Not important as a constraint	1	2	3	4	5	6	7	Very great constraint on growth

Shortage of managerial talent (e.g., to manage new or expanded ventures)

	Not important as a constraint	1	2	3	4	5	6	7	Very great constraint on growth

Lack of investment or growth opportunities (e.g., due to stagnant markets)

	Not important as a constraint	1	2	3	4	5	6	7	Very great constraint on growth

Lack of cooperation of white collar employees (e.g., interdepartmental squabbles, low motivation to work)

	Not important as a constraint	1	2	3	4	5	6	7	Very great constraint on growth

Shortage of technical manpower (e.g., shortage of qualified

	Not important as a constraint	1	2	3	4	5	6	7	Very great constraint on growth

engineers, scientists,
accountants, statisti-
cians)

| Government regula-
tions (e.g., price
control, control over
expansion or diver-
sification) | Not impor-
tant as a
constraint | 1 2 3 4 5 6 7 | Very great
constraint
on growth |

| Resistance to changes
needed for growth on
the part of managers
(e.g., too many tra-
dition-bound and
conservative man-
agers) | Not impor-
tant as a
constraint | 1 2 3 4 5 6 7 | Very great
constraint
on growth |

| Labor troubles (e.g.,
strikes, slowdowns) | Not impor-
tant as a
constraint | 1 2 3 4 5 6 7 | Very great
constraint
on growth |

8. What effect has *government* legislation, regulations, or actions, related to the following areas, had on your firm? If any item is irrelevant or has had no effect, circle 4. Government covers local, state or provincial, national, and where relevant, super-national governments.

| 1. Tariffs on im-
ports/exports | Very nega-
tive effect | 1 2 3 4 5 6 7 | Very posi-
tive effect |

| 2. Export aid | Very nega-
tive effect | 1 2 3 4 5 6 7 | Very posi-
tive effect |

| 3. Antitrust or anti-
monopoly regu-
lations | Very nega-
tive effect | 1 2 3 4 5 6 7 | Very posi-
tive effect |

| 4. Incentives for
operations in
designated areas | Very nega-
tive effect | 1 2 3 4 5 6 7 | Very posi-
tive effect |

| 5. Regulations for
protecting the en-
vironment from
industrial wastes | Very nega-
tive effect | 1 2 3 4 5 6 7 | Very posi-
tive effect |

| 6. Tax relief or sub-
sidies | Very nega-
tive effect | 1 2 3 4 5 6 7 | Very posi-
tive effect |

| 7. Special regula-
tory bodies or
legislation for
industry | Very nega-
tive effect | 1 2 3 4 5 6 7 | Very posi-
tive effect |

8. Labor legislation and legislation covering working conditions — Very negative effect 1 2 3 4 5 6 7 Very positive effect

9. Advertising and promotion regulation — Very negative effect 1 2 3 4 5 6 7 Very positive effect

Miscellaneous

Attempts at organizational change (such as a reorganization, or a program of better supervisory practices, or the introduction of a new, sophisticated management information system) often run into the problem of strong opposition and/or lack of commitment to it on the part of personnel. Management tends to use several methods for instituting change, overcoming this resistance, and getting the required commitment. These methods are not mutually exclusive, and there is no method that is best or worst under all circumstances. Please rate the use of each of these change methods in your firm.

1. Explain *concepts* underlying the proposed changes to those involved or affected by them—in other words, provide detailed *justification* for the changes to those affected by them before or after the changes are effected
   Seldom used   1 2 3 4 5 6 7   Used very commonly

2. Find or train line and staff *personnel* with the right drive and expertise to implement the proposed changes
   Seldom used   1 2 3 4 5 6 7   Used very commonly

3. Before taking action, direct *staff* or other internal groups to investigate scientifically the underlying problem with a view to formulating optimal action alternatives
   Seldom used   1 2 3 4 5 6 7   Used very commonly

4. Train supervisors in *human relations* skills or urge them to use them so that they can ease employees' opposition to the proposed changes and possibly even get their commitment to these changes. (Human relations skills involve better communications with subordinates, establishing personal relationships with them, lending a sympathetic ear to their problems, etc.)
   Seldom used   1 2 3 4 5 6 7   Used very commonly

5. Procure the services of *outside experts*, such as consultants, to investigate the problem and proposed changes
   Seldom used   1 2 3 4 5 6 7   Used very commonly

6. *Involve* fully those likely to be affected at each phase of the change process—in the articulation of the problem, gathering of pertinent information, formulation of action alternatives, and the implementation of the selected course of action—by means of participative, consensus-seeking, *democratic decision-making,* followed by feedback of results of change for group evaluation and further action

Seldom used   1   2   3   4   5   6   7   Used very commonly

7. Issue orders and implicitly or explicitly *warn* personnel of serious consequences of resisting management orders

Seldom used   1   2   3   4   5   6   7   Used very commonly

Researchers have indicated that decision-making in organizations takes place in three distinct (but not necessarily mutually exclusive) modes or styles. Please indicate how closely each of the following modes resembles the way decisions get made at the top levels of your firm.

1. Mode 1:

Adaptive mode, characterized by a cautious, pragmatic, one small step at a time adjustment to problems. Decisions are generally compromises between the conflicting demands of owners, unions, government, managers, customers, etc. They are made locally more often than centrally, and the primary concern is with stability and steady growth.

Little resemblance to   1   2   3   4   5   6   7   Very great resemblance
style of top level de-   to style of top level deci-
cision-making in firm   sion-making in firm

2. Mode 2:

Entrepreneurial mode, characterized by active search for big new opportunities; large, bold decisions despite the uncertainty of their outcomes; a charismatic decision maker at the top wielding great power and rapid growth as the dominant organization goal.

Little resemblance to   1   2   3   4   5   6   7   Very great resemblance
style of top level de-   to style of top level deci-
cision-making in firm   sion-making in firm

3. Mode 3:

Planning mode, characterized by systematic search for opportunities and anticipation of problems; a systematic consideration of costs and benefits of alternatives; and a conscious attempt to integrate programs of action to achieve specified goals efficiently. The accent is on profit maximization, long-term planning, very careful screening of investments to minimize risks, and the extensive use of expertise and solid research before making decisions.

Little resemblance to   1   2   3   4   5   6   7   Very great resemblance
style of top level de-   to style of top level deci-
cision-making in firm   sion-making in firm

3. Management often uses some or all of the following mechanisms for reducing conflict between different groups in the firm, or for improving coordination, or for effective collaboration between personnel. For example, if there are serious coordination problems between the Marketing and Operations fellows, or the Maintenance and the Operations people, or the Credit and Sales personnel, some or all of these could be used. Please rate the usage of each of these in your firm.

1. *Task forces* or *ad hoc* committees, whose objective is to examine a dispute and seek a solution that is optimal for the organization as a whole

   Not common at all   1   2   3   4   5   6   7   Very commonly used

2. *Standards and procedures:* Clear standards of job performance and detailed procedures for getting tasks accomplished, designed to minimize jurisdictional and other conflicts; explicit procedures for what to do in the event of disagreement between work groups

   Not common at all   1   2   3   4   5   6   7   Very commonly used

3. *Hierarchy:* Heads of groups in dispute refer to the executive with authority over both

   Not common at all   1   2   3   4   5   6   7   Very commonly used

4. *Human relations* training for managers to make them understand better their colleagues and subordinates and to help them communicate more effectively with them

   Not common at all   1   2   3   4   5   6   7   Very commonly used

5. *Behavioral science* techniques like confrontation meetings, sensitivity training, managerial grid type programs, are designed to raise the level of interpersonal competence and maturity of managers, and to create a climate of mutual trust in which conflicts may be discussed openly and settled amicably

   Not common at all   1   2   3   4   5   6   7   Very commonly used

6. *Liaison men:* Individuals or groups whose primary function is to help resolve conflicts between organizations and groups. Typically they explain to each group the other group's point of view and push for an accommodation by each side. For example, one or two senior executives experienced in Marketing as well as Operations are assigned the job of ironing out their differences, or a committee of the representatives of the groups is formed to improve coordination on a continuing basis

   Not common at all   1   2   3   4   5   6   7   Very commonly used

7. *Arbitration procedures:* Establishment of procedures for reviewing decisions on a complaint by an aggrieved party or group, such as is common in the field of labor relations

   Not common at all   1   2   3   4   5   6   7   Very commonly used

4. It takes all kinds of activities to run a modern firm. However, from a *strategic* viewpoint, certain activities may be more crucial to long-term profitability or growth than others. Please indicate the importance the *top management* of your firm attaches to each of the following:

1. Formalization of decision-making authority (i.e., of who makes what decisions)

    Little strate-gic impor-tance 1 2 3 4 5 6 7 Extreme strategic importance

2. A sophisticated management control and in-formation system

    Little strate-gic impor-tance 1 2 3 4 5 6 7 Extreme strategic importance

3. Executive or management training and development

    Little strate-gic impor-tance 1 2 3 4 5 6 7 Extreme strategic importance

4. Research and development of new products or processes

    Little strate-gic impor-tance 1 2 3 4 5 6 7 Extreme strategic importance

5. Forecasting sales, customer preferences, technology, etc.

    Little strate-gic impor-tance 1 2 3 4 5 6 7 Extreme strategic importance

6. The application of operations re-search tech-niques (such as linear program-ming and simu-lation) to opera-tions, distribu-tion, inventory and cash man-agement, etc.

    Little strate-gic impor-tance 1 2 3 4 5 6 7 Extreme strategic importance

7. Market research

    Little strate-gic impor-tance 1 2 3 4 5 6 7 Extreme strategic importance

8. Human engi-neering, job de-sign, job enrich-

    Little strate-gic impor-tance 1 2 3 4 5 6 7 Extreme strategic importance

ment (scientific
matching of jobs
and men; design
of more interest-
ing jobs)

9. Formalized, sys-
tematic search
for and evalua-
tion of opportu-
nities for acqui-
sitions, new in-
vestments, new
markets, etc.

	Little strate-gic impor-tance	1	2	3	4	5	6	7	Extreme strategic importance

10. Planning of
long-term invest-
ments and their
financing (long-
term capital
budgeting)

	Little strate-gic impor-tance	1	2	3	4	5	6	7	Extreme strategic importance

11. Participative de-
cision-making
at middle and
senior manage-
ment levels

	Little strate-gic impor-tance	1	2	3	4	5	6	7	Extreme strategic importance

12. Management by
objectives (goal
setting by sub-
ordinates with
their superiors'
help)

	Little strate-gic impor-tance	1	2	3	4	5	6	7	Extreme strategic importance

13. Formalization of
corporate strat-
egy and objec-
tives to guide de-
cision-making
by managers

	Little strate-gic impor-tance	1	2	3	4	5	6	7	Extreme strategic importance

14. Diversification

	Little strate-gic impor-tance	1	2	3	4	5	6	7	Extreme strategic importance

15. A sophisticated
incentive system
for increasing

	Little strate-gic impor-tance	1	2	3	4	5	6	7	Extreme strategic importance

the productivity of blue collar, line, and staff personnel	Little strategic importance	1 2 3 4 5 6 7	Extreme strategic importance
16. Vertical integration	Little strategic importance	1 2 3 4 5 6 7	Extreme strategic importance
17. Periodic brainstorming by senior management groups for novel solutions to problems	Little strategic importance	1 2 3 4 5 6 7	Extreme strategic importance
18. Development of good relations with the government and the public	Little strategic importance	1 2 3 4 5 6 7	Extreme strategic importance
19. Development of good labor relations	Little strategic importance	1 2 3 4 5 6 7	Extreme strategic importance

5. Has your firm undergone *major* changes in its environment, policies, structure, operations, or performances during the past 5 years? If so, please briefly describe these changes:

Environment (competition, technological change, government policies and regulations, needs of customers, etc.)

Policies (in the areas of marketing, finance, operations, personnel, labor relations, growth, etc.)

Organizational structure (reorganizations and changes in authority structure, divisionalization, new line and staff departments, etc.)

Operations (the nature of technology, controls, EDP, staff activities, etc.)

Performance (in terms of profits, growth, liquidity, morale, public image, market share, etc.)

If possible, please enclose or draw your *organization chart:*

Any comments or suggestions with respect to length, phrasing of the questions, relevance to your business, any notable omissions, etc.?

Please review the questionnaire for imcomplete items and return the completed questionnaire to *Dr. P. Khandwalla, Faculty of Management, McGill University, Montreal 101, Quebec, Canada.* If possible, please mail also your financial statements of the past few years.

How long did the questionnaire take to fill out?

[1] The data collection was funded by the University of Western Ontario's Associates Workshop for Research and Canada Council. Considerable support was provided by the Faculty of Management, McGill University.
[2] Jim C. Nunnally, *Psychometric Theory*, p. 193.
[3] *Ibid.*, p. 226.

Name Index

Ruggles, R. L., Jr., 407–08
Rush, H., 496–97
Rushing, William A., 139
Russell, Bertrand, 469

Sayles, Leonard, 22
Schermerhorn, John R., 275, 574
Schoenherr, Richard, 509
Scott, W. Richard, 22, 142, 144, 145,
    305–08
Seashore, Stanley E., 583, 584
Seiler, John A., 225
Selznick, Philip, 22, 84, 164
Shepard, Herbert, 561
Sherif, Muzafer, 547–48
Simon, Herbert, 6–7, 25, 62, 133, 201–
    06, 374, 453, 469, 483, 541–42
Skinner, B. F., 98, 99
Sloan, Alfred, 18, 149, 246
Smalter, D. J., 407–08
Smith, Adam, 4, 135
Stalker, G. M., 143, 148, 150–51, 236,
    238–39, 264, 274, 398, 412
Starbuck, W. H., 300, 302
Steiner, Gary, 275, 533, 534
Steuart, Sir James, 132
Stinchcombe, Arthur, 139, 303, 560
Straus, George, 138
Summer, Charles F., 150, 155

Talacchi, S., 535–36
Taylor, Frederick Winslow, 145–46,
    164, 177
Théoret, André, 213
Thibaut, J. W., 100, 101–02
Thompson, James D., 241–46, 332, 358,
    453, 457, 542
Toffler, Alvin, 80
Tregoe, B., 92
Trist, E. L., 133, 225, 228

Udell, Jon, 517
Udy, S. H., Jr., 141
Urwick, L., 148, 150, 151, 237, 483

Van de Ven, Andrew, 499–502

Walker, J., 560
Weber, Max, 53, 84, 133, 134–36, 141,
    164, 482–83
Wegner, R., 22
Weick, Karl, 24
White, Leslie, 80
Whitehead, Alfred North, 469
Whyte, W. F., 22, 107, 292–95
Williamson, Oliver, 25
Woodward, Joan, 133, 150, 237, 457,
    517–18

Subject Index

Academy of Management Journal, 12, 23
Accommodation, 83
Action research, 24–25, 26
Adaptive subsystem, 225, 227, 229
Administrative Science Quarterly, 12, 23
Age of organization, 272, 299–305
  goals and, 300–02
  industry traditions and, 302–05
  organizational change and, 300–01
  performance and, 573–74
Arthashastra (Kautilya), 59
Assembly line technology, 467–68
Assimilation, 83
Assumptions, 15
Authoritarianism, 110, 336. See also Coercive management
Authoritative model of organizational design, 188, 189
Authority:
  age of organization and, 302–03
  contingency theory and, 238–39
  delegation of, 148–49, 154–55, 367, 502, 503, 504. See also Decentralization
  environmental hostility and, 336, 337
  hierarchy of, see Hierarchy
  management process school and, 147, 148, 149, 154–55
  management style and, 435–38

  political, 53–54
  size of organization and, 64
Avoidance goals, 97, 118

Bargaining, 358, 541
Behavior, design of, see Human behavior, design of
Behavioral orientations in organization theory, see Carnegie (bounded rationality) theory; Human relations; Human resources
Behavioral variables, 273–76
Behavioristic psychology (reinforcement theory), 88, 98–105, 118
Brainstorming, 297, 298, 553–55
Bureaucracy, 133–34
  comparative study of organizations and, 141–44
  forms of, 138–41
  management process compared with, 163–65
  unanticipated consequences of, 136–38
  Weber on, 134–36, 164
Bureaucratic Phenomenon (Crozier), 22
Business Horizons, 19
Business organizations, 306, 308, 309, 315

Control (*Continued*)
  in participative model of organizational design, 189
  profitability goal and, 181
  size of organization and, 156–57
Control and information system (C.I.S.), 503–08
  capital intensive technology and, 464
  decentralization and, 509, 511
  defined, 505
  design of innovation and, 559–60
  determinants of sophistication of, 506–07
  diverse environments and, 338
  diversification and, 367
  hierarchy and, 517, 518
  high performance aspirations and, 382
  importance of, 505–06
  profitability goal and, 381
  standardized mass-output and, 468
  technologically complex environment and, 339, 506–08
Cooperation, 83, 541–51
Cooptive relationships, 358
Coordinated decentralization, 149
Coordination, 146–47, 157–58
  dependency and, 244–45
  divisionalization and, 495
  functional departmentalization and, 490–91
  high performance aspirations and, 382
  performance and, 589–90
  size of organization and, 295
Corporate management styles, 424–26
Cost function, 49–50
Craft technology, 246–48
Cultural constraints, 339–40
Culture, choice of design and, 265–66
Customized output, 466–67
Cycles of events, 226
Cyclical demand, 312, 314

Decentralization, 154–55, 508–11
  coordinated, 149
  defined, 508
  derived goals and, 374
  determinants of, 509–11
  implications for organizational design, 524
  importance of, 508–09
  management process school and, 148–49
  performance and, 589–90
  profit, 154

size of organizations and, 296, 509–11
  standardized mass-output and, 468
Decisions flow, 453
Definitions, 14–15
Demand, 312–14
Demographic characteristics of organizations, 270–72, 274–75, 291–322
  age, *see* Age of organization
  implications for organizational design, 320–22
  ownership, 272, 315–17, 573–74
  performance and, 573–76
  size, *see* Size of organization
  type of organization, 272, 305–15, 573–74
Demographic variables, *see* Demographic characteristics of organizations
Departmentalization, 483–502
  divisionalization, *see* Divisionalization
  factors affecting groupings of personnel, 487–89
  functional, 154, 246, 489–91, 498–99, 589–90
  importance of, 483–85
  management style and, 435–38
  matrix structure, 154, 246, 489, 495–97, 499
  organization charts, 483, 485–87
  size of organization and, 297
  standardized mass-output and, 468
  task environment and, 497–99
Dependency, *see* Interdependence
Derived goals, 363, 373–74
Design, 260–68
Deviant behavior, 83, 84
Differentiated environment, 338
Differentiation, 367, 484, 504
  on basis of status, 83–84
  derived goals and, 374
  environmental diversity and, 337–38
  management style and, 435–38
  open system, 226–27
  performance and, 241, 587–89, 595
  size of organization and, 296–97, 423
  task environments and, 239–41, 338
  See also Departmentalization
Discipline, 42
Discretionary performance programs, 203–04
Disorder, social, 75–77
Diverse environment, 337–38, 423
  coordinative mechanisms and, 549–51
  size of organization and, 337, 423
  workflow and, 456

Diversification, 50, 364–67
  concentric, 364–67
  conglomerate, 364, 365, 366
  profitability goal and, 381
  standardized mass-output and, 465–66
  See also Divisionalization
Division of labor, 4, 5, 56, 135, 502, 503, 504, 512–13, 541
  function of, 511
  management style and, 435–38
  size of organization and, 295
Divisionalization, 50, 154, 243, 366, 367, 489, 491–95
  defined, 491–92
  functional departmentalization compared with, 492–93
  growth and, 493–94
  management training and, 493
  performance and, 589–90
  problems with, 494
  by product or service line, 492, 498–99
  profitability goal and, 381
  task environment and, 498–99
  territorial, 366
Dynamic homeostasis, 226

Economic analysis of organizations, 41–51
  cost function, 49–50
  economics, defined, 43–44
  logic of optimal production, 44–45
  typology of market structures, 45–48
Economic constraints, 339
Economic forces, 228
Electronic data processing, 469–73
Emotional bonds, 6
Engineering technology, 246–48
Entrepreneurial management, *see* Risk-taking management
Environment of organizations, *see* External environment of organizations
Environmental pressure, 326–30
Equifinality, 227
Equilibrium model of society, 74–75
Expressive dispositions, 108
External environment of organizations, 326–49
  anatomy of, 332–33
  assessment of, 343–46
  as configuration of forces, 341–42
  design of top management style and, 429, 430
  diversity of, *see* Diverse environment
  environmental pressure, 326–30

hostility of, *see* Hostile environment
implications for organizational design, 347–49
information, organizational adaptation and, 330–32
inventive behavior and, 553–55
managerial interpretation of, 342–43
performance and, 576–77, 591–94
restrictiveness of, *see* Restrictive environment
technological complexity of, *see* Technologically complex environment
turbulence of, *see* Turbulent environment

Field studies, 22, 26
Field theory, 88, 93–98, 118
Flexibility dimension of management style, 398, 399, 409–12, 424–28
  See also Mechanistic management; Organic management
Force fields, psychological, 93
Forecasting, 146, 147, 151, 334, 335
Formal role behavior, 449
Formalization, 511–13
  function of, 513
  size of organization and, 296
Full bureaucracy, 139
Functional departmentalization, 154, 246, 489–91, 498–99, 589–90
Functional specialization, 4, 5, 483, 503, 504, 512–13
  function of, 511, 513
  goal conflict and, 361
  importance of, 502
  management style and, 435–38
  size of organization and, 296, 297

Gestalt psychology, 88–92, 118
Goal-means hierarchies, 375–77, 531
Goals, 355–87
  in authoritative model of organizational design, 189
  Carnegie theory and, 359–61
  choice of design and, 264–65
  conflict, 359–62, 544–48
  consequences of, 375–82
  demographic characteristics and, 300–02, 573–76
  derived, 363, 373–74
  in field theory, 93–98, 118
  formation of, 355–62
  group dynamics and, 180–81
  implications for organizational design, 386–87

Goals (*Continued*)
   operating, defined, 357–58
   output, 362–68
   in participative model of organizational design, 189
   performance aspirations, 377–82, 553–55
   product-characteristic, 363, 371–73
   serving social needs, 362–63
   stated, defined, 356–57
   system, 363, 368–71
   types of organization and, 308–09
   variety of, 362–75
Goods organizations, 310–13
Governmental regulation, 309
Group dynamics, 177–81
Group power, 54

Handbook of Organizations (March), 25
Harvard Business Review, 19, 20
Hegemonies, 62–63
Heuristics, 208–09, 212
Hierarchy, 2–3, 5, 6, 109–10, 135, 147, 157, 482–83, 504, 514–18, 550
   age of organization and, 302–03
   determinants of span of control, 517–18
   goal-means, 375–77, 531
   implications for organizational design, 524
   importance of, 515
   morale and, 538–40
   of needs, 534
   size of organization and, 296–97
   span of control, 514–18
Homeostatic activities, 8
Hostile environment, 335–37
   centralization of power and, 336
   performance and, 576, 591–94
Human behavior, design of, 530–67
   implications for organizational design, 567
   innovative behavior, 551–52, 555–64
   interunit conflict and cooperation, 541–51
   inventive behavior, 550–55
   motivation and morale, 533–40
   strategies, 530–31
Human inputs, 234
Human Organization, 12, 22
Human relations, 176–91, 214, 550
   critique of, 189–91
   evolution of theory, 212
   group dynamics, 177–81
   hostile environment and, 336–37

   management style and, 177, 183–87
   model of human being, 211
   nonformal organization, 177, 181–83
   organizational theory and, 187–88
   standardized mass-output and, 468
   strategic variables, 212
   See also Participative management
Human Relations in the Restaurant Industry (Whyte), 22
Human resources, 176–77
   founders of theory of, 192–94
   model of human being, 211
   programs, *see* Organization development
   strategic variables, 212
Hypotheses, 15–16

Identification activities, 8
Ideology:
   defined, 393
   development of, 393–94
   management style and, 394–97
Imperfect competition, 46, 49
Implicitly structured organization, 140–41
Inclusive hegemonies, 62
Industrial organization, 44
Industry traditions, 302–05
Information, environmental, 330–32
Information flow, 452–53
Information system, *see* Control and information system (C.I.S.)
Information technology, 446–47, 468–73
   computers, 469–73
   defined, 446
   implications for organizational design, 475–76
Initiating structure, 184–85
Innovation, 114, 115
   design of, 551–52, 555–64
   performance and, 577
Innovative management, *see* Risk-taking management
Input:
   open system, 225
   organizational, 234–35
   See also Operations technology
Institutional subsystem, 224
Institutionalized participative management, 422
Integration, 484, 504
   management styles and, 435–38
   performance and, 587–90, 595
   task environment diversity and, 240–41

Interdependence:
  coordination and, 244–45
  goal conflict and, 361
  grouping of personnel and, 487–89
  interunit conflict due to, 542–44
  reciprocal, 487–89
  workflow, 454–55
Interpersonal competence, *see* Organization development
Interpersonal response traits, 107–09
Interunit conflict, 83, 334, 335, 541–51
Interview, 22–23, 27
Inventive behavior, 550–55

Joint payoffs, 543
Journal of Applied Behavioral Science, 24
Journal of Management Studies, 12

Labor, division of, *see* Division of labor
Labor intensive technologies, 460
Laboratory experiments, 23–24, 26
Leadership, 146–47, 155–56
  in authoritative model of organizational design, 188
  dimensions of, 184–85
  learning theory and, 101
  in participative model of organizational design, 188
  performance and, 584–87
  psychoanalytic theory and, 109
  roles, 155–56
Learning theory, 88, 98–105, 118
Liaison personnel, 550
Linking pin concept, 180–81
Literature search, 25, 26

Maintenance subsystem, 225, 227, 229
Management:
  choice of design and, 265
  design function of, 261–62
  principles of, *see* Management process school
  top, *see* Top management style
Management by exception, 154
Management game, 24, 26
Management and Machiavelli (Jay), 59
Management by objectives, 154, 536, 537
Management process school, 143–65
  bureaucracy compared with, 163–65
  comparative management school, 158–63
  controlling, 146–47, 156–57
  coordinating, 146–47, 157–58

forecasting, 146, 147, 151
founders of, 145–47
leading, 146–47, 155–56
organizing, 146–47, 152–55
planning, 146–47, 151–52
principles of management, 146–51
Management style, *see* Top management style
Management and Technology (Woodward), 23
Managerial effectiveness, 581
Managerial grid, 197–98, 199, 267, 544
Managerial interpretation of environment, 342–43
Managerial subsystems, 224, 229–30
Marginal adjustments, 44
Market conduct, 47–49
Market research, 334, 335, 336
Market structures, typology of, 45–48
Mathematical model-building, 25, 26
Matrix structure, 154, 246, 489, 495–97, 499
Mechanistic management, 238–39, 264, 398, 409–12
  coordinative mechanisms and, 550, 551
  performance and, 579, 580, 591, 592, 594, 600
  structural mechanisms associated with, 437
Men Who Manage (Dalton), 22
Michigan Survey Research Center, 183
Microeconomic theory, 43
Models of Man (Simon), 25
Monopolistic competition, 46, 49
Monopoly, 47, 48
Morale, design of, 533–40
Motivation:
  in authoritative model of organizational design, 188
  design of, 533–40
  in field theory, 88, 93–98, 118
  human resources orientation and, 193–94
  in participative model of organizational design, 188
Mutual benefit organizations, 305, 308, 315, 316
My Years with General Motors (Sloan), 149

Nascent full bureaucracy, 140
Nascent workflow bureaucracy, 140
Natural experiments, 23, 26
Needs:
  field theory and, 93–94, 118

Needs (*Continued*)
  human relations orientation and, 178–79, 187
  organizational, 79–80
Negative entropy, 226
Negative feedback, 226
Nonroutine technology, 245–48

Ohio State Leadership Studies, 184
Oligopoly, 46–47, 48
Onward Industry! (Mooney and Reiley), 147–148
Open system, 225–27
Operating goals, *see* Goals
Operations technology, 446–48, 458–68
  capital intensity-labor intensity, 460–64
  customized output-standardized mass output, 464–68
  defined, 446
  implications for organizational design, 475–76
  role of, 458–59
Opinion formation, 83
Opportunities, as environmental pressures, 328, 331
Optimal production, logic of, 44–45
Optimization-oriented management, 398–99, 404–09
  combined with other styles, 424–29
  control and information system (C.I.S.) and, 508
  coordinative mechanisms and, 550, 551
  goal conflict and, 361–62
  matrix structure and, 497
  performance and, 578, 579, 582, 591, 594, 599, 600, 602
  restrictive environment and, 340, 341
  structural mechanisms associated with, 436
  technologically complex environment and, 339, 429, 591
Order, social, 74–75
Organic management, 238–39, 264, 398, 409–12
  capital intensive technology and, 464
  matrix structure and, 497
  performance and, 580, 582, 591, 592, 598–600, 602
  structural mechanisms associated with, 437
  turbulent environment and, 591, 598–99, 602
Organization charts, 483, 485–87
Organization development, 195–201

characteristics of, 195–96
critique of, 200–01
defined, 195
need for, 196–97
organizational design and, 199–200
strategies, 197–99
Organization and Its Environment (Lawrence and Lorsch), 23
Organization theory:
  behavioral orientations in, *see* Carnegie (bounded rationality) theory; Human relations; Human resources
  contingency approach to, *see* Contingency theory
  domain of, 17–18, 278
  evolution of, 132–34
  nature of, 14–20
  organizational design and, 19–21
  organizational laws, nature of, 16–17
  organizational practice and, 18–19, 20
  structural orientations in, *see* Bureaucracy; Management process school
  systems approach to, *see* Systems approach
  theory, nature of, 16
Organizational design, 260–68
Organizational functioning, model of, 268–80
  description of, 270–74
  properties of, 277–79
  relationship between variables, 274–76
Organizational inputs, 234–35
Organizational laws, nature of, 16–17
Organizational learning, 208
Organizational performance, *see* Performance
Organizational polities, 63–64
Organizational programs, 202–06
Organizational structure, 482–525
  committees, 518–19
  control and information system (C.I.S.), *see* Control and information system (C.I.S.)
  decentralization, *see* Decentralization
  defined, 482
  formalization, *see* Formalization
  hierarchy, *see* Hierarchy
  implications for organizational design, 523–25
  infrastructure, 502–19
  morale and, 538–39
  specialization, *see* Functional specialization; Role specialization

Organizational structure (*Continued*)
standardization, *see* Standardization
superstructure, *see* Departmentalization

Organizational Structure and Design (Dalton, Lawrence, and Lorsch), 22

Organizational type, 272, 305–15, 573–74

Organizations:
activities of, 7–9
age of, *see* Age of organizations
nature of, 1–15
properties of, 2–7
study of, 10–14, 21–26
as units of analysis, 9–10

Organizing, 146–47, 152–55

Output:
classification by nature of, 310–11
open system, 225
See also Operations technology

Output goals, 362–68

Ownership, 272, 315–17, 573–74

Participant observation, 22–23, 26

Participative management, 186–87, 192, 338, 398, 399, 417–23
capital intensive technology and, 463, 464
combined with other styles, 424–29
control and information system (C.I.S.) and, 508
coordinative mechanisms and, 550, 551
decentralization and, 510, 511
diversification and, 367
institutionalized, 422
matrix structure and, 497
morale and, 537–38
performance and, 578–79, 582, 589–90, 591, 598–602
performance aspirations and, 382, 537
size of organization and, 297–98
structural mechanisms associated with, 437
technologically complex environment and, 429, 591

Participative model of organizational design, 188, 189

Pathological systems, 239

Pattern variables, 587–95

Perception, gestalt psychology and, 88–92, 118

Perceptual differences, conflict and, 544–48

Perfect competition, 46, 49

Performance, 572–609
behavioral variables and, 583–87
concept of, 572–73
demographic variables and, 573–76
design of, 606–09
effect on organization, 597–602
environmental variables and, 576–77
measurability of, 308, 309
pattern variables and, 587–95
strategic variables and, 577–82
structural variables and, 583
type of organization and, 308, 309

Performance aspirations, 377–82, 553–55

Performance variables, 274, 277

Personality:
psychoanalytic theory and, 88, 106–11, 118
role and, 112–14

Personnel bureaucracy, 141

Planning, 146–47, 151–52
hostile environment and, 336
levels of, 152
scope of, 152

Planning-oriented management, 398, 399, 404–09
combined with other styles, 424–29
goal conflict and, 361–62
high performance aspirations and, 382
performance and, 578, 582, 591, 599, 600, 602
restrictive environment and, 340, 341
technologically complex environment and, 339, 591

Policies, 157

Political analysis of organizations, 41, 42, 51–65, 541–42
causes of politics, 60–61
forms of politics, 58–60
politics, defined, 51
polity, 51, 52, 61–64
power, *see* Power

Polity, 51, 52, 61–64

Polyarchies, 62

Portfolio Selection: A Simulation of Trust Investment (Clarkson), 24

Power:
of administrative units, 456–57
allocation of, 54–56
capital intensive technology and, 463, 464
centralization of, 336
management style and, 435–38
nature of, 52–54
restraints on exercise of, 57–58

Power (*Continued*)
sources of, 54–56
uses of, 56–57
See also Coercive management
Pre-workflow bureaucracy, 140
Price competition, 335, 336
Price leadership, 46
Principles of management, *see* Management process school
Private ownership organizations, 315–17
Problemistic search, 207–08
Problems, as environmental pressures, 328, 331
Procedures, 137, 296, 483
Producer goods, 312, 314
Product-characteristic goal, 363, 371–73
Production subsystem, 225, 227, 229
Professional management style, 423, 425
control and information system (C.I.S) and, 507–08
coordinative mechanisms and, 550, 551
design of innovation and, 561
performance and, 579–80, 582, 591, 598, 599, 600, 602
Professional organizations, 306, 307, 510–11
Profit decentralization, 154
Profitability, 370, 381
Progressive management, 581, 582
Psychoanalytic theory, 88, 106–11, 118
Public accountability, commonweal organizations and, 306–07, 308
Public ownership organizations, 315–17
Purposes, specificity of, 5–6

Quasi-resolution of conflict, 207, 209
Questionnaire surveys, 22–23, 26

Rebellion, 114
Recruitment, 153
Reinforcement theory (behavioristic psychology), 88, 98–105, 118
Research methods, 21–26
Restrictive environment, 339–41, 409
computer use and, 473
coordinative mechanisms and, 549–51
Retreatism, 114, 115
Reward and punishment, 98–105
Risk-taking management, 368, 398–404
combined with other styles, 424–29
diversification and, 365–66, 367
performance and, 579, 580, 582, 591, 592, 594
structural mechanisms associated with, 436

turbulent environment and, 334–35, 403–04, 429, 591, 598–99, 602
Ritualism, 114, 115
Role conflict, 111–13, 115–17
Role dispositions, 108
Role specialization, 512–13
defined, 512
size of organization and, 296
Role theory, 88, 111–18
Roles:
leadership, 155–56
personality and, 112–14
Routine system units, 500–02
Routine technology, 246–48
Rules, 3, 5, 6, 109–10, 135, 137, 157, 483

Satisficing, 404–05
Seat-of-the-pants management, 399, 404–05, 426, 427–29
performance and, 579, 592–93, 594, 600
structural mechanisms associated with, 437
Self-actualization, 192–93
capital intensive technology and, 463, 464
See also Organization development
Service organizations, 305–07, 310–11, 315, 316
classes of, 312, 315
dimensions of, 316
Situational expertise, management style and, 409–12
Situational variables, 270–72, 275–76, 277
See also Demographic characteristics of organizations; External environment of organizations
Size of organization, 272, 292–99
authority systems and, 64
choice of design and, 264
control and information system (C.I.S.) and, 508
decentralization and, 296, 509–11
differentiation and, 296–97, 423
diverse environment and, 337, 423
divisionalization and, 498–99
goal conflict and, 362
management style and, 297–98
motivation and, 535–37
performance and, 573–76, 595
structure and, 295–97
structuring of activities and, 513, 514
vertical integration and, 367
Social forces, 228, 235

Social interaction, learning theory and, 100–04

Social processes in organizations, 82–84

Social psychological analysis of organizations, 13, 42, 73, 86–119
  domain of social psychology, 86–88
  field theory, 88, 93–98, 118
  gestalt psychology, 88–92, 118
  learning theory, 88, 98–105, 118
  psychoanalysis, 88, 106–11, 118
  role theory, 88, 111–18

Sociological analyses of organizations, 41, 42, 71–86
  change, 80–82
  continuity, 77–80
  disorder, 75–77
  domain of sociology, 73
  order, 74–75
  social processes in organizations, 82–84
  sociological perspective, 74–82
  stability, 74–75
  structural factors, 76–82, 85–86

Sociometric dispositions, 108

Specialist system units, 500–02

Specialization:
  functional, *see* Functional specialization
  role, 296, 512–13

Stability, social, 74–75

Stable environment, 333–34, 403–04, 429, 430, 591

Staff-line conflict, 546

Standardization, 3, 5, 135, 502, 504, 511–13
  defined, 512
  function of, 513
  hostile environment and, 336, 337
  size of organization and, 296

Standardized mass-output, 464–68

Stated goals, 356–57

Strategic planning, 152

Strategic variables, 272–73, 275–77
  See also Goals; Top management style

Stratification, on basis of status, 83–84

Structural orientations in organization theory, *see* Bureaucracy; Management process school

Structural variables, 273–76
  See also Information technology; Operations technology; Workflow

Structure of organizations, *see* Organizational structure

Subordinacy, 586

Subsystems, *see* Systems approach

System goals, 363, 368–71

Systems approach, 223–25
  administrative uses of, 225, 232–35
  contingency theory compared with, 236, 249–50
  development of, 224–25
  evolution of, 249
  forces shaping systems and subsystems, 225, 228, 231
  interaction between subsystems, 225, 231–32
  major subsystems, 224–25, 227–30
  model of human being, 249
  open systems, 225–27
  strategic variables, 249
  system, meaning of, 223–24

Tactical planning, 152

Targets, 152, 263

Task environment:
  age of organization and, 304–05
  contingency theory and, 239–44, 248–49
  differentiation and, 239–41, 338
  diversity of, 239–41, 587–89, 595
  divisionalization and, 498–99
  form of departmentalization and, 497–99
  motivation and, 534–35
  performance and, 582

Task forces, 550

Technical forces, 228, 234

Technical subsystem, 224

Technical system units, 500–02

Techniques, 3–4, 5

Technocratic management, *see* Optimization-oriented management

Technologically complex environments, 338–39
  computer use and, 473
  control and information system (C.I.S.) and, 339, 506–08
  management style and, 339, 408, 429, 430, 591
  performance and, 591
  workflow and, 456

Technology:
  choice of design and, 265
  contingency theory and, 236–38, 246–48, 269
  defined, 457
  importance of, 457–58
  information, *see* Information technology
  morale and, 538–39

Technology (*Continued*)
  operations, *see* Operations technology
  scale for measurement of, 237–38
Theory, nature of, 14–16
Throughput, open system, 225
Top management style, 392–438
  coercive, *see* Coercive management
  corporate management, 424–26
  design of, 426–30
  design of innovation and, 561–64
  dimensions of, 398–99
  human relations orientation and, 183–87
  ideology and, 393–98
  implications for organizational design, 433–38
  mechanistic, *see* Mechanistic management
  morale and, 537–38
  optimization, *see* Optimization-oriented management
  organic, *see* Organic management
  participative, *see* Participative management
  performance and, 577–82
  performance aspirations and, 537
  risk-taking, *see* Risk-taking management
  size of organization and, 297–98
Training, 153–54
Turbulent environment, 333–35
  design of innovation and, 563–64
  diversification and, 367
  management style and, 334–35, 403–04, 429, 430, 591, 598–99, 602
  performance and, 591, 592, 598–99, 602

workflow and, 456
TVA and the Grassroots (Selznick), 22

Uncertainty, 241–42
Uncertainty absorption, 207, 209
  performance and, 589–90
  turbulent environment and, 335
Uncertainty avoidance, 207, 212
Uncertainty reduction, 504
  management style and, 435–38
  performance and, 589–90, 595

Vertical integration:
  in custom technology firms, 466–67
  performance and, 589–90
  size of organization and, 367
  standardized mass-output and, 467, 469
  turbulent environment and, 334, 335

Work units:
  morale and, 538, 540
  power of, 456–57
  types of, 499–500
Workflow, 8, 446–58
  defined, 446
  determinants of, 456
  dimensions of, 453–56
  implications for organizational design, 475–76
  morale and, 538–39
  nature of, 448–53
  power of administrative units and, 456–57
Workflow bureaucracy, 140

A 6
B 7
C 8
D 9
E 0
F 1
G 2
H 3
I   4
J 5